Auto Body Repair and Refinishing

Auto Body Repair and Refinishing

Robert P. Schmidt

Reston Publishing Company, Inc.
A Prentice-Hall Company
Reston, Virginia

Library of Congress Cataloging in Publication Data 346 1 4004

Schmidt, Robert P

  Auto body repair and refinishing.

  1. Automobiles—Bodies—Maintenance and repair.
I. Title.
TL255.S35   629.2′6′0288   80-26422
ISBN 0-8359-0247-1

© 1981 by Reston Publishing Company, Inc.
A Prentice-Hall Company
Reston, Virginia

10 9 8 7 6 5 4 3 2 1

Printed in the United States of America

To my wife, Estelle,
and to my children

Contents

This book is the result of my determination, with the encouragement of others, to put together all the materials gathered and used after many years of teaching auto body repair. It is the result also of many years of experience working in the trade and my efforts to gather together the most current information available in a rapidly changing automotive industry.

Before writing this text, I reviewed many auto body repair texts and found them lacking in some areas. I felt a more complete textbook was needed to suit the special interests of students and teachers alike.

Preface

This book is general in nature and does not favor any one manufacturer. Throughout, there is subject matter that is not covered in other books but is necessary in order to expose the student to as many repair procedures as possible.

Many times the bodyman is expected to do a variety of jobs and perform different operations that are not usually undertaken in an auto body shop. I have tried to supply information to help the student in these situations.

This book could not have been written without the help of a few important people. For their many hours of work in preparing the text and for their efforts in putting it together, I would like to express my gratitude and appreciation to my wife, Estelle, and to my children. I would also like to thank a close friend, Mr. Nick Contino of Prentice-Hall, Inc., who encouraged me to embark upon this project; the Reverend Stuart Suydam of the Callicoon Center Dutch Reform Church, who came to my assistance to take photographs; the administration and staff of the Sullivan County Board of Cooperative Educational Services, Occupational Division, for their help and assistance; and all my vocational teachers and friends for their support.

Robert P. Schmidt
Callicoon Center,
New York

Acknowledgments

General Repairs

part
1

In recent years, the number of lawsuits involving personal injuries has increased, and the amount of money awarded is staggering. Not only have employers been sued, but now, schools and instructors are being sued at an alarming rate.

Shop safety and accident prevention is very important and must be given serious thought. In the school situation, the development of good safety habits and an awareness of the potential dangers that exist in the body shop can help guide an individual through his or her life's work.

Carelessness or the lack of safety habits causes accidents. Accidents have far-reaching effects, not only on the victim but on the victim's family, the instructor, the school administration, the student body, and society in general. They result in lost time and wages to the employee. More importantly, they can cause serious injury, sometimes permanent, or even death. Therefore, it is the obligation of the instructor or employer to foster a safety program to protect the health and welfare of those involved. With reasonable care and common sense, the body shop can be a safe place to work.

Shop Safety

chapter 1

PERSONAL SAFETY

The following are some of the rules that are so very important for personal safety:

1. No horseplay, running, or fooling around should be permitted in any shop. One thing leads to another and eventually injuries may result. Horseplay is also distracting and wastes time in a body shop. The throwing of wet sponges, shutting off of another's welding tank, or disconnecting a painter's air lines are examples of horseplay.

2. To preserve eyesight or prevent eye injuries, clear protective goggles or face

shields must be worn when using a disc sander or bench grinder, when drilling overhead or removing shattered glass, or when there is danger of flying metal or other particles or chips.

CAUTION: We have been given only one pair of eyes, so protect them. It only takes a second to get the goggles.

3. Compressed air is one of the most important tools used in the body shop, but one that can be very dangerous if not used properly. A blow gun or dusting gun attached to the compressed air line is a dangerous tool. A compressed air stream should *never* be directed toward another person. An accidental gust of dust-laden air blown at someone's face can be misinterpreted as a practical joke. When using a blow gun or dusting gun to remove dust or dirt from a vehicle, make sure no one is in line with the air flow. Do not use a blow gun or dusting gun to remove dust or dirt from clothing or skin. Dirt or dust can be forced into the pores of the skin and cause infection. This is especially true if the dirt contains metal filings such as steel or lead.

4. In some states, the State Education Department enforces laws about wearing safety glasses when working in a body shop or when visiting a body shop while work is being performed. This law is mandated and must be strictly enforced.

5. Loose clothing, unbuttoned sleeves, loose ties, and shirts hanging out are very dangerous when a worker is using revolving equipment such as grinders, disc sanders, polishers, and large drills.

6. Shaded or colored goggles, either #5 or #6 shade, must be worn when welding or cutting with oxy-acetylene. These will protect the eyes from harmful light rays and flying molten pieces of steel. Sunglasses do not provide adequate protection.

7. When electric arc, TIG, or MIG welding, the proper helmet with at least a #10 shade lense must be worn. (Safety in electric welding will be discussed further in Chapter 5.)

8. Work shoes with heavy or thick soles should be worn. Sheetmetal edges are very sharp, and soft-soled shoes such as moccasins or sneakers do not provide adequate protection. Also, the worker's pants should be long enough to cover the top of the shoes. This prevents sparks from going down inside the worker's shoes, especially when he or she is using a cutting torch.

9. Avoid prolonged skin contact with thinners, paint, wax-removing compounds, rust-removing preparation, tinning compounds, and other chemicals. The mouth and eyes should be especially protected. After using such chemicals, always wash with soap and water before smoking or eating.

GENERAL SHOP SAFETY

With the type of materials used and the work performed in a body shop, the danger of fire lurks everywhere. By observing some simple precautions the risk of fire can be minimized.

The welding torch and the cutting torch produce very high heat, and sparks from the cutting torch travel a long distance. To prevent fires never weld or cut near paints, thinners, or other flammable liquids or materials. Be sure to cover open containers of thinners and paints or move to a safe area. Many body shops have one workbench which is also used for mixing paints. Never cut or weld a container before checking to see what was in the container.

When welding or cutting near car interiors, remove the seats and floor mats if possible. If not, cover them with a water-dampened cloth or towel. Always have a pail of water handy and a fire extinguisher nearby (dry chemical or CO_2 type, but not foam type). If at all possible, have a fellow worker fire watch. This person can alert you to any fires burning nearby.

You should never grind or weld near a battery. If the battery cannot be removed, disconnect the cables to prevent shorts and possible explosions. This also applies when you are working near electrical wires, especially under the instrument panel.

Fuel tanks should be removed, if necessary, to repair panels next to the filler tube or when the frame and floor is damaged near the tank. If the tank is removed, place it and the gasoline in a safe place. When grinding near fuel filler pipes, close them tightly and cover them with wet rags.

When working underneath cars, be sure the car is properly placed on stands or horses. Never rely on hydraulic jacks or bumper jacks.

All paint and thinners should be stored in steel cabinets or rooms away from the working area. Waste thinner should be kept in a suitable container and emptied frequently to prevent spontaneous combustion. Some local ordinances require that no more than three gallons of lacquer thinner be kept in the shop at any one time.

Electrical equipment and tools should be inspected frequently and stored in cabinets or on wall brackets and not on the floors. Never use frayed or defective cords and connectors. Be sure the equipment is properly grounded and the ground lugs on the plugs are not removed.

The exhaust fan must be large enough for the shop. An accumulation of paint and thinner fumes is very explosive.

Always keep the body shop clean and free from litter. Keep all the exits and passageways free from obstructions. Protect or cover jagged edges of body sections, such as torn fenders, to prevent serious injury.

All shops must have sufficient fire extinguishers, either dry chemical or CO_2 for paint and liquid fires. Water- and sand-filled buckets also come in handy.

Most accidents and fires are caused by carelessness. Care and common sense will make the shop a safe place in which to work.

Fire Extinguishers

Many shop workers do not know the location of the extinguishers or even know how to use them. When there is an emergency, many workers panic instead of staying calm and putting the fire out as soon as possible.

Fire is caused by three things: (1) something to burn, (2) air or oxygen, and (3) heat. Eliminate any one of these, and the fire will go out.

Fires are classified as **A, B, C,** and **D** (see Figure 1-1):

1. **A** fires involve wood, paper, cloth, plastic, or any similar materials.

2. **B** fires are liquid fires involving paint, thinner or reducer, oil, gasoline, grease, or other liquids.

3. **C** fires involve electricity including wiring, electrical motors, switches, and other devices using electricity.

Use the **RIGHT** Extinguisher!

FOR ORDINARY COMBUSTIBLES...CLASS A FIRES.

Put out a Class "**A**" fire by **LOWERING ITS TEMPERATURE** using a <u>water</u> or <u>water</u> <u>based</u> <u>extinguisher</u>— <u>wet</u> fire to cool—<u>soak</u> to stop smoldering ... or BY COATING the burning combustibles with "multi-purpose" dry chemical.

such as... trash, paper, cloth, wood, etc.

green*

FOR FLAMMABLE LIQUIDS...CLASS B FIRES.

Put out a Class "**B**" fire by "**SMOTHERING**" it. Use extinguisher giving a <u>blanketing</u>, <u>flame-interrupting</u> <u>effect</u>-- cover whole flaming liquid surface.

such as... gasoline, paint, oil, tar, etc.

red*

FOR ELECTRICAL EQUIPMENT... CLASS C FIRES.

When <u>live</u> <u>electrical</u> <u>equipment</u> (Class "**C**" fire) is involved ALWAYS use a **NON-CONDUCTING** extinguishing agent to prevent receiving an <u>electric</u> <u>shock</u> ! Shut off power as quickly as possible.

such as... motors, switchboards, etc.

blue*

FOR COMBUSTIBLE METALS... CLASS D FIRES.

Certain metals in finely divided forms (new Class "**D**" fire) require SPECIALLY designed extinguishing agent to provide **SMOTHERING BLANKET or COATING.**

such as... chips, turnings, shavings

yellow*

from magnesium, zirconium, titanium, etc.

Figure 1-1 Common types of fire extinguishers. (*Courtesy of National Fire Protection Association.*)

4. **D** fires involve metals such as magnesium which is found in some transmission assemblies or in other parts of certain automobiles.

To control these different types of fires requires different types of extinguishers. Some extinguishers are specially designed for a particular class of fire. Other extinguishers are multipurpose.

In **A** fires, the purpose is to lower the temperature of the burning material with either a water or water-based extinguisher. Some of these are pressurized water extinguishers—the soda acid type, alkali metal salt solutions and foam. When used on automobile interiors these can cause more damage than the fire itself.

A dry-type extinguisher, called *multi purpose ABC*, is probably the best. It coats the burning material, which cuts off the supply of air. Only a powder residue which can be vacuumed out is left.

Regular dry chemical with a sodium bicarbonate, called *baking soda*, is not as good but can be used in an emergency. The carbon dioxide (CO_2) is very ineffective as it evaporates very rapidly, and the burning material will just reignite.

If the fire is caught at the very beginning, it can be controlled very easily. The longer the fire burns, the more severe it gets. This is the purpose of using a co-worker to fire watch when welding around automobiles. The welder may not see the fire start, and it could get out of control very rapidly.

B-type fires are best put out by smothering. With the use of the proper type extinguisher, the extinguishing material will blanket the burning liquids and exclude the necessary air.

Water-type extinguishers must not be used on **B** fires as paint, thinner, or other liquids will float on the surface of the water and spread. Foam-type extinguishers should be avoided, especially when the fire involves the automobile interior, because it is very messy to clean up. Foam is good in the paint-mixing area or where solvents are in use. Carbon dioxide will put out the fire, but the fire will reignite after the CO_2 evaporates.

Dry chemical extinguishers such as sodium bicarbonate, potassium bicarbonate or *Purple K*, and the multipurpose-type extinguishers are the best and the most commonly used. These types blanket the area with a powder that smothers the fire and prevents it from reigniting. The jet stream of powder is directed at the base of the fire to cover the burning liquid.

Electrical fires, or Class **C** fires, are very dangerous because electrical shock may result if the extinguishing material is a conductor of electricity. Any water type or foam-type extinguisher must not be used. Shut off or cut off the source of electricity as quickly as possible. The dry powder-type of extinguisher is recommended. (After the electricity is shut off, the classification could change to **A** or **B**.)

The **D**-type fire is relatively new and requires a special dry powder extinguisher. In an emergency, dry sand can be used to control the fire. Water must never be used as the fire may flare up and create a greater hazard.

Each extinguisher has a special label. The extinguishers for Class **A** fires have a green triangular label with an **A**. **B**-type extinguishers have a red square with a **B** in it. **C**-type is a blue circle with a **C**, and **D**-type is a yellow star with a **D**. The multipurpose label would be **ABC** which can be used for all three classes of fires. The extinguishers with **A** & **B** are meant for **A** and **B** fires and not for **C** fires.

NOTE: Sodium bicarbonate, baking soda, is a very useful product for the shop and home. It can be used for cleaning batteries and cables and also for insect bites.

Questions

1. Why are clear goggles important when grinding or removing shattered glass?
2. Can loose clothing be dangerous when using a disc grinder?
3. What type of goggles must be worn when welding or cutting?
4. Can regular welding goggles be worn when electric arc welding?
5. What is the danger when using compressed air to remove dirt from skin?
6. What type work shoes are recommended when working in the shop?
7. What is the first precaution that should be taken before using a cutting torch in the shop?
8. What can be used to protect interior trim when welding nearby?
9. Where is the best place to store paints and thinners?
10. What damage may result when grinding near batteries?
11. What are the three elements that cause a fire?
12. What are the four classes of fires and name the materials involved?
13. What type extinguishing material should not be used on paint or oil fires?
14. What is the chemical used in dry chemical extinguishers?
15. What is the disadvantage of using a CO_2 extinguisher on a smoldering fire?

HAND TOOLS

Sheetmetal repair is only one of the many operations performed by the bodyman. He is involved also in removing fenders, aligning doors, adjusting bumpers, and so forth. These jobs entail the use of a fairly large selection of hand tools.

Hand tools, such as ratchet sets, screwdrivers, pliers, and chisels, are considered general-purpose tools and are essential in body shop repair work. Each bodyman should have his own tools to avoid wasting time in borrowing from someone else. Some body shops require that each bodyman possess a certain number of tools.

Within ten years, the metric system will replace the standard system of measurement. At the present time, prompted by the energy crisis, more and more imported vehicles are seen on the highway. Yet, it will be a long time before all of the present vehicles requiring standard measurement tools and equipment will be entirely off the highway.

Young people entering the auto body trade will have to consider purchasing both standard and metric tools. Most bodymen currently in the trade have added the metric wrenches and sockets to their already large selection of tools (Figure 2-1).

A list of the minimum requirements of a body shop follows:

Wrenches—open end and box end, $1/4$" to $11/8$" (6 mm to 24 mm) openings.

Ratchets and socket sets—$1/4$", $3/8$", and $1/2$" drive with shallow and deep sockets, standard and metric.

Screwdrivers—flat and Phillips blade assortment.

Punch and chisel—including long tapered punches for lineups.

Hammers—light and heavy weight, ballpeen and crosspeen, soft face, and rubber mallet.

Hand Tools and Fasteners

chapter
2

BODY SHOP MECHANIC'S SET

Set includes 1/4", 3/8" and 1/2" drive thin wall hand sockets plus special 3/8" and 1/2" drive power sockets. Socket sizes range from 3/16" thru 1-1/4". Wrenches from 1/4" thru 1". Detailed listing of set contents on page 220.
SET NO. 9091. 166 PC. SET AS SHOWN.
SET NO. 9090. SET WITHOUT TOP CHEST.

Figure 2-1 Box wrench set. Available in standard or metric sizes. *(Courtesy of Proto.)*

Metal cutting shears—left- and right-hand cut.

Pliers—needlenose, diagonal cutting, hose clamps, and general purpose.

Vise-grips—general purpose, welding clamps, sheetmetal clamps, and C-clamp type.

Door handle (inside) removing tools.

Hex wrench set and bits, standard and metric.

Body and fender tools—body hammers, dollies, selection of spoons, and file holders.
NOTE: These will be discussed more in Chapter 7.

Hand tools should be of good quality and should be kept in good condition. Worn tools damage parts and result in lost time. One of the most important things for beginners in the trade is to get acquainted with the various size fasteners and to learn to select the proper wrenches, sockets, or screwdrivers to be used. Time is lost if one has to return to the toolbox for another size wrench or if the screwdriver is too big for the slot in the screw. This generally happens when the car is some distance from the toolbox. Another problem arises if there is no room for an open end wrench or if a deep socket has to be used instead of a shallow one. The following discussion will focus on some of the most common hand tools used in auto body repair.

Wrenches

Open End Wrenches. These are very useful when working in a confined area and

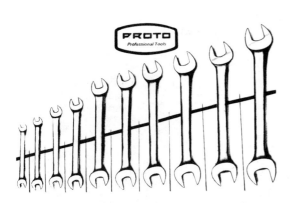

Figure 2-2 Open end wrench set. *(Courtesy of Proto.)*

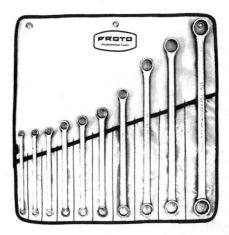

Figure 2-3 Box wrench set. *(Courtesy of Proto.)*

where movement of the wrench is limited. Each end is a different size; for example, ½" (12.7 mm) and 9/16" (14.2 mm). Also, the end of the wrench is about 15 degrees offset from the handle. Open end wrenches can be used to hold the bolt head while the nut is removed, to remove nuts from long rods, or to put over the top of the bolt or nut when there is no room for a box wrench. The main disadvantage of an open end wrench is that only two points of the bolts make contact with the wrench. There is a danger that the jaws of the wrench will spread or round off the corners of the nut or bolt.

Box Wrenches. Both ends of the box wrench are closed and encircle the nut or bolt (Figure 2-3). They are made in either 6 or 12 points or notches (Figure 2-4). Twelve-point ends are easier to use if the wrench must be slipped over the nut in a limited area but do not hold as well as 6-point ends if the nut is worn or rusted. The ends are generally offset, or made in a variety of angles and bends to suit a special purpose. The offset, normally 15°, gives ample fin-

ger clearance. Greater pressure can be applied to a box wrench because it does not readily slip off the nut or bolt. The box wrenches are far safer to use than the open end but cannot be used in tight areas. Also, the wrench must be completely taken off the bolt or nut for repositioning.

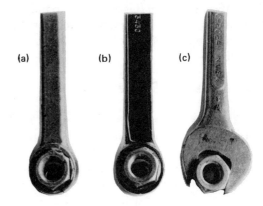

Figure 2-4 (a) 12-point box wrench; (b) 6-point box wrench; (c) open end wrench. Note the amount of contact area between the wrench and the nut. The 12-point has a tendency to strip if either the nut or wrench is worn. The open end wrench has a tendency to spread under pressure. *(Photo by S. Suydam.)*

Figure 2-5 Combination wrenches. *(Courtesy of Proto.)*

Combination Wrench. This is a wrench with one end open and one end closed. It serves many purposes but should not be bought in place of either the open end or box end sets (Figure 2-5).

Ratchet Wrench. This is a box end wrench on which the end rotates. This results in greater speed in removing or tightening bolts and nuts because the wrench does not have to be removed when repositioning for another swing. This wrench is especially useful when removing door hinges or bumper bolts or when working in a confined area.

SAFETY NOTE: It is advisable to pull on a wrench rather than push because if the wrench slips off, injury to the hands could result.

Ratchets and Sockets

Ratchets and sockets are used to save time when removing nuts and bolts or to gain access to an area too confined or too deep for a wrench. In body shops the most commonly used ratchet and socket sets are the $\frac{1}{4}$", $\frac{3}{8}$", and $\frac{1}{2}$" drives (Figure 2-6). For heavy equipment, the $\frac{3}{4}$" and 1" drive sets are available.

When reference is made to $\frac{1}{4}$" or $\frac{1}{2}$" drive sets, what is meant is the size stud on the ratchet and the sockets to fit the different drives. The $\frac{1}{4}$" drive sets usually consist of a ratchet, a flex handle for extra

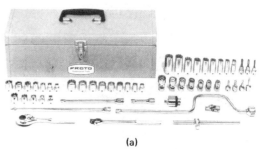

(a)

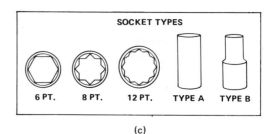

(b)

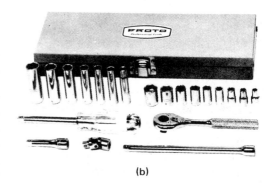

(c)

Figure 2-6 (a) $\frac{3}{8}$" drive socket set; (b) $\frac{1}{4}$" drive socket set; (c) socket types. *(Courtesy of Proto.)*

leverage and extension, and shallow sockets ranging from $\frac{1}{8}$" to $\frac{9}{16}$" (3 mm to 14 mm) and deep sockets from $\frac{3}{16}$" to $\frac{9}{16}$" (5 mm to 14 mm).

The $\frac{3}{8}$" drive sets range from $\frac{1}{4}$" to $\frac{15}{16}$" shallow and deep sockets or 6 mm to 24 mm in both shallow and deep sockets. The $\frac{1}{2}$" drive sets range from $\frac{5}{8}$" to $1\frac{1}{2}$" shallow and $\frac{7}{16}$" to $1\frac{1}{8}$" deep or 10 mm to 32 mm shallow or deep. The $\frac{1}{4}$" drive sets are very often used by bodymen for removing molding, emblems, door interior parts, or instrument panels. The $\frac{1}{2}$" drive sets are used for working on bumper brackets, front suspension parts, or for any job requiring extra leverage.

Most sockets are available in 6 or 12 point (Figure 2-7). The 6-point socket is the most popular because it will not slip as much on worn bolts or nuts. Eight-point sockets are used to remove square nuts or pipe plugs.

The ratchets are made to reverse direction for either loosening or tightening. The $\frac{3}{8}$" and $\frac{1}{2}$" drive ratchets are available with short, medium, or long handles. Some have flex handles for getting into difficult hard to reach areas. For example, they are very useful when removing spark plugs.

The shallow sockets are the most commonly used, especially in areas where there is limited clearance. The deep sockets are for nuts where the bolts extend through too far for shallow sockets.

NOTE: One way to avoid breaking sockets is to make sure the socket is placed

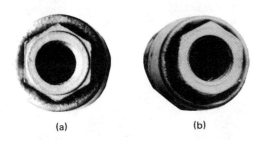

(a)   (b)

Figure 2-7 (a) 6-point socket; (b) 12-point socket. The 6-point socket has more contact area with the nut. The 12-point socket may slip if the wrench or nut becomes worn. *(Photo by S. Suydam.)*

squarely on the nut or bolt; otherwise, the socket may split.

For getting into recessed places, extensions of various lengths are available. Also, universal joints or universal sockets are useful when the opening or brackets obstruct the direct approach to the area. Long flex handles are made for loosening or tightening where extra leverage is needed. Many special sockets are available, such as Phillips, Clutch, or Torx drive for striker plates, seat belts, and so forth.

Screwdrivers

Perhaps the most common screwdriver used by bodymen is the *Phillips* (Figure 2-8). Most of the modern interior trim screws are Phillips. The No. 1 blade is used for small head screws and the large No. 4 blade is used for door hinges and striker plates. The No. 2 Phillips is the most popular size used for trim screws. Phillips screwdrivers are available in a variety of blade lengths for working in confined areas or in hard to reach spaces. The handles are made of wood or plastic, and each bodyman has his preference.

NOTE: Always select the right size screwdriver; one too small will damage the screwdriver and strip the head of the screw, one too large will also damage the screw. Always remove dirt or other material from the slots in a screw head to allow proper seating of the screwdriver.

The *standard* or *flat blade screwdriver* is used primarily for removing or installing slotted head screws. It comes in many different blade sizes and shank lengths for different purposes (Figure 2-9). The larger screwdrivers have square shanks which permit the use of a wrench to aid in the turning.

Figures 2-10 and 2-11 show the many

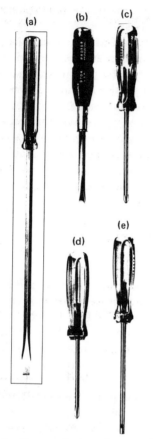

Figure 2-8 Types of screwdrivers: (a) extra long, standard tip; (b) square shaft, standard tip, steel cap; (c) Phillips tip; (d) Reed and Prince tip; (e) clutch head tip. *(Courtesy of Proto.)*

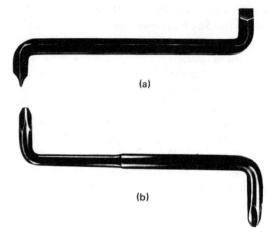

Figure 2-9 (a) Offset standard tip; (b) offset Phillips tip. *(Courtesy of Proto.)*

bars or chisels. Also, the handles on most of them are not made to be used as hammers.

Punches and Chisels

Punches are used for many different purposes, and a number of various types are

special types of screwdrivers available to the auto body repairman. It is very important to use a screwdriver that will fit the slot properly. A small blade will not hold properly and twist out of the slot. This will damage the screwdriver and the screw. Blades that are too large will not go in deep enough to permit a solid grip. Many times, the blades are ground off improperly (often called a rounded point), which results in damage to the screws and lost time.

Screwdrivers are not to be used as pry

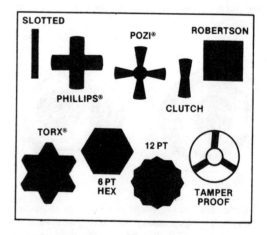

Figure 2-10 Special types of screwdrivers. *(Courtesy of Mac Tools Inc.)*

POSIDRIV
SCREW HEAD

IDENTIFICATION MARKS (4)

Figure 2–11 The Posidriv screw head is used on GM cars. The Phillips head or type 1A cross recess screwdriver can be used, but the type 1A is better. *(Courtesy of General Motors, Fisher Body Division.)*

available. The *center punch* is used for marking the location of parts before removal (Figure 2–12). Also used for marking a spot for drilling a hole to prevent wandering of the drill.

NOTE: Always keep the point sharp. Never use on hard metal because this will dull the point.

A *starter punch* is used to drive out bolts, pins, rivets, and so forth. The gradually tapered shaft is made to withstand heavy hammer blows (Figure 2–13).

NOTE: On any punch or chisel, if the head becomes mushroomed over or spread over like an umbrella, grind the mushroomed section off and taper in the head slightly. Otherwise, pieces from the mushroomed head could fly off and cause injury.

The *pin punch* is used to drive out pins and bolts when the starter punch is too large (Figure 2–14). The shaft is not tapered. The long *tapered punch* or *aligning punch* is very useful in lining up fender bolt holes and

Figure 2–12 Center punch. *(Courtesy of Proto.)*

Figure 2–13 Starter punch. *(Courtesy of Proto.)*

bumpers in order to put the bolts in. It is also used to line up body panels prior to welding.

The *flat chisel* or *cold chisel* is used very often in cutting off bolts and rivets, cutting welds, splitting nuts, or cutting sheetmetal and frames (Figure 2–15). Several sizes should be found in every toolbox for light- and heavy-duty cutting.

NOTE: Safety goggles should be worn when using punches and chisels to protect the eyes from flying metal or from the tools themselves.

Figure 2–14 Pin punch. *(Courtesy of Proto.)*

Figure 2–15 Cold chisel. *(Courtesy of Proto.)*

Hammers

A *ballpeen hammer* has a flat face on one end, and the other end is a peen or round end (Figure 2–16). This hammer comes in various weights ranging from two ounces to three pounds. It should be used to drive punches and chisels or in place of the body

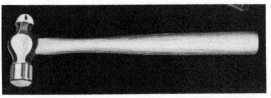

Figure 2–16 Ballpeen hammer. *(Courtesy of Snap-On.)*

Figure 2-17 Single-face or crosspeen hammer, available 2½ to 4 pound. *(Courtesy of Mac Tools Inc.)*

Figure 2-18 Aviation-type sheers. *(Courtesy of Proto.)*

Figure 2-19 Tinner snips. *(Courtesy of Proto.)*

hammer. When using this hammer, grip the handle at the end to get the most leverage and strike flat on the face. If hit on the edges, damage to the face of the hammer or the article being struck will result. Never use a hammer that has a loose head on the handle as it may fly off and seriously injure someone or damage something. Never hit a hammer on another hammer as chips from one hammer can cause injury.

The *crosspeen hammer* has a flat face on one end, but the other end tapers to an edge (Figure 2-17). This hammer is very useful in straightening bumpers, frames, and heavy sheetmetal. It is also used to shape damaged sheetmetal or when heavy hammering is necessary.

Metal Cutting Shears

A very important tool used for replacing sheetmetal panels or making a patch panel repair is the *metal cutting shears.* This tool can be used for trimming panels for proper fit, for cutting circular patterns, and for many other jobs. The *aviation-type shears* are made for left-hand cut, right-hand cut, and straight cut. These shears are often referred to as *compound shears* and produce the needed leverage for cutting metal (Figure 2-18). The *tinner snips* or *common shears* are good but have little cutting power. They are used only on thin sheetmetal (Figure 2-19).

Pliers

The most common pliers used are the *general purpose* or *combination.* This tool has a slip joint permitting the jaw to open very wide for gripping large objects. It is generally used for holding objects together or handling heated objects when welding. Pliers are not intended to serve as a wrench or to be used on hardened steel as this will dull the teeth. The *needlenose pliers* with the long tapered jaws are useful for working in small confined areas or tight places. The right tool for working with small springs or retaining clips or when doing ignition work is the *diagonal cutting pliers.* Most of these pliers are equipped with a wire cutting device. The jaw of the diagonal cutting pliers is set at an angle. These pliers are used for cutting heavy wire and small rods and for removing cotter pins.

The *hose clamp pliers* have notches in the end of the jaws for holding the prongs on

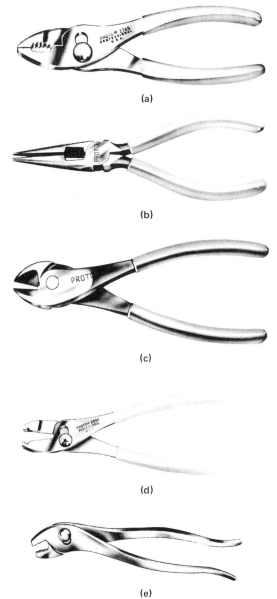

the spring-type hose clamps. This tool is very useful for removing clamps in tight places where general-purpose pliers will not hold.

The pliers just mentioned are but a few of the different types available but, they are perhaps they are the most important ones in any body shop.

Vise-Grips or Locking Wrenches

These wrenches are used for clamping various objects together and with the locking action of the handle, they stay together. A variety of different types are used when replacing a body panel to hold it in the proper position. Also, when welding objects together, they can be held firm without endangering the hands. Various types are listed as follows and shown in Figure 2–21.

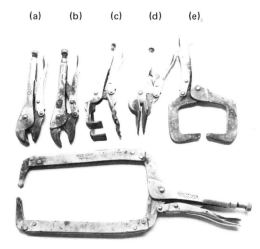

Figure 2-20 (a) Combination pliers; (b) long nose pliers with side cutter; (c) heavy-duty diagonal cutting pliers; (d) hose clamp pliers; (e) battery pliers. *(Courtesy of Proto.)*

Figure 2-21 Vise-grips or locking wrenches: (a) general purpose; (b) general purpose with wire cutters; (c) welding clamps; (d) sheetmetal clamps; (e) C-clamp type; (f) long reach type. *(Photo by S. Suydam.)*

General purpose—for all types of work, good in close quarters, made in various sizes.

Welding clamps—U-shaped jaws useful for working around offsets and for holding parts in alignment.

Sheetmetal clamps—useful for holding sheet-metal together with its wide jaws. Useful for shaping sheetmetal and when doing upholstery work.

C-clamp type—shape of jaws permits the clamping together of irregular objects in odd places where the general-type jaw cannot reach.

Long reach C-clamp—for hard to reach jobs.

NOTE: Most bodymen have several of each on hand. When replacing large panels a great number of vise–grips are needed.

Door Handle Removing Tools

Door handle removing tools are used for removing the inside door handles where a clip-type device is used to hold the handle of the shaft (Figure 2–22). The push plate type spreads the clip apart and releases the handle. The plier type removes the clip. These are very thin in order to slip in between the handles and escutcheon plate (a plastic disc used to protect the door trim panels). Ford and General Motors cars, late models, use the same type.

Hex Head Wrenches

Hex Head wrenches and sockets are used for removing or installing certain inside door handles, inside rear view mirrors, instrument panel knobs, and various other set screws. The sockets are used for larger set screws or special bolts like the disc brake calibers on some automobiles. The

Figure 2-22 Door and window handle clip removers. *(Photo by S. Suydam.)*

long hex wrenches are ideal for removing recessed parts and for removing or tightening the head assembly on certain types of spray guns (Figure 2–23).

Hacksaws

One of the important tools needed for sheetmetal work and very often abused is the hacksaw. With its many uses in a body shop, proper knowledge of the hacksaw and blade is necessary to obtain the desired results. One of its major uses is the cutting of sheetmetal when replacing panels because its cut is clean and smooth. Cutting panels with impact chisels leaves the edges wavy, and the torch generally warps the metal and leaves a rough edge that must be ground smooth. Improper methods generally result in broken or stripped blades. (The foregoing information does not represent the machinist's viewpoint but the bodyman's.)

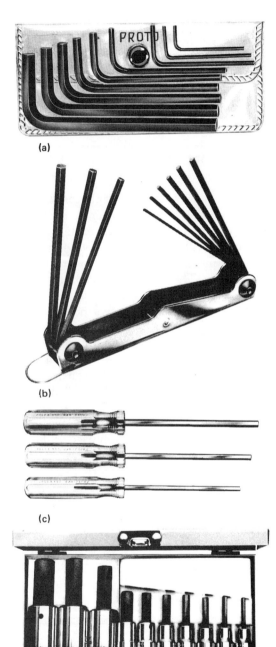

(a)

(b)

(c)

(d)

Figure 2-23 (a) Metric 9-piece hex key set; (b) 9-piece long hex wrench set; (c) hex drivers; (d) 10-piece hex bit set. *(Courtesy of Proto.)*

Figure 2-24 Hacksaw frame. *(Courtesy of Proto.)*

Hacksaw Frames. The pistol grip adjustable frame is the most common one used in a body shop. It adjusts to accommodate 8" (203 mm), 10" (254 mm), and 12" (305 mm) blades. Most are made so the blade can be set in four different positions for different types of cutting (Figure 2-24).

Hacksaw Blades. These are made of a tungsten steel alloy with about one percent carbon for hardness. The most common blades used in shops are flexible which have only hardened teeth.

Figure 2-25 Hacksaw blade. *(Courtesy of Proto.)*

The most important factor in selecting hacksaw blades is the teeth per inch (TPI). Cutting sheetmetal requires small or fine teeth (32 TPI or 32 teeth per 25 mm). Cutting heavy steel bars or soft metal requires coarse teeth (18 TPI or 18 teeth per 25 mm). At least two teeth must contact the surface of the metal to prevent stripping the teeth. Some blades are equipped with very fine teeth on both ends called *starter teeth*. These help to reduce chattering when starting to cut a piece of metal. When cutting soft metal like copper or aluminum coarse teeth will prevent clogging.

The teeth have what is called *set*. Some are standard set and others are wavy set to give the blade freedom of movement and

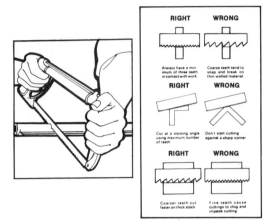

Figure 2-26 Cutting tips.

reduce binding. Standard set has one tooth tipped to the right and the next tooth tipped to the left. Wavy set has one pair of teeth tipped right and the next pair tipped left.

NOTE: Set is the amount the teeth are tipped left and right to permit freedom of movement of the blade when cutting through metal. The wearing of the set produces binding of the blade and possible breakage.

Tips for long life of the blade are listed as follows:

1. Properly adjust blade tension to prevent buckling or wandering.

2. Use an average of 40 strokes per minute.

3. Always face teeth away from person.

4. Pressure should not be excessive on forward stroke; relieve pressure on return stroke. Excessive pressure will generate too much heat and ruin the teeth.

5. Do not force the blade through metal, especially soft metal.

6. When cutting sheetmetal, do not hold the blade at a right angle to the metal; use about a 30° to 40° angle. This applies also when starting to cut on sharp-edged metal.

7. Always start the cut with slight pressure and a short stroke.

BLIND RIVETS

Not many years ago, the only method of fastening sheetmetal or other material together without heat was with either screws or bolts. Grills on some cars were factory riveted and to replace them meant using small bolts. This took time. Also, the bolts often loosened up and did not look factory original. (Sheetmetal screws have a tendency to loosen up through vibration.) With the appearance of blind or draw rivets some of the problems were solved, and the time involved for some repairs was shortened. Blind rivets are installed from one side only (Figure 2-27). Older rivets required both sides accessible.

The most common rivet used in body shops is the *hollow rivet*. It is available in several diameters from $\frac{3}{32}''$ to $\frac{3}{16}''$ (2.38 mm to 4.76 mm) although larger ones are used in industry (Figure 2-28). Recently, the $\frac{1}{4}''$ (6.35 mm) rivet has been used for

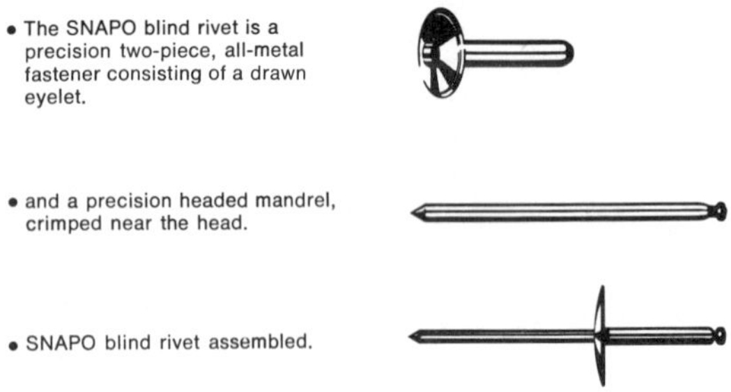

• The SNAPO blind rivet is a precision two-piece, all-metal fastener consisting of a drawn eyelet.

• and a precision headed mandrel, crimped near the head.

• SNAPO blind rivet assembled.

Figure 2-27 Blind rivet. *(Courtesy of Marsen Inc.)*

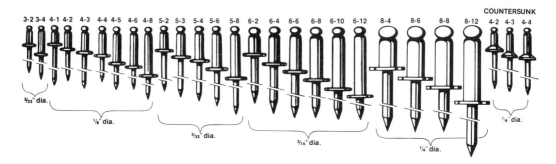

Figure 2–28 Hollow rivets are available in many sizes. *(Courtesy of Marsen Inc.)*

attaching the various door parts that are discussed in Chapter 18. The gripping range (the depth of the metal or material that the rivet will hold together) is from $\frac{1}{8}$" to $\frac{1}{2}$" (3.17 mm to 12.7 mm). The mandrel, or rivet stem, and rivet are made in several combinations such as steel rivet and mandrel, aluminum rivet and steel mandrel, aluminum rivet and mandrel. The head of the rivet is available in button or dome head, countersunk head, and flange head.

The *rivet tool* or *riveter* is a plier-type tool used in shops (Figure 2–29). When the handle is raised, the jaws inside open to receive the mandrel or stem. When the handle is lowered, the jaws clinch the mandrel and start to draw the mandrel through the rivet, expanding the rivet. The mandrel will break after a certain amount of tension is placed on it.

Air-operated or hydraulic guns are also available, but these are used more in a production situation.

Figure 2–29 Rivet hand tool. *(Courtesy of Marsen Inc.)*

Use of Rivets

If using $\frac{1}{8}$" rivets, use a $\frac{1}{8}$" or #30 drill bit and drill a hole. Be sure the pieces to be riveted are close together. Insert the rivet $\frac{1}{8}$" (3.17 mm) into the hole and lower or squeeze the handle of the riveter until the rivet mandrel breaks from tension.

Countersunk rivets are used in places where the head must be flush with the surrounding area (Figure 2–30). A good example is in installing a repair panel where the area that is riveted must be ground smooth and filled with a filler. When grinding the area, the heads on the dome-type rivets would be ground off and the panels would separate. Using countersunk rivets, the heads of the rivets would be flush or a little below the surface, and grinding would not hurt their holding.

Use a countersink drill made for rivets and carefully drill into the metal. As the small part of the drill goes down through the metal, the larger part of the drill will start to cut the countersink hole. The outside edge of the countersink drill should just start to cut the metal (less than $\frac{1}{64}$" or .40 mm). Do not let the large part of the drill cut the metal too deep as it will make the hole too large for the rivet. Install the

1 INSERT RIVET

Insert rivet in drilled hole.

2. APPLY TOOL

Place mandrel (stem) into nozzle end of rivet gun. Rivet gun jaws grip rivet mandrel.

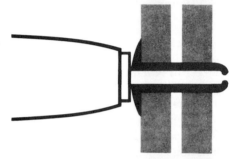

3. ACTUATE TOOL

The actuated tool grips the mandrel and exerts a strong pull, forcing the head of the mandrel into the rivet's hollow core. The protruding portion of the rivet expands thus forming the counterhead.

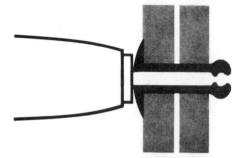

4. FASTENED!

At maximum pull, the mandrel breaks (at the pre-crimped section) and is withdrawn. The mandrel head remains locked in the rivet, forming a tight vibration-proof application.

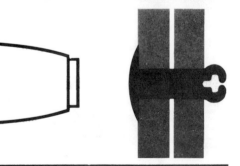

Figure 2-30 Installing a rivet. *(Courtesy of Richline Co., Inc.)*

countersunk rivet in the same manner as the dome rivet.

Blind rivets have unlimited application in the shop. They are used to install grilles, to help hold quarter panels in place for welding, to install rubber splash shields, and to patch holes in the floorpans. Rivets are very useful at home for repairing cabinets, furniture, toys, and so forth.

FASTENERS, NUTS, AND BOLTS

Each automobile assembled consists of a very large selection of fasteners not including the ones used for the assembly of the motor and powertrain. Each year brings some new types of fasteners or molding retainers and an increase in the use of plastic retainers. It would be very difficult to describe each and every type of fastener used today. Only the most common types and their uses will be discussed.

When a bodyman is assembling an automobile, it should be his aim to install the same type of fasteners that were originally used in production. One of the giveaways to the past history of an automobile is to see a slotted screw in place of a Phillips-head screw or to see a bolt and flat washer used where a washer-type bolt should have been used.

In order to be a good bodyman and to save time on the job, the correct identification of the types and sizes of fasteners is of the utmost importance (Figure 2–31).

Bolts are generally defined as devices which are used to fasten two objects together. In the body trade, bolts could be described as "cap-screws" because they are used in tapped (threaded) holes. In the machine trade bolts have a different meaning.

A bolt is inserted through two pieces of metal, and a nut is placed on the other end. The most common types of bolts range from $1/4$" to $1/2$" (6.35 mm to 12.77 mm) in diameter. The size is determined by the diameter of the body. The length of the bolt is measured from under the head to the end of the threaded portion. Most bolts are equipped with either fine (NF) or coarse (NC) threads. (Various types of thread will be further discussed later in this chapter.)

The bolts just described are the most common types, but there are many others which are commonly used today in the construction of automobiles.

DRILL BITS

On many occasions, various size holes must be made (for example, when installing moldings on a new door or when installing outside mirrors). The tool used in most body shops is the *high-speed twist drill*. Carbon steel drills are also used, but the cutting edges dull quickly.

The drill is divided into three sections:

1. The shank which fits into the chuck.
2. The body.
3. The point.

The body consists of the following parts:

Flutes—the spiral cut grooves in the length of the body. These allow the chips to escape from the hole and also permit lubricating oils to reach the point.

Margin—formed when the narrow surface that remains after the flutes are machined is undercut. The margin runs

NOMENCLATURE FOR BOLTS

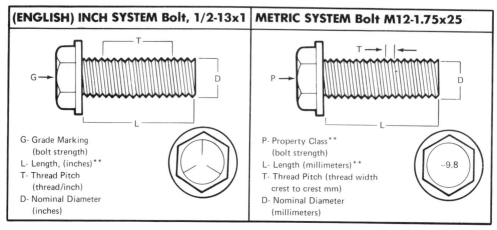

(ENGLISH) INCH SYSTEM Bolt, 1/2-13x1	METRIC SYSTEM Bolt M12-1.75x25
G- Grade Marking (bolt strength)	P- Property Class** (bolt strength)
L- Length, (inches)**	L- Length (millimeters)**
T- Thread Pitch (thread/inch)	T- Thread Pitch (thread width crest to crest mm)
D- Nominal Diameter (inches)	D- Nominal Diameter (millimeters)

*The property class is an Arabic numeral distinguishable from the slash SAE English grade system.
**The length of all bolts is measured from the underside of the head to the end.

BOLT STRENGTH IDENTIFICATION

(ENGLISH) INCH SYSTEM

Grade 1 or 2   Grade 5   Grade 8

(English) Inch bolts - Identification marks correspond to bolt strength - increasing number of slashes represent increasing strength.

METRIC SYSTEM

Metric bolts - Identification class numbers correspond to bolt strength - increasing numbers represent increasing strength. Common metric fastener bolt strength property are 9.8 and 10.9 with the class identification embossed on the bolt head.

Figure 2-31   Bolt and hex nut identification. *(Courtesy of Ford Motor Corporation.)*

HEX NUT STRENGTH IDENTIFICATION

(ENGLISH) INCH SYSTEM		METRIC SYSTEM	
Grade	Identification	Class	Identification
Hex Nut Grade 5	3 Dots	Hex Nut Property Class 9	Arabic 9
Hex Nut Grade 8	6 Dots	Hex Nut Property Class 10	Arabic 10
Increasing dots represent increasing strength.		May also have blue finish or paint daub on hex flat. Increasing numbers represent increasing strength.	

OTHER TYPES OF PARTS

Metric identification schemes vary by type of part, most often a variation of that used of bolts and nuts. Note that many types of English and metric fasteners carry no special identification if they are otherwise unique.

—Stamped "U" Nuts

—Tapping, thread forming and certain other case hardened screws

—Studs, Large studs may carry the property class number. Smaller studs use a geometric code on the end.

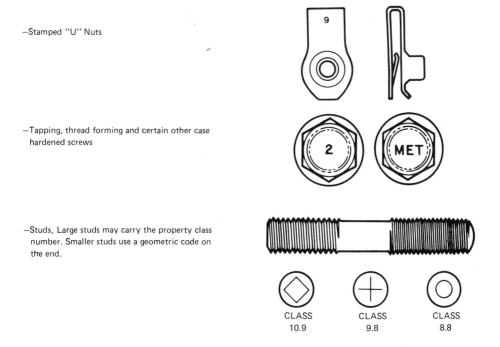

Figure 2-31 *(continued)*

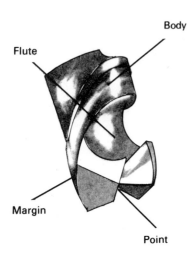

Body

Flute

Margin

Point

Figure 2–32 Parts of a twist drill.

the full length of the body and reduces friction when a hole is being drilled.

Body clearance—The undercut portion of the body between the margin and the flutes. Used to reduce friction.

Web—the thin partition in the center of the drill which extends the full length.

The point consists of the following parts:

Point—the cone-shaped cutting end of the drill.

Lips—the cutting edges of the drill that normally form about a 59° angle from the center line of the drill. For hard steel the angle is increased to about 75°, and for softer metals the angle is decreased. Both angles must be ground equal in order to drill a reasonable round hole. If the angles are unequal, the hole will be larger than the drill itself.

Lip clearance—the angle from the front edge of the lip on the flute to the back edge of the flute is called the *heel*. This angle will

vary with the hardness of the metal to be drilled. The harder the metal, the smaller the angle.

NOTE: This angle is very often ground wrong when sharpening drills without the use of a drill-sharpening attachment. Either the heel is ground at the same angle as the lip or the point between the heel and lip is higher.

Fractional drills are generally used in shops (Figure 2-33). They range from $\frac{1}{64}$" to over 1" (sizes increase in $\frac{1}{64}$" increments). For more precision-type work, there are *number* and *letter drills.*

Hints on Using Drill Bits

1. After selecting the proper size drill, check for sharpness.

2. Check shank for burrs. If any are found, remove before using.

3. Tighten chuck properly to prevent drill from twisting in chuck.

4. Turn drill on to check the trueness of chuck and drill bit.

5. If drilling sheetmetal, center punching or starting point may dent the metal. Turning the chuck by hand will make a starting point.

6. Use light pressure to start the hole and then apply more pressure. As the drill starts to cut through, ease off on the pressure so as not to shove the drill through. Also, the bit may catch as it breaks through and perhaps break the drill or stall the drill.
   CAUTION: Always be ready to release the switch to stop the drill as this could prevent injury.

7. When drilling through heavy metal, oil or a recommended lubricant should be

(a)

(b)

Figure 2-33 (a) High speed drill bits (fractional sizes $\frac{1}{16}$″ to $\frac{1}{4}$″; (b) large diameter drill bits for $\frac{3}{8}$″ chuck ($\frac{7}{16}$″ to $\frac{3}{4}$″). *(Courtesy of Mac Tools Inc.)*

used to aid in cutting and to preserve the drill bit.

8. When using large drill bits, caution must be observed when the drill cuts through or breaks through the metal because sometimes the bit will catch on the burrs. This could twist the drill from the operator's hands and cause injury. Using lighter pressure will reduce this risk.

9. When drilling small pieces of metal without the use of a drill press, place them securely in a vise or use locking pliers. Never attempt to hold the metal with the hands.

10. Never lay a drill down that is still turning. Never use a drill with loose shirt sleeves or unbuttoned shirts. The drill bit could catch the loose clothing and cause problems.

11. Always disconnect or unplug the drill before changing the bit. If drill chuck key is attached to the cord next to the plug with a short length of sash chain, the plug will have to be removed in order to change the bit.

12. Avoid using cut-down shank drill bits; smaller hand drills run too fast for larger diameter drill bits.

TAPS AND DIES

One type of tool set that is perhaps not used every day but is very important is the *tap and die set*. Many different types of special bolts, inserts, nuts, and other threaded fasteners are used in the manufacture of the modern automobile. On many occasions, these hard to obtain fasteners have damaged threads and are useless unless the threads can be repaired. Other bolts or inserted nuts have threads that are filled with rust or corrosion. These could be salvaged by means of a tap and die set. Also, a special job may require that holes be drilled in a heavy steel plate and the holes threaded on a rod of some type.

The following information is general in nature, but is not applicable to the machinist's trade.

Taps

Taps are tools used to cut internal threads in a drilled hole. They are manufactured in all of the standard sizes of threads. For body shop purposes, the machine screw sizes range from #6 screws to #12 and from $\frac{1}{4}$" (6.35 mm) to $\frac{3}{4}$" (19 mm) fractional screw sizes. Both are made for either fine or coarse threads. Each tap is marked with the size and threads per inch (TPI) and the type of threads (coarse or fine). For example, $\frac{5}{16}$ N.C. 18 means $\frac{5}{16}$" (7.93 mm) diameter, National Coarse threads, 18 threads per inch 25 mm).

Taps are made in several different styles (for example, tapered, bottoming, and plug), but the tapered is the most common. The tapered tap has the threads turned

Figure 2-34 Typical set of taps with handles and thread gauge. Thread size from #4–40 NC to $\frac{1}{2}$" NC and NF with $\frac{1}{8}$" pipe tap. *(Photo by S. Suydam.)*

down and tapered at the end of the tap for ease in starting to cut the threads. To assist in turning the tap, tap wrenches or T-handles are available. T-handles are made to accommodate the smaller size taps.

NOTE: For working in confined areas with taps, where standard handles cannot be used, square socket wrenches are good substitutes, generally those found in the $\frac{1}{4}$" (6.35 mm) drive sets.

How to Use Taps

1. If threads are to be repaired in a threaded hole, select the proper tap as to size and threads. Also select the proper tap wrench.

2. With sufficient pressure, start the tap through the damaged threads. Be sure the tap is started straight or squarely with the hole.

3. When the tap has started, turn approximately $\frac{1}{2}$ turn, then back up approximately $\frac{1}{4}$ turn. This will break the chip. Use steady and even turning motions so the tap does not break.

4. Continue with the tap until all of the threads are repaired. A lubricant should be used to assist in clearing the threads. Cutting oil is generally recommended for mild steel, but motor oil can be used.

Tapping New Threads

1. Check the chart, in the column under size of bolt and threads, to determine the size drill to use to make the hole. For example: if a $\frac{3}{8}$" (9.52 mm) 16 TPI bolt is used, a $\frac{5}{16}$" (7.93 mm) drill should be used to make the hole.

2. After making the hole, using the proper tap and tap wrench, start to thread the hole. Use sufficient pressure to

start the tap in the hole. Keep the tap squarely aligned with the hole.

3. With the tap aligned and started, the tap will feed itself into the hole. A lubricant should be used to aid in the cutting of the threads. Motor oil could be used if lard oil is not available.

4. Turn the tap approximately ½ turn, then back ¼ turn to break the chips. Be careful to do this with a steady motion and pressure in order to avoid breaking the tap. Do not force the tap.

5. Continue until the hole is completely tapped. Remove the chips from the hole before attempting to insert the bolt.

Dies

A die is used to cut external threads on rods, bolts, pipes, and so forth. Also, it can be used for repairing damaged or clogged threads on bolts and pipes. Dies are made in many different sizes and shapes, each for a purpose (Figure 2–35). The types normally used in body shops are the round adjust-

able, the round solid, hex shaped, and adjustable made in two halves. The round adjustable and the adjustable made in two halves can be made to cut threads over or under the standard depth. The hand-threading dies are very useful where precision threading is not required. The dies are held in a hold or stock when using. The hex-shaped dies can be used with a wrench or socket wrench.

Thread chasers or rethreading tools are made to restore damaged threads but are not intended to cut new threads. Die-like taps are tapered on one side to permit starting of the new threads. Adapters for round dies can be used in confined spaces. These can be turned with either ratchet or wrench.

How to Use Dies

Using dies is very similar to using taps. If using a solid-type die, the first step is to measure the diameter of the stock to be threaded or the size of the bolt to be threaded.

NOTE: Some bolt diameters are larger or smaller than the outside thread diameter which makes it impossible to cut additional threads satisfactorily. If the diameter is smaller, then the threads will be too shallow to permit the proper holding power. If the diameter is larger, it will damage the die or too much pressure will be needed to cut the larger diameter.

1. Select the proper die and holder or stock necessary. Be sure the lock or set screw is tight to prevent the die from turning in the handle. A small retaining hole is usually drilled in the die for the handle set screw.

2. Slightly bevel the end of the stock that is to be threaded. This will aid in starting the die.

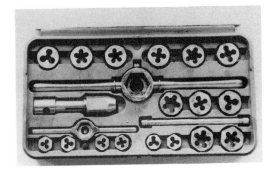

Figure 2–35 Typical set of hexagon dies with die holders from #4–40 NC to ½" NC and NF. Can be used with ⅝" and 1" wrenches or sockets. *(Photo by S. Suydam.)*

3. Place the chamfered side of the die against the stock or rod.

4. Using pressure, turn the die slowly to start the thread. Keep the die at right angles with the stock or rod.

5. Apply cutting oil to the die or stock. After the threads have started, little pressure is needed because the die will follow through. Turn about ½ turn, then backward for about ¼ turn to break the chips. Use plenty of cutting oil for better threads.

6. After cutting some threads, check their quality. If using an adjustable die, check the diameter of threads or fit with a nut or the piece of work it is to be used on.

7. After cutting a sufficient number of threads, run off the die. Clean the new threads and die of chips.

Cleaning or repairing threads is similar to cutting threads. After running the die back off, check the threads with a nut. Sometimes, certain rods or linkage, such as clutch or transmission linkage, require more threads. This can be performed in the same manner as threading a blank rod or stock. Once again, check the quality of threads and the fit. Hex dies prove excellent for cleaning threads on manifolds where a regular stock handle cannot be used.

Questions

1. What is the main disadvantage of using an open end wrench?
2. What type box wrench is best for rusted bolts?
3. What is the disadvantage of box wrenches in tight places?
4. Which is better, to pull or push a wrench?
5. What size ratchet set is best for removing emblems or instrument panel parts?
6. What type of socket is used on long bolts?
7. What size Phillips screwdrivers are most commonly used for trim screws?
8. What is the danger of using a small screwdriver on a large slotted screw?
9. What is a *mushroomed head* on a punch or chisel?
10. What is the danger of using a hammer with a loose head?
11. What is the difference between a ballpeen and a crosspeen hammer?
12. What type of hacksaw blade is better for cutting sheetmetal?
13. How many teeth must contact the surface to prevent stripping?
14. What is the average stroke per minute when using a hacksaw?
15. What is the advantage of using pop rivets?
16. What is a countersunk rivet?
17. What part of the bolt determines the size?
18. What two types of standard threads are used on bolts?
19. What are the three parts of the drill?
20. What should be used to make a starting point in heavy metal?
21. What can be used to lubricate the drill bit?

22. What is used to hold small pieces of metal to be drilled?
23. What are taps used for?
24. What are dies used for?
25. What does TPI indicate?
26. What is the most common type of tap style used?
27. What is the purpose of turning the tap or die ½" turn, then reversing for about ¼" turn?
28. What type of die is best for use in tight places?

The automobile has gone through many changes throughout the years from the horseless carriage to the well-proportioned luxury automobile of today. The older automobiles were designed for a purpose with simple lines and functions (Figure 3–1). Because of the slower speeds and poor roads, safety was not taken into consideration. Now, with the super highways and higher speeds, the thrust in engineering and design is toward a safer automobile, without the sacrifice of comfort.

Body Construction

chapter
3

CONVENTIONAL FRAME AND BODY CONSTRUCTION

Automobiles and trucks are made of two basic components, the frame and body (or passenger compartment). The frame forms the foundation of the vehicle with the powertrain, suspension, and body mounted to it. A front and rear bumper is attached for protection and beauty. The body is attached to the frame by a number of bolts with rubber bumpers to reduce the road vibration and noise.

The earlier frames, the ladder type, consisted of two U-shaped or channel-type side rails connected by a series of crossmembers where the most support was needed. This rigid frame plus the old type leaf springs gave a rather rough ride. This type of construction is still being used on trucks because of its strength. The frames were changed to accommodate the new types of front suspension, to lower the center of gravity, and to produce a more flexible unit that would ensure a comfortable ride.

The X-type frame is shaped like an elongated X. The frame narrows in the center which gives the vehicle a rigid structure. The perimeter frame forms a border around

Figure 3-1 Earlier vintage automobiles. Note the simplicity of design.

the passenger compartment. The forward and rear sections are narrower for the powertrain and suspension and are joined to the side rails, which are either box- or channel-type rails, by means of torque boxes. These torque boxes transfer the load to the frame and add flexibility to it.

Because of the construction of the side rails, the strength of the vehicle relies heavily on the body construction. One method to strengthen the center of the body is to increase the thickness of the rocker sill panel assembly.

With the perimeter frame, the frame side rails are up in between the rocker panels and floor side panel. This permits the vehicles to be lower in height but to have a higher tunnel in the center of the floor to accommodate the drive line and transmission.

UNITIZED FRAME AND BODY CONSTRUCTION

On some vehicles, the frame is incorporated or built into the body or welded together to form a single unit. This construction is called unibuilt or *unitized.*

There are many variations of this type of construction; for example, on certain models the unitized construction extends up to the front of the vehicle. The radiator support and fender aprons are welded together and to the frame rails. Some vehicles use a stub frame system where the stub frame bolts to the floor or front of the passenger compartment. The radiator support and fender aprons are fastened with bolts. A few of the vehicles have the front fender, aprons, radiator supports, and other panels or brackets welded to the frame and body. The rails and other critical areas are made of heavier metal for support, and a series of box-type structures are added for strength. The floor panels may be double layers of metal, with crossbeams and boxes for additional strength.

THE BODY

The automobile is divided into three parts, the front end assembly, the passenger compartment, and the rear end or section. The front end assembly, often called the *nose* consists of the hood front fender and aprons, radiator and support, the grille, headlights, and other brackets, the panels and trim parts. The nose section, a name commonly used by bodymen and salvage yards, is often sold as a unit for repairing front end wrecks. Otherwise, each part would need to be bought separately. The nose assembly on many automobiles can be removed easily by unfastening the bolts and disconnecting wires, hoses, and so forth.

The passenger compartment consists of the cowl, pillar, and dash assembly, the roof assembly, door openings and doors, floor and rocker panels, the glass, and many other trim parts.

The rear section consists of the quarter panels and wheelhouses, trunk lid, upper and lower rear body panels, the luggage compartment floor, and the numerous trim and other panels. The rear section, unlike the front end assembly, is welded to form a single unit. The trade name, *rear clip*, is often used to indicate the quarter panels and wheelhouse and everything from the rear window back to the bumper. The *side clip* means the quarter panel and wheelhouse and a section of the floor. *Full clip* indicates the complete rear section including the roof assembly. These are generally separated at the windshield and at the floor panel at the rear door opening. A *clip* involving a unitized body may be different because the frame is part of the body. There are many different variations of clip depending on what type body is involved, and all may have different names.

Nomenclature of Parts

It is important to be able to correctly identify the various parts or assemblies that make up the automobile (Figures 3-2 to 3-5).

MOLDING AND EXTERIOR TRIM

The exterior molding or trim parts are used to beautify or put the finishing touches to the automobile. Molding or trim parts are also used to cover body seams or finish off body openings such as windshield reveal moldings. Side moldings offer some protec-

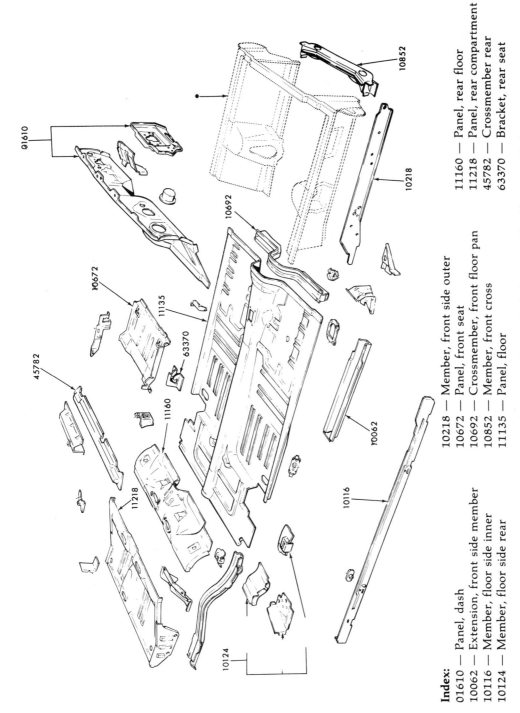

Figure 3-2 Typical exploded view of an underbody assembly. (*Courtesy of Ford Motor Corporation.*)

Index:

01610 — Panel, dash
10062 — Extension, front side member
10116 — Member, floor side inner
10124 — Member, floor side rear

10218 — Member, front side outer
10672 — Panel, front seat
10692 — Crossmember, front floor pan
10852 — Member, front cross
11135 — Panel, floor

11160 — Panel, rear floor
11218 — Panel, rear compartment
45782 — Crossmember rear
63370 — Bracket, rear seat

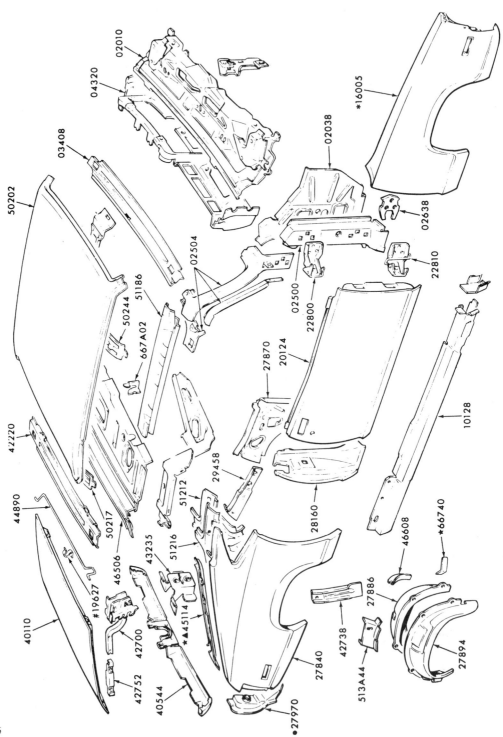

02010
04320
*16005
02038
03408
02638
50202
02504
22810
50244
51186
02500
22800
667A02
27870
20124
42220
27870
29458
10128
44890
51212
51216
28160
46608
*66740
40110
#19627
46506
43235
51216
27886
42700
*▲45114
513A44
42738
27840
27894
42752
40544
•27970

36

Index:

02010 — Panel, cowl top
02038 — Panel, cowl side — inner
02500 — Pillar assembly, front body
02504 — Pillar, front body — upper
02638 — Hinge attaching plate
03408 — Panel, w/s header
04320 — Panel, instrument
10128 — Panel rocker
16005 — Front fender
20124 — Door shell
22800 — Hinge, upper
22810 — Hinge and check, lower
27840 — Panel, quarter, hardtop
27870 — Panel, regulator, H.T.
27886 — Panel, wheelhouse — inner
27894 — Panel, wheelhouse — outer
27970 — Reinforcement, lamp opening
28160 — Pillar, latch

29458 — Pillar panel, quarter window
40110 — Deck lid
40544 — Panel, valence
42220 — Frame, back windows
42700 — Hinge to 4-1-71
42738 — Reinforcement, lock pillar
42752 — Attaching plate, deck lid
43235 — Bracket, latch striker
44890 — Bar torsion
45114 — Drip trough side
46506 — Panel, package tray
46608 — Reinforcement, quarter panel
50202 — Roof panel
50217 — Reinforcement, rear — w/vinyl cover
50244 — Reinforcement, center
51186 — Front outer and inner
513A44 — Reinforcement, wheelhouse to quarter
667A02 — Bracket, rear seat backrest
66740 — Reinforcement, wheelhouse to rocker panel

Figure 3-3 Typical exploded view of upperbody parts. (*Courtesy of Ford Motor Corporation.*)

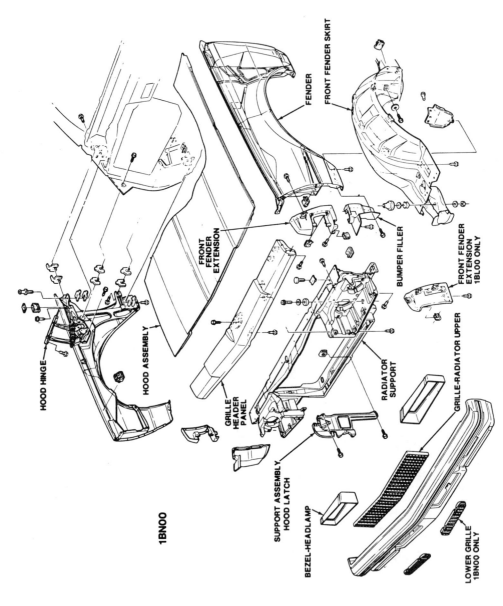

Figure 3-4 Front end sheetmetal components — B model. *(Courtesy of General Motors Corporation, Chevrolet Motor Division.)*

FRONT FENDER SKIRT

FENDER

FRONT FENDER EXTENSION

BUMPER FILLER

FRONT FENDER EXTENSION 1BLOO ONLY

HOOD HINGE

HOOD ASSEMBLY

GRILLE HEADER PANEL

RADIATOR SUPPORT

GRILLE-RADIATOR UPPER

SUPPORT ASSEMBLY HOOD LATCH

BEZEL-HEADLAMP

LOWER GRILLE 1BN00 ONLY

1BN00

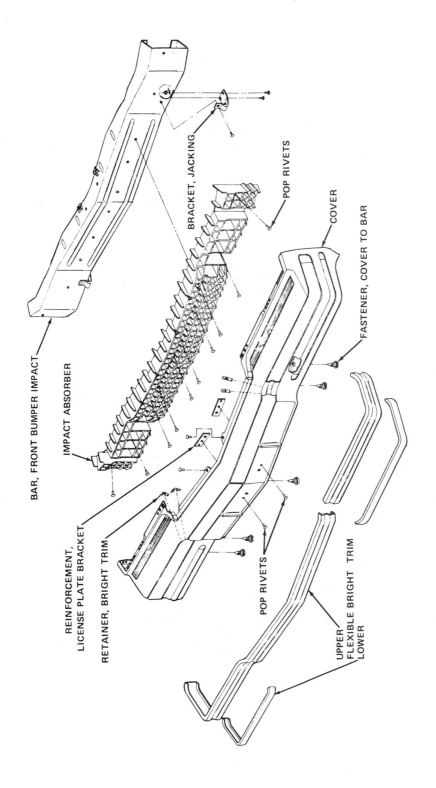

BAR, FRONT BUMPER IMPACT

BRACKET, JACKING

POP RIVETS

COVER

FASTENER, COVER TO BAR

IMPACT ABSORBER

REINFORCEMENT,
LICENSE PLATE BRACKET

RETAINER, BRIGHT TRIM

POP RIVETS

UPPER
FLEXIBLE BRIGHT TRIM
LOWER

Figure 3-5 Front bumper assembly — Monte Carlo. *(Courtesy of General Motors Corporation, Chevrolet Motor Division.)*

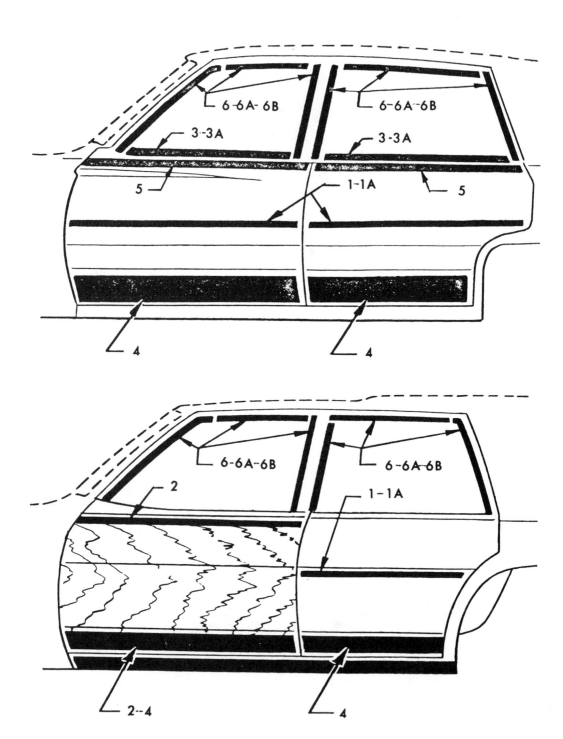

Figure 3-6 Typical door exterior moldings. *(Courtesy of General Motors Corporation, Fisher Body Division.)*

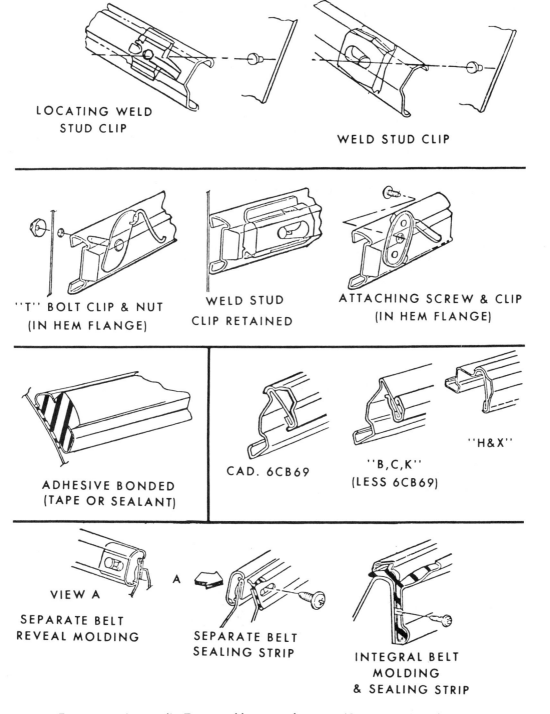

LOCATING WELD
STUD CLIP

WELD STUD CLIP

"T" BOLT CLIP & NUT
(IN HEM FLANGE)

WELD STUD
CLIP RETAINED

ATTACHING SCREW & CLIP
(IN HEM FLANGE)

ADHESIVE BONDED
(TAPE OR SEALANT)

CAD. 6CB69

"B,C,K"
(LESS 6CB69)

"H&X"

VIEW A

SEPARATE BELT
REVEAL MOLDING

A

SEPARATE BELT
SEALING STRIP

INTEGRAL BELT
MOLDING
& SEALING STRIP

Figure 3-6 *(continued)* Door molding attachments. *(Courtesy of General Motors Corporation, Fisher Body Division.)*

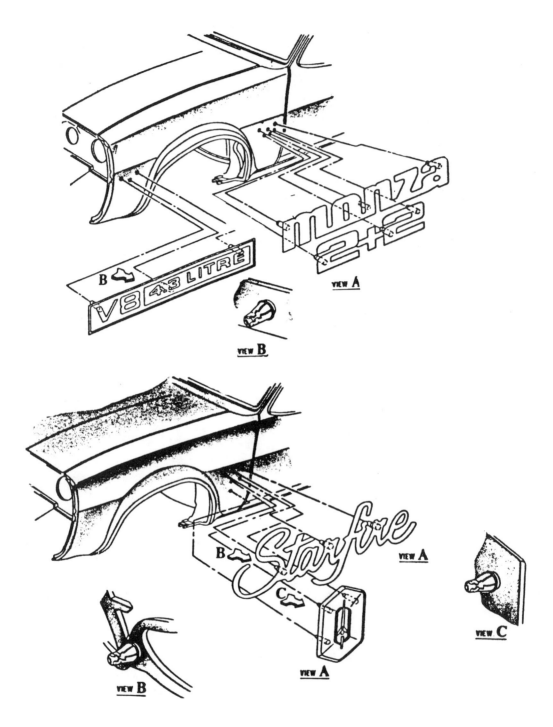

Figure 3-7 Emblem and nameplate attachments. *(Courtesy of General Motors Corporation, Fisher Body Division.)*

tion from nicks and chips or even small dents that occur in parking lots from careless drivers. Moldings are used to cover the edges of vinyl tops, for beauty, and to hold down the edges.

Moldings or trim parts are made of various materials such as aluminum, stainless steel, die castings, or plastics. These parts are chrome or silvery in appearance; some are flat black or colored to match the finish of the automobile (Figure 3-6).

The moldings are attached to the body in a variety of ways. Each automobile manufacturer uses a different method on some or the same on others. Because of the many varieties of moldings, or trim parts, it would be almost impossible to list them all or to show how each is fastened to the body.

There has been an increase in the use of adhesive-bonded moldings in the late model automobile. Some moldings only resemble the adhesive-bonded type but are held on by means of plastic clips. These clips are held on the panels by a welded stud or small sheetmetal screws. The reveal moldings around the windshield and back windows are generally held by some type clip attached to a welded stud or to small sheetmetal screws, or locked in a slot in the metal.

The name plates or letter strips are generally cast aluminum and are held on by a special clip or retainer, sometimes called a *barrel nut,* which is inserted in a hole in the metal (Figure 3-7). Some name plates or other casting with integral studs use a self-threading speed nut for attaching to the body.

Molding used on drip rails or upper door panel frames is a clinch type or self-retaining type that snaps on and is held on by tension. (See Figure 3-6 on attaching moldings.)

When it is necessary to reinstall any molding or trim part that involves a hole in the sheetmetal, sealer should be used to prevent water leaks. When straightening sheetmetal, replacing parts, or refinishing, molding or trim parts must be removed. Extreme care must be used to prevent damage to the parts when removing them. Many of the retainers are hidden by the molding or located where it is impossible to check whether the retainers are bolted, screwed, or pressed on. Attempting to pry them off will destroy them, and they will need to be replaced at the shop's expense.

If possible, check the appropriate service manual for the type of retainer used. Many trim parts require removing inner panels or loosening up fenders to gain access to the retainers. On some types, it is necessary to install the trim parts before installing the panels on the vehicle.

Removal of reveal moldings around windshields or stationary windows requires a special tool which will be described in the discussion of glass installation.

Questions

1. What is used to reduce the road vibration of the body?
2. What is a *perimeter frame?*
3. What is the purpose of using torque boxes in frames?
4. How does unitized construction differ from the conventional frame and body?
5. How are critical areas of the body strengthened?

6. What are the three major sections of an automobile?

7. What are some of the major parts in the nose section?

8. Name some of the methods used for attaching molding to the body?

9. Why is the welded stud better than the conventional screw or bolt for attaching moldings?

10. Besides appearance, what is another purpose for using side moldings?

In the body and fender trade, one of the most important pieces of equipment in the shop is the oxy-acetylene torch. With the types of body construction used in the modern automobile, welding has become very important. Although there are other methods of welding, such as the electric arc and spot welders, the oxy-acetylene torch is very useful for heating and bending metal, soldering, cutting, and for many other purposes. With the wide assortment of tips, the torch can produce sufficient heat for various thicknesses of metals (Figure 4-1). The flame of the oxy-acetylene torch can reach as high as 6300° F (3482° C). Because many repair jobs that come into body shops require oxy-acetylene welding, a good bodyman must be a good welder. It is very important for anyone entering the auto body field to become familiar with the oxy-acetylene torch and its operation.

There is much misinformation about the oxy-acetylene torch. Without proper instruction, injuries, gas explosions, and fires could result. Carelessness in handling the equipment and cylinders and failure to use precautions when working around inflammables could make the torch a very dangerous tool. However, with reasonable care and knowledge, the torch is as safe as a spray gun. Most injuries and damage are caused by man's failures rather than equipment failures.

Acetylene Welding and Cutting

chapter 4

HISTORY OF ACETYLENE AND THE OXY-ACETYLENE TORCH

The oxy-acetylene flame, the hottest flame known to man, is produced by the combustion of acetylene with oxygen. Acetylene gas was discovered by accident in 1836 and

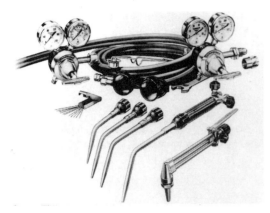

Figure 4-1 Oxy-acetylene torch and various tips. *(Courtesy of Marquette Division, Applied Power Inc.)*

was first used for illumination. Many buildings and streets used acetylene because of the brilliant light it produced. Some automobiles used acetylene gas for lights.

The oxy-acetylene process was discovered around the end of the nineteenth century in Europe. It was found that the combustion of equal parts of acetylene and oxygen produced carbon monoxide and hydrogen in the inner part of the flame. Gases that burned in the outer part of the flame (the envelope) combined with $1\frac{1}{2}$ parts of oxygen from the air to form carbon dioxide and water vapor. It was also discovered that welding metal with oxy-acetylene did not have injurious effects on the metal that was melted.

About the same time as the discovery of the oxy-acetylene flame, progress was being made to produce acetylene and oxygen on a commercial basis. Although by 1836 it was known that acetylene gas could be produced from calcium carbide, it was not until 1892, while attempting to make metallic calcium, that a means for commercially producing calcium carbide or acetylene gas

was found. The method involved fusing coke, produced from soft coal, and limestone in an electric furnace. The resulting gray stone-like material was crushed into crystals or granules. The acetylene gas was then produced by dropping calcium carbide in water to generate a chemical reaction. The bubbles that rose to the surface were acetylene gas.

The two common methods of producing oxygen are the liquifying of air and the electrolysis of water. The liquifying of air is the most commonly used process rather than the more costly electrolysis of water.

Methods for commercially producing oxygen were also developed, and this combined with improved methods of producing acetylene gas, led the way toward the rapid growth of oxy-acetylene welding and cutting.

In the early years of oxy-acetylene welding, many shops produced their own acetylene gas by means of low pressure acetylene generators, but eventually the present type acetylene cylinder became available.

NOTE: Because of the explosive nature of the gas, it must be handled cautiously.

CONSTRUCTION AND CONTENTS OF OXY-ACETYLENE CYLINDERS

The cylinders referred to in this discussion are those used in the average shop, not in large commercial firms. Because of the high pressure contained in the oxygen cylinders, they must pass the rigid requirements of the Department of Transportation (Figure 4-2).

Important information concerning the oxygen cylinder is presented in the following list:

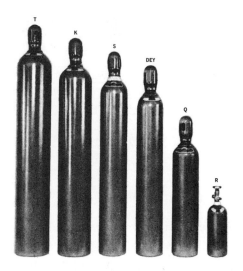

Figure 4-2 High pressure cylinders. Since gases have a relatively low density, a given volume of gas at atmospheric pressure can be considerably reduced by forcing it into a cylinder under greater pressure. Such cylinders must be strongly constructed to withstand the high pressures to which they are subjected. *(Courtesy of Linde Corporation.)*

1. Made of a seamless high-carbon steel and no less than 3/8" (9. 52 mm) thick.

2. The normal full tank of oxygen contains from 2,200 to 2,600 lbs (15,180 kPa to 17,940 kPa) per square inch depending upon the temperature and is tested periodically to over 3,300 lbs (22.770 kPa) per square inch.

3. A malleable iron neck is shrunk on at the top of the cylinder, and the tank valve is screwed into the neck.

4. The neck is threaded on the outside to permit a protective valve cap to be attached. This cap protects the valve if the cylinder is accidentally knocked over while being transported. If a valve was accidentally broken off and the cylinder pressure was about 2,000 lbs

(13,800 kPa), the very high pressure of the escaping oxygen would burn anything it came in contact with and the cylinder would be jet propelled.
NOTE: Never leave a cylinder, either empty or full, to stand by itself, without adequate support. Store in an upright position and away from heat. Always keep the cylinder valve closed, even when empty.

5. The tank valve is made of forged brass and made to withstand high pressure. It is called a *back seating* or a *double-seated valve,* which means the lower seat seals off the pressure from escaping from the cylinder.

6. The back seat or upper seat prevents oxygen from escaping around the valve threads when the valve is opened. This is why the valve must be opened all the way out when the cylinder is being used.

7. Each valve is equipped with a safety pressure disc which will burst when the pressure gets too high. This prevents a rupture of the tank.
CAUTION: Never use oil or grease on a cylinder or any part of the welding setup at any time because serious fire or explosion could result.

8. The cylinders are painted different colors, and they vary with each distributor or manufacturer (Figure 4-3).

ACETYLENE CYLINDERS

Acetylene, because of its nature, must be stored in a different type of cylinder than that used for oxygen. Acetylene cannot be stored in an open container (hollow cylinder) of over 15 lbs (103.5 kPa) per square inch, in a gaseous form, because of its

Spec'n	OXYGEN		ACETYLENE		MAPP GAS		PROPANE		NATURAL GAS	
	U.S.	Metric	U.S.	Metric	U.S.	Metric	U.S.	Metric	U.S.	Metric
Diameter	9 in.	.23 m	12 in.	.31 m	12 in.	.31 m	15 in.	.38 m	9 in.	.23 m
Height	55 in.	1.4 m	40 in.	1.02 m	44 in.	1.12 m	50 in.	1.27 m	55 in.	1.4 m
Capacity	244 cu ft	6.9 m^3	250 cu ft	7.1 m^3	600 cu ft*	17 m^{3*}	950 cu ft*	27 m^{3*}	220 cu ft	6.2 m^3
—	—	—	—	—	70 lbs*	32 kg*	115 lbs*	52 kg*		
@ Temp:	70°F	21°C	70°F	21°C	60°F	16°C	70°F	21°C	70°F	21°C
@ Pressure:	2200 psig	15,200 kPa	250 psig	1725 kPa	94 psig**	650 kPa**	125 psig	860 kPa	2200 psig	15,200 kPa

* Purchased by Weight
** Vapor pressure at 70°F or 21°C.

Figure 4-3 Cylinder data. *(Courtesy of Linde Corporation.)*

explosive nature. In order to store acetylene in a cylinder up to 250 lbs per square inch, the cylinders are filled with a porous material such as calcium silicate or wood pulp, depending on the manufacturer. Next, acetone is added and is absorbed by the porous material. Acetylene gas is then pumped into the cylinder to a pressure of about 250 lbs (1,725 kPa) per square inch (Figure 4-4). The acetone readily absorbs many times its own weight of acetylene. This method is the safest way to store acetylene. The porous material prevents pockets of acetylene gas from accumulating. The cylinders are constructed in accordance with Department of Transportation regulations.

Some cylinders have concave bottoms and two safety plugs which will melt out at around 220° F (104° C) to relieve the pressure in case of excessive heat.

Two types of valves are used for acetylene cylinders:

1. One type uses a hand wheel.
2. One type uses a square shank and key. NOTE: The key must be kept on the cylinder when it is being used to permit the valve to be closed in case of emergency.

The valves are of a simple construction because of the lower cylinder pressure as compared to the pressure in the oxygen cylinder.

1. The top of the cylinders vary with different manufacturers.
2. Some have recessed tops to protect the valve.

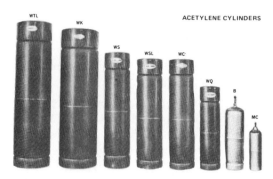

Figure 4-4 Acetylene cylinders. Acetylene is compressed into cylinders at a much lower pressure than other industrial gases. Acetylene in commercial cylinders is dissolved in acetone. At 70 degrees F and full cylinder pressure (250 psi), acetone will hold more than 400 times its own volume in dissolved acetylene. The acetylene-acetone solution is retained by a porous material that fills the cylinder interior. *(Courtesy of Linde Corporation.)*

3. Some have tops shaped like the oxygen cylinders. Acetylene cylinder outlets have left-handed threads to avoid putting on the wrong regulator.

CAUTION: Never attempt to transfer acetylene to another container.

Acetylene is sold by weight, not pressure. This is determined by weighing the cylinder after filling and subtracting the weight of the cylinder, when empty. The difference is multiplied by 14.5 cu. ft. (420.5 liters) which equals one lb (.4536 kg). Weight of empty cylinders are generally stamped on the side of the cylinder. Due to the nature of the acetylene, the gas is given off by the acetone at a slower rate at low temperatures. *Always store acetylene in an upright position* as acetone may enter the valves and gauges. Store away from heat.

Another fuel gas that can be used for welding, cutting, brazing, and heating is called MAPP gas. MAPP is a trademark of Airco, Inc. and is a mixture of stabilized methyacetylene and propadiene. The oxy-MAPP flames have a high flame temperature of 5301° F (2930° C) while the oxy-acetylene high flame temperature is approximately 6300° F (3482° C). MAPP gas can be used with the standard acetylene regulators; the cylinders have the same type threads as the acetylene cylinders. The same welding torch and cutting assemblies can be used for MAPP gas if one size larger tips are used. There are torches made especially for MAPP gas, and they are available at the MAPP distributors.

The oxy-MAPP flame is very wide and is excellent for welding of heavy plate and brazing. If fine pinpoint welding is required, acetylene is better than MAPP gas. MAPP gas will cut faster than acetylene and can be used at greater underwater depths, because of the higher available regulated pressure.

In the weight and safe-handling comparison, a filled acetylene cylinder weighs about 240 lbs (1,656 kPa) as compared to a cylinder of MAPP weighing 120 lbs (828 kPa). The acetylene cylinders are either rented (demurrage) or contracted, but the MAPP cylinders are generally customer owned.

OPERATION OF REGULATORS

In the previous discussion of cylinders, it was noted that the pressure of the oxygen cylinder is about 2,200 lbs (15,180 kPa) per square inch (psi) and the acetylene about 250 (1,725 kPa) psi. This pressure is too high to be used for welding. Therefore, some means must be used to reduce the pressure so that it is suitable for welding and also so that a constant pressure is maintained. Regulators are used to perform these two important functions.

1. The regulator will maintain a constant pressure at the torch even though the pressure of the cylinder decreases as the gas is consumed.

2. For example, with 2,200 lbs (15,180 kPa) pressure in the cylinder, 5 lbs (34.5 kPa) of oxygen needed at the torch, the pressure will remain constant.

3. After a prolonged period of welding or cutting, the cylinder pressure may drop to 400 (2,760 kPa) psi, but the torch pressure will remain at 5 lbs (34.5 kPa).

4. If a large cutting tip is used, the required pressure of oxygen may be 40 lbs (276 kPa) at the torch, but the pressure will be constant.

Regulators are high quality, sensitive instruments made for accurate regulation of pressure, but rugged enough for shop handling.

The basic operation of the *single-stage regulator* is fairly simple (Figure 4-5). By turning in the adjusting screw, pressure is applied to the spring. The spring depresses the flexible diaphragm which is connected to the valve. This opens the valve permitting the gas to flow. The pressure is regulated by the screw. The further the screw is turned, the more pressure is available at the torch. When the torch is turned off, the pressure will build up behind the regulator diaphragm, overcoming the tension of the diaphragm spring and thereby closing off the valve. The valve will remain closed until the torch valve is opened up. The two forces, the spring tension and the pressure of the gas, when balanced, provide an even flow of gas to the torch. On occasion, the

pressure will increase as indicated on the gauge after the torch has been shut off. This is caused by a worn out seat or needle or by dirt on the seat. If the pressure becomes excessive, it could rupture the diaphragm or possibly blow the bourdon tube in the gauge. This is generally called *creep*, and the regulator should not be used until repaired.

The *two-stage regulator* regulates the gas twice (Figure 4-6). In the first stage, which is preset, the oxygen pressure is reduced to about 250 to 400 (1,725 kPa to 2,760 kPa) psi. The second stage is similar to a single-stage regulator which reduces the pressure from 250 to 400 (1,725 kPa to 2,760 kPa) psi to the desired working pressure. In the acetylene, the preset stage first reduces the pressure to about 50 to 75 (34.5 kPa to 517.5 kPa) psi. All acetylene regulator hose connectors are left-handed and the oxygen connectors are right-handed.

Hoses are used to carry the gases from the regulator to the torch. Hoses must be of special construction to withstand pressure and to take abuse and of a material not affected by either the oxygen or acetylene gas. Hoses are made in three layers:

1. A high-quality gum rubber inner liner.
2. Two layers of strong fabric covering.
3. A tough rubber outer covering.

The oxygen and acetylene hose are fastened together by vulcanizing or with clips to avoid tangling. Most acetylene hoses are colored red with left-handed grooved ferrules or nuts. All acetylene fittings or ferrules are knotched or grooved to indicate gas. The oxygen hoses are either green or black and have right-handed ferrules or nuts (Figure 4-7). An acetylene hose must never be used for oxygen as a combustible

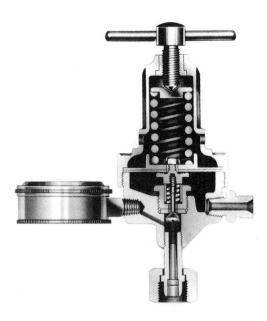

Figure 4-5 Single-stage regulator. *(Courtesy of Linde Corporation.)*

Figure 4-6 Two-stage regulator. *(Courtesy of Linde Corporation.)*

mixture could result. Avoid dropping sharp objects or hot metal on the hose. A rupture in the hose could cause fires. Kinking of the hose will hinder the flow of gases.

Hoses are made in several sizes, inside diameter (ID) $3/16''$, $1/4''$, and $5/16''$ (4.76 mm, 6.35 mm, 7.93 mm). The hoses are made up in various lengths. Never repair a broken line with a piece of copper tubing as it could cause a chemical reaction.

Safety Check Valves

A device that must be included with all oxygen and acetylene equipment is a backfire device called a *safety check valve*. This device permits gas to flow to the torch but not from the torch (called backfires). This device will reduce the danger to the torch, hoses, and regulators. It is either attached to the torch or to the regulators.

CONSTRUCTION AND OPERATION OF THE TORCH

The torch, a precision-engineered piece of equipment, is sometimes considered the most important part of the welding equipment because it directs the flame. In the torch, the oxygen and acetylene gases are

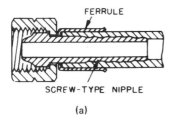

(a)

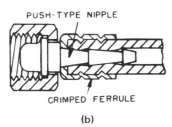

(b)

Figure 4-7 (a) Screw-type nipple and ferrule; (b) push-type nipple and crimped ferrule. *(Courtesy of Linde Corporation.)*

Figure 4-8 Reverse flow check valves. *(Courtesy of Linde Corporation.)*

mixed in the proper proportions. The mixture is burned at the end of the tip, and the operator can direct the flame to the work. The torch is divided into four parts:

1. Body—serves as a handle.
2. Valves—to control the amount of gases desired.
3. Mixing head or chamber—where the gases are mixed in proper proportions.
4. Tip—where the combustion takes place.

The torches are made of several different types of material such as brass, aluminum, and others. Size and capacities vary from small torches for welding sheetmetal or soldering to large ones used where great amounts of heat are necessary as in cutting heavy steel. Most body shops use either the small or medium size torches. The smaller the torch, the easier it is to handle in restricted areas.

There are two types of torches, the *injector* and *mixer* (equal pressure) type. The injector type has the acetylene at low pressure. The acetylene is carried through the torch by the higher pressure oxygen flowing from a jet (or venturi). The equal pressure has the gases pass through the torch at equal pressure and with enough pressure to force the gas through the mixing chamber (Figure 4-9).

All torches are equipped with a pair of needle or ball bearing–type valves which serve two purposes.

1. To turn the gases on or shut them off.
2. To make the proper adjustment to obtain the desired flame.

Care must be taken when shutting off the gas to ensure that the valve is not closed too tight. Otherwise damage to the valve needle or bearing and seat could result.

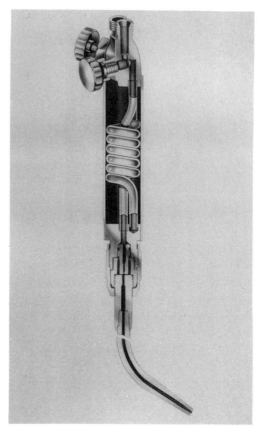

Figure 4-9 Mixer-type torch. *(Courtesy of Linde Corporation.)*

Sometimes, an operator may experience difficulty in holding the proper flame adjustment. If faulty gauges are not the cause and if the connections are tight, loose packing seal nuts are the problem. If the valve moves freely, slowly tighten the packing seal nut under the valve knob until there is a slight drag or stiffness. Occasionally, the seal nuts are too tight and it is difficult to turn the torch on. This can be remedied by backing off slightly on the seal nut.

Mixing Chamber

Some torches have the mixing chamber in the torch. Others have the mixing chamber combined with the tip and head assembly (Figure 4-10). Each time the tip is changed, the mixing chamber is changed also. This permits the mixing chamber to supply a sufficient amount of mixed gases for a certain size tip. Each mixing chamber is drilled with holes (or orifices) to match the size tip to be used. The tip size is stamped on the sides of the mixing chamber (either numbers or letters are

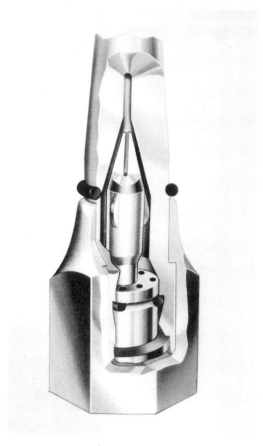

Figure 4-10 Mixing body. *(Courtesy of Linde Corporation.)*

used). The holes must not be altered or enlarged as they are precision drilled to permit the proper amount of gases to pass through.

Tips or Tubes

Tips or tubes are either permanently soldered or removable from the mixing head or chamber. They are made of copper and are rather soft. They are available in various sizes and are numbered or lettered according to the manufacturer (Figure 4-11). Tips are calibrated to permit a certain amount of mixing gases to pass through at a given pressure for a given length of time. Normally, the lower the number, the smaller the tip, but some are marked as to the size of the tip opening. Never attempt to enlarge the hole or orifice in the tip. If clogged, use a proper tip cleaner. The tip is soft, so handle it with care. Avoid dropping or using it as a pry bar or hammer.

Welding Goggles

The welder must wear some type of protective device to shield his eyes when welding, brazing, and cutting with a torch (Figure 4-12). The welding flame produces light and heat rays that can damage the eye tissue, and continued exposure will result in the loss of sight. Sparks and molten metal fly from the weld or cutting area and can cause painful eye injury. Brazing, although performed at a lower temperature, gives off harmful rays from the flame and the molten flux. Various protective devices are available: the goggle type, eye shields with 2″ x 4″ (51 mm x 102 mm) lenses that can be used with eyeglasses, or the full face shield. The full face shield is recommended

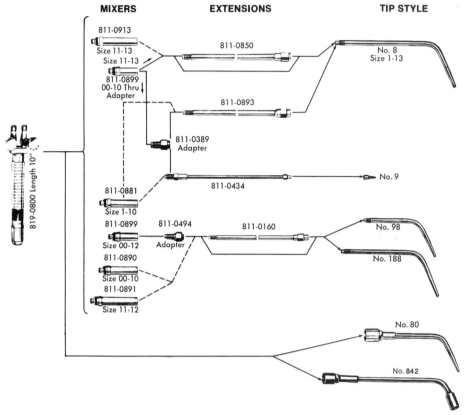

MIXERS

811-0913
Size 11-13
Size 11-13

811-0899
00-10 Thru
Adapter

811-0881
Size 1-10

811-0899
Size 00-12

811-0890
Size 00-10

811-0891
Size 11-12

819-0800 Length 10"

EXTENSIONS

811-0850

811-0893

811-0389
Adapter

811-0434

811-0494
Adapter

811-0160

TIP STYLE

No. 8
Size 1-13

No. 9

No. 98

No. 188

No. 80

No. 842

Figure 4-11 Tip—Mixer—Extension Guide. *(Courtesy of Airco.)*

**WHICH WELDING LENS/PLATE
SHADE TO USE
GAS TORCH CUTTING AND WELDING**

SHADE NO.	APPLICATIONS
2	SOLDERING
3 or 4	BRAZING
	CUTTING
3 or 4	Light/ up to 1"
4 or 5	Medium — 1" to 6"
5 or 6	Heavy — over 6"
	WELDING
4 or 5	Light — up to 1/8"
5 or 6	Medium — 1/8" to 1/2"
6 or 8	Heavy — over 1/2"

Figure 4-12 Protective eye devices used when cutting and welding. *(Courtesy of Linde Corporation.)*

for cutting and welding overhead to protect the face from flying sparks and metal. For most welding and cutting, lenses with a shade number from 5 to 6 are recommended. For welding and cutting heavy metal, shades numbered from 6 to 8 are recommended. Clear plastic lenses should be inserted in front of the welding lenses to prevent them from being damaged by flying sparks and molten metal. If welding lenses become severely chipped, the degree of protection will decrease.

Many welders wear eyeglasses, and the welding glasses hinder the line of sight, especially if the eyeglasses are bifocal. An equipment manufacturer has produced magnifiers that fit into the eye shield–type goggles. They are available in various strengths. Consult the local distributors for additional information.

Setting up the Torch

Securely fasten the oxygen and acetylene tanks in a welding cart or fasten to a sturdy wall or vertical column with chains, straps, or other mechanical means. Remove caps from tanks and crack open tank valves to clean out any dirt (Figure 4–13). Check

Crack the cylinder valve of the oxygen and fuel gas cylinders by opening each valve for an instant to blow dirt out of the nozzles. Do not stand in front of the valves when opening.

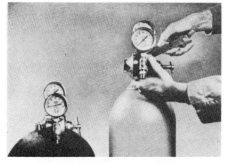

Attach a regulator for the fuel gas in use to the fuel gas cylinder and an oxygen regulator to the oxygen cylinder. Screw the nuts up tight with a close-fitting wrench.

Connect the black or green hose to the oxygen regulator and the red hose to the fuel gas regulator. Screw the nuts up tightly.

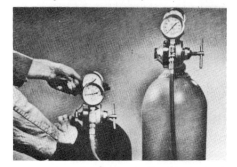

Bleed gas from the regulators by turning in then turning out regulator screws fully. After gas has been bled from regulators, slowly open cylinder valves.

Figure 4–13 Procedure for setting up the torch. *(Courtesy of Airco Welding.)*

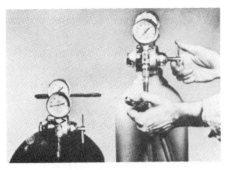

Hold thumb tightly over end of hose and adjust regulator to 1 psi. Release and replace thumb several times to cause short bursts of gas. Release regulator screw.

Connect the black or green oxygen hose to the needle valve stamped OX and the red fuel gas hose to the needle valve stamped AC or FUEL.

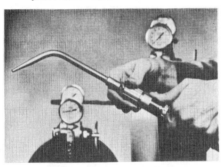

Slip tip-nut over mixing head, screw tip into mixing head and then screw tip-nut into torch handle. Hand tightening is all that is necessary.

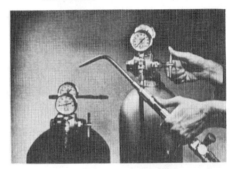

Adjust the pressure and purge the lines by opening the torch needle valves and adjusting the regulator screws for desired working pressure one at a time. TEST FOR LEAKS.

Figure 4-13 *(continued)*

tank outlet for damaged threads or chipped outlet seat. Use the wrench provided with the torch or use correct size wrenches. Do not use pliers, vise-grips, or pipe wrenches as they damage the soft metal fittings. After inspecting the regulator coupling, attach the proper regulator and tighten. With the regulator screw turned out, slowly open the tanks and check for leaks. Use soap suds and water for checking leaks. Attach the safety check valve on the regulator, if available. Inspect the hoses and coupling for damage. Attach the proper ones on the regulator (red on acetylene, green or black on oxygen) and tighten. Inspect the torch connection, attach to the

carrier hose, and tighten. With torch valves closed, slowly open the tank valve, turn in the regulator screws, and check for leaks with soap suds. With the proper tip installed, the torch is ready for use.

Another method of checking for leaks is to shut off the tank or cylinder valve with the torch valves closed. A drop in pressure or change in the gauge readings indicates a leak in the system. Then check further with soap suds.

How to Light a Torch

To light a torch the following steps are suggested:

1. Open the oxygen tank valve all the way, *slowly.* Do not stand facing the gauge, stand to one side, in case the diaphragm ruptures.

2. Turn the regulator screw in so the gauge reads about 5 lbs (3.5 kPa)

3. Open the torch valve to fill lines and shut off the torch valve.

4. Slowly open the acetylene valve $\frac{1}{4}$ turn. In case of fire, it is easier to shut off the tank.

5. Turn the regulator screw in so gauge reads about 5 lbs (34.5 kPa).

6. Open the torch valve to fill lines and shut off torch valve.

7. Put on welding goggles.

8. Crack open the oxygen torch valve and open the acetylene torch valve about $\frac{1}{2}$ turn.

9. Light the torch with flint lighter or striker (Figure 4–14). Do not use matches or cigarette lighters as burned fingers could result.

10. Open acetylene more until the flame starts to leave the tip, back off slightly. Open oxygen more until the desired flame is reached.

11. Turn off the acetylene torch valve first, then the oxygen valve. The purpose of the acetylene first is to avoid black smoke and to permit the oxygen to clean the torch of carbon. Also, the acetylene gas is very explosive.

Some welders may not agree with this procedure. For example, some may not understand the purpose of cracking the oxygen valve before opening the acetylene torch valve. But by following this procedure the carbon particles in the air will be eliminated when the torch is lit. After finishing welding, the following procedures should be followed:

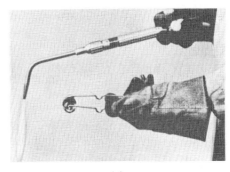

(a)

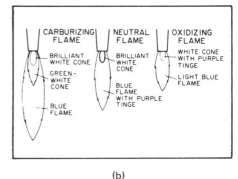

(b)

Figure 4–14 (a) Open the fuel gas needle valve and light the fuel gas with the sparklighter; (b) open and adjust oxygen needle valve for neutral flame. *(Courtesy of Airco Welding.)*

1. Close the acetylene tank valve.

2. Open the acetylene torch valve and drain lines.

3. Shut off the torch valve and relieve the regulator spring.

4. Close the oxygen tank valve.

5. Open the oxygen tank valve and drain line.

6. Shut off the torch valve and relieve the regulator spring.

7. Hang the hoses on cart or wall brackets. Keep hoses off floor and away from wheels.

SELECTION OF WELDING TIPS

The selection of welding tips is very important in body and fender work. Most of the welding is done on about 20–22 gauge sheetmetal. Much care must be exercised in welding to prevent burning holes in the metal. The orifice size (or size of the hole in the tip) determines the amount of acetylene and oxygen fed to the flame; therefore, the orifice determines the amount of heat produced by the torch. If the tip orifice is too small, not enough heat will be produced for the proper flow of the molten metal. If the orifice is too large, too much heat will be produced, and this will result in poor welds with excessive penetration. Occasionally, a certain size tip heats the metal to the melting point, but does not actually melt the metal or sustain the puddle. When this occurs, the welder must remember that the torch tip must be large enough to heat the metal but also to supply latent heat or heat of fusion. *Latent heat* is the amount of additional heat required to change a given object from a solid to a liquid

after the melting point is reached. One indication of a tip too small for a given job is the length of time needed to establish a molten spot or puddle. If too much time is needed, the tip is too small.

Each manufacturer of torches will state different pressure for a similar size tip. For welding 20-gauge sheetmetal, 5 lbs (34.5 kPa) of acetylene and 5 lbs to 7 lbs (34.5 kPa to 48.3 kPa) of oxygen will generally do the job. A number 0 tip from one torch is about the same as a number 2 tip of another torch. The heavier the metal, the more intense is the heat required. Experienced welders will have few problems in selecting tips. If you are not sure, consult the torch manufacturer for the correct tip and pressure. Table 4–1 lists several examples of tip size recommended for various thicknesses of metal (sheetmetal).

THE OXY-ACETYLENE FLAME

The oxy-acetylene flame does the work of the oxy-acetylene equipment. The flame has sometimes been called "the master of metals." The sole purpose of various parts of the welding equipment is to serve the flame by supplying the proper amounts of gases to the flame. The operator of the torch has full control as to efficiency, size, and quality of flame. Adjustment of the

Table 4–1 Tip Size Recommended for Various Thicknesses of Metal

Torch Manufacturing	20 ga	1/16"	1/8"	3/16"	1/4"
Airco	0	1	3	4	5
Smith	B60	B61	B63	B64	B65
Purox	4	6	12	15	20
Linde	2	3,4	5	7	8

*These tips average from 5 to 7 psi for acetlyene and oxygen (gauge reading).

flame can mean the welder's success or failure. Improper adjustment can destroy the metal characteristics.

Types of Flames

There are three types of flames, depending on the ratio of acetylene and oxygen (Figure 4-15). *Neutral flame* consists of approximately equal parts of acetylene and oxygen combined in the inner cone to produce a flame of about 5700° F (3154° C). It is called neutral because it does not have any chemical effect on the molten steel; it does not add or take anything from it. The inner cone of the flame is a light blue. This is surrounded by an outer envelope of

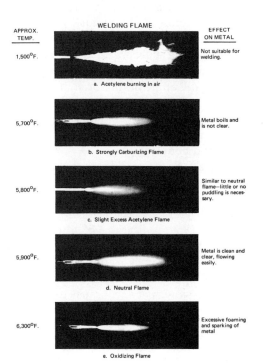

APPROX. TEMP.	WELDING FLAME	EFFECT ON METAL
1,500°F.	a. Acetylene burning in air	Not suitable for welding.
5,700°F.	b. Strongly Carburizing Flame	Metal boils and is not clear.
5,800°F.	c. Slight Excess Acetylene Flame	Similar to neutral flame—little or no puddling is necessary.
5,900°F.	d. Neutral Flame	Metal is clean and clear, flowing easily.
6,300°F.	e. Oxidizing Flame	Excessive foaming and sparking of metal

Figure 4-15 Types of welding flames. *(Courtesy of Airco Welding.)*

medium or darker blue. This outer envelope protects the molten steel from contamination by oxygen and other gases in the atmosphere. The neutral flame is used the majority of the time when welding mild steel.

The *carburizing or reducing flame* is one with an excessive amount of acetylene. This flame will cause a feather of pale blue extending from the inner cone. When welding with a carburizing flame, the excess carbon will combine with the molten metal, producing a very hard and brittle weld. The more acetylene that is added to the flame, the longer the outer envelope becomes. A carburizing flame with a long envelope is used when body solder is applied. Sometimes this is termed a *soft flame* because there is a great reduction in heat and a less concentrated flame. Some authorities recommend the carburizing flame for brazing or hard soldering; others disagree and use a neutral flame for brazing.

The *oxidizing flame* is produced by excessive oxygen in the flame. The inner cone is smaller and sharper. The outer envelope is shorter and produces a hissing sound. The flame is undesirable for welding because it has a tendency to oxidize the steel. This produces a noticeable foaming of the weld and a weld that is very weak. This flame can reach as high as 6300° F (3482° C), and with high heat the oxygen combines readily with other metals.

Chemistry of the Oxy-Acetylene Flame

In the oxy-acetylene neutral flame, the combustion of the acetylene and oxygen forms carbon monoxide. The carbon monoxide combines with the oxygen in the atmosphere to form carbon dioxide and water vapor. It may be noted that when welding in a very confined area, a torch may go out. This is caused by lack of oxygen in the area.

WELDING PROCEDURES— STEEL

After a person has become familiar with the welding equipment, including the practice of lighting the torch and adjusting the flame, the next step is welding. The oxygen-acetylene steel welding process is a method of joining or fusing metal by heating the metal to the melting point so that it will flow together or fuse. A good weld depends on several factors, including the proper selection of a tip, proper torch adjustment, correct movement of the torch, and correct speed. The most important thing in becoming a good welder and making strong welds is *practice*. Too many beginners feel that practice is boring and do not realize that it takes time to master the proper technique of moving the torch, making puddles, or running beads with filler rods.

Most welding books or articles show welding being done on flat surfaces and on clean metal. In the actual field, a welder cannot always hold the torch at a 40° to 60° angle and cannot follow many other procedures. A good bodyman is expected to weld in any position, in confined places, and on sheetmetal that is rusty or painted. This is why most practice welding should be done on old panels, and clean metal should be used only in the beginning.

Most of the welding performed by a bodyman is on auto body sheetmetal which is approximately 20–22 gauge metal, less than 1/16" (1.58 mm) thick. This is very thin metal and is more difficult to weld than heavier metal because of the danger of burning a hold through it or warping it with high heat. When starting to practice, the first step is to make puddles. This is called *puddling*. A puddle is a small spot of molten metal.

To puddle, light the torch and adjust it to a neutral flame. Hold the torch tip so that the inner cone is approximately 1/8" 3.175 mm from the metal. Hold the tip at a 45° to 60° angle in line with the direction of travel at the beginning. Hold the torch flame in one spot until a pool of molten metal forms—about 3/16" to 1/4" (4.76 mm to 6.35 mm) in diameter in light metal). Then move the puddle forward at an even speed in order to maintain a uniform width. A circular or weaving back and forth motion can be used. One of the objects in puddling is to move forward in a straight line. Observe the penetration of the puddle. If it is too deep, several things can be done to correct it: increase the speed, readjust the flame by decreasing the oxygen and acetylene, or decrease the angle of the torch. If penetration is too little, reverse one or more of these. Make four to five puddles the length of the metal. Observe the results, note width and penetration.

Look at the underside of the metal to check penetration. Use several pieces of metal until you have complete control of the torch and can produce even, straight puddles. One indication of the correct speed will be a puddle about 1/4" (6.35 mm) wide with even, half-round ripples. If the ripples are pointed, too much speed is being used. Too slow speed will cause extra wide puddles and excessive penetration. Vary the torch angle and note the results.

Fusion Welds

Another form of puddling is to make a butt joint, which is joining two pieces of sheetmetal placed end to end. Using the same technique as in puddling, with a round or weaving motion, melt both edges of the metal so that they flow together. Care must be exercised not to burn the edges through. Another exercise is to place two pieces of sheetmetal parallel with each other and fuse the edges together. Proper torch technique is important so that you do not melt the edges too much. The fusion weld should be even. Once again, the key to mastering the torch is *practice.*

Welds Made Using Filler Rod

After practicing running puddles and gaining torch control, the next step is adding filler rod to the puddle to form a bead. Filler or welding rod is used to add additional strength to metal where the weld is. It is also used when two pieces of metal do not fit closely together or in places where fusion welds cannot be performed. Filler rods are made in various sizes from $\frac{1}{16}$" (1.58 mm) for light metal to $\frac{1}{4}$" (6.35 mm) for heavy plate steel. They are generally made in 36" (914 mm) lengths. For general-purpose welding, the AWS number RG45 rod is used. This rod is copper coated and contains sufficient amounts of silicon and manganese to remove impurities from the molten metal. The AWS RG60 bare rod can also be used, but it will rust when exposed to moisture.

CAUTION: Always bend one end of the welding rod to avoid picking up the hot end and to avoid poking someone's eye out.

Selection of the proper size rod is very important in order to obtain a satisfactory weld. A filler rod that is too small will create problems. It will be difficult to control the puddle or to add enough filler rod to the puddle to make a good weld. On the other hand, if the rod is too large, it will cool down the puddle and the weld bead will lack proper penetration, which will make it higher than necessary. A good weld or bead should have good fusion (if welding on a flat surface). With the use of filler rod, proper coordination or manipulation between the torch and the filler rod is necessary.

The method of using filler rod is very similar to the puddling technique. Light the torch and adjust it to a neutral flame. Heat a spot to form a puddle, then place the rod into the puddle. Do not melt the rod with torch flames. Add just enough rod to form a slight convex or raised bead. Move the puddle forward, adding rod at a consistent rate. If the weld becomes too high, it means too much rod has been added. Also, the excess rod may have cooled the puddle too much. If the bead is too low, more rod should be added. Some beginners have a tendency to melt the rod with the torch rather than in the puddle. This generally results in poor penetration and poor looking welds. Run several beads. Check the height of the beads and the consistency of the width of the bead. As mentioned before, when making puddles, the ripples in the bead will give an indication of speed. Correct speed will result in even, half-round ripples with slightly convex beads and good penetration. If the speed is too fast, the ripples will be pointed, the bead will be higher than normal, and there will be poor penetration. If the speed is too slow, the bead will be lower than normal and there will be too much penetration and width.

Welding Joints

Most oxygen-acetylene welding involves joining panels. Some of the panels involved are called *butt, lap, and inside* or *outside corner.* These joints have to be made in various positions and on different sections of the body, such as lower body panels and vertical welds inside of door openings. Therefore, it is very important that a beginner practice these various joints on the same type of metal used on cars today. Some authorities recommend using clean metal for the first few joints, but then practicing on pieces cut from old panels.

Butt Joints

One very common type of joint is the *butt joint* (Figure 4–16). Because the sheetmetal is very thin, distortion from heat is a common problem. When practicing, the conditions are usually ideal—clean metal, proper gap, and welding on a bench. When doing the actual job which may involve, for example, splicing a rocker panel, the gaps between the two panels may be unequal and not ideal. This is where the previous practice and torch control will play a large part in the success of the welding operation. Also, the proper torch angle will be hard to maintain. When making any butt joint, a gap of at least $\frac{1}{16}$" (1.58 mm) should be present before welding to avoid any warping from the expansion of the metal.

(a)   (b)

Figure 4–16   (a) Butt weld; (b) lap weld. *(Photo by S. Suydam.)*

Position the metal together using either of two methods. The first is an equal gap of about $\frac{1}{16}$" (1.58 mm) and the second is a tapered gap, with one end closed and the other about $\frac{1}{8}$" (3.17 mm) apart. When using an equal gap, tack weld both ends and then tack weld about every 2" (50.8 mm). Then procede to weld the joint. When using a tapered gap, start from the closed end. Use vise grips to hold metal in position. The torch should melt both edges of the two pieces of metal evenly and the rod should be added at a uniform rate. After completing the weld, observe the bead and penetration.

When welding panels, it may be advisable to weld about 1" (25.4 mm), skip 2" (50.8 mm), and then weld 1" (25.4 mm). Another method is to quench the metal with cool water when it has changed from red to black. This will prevent the heat from expanding the surrounding panel. If the panel is miscut and there is an extra wide gap, several beads may be necessary to fill the gap.

Lap Joints

The *lap joint* is the most common joint used in the manufacture of cars (Figure 4–16). The lap joint is perhaps more difficult to weld because of the difference in the surface area of the two pieces of metal to be welded. The edge of the top piece requires less heat than the bottom one. Beginners have a tendency to apply insufficient heat to the bottom piece to form the puddle. The results are a good looking bead on the top piece with no fusion to the bottom one.

Many of the modern day automobiles have a heavy gauge rocker panel which serves as a frame, but the quarter panel which attaches to it is of much lighter gauge metal. This same situation is found in many areas of the unibuilt body where light and heavy gauge metal are welded together. Therefore, more heat must be applied to the heavier metal to form the needed puddle before too much heat is applied to the thinner gauge metal. This will prevent the lighter metal from melting away.

The torch should be aimed directly at the heavier gauge metal; the lighter metal will also heat up to the puddle stage. If the flame is directed toward the joint, the lighter gauge will melt away, but the heavier piece will be too cool to puddle.

In many cases involving lap joints on panels, the upper or lower pieces may separate due to expansion from the heat. Some bodymen use draw rivets or sheetmetal screws to hold the metal together before welding. (If force is used to hold the two edges together, the panel can be easily distorted.) Also, the bodyman should make welds of 1″ (25.4 mm), skip 2″ (50. 8 mm), and then cool the weld with water. This will help to eliminate distortion. Placing wet asbestos or cloths along the edge of the joint will keep the heat from traveling out into the surrounding areas of the panel. Once the panel is welded the full length, go back and weld in between the welds. When welding a panel, it is not advisable to weld a continuous bead the full length of the joint as severe warping could result.

T Weld or Fillet Weld

Another type of weld joint frequently performed is the *T-joint weld* or *fillet weld* (Figure 4-17). This weld is sometimes called the *inside corner weld.* Some of the precautions mentioned in lap welding also apply to the T-joint. The bottom plate will require more heat for forming a puddle than the vertical one. If too much heat is applied to the vertical piece, it will melt away before

(a)   (b)

Figure 4-17 (a) T-weld or fillet weld — also called inside corner weld; (b) outside corner or edge weld — a fusion weld without the use of a filler rod. *(Photo by S. Suydam.)*

the bottom one is hot enough. It is very important to establish a puddle on the lower piece before adding the filler rod. Otherwise, there will be little or no fusion. Add the filler rod near the vertical piece and tip the torch slightly toward it. The puddle will form on the vertical piece, and the filler rod will fuse to it. As the bead advances, be careful not to undercut the vertical piece. This can be avoided by adding the filler rod to the bead nearest the vertical piece. A slight weaving motion of the torch from the bottom to the top piece and back again, with a slight pause on the bottom, will aid in the proper formation of the bead. If a hole in the vertical piece should appear, immediately fill it with filler rod and move the torch back and forth to keep the hole from getting any larger.

On many occasions, a situation may arise where the vertical piece is heavier than the flat or horizontal one. Here, the technique will vary; that is, more heat is required to form the puddle on the vertical piece than on the flat one. Tip the torch toward the vertical piece to avoid melting a hole in the flat piece. With practice and experience, the different situations that arise will cause fewer problems.

Repairing a bicycle frame or welding a piece of vertical pipe to a flat piece of metal will present a little variation in technique because the bead will be circular rather than straight. The proper torch angle should be maintained with the constant change around the circle.

NOTE: Welding in corners may result in improper torch flame action caused by the lack of sufficient oxygen in the corner, sometimes called *spitting*. Increasing the oxygen slightly will sometimes eliminate the problem, but when the corner welding is complete, the oxygen must be reset or else oxidation of the future welds could cause problems.

Welding Sheetmetal—Vertical, Horizontal, and Overhead Positions

During the previous discussion of butt, fillet, and lap weld joints, the position of the welded area was frequently mentioned. Unfortunately, many of the areas to be welded on an automobile are either in a vertical, horizontal, or overhead position. But if a welder has mastered the proper joint welding techniques, welding out of position will not create serious problems. However, there are a few points that should be remembered.

Gravity will have a tendency to force the molten steel to run down. When welding out of position, keep the molten puddle to a smaller size than when welding on a flat surface. The proper penetration and rod will help to control the size of the puddle. A low heat setting on the torch or one size smaller tip may be necessary to control the size of the puddle while maintaining the proper penetration.

In vertical welding, welding downward will cause problems because the molten metal will try to run ahead of the puddle. Also, a vertical down bead will generally be smaller in size. Vertical welding up beads are generally a little wider in size and sometimes become too large because the molten metal will try to run back over the bead. Both up and down vertical welds will become easier with practice.

When welding horizontally, the molten metal will have a tendency to run down, overlapping the lower edge of the joint, but will lack the proper penetration and fusion. Keeping a smaller puddle and pointing the torch tip a little bit upward will help to keep the metal in place. Also, using the next size heavier welding tip and adding the rod to the upper edge of the puddle will help to keep the molten metal in place.

CAUTION: When welding out of position, be careful of falling molten metal or sparks, especially when the situation requires the welder to lay on a creeper to do the necessary repair work. Remove all loose dirt, rust, and undercoating in the weld area to avoid being burned.

Overhead welding requires a smaller puddle yet one large enough to get the desired penetration and fusion. This can be done by reducing the size of the welding flame or using the next size smaller welding tip. Using a little larger welding rod will help to keep the molten metal in place. Many welders are afraid of welding overhead but with a little care, it is a pretty safe operation.

CAUTION: Never position yourself directly beneath the welding area if the situation demands that the welder lay on a creeper while making repairs. Move off to one side and avoid having the arm underneath the area. Remove as much loose dirt, rust, or undercoating as possible. Sparks and molten metal will fall and could cause serious burns. Bend the welding rod in the middle at right angles to bring the hand holding the rod out of the way of falling metal and sparks. Gloves should be worn if possible and a full face shield rather than goggles.

BRAZING

Brazing is another method of joining metal together. It is very popular in the automotive trade and is used widely for repair work in many areas. Some of the reasons for its popularity and widespread use are the ease with which the process can be performed, especially by beginners; the relative high strength of most of the joints; and the much lower temperature required as compared to steel welding. However, many repair jobs are ruined or fail because of the improper use of brazing materials.

Brazing is defined as a group of welding processes where adhesion is produced by heating the metal to a suitable temperature —above 800° F (426° C)—and adding a nonferrous filler which has a melting temperature below that of the base metal. (*Nonferrous* means any metal that does not contain iron and steel.) The molten filler rod is distributed by capillary action between the closely fitted surfaces of the joint.

Brazing is considered hard solder or solder that is applied with a torch. Normally, when brazing is mentioned, it generally means the use of brass or bronze filler metal. But, in the same category, is silver solder, some aluminum soldering processes, phos-copper, and many more.

Under the proper conditions, adhesion between the molten filler metal and the base metal, together with surface tension of the molten filler, causes the filler metal

to be distributed between the two closely fitted surfaces of the joint to be brazed. This process is very similar to that of soldering copper pipes with wire solder. The wire solder melts at approximately 400° F (204° C), and the copper melts at 1100° F (593° C).

One error that many welders make is to use the expression "bronze rod (copper and tin)," when talking about brazing; they really mean "brass rod," which is copper and zinc.

Another common error occurs when a particular repair job, for example, joining two pieces of heavy metal together, is referred to as brazing when it is really *braze welding.* (One of the most common cast-iron jobs involves beveling the broken or cracked edges and filling the affected areas with brass.) In braze welding the filler metal is not distributed by capillary action. The process involves a groove, slot fillet, or plug weld which is made by using a nonferrous filler metal having a melting point below that of the base metal but over 800° F to 900° F (426° C to 481° C).

In either case, brazing or braze welding, the base metal is not melted but brought up to a tinning temperature. If the base metal is permitted to melt, it will mix with the filler metal causing a weak spot. Also, because the temperature far exceeds the normal brazing temperature, applying the brass rod to the surface will cause a flareup. This is caused by the decomposition of the zinc, noticeable by a trace of white powder in the area. This is the same white powder found when brazing or cutting galvanized steel.

Most brazed joints, when properly brazed, are very strong. In some cases they are as strong as steel-welded joints. The weakest joint in the brazing process is the butt joint and should be avoided because of its frequent failure. To correct a broken brazed joint requires the complete removal of the brass deposited on the base metal in order to reweld it with steel filler rod. Many inexperienced welders have made this mistake when trying to repair old type fenders where cracks were caused by stress or vibrations.

When working with sheetmetal on car bodies, heat can cause problems such as warping because of the large surface area of the body panels and the thinness of the metal. This is why many bodymen prefer the brazing method over the steel welding method. That is, most of the brazing performed by the bodyman is actually braze welding. Installing repair panels or patches with poor fitup, for example, can be easily brazed.

Brazing Rods for General Body Work or Repairs

There are many different types of brazing rods available. The most common is the brass rod containing copper and zinc with approximately 70 percent copper and 30 percent zinc. This ratio will vary considerably according to the strength of the joint desired and where temperature is a critical factor. Also, brazing rods can contain small amounts of tin, manganese, iron, lead, or silver. Lower melting temperatures can be obtained by adding tin and silver.

Brass and bronze are available either plain or flux covered and common sizes are from $\frac{1}{16}''$ (1.58 mm) to $\frac{1}{8}''$ (3.17 mm) and larger. Lengths of either 18″ or 36″ (457.2 mm or 914.4 mm) are also available.

Brazing Flux

When steel welding, the base metal and the rod are melted and fused together.

During the brazing process, the base metal is not melted, and the brass will not adhere to the surface without the addition of a cleaning compound. A flux is needed to promote adhesion, to prevent oxides from forming while the metal is heated, and to permit the filler material to flow or wet the surface of the metal. The molten flux will also carry away impurities and prevent them from becoming imbedded in the brazed metal. Most of the popular fluxes contain borax or boric acid with small amounts of other chemicals such as bromides, fluorine, chlorine, and other compounds. Common household borax can be used for brazing but does not have as good a cleaning action as the regular flux. Brazing fluxes are made for different types of metals (for example, one for general repairs on steel or iron, one for cast iron, one for copper or brass).

CAUTION: Some fluxes will give off very toxic fumes when heated. Use them in a well-ventilated place. When removing flux residue, wear safety glasses as the residue will cause eye infection or damage.

There are various opinions as to what type flame should be used for general-purpose brazing. Some favor a reducing or carburizing flame, others favor a neutral flame or a slightly oxidizing flame.

The following discussion of brazing procedures will focus on body work and working with 20- to 22-gauge sheetmetal. Many of the brazing operations will not be under ideal conditions. Most of the metal being brazed will be covered with paint, rust, undercoating, galvanizing, and other materials. This makes brazing very difficult. Also, at times it is too expensive to remove all of the material covering the metal that is to be brazed. But as much as possible should be removed by wire brushing, grinding, or scraping.

The sooner beginners practice brazing

under these difficult conditions the better. At first, they can use clean bare metal to learn the proper procedures and to see the results. After this, the practice should be on old panel sections that have small traces of paint, rust, or other materials. This will show that it is impossible to remove all foreign material on the actual job.

Select the piece of sheetmetal and light the torch. Adjust the torch to a neutral flame. Bend over one end of the brazing rod for safety. Gently heat the end of the brazing rod and dip it into the can of flux. Notice that the flux will cling to the heated rod. Heat the metal to a dull red. Place the end of the rod on the heated area and melt off some flux. Immediately melt a small amont of rod. Note whether the brass flows freely on the surface, if the metal is clean, and if the proper temperature has been reached. Add additional rod in order to build up a bead and advance the torch to make a bead. Notice how the molten flux will run ahead of the bead. Add additional flux to the rod when the molten flux no longer precedes the bead. By proper torch manipulation, the bead will resemble that of steel welding as to contour and ripples. The width of the bead can be increased by adding more or using a heavier rod or by an oval or weaving torch motion. If the bead is too high and the edges of the bead curve inward, the cause is either not enough heat or not enough flux to properly clean the metal. Run several beads across the metal and check for uniformity in width (about 1/4" [6.35 mm] wide), in height (1/16" [1.58 mm], and in ripples. Next, try a dirty piece of metal without flux and notice the difference in flow.

Brazing Joints

Butt joint brazing should not be done. If a butt joint is necessary when making some kind of repair, use a strip of metal under the joint for reinforcement; then it will be a lap joint. Experienced welders will confine their brazing to the lap and fillet in all positions.

Lap joint brazing is very frequently used when replacing panels (such as quarter panels, fender patch panels) or when making floor repairs (Figure 4–18). The panel can be brazed very easily using the same method as desribed for steel welding. (Hold the panel in place with rivets or screws.) Due to the reduced amount of heat, the distortion of the panels will be less. With the reduction of heat, the seam or joint can be brazed completely, thus making it watertight. The chance of distortion will be further reduced by using asbestos along the joint and water to cool the bead after it has hardened and is no longer red. If the panel is hand held together while brazing, do not release the pressure until the brass had hardened or else it will crack.

Next try strips of metal of different thicknesses, remembering that the heavier piece or the one with a greater surface requires more heat. The bead or amount of brass deposited in the joint will vary with the thickness of the metal used.

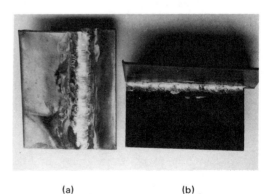

(a)   (b)

Figure 4-18 (a) Typical lap joint; (b) inside corner or fillet joint. *(Photo by S. Suydam.)*

Inside Corner or Fillet Joints

Inside corner joints such as those found around the trunk opening and door opening edges on the quarter panels do not present a serious problem of distortion (Figure 4–18). Sufficient heating of both pieces is important with the larger area requiring the most heat. The proper manipulation of the torch and the addition of filler rod is important to give the necessary strength to the joint. The filler material should be distributed equally on both sides, and the resulting bead should be concave.

Horizontal, Vertical, and Overhead Brazed Joints

These joints will be either lap or fillet joints when doing repair work. The biggest problem is gravity. Because the improper use of heat will cause the brass filler to run, avoid heating the metal beyond a dull red. The use of a large filler rod will help to eliminate the problem of the filler running down or away from the joint. Many of these joints are in a bad location where the welder is in danger of being burned by the filler that runs away from the joint. The inside of the wheelhouse and the bottom of the automobile generally present the greatest challenges to the welder. The use of flux-coated rods is recommended for these out of position joints because it may be difficult to properly locate the can of flux for easy access.

CAUTION: Many shops use galvanized metal for repair work because it is easy to braze and in many places it can be obtained free as scrap. Use with caution and in a well-ventilated place. Avoid inhaling the fumes given off when heated as they can cause serious illness.

Aluminum Brazing

For many years, welders have shied away from repair involving aluminum. Today, however, the trend is toward the use of aluminum body parts because of the weight factor and the need to conserve energy. Several car manufacturers are using aluminum hoods on some of their automobiles, and the forecast is for additional use in the future. Perhaps the easiest way to weld aluminum is the TIG or the MIG welder. Aluminum can also be brazed or welded with the oxy-acetylene torch.

Aluminum possesses several unusual properties, and once we understand them the process becomes a little easier. The brazing or welding of aluminum is similar to that of iron with its great affinity for oxygen. Once aluminum is cleaned, it immediately reacts with oxygen to produce a thin, glasslike, hard film of aluminum oxide on the surface. This film of oxide gives the aluminum its bad reputation. Immediately, before the aluminum is welded or brazed, the oxides must be removed by scraping, wire brushing, sandpapering or other mechanical means. The oxides can be removed chemically by the use of a flux.

One factor that makes aluminum different from steel is its high heat conductivity. Aluminum has a conductivity almost five times that of steel or iron depending on the type of alloy. This means that it takes more heat to bring it to the proper welding or brazing temperature.

NOTE: Take a piece of sheetmetal and a piece of aluminum of the same size and thickness. Heat one corner of both pieces for a few seconds. On the piece of sheetmetal, the heat will be concentrated at the corner while the heat will travel across the aluminum piece very rapidly.

The biggest difference between steel and

aluminum is the color change. When steel or iron is heated, it will gradually turn red, then a bright red, until it melts. Aluminum, on the other hand, will not change color until the melting point is reached, then it will simply fall away. Using a special crayon that will melt or become liquid at a certain temperature is one method of determining the amount of heat being generated.

When brazing or soldering aluminum, a flux is used to obtain the proper adhesion. The flux is available in powder or paste form. The most common is the paste form. When applied to the surface of the repair area, the flux will dry out as the temperature is raised. As the correct brazing temperature is reached, the flux will turn to glossy liquid.

When welding aluminum, as the critical temperature is reached, a small wet spot will appear as the aluminum starts to melt. The time between the appearance of the wet spot and the falling away of the aluminum is very short. The welder should watch for this first indication of the wet spot. Then he or she can remove the heat or move the torch on and off the area to avoid the complete melting of the aluminum.

Aluminum has a tendency to become very soft around the weld area, and this could lead to distortion and warping if the surrounding area is not supported by some method. This could be a major problem when repairing body panels which cannot be properly supported.

The field of aluminum welding, brazing, and soldering is very large because of the many different types of aluminum alloys and the many different types of aluminum shapes (tubing, forgings, sheets). Aluminum alloy may contain as many as six different elements to give it some desired property such as hardness or softness. The weldability of aluminum will change with each type of aluminum. The particular type of iron or steel being worked on can be determined by the spark or chipping method. With aluminum, it is very hard to determine what type is involved. When working in the repair business, most of the parts or sheets have the code numbers removed or hidden, so it is experience that helps determine what process is the best.

Post-cleaning of the welded area is very important because the flux has a corrosive action. If left on the aluminum, oxidation or corrosion will immediately take place. Also, if the part is painted, any remaining flux residue will cause the paint to peel off. There are several different chemicals used by manufacturers, but boiling hot water and scrubbing with a brush will remove most of the flux. Then the part should be rinsed with cold water.

CAUTION: Aluminum flux may give off toxic fumes when heated. Use in a well-ventilated area. If necessary to mix powdered flux and apply to the surface, wash hands immediately and avoid getting flux in eyes.

The following procedures will be limited to brazing sheet and tubing, as most castings are very difficult to repair with a torch. Other methods such as TIG will give more satisfactory results and are less difficult.

Procedure for Brazing Aluminum

Remove oxides from the brazing area by one of the previously described methods. Butt the two ends of aluminum together; leave about 1/32" (.79 mm) gap. Brush a small amount of flux on the aluminum metal. Also, brush a small amount of flux on the aluminum rod. Adjust the torch flame. (The flame should have a slight excess of acetylene.) Heat one end of the butt with the blue cone about 1/8" (3.17 mm) away from the torch at about a 30° to

40° angle with the joint. Watch as the flux turns to a powder then to a liquid. Touch the rod to the area. If the rod flows, the proper temperature has been reached. If not, apply more heat and move the torch to and from the area to avoid melting away the edges. As the rod starts to flow, keep the torch moving and dip the rod rather than feeding the rod steadily. This will control the size bead. Continue across the joint.

This is a difficult method, but with practice it becomes easier. The biggest problem is the melting away of the edges. By moving the torch continually, this problem is minimized. Using a pair of pliers, scrub off the flux with a brush and hot water. Rinse in cold water. Observe the appearance and contour of the bead. Aluminum is more difficult than brass brazing but can be mastered.

Lap Joints

Repeat the same steps as in the butt joints, except for one difference. The bottom plate will require more heat than the top one. There is danger of melting away the edge of the top layer before the bottom has reached the proper brazing temperature. Tip the torch a little toward the bottom piece until the temperature is reached. Capillary action will carry the molten rod into the joint.

Inside or Fillet Braze

Use the same method as for butt joints. Keep the torch moving to avoid melting away the edges, especially the vertical one. With the proper temperature, capillary action will carry the molten rod along the joint.

OXY-ACETYLENE CUTTING

In the normal course of repairing collision wrecks, the metal is often mangled to a point where the bolts cannot be removed or original panels, having been welded on, cannot be dislodged. Therefore, mechanical means of removing the sheetmetal must be used. Although the impact cutter, metal sheers, or sheetmetal saw are helpful, the cutting torch is the fastest method. Also, reinforcement or heavy metal brackets will hinder the mechanical cutters. Although the cutting torch is the fastest way to cut metal, there are two main objections to its use: the width of the cut is very wide and the edges of the metal must be cleaned off in order to make a good weld and eliminate the danger of fire. The cutting torch is widely used throughout industry, either by manual operation or automatic machine cutting using many torches at one time.

Oxy-acetylene cutting is actually a burning process. It is the severing of ferrous metal by heat and oxygen. After the ferrous metal is heated to the kindling temperature the addition of oxygen will cause the metal to burn at a very rapid rate. This process is called *oxidation of ferrous metal*. This is the same basic process that destroys many thousands of automobiles each year. The more common term is *rusting*, a process that occurs at a much slower rate. For example, just heat a piece of ferrous metal and then expose it to a moist atmosphere and immediately, the metal will start to oxidize. Oxy-acetylene cutting is a chemical process involving the affinity of oxygen for ferrous metals which increases when the metal is heated. The hotter the metal, the greater the affinity.

The Cutting Torch

Most of the torches used are welding torches with a cutting head installed in place of the welding tip. Also, many of the cutting torches, especially the larger ones, are combination torches. These have only one oxygen valve which controls both the volume and the final adjustment of the flame. All cutting torches have a high pressure lever that is used to feed the high pressure oxygen to the cut area.

The tip of the cutting torch has a series of orifices around the outside of the tip. The average cutting tip has either four, six, or eight orifices which are called *preheat jets*. The size of the jets will vary depending on the thickness of the metal to be cut (Figure 4–19). The center jet, which is generally larger than the outside ones, is the *cutting* or *oxygen jet*. The tip also comes in different shapes, angled and jet arrangement for special cutting, scaling for other special cutting operations. A tip used for cutting steel plate will have one preheat jet and one oxygen jet.

Proper Cutting Pressures

The amount of acetylene and oxygen pressure to be used is determined by the size tip that is necessary to cut a particular thickness of metal. Most tips found on the average cutting torch will cut up to about 2" to 3" (50.8 mm to 76.2 mm) of steel. The small torches, called *aircraft torches,* will cut up to about 3/4" (19 mm) of steel. The average cutting job will be under 1/2" (12.7 mm).

The pressure setting for oxygen and acetylene should follow the torch manufacturer's recommendations, if known. But for

Style	Number of Preheats	Size
144	4	00
	4	0-8

Medium preheat, for rusty or painted surfaces and steel castings.

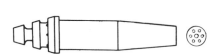

Style	Number of Preheats	Size
164	6	00
	6	0-8

Very heavy preheat, for general cutting. Also for use in cutting cast iron and stainless steel.

Figure 4–19   Number of preheats vary with material to be cut. *(Courtesy of Airco.)*

the average torch, 20 lbs of oxygen and 5 lbs (34.5) of acetylene can be used for ordinary cutting. Cutting metal over 1" (25.4 mm) thick may require additional oxygen. Many medium size torches will cut up to 6", but the oxygen may have to be raised to 100 lbs. When cutting heavy pieces of metal, over 1" thick (25.4 mm), the cut must be made all the way through. It is very difficult to start the cut again if stopped in the middle.

The approximate four to one ratio (20 lbs [138 kPa] of oxygen to 5 lbs [34.5 kPa] of acetylene) produces a fine cutting or burning action. In lighting the torch, 5 lbs (34.5 kPa) of oxygen and 5 lbs (34.5 kPa) of acetylene are used to produce a neutral flame for preheating the metal. The remaining 15 lbs (103.5 kPa) of oxygen is needed for the burning or oxidation of the metal and to ensure enough velocity to wash or blow out the oxidized metal from the cut area. One of the most common mistakes made by inexperienced torch operators is that they do not set the oxygen pressure high enough. This generally produces a poor cutting action, and most times the molten metal flows back in behind the tip, refusing the two pieces together again. When cutting thicker pieces, there is difficulty cutting through the metal. There is also a problem of using too much oxidized metal or slag especially at the bottom of the cut. Also, the cut, or *kerf*, becomes too wide and is uneven.

NOTE: A *kerf* is a cut or slot from which the metal has been removed by the cutting torch in a flame-cutting operation.

Selection of the Proper Cutting Tip

As stated before, most of the common cutting tips have either four or six preheat jets. When using a four-jet tip, two jets and the center jet must be in line with the cut. With a six-jet tip, the arrangement of the jets in relation to the line of the cut is not important.

Safety in Cutting

Using a cutting torch presents two major problems—fire and molten metal. Before using the cutting torch, check the surrounding area for any inflammable material such as thinner, gas-soaked rags, paper, open containers of flammable liquids, or car batteries. *Remember that the sparks and molten metal will travel as far as 30 feet (9.14 m), from the torch.* The person using the torch will be preoccupied with cutting and not notice anything burning nearby. Cutting off body panels can present a problem due to the large amount of flammable material on an automobile, such as upholstery, body sealer, and wiring. Remove as much as possible and cover the rest with wet rags. Undercoating and sealer should be scraped off. Some sealers and like material found in modern automobiles give off toxic fumes when burned.

The torch operator must wear welding goggles and/or face shields. Sneakers or fabric shoes are not recommended because of the molten metal being blown from the cut. Pants without cuffs are recommended. Shirt pockets should be buttoned, and all bookmatches removed. Gloves should be worn because of the hot metal and undercoating dripping from around the cut area. Keep welding hoses clear of falling metal and burning materials. Double-check for any smoldering material before leaving the area. Many fires have started after the worker has left for home. Mark HOT on any recent cut metal to avoid having other persons burn their fingers. Keep welding tanks away from the line of sparks and molten metal. *Safety precautions are not foolish notions.* Keep a fire extinguisher and water handy.

When attempting to cut apart a container, be sure that you know what type liquid was stored in it. Many different types of flammable liquids leave a residue after the liquid has been removed. The heat from the cutting torch will cause this residue to give off an explosive vapor. There are certain methods to make the container safe to cut, but that should be left to the professionals. Cutting galvanized metal, such as old water tanks, can be dangerous. When it is necessary to cut them, make sure it is in a very well-ventilated area, preferrably outside, and if possible, make sure that the wind is against your back. *Inhaling fumes can cause very serious respiratory illness.*

It is very difficult to start the cut. Many times, it must be started away from the edge of the plate, like cutting out round or odd-shaped pieces or cutting holes for bolts.

Install cutting assembly on torch handle. Select the proper cutting tip and line up the jets if using a 4 preheat jet tip. (Most cutting assemblies have one tip supplied with the purchase, but other tips are available from the supplier. Medium size cutting torches are equipped with a tip that will cut up to 1-1/2" while the light duty torches are equipped with a tip for a thickness of up to 3/4" (19 mm).)

Open up the oxygen tank all the way and set regulator at 20 lbs (138 kPa). Open acetylene tank valve 1/4 turn and set regulator at 5 lbs (34.5 kPa). Crack open both torch valves to purge the lines and recheck the regulator settings. Open the acetylene valve about 1/2 turn and light torch with a striker. Continue opening the acetylene valve until the flame starts to leave the tip; then close valve slightly until flame returns to the tip. Open the oxygen torch valve all the way. Next, open the cutting assembly oxygen valve until a neutral flame appears. Then depress the cutting lever slightly and check the flame. If the flame is still neutral, the torch is ready for cutting. If a carbon feather appears, add additional oxygen until the neutral flame reappears.

If the torch has one oxygen valve, open until the neutral flame is reached.

With soapstone, mark a line about 1" (25.5 mm) from one end of a piece of steel plate. Center punch the line if the plate is rusty.

NOTE: Remove most of the rust and paint before cutting.

Position the plate so that the line is off the edge of the bench or table. Put on the welding goggles and relight the torch and adjust to a neutral flame. Hold the torch vertical to the edge of the plate above the soapstone line with the blue flame cones about 1/8" (3.17 mm) from the metal. Preheat the metal to a bright red and slowly depress the oxygen lever until the metal starts to burn away. Move forward slowly, making sure that the metal burns and is blown out of the cut or kerf. Tilt the tip of the torch forward about 5° to 10° and continue across the plate to the other end. The cut piece should drop on the floor. If the piece appears to be cut but does not fall off, tap with a hammer, as some slag may have remained in the cut. Do not use the torch as a hammer.

NOTE: Only use as much oxygen as is necessary to cut the metal. There is no need to depress the lever all the way down if 1/4 of the way is doing the job.

Observe the cutting marks on the edge

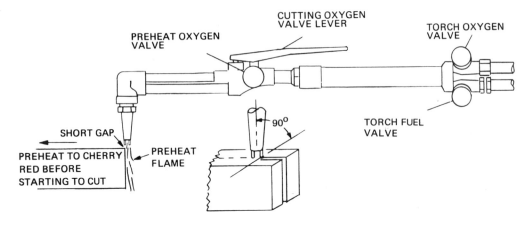

Figure 4-20   Parts of torch. *(Courtesy of Airco.)*

of the plate. They should be in a fine, even line. The cut itself should be straight and the side even. If the side appears ragged, this generally indicates that the speed is too slow.

Mark another line and cut the plate again to develop the proper speed and straightness. Also, use plates in different thicknesses to further improve the cutting technique. For really straight cuts, clamp a piece of angle iron on the plate and use it as a torch guide.

Hold the torch in one spot until the metal starts to turn red (Figure 4-20). Then raise the torch tip to about 1/2" (12.7 mm) away and then depress the oxygen lever slowly to establish a hole. After the hole is burned through, move the torch tip back to the normal distance. If the tip is too close as the hole is being burned through, the slag will clog up the jets.

The cutting torch is a real time saver when used to make bolt holes and if the bolts do not require a close fit. With care and practice and using a bolt to check the hole size, it is much quicker than using a drill (Figure 4-21).

Beveling Plates

With plates over 3/16" (4.74 mm) thick, in order to secure the proper penetration when welding the edges, the edges of plates should be beveled. When using a four-jet tip, the line of travel should be between the two pair of jets.

In some instances where a lot of beveling must be done and there is difficulty in clamping the angle to the plate, a small

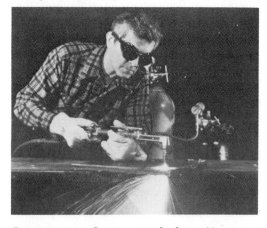

Figure 4-21   Cutting steel plate. *(Courtesy of Airco Welding.)*

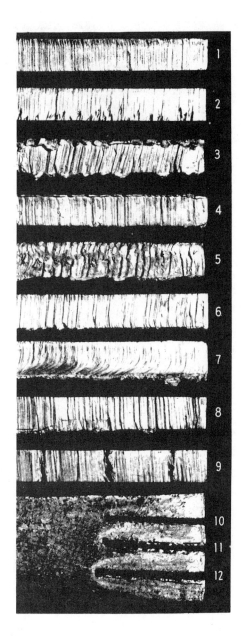

(1) Correct Procedure
Compare this correctly made cut in 1-in. plate with those shown below. The edge is square and the drag lines are vertical and not too pronounced.

(2) Preheat Flames Too Small
Result: cutting speed was too slow, causing bad gouging effect at bottom.

(3) Preheat Flames Too Long
Result: top surface has melted over, the cut edge is irregular, and there is too much adhering slag.

(4) Oxygen Pressure Too Low
Result: top edge has melted over because of too slow cutting speed.

(5) Oxygen Pressure Too High; Nozzle Too Small
Result: entire control of the cut has been lost.

(6) Cutting Speed Too Slow
Result: irregularities of drag lines are emphasized.

(7) Cutting Speed Too High
Result: there is a pronounced rake to the drag lines and the cut edge is irregular.

(8) Torch Travel Unsteady
Result: the cut edge is wavy and irregular.

(9) Lost Cut Not Properly Restarted
Result: bad gouges were caused where cut was restarted.

(10) Good Kerf
Compare this view (from the top of the plate) of a good kerf with those below. This cut was made by using correct procedures.

(11) Too Much Preheat; Nozzle Too Close
Result: bad melting occurred over the top edge.

(12) Too Little Preheat; Nozzle Too Distant
Result: heat spread has opened up kerf at top. Kerf is too wide and is tapered.

Figure 4-22 Correct procedures vs. common faults in hand cutting. *(Courtesy of Airco.)*

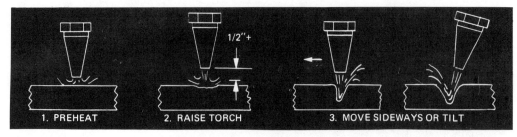

Piercing to Start Cut Away from Edge

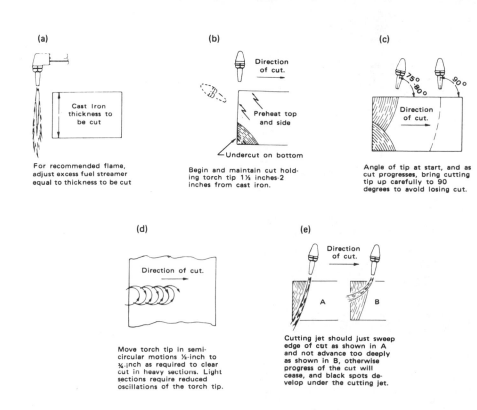

Figure 4-23 Cutting procedure. *(Courtesy of Airco Welding.)*

piece of plate can be tack welded to the opposite angle and a clamp on the tacked pieces will hold the angle iron from moving.

Round Bar or Stock

Round stock or bar can be easily cut by holding the torch at a 90° angle. As the cut is started, follow the contour of the bar keeping the torch vertical to the surface. Close observation is needed to make sure the bar is being cut all the way through, especially when cutting through the thickest part (Figures 4-22 and 4-23).

1. What is the highest temperature that the oxy-acetylene flame can reach?
2. What is the most commonly used process for obtaining oxygen?
3. What type steel is used in the manufacture of oxygen cylinders and what is the minimum thickness allowed?
4. To what pressure is an oxygen cylinder filled?
5. The oxygen cylinder uses a special valve; what type is it and why is it used?
6. What safety device is used on the oxygen cylinder?
7. Why is it dangerous to use oil or grease around the cylinder valve or near any part of the welding equipment?
8. What is acetylene gas made from?
9. What is the highest pressure at which acetylene gas can be stored in an open container?
10. What materials are used in the acetylene cylinder?
11. What chemical is inside the cylinder and what is it used for?
12. What safety device is used on the acetylene cylinder to prevent any excessive heat buildup?
13. Acetylene cylinders are available in what two basic shapes?
14. How is a cylinder of acetylene gas sold?
15. What other type of welding fuel gas is less explosive?
16. Name one advantage of using this new welding fuel gas.
17. What is the purpose of using a regulator?
18. What causes the regulator pressure to increase after the torch valve is closed?
19. What type of threads are used on the acetylene regulator and why?
20. What is the difference between a single- and two-stage regulator?
21. How can the ferrules or nuts of the acetylene hose be identified?
22. What safety device is used to prevent damaging backfires in the torch and hoses?
23. What are the four parts of the welding torch?
24. Why must welding goggles be worn when welding, brazing, or cutting?
25. What number shaded lens is recommended for welding or brazing?
26. How far open should the acetylene and oxygen valves be when the torch is in use? Why?
27. What is one method of avoiding black smoke when lighting the torch?
28. What is the safest method for lighting the torch?
29. What determines the size tip to be used when welding?
30. What is *latent heat?*
31. Name the three types of flames.
32. Which flame is used for welding?

33. Which flame causes the metal to foam and become porous and brittle?
34. Which flame adds too much carbon to the metal?
35. What is a *puddle* in welding terms?
36. What is *fusion welding?*
37. Why is it necessary to bend one end of the welding rod?
38. Is the welding rod melted by the torch or melted in the puddle?
39. What is one indication of the correct welding speed?
40. When making a butt weld, why should the metal be spaced apart before welding?
41. When making a lap weld, which piece of metal requires more heat, the tip or bottom piece of metal?
42. If the vertical piece of metal is heavier than the flat piece in a T-joint, which piece requires the most heat?
43. What force makes it more difficult to weld in a vertical or overhead position?
44. What are some of the dangers present when welding underneath a car?
45. What is the chief difference between steel welding and brazing in regard to the metal to be repaired?
46. What do *nonferrous filler rods* mean?
47. Brazing is considered to be what type of solder?
48. What is the difference between brazing and braze welding?
49. What color should the metal be before adding the brazing filler rod?
50. What is brass and bronze made of?
51. What is the danger of overheating the metal when brazing?
52. Name a compound or chemical used in brazing flux?
53. Why is it necessary to use flux when brazing?
54. What can be used to control the heat in the surrounding area?
55. What precaution should be used when brazing on galvanized metal?
56. What are two characteristics of aluminum which make it hard to braze or weld as compared to steel?
57. What is used to prevent oxides from forming on aluminum just before brazing?
58. Why is it important to remove the residue after brazing aluminum?
59. What type flame is used for aluminum?
60. What is the oxy-acetylene cutting process?
61. What are the four or six outer holes in a cutting tip called?
62. What is the average oxygen and acetylene pressures used for cutting?
63. When using a tip with four door holes, how should the holes and cut be aligned?
64. What are some of the problems involved when using a cutting torch in the shop?

WELDING SAFETY

Before a person uses one of the electric welding processes for the first time, he or she should be aware of the potential hazards involved. Of the five methods discussed in this chapter, the electric arc, the TIG, and the MIG are considered to be the most hazardous, if used improperly. However, by using common sense and observing the safety rules, these electric welding processes can be safe and useful methods.

There are several factors to be considered when using these processes. These include the high voltage and amperes used, the ultraviolet and infrared light rays given off by the arc, the molten metal, the sparks and molten metal globules that fly from the arc, the presence of hot metal, and the fumes given off when welding. These are but a few of the things that may cause injury to the welder and others nearby.

The Welding Helmet

The welding helmet is a must when using any electric welding process involving an open or visible arc. The helmet protects the eyes from being burned by the ultraviolet and infrared rays given off by the arc (Figure 5–1). The dark lenses in the welding helmet will filter out about 99 percent of the harmful rays. The arc rays are considered harmful at even 50 feet (15.2 m) from the source. Looking at the arc at a close distance for a few seconds can cause serious injury to the eyes and prolonged exposure to the rays could cause blindness. Also, the helmet protects the welder's face and neck from the rays and hot sparks coming from the arc. The rays will cause serious burns to these areas if they are not covered by the helmet.

The use of dark sunglasses or oxyacetylene welding goggles for arc welding

The Electric Welding Processes

chapter 5

MAGNIFIER LENS

COVER PLATE

FILTER PLATE

Figure 5-1 Welding helmet. *(Courtesy of Linde Corporation.)*

another clear lens to protect the filter lens. *Never* use a helmet with a cracked filter lens or one without a clear lens in front of the filter. A chipped filter lens is not effective in filtering out harmful rays.

Safety Glasses or Chipping Goggles

Safety glass or chipping goggles must be worn when chipping the slag from the weld or when handling freshly welded metal because of the hot slag or globules of metal in the welded area (Figure 5-2). The hot slag can cause serious eye damage when hot or even when cold because it contains oxides that cause eye irritation and infection. The flexible cover goggles are preferred to safety glasses because the entire eye area is covered.

do not give adequate protection to the eyes and head and, therefore, must not be used.

Helmets are made of compressed fiber or plastic and equipped with an adjustable headband. Helmets are available in two different size lenses, either 2" x 4¼" or 4½" x 5¼" (51 mm x 108 mm or 114.3 mm x 133.4 mm).

The lens assembly consists of a clear, inexpensive plastic or glass lens in front to protect the filter lens from flying sparks or metal globules. These are changed frequently when they become coated with spatter and visibility is impaired.

The filter lens is available in different shades. The shade #10 or #11 is used for small electrodes, shade #12 for gas-shielded arc 3/16" to 1/4" (4.76 mm x 6.35 mm) electrodes, shade #14 for carbon arc. The higher the number shade, the darker the lens. Behind the filter, is a gasket and

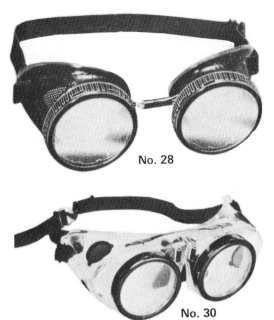

No. 28

No. 30

Figure 5-2 Chipping goggles. *(Courtesy of Linde Corporation.)*

Clothing

Shirts made of heavy material but free of oil, grease, or other flammable liquids, and with long sleeves, offer a safe amount of protection if leather clothing is not available. Avoid fuzzy sweaters, new flannel shirts, short-sleeved summer shirts (particularly those of man-made materials), and open pockets especially with matches or combs in them.

NOTE: Some of the man-made materials will not burn but melt, clinging to the skin and causing painful burns. This material, when melted, is difficult to remove from the skin.

Pants should be of the work type and not of man-made materials, without cuffs as cuffs serve as a spark catcher. The pants should be long enough to cover the tops of the shoes. Pants with frayed bottoms are also a hazard.

Work shoes with high tops, preferrably the steel toe–type are recommended. Sneakers or low oxfords or shoes constructed of man-made materials are dangerous because of the heavy hot metal being handled.

Work gloves with cuffs or gauntlet-type gloves should be worn. Some welders find it hard to work with gloves, and they have to be extra careful to avoid burning their hands.

Most industrial shops require that protective clothing be worn: leather aprons, sleeves, anklets, gloves, steeltoe shoes, safety goggles, and skullcaps (Figure 5–3). Unfortunately, the average body shop has little or nothing in the line of protective clothing.

Checking the Machine and Cables

Before turning on the machine to start welding, check over the welding cables for

CHROME LEATHER COAT

Figure 5–3 Protective clothing. *(Courtesy of Hobart Brothers.)*

bad spots in the insulation. Check the electrode holder for loose jaws, defective insulated handles, or set screws for the cable protruding through the handle. Check the ground clamp for positive grip jaws and a tight cable connection. A poor ground is one of the causes of welding problems.

If the welder is moved around the shop often, check the power feed cable for broken or loose plugs. Also check to see if the cable is securely fastened in the machine.

Proper Ventilation

When the electrode coating is burned or when metal with paint or other materials is welded, toxic fumes are given off. Some electrodes are worse than others, so be sure to weld in a well-ventilated area to avoid injury to the respiratory system. If the shop lacks an exhaust and the work cannot be moved, a regular household fan will disperse the fumes.

NOTE: If working on galvanized metal, good ventilation is a must for the welder's safety.

Hot Metal

Metal will be very hot after welding. Wearing gloves and using tongs or vise grips are recommended. Most welding should cool naturally; sudden chilling may destroy the metal. If it is necessary to leave the area after welding, mark the metal HOT with soapstone so someone else does not touch it. If possible, place the hot metal under the bench or someplace out of the way.

Surrounding Area

Before welding, check the surrounding area for combustible materials such as oily rags or anything that will burn. Special care must be taken when welding on bodies due to the large amount of plastic material, either interior or exterior, that could be damaged. Floor mats, for example, can be easily ruined if they are hit by flying sparks or metal globules.

Move any material that could be damaged or ignited away from the area or cover with wet cloths or asbestos blankets. Always keep a fire extinguisher and water handy. Also, a helper willing to fire watch is a good idea. If welding on floor pans and frames, check the location of the fuel lines and brake lines. If welding in the vicinity of a fuel filler neck, check the cap for tightness and cover it with a wet cloth or asbestos material.

CAUTION: It is very easy to have a fire start alongside the welder without his being aware of it. The welder's vision may be impaired by his helmet, and if there is a ventilating fan operating, this will draw the smoke away, and the welder will not see the fire in time. A few minutes of preparation may save hours later on.

A portable welding curtain, the folding type, should be considered to shield the other workers or customers from the harmful rays.

Wet Floors

It is recommended that welding be done only in areas where the floors are dry. However, many times in the repair field, welding must be done on equipment that is wet or in areas where the floor or ground is damp. If the cables are in good condition, if there is a good insulated electrode hold and a properly attached ground clamp near the weld area, and if the machine is properly grounded, there is little danger of severe injury. Good rubber boots and gloves will help in this situation, but extreme caution must be exercised nevertheless. (One cause of shock is putting a new electrode in the holder, so shut off the machine before getting a new electrode.

Accidents do not just happen. They happen because someone gets careless, ignores the safety precautions, and doesn't use his or her common sense.

ELECTRIC ARC WELDING

The electric welding processes play a major part in the manufacture of the modern automobile. The many outer panels, inner panels, and reinforcements are all welded together to form a rigid body. Very few, if any, welds are made with an oxy-acetylene torch. The electric welding processes are much faster and less heat is produced to cause distortion. However, the electric welding process has its limitations, and these will be mentioned later in the chapter.

With the introduction of aluminum in the manufacturing of body parts, two electric welding processes, TIG (tungston inert gas) and MIG (metallic inert gas) welding, will be more in demand. The electric welding processes now being used most often are as follows: the electric arc or stick electrode, the spot welder, and the resistance welder. The arc welding process is mainly used for welding heavy steel brackets and frames, for fabricating trailer hitches and for many other purposes, but it is rarely used for welding sheetmetal.

The electric arc welding process uses an electric arc to produce sufficient heat to melt the metal and promote fusion. The arc is formed by current flowing through an air gap between the electrode and the object being welded.

The most common welding machine used in auto body repair is the transformer type which operates on 208 or 230 volts which is available in most shops or buildings (Figure 5–4). There are some light-duty welding machines that operate on 110 volts.

The transformer-type machine is made to produce ac (alternating current) and some will produce ac and dc (direct current) (Figure 5–5).

Figure 5–4 Transformer-type welding machine. *(Courtesy of Lincoln Welding.)*

Figure 5–5 Transformer-type welding machine — ac/dc. *(Courtesy of Airco Welding.)*

The ac machine's current output (welding current) ranges from 150 to 275, although some have greater output. However, the 225 ampere welding machine is about the most popular for general-purpose welding and is fairly low priced.

Most of the transformer welding machines are very simple in construction, consisting of a step-down transformer, a selector dial type or tap-in type or a movable coil with a crank for selecting the desirable welding current, a fan for cooling the transformer, and a set of welding cables or leads (Figure 5–6). The welding cables or leads are either with tap in lugs or permanently attached to the machine. The transformer machine input (current coming into the machine) is 208 or 220 volts at about 25 to 60 amperes depending on machine and output amperage. The output current (welding current) ranges from 20 to 275 amperes at 15 to 40 volts depending on the type of machine.

All welding machines must comply with the National Electrical Manufacture Association standards in regard to safety.

The welding cables or leads are insulated heavy copper wire made to withstand high welding currents. One cable is used for a ground with either a heavy clip or clamp for attaching the cable to the work or object to be welded. The other cable has an insulated electrode holder on the end. This is often called the *stinger*.

Other Types of Welding Machines

Portable

The portable welding machine is operated by a gasoline motor and can be used when electricity is not available (Figure 5–7). This machine is often used for repairing heavy construction equipment or farm machinery that cannot be moved to the nearest power supply. Many of these machines are mounted on small trailers.

AC (or alternating current) is normally 60 cycle (the current changes direction in

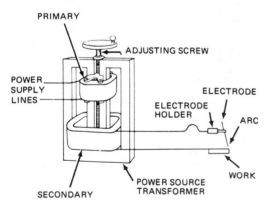

Figure 5–6 Parts of transformer welding machine. *(Courtesy of Airco Welding.)*

Figure 5–7 Portable welding machine. *(Courtesy of Lincoln Welding.)*

its flow 120 times a second). DC means direct current (the current will flow in one direction). When welding with a dc machine, certain electrodes will operate on dc plus (or positive) current and some will operate best on dc minus (or negative) current.

In welding terminology, the dc+, or positive, is referred to as dcrp, or direct current reversed polarity and dc–, or negative, is referred to as dcsp, or direct current straight polarity.

The original dc welding machine was the motor generator type, that is, an electric motor driving a generator to produce dc current. With the advancement in technology, it was found that the transformer welding machine which produces ac current could be converted to produce dc current. These machines are a lot lighter in weight and less expensive than the old type dc motor generator. Many of the ac–dc machines can be switched to dc by means of a lever or by placing the welding cable ends into the dc receptacles. Likewise, when necessary, the dc current can be switched to dcsp (or negative) or dcrp (or positive) by a lever or by placing the cable ends in the plus or minus receptacle.

Arc Blow

One of the disadvantages of the dc welder is a phenominal condition called *arc blow*. When an electrical current, such as the welding current, passes through the welding area of the work piece, magnetic lines of force build up to form a magnetic field. When these lines of force become concentrated at the end of the weld (or bead) or as the electrode nears a corner, they cause the arc to wander or deflect from the normal path of travel. This can be remedied by changing the location of the ground cable or placing a piece of metal against the edge of the metal being welded.

Difference Between Reversed and Straight Polarity

Reversing the flow of current between the electrode and the ground (work piece) combined with the correct electrode can be beneficial.

In some welding applications, a deep penetration of the base metal is desired. The dc machine should be set at dcrp. When using dcrp (or electrode positive) and with the ground (work piece) negative, approximately $2/3$ of the heat generated in the arc is at the electrode and $1/3$ at the work piece. The molten metal from the electrode travels at high velocity across the arc gap. This results in deep penetration of the work piece.

If the material to be welded is thin or light metal, deep penetration would be undesirable. By changing to dcsp (or electrode negative), $2/3$ of the heat of the arc is released at the base metal and $1/3$ at the electrode. This results in a shallower penetration which is desirable for welding light metal.

Selection of Electrodes

One of the most important factors in a good welding job is the proper selection of electrodes. The original electrodes produced were bare wire or lightly covered electrodes. This made arc welding very difficult, and the quality of the welded joints was less than desirable. With the introduction of the extruded coating on the electrodes plus advancement in manufacturing technology, modern electrode arc welding was made easier.

COATING COLOR	AWS Number on Coating	(L)LINCOLN	ELECTRODE	ELECTRODE POLARITY	SIZES AND CURRENT RANGES (Amps.) (electrodes are manufactured in those sizes for which current ranges are given)					
					3/32" SIZE	1/8" SIZE	5/32" SIZE	3/16" SIZE	7/32" SIZE	1/4" SIZE
Light Tan	6010		FLEETWELD 5	DC+					200-275	250-325①
Brick Red	6010		FLEETWELD 5P	DC+	40-75	75-130	90-175	140-225		
Light Tan	6011		FLEETWELD 35	AC DC+		75-120 70-110	90-160 80-145	120-200 110-180	150-260 135-235	190-300 170-270
Red Brown	6011	Green	FLEETWELD 35LS	AC DC±		80-130 70-120	120-160 110-150			
Brown	6011		FLEETWELD 180	AC DC+	40-90 40-80	60-120 55-110	115-150 105-135			
Pink	7010-A1		SHIELD-ARC 85	DC+	50-90	75-130	90-175	140-225		
Pink	7010-A1	Green	SHIELD-ARC 85P	DC+				140-225		
Tan	7010-G		SHIELD-ARC HYP	DC+		75-130	90-185	140-225		160-250
Tan	7010-G	Green	SHIELD-ARC 65+	DC+		75-130	90-185	140-225		
Tan	8010-G		SHIELD-ARC X70	DC+		75-130	90-185	140-225		160-250

①Range for 3/16" size is 280-400 amps. DC+ is Reverse Polarity; DC— is Straight Polarity.

TYPICAL MECHANICAL PROPERTIES

Test procedures per appropriate AWS spec. Other specs may have different min. requirements and test procedures. ②

Low figures in the as welded ranges below are AWS minimum requirements.

Low figures in the Stress Relieved ranges below are AWS minimum requirements.

	FLEETWELD 5	FLEETWELD 5P	FLEETWELD 35	FLEETWELD 35LS	FLEETWELD 180	SHIELD-ARC 85	SHIELD-ARC 85P	SHIELD-ARC HYP	SHIELD-ARC 65+	SHIELD-ARC X70
As Welded Tensile Strength—psi	62-69,000	62-69,000	62-68,000	62-67,000	62-71,000	70-78,000	70-78,000	77-83,000	75-87,000	92-93,000
Yield Point—psi Ductility—% Elong. in 2"	50-61,000 22-36	50-62,000 22-33	50-62,000 22-30	50-60,000 22-31	50-64,000 22-31	57-71,000 22-26	57-63,000 22-27	65-73,000 20-23	66-79,000 16-25	82-86,000 19-23
Charpy V-Notch Toughness—ft. lbs.	20-80 @ -20°F	20-60 @ -20°F	20-90 @ -20°F	20-57 @ -20°F	20-54 @ -20°F	68 @ 70°F	68 @ 70°F	55 @ 70°F	34 @ -50°F	58 @ 70°F
Stress Relieved @ 1150°F Tensile Strength—psi	60-70,000	60-70,000	60-70,000	60-65,000		70-80,000	70-74,000	70-85,000	70-83,000	80-96,000
Yield Point—psi Ductility—% Elong. in 2"	46-56,000 28-36	46-56,000 28-36	46-56,000 28-36	46-51,000 28-33		57-69,000 22-25	57-64,000 22-26	57-79,000 22-29	57-75,000 22-28	67-85,000 19-23
Charpy V-Notch Toughness—ft. lbs.	88 @ 70°F	71 @ 70°F		120 @ 70°F		64 @ 70°F	68 @ 70°F	68 @ 70°F	28 @ -50°F	69 @ 70°F

② Other tests and other procedures may produce different results (see "Properties vs. Procedures"—page 2).

CONFORMANCES AND APPROVALS

See Lincoln Price Book for certificate numbers, size and position limitations and other data.

Conforms to Test Requirements of AWS—A5.1 and ASME—SFA5.1 AWS—A5.5 and ASME—SFA5.5	FW-5 E6010	FW-5P E6010	FW-35 E6011	FW-35LS E6011	FW-180 E6011	SA-85 E7010-A1③	SA-85P E-7010-A1	SA-HYP E7010-G	SA-65+ E7010-G	SA-X70 E8010-G
ASME Boiler Code { Group { Analysis	F3 A1	F3 A1	F3 A1	F3 A1	F3 A1	F3 A2	F3 A2	F3 A2	F3 A2	F3 A2
American Bureau of Shipping & U. S. Coast Guard	Approved	Approved	Approved	Approved		Approved				
Conformance Certificate Available④	Yes	Yes	Yes	Yes	Yes	Yes	Yes	Yes	Yes	Yes
Lloyds	Approved	Approved	Approved							
Military Specifications			MIL-QQE-450	MIL-QQE-450		MIL-E-22200/7				

③ Also meets the requirements for E7010-G and E6010 in 3/32" size.
④ "Certificate of Conformance" to AWS classification test requirements is available. These are needed for Federal Highway Administration projects.

Figure 5-8 Electrode indentification and operating data. *(Courtesy of Lincoln Welding.)*

The coating on the electrode provides a gaseous shield around the arc and the molten metal. The purpose of the gaseous shield is to prevent oxygen or any impurities from combining with the molten metal. It also acts as a cleaning agent to prevent impurities from remaining in the molten metal. (The presence of impurities may cause weakness in the weld.) The coating also provides a shield in the form of slag on top of the weld until the metal cools. (Slag results from the oxidation of the coating.) This prevents impurities such as oxygen from entering the hot metal.

Classification of Electrodes

The electrodes must meet certain standards as set down by the American Welding Society (Figure 5-9). The electrodes are

AWS Numbering System

a. The prefix "E" designates arc welding electrode.
b. The first two digits of 4 digit numbers and the first three digits of 5 digit numbers indicate minimum tensile strength:

E60xx	60,000 psi Tensile Strength
E70xx	70,000 psi Tensile Strength
E110xx	110,000 psi Tensile Strength

c. The next-to-last digit indicates position:

Exx1x	All Positions
Exx2x	Flat position and horizontal fillets

d. The last two digits together indicate the type of coating and the current to be used (See "Electrode Groups" below).
e. The suffix (Example: EXXXX-**A1**) indicates the approximate alloy in the deposit.

-A1	$\frac{1}{2}$% Mo
-B1	$\frac{1}{2}$% Cr, $\frac{1}{2}$% Mo
-B2	$1\frac{1}{4}$% Cr, $\frac{1}{2}$% Mo
-B3	$2\frac{1}{4}$% Cr, 1% Mo
-C1	$2\frac{1}{2}$% Ni
-C2	$3\frac{1}{4}$% Ni
-C3	1% Ni, .35% Mo, .15% Cr
-D1 & D2	.25-.45% Mo, 1.25-2.00% Mn
-G	.50 min Ni, .30 min Cr, .20 min Mo, .10 min V

(Only one of the listed elements is required)
E11018-M 1.3-1.8 Mn, 1.25-2.50 Ni, .40 Cr., .25-.50 Mo, .05 max. V.

Figure 5-9 AWS numbering system. *(Courtesy of Lincoln Welding.)*

classified by numbers and must meet or exceed certain mechanical properties used for certain positions, the type of penetration and the type of current used. The code or classification number is a four- or five-digit number prefixed by an E to signify electrode used for arc welding; for example, E6011 or E7024. The number, E6011, can be broken down as follows:

E — electrode for arc welding.

60 — the minimum tensile strength of the weld metal in thousands of pounds per square inch (60,000 psi or 414,00 kPa). This number could also be in one hundred thousands.

1 — (the third or fourth number), the position that can be used. The number *1* indicates the electrode can be used in all positions; the number *2*, flat or horizontal; and the number *3*, flat only.

1 — the type of coating, type of current, and welding characteristics.

Certain electrodes can be used by both ac and dcrp or ac and dcsp, or by all three. The E6010 electrode is made for dcrp only.

Most of the electrodes are stamped with their classification on the coating on the grip end of the electrode. A few manufacturers still use color codes or spots for electrode identification, but this type of identification is on the decline.

In the body shops, where there is a limited amount of arc welding being done, the E6011, E6013, and perhaps the E7014 are generally used for all-purpose welding of mild steel. These electrodes produce good results when used with the ac welder.

There are many other types of electrode, such as iron powder coating (including E7014), low hydrogen type, alloy steel electrode, cast iron, and aluminum, but these are not commonly used in body shops. The smaller shops, especially in the rural areas, will do a lot more arc welding for extra revenue.

The size of the electrode is determined by the diameter of the steel core or wire, not including the coating. The rods are available from 1/16″ to 5/16″ (1.58 mm to 7.93 mm) in diameter with the 3/32″ and 1/8″ (2.38 mm and 3.17 mm) diameter electrodes being the most common. The electrodes vary in length, depending on the diameter. The 1/16″ (15.8 mm) is 9 inches (229 mm) long, the 3/32″ (2.38 mm) is 12″ (305 mm) long, the 1/8″ (3.17 mm) is 14″ (355 mm) long, and the 5/16″ (7.93 mm) is 18″ (457 mm) long.

Current Setting

The amount of current used for welding depends on the diameter of the electrode, the thickness of the metal to be welded, and the type of electrode being used. A 1/8″ (3.17 mm) E6011 electrode current ranges from 60 to 120 amperes while a 1/8" (3.17 mm) E6013 electrode ranges from 100 to 150 amperes. The thinner the metal, the lower the amperage to prevent burning through the metal. To get the proper penetration on heavier metal, the amperage would be higher.

Follow the electrode manufacturer's recommendations on selecting the proper current or amperage. Also, the diameter of the electrode should not exceed the thickness of the metal to be welded. However, there are times when smaller electrodes are not available. In this situation adjust the amperage and travel speed to prevent burning holes in the metal.

The use of excessive amperage could cause excessive penetration with a large and uneven bead. Using current that is too low will cause the bead to be too high and lack penetration because there is not enough heat to melt the base metal properly.

Arc Length

The arc length or the distance from the electrode to the metal is very important. If the electrode is held too close to the metal, the voltage will be too low, with not enough heat to melt the base metal properly. The bead will be too high and uneven, and the electrode may stick to the metal. If the electrode is held too far away, the arc length will be too long and the voltage will be excessive, which will cause the arc stream to wobble. The metal from the electrode will melt in globules causing a wide bead, excessive splatter, and decreased fusion of the base metal.

The proper distance or arc length should be approximately the same length as the diameter of the electrode. The sound is another way of determining the correct arc length. The sound should be sharp and crackling.

The arc length will vary when welding in vertical, horizontal, and overhead positions.

Speed of Travel

If the speed of travel is too fast, the bead will be too narrow (with pointed ripples), and the pool of melted metal will solidify too fast and trap impurities in the metal. The beads will be too high and lack the proper penetration.

If the speed of travel is too slow, the beads will be too wide, too much metal will be deposited, and there will be excessive penetration.

Preparing to Arc Weld

Before starting to weld, make a quick survey of the surrounding area for hazardous materials. Check the machine and equipment (cables, personal clothing, safety goggles, and welding helmet). Correct anything that violates the safety rules and recommendations.

Select several pieces of plate steel, for example $3/_{16}$" x 6" x 6" (4.76 mm x 152 mm x 152 mm) or thinner or heavier, depending on whatever is available. Sections of auto frames are ideal for practice. Remove paint and rust from surfaces with a disc grinder or wire brush.

Depending on the thickness of the practice metal, use a $1/_8$" (3.17 mm) electrode on metal thicker than $1/_8$" (3.17 mm) or $3/_{32}$" (2.38 mm) electrodes on lighter metal.

Either E6012 or E6013 electrode is preferred for practice rather than E6011 as the beads are more defined and it is easier to check the progress of beads. Select the amperage setting depending on the size of the electrode and the manufacturer's rec-ommendations. Some ⅛″ (3.17 mm) elec-trodes work well at 85 to 100 amperages while others require higher amperage set-tings. Using current or amperage that is too high will cause the electrode to melt too fast creating a large and irregular bead, sometimes with excessive penetration. Low amperage will cause a narrow, high bead with poor penetration.

Before turning on the machine, practice using one of two methods of striking an arc. Use either *tapping* or *scratching*.

The scratching method involves scratch-ing the electrode on the surface of the metal using short strokes (Figure 5-10). The tapping method is striking the metal with the electrode at a 90° angle, then mov-ing the electrode up about ³⁄₁₆″ (4.76 mm) from the surface.

Connect the ground cable to the metal or bench and check for good contact. Put on the helmet and other accessories such as gloves and apron. Place the electrode in the holder and turn the machine on. Remem-ber the location of the power switch on the machine in case of emergency. Lower the electrode within 1″ to 2″ (24.4 mm to 50.0 mm) from the surface and lower the helmet.

Strike the electrode on the plate with either the scratching or tapping motion to establish the arc. Don't move the rod too fast or else the arc will stop. As the arc starts, raise the electrode up a little to about ³⁄₁₆″ (4.76 mm) (long arc) for a mo-ment to establish the arc and form a molten pool of metal. Then lower the electrode to about ⅛″ (3.17 mm) from the surface and start to move forward. Keep the electrodes at a 90° angle to the surface and tipped at a 15° angle in the direction of travel.

If the welder is right-handed, move the electrode from left to right. A left-handed welder would move the electrode from

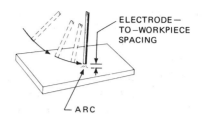

Scratch Start

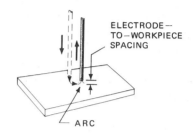

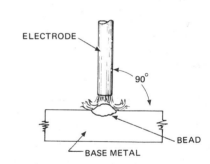

Looking in Weld Direction

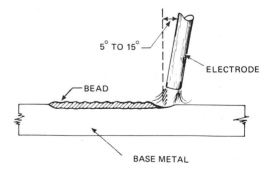

Figure 5-10 Scratching method. *(Courtesy of Airco.)*

right to left. This way, the welder can observe the puddle of molten metal and the formation of the bead as the metal solidifies or hardens.

Move the electrode forward at a steady rate, observing the bead formation (Figure 5–11). Using an even rate of speed, the bead will be formed evenly. An unsteady rate of speed will result in a bead with wide and narrow sections. The bead should be about 1/4″ (6.35 mm) in width and have a slightly convex or raised contour, with even half-moon ripples.

NOTE: The width of the bead will vary depending on what size electrode is used. The 1/8″ (3.17 mm) electrode is very commonly used for practice welding.

Beads with pointed ripples and narrow in width are generally an indication of having gone too fast. Wide and high beads result from going too slow. The shape of the bead is also affected by the length of the arc gap, (or distance between the electrode and the metal). If the electrode is held too close to the metal, the arc will fail to generate enough heat to properly melt the base metal and the bead will be too high and uneven. This causes the electrode to stick to the metal. A long arc, or holding the electrode too far away from the metal, will cause the metal from the electrode to melt off in globules. The bead will be wide and

covered with spatter. There will be poor fusion between the electrode metal and the base metal.

After making several beads, put on safety glasses, remove the slag, and check the size and shape of the beads. Check the chart for welding bead defects. The best method of learning how to arc weld is practice. A few good beads does not mean that one has mastered the art.

Before attempting to weld joints, practice running straight beads until all of them have the proper size and contour. Use the electrode until about 1 1/2″ to 2″ (38.1 mm to 50.8 mm) is left in the holder. Discarding stubs of electrodes longer than 2″ (50.8 mm) is wasteful. Place all stubs in a can or put them on the bench. Do not put them on the floor as someone may slip on them.

When the arc comes in contact with the metal, a pool of molten metal is formed and will be filled with the electrode as the electrode is moved forward to form a bead. This pool, or depression is called a *crater* and will remain at the end of the bead when the arc is broken. The crater is a source of weakness in the welded bead if stress is applied, especially in a joint. To avoid craters at the end of a bead, pause a second or two at the end to fill the crater, then move the electrode back over the bead, increasing in arc length until the arc is broken.

To fill a crater in a previously welded bead, start the arc just ahead of the crater and bring it back to the crater, then move forward. This method allows sufficient heat to be built up and ensures proper fusion on the crater. Start at the crater, especially with a new electrode, or the metal will not fuse properly.

Another method of developing the proper welding technique is to run parallel beads, evenly spaced and of considerable

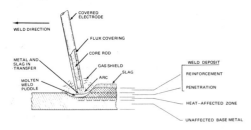

Figure 5–11 For good bead formation move the electrode forward at a steady rate. *(Courtesy of Airco.)*

length. Prepare a piece of metal and draw lines with soapstone about ½" to ¾" (12.7 mm to 19.0 mm) apart across the metal. The metal should be abut 4" x 6" (101.6 mm x 152.4 mm) or similar in size. After running beads on all of the lines, remove the slag and observe the results. An alternate method is to draw lines at right angles to each other so that the welder must change directions yet form a continuous line.

Arc Welding Joints

The joints mentioned in the discussion of oxy-acetylene are basically the same as used in arc welding, but with different thicknesses of metal. The *butt joint* is where two pieces of metal are in line with each other and, when welded, form a flat surface (Figure 5–12). To obtain maximum strength, the joint must have 100 percent penetration. When welding a butt joint with only one side accessible, the penetration is more critical.

On metal plates up to ⅛" (3.17 mm), sufficient penetration can be achieved by spacing the plates apart, equal to ½ the thickness of the plates. This spacing is also recommended to prevent distortion from expansion and contraction of the welded joint.

When welding heavier plates, the edges must be beveled to a 30° angle and a ¹⁄₁₆" to ⅛" (1.58 mm to 3.17 mm) root face or land must be left on the bottom of the plate. NOTE: The *root* is the part of the weld which is farthest from the application of the weld heat.

If both sides of the plate are accessible, a double bevel or double V bevel can be used. When beveling a joint, an excessive angle such as 45° can cause a problem because if the weld contracts, excessive warping could

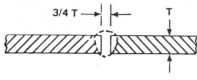

A. Square Edge (T = Thickness)

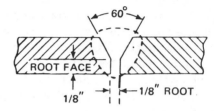

B. Single V - Groove

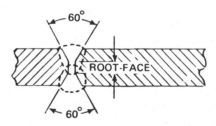

C. Double V - Groove

Figure 5–12 Butt joints. *(Courtesy of Airco.)*

take place. Heavier plates may require more than one pass or bead.

Distortion can be a major problem when welding thin plates with long continuous beads. This is called *lengthwise* distortion, and the plates will bend upward in the direction of the weld.

Clamping the plates to a bench or some rigid object will help prevent distortion, but at times, this is not possible. The use of skip welds or backstep weld techniques will help to eliminate distortion.

NOTE: *Skip welding* — weld a series of

beads, starting about 2" (50.8 mm) from the end of the plate. Weld back to the end. Start the next bead about 6" (152.4 mm) from the end and weld backwards for 2" (50.8 mm). Continue this procedure to the end of the plate. Then, after cleaning off the welds, fill in the remainder of the bead.

Backstep welding — start about 2" (50.8 mm) from the end and weld back to the edge. Clean the weld and start about 4" from the end (101.6 mm) and weld backward to the first bead. Continue this procedure to the end of the plate.

When welding butt joints, properly space the plates and tack weld each end to prevent the plate from shifting. Long plates should be tack welded several times in the middle.

Excessive amperage or current when butt welding could cause excessive penetration, burning holes, and too much contraction when the weld is cooling. After making a butt weld, check the bottom of the plate for penetration. Place one piece in a vise and bend it back and forth with a large hammer until it breaks. Check the weld joint for slag inclusion, porosity, incomplete fusion, and penetration.

Lap Joints

The *lap joint* is one of the most commonly used joints. The lap joint requires very little preparation since the edges do not have to be beveled (Figure 5-13). The amount of overlap depends on the strength requirement, the thickness of the metal, and the direction of the stress on the joint. The greatest strength in the lap joint results when both sides of the joint can be welded.

When replacing automobile frame sections or reinforcement members, one side of the joint is generally accessible. In preparing to weld the joints, bring the lap edge down as close as possible to the bottom

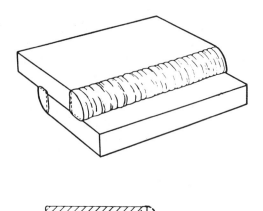

Figure 5-13 Lap joint. *(Courtesy of Airco.)*

piece to avoid burning away the top edge.

The electrode should be held at a 45° angle with the bottom plate. Tip the electrode at a 20° to 30° angle toward the line of travel. If the top edge starts to burn away, direct the arc toward the bottom plate, especially if the top plate is thinner.

Lap joints involving heavier plate, for example 3/8" (9.52 mm), would require a series of beads. The first bead would be the *root bead* (or *pass bead*) with complete fusion of the plates. After removing slag, the second bead would require a weaving motion resulting in a wider bead. Heavier plate would require more beads, depending on the thickness of the metal.

NOTE: Slag inclusion may be a problem for inexperienced welders. This is often found when using E6013 or E7014 electrodes. The slag becomes trapped in the root of the weld thus preventing the fusion of the top and lower plates. This is caused by holding the arc too short or too close and improper electrode manipulation. Some welders prefer to use E6011 electrodes to reduce the chance of slag inclusion because of a forceful arc and light slag.

Fillet Weld (Inside Corner or T Welds)

The *fillet weld* is similar to the lap weld. It is very commonly used in fabrication of various structures. If stresses are placed in the opposite direction of the welded joint, the joint is too weak. By adding a weld on the other side of the joint, sufficient strength is added to the joint (Figure 5-14).

A common defect in fillet welding is the undercutting of the vertical plate which could cause failure under stress. The *undercut* is a groove or ridge at the upper edge of the fillet weld or bead; therefore, the upper plate is thinner which causes weakness. Undercutting is caused by several reasons but two of the common ones are incorrect electrode angle and improper electrode manipulation.

When fillet welding, the electrode should be held at a 45° angle from the bottom plate and tipped forward in the line of travel.

Little or no weaving motion with the proper speed will deposit enough metal to form a ¼" (6.35 mm) bead. The fillet weld is another type of joint where slag inclusion occurs frequently. To obtain a stronger inside corner or T-weld, especially when using a heavier plate metal, a series of beads can be used.

When welding fillet welds, the contraction of the welded metal when cooling, causes the vertical plate to tip. This is very common when using a multi pass bead on one side of the vertical plate or when using excessive weld material when making one pass. One way of overcoming this problem is to tip the plate out of alignment before welding, and as contraction during cooling takes place, the plate will be pulled back to the proper position.

If the plate is accessible on both sides, use a staggered method of welding; that is, a short bead on one side of the vertical, then a short bead just ahead of the other bead on

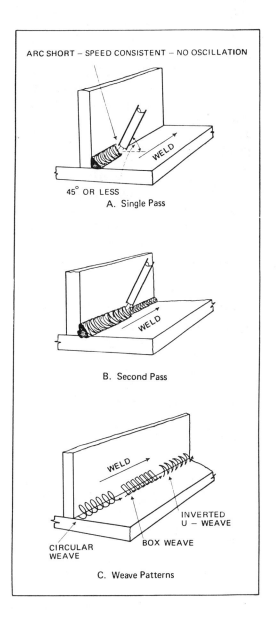

Figure 5-14 Fillet weld. *(Courtesy of Airco.)*

the opposite side. Continue this procedure the length of the joint. In cases where additional strength is required, fill in between the short beads.

CAUTION: Remove slag before filling in between the beads.

Another method to control distortion is to weld one short bead on one side then a short bead on the other side. One bead will counteract the other.

Outside Corner Joint Welds

Outside corner joint welds are used very frequently in the manufacture of rectangular tanks and other structures where the corner must have a good appearance (Figure 5–15). Some of the basic outside corner joints are the *open corner*, *half-open* and *closed* joint.

The open outside corner joint is where the root of the plates are touching each other or close together forming a V-joint. The half-open joint is where one plate covers half of the width of the other plate. The closed corner joint is where the one plate is flush with the other. It is generally used on light gauge metal and is the weakest of the three. If heavy plates are involved, the edges must be beveled in order to get adequate penetration. If the plates are under load or stress, then, the inside corner must be welded.

Depending on the thickness of the plates, the open and half-open joints may require more than one bead or pass. In places where appearance is important, an E6013 or E7014 is preferred over E6011.

Horizontal Welding

A weld in a horizontal position is welded on a vertical plate or structure which is parallel to the ground or horizontal plane. Horizontal, like vertical and overhead welds, are affected by the force of gravity acting on the molten metal. The molten metal has a tendency to run down, overlapping the adjoining metal without actually penetrating or fusing the metal. The upper

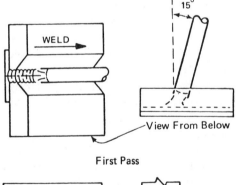

First Pass

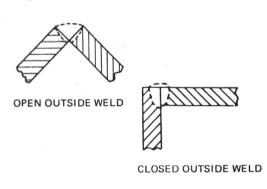

Figure 5–15 Outside corner joint weld. (Courtesy of Airco.)

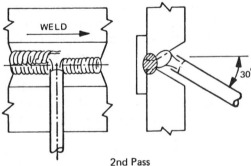

2nd Pass

Figure 5–16 Horizontal butt weld. (Courtesy of Airco.)

part of the bead is usually undercut, which can cause weakness of the joint.

Two important factors will help to control the molten metal in the puddle: a slight reduction in amperage to reduce the amount of molten metal and the use of a short arc (one that is shorter than that used in a flat position).

The electrode angle should be about 15° to 20° in the line of travel with the electrode pointed up about 5°. A slight weaving motion will help to distribute the heat more evenly, thus reducing the tendency of the molten metal to sag or run down.

The force of the arc has a tendency to undercut at the top of the bead. Tip the electrode upward at a greater angle.

For horizontal welding of butt joints in plates 1/4" (6.35 mm) or thicker, the edges of the plates must be beveled. The bevel should be the same as butt joints in a flat position. For the first bead (or root weld) the electrode is tipped up at about a 5° angle.

NOTE: Remove the slag before applying the next bead or any additional beads.

The second bead should be on the bottom plate, fusing the second bead with the first and the bottom plate. Tip the electrode down at about a 5° to 10° angle. The third bead should fuse with the first two beads and the upper plate. The electrode should be tipped up at about a 10° to 15° angle. The amount of bead necessary will depend on the thickness of the metal and the size electrode being used.

If smoothness and appearance is important, a *cover bead* can be applied using a wide weaving motion to cover the entire surface of the previously deposited beads.

Vertical Welding

Welding beads in a vertical position is very difficult because gravity tends to pull the molten metal downward from the weld area (Figure 5–17). Many welders experience more difficulty when welding up vertical than down and require more skill to master it than any other position.

For maximum strength of a joint, in a vertical position, welding upward will deposit more metal than downward. Vertical down welding is suitable for thinner plates because the penetration is not as deep, thus preventing burn through holes but forming adequate welds. The fast-freeze electrodes are recommended for vertical welding because the weld metal will solidify faster, thus preventing the molten metal from running out of the weld area.

The use of the E6011 electrode will be easier than the E6013 because of the forceful action of the arc. The E6013 electrode produces a softer arc, and the slag is heavier.

The angle of the electrode for vertical up and down welding is very important in helping to control the molten puddle. When welding downward, the electrode should be pointed up at about a 10° to 25° angle. The arc should be rather short, and the speed must be fast enough to prevent the molten steel and slag from running ahead of the puddle.

When welding upward in a vertical position, the electrode is pointed up at about a 10° to 15° angle. A whipping or rocking motion is used to control the molten metal in the puddle. The whipping or rocking motion involves tipping the electrode upward out of the puddle or crater and back to the puddle. This is simply a slight twist of the wrist and allows the molten metal to solidify. Repeat the procedure the full length of the vertical bead. Do not break the arc. The solidified metal will provide a shelf for additional weld metal.

A U-shaped or figure 8 weave-type bead

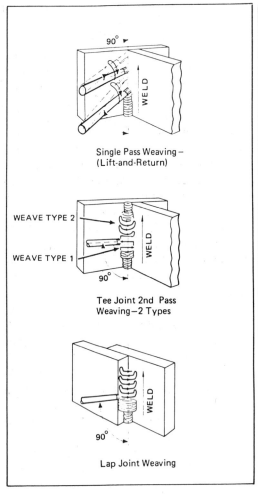

(a)

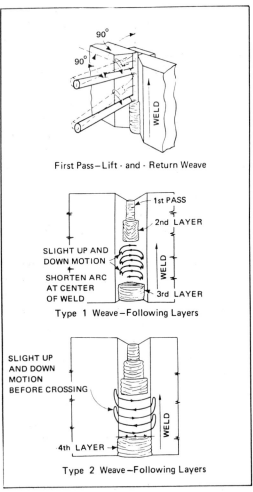

(b)

Figure 5-17 (a) Vertical fillet welds; (b) vertical butt welds. *(Courtesy of Airco.)*

is used very often when welding vertical fillet welds. It requires a lot of practice to master the vertical up welding technique. When welding heavy plate, the first bead (or root bead) is a whipping type followed by a weave-type bead or beads.

The use of low hydrogen electrodes such as the E7018 is increasing for general repairs. Some modification must be made when using low hydrogen electrodes in all positions. A very short arc must be maintained in order to secure the proper shielding of the molten metal. Therefore, these electrodes should not be whipped when welding vertical. Small weaves are better than wide ones. A slight weaving motion such as a triangular or figure 8 produces a satisfactory bead. A slight reduction in amperage will assist in the proper bead formation.

Overhead Welding

Overhead welding is somewhat difficult because of the force of gravity that acts against the molten metal in the puddle (Figure 5-18). Also, the welder is placed in an awkward or uncomfortable position because of the sparks and falling droplets of molten metal coming from the weld area. In many cases, the welder is lying flat on his back when welding overhead on vehicles and machinery.

The E6010 or E6011, or low hydrogen electrodes, work well in the overhead position. A few precautions should be taken before starting to weld overhead: (1) wear a cap to protect the head and hair; (2) button pockets and make sure the tops of the shoes are covered by the pants legs; (3) wear leather sleeves and shoulder covers if available; and (4) button shirt collar. If possible, drape the welding cable over the shoulder to help eliminate arm fatigue if standing.

Aluminum Welding

Aluminum will be used in greater quantities in the automotive industry in the future. Aluminum can be welded with electrodes but it is difficult on thin gauge. Other methods, such as MIG and TIG welding of aluminum are easier, and the welder has better control.

MIG

The MIG welding process is expected to play a greater role in auto body repair in the coming years. It is forecast that the majority of automobiles produced in the 1980s will be unitized construction with MIG being the recommended welding process.

The MIG welding process offers several advantages such as the high speed of welding and metal deposit, less distortion, a narrow heat zone or weld zone, no slag to remove, and little waste of filler material (Figure 5-19).

The MIG (metal inert gas) or GMAW (gas metal-arc welding) uses a consumable electrode in the form of a continuous wire. The system is semiautomatic with the current setting, gas flow, and wire speed being preset and the torch or gun operated manually.

There are several different types of MIG, with the spray arc and short arc being the most common. The spray arc uses a high current which is unsuitable for repairing light gauge metal. The short arc, also called short circuiting transfer welding, is a process where the wire is in contact with the work piece. This creates a short for a fraction of a second, and the heat produced

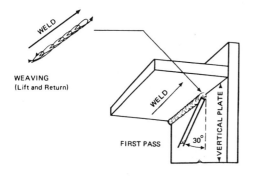

WEAVING
(Lift and Return)

WELD

WELD

FIRST PASS

30°

VERTICAL PLATE

Figure 5-18 Overhead welds. *(Courtesy of Airco.)*

Figure 5-19 Auto body repair using MIG welding. *(Courtesy of Airco.)*

melts the wire. The metal is deposited, the arc is reestablished, and the heat produced forms a puddle. Once again, the wire approaches the work piece and creates another short, melting the wire once again. This all happens in a fraction of a second.

This type of metal transfer produces a small puddle which is easier to control in all positions. The number of short circuits per second is controlled by the wire speed. For thin gauge metal like 24 gauge (0.6 mm) the wire speed is approximately 12″ to 20″ (304.8 mm to 508 mm) per minute to approximately 290″ (7,366 mm) per minute for 1/4″ to 5/16″ (6.35 mm to 7.94 mm) plates. The wire for machines used for sheetmetal is either .030″ or .035″ (0.8 mm or 0.9 mm) in diameter and is available in 8″ to 12″ (203.2 mm to 304.8 mm) spools.

Like the TIG, the MIG uses an inert gas

for shielding the weld area. Either a mixture of 75 percent argon and 25 percent CO_2 (carbon dioxide) or 100 percent CO_2 can be used. Carbon dioxide is being used more frequently. The argon and CO_2 mixture produces a neater bead, with greater welding speeds and less splatter while CO_2 has excellent penetration qualities.

The MIG welding machine is a highly specialized and expensive piece of equipment. The MIG welding equipment consists of a power source, a wire feed unit, a gun and welding cable assembly, and a gas supply with a regulator flow meter.

In some models, the wire spool is inside the cabinet, away from the dirt and grinding dust, while other models have the wire spool and wire control mounted outside the cabinet where it can be attached to a suitable power source.

The power source generally used for body repair is constant potential power with about 150 to 160 ampere output with either selected current taps or variable current control. These machines have basically two controls: the amperage and the wire speed. Some machines have a chart on the amperage control to indicate the differ-

ent thicknesses of metal. The wire speed control also has a chart to indicate the metal thickness.

The MIG gun is generally air cooled because of the lower amperage used. The high current gun is water cooled. The wire feed mechanism or drive unit is located inside most units on top (called a push-type unit). Where fine wire or soft aluminum is used, a pull-type unit is located in the handle of the gun.

When the trigger of the gun is depressed, the wire drive unit and the shielding gas solenoid are activated, as well as the current to the gun. These guns are available with different nozzle designs and contact tips for different size wire. The nozzles direct the flow of shielding gas to the weld zone and must be cleaned frequently of spatter which restricts the flow of shielding gas. A spray or liquid is available to decrease the buildup of spatter on the nozzle.

The contact tips, which carry the current, are subjected to wear and must be changed if the holes become egg shaped. Avoid dropping heavy objects or hot metal on the MIG cables in order to prevent dam-

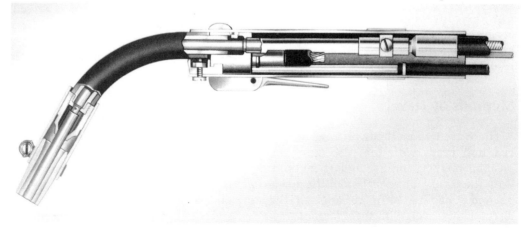

Figure 5-20 MIG gun. *(Courtesy of Linde Corporation.)*

age to the wire liner, power cable, or shielding gas lines.

Welding Wire

The welding wire (or consumable wire electrode) should be similar to the type of metal being welded. Like the stick electrode classification numbers, the welding wire is similar in classification. For example, welding wire for general-purpose welding is E-70S-3. The E identifies it as an electrode, the 70 represents the tensile strength in thousands (70,000), the S indicates solid bare wire, and the 3 specifies the chemical composition of the particular wire in accordance with the AWS specifications.

Wire Stickout or Work Distance

The wire *stickout* is the distance between the nozzle and the work piece. The distance may vary with different machines but the average is about $\frac{1}{2}$" (12.7 mm). If the distance is too short between the nozzle and work piece, the wire will fuse to the contact tip or the spatter will restrict the wire from running freely.

An excessive stickout will decrease the penetration of the weld metal, will cause improper melting of the wire, and will result in poor looking beads.

Methods of Travel

There are two methods of traveling (or running) beads with the MIG gun: the pushing method and the pulling method. With the *pushing* (or *leading*) *method* the gun is pointed at about a 10° to 20° angle, in the direction of travel. With the *pulling* (or *dragging*) *method*, the gun is pointed at a 10° to 20° angle, away from the direction of

travel. The gun is held at a right angle to the flat surface. Tipping the gun at an excessive angle will cause air to be drawn into the weld area due to the distorted gas shield.

Starting to Weld

The following procedure may vary with different makes of MIG welders. With the machine turned off, check all electrical connections, remove spatter from the nozzle, and check the contact tip for wear (replace if necessary). Check the wire supply, rollers, and gas line inside the cabinet or the externally mounted wire control units. Set the wire speed and current in relation to the thickness of metal to be welded. Many of the MIGs made for body work do not have a voltage control that can be adjusted. It is preset at the time of manufacture. On large machines, with voltage control, set between 15 and 17 volts.

Turn the machine on, open shielding gas tank valve, and check the gas flow. The gas flow will vary with different machines and MIG guns. Some average between 15 to 30 cu ft per minute ($7\frac{1}{2}$ to $14\frac{1}{4}$ liters/min) using either CO_2 or a mixture of 75 percent argon and 25 percent CO_2. Depress the trigger and check the wire feeding out of the nozzle and the shielding gas flow. Turn off the machine and secure adequate clothing and a good welding helmet with the proper arc welding lens. Pick out some practice metal, the same type and thickness that will be used later. Remove oil and dirt; if painted, remove paint.

NOTE: Some shops will use old panels to get the new operator accustomed to welding on that type metal.

Review safety practices and procedures, taking into consideration the surrounding area. Securely attach the ground cable to the work piece and turn the machine on. Be aware of the machine switch and the master switch for the welder current in case of an emergency.

To start the arc, two methods can be used with most machines. With one method, the MIG gun is held just above the starting point without the wire touching the work piece. By squeezing the trigger, the current, gas flow, and wire feed is activated. When the wire nears the work piece, the arc will start. Bring the gun to proper stickout distance and hold it at the recommended angle as previously mentioned.

With the other method, the wire is in contact with the work piece before the trigger is squeezed. Practice running beads while maintaining the proper distance and angle. Move the gun at a uniform rate.

On light gauge metal, use the pull or drag method and the push method on heavier metal or use both methods to see the different results. At the end of a bead, move the gun back over the bead a short distance, then break contact to eliminate the craters.

The new operator should master the simple flat beads or welds before attempting to weld the different types of joints. Check the beads for uniformity and appearance.

At times, it may be necessary to adjust the wire feed and/or current to obtain a better bead: for example, when welding in different positions or on two different thicknesses of metal at one time, when welding poor fitting panels, or when welding under other conditions that may affect the weld.

When welding the different types of joints, the vertical angle is basically the same as in stick electrode with the pulling or pushing angle ranging from 10° to 20°. However, there will be many occasions when welding body panels that the proper

angles of the gun cannot be maintained due to the location of the joints or their inaccessibility.

MIG Spot Welding

Some makes of MIG machines have an optional spot-welding kit that can be installed to convert the MIG to a spot welder. These kits consist of a set of MIG gun nozzles and a control panel with a spot timer and a burn back control (Figure 5-21).

This is ideal for torch welding panels together prior to finish welding with the wire weld. Spot together where finish welding is not required.

Arc Spotter

Another type of spot welder used for attacking body panels is called an *arc spotter*. The arc spotter uses a special electrode held in a gun-type frame or holder (Figure 5-22). The frame or holder uses a sliding handle so the proper amount of electrode to be used on the spot weld is preset. The

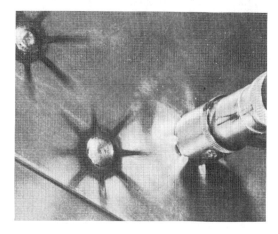

Figure 5-21 MIG spot welding. *(Courtesy of Linde Corporation.)*

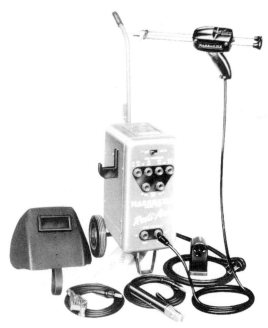

Figure 5-22 Arc spotter. *(Courtesy of Marquette Division, Applied Power Inc.)*

electrode will advance downward until it reaches the setting and then stop when the spot weld is finished.

This type welder is limited to lap or flange welds on light gauge body panels. The area to be welded must be free of all paint, dirt, oil, or any other foreign materials. The two pieces of metal to be joined must be tight together in order to get the proper penetration.

The power unit has three heat or current settings — high, medium or low. To use, install the electrode in the holder through the brass nozzle and lock it in place. Slide the gun handle until the tip of the electrode is just inside the nozzle. Obtain two pieces of light gauge metal and clean them, then form a lap joint. Connect the ground to the metal and the current power unit to the power supply. Start with the heat selector in the medium tap. Put on the arc welding helmet and switch on the power unit.

Place the nozzle against the metal and push the gun handle toward it. When the electrode touches the metal, the arc will start. Pull the trigger, hold down, and continue pushing the handle toward the metal. The arc will stop automatically when the preset setting is reached and the proper amount of metal is deposited. Check the weld for penetration. This can be done by prying apart the two pieces of metal.

RESISTANCE SPOT WELDER

The resistance spot welder, or panel spotter, is used for joining light gauge metal or body panels (Figure 5-23). This type welding creates less heat than any other welding method and is used extensively in the production of automobile bodies. The panel spotter is limited to mostly lap welds or flange welds and cannot be used for panels with poor fitup.

Figure 5-23 Resistance spot welder. *(Courtesy of Lenco Inc.)*

Two disadvantages are that the metal surfaces must be absolutely clear (i.e., bare metal) and the two pieces of metal to be joined must be tight together. If an air gap exists between the two pieces, the welder electrodes will burn holes in the metal.

The panel spotter is portable, and some are equipped with a long power supply cord for movement around the automobile. The unit consists of a power supply with a timer control and two heavy welding cables with electrode holders. The electrodes are made of copper and the tip ends should not exceed $\frac{1}{8}$" (3.17 mm) in diameter. When the tips become worn or coated with body steel, they must be ground to the proper diameter and must be flat at the point of contact. Worn or coated tips will cause poor, weak welds with decreased penetration. The electrodes are easily removed by just tapping the holder.

The timer is adjustable and may have to be adjusted for each job. If the timer is set too low, the welds will not have the proper fusion. A high timer setting will cause too much heat and will result in holes in the metal, thus coating the tip with steel which will require additional grinding.

To weld with the panel spotter, clean the metal edges to be welded and form a lap joint. Check the electrode tips for the proper diameter and condition. The edges where the metal laps should be sanded with a disc sander to the bare metal. The surfaces must be free of paint, primer, or dirt, about 1" (25.4 mm) beyond the lap joints. Also, the area where the electrodes are used must be sanded to bare metal to prevent burning holes in the metal. Because little or no flash is present during panel spotting, flash glasses are suitable. Gloves are optional because of the low heat. Set the timer at about 20 and connect the power cable.

Space the electrodes about 2" to 4" (50.8 mm to 101.6 mm) apart and about $\frac{1}{4}$" (6.35 mm) from the edge of the lap joint edge.

Press the two electrode handles tightly against the metal and depress the ON switch in the handle. The welder will turn off automatically with the timer setting. Move the electrodes over from 1" to 2" (25.4 mm to 50.8 mm) and repeat this procedure. The spot welds can form close together or up to 2" (50.8 mm) apart (Figure 2–24).

One of the problems that exists when using a spot welder is the distortion of certain panels; that is, pressure must be exerted to hold the two pieces together, and this pressure will bend the panels. This can be eliminated by the use of pressure from behind the panel to prevent it from bending.

NOTE: The panel spotter can be used for attaching stove bolts, screws, and washers to panels. The washers are welded to a dented area, and with the use of a slide hammer the dent can be pulled out. After straightening, the washers are twisted off with a pair of pliers. This method is better than drilling holes in the panels to remove dents with a slide hammer. Some auto repair equipment suppliers have these type attachments to be used with the panel spotter. The preparation of the panels is the same as for panel spotting; that is, the surface must be clean.

PLASTIC WELDING

The later model automobiles contain more hard and soft plastic parts than ever before. These parts are expensive, and many of them can be repaired by using a plastic welder.

There are approximately 16 different

Completely welded panel shows perfect contour which is free of distortion. Joint is ready to feather edge and receive body filler material. Weld spacing is about ¾ inch.

Soldered joint ready to finish off. 40% less body filler needed. Total job time is 50% of normal time.

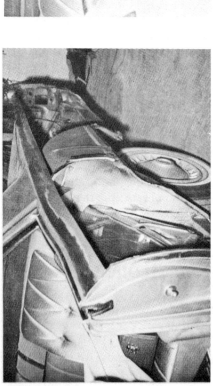

Quarter panel is cut off approximately 2″ below the peak crown. Operator grinds off paint to bare metal before cutting off old panel.

PANELSPOTTER welder in action. Operator simply presses both electrodes against the work and pulls trigger on the gun. Machine automatically turns on and off. Welds are complete.

Figure 5-24 Procedure for welding with a panel spotter. (*Courtesy of Lenco Inc.*)

plastics and variations of plastics used in the manufacture of automobiles and trucks. These are either *thermoplastic* or *thermosetting-type plastics*. The thermoplastic can be softened by the use of heat, and many of them can be welded without real problems. The thermosetting-type plastic will not soften after the plastic is made and therefore cannot be welded, although some can be repaired by other methods. A good example of thermoset material is the polyester in fiberglass.

The plastic currently in use is coded with an international code number which is generally stamped on the back side of the panels; for example, polyvinyl chloride (PVC) which is used for filler panel and is weldable or polypropylene (PP) which is used for inner fender panels and radiator shrouds.

The plastic welding kits consist of a heat element, generally 500 watts, an air regulator and pressure gauge, three welding tips and a selection of various types of plastic welding rod to match the type plastic to be welded (Figure 5–25).

The air regulator should be set at 3 psi (20.7 kPa) for most repair jobs. The welding temperature will vary from 500° F to 575° F (260° C to 298° C) depending on the type of material. Follow the equipment manufacturer's recommendations.

Welding plastic is similar to welding with an oxy-acetylene torch in that there is a feel or knack to be learned which takes practice.

The three tips supplied with the set are used as follows:

The *tack welding tip* is used for tacking the broken pieces together for welding. To tack weld, draw the tip along the joint, and the tip will fuse a thin line along the joint.

The *round tip* is used for sharp corners and filling small holes. To weld, select the proper welding rod and cut the end to a 60° angle. Position the rod at a 90° angle to the work piece. Heat the work piece and rod

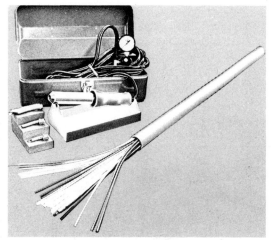

Figure 5-25 Auto body starter kit. Kit includes color-coded starter kit of rod, #10 speed tip, #4 tacking tip, #5 round tip, air regulator, pressure gauge, welder stand, carrying case, and 500 watt element. *(Courtesy of Seelye Inc.)*

until the material is tacky or softened, then press the rod firmly into the joint with the point of the rod away from the direction of travel. After the material is properly bonded, heat the rod and work piece with a slight fanning motion in line with the weld. Keep pressure on the rod at all times and maintain the 90° angle of the rod.

The *high speed welding tip* is best for long straight cracks or joints. Use a welding rod cut at a 60° angle and place in the feeder tube of the tip. Hold the welder at right angles to the section to be repaired. Using the curved end of the tip, press the rod into the weld. Move the welder forward, lower the angle to about 45°, and feed the welding rod into the feeder tube. Keep moving across the length of the weld. Watch the bead formation and adjust the speed or heat as necessary. If any of the rod remains, draw it through the tip and cut it off.

NOTE: Remove the rod from the tube to prevent clogging the opening.

PLASTIC IDENTIFICATION
CHEVROLET

SYMBOL	PLASTIC MATERIAL
ABS	ABS
ABS/PVC	ABS/Vinyl
PA	Nylon
PC	Lexan
PE	Polyethylene
PP	Polypropylene
PPO	Noryl
PUR	Thermoset Polyurethane
PVC	Polyvinyl Chloride (Vinyl)
SAN	SAN
TPUR	Thermoplastic Polyurethane
UP	Polyester (Fiberglas)
TPR	Thermoplastic Rubber
EPDM	Ethylene Propylene Diene Monomer

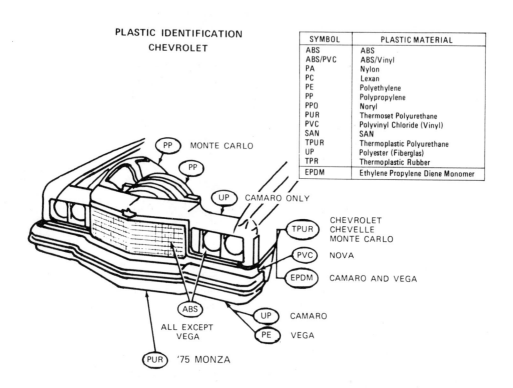

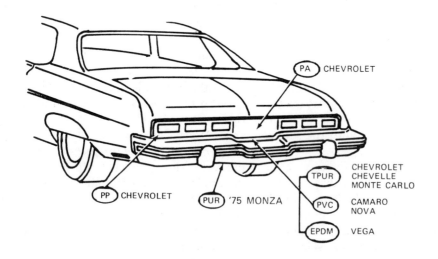

Figure 5-26 *(Courtesy of General Motors Corporation.)*

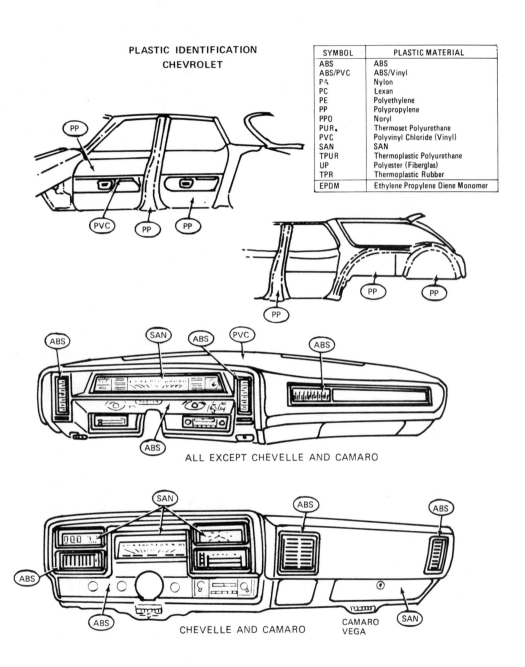

PLASTIC IDENTIFICATION
CHEVROLET

SYMBOL	PLASTIC MATERIAL
ABS	ABS
ABS/PVC	ABS/Vinyl
PA	Nylon
PC	Lexan
PE	Polyethylene
PP	Polypropylene
PPO	Noryl
PUR.	Thermoset Polyurethane
PVC	Polyvinyl Chloride (Vinyl)
SAN	SAN
TPUR	Thermoplastic Polyurethane
UP	Polyester (Fiberglas)
TPR	Thermoplastic Rubber
EPDM	Ethylene Propylene Diene Monomer

ALL EXCEPT CHEVELLE AND CAMARO

CHEVELLE AND CAMARO

CAMARO
VEGA

Figure 5-26 *(continued)*

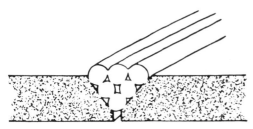

No bond — weld can be
pulled apart

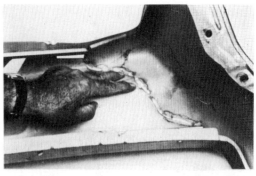

Reverse side of decorative polyurethane bumper
cover showing application of weld in short sections
to align crack with round welding tip.

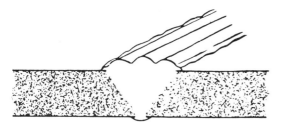

Proper weld

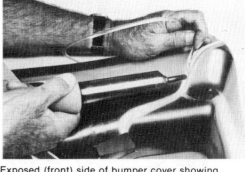

Exposed (front) side of bumper cover showing
application of a continuous weld with round tip. No
tacking is necessary on this side of bumper cover.
Paint has been "feathered" back.

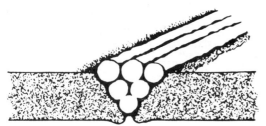

Burned weld and material
charred — weak weld

Figure 5-27   Welding analysis. *(Courtesy of Seelye Inc.)*

Identification of Some Plastics

To test, remove a small sample from a
hidden area, hold with pliers, and ignite.
Watch the burning plastic and compare the
odor of the piece with the odor of a color-
coded welding rod.

1. *Polyethylene (PE)* — the smell resembles
   burned wax and will burn after flame is
   removed.

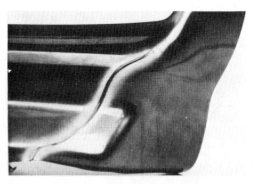

Completed polyurethane weld. Elapsed time:
including preparation approximately 30 minutes.
Next steps are to fill voids and pinholes with a
structural adhesive, sand down and paint.

Figure 5-28   Typical plastic repairs. *(Courtesy of Seelye Inc.)*

Typical torn out bolt hole damaged on collision impact.

Using high speed welding tip to lay a welding rod across damaged and missing edge of bolt hole. Note that two rods are being laid. A ribbon rod may be used instead of two round rods.

Finished bolt hole repair, ready for reassembly. Elapsed time: 15 minutes. This type of repair can also be done by replacing/ welding a piece of the damaged material as described earlier.

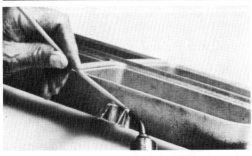

Welding of ABS plastic auto grille bolt lug using round tip for tight corners. Welding is done following grooving and tacking procedures covered earlier.

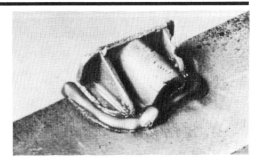

Welding grille attachment lug. Elapsed time: approximately 15 minutes.

Figure 5-29 Plastic repairs. *(Courtesy of Seelye Inc.)*

2. *Polypropylene (PP)* — little smoke produced, has an odd smell, and will burn.

3. *Polyurethane (TPUR)* — produces a yellow orange flame with black smoke.

4. *Polyvinyl chloride (PVC)* — is self-extinguishing, has its own distinguishing smell. Gives off gray smoke and forms a char.

5. *ABS* — will burn, produces a heavy black smoke.

CAUTION: Some types of plastic give off obnoxious odors and poisonous fumes when burned or heated, especially polyvinyl chloride. Avoid inhaling these fumes.

A good weld cannot be pulled apart even when hot because the rod and base material flow together. Avoid overheating the material to prevent charring or discoloration. A small amount of juicing should form on each side of the bead or weld. *Juicing* means that the plastic has reached the melting point along the edge of the weld. Repair procedures may vary with different manufacturers (Figure 5-28 and Figure 5-29).

Questions

1. What type of dangerous rays are given off when electric welding?
2. Why must a welding helmet be worn instead of goggles when arc welding?
3. What shade lens should be used for small electrodes?
4. Why is it important to have a clean lens in front of the welding lens?
5. Why must chipping goggles or cover goggles be worn when chipping slag?
6. What type of clothing is recommended when arc welding?
7. Can an improper ground cable cause welding problems?
8. Why is a well-ventilated work area important when arc welding?
9. What safety precautions should be followed before welding in an automobile?
10. List some of the most common methods of selecting proper welding current used on some of the welding machines.
11. What is the average input and output voltage of the most common welding machines?
12. What is one advantage of a portable welding machine?
13. What is ac and dc current?
14. What is dcrp and dcsp?
15. What is *arc blow*?
16. Which gives deeper penetration, dcrp or dcsp?
17. What is the AWS?
18. What does *70* mean in an E7014 electrode?
19. Does the thickness of the metal to be welded have any effect on the amperage setting?
20. What causes the ripples in a bead to be pointed?
21. What is a *crater* in a bead?
22. What causes excessive spatter and poor fusion when running beads?
23. What is the *root* of a bead?
24. Why must heavier plates bevel?
25. What is *skip welding* and *backstep welding?*
26. When butt welding, why should the plates be spaced apart?
27. What two methods are used for starting the arc?
28. What is *slag intrusion?*
29. What is *undercutting?*
30. What force acts on the molten metal when horizontal or vertical welding?
31. Which type welding gives the most penetration, vertical up or vertical down?
32. Name some of the advantages of MIG welding over electric arc welding.
33. What electrode is used in MIG welding?

34. What types of shielding gases are used for MIG welding?
35. What is wire *stickout*?
36. What are two methods of running beads?
37. What is a *resistance spot welder*?
38. What are two disadvantages of the resistance spot welder?
39. How can different types of plastic panels be identified?

Power Tools

chapter

6

DRILLS

Portable electric drills or air drills are used frequently by the bodyman for drilling holes for rivets and moldings, for cutting holes for antennas and for a variety of other repair jobs (Figures 6–1 and 6–2).

The air-powered drill is more useful and safer to use if there is an adequate air supply. The speed of the drill can be controlled by the air pressure. You can get into tighter spaces because of its size, and it can be used safely on wet floors.

NOTE: Always use safety goggles or glasses when operating power equipment.

The size of the drill is determined by the largest drill bit that will fit in the chuck. The drills are generally available in $\frac{1}{4}$", $\frac{3}{8}$", and $\frac{1}{2}$" (6.35 mm, 9.52 mm, and 12.7 mm) sizes, light to heavy duty. Some electric drills offer variable speeds. For larger holes, drill bits are made with $\frac{1}{2}$" shanks (12.7 mm), and the bit sizes are from $\frac{17}{32}$" to 1" (13.49 mm to 25.4 mm). The drill bits with $\frac{1}{4}$" (6.35 mm) shanks range from $\frac{9}{32}$" to $\frac{1}{2}$" (7.14 mm to 12.7 mm) bits (Figure 6–3).

Most drill chucks are three-jaw types and hold the drill bit securely. The chuck is loosened or tightened by a chuck key. The key should be taped or chained to the plug end of the electric cord to prevent it from being lost. The key of the air-powered drill can be attached to the handle of the drill.

CAUTION: Remove the key from the chuck before starting the drill; otherwise, the key will fly from the chuck causing injury to the operator or someone nearby. Some keys are spring loaded and come out of the chuck when the pressure is released. (See Chapter 2 for drilling information.)

Figure 6-1 Hole saws are used for cutting holes in sheetmetal for antennas or other pieces of equipment. *(Courtesy of Milwaukee Tools, Division of Amstar Company.)*

BENCH GRINDERS, PEDESTAL GRINDERS

The electric bench grinder is used for grinding operations such as sharpening drill bits and chisels, removing excess metal, or smoothing welds.

All grinders must be equipped with an eye shield, wheel guards, and a tool rest. The tool rest should be located at the center or just below the center of the wheel and within $\frac{1}{8}$" (3.17 mm) of the grinding wheel. The tool rest is used to support the object being ground (Figure 6-4).

CAUTION: Always stand to one side when turning on the grinder until it has

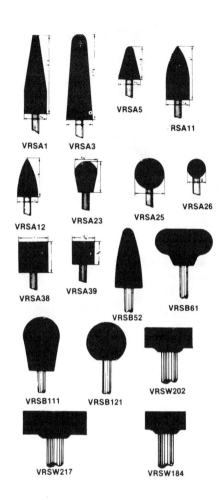

Figure 6-2 Vitrified rotary stones, used with either air or electric $\frac{1}{4}$" drills. *(Mac Tools Inc.)*

reached full speed. The wheel could have an unseen crack in it. Safety glasses or goggles must be worn at all times when using the grinder.

Grinding wheels are made of either silicone carbide or aluminum oxide, which

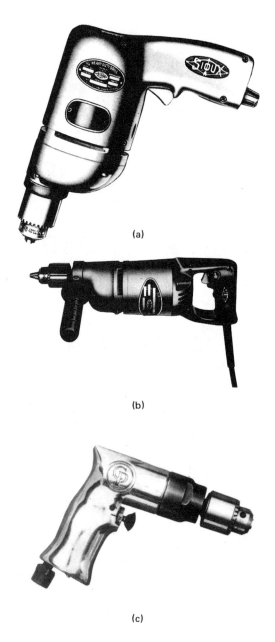

(a)

(b)

(c)

Figure 6–3 (a) $\frac{1}{4}$″ electric drill; (b) $\frac{1}{2}$″ electric drill. *(Courtesy of Sioux.)* (c) Heavy-duty air drill. *(Courtesy of Chicago Pneumatic.)*

Figure 6–4 Bench grinder. *(Courtesy of Sioux.)*

have replaced the softer materials such as sandstone, emery, and carborundum. Both of these man-made materials are produced in electric furnaces. Silicone carbide is made from sand and carbon (coke), and aluminum oxide is made from aluminum ore, called *bauxite*.

The grinding wheels will vary in size, shape, size of grit, and grade depending on what they are used for. The grit or grain size will vary from coarse to very fine. Generally, the coarse wheels are used for rough grinding and quick removal of metal. The medium wheels are used for general grinding, and the fine wheels are used for sharpening tools or grinding to close limits.

Always keep the work moving across the face of the wheel. If work is held in one spot, a groove will form in the wheel or the face will be worn crooked. The face can be restored by using a dressing tool. To dress the wheel, turn on the grinder and wait until the grinder reaches top speed. Press the dressing tool against the wheel and move the tool back and forth across the face of the wheel until the face or surface is smooth and square to the sides. Avoid grinding on the sides of the wheel as much as possible.

Wire wheels can be used on the grinders.

Many grinders come equipped with one medium abrasive wheel and one wire wheel. The wire wheels are used for removing rust or corrosion from metal as well as paint and dirt.

Wire wheels are available in coarse wire for rough general cleaning, fine wire for fine finishing and polishing, and some for high speed buffing.

CAUTION: Wire wheels are very dangerous to use because pieces of wire have a tendency to break off after the wheel has been used for awhile. It is advisable to use a vise grip or pliers when wire buffing small parts or objects. If the fingers come in contact with the wheel, serious injury can result. Wear leather gloves.

Figure 6-5 Air sander with 5" sanding disc and backing plate. *(Photo by S. Suydam.)*

DISC GRINDERS, AIR OR ELECTRIC

The disc grinder, either air (Figure 6-5) or electric, is an important tool for doing body work. The grinder is used for removing paint and rust, cutting off damaged door panels, removing surplus weld material, and many other purposes. Generally, the electric disc grinder is used for removing paint or rust from large areas, and the air grinder is used for smaller areas.

The sanding discs are made in various grit and types of coating. The coatings are either open or closed. This means that the grit on an open coat disc is spread farther apart to reduce clogging when grinding paint on soft materials. The closed coat disc is used for metal finishing.

The size grits range from #16 (4), a very coarse grit and #24 (3) a coarse for rough sanding to #36 (2) and #50 (1) for medium

sanding, to #80 ($\frac{1}{0}$) for fine sanding and metal finishing (Figure 6-6).

The electric disc grinder, with no-load speeds up to 5,500 RPA is very powerful and must be handled with care.

Figure 6-6 Sanding discs: top — 16 (4) and 24 (3) grit, open coat 5" (127 mm) and 7" (177.8 mm) disc; bottom — 24 (3), 50 (1), and 80 (1/0) grit, closed coat disc.

NOTE: Before attempting to use a disc grinder, especially the heavy type, a person should receive instructions. The disc grinder is one of the leading causes of injury in the body shop.

Light-, medium-, and heavy-duty disc grinders are available. The heavy-duty grinders can operate under pressure for a long period of time without overheating. Because of their power, they are practically impossible to stall.

The disc grinder uses either a 7" or 9" (178 mm or 229 mm) disc with the 7" (178 mm) being the most popular (Figures 6-7 and 6-8). The grinder can also be fitted with a wire cup brush for removing rust and scale, a cone-type attachment for getting into curved surfaces, and a depressed center abrasion wheel for heavy grinding of metal and welds (Figures 6-9 and 6-10).

The disc grinder must be used with caution when grinding on sheetmetal edges or body gaps between panels or near moldings. If the grinder catches, it can be easily

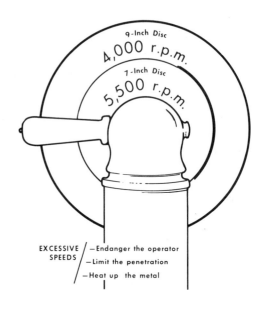

Figure 6-8 Maximum tool speeds. *(Courtesy of 3M Company.)*

knocked from the operator's hands. Keep the grinder away from the body to avoid catching on the clothing.

Because it is electrical, it should not be operated on wet floors. Also, check the electrical cord for proper grounding. Wear safety glasses or goggles and, if necessary, a dust mask.

When using the disc grinder, tilt the grinder about 5° from the surface with just enough pressure to bend the disc, until about 1" to 1½" (25.4 to 12.7 mm) of the disc makes contact with the surface of the metal. If the grinder is held at a greater angle, only the edge or a small part of the disc makes contact with the surface causing deep gouges and burrs. If the disc grinder is held flat on the surface, it will be too hard to control and the cutting action will be irregular. Keep the disc grinder moving at all times when in contact with the surface. It can cut through the sheetmetal in a few

Figure 6-7 Backing disc for sanders, available in 5", 7", and 9" sizes. *(Courtesy of 3M Company.)*

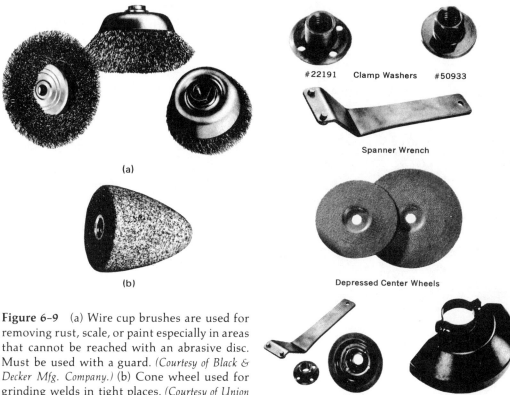

#22191 Clamp Washers **#50933**

Spanner Wrench

Depressed Center Wheels

Disc Wheel Adapter Guard

Figure 6-9 (a) Wire cup brushes are used for removing rust, scale, or paint especially in areas that cannot be reached with an abrasive disc. Must be used with a guard. *(Courtesy of Black & Decker Mfg. Company.)* (b) Cone wheel used for grinding welds in tight places. *(Courtesy of Union Carbide.)*

Figure 6-10 Depressed center wheels are used for grinding welds, trimming frame sections, or other heavy grinding operations. *(Courtesy of Black & Decker Mfg. Company.)*

seconds, especially on a crease (Figure 6-11).

NOTE: If grinding must be done on aluminum, use extreme caution. First use a #36 grit (2) disc — #24 and #16 (3 and 4) grit disc will cause extreme damage to the soft aluminum. Carefully remove the paint and avoid removing or grinding away the metal. Keep grinder moving and avoid heat build-up. Cool metal at intervals if necessary.

When preparing to use the grinder, select the proper grit disc. Use a #24 (3) grit disc open coat if it will do the job rather than a #16 (4) because the #16 (4) leaves deeper grooves in the metal.

NOTE: Always disconnect the power

cord before changing the disc to prevent accidents.

Check surrounding area for flammables, the sparks carry a long way. When grinding panels, grind along the contour in a long sweeping motion, back and forth. Grinding across the contour will leave valleys or low spots. At the end of each stroke, slightly release the pressure of the grinder on the surface and immediately start the return stroke adding light pressure. Do not let the grinder remain in one place, keep it mov-

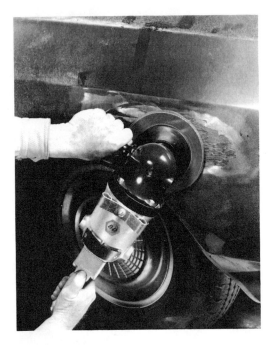

Figure 6-11 Disc grinder. *(Courtesy of Black & Decker Mfg. Company.)*

ing. Never go to the very edge of the panel. Grind the edges separately. On the edges, make sure the disc is turning off the panel or the sparks are flying away from the panel. This also applies when grinding pieces of sheetmetal to avoid catching the disc on the edge of the panel. When grinding along sharp crease lines or edges, use very light pressure to avoid grinding off too much metal.

If no further body work is to be performed, replace the disc with a #50 (1) disc and go over the entire surface to remove the heavy grinder marks. If possible, move the grinder at right angles to the first grinding. This is called *cross-grinding.*

For grinding small areas and in tight spaces, the air sander is very popular because of its ease in handling and its size. The air sander is available with 4", 5", and

7" (102 mm, 127 mm and 178 mm) grinding discs and with different size backing plates to accommodate the different size discs.

The free run speeds range from 5,000 to 25,000 RPMs. Air grinders are available in light-, medium-, and heavy-duty models. The lightweight air grinder with a 5" (127 mm) grinding disc is the most popular model. The speed of the air grinder can be controlled with a regulator to make it more versatile. A drill chuck can be installed on some models to convert them to air drills. Many wire brushes and small grinding stones are available to work in confined areas. Because the grinder is air operated, it is a safe tool to use when working on wet floors.

The air grinder procedure for removing paint and rust is the same as for the electric grinder.

USE OF SANDERS

Air-Operated Sanders

Sanders are either electric or air operated. Although the electric sander or orbital sander can be used in body shops, most shops prefer to use the air operated. Electric sanders cannot be used for wet sanding and cannot be used safely on wet floors. The electric sander is also larger and heavier as compared to the air-operated model.

The sanders are available in two different types. One is the popular orbital sander, often called a *vibrator sander* (or the *jitterbug*). The other type is the *orbital disc sander* (or *dual action sander*) (Figure 6-12).

NOTE: Because of dust conditions, lubricate the sander with the recommended lubricant or oil.

Figure 6–12   Orbital sander. *(Courtesy of Chicago Pneumatic.)*

Figure 6–13   Air sanding board. *(Courtesy of Chicago Pneumatic.)*

The orbital sander is available in three different size pads, for 3″ × 8″ (76 × 203 mm), 3²/₃″ × 9″ (92 mm × 229 mm), and 2³/₄″ × 17¹/₂″ (70 mm × 445 mm) sandpaper.

The short sanders are used for feather-edging paint, sanding plastic, and fine sanding with either wet or dry sandpaper. Most of the sanders operate at about 80 psi (550 kPa). Operating these sanders at full line pressure will damage them. Some of the sanders are equipped with a vacuum to pick up most of the dust caused by sanding.

When operating the air sander, hold it flat against the surface with just enough pressure to control it. Keep the sander moving back and forth across the surface to be sanded. The sander cuts very fast on plastics, so keep it moving and check for smoothness frequently. The long sander (Figure 6–13), often called a *speed file* or *speed sander,* is used primarily for rough and finish sanding of plastic. This sander is ideal for large areas because of the large surface area of the pad.

Orbital Disc Sanders

The orbital disc sander operates with an off-center rotary motion. Most of these sanders are called *random orbit,* that is, the pad assembly is free turning or free spinning and is not turned by the motor shaft. This type motion helps keep the sanding disc from clogging and does not leave sanding rings (Figure 6–14).

Figure 6–14   Orbital disc sander. *(Courtesy of Chicago Pneumatic.)*

The dual action orbital sander can be converted to a regular sander by engaging a clutch or lock which locks the pad to the shaft of the motor.

This type disc sander uses a glue on–type sanding disc, generally in 5" or 6" (127 mm or 152 mm). A special glue or adhesive is used so several discs can be used and then removed without having to apply adhesive on each disc. A special pad is available to use with preglue sanding discs. The sanding discs come in rolls with a dispenser that accommodates two rolls at one time.

Many of the random orbit sanders are equipped with an air-regulating valve and come either with or without a vacuum system.

With light pressure hold the pad flat on the surface to be sanded. Keep the sander moving back and forth on the surface. This sander is ideal for featheredging, sanding large flat areas, and finish sanding of body plastic. The dual action sander can be used first as a regular sander to remove the rough material and then switched to random orbit for featheredging.

Rotary Sander

The rotary sander is used primarily for rough sanding of body plastic. The sander has a revolving long cylinder with a standard sheet of 9" × 11" (229 mm × 279 mm) abrasive paper attached to it. Normally, #36 (2), #40 (1½) or #80 (⅛) grit paper is used, but finer paper can be used if desired. After the plastic is cut down to about the right level, other types of sanders (the orbital or random orbit sander) are used for the final sanding.

Because of the round cylinder, the rotary sander can be used on almost any contour. The advantage of this sander is that it creates less dust because of the revolving

motion and cuts fast. This sander can be used on fiberglass and other types of materials.

IMPACT HAMMER

The impact hammer, or air chisel, is another useful tool for a variety of different operations. The tool is used for removing damaged or rusted out panels, cutting apart spot-welded body joints, driving out door hinge pins, removing ball joints and tie rods, and many other useful operations (Figure 6–15).

The different types of chisels are inserted in the end of the tool. They are held in place with either a spring, a spring with safety jaws, or a safety chuck. The spring with safety jaw and safety chuck are recommended to keep the chisels from accidentally flying out of the tool. If the chisel comes out accidentally, it could cause injury to the operator or to a bystander and could possibly damage the body or break a window.

The tool is operated by a piston, called the *hammer,* which strikes the end of the chisel. The movement of the piston is con-

Figure 6–15 Air hammer. *(Courtesy of Chicago Pneumatic.)*

trolled by the amount of air and pressure entering the tool. The tool, depending on make and size, may vary from 2,000 to 4,000 maximum hammer blows per minute. This is why the tool must be used with care.

When cutting sheetmetal, the operator must be alert because the air chisel cuts very fast. A wrong cut or cutting too far will result in extra labor to repair the damage. For example, cutting off a quarter panel with a panel cutter chisel could lead to extra work if the chisel cuts into the wheelhouse. Use gloves when cutting off sheetmetal because the edges are very sharp. Never allow the tool to run free. Hold the tool against the work before pressing the switch. The chisel could fly out or possibly break the piston. Use the recommended air pressure and oil frequently.

Figure 6-16 Heavy duty metal cutting shears. *(Courtesy of Milwaukee.)*

USE OF METAL CUTTING SHEARS

There are many different types of hand held metal cutting shears, available either electric or air operated (Figure 6-16).

With shears the bodyman can cut much quicker than by hand and with more accuracy. Most of the shears leave a smooth straight edge, with less distortion as compared to the edge cut with the air impact chisel. Because of the construction of some of the shears, not all types are suitable for cutting off or trimming body panels.

These shears are ideal for cutting out panels from flat sheets for patching. When cutting sheetmetal with the shears, wear gloves because the edges are very sharp.

Questions

1. Which is safer to use on wet floors: air- or electric-powered tools?
2. What determines the size of the electric drill?
3. Where should the tool rest be located on a bench grinder?
4. What are grinding wheels made of?
5. What can be used to restore the correct shape of a grinding wheel?
6. What should be used when cleaning small objects with a wire wheel?
7. Why are disc grinders dangerous around body gaps or new moldings?
8. What is the proper angle when using a disc grinder?
9. What must be done before changing a grinding disc?
10. Why must the grinder be kept moving on the surface of a panel?

11. Which type grinding disc leaves deeper grooves in the metal, the #16 (4) or #50 (1) disc?

12. What is the normal operating pressure of the vibrator sander (or jitterbug)?

13. What is a *speed file?*

14. What is a *random orbit sander?*

15. What power tools are ideal for featheredging?

16. What is a *rotary sander?*

17. What controls the speed of the air chisel?

18. Why is it dangerous to let the air chisel run free?

PROPERTIES OF AUTO BODY SHEETMETAL

The automobile is in the process of going through drastic changes in design, construction, and weight. The early automobile was rather simply constructed and contained large amounts of wood. Some roof panels, for example, were metal-covered wood frames with the center covered with canvas. As time went on the automobile became larger and more complex. During the 1930s, the automobile looked like a box with wheels.

As technology advanced, the automobile came to have an all-steel–constructed body. It no longer had simply a functional purpose but became a thing of beauty. Long sleek contour lines replaced the box-like features. About the same time road speeds increased so the automobile had to be designed accordingly. With the higher speeds, safety of the passengers became an important factor in the designing.

Now the automobile is beginning to grow smaller and lighter to meet the needs of fuel conservation. The new safety rules and regulations have had an important impact on the design and construction of the automobile. Auto manufacturers have had to design major components that are economical to produce on a large scale.

As the automobiles change in design, the methods of straightening also change. Up to the late 1940s, most of the body panels were accessible from the underside. Therefore, the metal could be straightened with a hammer and dolly, and high and low spots could be checked with a body file. As time went on, many of the panels became sealed from the underside and not easily accessible. For example, to straighten out some areas of a fender meant removing the fender skirt or the fender from the automobile. With the introduction of the reinforcement in the door, often called the *steel*

Basic Sheetmetal

chapter
7

beam, it became more difficult to straighten the panel without the use of a filler material. Some of the automobiles that are now being produced are constructed of thinner gauge yet harder metal than the older models. The straightening techniques will have to change because this hard metal will be affected more by heat and hammering.

The metal of today is made of low carbon steel or mild steel, which must be soft enough to be shaped in many different forms. A flat piece of sheetmetal is rather weak by itself. By adding creases, crowns, or sharp ridges, the piece of sheetmetal becomes strong. Locate an automobile with a large roof panel and push down in the flat area. The roof will bend in readily, yet the edges around the panel are rigid.

The steel is made up of grains which are formed together, called *grain structure*. The grain structure will determine how much the steel can be formed or shaped without cracking or splitting. When a flat sheet is formed into a panel, the grains are compressed into a smaller area or stretched out.

The sheetmetal used in production must have a smooth surface. Also, the dies used to shape the metal into panels must be free of nicks or gouges. If the panels were rough, it would require more work to get them ready for painting. Compare the smoothness of a trunk lid outer panel with the inner panel. The inner panel has a rough surface covered with small grooves or lines. The inner panel is used to strengthen the outer panel, and the smoothness of the surface is not important.

The sheetmetal used in the production of automobile surface panels must contain certain properties or qualities.

Plasticity. The metal must be capable of being formed or shaped without splitting while tremendous forces are exerted on it. The sharp ridges, high crowns, and re-versed crowns are good examples of what the sheetmetal had to withstand while being stamped into the different shapes from a flat sheet.

Elasticity. The ability of the metal to regain its shape when the force that caused the metal to bend is removed. As previously mentioned, when a fairly flat roof panel is pressed down the metal bends and then returns to its original shape when the pressure is removed. If too much pressure is exerted on a flat surface or other surfaces, a dent or depression will remain after the pressure is released. In this situation, the elastic limit or limit of nondestructive bending is reached, and the metal can not return to its original shape. When a strip of sheetmetal is bent, it will spring back to its original shape unless the elastic limit has been reached. Then the sheetmetal will remain bent until a corrective force is applied to remove the bend.

Work Hardening. A condition where the metal becomes harder as it is worked. The metal will increase in stiffness and be somewhat stronger. Work hardening first occurs in some areas of the panels as they are formed in the dies. It also occurs during the course of collisions where the panels are bent, upset, or stretched. Excessive forces exerted on the sheetmetal from hammering, constant bending, or vibrations will cause the metal to crack or split. This is called *metal fatigue*. This can be tested with a thin piece of sheetmetal. Bend it back and forth until it breaks off. Note that if the metal is kinked from excessive bending, it is hard to bend back in the same spot. This condition occurs when work hardening has taken place.

The exterior sheetmetal panel used on the automobile consists of a wide variety of sizes and shapes. Some of these are strong and rigid and some are fairly unsupported. A force striking a panel or a panel striking an object will affect the sheetmetal in different ways.

The direction from which the impact strikes the panel will have a definite effect on how the sheetmetal is damaged. Damage to the body sheetmetal can be classified as either *direct* or *indirect.*

Direct damage results from the impact of an object striking the sheetmetal. The area of damage is called the *point of impact.* The amount of direct damage is related to the amount of pressure exerted on the sheetmetal. Direct damage can be in the form of deep scratches, gouges, tears in the metal, or in the case of severe impact, crumpled or mangled sheetmetal.

Indirect damage is caused by the direct damage. The force of the direct damage is transmitted or transferred from the impact area to different parts of the panel. For example, direct damage to a lower door panel could cause indirect damage to the upper part of the door panel. The amount of indirect damage will vary depending upon the amount of force exerted in the impact area.

Indirect damage is generally in the form of roll buckles, valleys, or sharp ridges. The ridges or roll buckles are formed by the force bending the sheetmetal beyond its elastic limit and, depending on the sharpness of the ridges, may become work hardened. The indirect damage is often more difficult and time consuming to repair than the direct damage because it is more widespread. Direct damage is very often limited to a crease or gouge which can be brought out and filled.

Also, indirect damage can be caused by direct damage, yet no direct damage in the impact area is apparent. This is due to the fact that the object that struck the panel was soft, yet, the object struck with enough force to cause indirect damage. After the force was removed, the impact area returned to its original shape. Accidentally bumping against a door or quarter panel will cause the panel to flex inward and then spring back out again, but indirect damage results, generally at the upper part of the panel.

Another common example occurs when a heavy object is laid in the center of a roof panel. The indirect damage could appear around the edges and form small roll buckles where the more flexible center part of the roof panel meets the crown (or the more rigid part of the roof panel).

When straightening a panel with direct and indirect damage, normally the indirect damage is straightened first.

Stretching and Upsetting. Two conditions that are very common during collisions or when metal is damaged. Stretching is a condition that occurs when the metal has been thinned out as a result of a force exerted on the metal. Upsetting is a condition that occurs when the metal becomes thicker because of some force exerted on it. Stretches and upsets are very common when a panel becomes gouged or sharply creased. (Correcting stretched metal is discussed later in the chapter.)

SELECTION OF PROPER HAMMERS AND DOLLIES

Body Hammers

There are many different types of body hammers available and they are called by many different names. Also certain hammers are called by different names by different bodymen. A hammer used to remove the majority of the dented metal is called either a *roughing* or *bumping* hammer. These hammers are generally heavier in weight with a round and square face. The surface of the faces are nearly flat and average about 1½" (37 mm) wide. The wide face will spread the force of the hammer blows over a wider area than a small-faced hammer. The roughing or bumping hammers are also used for straightening inner panels or for reinforcing areas that require more force (Figure 7-1).

Another type of roughing hammer or bumping hammer is the *long neck hammer*. It is used for reaching into areas where the conventional-type body hammer cannot reach. Some makes are called *fender bumpers*.

Finishing Hammers

The finishing hammer is sometimes referred to as a bumping hammer but it is lighter in weight and is used to finish straightening a dent. These hammers are available in many shapes. Some have a large and small round face, some have a round and square face, others have a round face and a pointed end and are called *combination hammers*. The combination hammers are often called *pick hammers*. The pick ends range from short to long, straight to curved, from sharp to blunt ends, chisel and cross-peen. The pick ends are used to raise small low spots in the metal, for reshaping beads, or working in close corners.

The face of the finishing hammer is smooth with a slight crown. Many bodymen will select a combination finishing hammer or pick hammer and keep the face of the hammer highly polished and free of nicks. This hammer will be used for most of the final metal work and will not be used for any other purpose. If a face is nicked or gouged, the nick or gouge will be transferred to the panel being worked on. Then

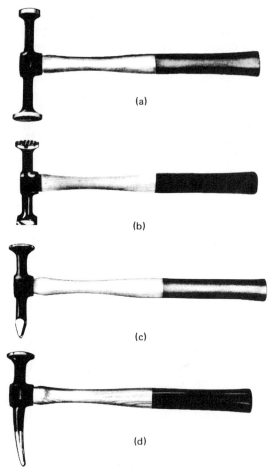

Figure 7-1 (a) Dinging hammer or bumping hammer; (b) shrinking hammer — serrated face; (c) finishing hammer; (d) pick hammer. *(Courtesy of Proto.)*

more work will be required to get the surface smooth.

Other types of body hammers are the *reversed* (or *high crown bumper hammer*) and *the shrinking hammer*. The reversed crown hammer has one crown parallel with the hammer and the other crossed. These hammers are available in a heavier style with the faces about 1½" (37 mm) in diameter. The lighter ones have faces about 1" (25 mm) in diameter. These hammers are used for straightening reversed crowns or panels where flat hammers will not fit the contour.

Shrinking hammers are used for shrinking metal without the use of heat. The faces are either cross-grooved or serrated. This hammer must be used carefully because the panel can be overworked, and more problems will then result.

Selection of the proper body hammer depends on what type dent is to be straightened and where it is located. Many dents can be straightened with just one hammer and a dolly. Some dents may require a variety of different types of hammers. It is very important to keep the faces of the hammers in a smooth condition free from nicks and gouges.

Dollies or dolly blocks

Dollies or dolly blocks are used underneath the dents or the underside of the panel. The dolly is often referred to as the *anvil* and is used as a backup for the body hammer. The dollies vary widely in shape, size, and weight. As in the case of body hammers, some of the dollies have several names such as the *all-purpose dolly* which is also called the *general-purpose dolly*, the *utility dolly*, or the *rail dolly*.

One of the most important factors when choosing a dolly is that it fit the contour of the panel. The crown should be the same or a little higher than the crown of the panel. Using a low crown or flat dolly on a high crown fender can create more dents.

The general-purpose dolly has an assortment of curves or crowns. This is the most popular dolly used (Figure 7–2).

The *toe and heel dollies* are ideal for working in close places and have a large surface area. The right angles of the dollies are used for forming flanges. The dollies are often used for metal bumping and to raise low spots.

Another tool which serves as a dolly as well as a spoon is called the *spoon dolly*. This general-purpose tool is used in places that are beyond the reach of the hand. With the long handle, it works well for raising low spots when a regular dolly or hammer cannot be used.

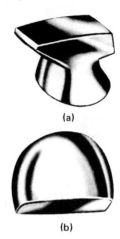

(a)

(b)

Figure 7–2 (a) General-purpose dolly; (b) heel dolly. *(Courtesy of Proto.)*

OTHER STRAIGHTENING DEVICES

Use of Body Spoons

Body spoons cover a large variety of body-straightening tools. Spoons are available in many different shapes and sizes and are designed to do a specific job.

The spoons are used for getting into confined areas which cannot be reach with a hammer or dolly. With their large flat surfaces some spoons are used as dollies where there is limited space. The *dinging spoon* is used for working down creases in the metal because it spreads the hammer blow over a larger area.

The *spoon dolly* is really a combination tool because it serves as a dolly for places beyond arms reach. Also, it is used for removing dents in confined places. Because of its weight, it makes an excellent driving tool when used with a hammer.

General-purpose spoons with flat sections on both ends, generally bend at different angles. Some general-purpose spoons are long for exerting tremendous pressure in prying out dents. The flat ends also serve as dollies (Figure 7–3).

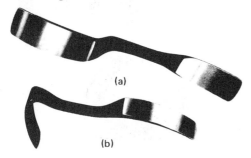

Figure 7–3 (a) Double end lower back panel and quarter panel spoon; (b) general-purpose spoon. *(Courtesy of PF Division, H.K. Porter.)*

Another type of general-purpose spoon has a slightly curved section on one end, right angled to the shaft. This serves as a dolly for prying and as an offset driving tool.

These are only a small sample of typical spoons that are available. On numerous occasions, a bodyman will shape a piece of spring leaf to serve as a spoon for removing a particular dent.

Picks

Picks, like spoons, are used to reach into confined and tight places. However, picks are only used for prying. They vary in length from short to long and have curved ends. The one end is U-shaped, is used as a handle, and is made out of spring steel (Figure 7–4).

In the same category as picks, we could include screwdrivers and metal rods of different shapes.

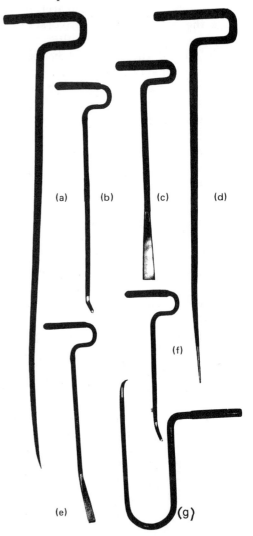

Figure 7–4 (a) Curved pick — long; (b) 18″ round point pick; (c) long tee handle chisel bit pick; (d) curved pick — short; (e) 16 ½″ chisel point pick; (f) 12″ round point pick; (g) deep throat straight pick. *(Courtesy of PF Division, H.K. Porter.)*

Picks are most commonly used for picking out dents in doors, quarter panels, and other sealed panels. Some bodymen prefer to use picks instead of slide hammers or pull rods because both require drilling holes in the panel (Figure 7-5).

Pull Rods

Pull rods can be used for removing small creases and dents (Figure 7-6). A series of

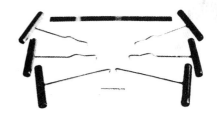

Figure 7-6   Pull rods. *(Courtesy of Mac Tools Inc.)*

holes are drilled in a crease. Anywhere from one to four pull rods may be used at one time. Rods are inserted in the series of holes, and the crease is pulled out.

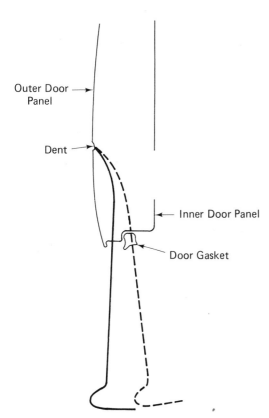

Outer Door Panel

Dent

Inner Door Panel

Door Gasket

Figure 7-5   Removing a dent with a pick without removing trim or making holes in the outer panel for the dent puller. The pick is inserted through a drain hole at the bottom of the door or through a hole made under the door gasket.

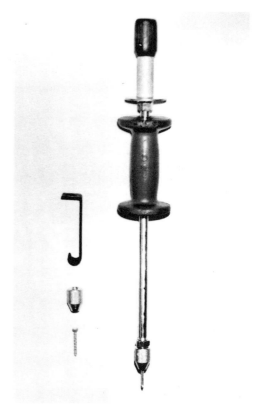

Figure 7-7   Slide hammer. *(Courtesy of Unican Corporation.)*

Slide Hammers

The slide hammer consists of a steel shaft with a handle and a sliding weight or hammer. The weights are available in several different sizes (Figure 7-7).

A variety of different pulling devices are available from screws to a door edge puller.

For straightening panels, holes must be drilled in the panel to accommodate the screw.

CORRECT USE OF BODY HAMMERS

Before using a body hammer, check the head of the hammer for tightness. If the hammer is to be used for finishing sheetmetal, take a look at the face of the hammer. If the head is nicked, file and sand it to a smooth finish (Figure 7-8).

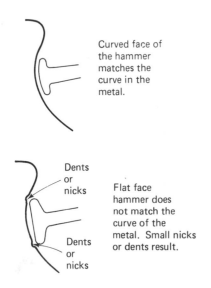

Curved face of the hammer matches the curve in the metal.

Dents or nicks

Flat face hammer does not match the curve of the metal. Small nicks or dents result.

Dents or nicks

Figure 7-8 Selecting the correct type of body hammer.

When using a body hammer, hold the hammer loosely, at the end of the handle. Never choke up or hold the hammer near the head.

When roughing out a panel, heavier strokes of the hammer can be used within reason and with sound judgment. Never hit the metal too hard as this will cause more damage.

When finished hammering or dinging, use light fast blows. Remember, the metal is thin, relatively soft, and will readily respond to hammering. Whether using a hammer with or without a dolly, hit the surface of the metal squarely. Letting the hammer rock on the edges will cause additional nicks or small dents.

On-Dolly and Off-Dolly Method

Before starting to straighten a panel with a hammer and dolly, check the condition of the surfaces involved, both the outer and inner sides of the panel.

The underside of the panel should be free of undercoating and other foreign matter. Undercoating, in this situation, refers to sound deadness, rustproofing, and other like material applied during manufacture or by a dealership. This can be removed with a torch with a long feather flame, a putty knife or scraper, and wire brush. It is recommended that gloves be worn to protect the hands from the hot undercoating or tar. If undercoating is left on, the shape of the undercoating could be transmitted to the panel, causing roughness in the metal.

The outerside of the panel may contain excessive rust or previously applied body filler or putty which will have an effect on the use of the hammer and dolly. Remove this material first before starting to straighten the panel.

The use of the body hammer and dolly in

combination requires coordination because the dolly will be hidden from sight. The object of using the dolly method is to place the dolly on the underside of the panel and strike the hammer on the surface directly above it. This technique requires practice in order to be able to place the dolly exactly under the area to be straightened.

When using the *on-dolly method*, the bodyman must remember not to strike the metal too hard or use a follow through method of hammering (Figure 7-9). The metal between the hammer and dolly will have a tendency to be thinned and a stretched situation could develop.

A light to medium hammer blow should be used with the hammer held lightly. The hammering action should be done more with wrist action rather than with full arm movement. With lighter or thinner metal being used in the late model automobiles, in most cases, light hammering action is sufficient.

Place the thumb on the top of the hammer handle and the fingers on the bottom. The thumb will direct the hammer blows downward, and the fingers will lift or bring the hammer back off the panel. The dolly should be held with variable pressure against the underside of the panel. When the dolly is held lightly against the panel, the hammer blows will force the dolly away from the panel, and the hand pressure will bring it back again. As the hammer hits the panel, the metal will be forced down, and the rebounding dolly will bring it back up again.

The amount of metal to be raised by the rebounding dolly depends on the amount of hand pressure and the weight of the dolly used. Too much hand pressure is not advisable as stretching could result. The amount of metal raised will also depend on the type of crown in the metal. A high

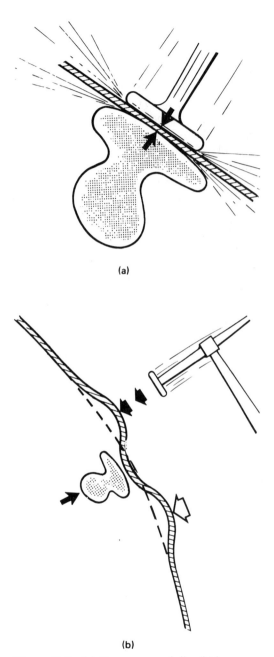

Figure 7-9 (a) Hammer on-dolly; (b) hammer off-dolly. *(Courtesy of 3M Company.)*

crown will not react as much as a panel with a low crown.

The on-dolly method requires much practice in order for the beginner to develop coordination and to observe how the metal will react.

An important thing to remember is to select the right dolly or dollies to match the contour of the panel to be straightened (Figure 7-10). Move the hammer and dolly back and forth across the damaged area until it is smooth. Avoid excessive hammering to eliminate stretching. It is much harder to lower the metal than to raise it.

The *off-dolly method* is used to straighten metal with a series of high and low sections or spots, such as creases.

During these procedures, the dolly is held under the low spot, and the hammer is used to lower the high spot on the section next to the low spot. Therefore, this hammer does not strike the area under the dolly but next to it. This could be a short distance away depending on the type dent involved.

As the hammer drives the metal down, the rebounding of the dolly raises the metal by the dolly. For a dent covering a large area, the bodyman should start on the least dented area and work toward the deeper dent.

This may not hold true in all straightening situations because the area may be severely gouged, the distorting force may have been exerted on the panel, or the damage may be close to the edge or near a body reinforcement.

Some dents can be straightened readily by bringing down the high ridges surrounding the dent. To do this, hold the dolly under the dent and work down the ridges.

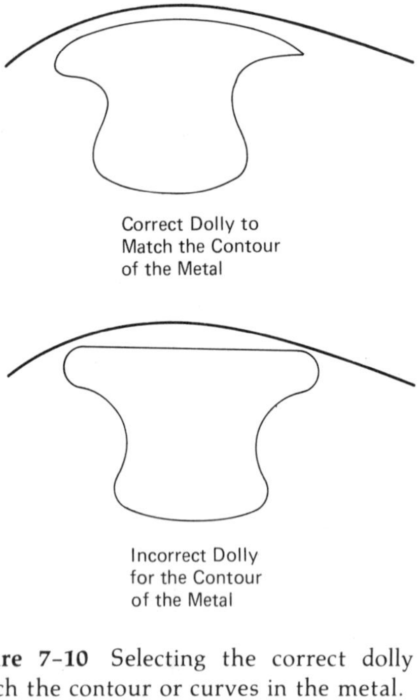

LOCATING HIGH AND LOW SPOTS WITH A BODY FILE

Body files are used to locate high and low spots in the panel during the straightening operation.

During the time when body solder was used for filling dents, the file was used for smoothing the body solder. Some bodymen still use the body file for smoothing the plastic filler.

There is a misconception as to the true purpose of the body file. It was never intended to be used as a means of removing metal but rather as a method to assist the bodyman in locating high and low spots in the panel (Figure 7-11).

Flat body files, also called *flexible files*, are generally mounted on wooden handles of

Correct Dolly to
Match the Contour
of the Metal

Incorrect Dolly
for the Contour
of the Metal

Figure 7-10 Selecting the correct dolly to match the contour or curves in the metal.

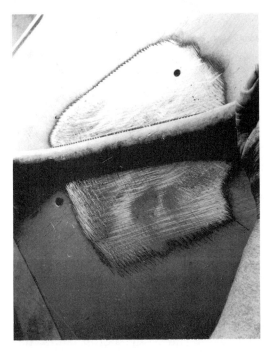

Figure 7-11 Using a body file for locating high and low spots. Note the dark areas. These are low spots in the fender. *(Photo by S. Suydam.)*

clogging. The number of teeth range from 8 to an inch (25.4 mm) for soft materials such as body plastic to 12 per inch (25.4 mm) for body steel.

NOTE: Because the body metal is relatively thin, about $\frac{1}{32}$" (.79 mm) and getting thinner, excessive filing will cut through the metal, creating more problems.

When cleaning files, use a file card or brush. Do not use a wire wheel because it will dull the teeth.

When using a body file, pass the file over the area at about a 30° angle. This will give a larger area of coverage than passing or pushing the file straight ahead. Always file *with* the contour *not across it* in order to avoid forming low spots or gullies. Immediately, the file will locate the high spots. If the high spots are excessive, work them down with a hammer and dolly or just a hammer, gently tapping the high spots. Continue filing and notice that the low spots begin to appear as the file bridges them. After the panel is finished, cross-file at a 90° angle carefully and lightly to reduce any ridges.

various designs. Metal files are available but unless a pad is placed under the file, this metal will dull the teeth.

An adjustable file holder is used with the flexible file for different contours of the panels. After using an adjustable file, with the file bent either inward or outward, the file should be returned to the flat position before storing. The file blade could snap if it is left in a bent position.

Body files are available in half-rounds, called *shells,* formed blades of different angles, and small file blades of different shapes and sizes for special jobs *(reveal files).*

The teeth on the file blades are U shaped with a groove between the teeth to reduce

METAL BUMPING

Metal bumping or *roughing* means bringing the metal of the panel out almost to its original shape so it can be metal finished. This discussion will be basic and will focus on small dents or body damage. More serious damage involves the use of hydraulic jacks or other methods.

Before attempting to repair any sheetmetal or body damage, a thought must be given to how the damage happened and from what direction the destructive force came. The direction is very important because the metal has been shifted to a certain degree. Another point to remember is that the damage to the panel is not confined to the impact area but is transmitted outward to other parts. As previously discussed, direct damage is damage at the point of impact. Indirect damage is damage caused by the impact and is apparent in the surrounding area.

A typical example would be an object hitting a door or fender panel. The point of impact is creased or dented. At the time of impact, the whole panel was sprung inward. The surrounding area sprung back out after the force was removed because of the elastic quality of the panel. Small creases, high ridges, or buckles will hold some of the metal from returning to its original shape.

Place a dolly against the dented area, after the underside is properly cleaned, and lower the ridges and creases by hammering. This will bring the panel out nearer to its original contour.

Sometimes it is necessary to use force such as hammering or bumping with a dolly to further reduce the damage. Bumping should start at the smallest area of the dent, not at the deepest area.

In many cases, by using the off-dolly method, the whole panel will spring out leaving a small area to be finished.

Direct damage to a panel edge will be different from damage resulting from an impact to the center. Every dent is different, and the method of bumping will vary with each one.

METAL DINGING OR FINISHING

Metal dinging or finishing is the final stage in straightening a panel to its original contour and shape. The high and low spots must be taken care of and a smooth finish must be the end result. A great deal of patience and skill is needed along with a good sense of touch.

A bodyman must develop a keen sense of touch. By moving the flat hand over the surrounding area of the panel, he can locate any high or low spots and detect any unwanted ridges. By using a body file, his hand, and a straight edge, the bodyman will know what work remains to be done.

High spots must be tapped down gently, and the low spots raised up. Using hard hammer blows will ruin what work has been accomplished. After filing, a disc grinder should be used to remove any remaining file marks.

When raising low spots, a pick hammer is very useful. However, beginners often find it difficult to locate the low spots without making the panel full of little knobs.

Do not hit the panel too hard or high spots will result. Using a drop light so the light reflects on the panel will help. Then, when the pick hammer hits the panel from underneath, the movement of the metal can be seen.

Hitting the exact area when needed requires much practice. Try working on an old panel before trying the technique on something good.

UNLOCKING METAL

Removing Creases with a Hammer

When the metal has reached its elastic limit, it cannot return to its original shape. The metal is then *locked*. These locks are in the form of creases or buckles which hold the metal in a distorted position. Each crease or buckle is work hardened to a certain degree, depending on the amount the metal is bent, and is harder than the area alongside. The sharper the crease, the harder the metal.

Many of the creases can be removed, and the panel restored to its original contour by working the creases down with a hammer. The hammer alone, the hammer and dolly method, or the hammer and spoon method could be used depending on the type and size of the crease (Figure 7-12).

Many of the creases can be removed with a cloth or masking tape on the face of the hammer without damaging the finish of the panel.

Another method is to use a hammer and a dinging spoon covered with layers of tape. Place the spoon on one end of the crease and tap the spoon with the hammer or work on both ends of the crease, alternating back and forth. Work toward the center. These two methods are often used if the creases are a distance from the impact area separated by a molding.

Exerting pressure on the impact area, either with a dolly or by some other means (hydraulic jacks or tension plates), will help in the removal of creases.

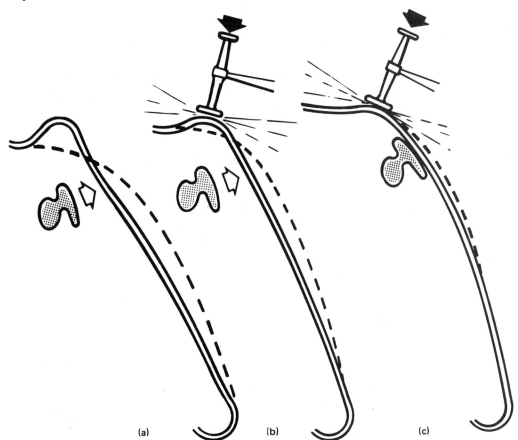

Figure 7-12   Simple rolled buckle: (a) dolly position for first rough-out blow; (b) hammer on high break-over point; (c) final buckle condition. *(Courtesy of 3M Company.)*

Unlocking Metal with Heat

Areas with creases or buckles that are severely kinked or bent can be unlocked by the use of heat.

As previously mentioned, work hardening of the metal takes place when the metal is bent. Attempting to straighten a sharp crease by hammering alone can cause upsetting in the crease area. The application of heat will soften the metal and relieve the tension in it.

Before using heat, a force must be exerted on the impact area in order to help the metal return to its original contour. Using heat alone will only make straightening the panel more difficult because the useful tension in the panel will be relieved and, in some cases, create more metal distortion.

Heat must be applied with care, especially in the newer types of bodies. Never heat the metal beyond a dull or dark red.

Removing Dents with Heat

Some of the small, shallow creases can be removed with heat. However, caution must be used not to overheat the panel as this creates buckling or caving in of the panel.

Because of the different types of body designs, some creases cannot be removed by heat. Also, there is a limit as to how deep a crease can be removed. Generally, a small welding tip is used, plus a body file.

Heat the shallowest end of the crease with the torch facing toward the length of the crease. Gently heat about ½" (12.7 mm) and watch for the metal to raise. Immediately file the heated area with a body file. Then heat another small area and file across the length of the crease. If the metal starts to sink, stop and let it cool. Reheating the area may raise the metal. If not, the rest must be straightened by other means.

After the crease has been heated and filed, check the contour for correctness.

Removing Dents with Spoons

Body spoons are very useful for getting into confined areas and for removing or roughing out dents. Spoons are also useful in areas beyond the reach of the hammer and dolly, such as the trunk area.

Many dents can be removed from the quarter panel with a spoon dolly and a long spoon serving as a dolly. In the lower sections of many quarter panels, the flat blades of the spoons are ideal for reaching down into the confined areas.

In the event that the dents are deep, the spoon can be used as a driver to drive the metal out. Using a spoon like a dolly or pry bar is very useful for straightening doors (Figure 7-13). In some cases, the spoon will fit between the door panel and the reinforcement (Figure 7-14).

The spoon dolly, because of its weight and length, can be used as a dolly or used in place of a pick hammer where space is limited. It can also be used for tapping out small dents.

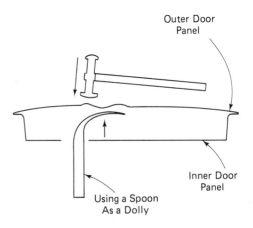

Outer Door Panel

Inner Door Panel

Using a Spoon As a Dolly

Figure 7-13 Roughing out a door.

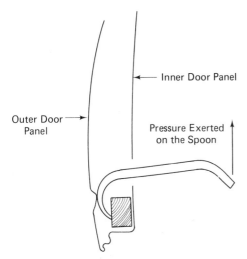

Figure 7-14 Removing a dent with a spoon and a block of wood.

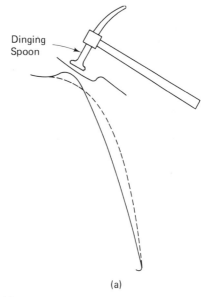

(a)

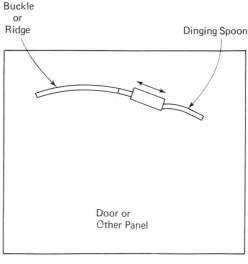

(b)

Figure 7-15 (a) Removing a buckle or ridge with a dinging spoon and hammer; (b) work dinging spoon back and forth along the buckle or ridge until smooth to avoid damaging paint. Put masking tape on the spoon or wrap a cloth around it.

The dinging spoon, also called a *bumping spoon*, is not made for prying and is not heavy enough to be used as a dolly. The dinging spoon is used to remove creases or high ridges near a dent or impact area. The dinging spoon used with a hammer will flatten a crease or ridge much smoother than a hammer used alone due to the surface area of the spoon (Figure 7-15).

The face of the spoon should always be kept free of nicks or burrs and in a polished state. The application of a strip of heavy protective tape or several layers of masking tape will keep the spoon's finish from becoming marred, thus saving time in some cases.

To remove a crease, start at one end of the crease and place the spoon lengthwise on the crease. Tap the spoon with a hammer using a zigzag motion across the length of the crease. It may be necessary to repeat the procedure to get a smooth finish but do not lower the metal too far. Some sharp creases or buckles may not be removed by the dinging spoon, depending on the location of the crease.

In cases where the dent covers a large area, the removal of the creases will cause large areas of the panel to snap out to their original contour. This method of removing creases is sometimes referred to as *spring hammering.*

There are many other uses for spoons, either manufactured or homemade. The type spoon to use is often determined by the supply of spoons available to the bodyman or his ability to create new ones, when needed.

Removing Dents with Picks

Picks are used for getting into confined areas, for prying, and for straightening doors.

Most doors have drainage holes on the bottom inner panel. These holes provide access for the pick, and the bodyman is thus saved the time of having to remove the inner door trim. Another method of gaining access is a punch a hole underneath the door gasket. When finished with the pick, seal the hole and reattach the gasket.

Quarter panels present a problem in the wheelhouse area. Holes can be punched in the wheelhouse panel in order to remove the dent with a pick. The holes should be plugged up to prevent water and mud from getting inside. Many jobbers or wholesalers carry plastic or rubber plugs that can be used to seal up the holes.

Dents in rocker panels can be straightened by making holes underneath the step plate. Some rocker panels are made of heavy gauge metal, so picks may not be strong enough. Heavy metal rods can be used as picks.

Picks can be used in many other places such as deck lids, hoods, fenders, or roof panels and save the bodyman a lot of time in dismantling parts.

When using picks, do not distort or stretch the metal by exerting too much pressure. Check contour with a straight edge for height. Move the pick slowly along the crease and raise it up gently. Use a flat-bladed pick rather than a pointed one to spread the force over a larger area. Tap the area around the dent with a hammer to help in raising up the metal. Care must be exercised to avoid creating more work by careless use of the picks.

Screwdrivers and long tapered punches can also be used as picks. Some bodymen shape old screwdrivers into desirable picks. Many good bodymen prefer to use picks instead of slide hammers and pull rods because picks do not leave holes in the outer panel surfaces. It is much faster to seal or close a few holes in the inner panels than a number of holes in the outer panels.

Pull Rods

Pull rods can be used to remove small creases and dents. To use, holes must be drilled with a $9/_{64}$" (3.57 mm) drill bit about $1/_2$" to 1" (12.7 mm to 25.4 mm) apart in the bottom of the crease. The dent can be removed by starting at the shallowest part of the dent, inserting one or more pull rods, and pulling outward. Work the metal out gradually. As pressure is applied to the pull rods, tap the metal alongside of the pull rods, lowering the ridges. Pull but do not pry on the pull rods. After the straightening operation is complete, solder the holes shut with a long pointed solder gun or iron.

The use of pull rods saves the bodyman from having to dismantle the interior trim. Do not overpull on the pull rods because there is a possibility of raising the metal too high. Check the surface with a straight edge for proper contour. A little low is better than too high.

Slide Hammer or Dent Pullers

The first slide hammer used screws that were inserted into a hole in the metal. The weight sliding back provided the necessary pressure.

To remove a crease or dent, a series of holes must be made. The dent or crease should be worked out gradually, starting from the shallowest end and working toward the deep end or section.

Do not attempt to pull the dent out all at once, do it gradually. Work down the ridges in the area at the same time. Avoid using excessive pressure because there is a danger of making small stretched areas surrounding each hole. Check the contour with a straight edge to avoid overpulling. After the dent is removed, solder the hole shut with a long-nosed solder gun or iron.

Other types of attachments are made to use with a slide hammer including a hook-like device for pulling out edges of fenders or doors. The slide hammer saves time because it eliminates the need for dismantling interior trim, but its use must be restricted to relatively shallow dents. Excessively sharp deep creases must be removed by some other method. The slide hammer is an excellent tool if used in the right way, but it can create problems if improperly used.

Another method of removing dents with a slide hammer was introduced recently. This involves spot welding flat washers on the panel and using a slide hammer to remove the dents. To accomplish this, the area to be straightened must have the paint ground off to bare metal. A spot welder with a special attachment is used, and washers are spot welded to the area. Then,

with a slide hammer and a hook attachment, the metal is gradually worked out starting from the shallowest part to the deepest and using a back and forth motion across the dent.

After the dent is removed, twist off the washer and grind off surplus metal from the washers. Occasionally, the washer may create a hole when removed. Solder the hole shut.

NOTE: Bare steel washers are recommended rather than plated-type washers.

USE OF HYDRAULIC EQUIPMENT

Some types of body damage cannot be corrected with the use of hand tools alone, so other methods must be used.

Hydraulic body jacks, along with hand tools and sometimes heat, are used to restore the damaged sections to their original shape.

In a collision, the outer panel is distorted and this most likely involves damage to inner panels or construction as well. When correcting the damage, both inner construction and the outer panel must be straightened and aligned at the same time (unless the outer panel is replaced).

The hydraulic body jacks are available in 4-ton (3,629 kg) models for light-duty work and 10-ton (9072 kg) models for average and some heavy-duty work (Figure 7-16). For frame straightening racks or extra heavy-duty work, body jacks have the capacity of up to 50 tons (45,360 kg).

Hydraulic jacks are made for pushing only or pulling only although there is a combination push-pull type which will be discussed later.

The basic hydraulic unit consists of a

Figure 7-16 Four-ton hydraulic body jack set with threadless tubing. Push-type. *(Courtesy of PF Division, H.K. Porter.)*

pump, either manual or air powered, a special heavy-duty hydraulic hose, and a ram. Rams are available in various lengths from about $2\frac{5}{16}''$ (58 mm) for confined areas to $16\frac{1}{4}''$ (412 mm) with the average being about 12″ (308 mm). Included under rams are two wedge-type or spreader rams used for getting into tight places.

The small spreader ram is used for straightening doors and quarter panels and for getting in other tight places. The large ram, which is more powerful, is used for heavier straightening of body panels, inner construction, and some frame work.

To perform the many different straightening operations involving pushing or pulling, a large assortment of attachments can be obtained. The hydraulic jacks are generally sold in sets or kits for general work. There is also a body work set, a mechanical set, and even a rescue set which is used during vehicle accidents. Most sets consist of basic attachments including an assortment of tube extensions or pipes with push-on type connections, an assortment of connectors, and male and female adapters. The older type sets with all threaded pipe connections are still available and can be used with the push-on types. The push-on type tubing uses a lock pin to lock the tubes and connectors together.

The end attachments are made for particular types of pushing or pulling. These attachments include a flat base, a rubber flexhead, a U-base, a fender clamp, a chain plate, and many more. Many attachments can be obtained separately for use in a particular straightening situation. Some types of pulling operations can be accomplished with the use of chains and clamps.

The rams or spreader attachments can be changed by the use of a quick-change coupling when the hydraulic hose joins the ram.

Operation-Manual Type

These rams are single action meaning that they move in one direction under pressure.

Push-Type Ram

The hose of the push-type ram is attached to the base of the ram or opposite the plunger end. To operate the ram, close the valve located at the hose end of the pump. Rotate clockwise until tight. Then, pump the handle up and down, and the oil from the pump will force the ram plunger out a short distance with each stroke of the handle.

To release the plunger, turn the valve counterclockwise, and a spring inside the plunger will retract the plunger, forcing the oil back to the reservoir of the pump. The distance traveled by the plunger varies with the length of the ram, a $2\frac{5}{16}''$ (58 mm) ram has a 1″ (25.4 mm) plunger travel and the $16\frac{1}{4}$ (412 mm) ram has a 10″ (254 mm) plunger travel.

Pull-Type Ram

The hose of the pull-type ram (single action) is attached to the plunger end of the ram. Without hydraulic pressure on the ram, the plunger is held out by the spring inside the pumper.

To operate, close the valve with a clockwise rotation until tight. When the handle is pumped, the oil will force the plunger inward (a pulling action). When the valve is opened counterclockwise, the spring inside the plunger will pull the plunger out forcing the oil back to the reservoir.

Operation of Push-Pull Hydraulic Jack

The push-pull hydraulic jack operates a little differently. There are two hoses from the pump to the ram, and they are attached to the ram in different places (Figure 7-17). The hose that attaches to the bottom of the ram is used for pushing. The hose that attaches to the plunger end of the ram is the pull hose. Unlike the previously discussed ram, these hoses are not the quick-couple type.

To operate, close the valve by turning it clockwise. Pumping the handle will force the oil through the push hose to the plunger, forcing it out. To retract the plunger, turn the valve counterclockwise and pump the handle. The oil will enter the top of the ram, forcing the plunger down. In either direction, the plunger must be moved by the pump.

Although this type is very versatile, it has disadvantages: for example, it takes a long time to move the plunger because it is two way; it weighs more than the single-action type, making it harder to handle

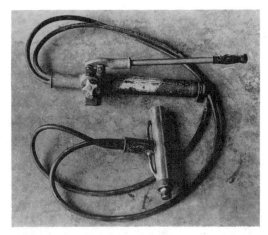

Figure 7-17 Push-pull hydraulic body jack unit. *(Photo by S. Suydam.)*

with one hand under fenders; and it is available in just one length ram (Figure 7-18).

The air-operated hydraulic pump is a quick way to operate the hydraulic body jack. Instead of operating the pump manually, the pump is operated by air (Figure 7-19).

The air hydraulic pump can be operated by the hand, the foot, the knee, or even the arm if necessary. Operating the pump with the knee or foot will leave both hands free to hold the ram and attachments in place. It is also possible to hold the ram in place with one hand and hammer down the ridges or use a torch with the other hand.

To operate, connect the air supply to the pump. Tip the top plate or pedal down on the air inlet side. The air entering the pump will activate the hydraulic pump and will pump as long as the pedal is depressed or tipped down. Release the pressure on the pedal, and the pump will stop. The pressure on the hydraulic side will hold until released. To release the hydraulic pressure, tip the forward part of the pedal down.

NOTE: On most air-operated hydraulic pumps, the pump end of the pedal is larger and lower than the release end of the pedal. Also, most of them are marked "pump" and "release."

CAUTION: The air-operated hydraulic pump works very fast and is powerful. Do not hold the pedal too long because there is a danger of overpulling (or using excessive pressure). This can create more damage to the vehicle. It is better to use in short spurts and observe what is happening.

In some cases, it is better to take frequent measurements. On bodies and unibuilt bodies, be on the lookout for popping spot welds. Never extend the plunger of the ram to the maximum travel under pressure as danger to the plunger stop could result (Figure 7-20).

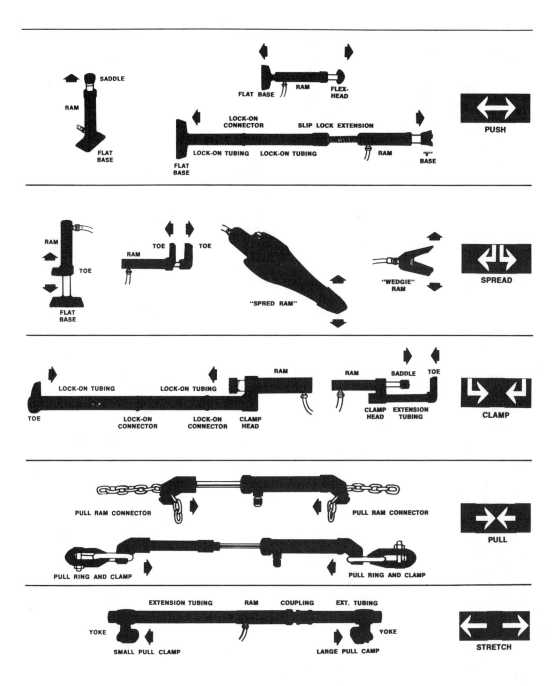

Figure 7–18 Basic setups using rams and attachments. *(Courtesy of Porto-Power, Applied Power Inc., Blackhawk Manufacturing Division.)*

Figure 7-19 Air-operated hydraulic pump. *(Courtesy of Applied Power Inc., Blackhawk Manufacturing Division.)*

Use of Tension Plate and Clamp

Another method of straightening panels is the use of tension; that is, a pulling force is used to relieve tension on a panel.

It is more effective to use a pulling force than trying to push out a dent in a panel (Figure 7-21).

To understand the reason for the use of tension, it is necessary to know what takes place when the metal has been distorted. If, for example, a door is hit by an object at a right angle to the surface of the panel, the outer panel will have a large dent. But notice the alignment of the door edges. The gap at the front and rear of the door will be larger than before the impact; therefore, the door is actually shorter.

Using other methods to push out the dent will not bring the door back to its original length. Also, the inner door panel or door frame will probably be damaged. With the use of tension, the door frame will be straightened as will most of the dent in the outer panel.

NOTE: In many cases, the door or outer door panel can be saved by an experienced bodyman. However, an inexperienced bodyman will often use the wrong technique or replace the door.

When using a pulling method, the door must be removed from the vehicle. Attach pull clamps or fender clamps to the front and rear sections of the door edges or pinch welds. The clamp should be placed directly in line with the deepest part of the dent.

Using the 10-ton (9072 kg) hydraulic body jack, the necessary extension tubing, and attachments, connect the jack to the two clamps. It is advisable to attach most of the tubing to the ram rather than to the movable plunger. Excessive amounts of tubing and connector attached to the plunger may damage it if the tubing bends under pressure.

Slowly apply hydraulic pressure to the clamp. As the dent starts to raise, use a dinging spoon and hammer. Work the creases or ridges downward relieving the tension. Continue applying pressure until most of the dent is removed and the inner door panel is restored to its original shape.

NOTE: If the inner door reinforcement (or *beam*) is still bent, use force with a hammer or use heat if necessary to return it to its original position.

All dents are different and various techniques are required to straighten them. In areas where clamps cannot be attached, heavy gauge metal tabs can be brazed on and attached to the clamps.

In some areas clamps are not applicable. Rather than removing the door, the tension plate method can be used. Areas like doors, fenders, roof panels, deck lids, and quarter panels can be straightened with tension plates, depending on the type of damage.

Removal of the tension in the metal created by the impact will greatly assist in the straightening. To use tension plates, a small area just beyond the dent on both sides must be ground down to bare metal. Tin the bare area with solder or soldering compound but do not wipe.

NOTE: Materials used for tinning may

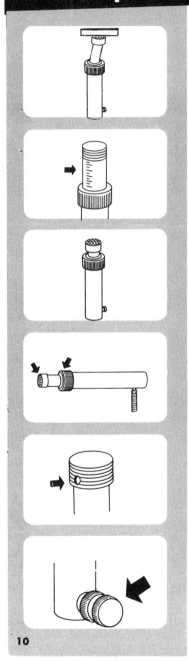

how to protect

do not overload ram
Never attempt to lift a load that exceeds the capacity of your ram. Overloading causes cracked cylinders, blown cups, bent plungers.

do not overextend ram
Because of the tremendous force of hydraulic power it is possible to push plunger out of top of ram. Be extremely careful not to overextend plunger.

do not adjust spring retaining screw
The spring retaining screw, located in cylinder wall near bottom of 20 and 50 ton rams should never be tampered with. It anchors spring which pulls back plunger. Adjustment will cause spring to jump out of position.

protect threads
Whenever possible guard ram threads with protector ring. Also protect ram plunger thread by using serrated saddle or pusher head.

repair damaged threads
Chase or file bent or marred threads for perfect fit. It's easy to replace threaded saddle on ram plunger. Simply drill out retaining pin (some saddles have no pin) with under-sized drill diameter. (Do not drill deeper than thickness of saddle wall). Then press saddle off end of plunger. Press fit new threaded saddle. A new pin is not required.

keep oil lines clean
When coupler halves are disconnected always screw on dust caps. Use every precaution to guard unit against entrance of dirt because dirt and foreign matter may cause pump failure.

10

Figure 7-20 How to protect ram. *(Courtesy of Porto-Power, Applied Power Inc., Blackhawk Manufacturing Division.)*

off-center loads

Be careful whenever load is not centered on ram plunger. Loads will be off-center, for example, when you use the following attachments: Notched-Pull-Toe, Edge-Clamp-Pusher-Head, Adjustable Body Spoon, Toe Lift. IMPORTANT: Pump carefully! When you feel that you have to pump unusually hard — stop operation. Adjust set-up so that off-center load is not as great. Excessive off-center loads produce considerable strain on the ram plunger and extension tubes.

do not drop heavy objects on hose

A sharp impact may kink wire strands on which the strength of the hose depends. Subsequent applications of pressure subject the kinked wires to a bending and unbending process which eventually causes hose to break. Do not carry Porto-Power unit by hose.

avoid sharp kinks in hose

Never apply pressure when hose is swung in sharp curves. Your Porto-Power hose will last longer with proper care.

provide clearance

Always position set-up so that hose and Spee-D-Coupler have clearance when ram extends. Avoid setting near obstructions as shown.

keep away from fire and heat

Keep your Porto-Power equipment away from excessive heat which tends to soften packings and cause leakage. Heat also weakens the structure of Porto-Power hose and Flex-Heads.

**A Network of
AUTHORIZED REPAIR DEPOTS**

serves Porto-Power Users worldwide

For quality workmanship with genuine Porto-Power parts select an authorized Blackhawk Service Depot for your repair work. Only repairs performed by an authorized service depot are backed with full factory guarantee.

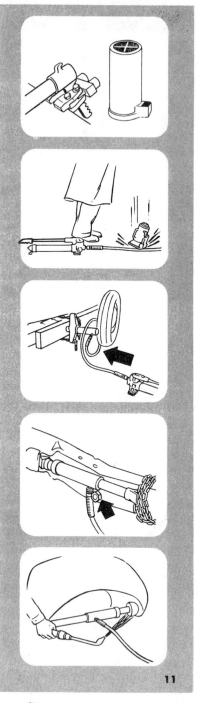

11

Figure 7-20 *(continued)*

(a)

(b)

Figure 7-21 (a) Straightening a door panel using soldered on tension plates with a hydraulic body jack and extension tubing; (b) straightening a door panel using body sheet metal clamps with a portable frame straightener. Note safety blanket has been removed.

vary according to what is on hand. For tinning information, see Chapter 9.

Before tinning the tension plate, make sure the plate matches the contour of the panel where it is to be attached. Clean and tin the plate thoroughly. Leave a surplus of solder on the plate and reheat the tinned area of panel until the solder is soft.

Using a glove or vise grip to hold the plate, press the plate in position and reflow solder on both plate and panel. As the solder starts to harden, cool with water. It

may be necessary to add more solder for improved bonding. Do not overheat as the plate will fall off especially if the plate is attached in vertical position.

Cool the plate with water and check the joint. Install the hydraulic body jack with necessary fitting and check the alignment of the plate. The jack should be parallel with the plates. If it is not, the body jack may have a tendency to lift the plates and break the solder connection.

As pressure is applied to the panel, lower the ridges with a dinging spoon and a hammer. Leave the pressure on the panel as long as possible while continuing the straightening process.

Release the pressure slowly and check the panel for alignment. To remove plates, heat the plate with a torch, just enough to soften the solder.

NOTE: Wash the plates with soapy water to remove acid. Dry and spray with a silicone lubricant to prevent corrosion of the plates when not in use.

SUMMARY OF CORRECT JOB PROCEDURES

Before attempting to correct damage caused by collision or other distorting forces, the first step is to determine in what direction the force was applied. The damage created by a head-on impact will differ from an angle impact or side hit.

The amount of damage shown by this impact is called *direct damage. Indirect damage* results from the impact but is manifested in the surrounding areas. Damage to the panels or body construction behind the outer panels and the adjoining panels must be considered. Often, the force of impact will cause damage well away from the area hit. Many times this damage goes undetected until repairs are well under way. This is often referred to as *hidden damage.*

The theory of correcting body damage is to exert a force in the opposite direction to which the impact occurred. However, in many cases, mostly due to the lack of equipment, the damage cannot be corrected in the proper manner.

One of the most important factors in determining the procedure to follow is what type equipment is available at the time. Then, after a careful analysis of the damage, proceed with the correcting operations.

Several correcting forces either pushing or pulling at the same time may be necessary.

Each repair job will be different from the next even though two autos may appear to have been hit in the same manner. Experience will confirm this.

ALUMINUM

The use of aluminum body panels is increasing, and as a result auto body repair men will need to become very familiar with the distinctive properties of aluminum and with proper repair techniques.

Several things must be understood about aluminum sheet (or sheetmetal) before damaged aluminum panels can be successfully repaired. Aluminum is a very soft metal as compared to steel. When grinding the paint from aluminum, care must be exercised to ensure that the panel is not destroyed or the job made more complicated.

Use a sharp #36 grit disc and be careful to remove only the paint and primer but not the aluminum metal. Remember, the disc will cut through the aluminum panel very fast. If the areas involved are small, use a finer disc like a #50 grit.

If large areas must be ground off, avoid overheating the panel because it may buckle or warp. It is better to make a pass or two, then let the panel cool or cool it slowly with water.

When sanding down plastic filler, avoid using a #40 grit as much as possible or confine it just to the plastic area; then use a #100 grit paper for featheredging. Once again, avoid sanding off too much of the aluminum. Remember it is soft.

Plastic filler will adhere to the aluminum just as well as it does to steel if the surface is prepared correctly. If a *cheese grater* is used to shape the plastic filler, avoid gouging the metal with it.

Polyester filler can be used to attach tension or pull plates to straighten panels with the hydraulic body jack, but it has its limitations as to the amount of pressure that can be applied. The polyester filler is not as strong as steel with soldered or tension plates.

While the panel is under pressure from the hydraulic body jack, heat can be used to relieve the buckles but avoid overheating.

NOTE: Aluminum does not change color as steel does. It is possible to melt the aluminum, or it may become soft and just drop away.

The aluminum panel can be picked, spooned, or spring hammered like steel while the correct force is applied, but care must be exercised to ensure that additional damage does not result. The aluminum can be shrunk but not as much as steel. The aluminum must be heated beyond 1200° F (648° C) and must be cooled or quenched gradually with water to avoid distortion or buckling.

Aluminum is sensitive to heat and hammering, so proceed with caution when repairing aluminum panel to avoid getting into a more difficult situation.

As more aluminum panels appear, new techniques will be developed. If the paint must be removed, sand with a #36 grit open coat disc. Then use a paint remover that only removes the color coat. Avoid using any caustic paint stripper because it may damage the aluminum.

For aluminum panel refinishing, where the bare metal is involved, refer to Chapter 11 for the correct procedure.

Questions

1. What are some of the factors that determine the design and construction of the automobile?
2. Has the new type automobile had any effect on repair procedures?
3. What is used to strengthen a piece of sheetmetal?
4. What is the difference between the metal used on the outer and inner panels of a trunk lid?
5. What are two of the properties that body sheetmetal must contain?
6. What is a simple demonstration of work hardening?
7. What is *direct* and *indirect damage?*
8. What is *stretching* and *upsetting?*
9. What is the difference between a bumping hammer and a finishing hammer?
10. What is a *pick hammer?*
11. What is a *crowned face hammer?*
12. What is a *dolly?*
13. What is a *spoon dolly?*
14. What are spoons used for?
15. What are picks used for?
16. What is the result of using too much force when using a hammer and dolly?
17. What are the *on-dolly* and *off-dolly* methods?
18. What is a body file used for?
19. When removing a dent, where does the process start?
20. Is it important to know how the dent in the panel occurred?
21. What is the disadvantage of using a slide hammer for removing dents?
22. What are the basic parts of a hydraulic body jack?
23. What type hydraulic body jack attachment can be used inside a door?
24. To what end of the ram should the extension tubing be added?
25. What is the danger of carelessly using the air-operated body jack?
26. What are tension plates and what are they used for?
27. Why is it important to analyze the job before attempting to straighten it?

28. What is the chief difference between an aluminum panel and a steel panel when grinding off paint?

29. Can the #40 grit production paper be safely used on an aluminum panel?

30. What danger results from grinding an aluminum panel?

Metal shrinking is one of the important processes used to reshape the metal in a panel that has been damaged by impact or made thin by excessive hammering. Impact damage is usually a gouge, crease, or groove. Each of these abrasions and excessive hammering cause the metal to stretch. When metal is stretched it becomes thin and too large in area to fit back into the space it occupied originally (Figure 8-1). Since the excess area of metal must go some place, the result is a dent or a bulge.

If the damage is not too severe, the metal will have a natural tendency to return to its original shape, if properly worked. Since metal has a certain amount of elasticity, the arrangement of the molecules will not be permanently disturbed even though the metal has been dented or bent out of shape. It is this characteristic of metal that body and fender repairmen must endeavor to preserve.

Several methods are employed to shrink stretched metal in the process of reshaping damaged panels.

1. *Hot shrinking* — a torch is used to soften and upset the metal.
2. *Cold shrinking* — a hammer with a serrated face is used to cut grooves and dots in the metal, which tends to draw the metal together.
3. *Cutting and slicing* — the metal is cut, lapped, and welded or brazed together.
4. *Grooving method* — indentations (such as grooves or valleys) are made in the surface of the metal to draw it together. The grooves are filled with solder or plastic.

The use of heat to upset the metal is the fastest method and the one generally used by experienced craftsmen when repairing grooves, gouges, and creases in panels. Since red hot metal is easier to reform and shrink than cold metal, the hot shrinking

Metal Shrinking

chapter
8

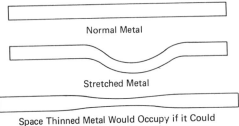

Normal Metal

Stretched Metal

Space Thinned Metal Would Occupy if it Could
Stretch to Full Length

Figure 8-1

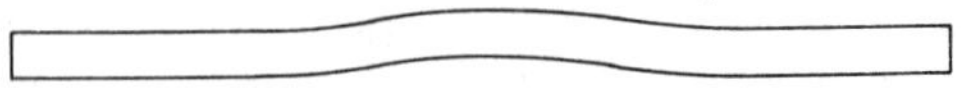

Area stretched or thinned due to excessive use of
body hammer or impact, resulting in bulges

Figure 8-2

method produces much better results with less time and effort.

True stretch — a stretch or condition where the metal has been increased in surface area, caused either by excessive hammering or by impact.

False stretch — an unstable area or a raised bulge in the metal near an area that has been upset. Most of the false stretches remaining after the adjoining area has been straightened is a result of poor straightening techniques. Some may have to be shrunk to eliminate this condition.

METAL SHRINKING WITH INSIDE OF PANEL ACCESSIBLE

When it is possible to use equipment on both sides of a panel, such as a door, hood, or fender, the metal shrinking procedure is less complicated since dollies, spoons, and other tools can be used to support the inside of the panel while the bodyman works the outside surface (Figure 8-2).

Service Procedure

1. Remove any undercoating that is present on the inside of the panel and grind off as much paint as required on the outside of the panel.

   NOTE: Undercoating will make the metal very rough to the touch, and hot undercoating will burn your hands. Always wear gloves when necessary, to avoid injury to your hands.

2. Straighten as much metal as possible with a hammer and dolly before shrinking.

3. Examine the panel and determine the area that requires shrinking (Figure 8-3).

4. Place a #1 or #2 tip on the torch. Light the torch and adjust it to a neutral flame. Heat a small spot in the center of the stretched area to red hot. Notice how the metal will raise in the center.

   CAUTION: Be careful with the torch. If you hold it too close to the panel, the metal may melt.

5. When the metal has risen, immediately hit the red area with a body hammer or wooden mallet to drive the center down.

6. Hold the dolly underneath and work the immediate area smooth with a few light hammer or wooden mallet blows.

7. Strike the blows in a circular pattern working from the edges of the hot area toward the center of the spot. In this way, you can smooth out the bulge and bring the metal back to its original shape.

   CAUTION: Be particularly careful to keep the dolly in the correct position under the metal during this straight-

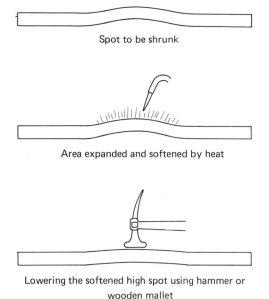

Spot to be shrunk

Area expanded and softened by heat

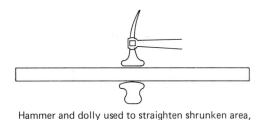

Lowering the softened high spot using hammer or wooden mallet

Hammer and dolly used to straighten shrunken area, cool with water if neccessary

Figure 8-3 Shrinking operation.

the panel back to normal size. Remember, sheetmetal expands with heat.

8. If the spot appears to be slightly higher than the surrounding area, let it cool normally. If not, quench with water.

CAUTION: Always allow metal that has been red hot to cool until it becomes black before applying water with a sponge.

9. When the metal is cool, feel the panel with your hand to find irregular spots. Use a body file to check for high and low spots. Also, a straight edge can be used on flat surfaces to check for high and low spots.

10. If the surface is not satisfactory, continue to shrink until it is. Take the next highest spot in the stretched area and reduce it. Continue until you are able to bring the surface of the whole panel back as nearly as possible to its original condition.

11. Finish the area with a body file. Avoid additional excessive grinding with disc grinder. This is important, since the metal has been softened with heat and will therefore stretch more readily than before.

ening process. Remember, excessive hammer blows will make the metal stretch more readily as it is softened with heat. Also, while you are using the hammer and dolly the panel will cool rapidly and the metal will start to harden. If it is possible, have someone assist you with the heating.

NOTE: In some cases, it may be necessary to alternate some of the metal work with the shrinking process. Always cool a panel before making another shrink to limit the heat accumulation in the panel and to bring

METAL SHRINKING WITH THE INSIDE OF PANEL INACCESSIBLE

With the modern design of bodies and fenders, it is impossible to reach the underside of some panels. This is especially true of most quarter panels. With these new designs, and the large expanse of metal, the damaged area must be repaired from one side only.

Service Procedure

1. Remove the paint from the work area.
2. Heat small spots red hot. This will cause the area to raise.
3. While the area is red, tap the spot down with light hammer blows.
4. If the area, after being hammered into place, is similar to the surrounding area, let it cool. If it is not, cool it with a wet sponge.

    CAUTION: Always allow metal that has been red hot to cool until it becomes black before applying water with a sponge.
5. Examine the results.
6. Shrink more if necessary, but not too much, as this will cause buckling of the surrounding area which can cause problems.
7. Continue to shrink small areas of the damaged part until the whole panel is restored.
8. Finish the area with a body file.

SHRINKING GOUGES WITH THE UNDERSIDE OF THE METAL ACCESSIBLE

Shrinking gouges or deep grooves is similar to shrinking stretched areas. The only difference is that the dolly plays a more important part.

A gouge or groove is a deep depression in the metal (Figure 8–4).

Service Procedure

1. Heat a small spot in the damaged area until it is red hot.

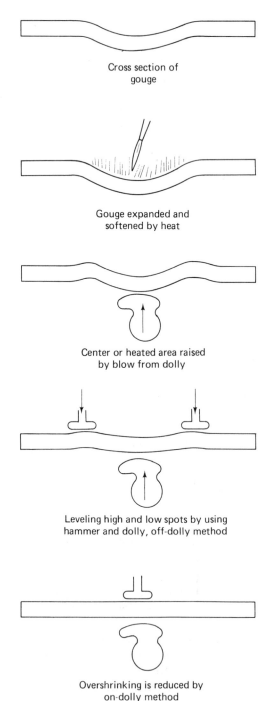

Cross section of gouge

Gouge expanded and softened by heat

Center or heated area raised by blow from dolly

Leveling high and low spots by using hammer and dolly, off-dolly method

Overshrinking is reduced by on-dolly method

Figure 8–4 Shrinking gouges.

2. Using a dolly as a hammer, tap the spot upward.

3. Hold the dolly directly under the groove and strike the metal on both sides of the dolly with carefully placed hammer blows. This will drive the metal upward, over the dolly and the small ridges along the sides of the groove downward.

   NOTE: The off-dolly method of working metal consists of placing hammer blows on both sides of a groove while the dolly is held firmly in position directly under the groove. Sometimes it is advisable to start at each end of a gouge and work toward the middle. Also, on long grooves, a long narrow section may be heated at one time, but only as much as you can work before the metal gets cold.

4. Correct overshrinking by using the on-dolly method.

CAUTION: Use extreme care when leveling metal that has been heated red hot as it is soft and may become too thin and bulge.

NOTE: The on-dolly method of working metal consists of holding the dolly directly under the work area, while striking hammer blows on the metal surface as near the central part of the dolly as possible.

Cooling normally is not necessary when shrinking grooves as tension may set up. Also, the on-dolly method tends to reduce tension in the groove caused by impact.

Cooling may be used under certain conditions or on certain areas of panels, but remember, every groove is different and must be treated accordingly. This is true with all shrinking operations and all metal repairing.

Questions

1. Why is shrinking considered a precision job?
2. What is the result of overshrinking a panel?
3. What is the purpose of heating the metal red hot?
4. Is quenching the shrunken area always necessary? Explain your answer.
5. What determines the size of the spot to heat red hot?
6. Why is speed important when shrinking an area?
7. Is the dolly method the same for stretched areas as it is for gouges? Explain your answer.
8. Why is it necessary to remove existing undercoating from the underside of the panel?
9. What could result if the torch is too close to the metal during the heating process?
10. Give several reasons why dollies are used in the metal straightening and shrinking process.
11. Explain why the off-dolly and the on-dolly methods of working metal are used in two of the service procedures.
12. Explain why a wooden mallet is sometimes used instead of a metal hammer.

13. Why is it important to allow red hot metal to turn black before cooling with water?

14. What precautions should be taken when using a body hammer on sections of metal that have been straightened by the shrinking process?

15. Why does bent metal have a natural tendency to return to its original shape?

There are many areas of the body that are inaccessible and cannot be straightened in the usual manner. These areas include sections of doors, fenders, hoods, decks, and quarters that are double paneled, with reinforcement and other obstructions that prohibit the proper use of metal-straightening tools. Also, when repairing rust damage with metal patches, something must be used to finish off the area to a smooth surface. In these situations the most common procedure is to use body filler (plastic) or body solder (the older method). Plastic body filler is a very durable material if it is applied in the proper way.

PLASTIC BODY FILLER

During the late 1940s, little was known about the use of plastic as a substitute for conventional body solder. But changes in body styles and construction made it necessary to find an alternative filler for repairing auto bodies. A material was needed that would be inexpensive, would reduce the cost of labor, and would make it easier to repair body damage without the use of heat. One of the first types of filler to be used was aluminum powder mixed in a liquid plastic compound which used a type of hardener similar to the type used today. But this early plastic had the disadvantage of having to be applied in thin layers on a properly prepared surface and of requiring considerable time to harden. The adhesion was fair, but if applied to heavy layers it would not harden. It was found, however, that a special fabric saturated with a chemical compound to harden the material could be used to cover holes, then a plastic filler could be used to finish the job.

By the late 1950s, the present plastic or similar types were available but many were very brittle, and holes had to be drilled in the panel to increase the adhesion to the metal.

Plastic and Lead Filling

chapter
9

The plastics (or body fillers) available today are easy to use, harden in a short time, can be sanded to a fine edge, and adhere well on properly prepared surfaces (Figure 9–1). There are three basic compounds used in the plastic body filler: resin, the filler material, and the hardener.

The *resin* is a heavy liquid plastic (such as polyester resin) that is used for repairs on fiberglass and on similar materials. The resin does not have the necessary filling qualities needed for body filler and is hard to sand. However, it is used as a binder for the filler material and to promote adhesion to the body panel. Different compounds are used or added to the resin to give it the necessary filler characteristics. Depending on the manufacturer, some of the filler compounds used are powdered fiberglass, magnesium silicate, nylon, powdered metal, and others (Figure 9–2).

The plastic body filler will not harden or cure by itself unless a catalyst or curing agent is added. This catalyst is called the *hardener* and it is available in a liquid or a cream. (The cream hardener is the most popular.) It changes the color of the plastic

(a)

(b)

(c)

Figure 9–2 Different types of plastic fillers: (a) plastic filler with nylon; (b) plastic filler reinforced with chopped fiberglass. *(Courtesy of Unican Corp.)*; (c) plastic filler with powdered aluminum. *(Courtesy of Bond Tite, Oatey Corporation.)*

Figure 9–1 Typical plastic body filler. *(Courtesy of Bond Tite, Oatey Corporation.)*

filler, depending on the amount used. Some manufacturers use a color patch on the filler can to indicate the correct mixture.

CAUTION: Many of the hardeners contain benzoyl peroxide, an oxidizing agent which must be handled with care.

The hardener and plastic filler should be kept away from heat, fire, and combustible materials. Avoid contact with skin, eyes, and hands. In the event of contact, flush with water. If the eyes are involved, seek medical attention.

NOTE: A certain amount of heat is given off during the curing stage. (This heat is caused by a chemical reaction.) Avoid disposing of waste plastic in containers holding combustible materials because there is a chance of fire.

Too much hardener added to the filler is wasteful because the filler will harden before it can be used and the added heat from the curing can cause the loss of the filler's adhesive quality. One of the causes of pinholes in plastic filler is the use of too much hardener, which causes small gas bubbles to form during rapid curing.

Adding too little hardener to the filler may prevent the filler from curing or hardening properly, and as a result valuable time is lost in the repair process.

During cold shop conditions, a little more hardener can be used to speed up the curing and less can be used during hot days. Always follow the recommendations listed on the plastic containers.

NOTE: After using plastic filler, thoroughly wash the hands and properly close the container.

The plastic fillers are available in a wide variety of different types, depending on the manufacturer. The plastic filler can be purchased in pints, quarts, gallons, and five-gallon pails. It is also available in three-gallon pressurized container cartridges (Figure 9–3). Possibly, in the future, plastic will be in metric measured containers.

Plastic filler has the advantage of being a quick and easy method for correcting body damage. It is easy to sand, prime, and paint when properly prepared. The repairs done with plastic filler will last a long time if not affected by rusting from under the surface.

The main disadvantage of using plastic is the amount of dust it creates, often affect-

Figure 9–3 A typical body filler dispenser which uses air pressure. This system cuts down plastic filler waste and prevents filler from drying out. Eliminates the possibility of contamination from hardener being left on the putty knife. *(Courtesy of Bond Tite, Oatey Corporation.)*

ing the whole shop area. One of the problems is keeping the plastic filler dust out of the paint area.

Surface Preparation

The preparation of the surface for applying plastic is similar to that for body solder. Here are some of the steps and precautions to follow:

1. Remove all wax and grease in the area. Grind off *all* paint and rust from the

Figure 9-4 Initial grinding to remove paint and rust using either 24 (3) or 16 (4) grit, open coat disc. *(Courtesy of 3M Company.)*

area to be filled and about 2" or 3" (50.8 mm or 76.2 mm) beyond. Use a #24 grit disc or if necessary a #16 grit disc (Figures 9-4 and 9-5). This will give

Figure 9-5 Using 50 (1) grit, closed coat disc, to remove the deep scratch marks or grooves from the 24 (3) or 16 (4) grit disc. *(Courtesy of 3M Company.)*

the plastic filler a better bond to the metal.

2. Featheredge the paint around the area before applying plastic. This will help to prevent undercutting the plastic later when featheredging. Straighten the panel as near as possible to its normal shape and smoothness.

3. Check contour and lower all high spots. Low spots should not exceed 3/16" (4.7 mm). High spots should be lowered before applying plastic, otherwise hammering on plastic could crack it. .

Application of Plastic

Use glass or sheetmetal for a mixing tray. Measure out the required plastic. Never use cardboard or other porous material as it will absorb the hardener. (One ounce is roughly the size of a golf ball.) Add the hardener as recommended on the can's label. Mix the plastic thoroughly and evenly but do not waste time or the mixture will start to harden before you can use it (Figure 9-6). Apply plastic evenly to the surface

Figure 9-6 Mixing plastic body filler. *(Courtesy of 3M Company.)*

Figure 9-7 Plastic spreaders for applying plastic body fillers or glazing putty. *(Courtesy of Unican Corporation.)*

with a squeegee or plastic spreader (Figure 9-7). Use some pressure to ensure good contact with the metal. Put enough on to avoid repeating the application (Figure 9-8). The smoother it is applied, the easier it is to sand or file. It should be slightly above the surrounding area in order to prevent low spots. Clean all the tools and equipment you use immediately with lacquer thinner before the plastic hardens.

Proper Selection of Finishing Files

When the plastic has cured or hardened, it can be made into a smooth surface by various means. Following are some of the methods most frequently used by auto body repairmen.

A disc sander with #36 or #50 grit disc can be used, especially on flat or slightly curved surfaces (Figure 9-9). A low speed grinder or polisher with 1,750 RPMs does a better job than a grinder with 5,000 RPMs. It takes a lot of practice to use a grinder on plastic efficiently and without undercutting the plastic. After grinding, finish sanding by hand or with a vibrator sander or sanding board. The one main objection to using grinders on plastic is the large amount

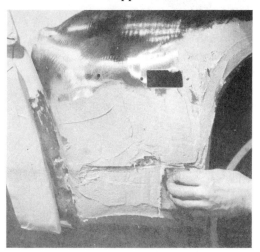

Figure 9-8 Applying mixed plastic body filler. *(Courtesy of 3M Company.)*

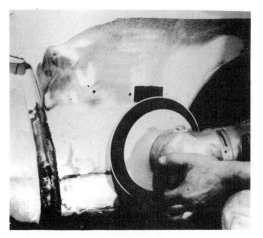

Figure 9-9 One method of smoothing plastic filler using a 36 (2) grit, open coat disc to remove surplus body filler. *(Courtesy of 3M Company.)*

of plastic dust created. This holds true for air-driven revolving sanders or grinders.

CAUTION: Wear a respirator or dust mask to avoid inhaling the dust.

Another method very commonly used is the vibrating (or oscillating) sander, air or electric driven. It is available in various size pads. Dust is a problem and the chances of undercutting the plastic are great, especially at the hands of an inexperienced bodyman. Most bodymen start with #36 or #40 grit paper, and final sanding is done with #80 or #100 grit paper.

Hand sanding or the use of sanding boards is slower, but the results are better (Figure 9–10). Undercutting the plastic is less frequent with this method. Some bodymen use body files that are made for plastic and have coarse teeth (Figure 9–11). A grater-type file is also used on plastic, but the plastic must be semi-cured, or a little soft (Figures 9–12 and 9–13). Hard plastic cannot be filed efficiently and soft plastic may be pulled loose from the panel.

A second application of plastic filler may be necessary to fill in low spots. The plastic

Figure 9–11 Hutching files, often called sanding boards, used for rough sanding of plastic filler with 40 (1 1/2) grit production paper and finish sanding with 80 (1/0) or 100 (2/0) grit production paper. *(Courtesy of Unican Corporation.)*

Figure 9–12 Replacement grater file blades, flat or half-round. Some prefer to use them without the holders for shaping the filler while it is curing. *(Courtesy of Bond Tite, Oatey Corporation.)*

Figure 9–10 Sanding board. *(Courtesy of 3M Company.)*

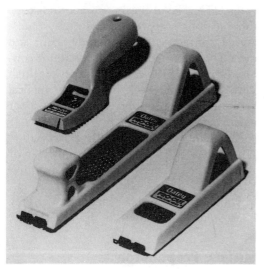

Figure 9-13 Grater files and holders can be used for shaping or removing surplus plastic filler while the filler is curing or hardening. *(Courtesy of Bond Tite, Oatey Corporation.)*

Figure 9-14 Finish sanding plastic filler using an air-powered sander with 80 (1/0) or 100 (2/0) grit production paper. *(Courtesy of 3M Company.)*

should blend in with the surrounding area. After the final sanding, prepare the panel for painting using the same method as for steel panels (Figure 9-14).

CAUTION: Do not oversand or overfile. This could create low spots and the need to add more plastic. Check the surface frequently for smoothness and correct contour. The plastic is softer than the surrounding area. Avoid using plastic in a poorly ventilated area. Avoid skin contact with the liquid plastic as irritation could result. Wear a face mask when grinding or sanding plastic to avoid inhaling the dust. Wash hands before eating or smoking. Remember, *the plastic is poisonous.*

METAL FILLING — BODY SOLDER

Like plastic filler, body solder is used to restore the body metal to its original contour. Body solder can be used to finish off quarter panel joints and to repair rust around the back window opening or other areas.

Body solder is not used as much as it was before plastic filler became available. Some shops still use it for special jobs such as customized or restoration work.

The *disadvantages* of body solder are the cost of materials, primarily the tin, the amount of time needed for the application process, and the fact that certain body panels react readily to the use of heat (that is, they buckle).

The main *advantages* of body solder are as follows: it is a permanent repair if applied correctly; it will not crack; it is not affected by moisture; and it can be shaped and sanded easily.

Body solder requires a reasonable amount of skill to apply, especially when working on a vertical surface.

Contents of Solder

Body solder is a mixture of lead and tin with the average ranging from 40 to 30 percent tin and 60 to 70 percent lead. (The percentage of tin is stated first, then lead.)

This combination of lead and tin has one important property: it is able to go from a solid to a plastic (soft) state without melting into a liquid. This makes it easy to apply and to be smoothed out. The melting point, or the point at which the solder becomes plastic (soft), of a 50-50 combination of solder is 361º F (182º C). It flows (or runs) at 420º F (216º C). This gives an approximate work range of 59º F (14.9º C). This working range is too narrow, and as a result a 50-50 solder is ordinarily used for general repairs and by plumbers because it is stronger than a 30-70 combination.

Tinning Compound

In the soldering process *tinning compounds* are used to clean the metal so that the body solder will adhere to the surface of the panel. The acid (or cleaning agent) removes oxides from the surface and excludes oxygen from contacting the heated metal. Tinning compounds are availabe in either a liquid or paste form.

Tinning liquids are basically muriatic acid (hydrochloric acid), but other chemical compounds can be used such as zinc chloride and ammonium chloride combinations.

Tinning paste is a combination of muriatic acid (or another acid) mixed with powdered solder and is formed into a 1" (25.4 mm) square stick. Many times, an acid core solder can be used as a tinning compound.

CAUTION: All tinning compounds contain acid or very corrosive compounds. Avoid contact with the hands, skin, and eyes. Flush immediately with water if contact is made. If the eyes are involved, flush with water and seek immediate medical attention. Thoroughly wash hands after soldering.

Keep the container tightly closed when not in use and store away from heat or flame. Store where it cannot damage anything in the near vicinity.

Tools and materials used for applying body solder are shown in Figure 9–15.

Surface Preparation

Straighten the panel as near as possible to normal shape and smoothness. In order

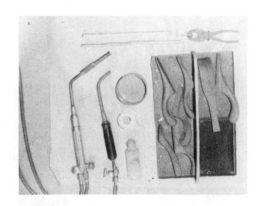

Figure 9-15 Tools and materials used for applying body solder: (top) bars of solder; pair of pliers made to hold short pieces of solder; (lower, left to right) welding torch with soldering tip attached — air and acetylene; air and acetylene soldering torch; bottle of tinner's acid; acid core solder; container of powdered solder and tinning compound; tray of assorted soldering paddles for different body contours; sheet-metal tray with motor oil used as a paddle lubricant. *(Photo by S. Suydam.)*

to apply solder, grind off all paint and rust on the surface. The metal must be clean. A few remaining spots can be hand sanded or wire brushed. Also, small grinding stones mounted in a 1/4″ (6.35 mm) drill may be used. When metal is cleaned, the area is ready for tinning.

The following is the general procedure for applying tinning compounds. There will be some variation for different types of applications.

With the area clean of any paint or other impurities about 2″ (50.8 mm) beyond the damaged area, gently heat the metal with a torch. Use an excess acetylene flame with a 3 or 4 tip. Avoid overheating the panel to prevent warping. Apply the acid core solder to the area to be soldered (Figure 9–16). While the solder is in a liquid state, use a wire brush to make sure the area is completely covered. Then wipe off all the surplus acid and solder with a rag. Now the surface is ready for the application of body solder.

If a paste-type compound is used, brush on the compound before heating, then heat the panel until the paste turns to a liquid. Use a wire brush and wipe the excess off with a rag.

When using a liquid-type compound, heat the surface, then apply the compound with a brush. Continue to heat until the flame melts a bar of solder. Coat the area with solder. While solder is melted, wipe with clean rag to remove the excess (Figure 9–17). Now the panel is ready for solder filling.

CAUTION: Tinning compounds contain acid and operation involves molten metal; therefore, use with care and always wear gloves.

Application

Hold the torch in one hand near the panel and hold the bar of solder in the other hand. Heat up the end of the solder until it becomes soft or plastic, then apply it to the panel (Figure 9–18). Continue heating the bar of solder while gently pressing on it.

Figure 9-16 After the paint and rust are removed by means of a disc sander, the damaged area is tinned using acid core solder. A wire brush is used to remove all traces of dirt and rust. *(Photo by S. Suydam.)*

Figure 9-17 The solder is remelted and a cloth is used to remove all the acid residue and impurities. *(Photo by S. Suydam.)*

Figure 9-18 The bar solder is applied to the surface. *(Photo by S. Suydam.)*

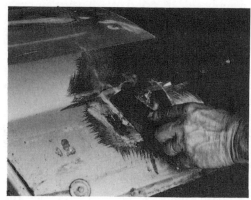

Figure 9-19 After the solder is applied, it is smoothed with a wooden paddle to the proper contour. *(Photo by S. Suydam.)*

Take care not to get the solder too hot. If the bar becomes too short, use pliers to hold it. While still plastic (soft), take a wooden paddle and using heat, carefully smooth out the solder. The wooden paddles are made of hard maple or hickory. Continue doing this until the lead is a little higher than the surrounding area, remembering that the heat has expanded the panel. Be careful not to heat the solder too many times or it will become sandy. If the panel starts to cave in or buckle, stop the operation and let the panel cool as this would indicate that there was too much heat being applied (Figure 9-19). Always point the torch upward if possible; this will distribute the heat over a larger area of the panel and decrease the chance of buckling. Occasionally dip the paddles in motor oil or beeswax to prevent the solder from sticking to the paddles. Always keep the torch moving to avoid melting the solder off the panel. If the metal turns black, it is too hot — the tinning has burned off and the surface must be retinned.

After the panel has cooled and before filing or grinding the solder, remove the oil, beeswax or other lubricants with enamel reducer or lacquer thinner.

If you notice a low spot when you are filing the solder, you can just reheat the solder and add it without any trouble unless you have bare metal showing around the low spot (Figure 9-20). If so, you will have to retin that small area, then continue to fill the low spot. High spots can be tapped down without damaging the solder.

Figure 9-20 After the solder has cooled, it can be filed to a smooth finish with a body file. *(Photo by S. Suydam.)*

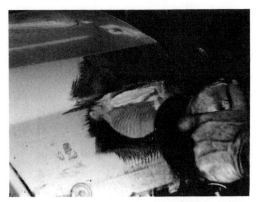

Figure 9-21 Using a disc grinder to smooth the solder. Final sanding and blending in the solder with the surrounding area can be done with an orbital sander. *(Photo by S. Suydam.)*

Figure 9-23 Repairing radiator neck with a soldering iron and solder. *(Photo by S. Suydam.)*

Continue filing until the solder blends in with the panel and the panel is smooth. Be careful when using a file on solder because

it is softer than the surrounding area and you may undercut the solder. Also, the file will cut deep grooves in the lead if it is rocked sideways. Avoid using a new file blade as it will have a tendency to gouge the solder. A disc grinder with #50 grit disc can be used to partially remove excess solder (Figure 9-21). Then finish with a file.

(a)   (b)   (c)   (d)

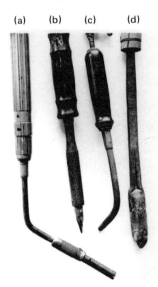

Figure 9-22 Devices used for repairing objects with solder: (top to bottom) (a) soldering tip attached to welding torch; (b) electric soldering iron; (c) air-acetylene soldering torch; (d) soldering iron (often called a soldering copper) heated with a torch. *(Photo by S. Suydam.)*

Figure 9-24 Repairing radiator neck with a welding torch using a carburizing flame (excessive acetylene) and acid core solder. *(Photo by S. Suydam.)*

A solder-filled dent is the most permanent in nature and more durable than plastic. After the solder has been filed and sanded, the area should be cleaned again with reducer or thinner. The area is then treated with a metal conditioner to neutralize any remaining acid that is on the surrounding panel area. (Refer to Chapter 25 for information on the use of metal conditioners.)

Questions

1. What chemical is used as a binder and to promote adhesion in body filler?
2. Name a few of the compounds that give the body plastic the filling qualities?
3. What is needed to ensure that the body filler hardens or cures?
4. Loss of adhesion is caused by too little or too much hardener?
5. What is the main disadvantage of using plastic body filler?
6. Why is cardboard not recommended for mixing body filler?
7. What is the biggest problem encountered when using air tools on plastic?
8. What are some of the disadvantages of using body solder?
9. What are some of the advantages of using body solder?
10. What is the average combination of body solder?
11. Why is this combination of body solder the best?
12. Why is it difficult to use 50-50 solder?
13. What is *tinning* and why is it important?
14. How clean must the surface be before solder can be applied?
15. What type of flame is used for soldering?
16. What causes the tinned area to turn black?
17. What must be used to neutralize the acid before paint preparation?

In spite of all present day efforts to rust-proof the automobile, there are still certain areas where rusting takes place. On some of the later model cars, the lower rear section of the front fender is affected. On other models, rusting may be noticeable on areas such as door legs and tops of front fenders.

It is not the purpose of this chapter to describe the repair procedure for major rust damage, but to focus on the correction of small problem areas. These repairs could involve, for example, closing the large hole that remains after the antenna has been removed or the hole in the trunk area that is left after a trailer wiring harness has been removed. With the proper planning and procedure this type of job can be done quickly and easily.

SURFACE PREPARATION AND INSTALLATION

When a small patch is needed (for example on the lower front fender), first grind off the paint from the surrounding area. Check the extent of the rusted area. Cut out the rusted area and into the solid metal using hand or power cutters. Straighten and prepare the edges of the base metal. Select the type of patch best suited. Cut the sheet-metal and fit it into place. Use paper or light cardboard to make a pattern. Use asbestos paste to control the heat. Hold the patch in place and tack weld on opposite ends. Use vise-grips or C-clamps. Keep the patch below or even with the surface of the base metal. Grind down the welds or brazing area to prepare for the solder or plastic filler (Figure 10-1).

Another method of repairing minor rust damage (or, perhaps, crushed sheetmetal) is to use partial replacement panels. These are generally sections of lower quarter

Small Patch Repair

chapter
10

Figure 10-1 A typical repair patch to the panel. *(Photo by S. Suydam.)*

panels, lower sections of front fenders, or headlight panels. Sometimes it is cheaper to replace only a small section of the panel rather than the whole panel. Replacing a section depends on whether or not it is less expensive than straightening and also on the availability of the replacement panel.

The procedure is similar to making a small patch repair. Place the new panel over the affected area and mark the outline of the new panel. Straighten the surrounding area if necessary. An alternate method is to cut out the affected area first and then cut the panel to fit. Cut out the affected area about 1/2" to 3/4" (12.7 mm to 19 mm) smaller than the cutout section. This leaves an edge to overlap the replacement panel on the surrounding metal. Grind off the paint from the surrounding area. (Be careful when grinding near sharp edges of the sheetmetal.) Use a metal crimper, if available, on the surrounding area or on the replacement panel, depending on which method you decide to use to install the panel. Grind the edge of the replacement panel; this aids in making better and faster welds if the panel is to be welded in. With the panel in the proper place, clamp wherever possible. Depending on conditions,

the panel can be either welded or riveted in place. If riveted, use countersunk rivets. If the panel is welded or brazed into place, the use of asbestos and water will help to control expansion from heat. Grind the seam and apply either plastic or body solder. Prepare the surface for painting.

Sometimes the joints or seams can be covered by molding if they are nearby. It is advisable to remove the old panel rather than place one on top of another. With two panels placed close together, rusting is likely to start and produce the same condition as before even though the new panel is primed on the inside.

Solder is recommended over seams of patches and partial panel repairs because there is a chance of rust forming under the plastic if the seams are not thoroughly welded. Rust can also be a problem if the panel has been riveted.

ALTERNATE METHOD OF BODY REPAIR

Rusting of body panels is a severe problem especially in some areas of the country. In most cases, the rusting goes undetected until it appears on the outside surface of the automobile. Quite often, the average automobile owner will confuse outside rust with inside rust. Most outside rust, or surface rust, comes from fractured or damaged paint film that permits moisture and chemicals to attack the steel panels. Very rarely will surface rust completely rust through the panel under normal conditions. The owner is most concerned about the outside appearance and believes wax and polish will prevent rusting. However, the real problem comes from the inside of the panels where water, chemicals, and dirt become trapped. Many areas are very difficult to reach and removing the dirt and chemicals even with additional drain holes requires time and effort.

Most automobile owners and used car dealers cannot afford to properly repair rust damage and must find an alternative repair procedure. Some of these methods are only temporary, and many first-class shops or bodymen will not use them. They would rather make a permanent repair that will last a long time.

Some automobile owners will ask for temporary repairs in order to have their automobile look nice for trade-in purposes or, on occasion, to prevent water and dirt from being thrown up through a hole on a front fender and onto the windshield.

There are many materials available to make temporary repairs, such as fiberglass and resin, aluminum contact tape, sheetmetal, and pop rivets.

Figure 10-2 Rusted out fender. *(Courtesy of Unican Corporation.)*

When using fiberglass and resin, all the paint and rust must be removed by means of a grinder. The area is then lowered by hammering to allow for the proper buildup of the repair material (refer to Figures 10-2 to 10-10). Depending on the brand of material to be used, the area is either covered with a saturated resin and fiberglass material or a repair compound is spread over the area and the fiberglass is put in place. More repair compound or premixed fiberglass and resin is added for additional coverage of the fiberglass material. After the proper curing, the area is ground off to remove the rough areas or edges. A plastic body filler made for fiberglass or a premixed fiberglass filler is added to bring the repair area up to the right contour of the panel. The area is finished, sanded, primed, and painted.

Aluminum contact tape can be cut and fitted over a rusted area, and plastic body filler or premixed fiberglass material used for the proper buildup. Some bodymen use a piece of sheetmetal and pop rivets for

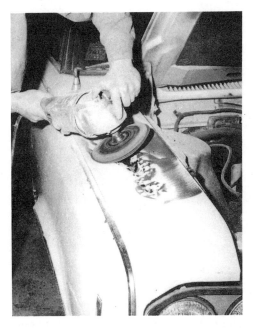

Figure 10-3 Removing old paint with grinder. *(Courtesy of Unican Corporation.)*

Figure 10-4 Applying rust out repair compound. *(Courtesy of Unican Corporation.)*

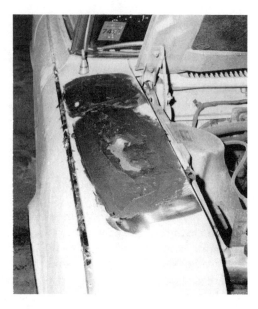

Figure 10-6 Note that the center section is still low. *(Courtesy of Unican Corporation.)*

Figure 10-5 Using fingers to spread out repair compound. Use gloves to protect hands. *(Courtesy of Unican Corporation.)*

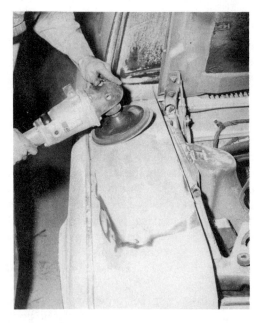

Figure 10-7 Use coarse grinder to grind off surplus. *(Courtesy of Unican Corporation.)*

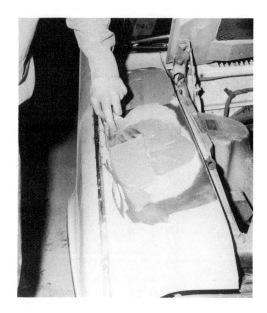

Figure 10-8 Auto body filler spread on rust out repair. *(Courtesy of Unican Corporation.)*

Figure 10-10 Finished product. *(Courtesy of Unican Corporation.)*

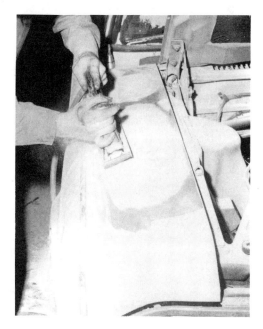

Figure 10-9 Standard refinish technique. *(Courtesy of Unican Corporation.)*

making rust repairs. Before installing the sheetmetal, the area is tapped down a little to bring the sheetmetal just below the level of the surrounding area. It is advisable to use a countersink drill for the pop rivets to avoid grinding off the heads in preparation for adding plastic body filler or premixed fiberglass. Sand material to the proper contour, prime, and paint.

NOTE: Do not use aluminum rivets when patching where there is a lot of moisture. The rivets will corrode due to a chemical reaction between the steel and aluminum.

If possible, spray on a rustproofing material to the underside of the patched area. This will protect the repaired area for a while.

There are many other methods and materials that can be used. Only a few have been mentioned here.

Questions

1. How much of the rusted area should be cut?

2. What can be used to control the heat?

3. What determines whether a panel section should be straightened or replaced?

4. If rivets are used for the patch, what type is recommended?

5. Name some of the temporary repairs that can be made.

6. Why must bulges of the rusted out area be tapped down before applying the repair material?

As a result of collisions, panels become creased, torn, and caved-in. In many cases, these panels can be straightened by hammers, picks, spoons, and hydraulic jacks. One of the jobs of a bodyman is to determine whether it is cheaper to straighten and repair the damaged section or to replace it. Is the cost of repair more or less than the cost of replacement parts plus the cost of installation?

To beginners in the trade, replacing parts of a quarter panel is a difficult job. However, with the proper planning and procedure, it becomes a rather routine matter.

One of the most important things to do before starting to remove the damaged panel is to observe how the damage occurred.

1. From which direction did the force of impact come?
2. Did the force of impact carry into the adjoining panels?
3. How did it affect the door, hood, and trunk openings?
4. Do the door and trunk lid close properly?
5. How many panels have to be replaced and which can be straightened?

In some cases, crown molding, sharp body creases, or other breaks in the body formation tend to make it easier to replace the panel or make joints at these spots. Observing how the new panel is shaped will help determine where the joining seams will be made. Another factor that must be taken into consideration is the type of welding equipment available in the shop where you are working. If only an oxyacetylene torch is available, problems of heat must be taken into consideration especially when joining a panel in the midsection. If a spot welder is available, these problems will be considerably less.

There have been cases where panels

Panel Replacement

chapter
11

were fastened together by pop rivets followed by an application of plastic. This is a fast method of replacing a panel but a poor one. Rivets have their place in the body and fender field but should not be completely relied upon for installation of, for example, quarter panels. The normal vibration of the car traveling on the road will result in cracked plastic and loosened rivets. This is a sure sign of poor craftsmanship. The real objective of a bodyman is to restore the car as near to its original shape and condition as possible. Craftsmanship and quality work should be foremost in the bodyman's mind.

GENERAL PROCEDURES

After carefully looking over the job to be undertaken and after the proposed method or procedure to follow is settled in your mind, the job can begin. In the following paragraphs, a general procedure will be described for the various panels or sections being replaced.

One of the most common jobs that a bodyman must undertake is the replacement of the cowl side panel and/or adjoining panel (sometimes involving the front hinge pillar) on the front section of the body. Damage to the cowl area could mean simply replacing the panel as long as there is no damage to an adjoining section. In cases of severe impact from the front or sideswipe, hydraulic jacks or even a frame straightener (stationary or portable) must be used to correct the damage in the adjoining section. It is generally advisable to use pressure, either push or pull, to partially straighten the damaged panel before cutting it out. This aids in applying the corrective force, generally in the opposite direction of the impact. One mistake a bodyman makes is to cut out the damaged panel before applying a corrective force to realign the adjoining section. Only when the section is aligned, should the panel be removed. Rocker panels are somewhat easier to replace than other major body panels. Note that on most cars, the cowl and quarter panel are mounted on top of the rocker panel.

If only the rocker panel is being replaced and not the quarter panel, the panel has to be cut to fit. That is, do not try to remove the panel that is under the cowl and quarter panel unless there is damage in that area. Measuring and cutting the panel out and fitting the new panel in must be done with care. If the adjoining floor panel is damaged in that area, along with the rocker panel, a pulling or pushing force can be exerted against the rocker panel to assist in partially straightening the floor panel. A variety of clamps or anchors can be attached to the rocker panel rather than to the floor panel itself.

The quarter panel can be approached in several different ways. If the impact resulted from a rear end collision, the quarter, lower rear, and trunk floor panels could be damaged. Also, the rear section of the frame could be damaged. In this case, the body and frame could be pulled as a unit which would save a lot of time in aligning the adjoining panel. This, of course, depends on the severity of the impact.

The frame must be straightened before any panels or body openings can be aligned. Several pulling forces can be exerted on the body and frame at the same time. Once again, the quarter panel should be partially straightened before removal. Pull plates or anchors can be safely attached to the panel since it is to be removed. In some cases, a quarter panel is cut out before the door openings are checked. This results in more time lost trying to align the opening.

Damage resulting from sideswipe and involving the quarter panels, could also involve the wheelhouse, rear lock pillar, inner panels, and so on. A pulling or corrective force should be applied with either a portable frame straightener or hydraulic body jacks.

One of the most difficult panels to replace and one that is avoided by many bodymen, is the roof panel. However, if a roof is damaged to the point where it has to be replaced, normally the car is considered a total wreck. But at times, a roof must be replaced.

Often the door and window openings are distorted and must be checked. Depending on the direction of impact, generally the upper hinge pillar and header panels are damaged. Also, check the center door post, if any, roof side rails, and a number of other panels. On some jobs, one or more hydraulic body jacks are used to partially correct the damage, and this will assist in aligning the various openings. In some cases, a frame straightener can also be used to aid in correcting the damage. The bodyman should realize, however, that hydraulic body jacks and frame straighteners will not completely align the various panels even if they are applied before the panels are removed. The damaged panels serve as a method of attaching the various devices used to apply a force to correct *some* of the damage caused by impact. Cutting out the panels too soon can result in time lost in aligning and fitting a new panel.

On certain makes of cars, the fenders, aprons, and front panels are all welded together. Replacing a front fender has to be approached in the same manner as replacing a quarter panel. On certain models, the rear edge extends into the windshield opening. Unless the damage is severe at the windshield opening, some bodymen prefer to splice the fender about 6" (15.2 mm)

from the windshield. This saves time in removing the glass and minimizes the risk of breaking it. The proper gaps between the luggage compartment to fender and the fender to door must be maintained.

As a result of head-on impact, the front panel and perhaps both front fenders will be damaged, and the damage will often extend back into the engine compartment. In most of these cases, a frame straightener is used to partially remove some of the damage before these panels are removed. On this type of body construction, it is advisable to check the manufacturer's underbody specifications. Some of the correction to the underbody can be made prior to removing the fenders. Replacing both fender and front panel involves the alignment of the whole assembly, and care must be taken to maintain the proper body openings.

METHODS FOR REMOVING PANELS

There are various methods for removing panels. After the necessary jacking is completed (if needed), the next step is to determine where to cut out the damaged panel. With some panels, there is no question about where the joints will be. When replacing quarter panels, especially those that extend up into the roof area, a splice joint can be made across the panel just below the window line. Many cars today are equipped with a vinyl top covering, and the joint can be made just underneath the lower part of this covering. A joint should be made where it will cause the least problems, especially if an oxy-acetylene torch is used for welding. Some bodymen like to splice at a crowned or concaved area. Try to avoid having the splice end up in a corner of a window where it will be difficult to finish off. If a spot welder is available, the joint could be made in an area not ordinarily accessible when using an oxy-acetylene torch. Mark the joint line and start to cut out the panel. Grind off paint before cutting in the area of the splice joint. There are various methods of cutting out panels, depending on what type equipment the shop owns.

Cutting Out Panels with the Oxy-acetylene Torch

The oxy-acetylene cutting torch is often used to cut out panels. The torch is a very fast method and the best for removing crumpled metal, bolts, and so forth. However, there are several disadvantages to using the torch. (1) There is the danger of fire and the necessity of having to disassemble wires, floor mats, interior cloth trim, etc. in order to ensure that they are not destroyed. (2) All body seams are filled with a sealer and are undercoated. They burn easily and rapidly. (3) The edges of metal are generally rough and require further trimming by hand. (4) The heat causes distortion of the remaining panels.

Air Impact Chisel

The air impact chisel is one of the safest methods used to cut out panels. Because of the speed of the cut, care must be taken not to cut too deep. This is especially important when cutting along the wheelhouse, as both panels may be cut. When cutting spot welds, for example, around door post and trunk side gutters, there is a risk of cutting into the post and gutters while trying to remove the panel. One way to avoid this problem is to drill out the spot weld with an electric drill before using the impact chisel.

Power Shears

Power shears or nibbler-type machines are used often and make generally neat edges across open panels but are limited to corners or to areas where several panels are joined together. Also, a starting hole must be made. Regardless of what method is used to cut out the damaged panel, care and accuracy are essential.

ALIGNMENT AND FITTING WITH ADJACENT PANELS

After the panel has been cut out, the following procedure should be followed. All spot welds, jagged edges, or rough spots where the new panel will be placed must be ground smooth to ensure a close and even fit. All edges must be straightened as well as the adjoining panels. If the new panels have to be trimmed, especially when splicing a quarter panel, do it carefully and accurately. Use a measuring tape, if necessary. It is better to cut the panel a little longer the first time, check the fit, and trim again. This will avoid cutting the panel too short and having to add a small piece of metal to close the hole. On quarter panel splice joints, the new panel should overlap the remaining panel about 1/2" (12.7 mm). If panels involve door or trunk openings, check these openings as additional alignment or straightening may be necessary. Check the width of the gap in the opening with the opposite side of the car or check another car of similar make. Normally, a door opening or trunk will vary from 1/8" to 1/4" (3.175 mm to 6.350 mm). Some new cars have even greater gaps. Make sure the gap is even, not tapered along the entire edge of the new panel. It may be necessary to use a hydraulic body jack or even a turnbuckle to maintain alignment of the the opening until the panel is welded in place. Vise-grips and C-clamps can be used to hold the panel in place while checking the alignment. The use of pop rivets will also help to hold the panel in place (Figure 11-1). With the panel in place, again check body opening gaps, body contours, especially on door, door or hood closing, and so forth. With everything in alignment, the panel can be welded in. If a spot welder is to be used, all areas to be welded must be free of paint and primer. Blow through holes will result if the metal is not clean.

If available, a crimping tool can be used to make an offset on either the new panel or remaining panel in order to ensure an even joint or seam. This is done generally when splicing a quarter panel or installing a section of a quarter panel.

INSTALLATION TECHNIQUES

There are various methods of installing or welding in a quarter panel or other panels. Which one to use depends upon what is available in the shop. Some have advan-

Figure 11-1 A replacement quarter panel, trimmed and held in place before welding.

tages over others. The oxy-acetylene torch is the most popular because every bodyman has one. The question as to whether to steel weld or braze is left up to the individual although some bodymen feel that brazing is a poor method. But brazing, if done properly, makes a very strong joint, requires less heat, and can be done faster.

Regardless of what panel is being installed, tack weld or braze in various places, then check the alignment. Quarter panels and roof panels require more care in the welding process. On lap joints, weld or braze about 1/4" to 1/2" (6.35 mm to 12.7 mm) at a time and cool with water; skip about 1 1/2" to 2" (38.1 mm to 50.8 mm) and weld or braze again. Never weld a continuous bead because distortion may occur. The use of asbestos paste around or along the joint will help to control heat distortion. In the trunk side gutter and around taillight openings, weld and skip or tack weld and skip. Frequently check alignment and gaps as welding will tend to draw the panels. In door openings, to make them look original and simulate a spot weld, drill 3/16" (4.76 mm) holes (or slightly smaller) about 1" (25.4 mm) apart along the inside flange of the panel. The purpose is to make buttonhole welds (refer to Chapter 4 on acetylene welding and cutting).

Complete the welding process. If the wheelhouse panel does not line up with the new panel, use body jacks. Do not attempt to use a clamp to draw them together as it will damage the outer panel. After welding or brazing, grind down welds or braze if the repair area will be visible (for example, inside door openings, on certain areas of rocker panels). Spot welders are capable of doing a very fast job of welding in panels, and one of their big advantages is that the amount of heat produced is much less than when using a torch. The two pieces must be held tightly together and be free of dirt or paint. Like torch welding, spot several areas together and check alignment. If panels are slightly apart in an area and cannot be clamped, prick punch the metal, then use the spot welder.

There are several types of spot welders available and it is best to follow the manufacturer's procedures (Figure 11-2). The electric arc welder can be used to install panels, but few shops have a welder suitable for sheetmetal. Some shops use pop rivets to install panels, but this method is not considered good quality workmanship. (It is a cheap method.) Pop rivets are used on a limited basis, primarily in areas where

the rivets will not show after the job is finished.

Metal Finishing

After the panel has been welded in place, the next step is to conceal the splice joints, if any. The first step is to grind the welds and grind the sheetmetal to a shiny finish, removing all paint and welding scales. Fill with either plastic or solder as described in Chapter 9. Grind off welds or tack welds that will be exposed. Neatness and a likeness to the original are important.

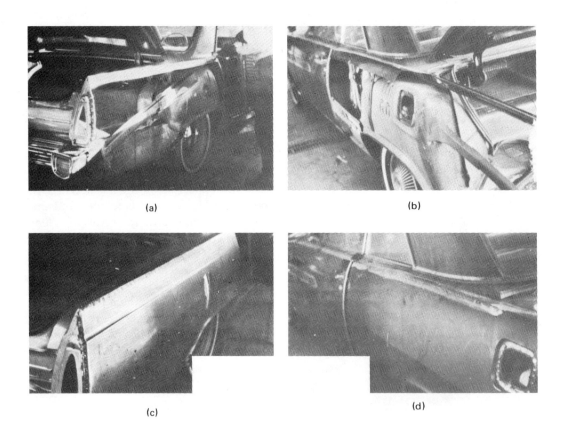

(a)

(b)

(c)

(d)

Figure 11-2 Panel replacing: (a) badly damaged panel; (b) panel removed and trimmed; (c) spot welded in place; (d) ready for finishing. *(Courtesy of Lenco Inc.)*

Necessary Holes for Chrome and Hardware

Any necessary holes for chrome and hardware should be made before priming or painting. This is to prevent accidental damage from occurring; for example, when drilling antenna holes, the drill could slip or the paint could be burned. Seams should be sealed after priming. Body deadeners should be applied if the old panel was so equipped. All lower body seams should be sealed if they were sealed before to prevent dust from coming through.

REPLACING DOOR PANELS

Doors could be considered in a class of their own in regards to repairing damage caused by impact. Like other panels, they are straightened if damage is not too severe and replaced if they are badly damaged. If the outer panel or surface is damaged and the inner panel or frame is in good condition, just the outer panel or surface can be replaced. One of the problems a bodyman faces is to determine if the door can be repaired by just replacing the door skin or if the entire door must be replaced. A complete door, which is called a *door shell,* costs an average of $300 plus the labor to change over the necessary parts. A door skin costs $75 plus 4 hours extra labor to install. This is why door skins are frequently replaced. The procedure for replacing a panel is similar for most makes of cars (Figure 11-3). Doors that contain power windows, locks, exterior moldings, and so forth require a little more time to replace than the lower priced car doors. Late model cars equipped with crashbars inside the door must be examined more closely.

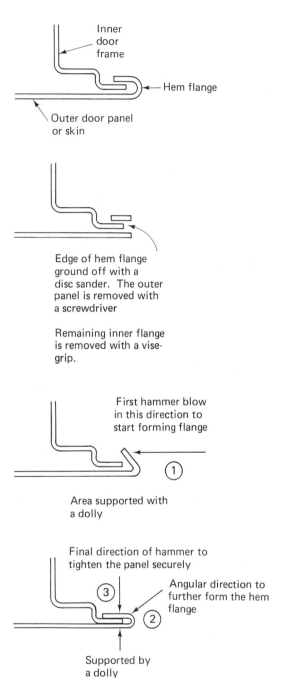

Figure 11-3

Before removing the door from the car, observe the alignment of the door in the opening and decide if the hinges are sprung. Some bodymen claim they can replace a door skin without removing the door from the car or removing the windows. The following is done with the door removed from the car. With the new panel close by, observe how the top of the panel is fastened. This will determine how much interior hardware must be removed from the door. Remove trim panel and disconnect the battery if the door has power windows and/or a cigarette lighter. Remove all hardware. (It is easier to remove while the door is still on the car.) Place parts and pieces in the car, especially the door glass. A body jack or other device can be used to partially remove some of the damage and will aid in straightening out or aligning the inner door frame. Door glass could be broken or chipped if it is left in the door while the panel is being replaced. Remove door and place on a suitable bench or stand.

About the fastest method of removing a door skin is to grind off the edge of the hem flange using a disc grinder. Just grind enough so that the panel separates from the inner flange around the entire edge. A screwdriver will aid in separating the panel. Use of a cutting torch to remove the outer panel will distort the inner panel. An air chisel is also not advised because the inner panel may be accidentally cut.

On the top of the panel, especially those doors with vent glass assemblies, separate the reinforcing strip. The panel should then be free to remove. Remove the remaining inner hem flange using either a pair of pliers or vise-grips. Grind off the remains of the spot welds. Straighten the inner panel edges if necessary. Place the new panel on the door frame and check for alignment. With the panel in place and using a hammer and dolly, start to bend the edges of the panel over the door frame edge. It is advisable to bend a small section on both sides and bottom to center the panel. Continue to bend and form the hem flanges. Always keep the dolly underneath where the hammer blows are to avoid bending or denting the outer panel.

After the flanges are completed, weld in the upper reinforcement, if any. Tack or spot weld about 2" or 3" (50.8 mm or 76.2 mm) apart and grind off the welds if necessary. Check the outer panel for knicks or dents. Necessary holes for moldings should be drilled before painting. At this point, people who like to gamble will continue to prepare the panel for painting. Others will place the door on the car to check its alignment. Prepare for painting and reinstall.

Properly sand and prepare the inner panel for priming. Mask off the door gasket if necessary, the door latch, or any other pieces of hardware or glass that should not be painted.

After applying the primer, let it dry, then apply a recommended seam or joint sealer to the welded joint. Allow the sealer to dry and paint the inner panel with the correct color. It is easier to paint with the door on the bench than on the vehicle.

At this point, those who enjoy taking risks will continue to prepare the outer panel, then prime and paint it. Others will prepare and prime the outer panel, then install the door.

Install the glass, if it was removed, to keep overspray from getting on the interior. Align the door with the adjoining panel and check for proper latching.

Finish the paint preparation and paint the outer panel. Apply rustproofing to the inside of the door panel before installing the necessary trim and hardware.

1. What is the first step in planning to repair a damaged section?

2. Is it better to use force to align the adjoining panel before or after the damaged panel or panels are removed?

3. When replacing a rocker panel, is it advisable to disturb the quarter panel if it is not damaged?

4. In a rear end collision, is it possible to straighten the body and frame together?

5. What is the most difficult panel to replace?

6. If the rear section of the welded on fender is intact, is it necessary to disturb the windshield?

7. What is the advantage of using a spot welder over an oxy-acetylene torch when replacing quarter panels?

8. What is the main disadvantage in using the oxy-acetylene torch for removing damaged parts?

9. What is the problem with using the air chisel for removing damaged parts?

10. How should the edges of the remaining panels be prepared before installing a new replacement panel?

11. What methods are used to hold the new panel in alignment before welding?

12. How much welding should be done before rechecking the alignment of the new panel?

13. How should the visible welds or brazing be prepared after the panel is secure?

14. How can a splice joint be concealed?

15. Is it necessary to seal the lower body joints?

16. What determines whether or not a door panel is replaced?

17. What is the fastest way to remove an outer door panel?

18. Is it necessary to check the door before painting it?

Bolt-On Replacement Assemblies

ALIGNING AND STRAIGHTENING ADJACENT PANELS

During a collision, many of the bolt-on panels or assemblies are damaged or shifted out of position. There may also be damage to the nonmovable or stationary panels. To complete the repairs and restore the automobile to its original condition, the bolt-on and the stationary panels must be aligned.

If a stationary panel or movable panel is damaged, the bolt-on panel attached to it cannot be aligned. An alert bodyman will inspect the panels beyond the damaged area for indirect damage caused by the impact. For example, a force hitting the front fender could possibly be hard enough to push back the door post. Then, the door is out of alignment and will drop a little when it is opened.

After removing the damaged bolt-on panel, a thorough check should be made of body openings, shifted bolts and brackets, or signs of shifted metal. Most of the bolt-on panels may have shifted without disturbing the stationary panels and can be readjusted.

REPLACING AND ALIGNING BOLT-ON ASSEMBLIES

The bolt-on panel or assembly includes fender hoods, doors, bumpers, trunk lids, tailgates, radiator supports, fender skirts, and other panels (Figure 12-1). When removing doors, hoods, or lids, wherever possible, mark the location of the hinges before loosening bolts. It may help when putting the assembly back on.

Many of the panels can be adjusted by loosening the attaching bolts and moving the panels to the desired location. Hoods,

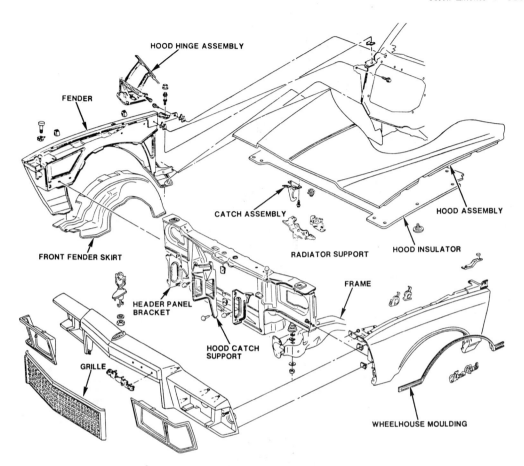

Figure 12-1 Front end sheet metal components. *(Courtesy of General Motors Corporation, Chevrolet Motor Division.)*

for example, can be adjusted by loosening the bolts attaching the hood to the hinge or the hinge to the body.

Before attempting to align or adjust a panel, the adjacent or surrounding panels must be straightened first. Where the inner fender shield (or skirt) or the radiator support are welded together, such as in the unitized bodies, hydraulic equipment must be used. One indication of damaged inner panels is that the bolt holes do not line up with the holes in the new panels. Checking the gap between the hood and fenders will give an indication of alignment. With the hood aligned with the cowl area, a tapered hood and fender gap would indicate that the attaching panels on the fenders are out of alignment.

HOOD LATCHES

Before adjusting the hood latch, be sure that the hood is aligned with the fender, side to side, and the front edge of the hood

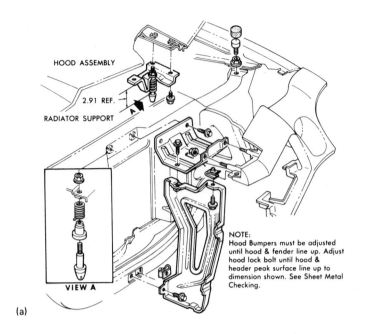

HOOD ASSEMBLY

2.91 REF.

RADIATOR SUPPORT

VIEW A

NOTE:
Hood Bumpers must be adjusted
until hood & fender line up. Adjust
hood lock bolt until hood &
header peak surface line up to
dimension shown. See Sheet Metal
Checking.

(a)

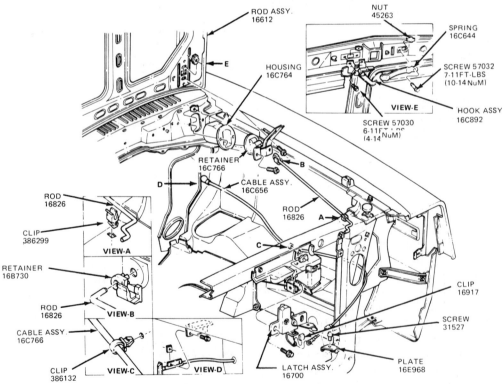

ROD ASSY.
16612

NUT
45263

SPRING
16C644

HOUSING
16C764

SCREW 57032
7-11FT-LBS
(10-14 NuM)

VIEW-E

HOOK ASSY
16C892

SCREW 57030
6-11FT-LBS
(4-14 NuM)

E

RETAINER
16C766

D

CABLE ASSY.
16C656

B

ROD
16826

CLIP
386299

VIEW-A

ROD
16826

A

C

RETAINER
16B730

ROD
16826

VIEW-B

CABLE ASSY.
16C766

CLIP
386132

VIEW-C

VIEW-D

LATCH ASSY.
16700

PLATE
16E968

CLIP
16917

SCREW
31527

(b)

Figure 12-2 Typical hood latch assemblies. (a) *(Courtesy of General Motors Corporation, Chevrolet Division.)* (b) *(Courtesy of Ford Motor Corporation.)*

is even with the front edge of the fender. On those vehicles with a front header panel, the gap must be even between the hood and header. On other models the rear edge of the hood and the cowl grille must be aligned with the proper gap (Figure 12–2).

NOTE: On some models, the protruding adjustable bolt, located on the top of the cowl must be adjusted so the head of the bolt extends into the opening provided in the hood inner panel. If adjusted properly, it will prevent the hood from hitting the windshield during a front end collision.

One method of checking the alignment is to remove the hood latch and lower the hood. This is often called the *free fall method* for checking hoods. If all of the gaps are aligned, install the latch and lower the hood until it contacts the first latch or auxiliary latch or hook (Figure 12–3). Try to raise the hood and if it does open, adjust the auxiliary latch so it catches. The latch must hook properly to prevent the hood from flying open in the event of a collision.

Lower the hood slowly and check whether the hood shifts to one side or the other as it locks. Adjust the latch or latching device, depending on the make and model. When the hood is latched, it should be even with the surrounding surfaces and fit tight.

Some models use an adjustable bolt with a rubber tip located on the radiator support to adjust the left and right front corner of the hood. This will help keep the hood from vibrating.

NOTE: Be sure that the side bumpers are in place and in good condition.

ADJUSTING FENDER WITH SHIMS

The rear part of the fender on some vehicles can be adjusted with the use of shims to line up with the door, by moving the fender higher or lower and inward or outward. Also, some fenders can be moved backward or forward to reach the desired fender to door gap by adding or removing the desired number of shims (Figure 12–4). (Many vehicles have shims installed at the time of assembly in the factory.)

When removing a fender, note the number of shims at the different locations and the thickness of the shims. During the installation of the fender, put back the same number of shims or thickness as removed. The final adjustment of the fender may require more or less shims.

Shims are sometimes added in other places in order to correct improper alignment due to defective parts or sheetmetal distortion.

Depending on the type of hinge used some hoods can be raised up at the rear section to match the height of the fender. This is done by adding a shim between the hood and hinge at the rear bolt if there is no adjustment in the hinge slots.

NOTE: If the standard type of shims are not available, some front end alignment shims can be used or a slot can be cut in a flat washer so it can be slipped over the bolt.

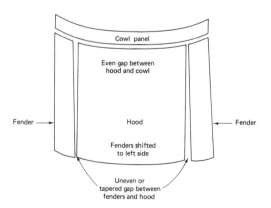

Figure 12–3 Fenders and hood misaligned.

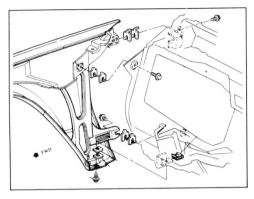

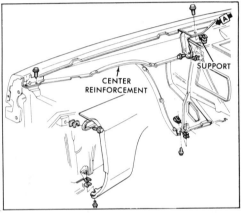

Figure 12-4 Fender shimming. *(Courtesy of General Motors Corporation, Chevrolet Motor Division.)*

All of the gaps on hoods, fenders, doors, gates, and trunk lids should be even and within the manufacturer's specifications (Figure 12-5). Also, the panels should be flush or even with the adjoining panels. Doors with narrow gaps may rub on the fender, and doors that are not flush with the fender may also rub. Excessive door gaps will cause rattles and dirt and water leaks. Most doors with bolt-on hinges can be adjusted up and down, backward and forward, and in or out. Some of the newer doors present more problems because the hinges are welded on the body and/or doors

(Figure 12-6). If hinges are damaged, it may require bending the panels for adjustment. If replacing the hinges is necessary, care must be used to properly locate the hinges before welding (Figure 12-7). The amount of effort to close the door is one indication that the door is not properly adjusted; in the case of hardtop doors, the glass adjustment could be the problem.

An improperly fitted trunk lid and misaligned body panels adjoining the trunk lid are a source for water and dust leaks. For proper sealing, the lid must make proper contact with the rubber gasket. If the lid is damaged, there is no doubt that the adjoining panels will be damaged or out of alignment. Many trunk lids can be adjusted at the hinges and at the striker plate or lock (Figure 12-8). A striker plate or lock that is too loose will cause the lid to rattle and if the striker plate or lock is set too tight too much effort will be required to close the lid. The gap between the body and trunk lid must be even with the edges flush with the adjoining panel. Automobiles with hatchlike lids are most difficult to align because of their size, and many of them are nearly horizontal which makes them more susceptible to water leaks. Some models have adjustable hinges while others are welded (Figure 12-9).

The body or adjoining panels surrounding the hatch lid must be in perfect alignment with correct contact with the rubber gaskets and all the gaps even. Many of the tailgates used today open as a door or as a gate, and the proper alignment is very critical for proper operation. Because of the large variety of adjustments, it is recommended that the factory service manual be consulted for the proper procedures.

NOTE: Caution must be used due to the gas cylinders and torque used in some tailgate assemblies (Figure 12-10).

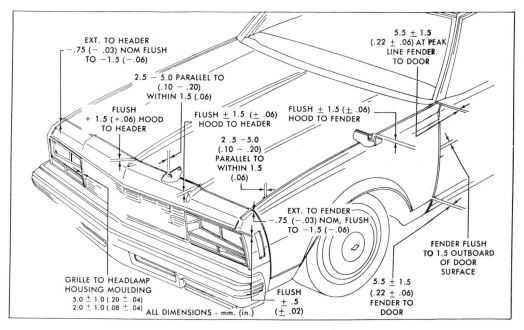

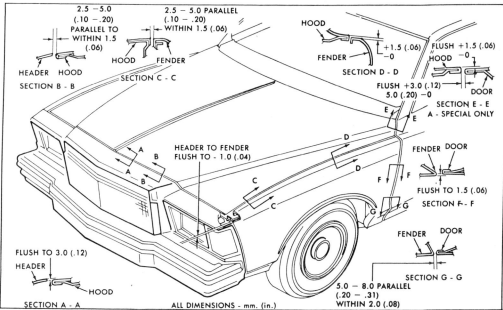

Figure 12-5 Clearance gap dimensions. *(Courtesy of General Motors Corporation, Chevrolet Motor Division.)*

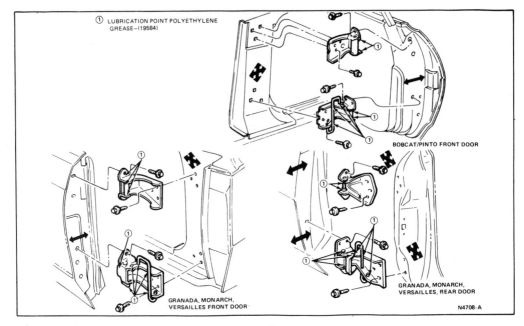

Side Door Hinge Adjustments—All Except Mustang/Capri

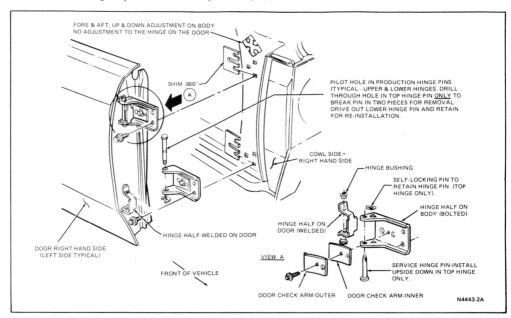

Front Door Hinge System—Mustang/Capri

Figure 12-6 Side door hinge adjustment. *(Courtesy of Ford Motor Corporation.)*

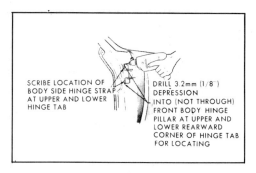

SCRIBE LOCATION OF
BODY SIDE HINGE STRAP
AT UPPER AND LOWER
HINGE TAB

DRILL 3.2mm (1/8")
DEPRESSION
INTO (NOT THROUGH)
FRONT BODY HINGE
PILLAR AT UPPER AND
LOWER REARWARD
CORNER OF HINGE TAB
FOR LOCATING

Body Side Door Hinge Strap Removal - H Styles

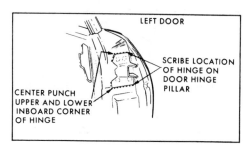

LEFT DOOR

SCRIBE LOCATION
OF HINGE ON
DOOR HINGE
PILLAR

CENTER PUNCH
UPPER AND LOWER
INBOARD CORNER
OF HINGE

Locating Hinge on Door Hinge Pillar - X Styles

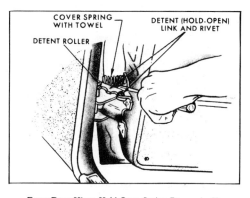

COVER SPRING
WITH TOWEL

DETENT (HOLD-OPEN)
LINK AND RIVET

DETENT ROLLER

Front Door Hinge Hold-Open Spring Removal - X
Styles

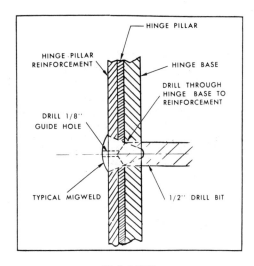

HINGE PILLAR

HINGE PILLAR
REINFORCEMENT

HINGE BASE

DRILL THROUGH
HINGE BASE TO
REINFORCEMENT

DRILL 1/8"
GUIDE HOLE

TYPICAL MIGWELD

1/2" DRILL BIT

Typical Weld

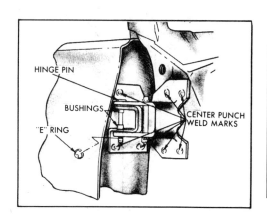

HINGE PIN

BUSHINGS

"E" RING

CENTER PUNCH
WELD MARKS

Front Door Hinge E Ring Removal - X Styles

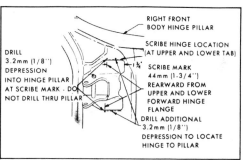

RIGHT FRONT
BODY HINGE PILLAR

SCRIBE HINGE LOCATION
(AT UPPER AND LOWER TAB)

DRILL
3.2mm (1/8")
DEPRESSION
INTO HINGE PILLAR
AT SCRIBE MARK - DO
NOT DRILL THRU PILLAR

SCRIBE MARK
44mm (1-3/4")
REARWARD FROM
UPPER AND LOWER
FORWARD HINGE
FLANGE

DRILL ADDITIONAL
3.2mm (1/8")
DEPRESSION TO LOCATE
HINGE TO PILLAR

Locating Hinge Position on Body Hinge Pillar - X
Styles

Figure 12-7 Installing welded-on door hinge. *(Courtesy of General Motors Corporation, Fisher Body Division.)*

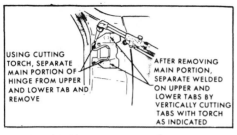

Body Side Hinge Strap Removal - X Styles
Shown, H Styles Similar

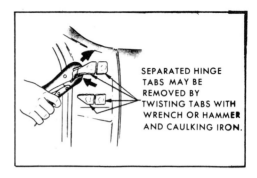

Body Side Hinge Strap Removal

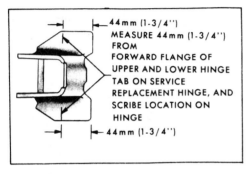

Body Side Hinge Strap Installation - X Styles

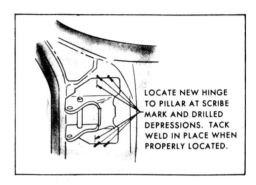

Body Side Hinge Strap Installation - X Styles

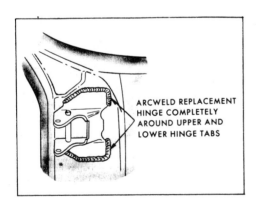

Body Side Hinge Strap Installation - X Styles
Shown, H Styles Similar

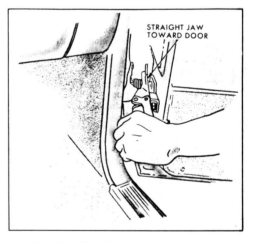

Front Door Hinge Hold-Open Spring Installation
Using Tool J-23497 or Equivalent - X Styles

Figure 12-7 (continued)

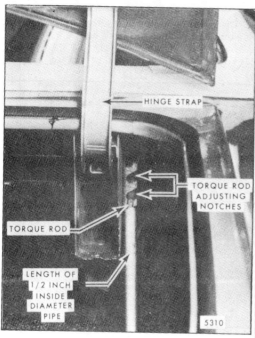

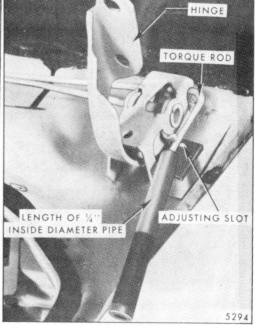

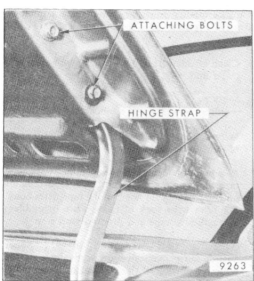

Figure 12–8 Rear compartment torque rod and hinge adjustments. *(Courtesy of General Motors Corporation, Fisher Body Division.)*

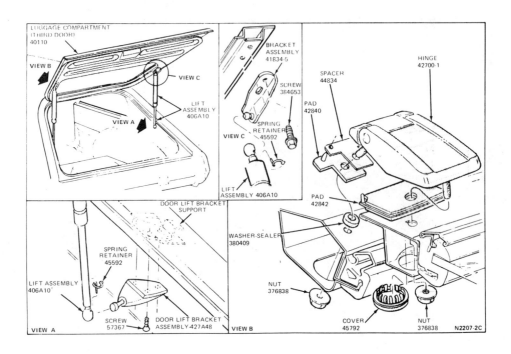

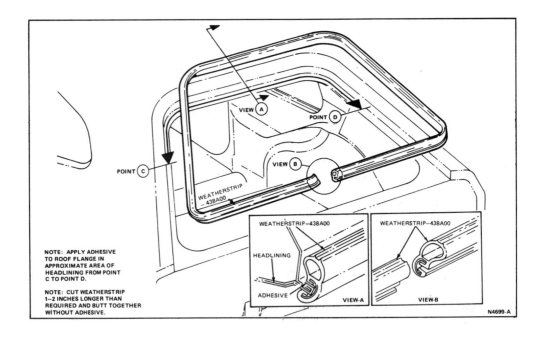

Figure 12–9 Luggage compartment door. *(Courtesy of Ford Motor Corporation.)*

DISPOSAL PROCEDURE

GAS OPERATED COUNTERBALANCE SUPPORT ASSEMBLY

Refer to instructions in this Manual for removal and installation information. When removed, depressurize the support assembly as described below before discarding.

> CAUTION: PROTECTIVE EYE COVERING MUST BE WORN WHILE PERFORMING THE FOLLOWING STEPS.

1. Place support assembly horizontally in bench vise and tighten vise.

2. Place several layers (4 layers minimum) of shop towels or rags over end of cylinder in vise (Fig. 1).

3. Measure 38.10 mm (1-1/2") in from fixed end of cylinder and, using a scratch awl or pointed center punch and hammer, drive awl or punch through the towel and into the cylinder until the gas begins to escape (Fig. 1).

4. Hold the towel and scratch awl in place until all gas has escaped (a few seconds). Then, slowly remove scratch awl. Escaping oil will be absorbed by the towel.

5. While still holding towel over hole, push bright shaft completely into black cylinder to purge remaining oil (Fig. 2).

6. Remove from vise and discard.

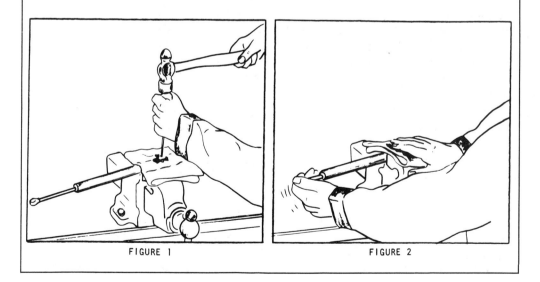

FIGURE 1   FIGURE 2

Figure 12-10 Disposal procedure for replaced gas spring support assembly.
(Courtesy of General Motors Corporation, Fisher Body Division.)

Front and rear bumpers are constructed differently today as compared to ten years ago (Figure 12–11). The older type bumpers were fixed or bolted directly to the frame or body by means of brackets. The brackets allowed adjustment to match the body contours. Bumpers that formed part of the front grille or extended into the body contour required more exacting adjustment to match the contour.

Wraparound bumpers should be evenly spaced (equal distance between bumper and body panel on both sides). Some bumpers have large shimplates to keep the bumper away from the body.

Since the mid-1970s, bumpers have been attached to the frame by means of an energy-absorbing device (Figure 12–12). This device is used to protect the automobile and passengers during minor impact.

To check energy absorbers, position vehicle in front of a suitable wall or pillar. Put vehicle in PARK with the ignition switch off. Set parking brake and apply service brake. Position a hydraulic body jack or other suitable jack between anchor and bumper in line with energy absorber (Figure 12–13).

Apply pressure to compress the absorber about 3/8" (9.52 mm) and release the pressure. If the absorber does not return to its original position, replace the absorber.

The absorber can be tested by using a hydraulic press. Do not apply heat or weld near the absorber.

CAUTION: Do not weld or use heat near the gas-filled–type cylinders. Damaged cylinders should be discarded rather than fixed.

If the absorber is to be discarded, relieve the gas pressure prior to discarding. To relieve gas, center punch the small cylinder and drill a 1/8" (3.17 mm) hole through the cylinder wall (Figure 12–14). Wear safety glasses to protect eyes. When cylinder is bound up due to a collision, hold in position and drill hole to relieve the gas.

While installing a new bumper, place the bumper on a blanket or a piece of cardboard to avoid scratching the chrome. Install all bolts in the exact place from which they were taken and do not mix them up. If a chrome head bolt is damaged or broken, replace it with an identical bolt.

When repairing wrecks, sometimes rechromed bumpers are used instead of new ones because of the price difference. Rechromed bumpers are damaged bumpers that have been straightened and rechromed. These bumpers do not always fit exactly as new ones, and occasionally the chrome plating peels off. Bumpers can be straightened if the damage is not too severe, but in most cases the chrome plate is scratched or marred.

Most trucks use a painted type or no chrome bumper which can be straightened, heated, filled if necessary, and painted in the same manner with regular vehicle paint.

Before removing a bumper, be sure to disconnect all wiring before loosening the bolts to avoid damaging the wires. If the bumper was damaged, check all brackets and braces for damage. Before installing the new bumper, check the frame for damage or torn bolt slots.

TRANSFERRING HARDWARE

When replacing doors, gates, fenders, or other panel assemblies, it is necessary to transfer the numerous parts from the old panel assembly to the new one. Doors and gates present the greatest problem because of the many parts involved in the window glass assembly and the lock system. It is

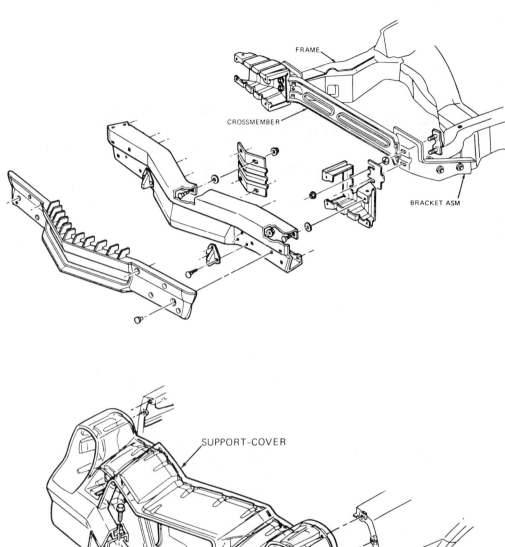

FRAME

CROSSMEMBER

BRACKET ASM

SUPPORT-COVER

IMPACT BAP

LOCK SUPPORT

IMPACT BAR

Figure 12-11 Front bumper assembly. *(Courtesy of General Motors Corporation, Chevrolet Motor Division.)*

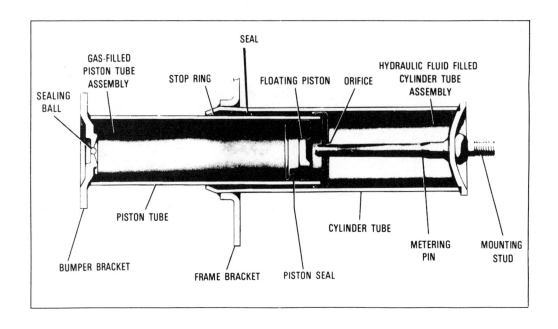

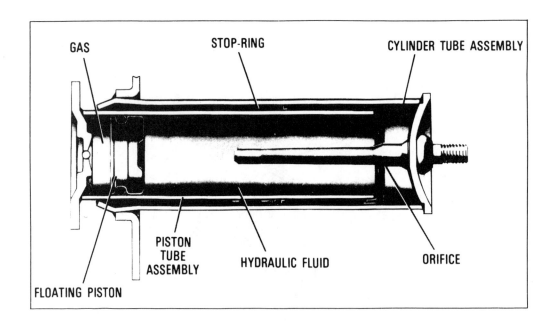

Figure 12–12 Energy absorber. *(Courtesy of General Motors Corporation, Chevrolet Motor Division.)*

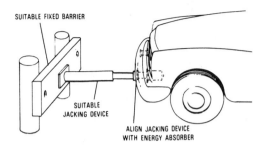

Figure 12-13 Typical test facilities for energy absorbers. *(Courtesy of General Motors Corporation, Chevrolet Motor Division.)*

difficult to reassemble the hardware if the old door or gate is dismantled long before the new part is installed. Many times, if the numerous small parts, clips, bolts, and screws are left lying around in the shop, the pieces get lost.

The recommended procedure is to leave the old panel intact until the new panel is installed. Then, the parts can be trans-

Figure 12-14 Relieving pressure. *(Courtesy of General Motors Corporation, Chevrolet Motor Division.)*

ferred easily and in the right sequence (Figure 12-15). If the panel must be dismantled ahead of time, tape the bolts and small pieces together and mark them. Then place all of the parts in a box in the car. Special care should be taken with the window glass, trim parts, and moldings. A lot of valuable shop time is lost looking for small parts that are lost.

On some automobiles, various hardware parts are riveted and must be installed with rivets. Likewise, those parts must be installed in the exact location due to the many variations of window setups using the same door shell. The manufacturer's service manual should be used as a guide for the proper location of the parts, especially the window guides and stops (Figure 12-16).

After all of the parts are assembled, the operation should be checked before the trim panels are installed.

NOTE: Be sure to properly tighten all bolts after the operation is checked to avoid possible failure due to loose bolts. This is a common occurrence with new cars because of improper tightening of the bolts during the factory assembly.

Necessary Holes for Hardware and Chrome

During the installation of new panel assemblies, holes must be drilled to install various parts such as chrome trim mirrors and new hinges. Unless the panel assembly is badly damaged, the location of the parts on the damaged panel can be used as a guide to install them on new panels. One method is to use a piece of masking paper or wide tape with a pencil or a sharp punch. Then place the paper or tape on the new panel in the same location and mark the panel.

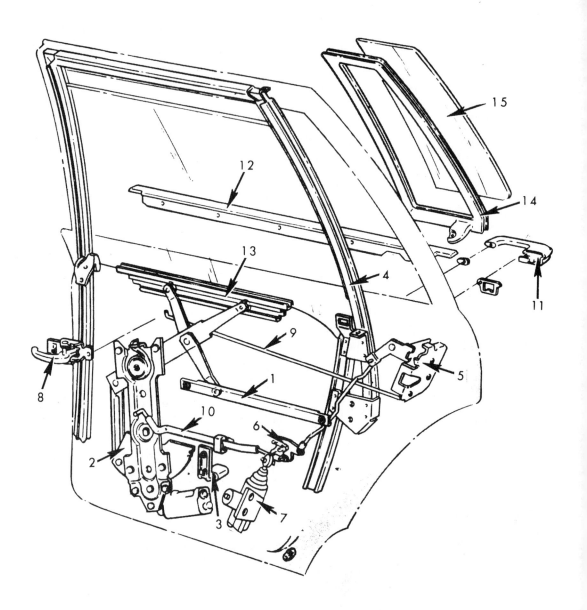

1. Inner Panel Cam	5. Door Lock	8. Inside Remote Handle	13. Lower Sash Channel
2. Window Regulator	6. Locking Rod Bell	9. Handle to Lock	Cam
3. Down Stop	Crank	Connecting Rod	14. Vent Glass Rubber
4. Vent Division	7. Power Door Lock	10. Inside Locking Rod	Channel
Channel	Actuator	11. Outside Handle	15. Stationary Vent Glass
		12. Outer Belt Sealing	
		Strip	

Figure 12–15 Rear door hardware, K style. *(Courtesy of General Motors Corporation, Fisher Body Division.)*

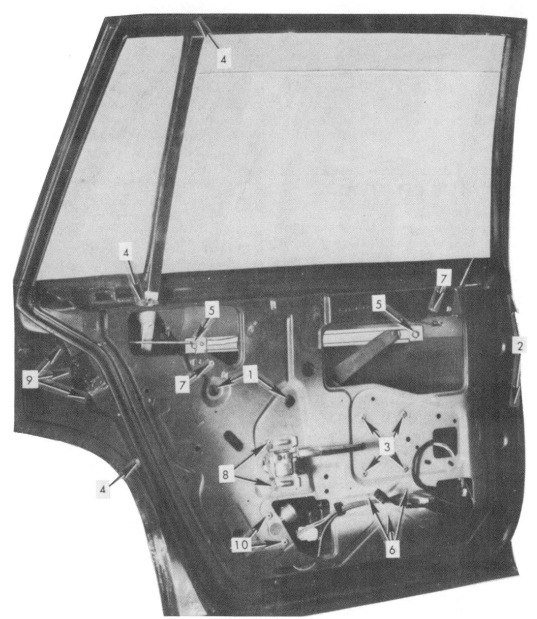

1. Inner Panel Cam
   Screws
2. Run Channel Retainer
   Screws (on Hinge
   Pillar)
3. Window Regulator
   Rivets
4. Division Channel
   Screws (3)
5. Sash Channel Cam
   Screws
6. Window Regulator
   Motor Bolt Locating
   Dimples
7. Bell Crank Rivets
8. Inside Remote Handle
   Rivets
9. Door Lock Screws
10. Power Door Lock
    Actuator Rivets

Figure 12-16 Reardoor hardware attachments. *(Courtesy of General Motors Corporation, Fisher Body Division.)*

If holes for small letters are needed, avoid punch marking the holes too hard as this will dent the panel. When installing some types of door hinges, care must be used to install the hinges in their proper locations or else the door will not align with the body.

RADIATOR REMOVAL

Many front end wrecks involve the radiator. In many automobiles the radiator is mounted on a removable radiator core support; in others the radiator is held in place by means of bolts attached to welded panels.

When the radiator is damaged beyond repair, the coolant is generally lost. But many times, the radiator is not damaged, but the core support or adjoining panels must be replaced or straightened; therefore, the radiator must be removed.

Unless the owner of the automobile requests it, new coolant does not have to be used. Drain the coolant and place in a clean container. Many automobiles with automatic transmission have cooling coils in the radiator. These lines must be removed when taking out the radiator. During the course of repair, if the automobile must be started up and moved without the radiator, connect the two transmission lines together with a short length of rubber hose. If the rubber hose fits snuggly on the cooling lines, there is no need to put a clamp on the hoses as the pressure on the line is low.

When replacing a radiator core support on many automobiles, it is not necessary to disconnect the hoses or cooling lines. After the radiator support is unbolted, the radiator can be held up by the helper as the radiator support is replaced. With the support out, the radiator can be placed on a wooden box or a short board laid on the frame. This can be done to the air conditioner condenser core which is in front of the radiator. Handle it with care to avoid poking holes in the cores.

Many radiators with small holes can be repaired easily with a small welding tip and solder. When in doubt, send the radiator out to a radiator repair shop.

After reinstalling a radiator, properly connect the hoses and lines. If the hoses are in poor condition, including the heater hoses, inform the owner as to the necessity of replacing them before they break. Fill with used or new coolant and replace the radiator cap. Start engine and let it warm up, then shut off the engine. Check all hoses and lines for any leaks.

Carefully remove radiator cap and check the level of the coolant. Fill to recommended level and fill coolant reservoir to hot or warm level.

NOTE: In cold climates, check the coolant with a tester and mark the protection degrees on the radiator. It is recommended that the coolant be set at a low temperature because it may be forgotten when cold weather arrives.

AIR CONDITIONING SYSTEM

As mentioned previously, the air conditioner condenser core is in front of the radiator and many times it may be damaged. If the core is cut open, or punctured, the refrigerant called *Freon* is leaked out. The air conditioning system is under high pressure, and if a line is accidentally broken or the core punctured the Freon will spray out and will freeze anything it touches. This is why it is important to wear safety glasses when dismantling or straightening damage with the air conditioner system under pressure.

There are times when the air conditioner condenser core must be removed or replaced if the lines are badly kinked but not broken. If the shop has an air condition mechanic, let him bleed down the system with the proper equipment. The system can be bled down or the pressure released by cracking open one of the line couplers. This should be done in a well-ventilated area, away from any open flames. Place a cloth over the coupling to prevent the Freon from damaging the surrounding area.

If the Freon is permitted to escape very rapidly, some of the lubricating oil in the system will be lost and must be replaced when recharging the system after repairs.

All open lines should be temporarily plugged shut to prevent moisture from entering the system during repairs. Recharging the system should be done by an experienced air condition mechanic using the proper equipment.

Failure to add or replace the lubricating oil can cause the system to fail.

Questions

1. What are some of the indications of damage to the adjoining panel?
2. How can most types of hoods be adjusted?
3. On some models, what is used to prevent the hood from hitting the windshield?
4. What is used to control the height of the front corners on some hoods?
5. What does a tapered hood to fender gap indicate?
6. Do all doors have adjustable hinges?
7. If too much effort is required to close a trunk lid, what is the problem?
8. What can be used to adjust the rear part of the fender to match the door?
9. What is the result of a misaligned hatch-type lid?
10. Is it safe to weld or use heat near the energy-absorbing devices?
11. What must be done first before loosening the bumper attaching bolts?
12. Where should the parts and pieces of a door assembly be placed while waiting for a new door?
13. When should molding holes be drilled, before or after painting?
14. What should be done before discarding energy-absorbing devices?

Unitized Correction

chapter 13

CHECKING WITH GAUGES

Before repairing sheetmetal damage, the underbody (or the unitized frame section) must be checked for alignment. If the underbody is damaged during an impact or collision, it will affect the alignment of the upper body parts. The underbody alignment is important to the steering and suspension system, for proper handling of the vehicle, and for passenger safety.

One method of checking the underbody is with the use of self-centering frame gauges.

NOTE: A self-centering frame (or centering frame gauge) is attached to different points on the frame or underbody by means of different adapters. The center point of the gauge will remain in the exact center of the frame regardless of the width of the frame or underbody.

Three or four gauges are used and generally placed in four areas, the front crossmember, the cowl area, the rear door area, and behind the rear wheels, if necessary.

The gauges must be installed at the same location and in the same position on both sides of the underbody; that is, the inner or outer edge of a hole in the subframe or the same edge of a rail (Figure 13–1).

Never attach the gauges to any movable parts such as control arms or springs (Figure 13–2). For better sighting of the center pins or pointer, the gauges should be on the same parallel or horizontal, if possible; that is, each gauge should be the same distance from the surface of the rack platform or floor (Figure 13–3). If any sag or pushup is present, it will be easier to see if the gauges are at the same level.

For the best sighting, eye the gauge from the opposite end of the automobile from where the damage is.

The gauges can be moved closer together, especially for front end damage, to pinpoint the damaged area. All the pins or gauges

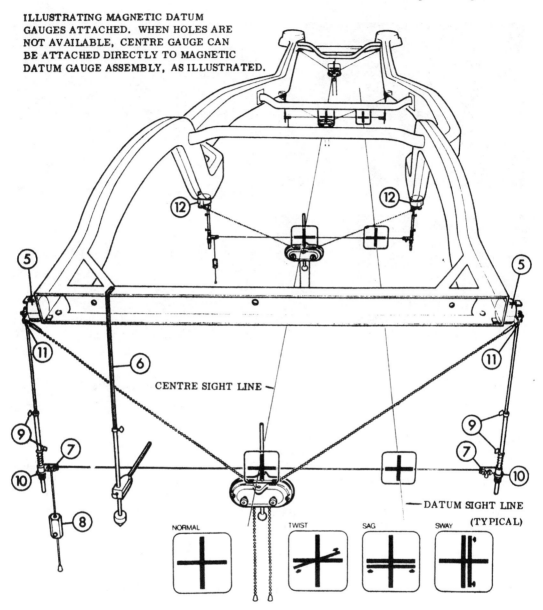

ILLUSTRATING MAGNETIC DATUM
GAUGES ATTACHED. WHEN HOLES ARE
NOT AVAILABLE, CENTRE GAUGE CAN
BE ATTACHED DIRECTLY TO MAGNETIC
DATUM GAUGE ASSEMBLY, AS ILLUSTRATED.

CENTRE SIGHT LINE

DATUM SIGHT LINE
(TYPICAL)

NORMAL   TWIST   SAG   SWAY

Figure 13-1   Typical frame gauges. *(Courtesy of Guy Chart Tools Ltd.)*

must be in line. Some gauges use a circular loop at the top of the pin. If the underbody is in perfect alignment, all of the circles will line up with each other.

Checking the side, the width, or making diagonal measurements may be impossible due to obstructions, such as exhaust systems, transmissions, or front suspensions. The tram gauge can be used for checking diagonals, width of underbody, or side

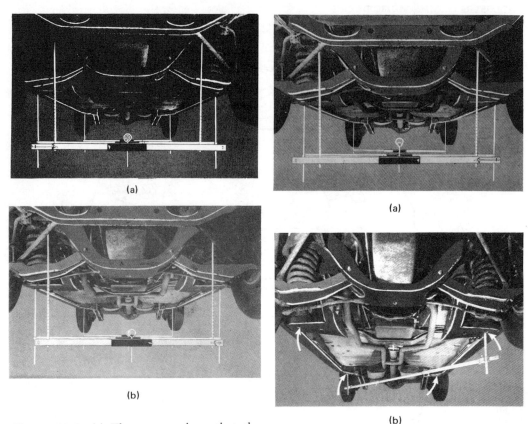

(a)

(a)

(b)

(b)

Figure 13-2 (a) The gauges show that the understructure of this car is in perfect alignment. The horizontal bars are parallel to each other and the round center line pins form concentric circles like a bullseye target; (b) swayed condition: centerline pins are parallel to each other but the front pin is off to the side, indicating that sway is present. *(Courtesy of Applied Power Inc., Blackhawk Manufacturing Division.)*

Figure 13-3 (a) Sag condition: center gauge is lower than the other two gauges; (b) diagonal dimensions are checked with a tram gauge to determine if the frame is symmetrical. *(Courtesy of Applied Power Inc., Blackhawk Manufacturing Division.)*

rails. The tram gauge is adjustable to any length and can be used for checking wheel bases, long diagonal measurements, and the width of the front frame section. Due to the different heights at the various measuring or reference points, the pointers should be adjusted so that the tram gauge bar is horizontal. If a tram gauge is not available, a plumb bob is used at each reference point and marked on a level floor. Then the marks are measured using the specification sheet as a guide.

When using a plumb bob, it is only necessary to have a piece of string and a piece of gas welding rod or similar material. The welding rod can be cut and fashioned into hooks or a hanger, depending on the type of underbody construction. The vehicle should be level and high enough to work under. Attach the hook to a reference point on the underbody and adjust the string with the plumb bob attached so it just barely clears the floor. Mark the spot with an X or dot with chalk or a marking crayon. Attach the hook to the opposite reference point and mark in the same way. Mark all of the reference points and measure with a steel tape.

NOTE: When attaching the hooks, be sure the hooks are placed in the same position on the opposite reference points; for example, the front or rear of a hole in the subframe, *not* the front of one hole and the rear of another.

Datum Line

Another method of checking the underbody or frame for the correct height is to use a *datum line*. The datum line is an imaginary horizontal line which is at the bottom or below the underbody and is used for vertical measurement. The position of the datum will vary with different manufacturers. (The datum line will be further discussed in connection with using manufacturer's specifications.)

Some of the damage can be seen, such as bent braces, wrinkled metal, or pulled spot welds. During front end collision damage frequently occurs to the floor board area where the underbody rails are spot welded to the floor area. Peeled paint or body deadener in the underbody is an indication that the metal has been disturbed.

USE OF MANUFACTURER'S SPECIFICATIONS

The use of the manufacturer's specifications is important for determining the extent of the damage. By using a tram gauge and the frame charts, measurements can be taken. The measurements (or tram gauge setting) must be exactly as stated in the specifications and the correct reference points must be used (Figure 13–4).

When using the manufacturer's specifications, it is important to note the way the measurements are specified or from which points the measurements are taken (Figure 13–5). Some are made from the edge of a hole, the center of a bolt hole or bolt, the outside or inside edge of a rail or crossmember. On later models, the specifications are stated in inches or millimeters or both. On some of the 1979–1980 models, the specifications are listed in millimeters and have to be converted to inches unless the new measuring devices are available. Some manufacturers allow a certain amount of tolerance (or leeway) in measurement.

The datum line should be established as specified in the manufacturer's charts. As noted, some of the lines are established through the top of the mid-side rails or immediately below, which makes it impossible to set up the center gauges for sighting. One method is to add an equal number of millimeters or inches to bring the line low enough so the center gauges can be sighted across. The meaurements are made from the reference points to the bar of the center gauges, if the bar type is used.

If a frame rack or platform is used, the car can be positioned in height and the datum line can be extended to the surface of the rack or platform. Any measurement that is above or below the recommended specification indicates the damaged area.

CHECK FOR SWAY

When a vehicle receives an impact from the side or at an angle in the front or rear, the sway condition may result. Depending on

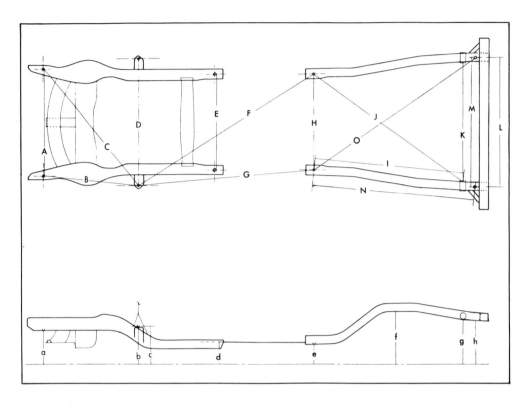

HORIZONTAL DIMENSIONS - X Styles

Fig.
Ref.	Dimension	Location
A	31-3/4" 806.5 mm	Between centers of front stabilizer bar U bracket front attaching holes.
B	33-1/16" 839.8 mm	Center of front stabilizer bar U bracket front attaching hole and center of master gage hole adjacent to no. 1 body mount on same side of body.
C	50-1/16" 1 271.6 mm	Center of front stabilizer bar U bracket front attaching hole and center of master gage hole adjacent to no. 1 body mount on opposite side of body.
D	44-9/16" 1 131.9 mm	Center of master gage hole adjacent to no. 1 body mount

Fig.
Ref.	Dimension	Location
E	33-3/4" 857.3 mm	Rear edge at centerline of no. 2 body mount bolt hole.
F	79-1/16" 2 008.2 mm	Center of master gage hole adjacent to no. 1 body mount and center of master gage hole in side rail on opposite side of body.
G	69" 1 752.6 mm	Center of master gage hole adjacent to no. 1 body mount and center of master gage hole in side rail on same side of body.
H	33-11/32" 846.9 mm	Between centers of 5/8" master gage holes in compartment side rails.
I	54-7/8" 1 393.8 mm	Center of 5/8" master gage hole in side rail and a point at inboard edge of same side rail at centerline of shackle bolt hole (Fig. 3-13).

Figure 13-4 Horizontal and vertical checking dimensions. *(Courtesy of General Motors Corporation, Fisher Body Division.)*

Fig. Ref.	Dimension	Location
J	66-9/16" 1 690.7 mm	Center of 5/8" master gage hole in side rail and a point at inboard edge of opposite side rail at centerline of shackle bolt hole (Fig. 3-13).
K	42-3/4" 1 085.9 mm	Between inboard lower edges of compartment side rails on centerline of shackle bolt hole (Fig. 3-13).
L	40-1/4" 1 022.4 mm	Center of rear bumper lower attaching bolts.
M	45" 1 143 mm	Between centers of 11/16" hole in compartment side rails for rear bumper energy absorbing unit front attaching bolt.
N	61-7/16" 1 560.5 mm	Center of 5/8" master gage hole in side rail and center of 11/16" hole for rear bumper energy absorbing unit front attaching bolt on same side of body.
O	72-3/8" 1 838.3 mm	Center of 5/8" master gage hole in side rail and center of 11/16" hole for rear bumper energy absorbing unit front attaching bolt on opposite side of body.

VERTICAL DIMENSIONS - X Styles

Fig. Ref.	Dimension	Location
a	5-5/32" 131 mm	Front stablilzer bar U bracket front attaching hole or center of bolt head.
b	10-15/16" 261.9 mm	Master gage hole adjacent to no. 1 body mount in frame.
c	11-13/16" 300 mm	Master gage hole adjacent to no. 1 body mount on body.

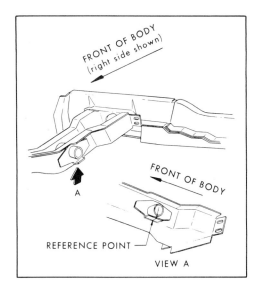

Side Rail at Rear Spring Rear Shackle Bushing - X Styles

Fig. Ref.	Dimension	Location
d	3-21/32" 92.9 mm	No. 2 bar adjacent to no. 2 body mount bolt cage nut.
e	1-7/8" 47.6 mm	5/8" master gage hole in side rail.
f	13-7/16" 341.3 mm	Lower surface of side rail at kick-up either side of rear axle housing.
g	9-21/32" 245.3 mm	Lower surface of side rail at centerline of shackle bolt hole (Fig. 3-13).
h	9-3/32" 231 mm	Lower surface of side rail at 11/16" hole for rear bumper energy absorbing unit front attaching bolt.

Figure 13-4 (continued)

the type and force of the impact, a visual check can be made before using the self-centering gauges. In many cases, the hood or deck lid will be out of alignment. The door to fender gap on the rear door and the quarter panel gap will be wider on the side of the impact. Also, the gap will be decreased on the opposite side.

The three frame gauges may line up horizontally, but the pin or circular pin in the impact area will be out of alignment with the other pins. The gauges can be

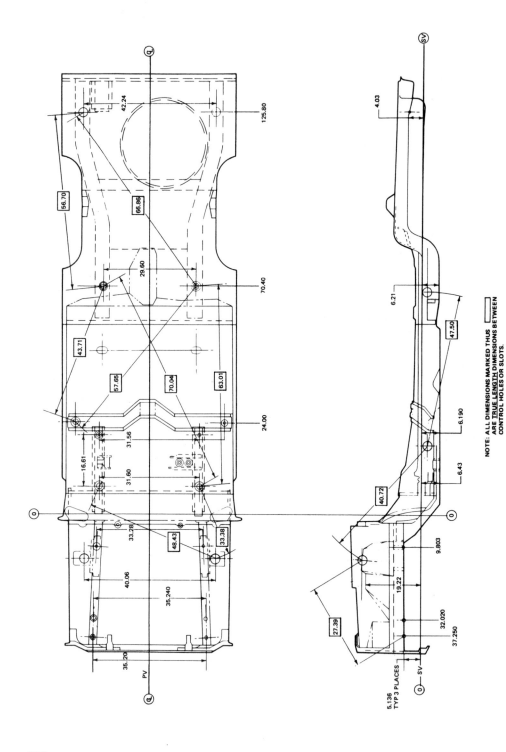

Figure 13-5 Underbody dimensions—Thunderbird/Cougar XR-7. (*Courtesy of Ford Motor Corporation.*)

NOTE: ALL DIMENSIONS MARKED THUS ▭
ARE TRUE LENGTH DIMENSIONS BETWEEN
CONTROL HOLES OR SLOTS.

moved to determine the area of the greatest damage.

A front or rear impact can cause damage to the underbody. Depending on the force of impact, a visual inspection will indicate a sag in the underbody. A sag is often caused by hitting a curbstone or rock or by running into a deep ditch. Yet, the outer sheetmetal may not be damaged. One indication of a sag is the gap or space between the fender and door; that is, the gap is narrower at the top or the fender overlaps the door and the gap is wider at the bottom of the fender and door.

This condition can occur on one side or both sides of the vehicle. If the vehicle is hit in the front, the sag can be detected by using bar gauges. The front gauge will be higher on the side of the sag, and the gauge on the cowl area will be much lower. Very often, the vehicle will have sag and sway at the same time. Another method of detecting a sag is to use the datum line with the manufacturer's specification sheets.

The Mash Condition

The mash condition is caused by a direct head-on collision. The damage is generally centered in the forward cowl area (or where the frame rails join the floor pan). The floor pan metal will be wrinkled or distorted, and in some cases the spot welds will be stretched or broken. The extent of the damage can be determined by the use of a tram gauge using the manufacturer's specifications as a guide.

JOB PLANNING

Once the damage is inspected, the next step is to determine from which direction the damage or impact occurred. The correction force should be applied in the opposite direction of the impact. When using corrective force, a series of pulls is better than trying to make one big pull. Spread out the pulling force and, if possible, make several pulls at one time. Remember, the unitized underbody is basically made of sheetmetal construction, and damage could result if too much force is applied at one point.

When determining the cost or time involved to make the repairs, additional time must be added to cover the removal of the necessary parts, not including the damaged area. For example, if the damage is extended to the floor pan of the passenger compartment, removal of the floor mats, perhaps the front seat, and various other interior parts may be necessary. This time should be added to the estimate.

In cases of curb damage, the bumper and other parts have to be removed to allow for straightening. The time necessary to straighten the damage will depend on the type of straightening equipment that is available. Setting up the equipment or attaching the necessary equipment takes more time than the actual straightening.

PORTABLE FRAME STRAIGHTENER

The portable frame straightener works well in unitized bodies because it can pull at different angles (Figure 13-6). Because the unitized body does not have a frame to anchor on, pinch weld clamps must be attached to the pinch weld of the underbody. With the proper hookup using the clamp, rail, and chains, the portable straightener can be used at various angles. The automobile should be mounted on

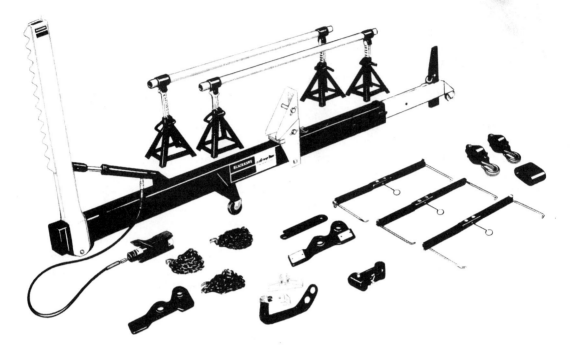

Figure 13-6   Typical portable frame straightener. *(Courtesy of Applied Power Inc., Blackhawk Manufacturing Division.)*

safety stands; this will allow ample space for working on the automobile.

CAUTION: Never stand in line with the pulling force. There is always the possibility of the chain slipping, the clamp slipping, or the clamp tearing the metal (Figure 13-7). Also, it is advisable to use a blanket or tarpulin on the chains when pulling. This will prevent the chain from traveling or whipping in the event that it slips or breaks.

Using chains wrapped around a rail or crossmember, cover the area under the chain with plate steel or angle iron to prevent the section from being crushed or bent (Figures 13-8 and 13-9). The portable straightener can be anchored against the cowl (or where the front suspension sec-

tion and body side rails meet at the offset). Once again, to spread out the force of the angle, insert a heavy piece of plate steel between the anchor and the body. In some damaged areas, there is not a suitable place to attach a clamp or other anchor. A heavy sheetmetal tab can be welded on the underbody to attach the clamp and then removed when the panel is straight.

Never anchor the straightener against the front or rear suspension units or other movable parts. These units could be damaged or forced out of alignment. Careful planning is necessary when anchoring and attaching pulling devices to avoid creating additional damage (Figures 13-10 and 13-11). Most of the portable straighteners will develop 10 tons (9,073 kg) of pressure,

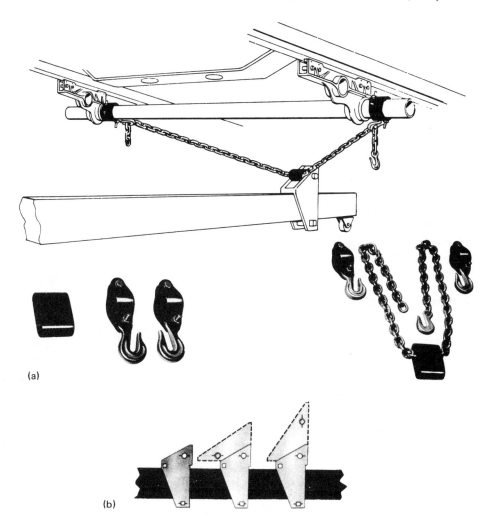

(a)

(b)

Figure 13-7 (a) Cross-tube anchor system; (b) multi-position anchor post. *(Courtesy of Applied Power Inc., Blackhawk Manufacturing Division.)*

and if hooked in the wrong place additional damage could occur or the spot welds could be torn loose. It is necessary to check measurements as the panels near specifications to avoid overpulling. When the area being straightened involves the windshield, doors, fender, or other panels, these should be tried for alignment.

USE OF COMBINATION AND MULTIJACK SYSTEMS

At times, the portable frame straightener is not sufficient to correct the damage so an additional force or forces are needed (Figure 13-12). Hydraulic body jacks can be

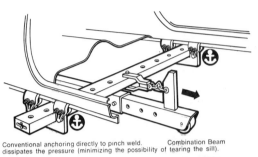

Conventional anchoring directly to pinch weld. Combination Beam dissipates the pressure (minimizing the possibility of tearing the sill).

When no pinch welds are available, a section of angle iron must be installed. (the angle iron can also be welded to a conventional frame. This allows you to use the Combination Beam and anchor the Power Pull in any given position).

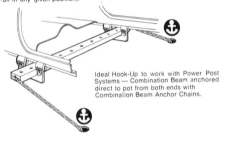

Ideal Hook-Up to work with Power Post Systems — Combination Beam anchored direct to pot from both ends with Combination Beam Anchor Chains.

Figure 13-8 Unitized body hook-up. *(Courtesy of Guy Chart Tools Ltd.)*

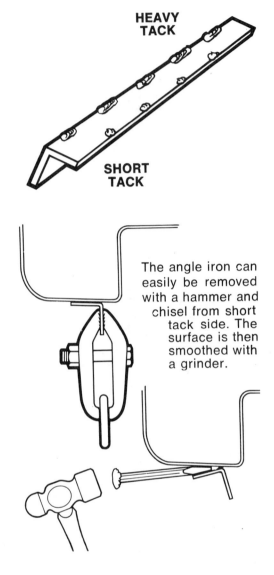

The angle iron can easily be removed with a hammer and chisel from short tack side. The surface is then smoothed with a grinder.

Figure 13-9 Use of angle iron for anchoring. *(Courtesy of Guy Chart Tools Ltd.)*

used in combination with the portable straightener or they can be used to straighten the interior part not accessible to the portable straightener. When using hydraulic body jacks, it is sometimes necessary to use wood blocks to spread out the force and prevent damage to the panel used as an anchor.

The hydraulic body jack can be used to hold one area in position while force is being exerted in another area. Or, using a push-pull body jack, a second pull can be made from the same upright of the portable straightener.

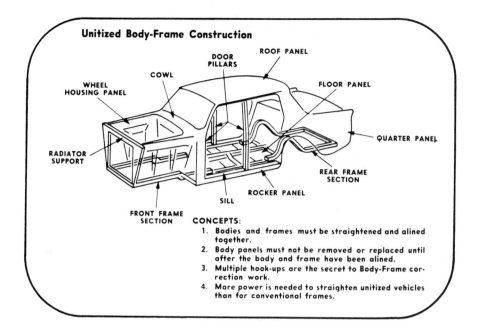

Unitized Body-Frame Construction

ROOF PANEL

DOOR PILLARS

COWL

WHEEL HOUSING PANEL

FLOOR PANEL

RADIATOR SUPPORT

QUARTER PANEL

REAR FRAME SECTION

FRONT FRAME SECTION

SILL

ROCKER PANEL

CONCEPTS:

1. Bodies and frames must be straightened and alined together.
2. Body panels must not be removed or replaced until after the body and frame have been alined.
3. Multiple hook-ups are the secret to Body-Frame correction work.
4. More power is needed to straighten unitized vehicles than for conventional frames.

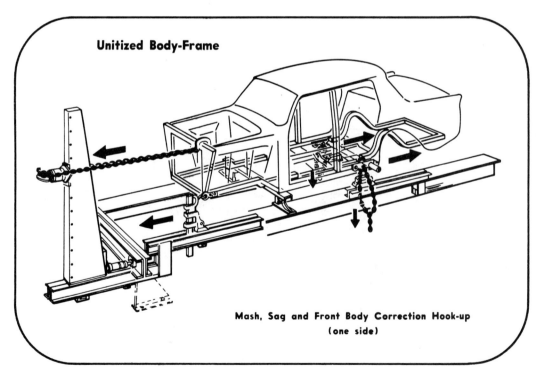

Unitized Body-Frame

Mash, Sag and Front Body Correction Hook-up
(one side)

Figure 13–10 Unitized body-frame. *(Courtesy of Applied Power Inc., Bear Manufacturing Corporation.)*

Unitized Body-Frame

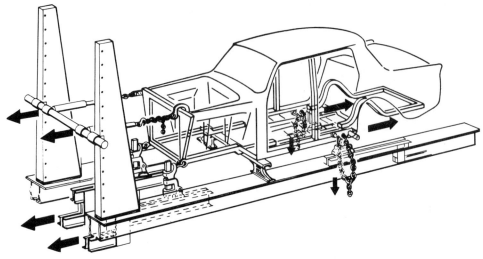

Double Mash, Sag and Front Body
Correction Hook-up
(Both sides)

Unitized Body-Frame

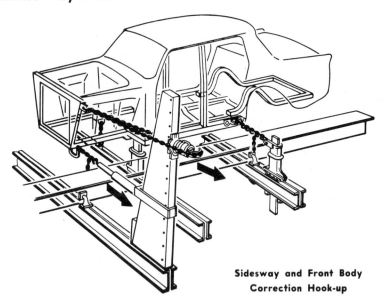

Sidesway and Front Body
Correction Hook-up

Figure 13-11 Unitized body-frame. *(Courtesy of Applied Power Inc., Bear Manufacturing Corporation.)*

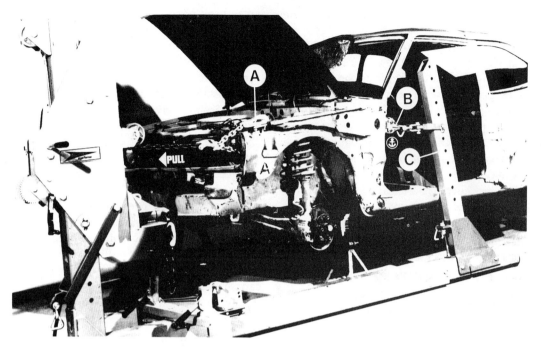

Figure 13-12 Pulling front fender skirt or apron: (a) lock clamps, top one bolted to top of the fender skirt or apron flange and the lower one through the side of the apron. The metal is secured on both sides. (b) clamp secured to the door post pinch weld or hinge plate to serve as an anchor; (c) bracing tower beam. *(Courtesy of Guy Chart Tools Ltd.)*

There are many more combinations that can be used to fit each individual underbody straightening operation.

Occasionally, the side rails may be severely wrinkled after the underbody is straightened. The section can be cut out, straightened, and welded back in position for appearance sake. Also, a door can be cut in the frame section; that is, a section cut on three sides and folded outward. This will permit the straightening of sharp kinks or distorted metal. Often, the section is straighened, the door is folded back into position, and welded.

Heat should be applied only when necessary to avoid weakening the metal, especially on the newer models.

When the pressure is applied, hammering the creases and the distorted metal will help to relieve the pressure.

If the metal must be heated in order to be straightened, heat it to a cherry red, about 1200°F (650°C).

After correcting the damage to the unitized underbody, not including the exterior sheetmetal, the bare metal should be properly prepared, treated with a metal conditioner, and primed. Several coats of a good quality air dry enamel primer, such as a rust inhibitor primer or equivalent, should be applied to the surfaces. The lacquer-type primer-surfacer is not recommended.

Any seams should be sealed if the sealer has been destroyed, removed, or disturbed.

The seams should be in factory new condition.

If the subframe or underbody parts were originally painted, these parts should be repainted. Finally, the underside should be rustproofed with a good quality rust-proofing.

Each panel contributes to the overall strength of the body. If the panels are permitted to rust, the body is then weakened and could become dangerous. Erratic steering is known to be caused, at times, by badly rusted underbody parts.

STRAIGHTENING EQUIPMENT FOR X-BODIES OR STRUT EQUIPPED BODIES

Automobile construction is going through a period of rapid change. Some auto manufacturers predict that within five years, the majority of the automobiles produced will be unitized construction. Some of these unitized constructed automobiles with the strut suspension are on the roads today. They are very similar to the imported automobiles which have used a strut-type suspension for some time (Figure 13-13).

At present, the strut-type suspension has little or no adjustment for caster or camber. On some automobiles, the correct caster and camber is built in at the time of manufacture. This type unitized construction demands more accuracy when the underbody is straightened or new panels installed. Some body specifications require exact measurements with no leeway (Figure 13-14).

Several manufacturers of frame and body equipment have introduced new types of straightening and alignment equipment to help eliminate the repair problem.

Another problem to consider is the front wheel drive automobile that uses a cradle-type removable frame. This frame bolts to the unibody subframe and has the motor, transmission, drive axle, and lower suspension parts attached to it.

During some front end collisions, the cradle may be damaged and need to be replaced. The bolt holes of the subframe or side rail must line up with the holes in the cradle arms. With the cradle out of position, the wheel alignment, mainly the caster, will be affected causing erratic steering, poor handling, or pulling to one side. The cradle-type suspension does have a camber adjustment.

The caster is also affected by improper straightening or improper alignment of new panels around the shock tower or fender skirt assembly. If the fender skirt is pushed backward in the cowl panel, this will have an effect on the wheel alignment.

With the front wheel drive and the strut suspension, more load-bearing parts and thinner, higher strength steel will be used in construction.

NOTE: General Motors recommends the use of MIG welding for welding in new front end body panels because of the new type steel being used. They do not recommend the use of the oxy-acetylene torch because of its excessive heat (Figure 13-15).

When straightening or replacing posts on these new type bodies, the old method or measuring could be misleading; there is too much leeway for error. One particular new type of unitized body straightener and aligner uses a large table to which the vehicle is anchored.

To check the alignment of the front panels, various fixtures are used (Figure 13-16). When the fixture dowl (or pin) matches the

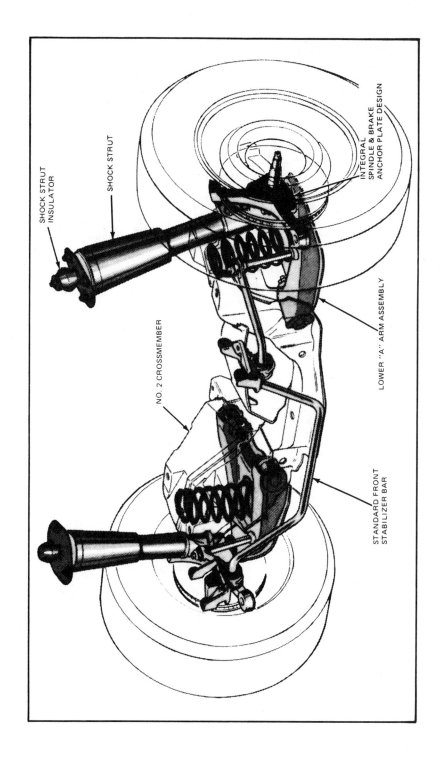

SHOCK STRUT INSULATOR

SHOCK STRUT

INTEGRAL SPINDLE & BRAKE ANCHOR PLATE DESIGN

LOWER "A" ARM ASSEMBLY

NO. 2 CROSSMEMBER

STANDARD FRONT STABILIZER BAR

Figure 13-13 A modified MacPherson Strut design. Camber and caster angles are factory set and cannot be adjusted. (*Courtesy of Ford Motor Corporation.*)

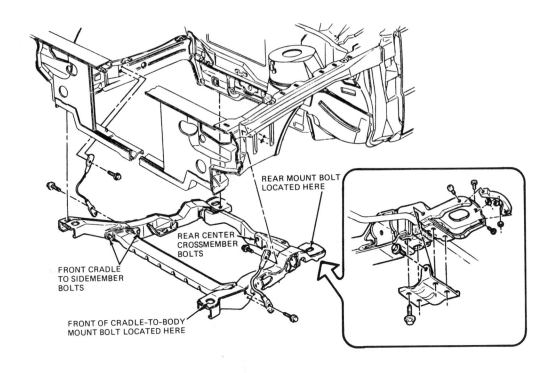

REAR MOUNT BOLT
LOCATED HERE

REAR CENTER
CROSSMEMBER
BOLTS

FRONT CRADLE
TO SIDEMEMBER
BOLTS

FRONT OF CRADLE-TO-BODY
MOUNT BOLT LOCATED HERE

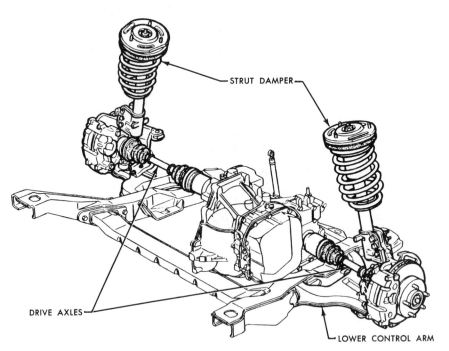

STRUT DAMPER

DRIVE AXLES

LOWER CONTROL ARM

Figure 13-14 Front end and strut assembly. *(Courtesy of General Motors Corporation, Chevrolet Motor Division.)*

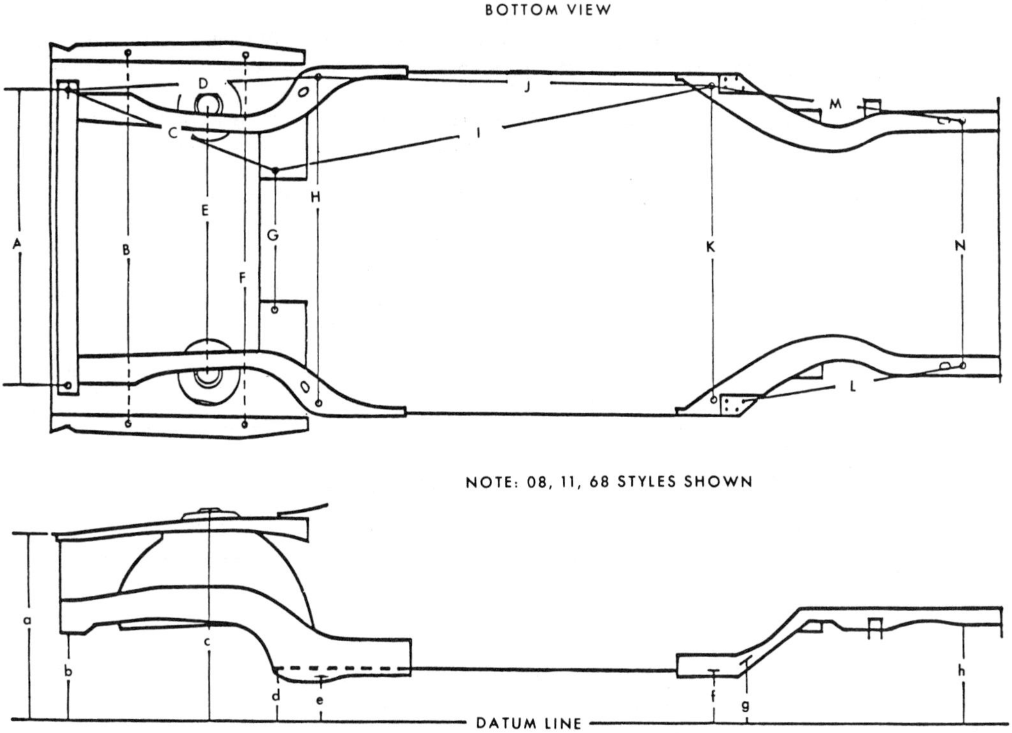
BOTTOM VIEW
A
B
C
D
E
F
G
H
I
J
K
L
M
N
NOTE: 08, 11, 68 STYLES SHOWN
a
b
c
d
e
f
g
h
DATUM LINE

Figure 13-15 (a) Diagram for X body dimensions. *(Courtesy of General Motors Corporation, Chevrolet Motor Division.)*

UNDERBODY HORIZONTAL DIMENSIONS

Reference and Dimension Location

A-1146 mm (45.1") Center of 16 mm (5/8") gage holes in the lower motor compartment front panel just outboard of engine cradle attaching bolts.

B-1421 mm (55.9") Center of 9 mm (23/64") holes located in depressions of upper motor compartment side rail. Measure from top side.

C-910 mm (35.8") Center of 16 mm (5/8") gage hole in lower motor compartment front panel to center of 16 mm (5/8") hole inboard of cradle attaching hole.

D-1029 mm (40.5") Center of 16 mm (5/8") gage hole in lower motor compartment front panel to center of 16 mm (5/8") hole located rearward of front wheelhouse opening.

E-1054 mm (41.5") Center of each shock tower hole. Measure from top side.

F-1440 mm (56.7") Center of 9 mm (23/64") holes located in depressions of upper motor compartment side rail. Measure from top side.

G-581 mm (22.9") Center of 16 mm (5/8") holes inboard of cradle attaching holes.

H-1183 mm (46.6") Center of 16 mm (5/8") gage holes located rearward of front wheelhouse openings.

I-1893 mm (74.5") Center of 16 mm (5/8") holes inboard of cradle attaching holes to 19 mm (3/4") hole located in rear compartment pan rail forward of rear wheelhouse opening.

J-1716 mm (67.6") Center of 16 mm (5/8") gage holes located rearward of front wheelhouse opening to 19 mm (3/4") hole located in rear compartment pan rail forward of rear wheelhouse opening.

K-1142 mm (45.0") Center of 19 mm (3/4") holes located in rear compartment pan rail forward of rear wheelhouse openings.

L-926 mm (36.5") Center line of rear control arm attaching hole to 19 mm (3/4") gage hole in rear compartment pan rail rearward of rear wheelhouse opening.

M-1040 mm (40.9") Center of 19 mm (3/4") hole in rear compartment pan rail forward of rear wheelhous opening to 19 mm (3/4") gage hole in rear compartment pan rail rearward of wheelhouse opening.

N-978 mm (38.5") Center of 19 mm (3/4") gage holes in rear compartment pan rail rearward of rear wheelhouse openings.

UNDERBODY VERTICAL DIMENSIONS

Reference and Dimension Location

a-732 mm (28.8") Datum line to top of front end upper tie bar.

b-333 mm (13.1") Datum line to lower motor compartment front panel.

c-824 mm (32.4") Datum line to upper surface of shock tower.

d-204 mm (8.0") Datum line to surface of rear engine cradle attaching bolt holes.

e-182 mm (7.2") Datum line to 16 mm (5/8") gage hole in motor compartment side rail.

f-207 mm (8.1") Datum line to surface of rear compartment pan rail at 19 mm (3/4") hole.

g-258 mm (10.2") Datum line to surface of rear compartment pan rail at rear control arm attaching hole.

h-388 mm (15.3") Datum line to rear compartment pan rail at 19 mm (3/4") gage holes.

Figure 13-15 (b) Dimensions to gauge hole are measured to dead center of the holes and flush to adjacent surface metal unless otherwise specified. (*Courtesy of General Motors Corporation, Chevrolet Motor Division.*)

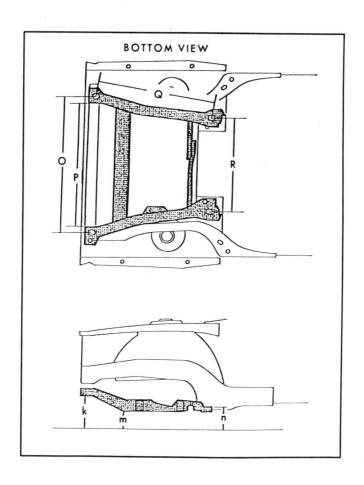

ENGINE CRADLE HORIZONTAL DIMENSIONS

Reference and Dimension Location

O-1040 mm (40.9″)	Center of front engine cradle attaching bolt holes.
P-952 mm (37.5″)	Inner edge of engine cradle surfaces.
Q-904 mm (35.6″)	Center of front engine cradle attaching hole to center of rear attaching hole.
R-700 mm (27.6″)	Center of rear engine cradle attaching holes.

ENGINE CRADLE VERTICAL DIMENSIONS

Reference and Dimension Location

k-250 mm (9.8″)	Datum line to lower surface of the engine cradle at front attaching holes.
m-136 mm (5.4″)	Datum line to lower surface of engine cradle at cross member.
n-177 mm (7.0″)	Datum line to upper surface of engine cradle at rear leg.

Figure 13–15 (c) Engine cradle dimensions. *(Courtesy of General Motors Corporation, Chevrolet Motor Division.)*

HORIZONTAL SHOCK TOWER DIMENSIONS

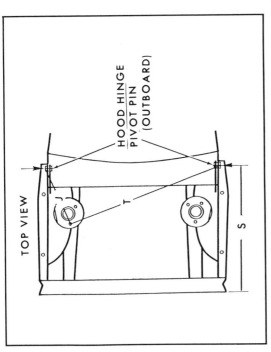

Reference and Dimension Location

S-1042 mm (41.0") Leading edge of upper motor compartment tie bar to center of hood hinge pivot pin.

T-1282 mm (50.5") Center of front shock tower attaching hole to center of outboard edge of hood hinge pivot pin on opposite side of the body.

U-458 mm (18.0") Center of front shock tower attaching hole to center of outboard edge of hood hinge pivot pin on the same side of body.

Figure 13-15 (d) Specifications for the X body shock tower. (*Courtesy of General Motors Corporation, Chevrolet Motor Division.*)

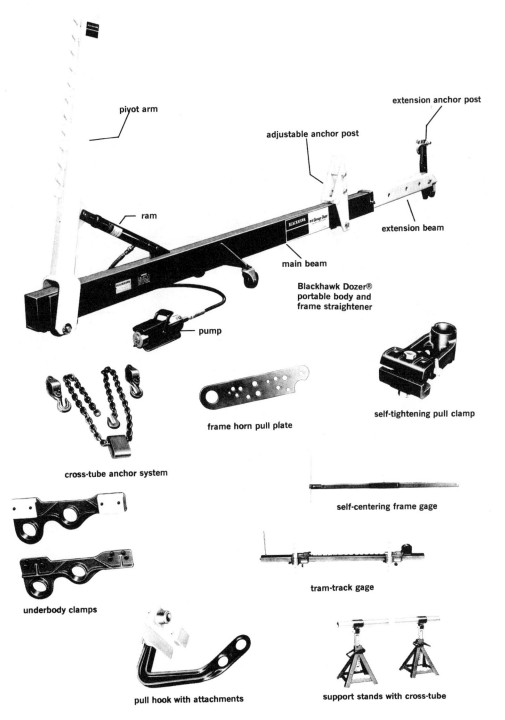

pivot arm

extension anchor post

adjustable anchor post

ram

extension beam

main beam

Blackhawk Dozer®
portable body and
frame straightener

pump

frame horn pull plate

self-tightening pull clamp

cross-tube anchor system

self-centering frame gage

underbody clamps

tram-track gage

pull hook with attachments

support stands with cross-tube

Figure 13-16 (a) Portable frame and body straightener with attachments and air operated pump. *(Courtesy of Applied Power Inc., Blackhawk Manufacturing Division.)*

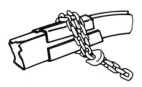

Box frames and channel sections should be padded with short pieces of angle iron to prevent damage to the corner of the section when a chain is wrapped around the frame section.

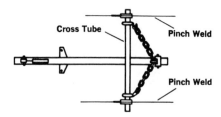

Proper anchoring for a heavy fore and aft pull utilizes the underbody anchoring system as shown here.

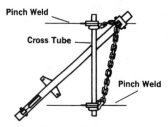

For a diagonal pull, the underbody anchoring system provides attachment to both rocker panels, for better efficiency and less damage. The anchoring loads are spread across both sides of the car.

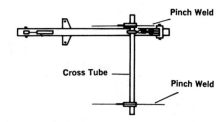

For pulling on one side only, it is best to attach the cross tube to both rocker panels. Anchor your Dozer to the cross tube. This will prevent undue rolling of the underbody clamps on the pinch weld.

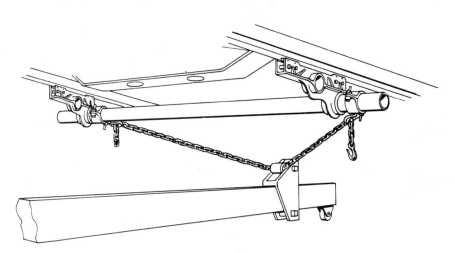

The underbody anchoring system fastens to the pinch welds and provides full load capability plus versatility in positioning your Dozer portable body and frame straightener.

Figure 13-16 (b) Recommended anchoring procedures. *(Courtesy of Applied Power Inc., Blackhawk Manufacturing Division.)*

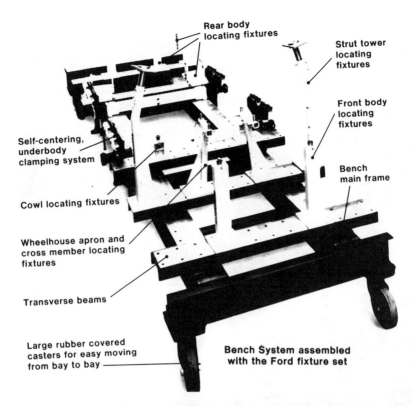

Rear body
locating fixtures

Strut tower
locating
fixtures

Front body
locating
fixtures

Self-centering,
underbody
clamping system

Bench
main frame

Cowl locating fixtures

Wheelhouse apron and
cross member locating
fixtures

Transverse beams

Large rubber covered
casters for easy moving
from bay to bay

**Bench System assembled
with the Ford fixture set**

Figure 13-17 Demonstration model of the bench system with the fixtures in place. *(Courtesy of Applied Power Inc., Blackhawk Manufacturing Division.)*

Figure 13-19 X-type body front under body sections tack welded in position prior to final assembly of other sections and alignment. Note damage to cradle assembly by the vise grip. *(Courtesy of Applied Power Inc., Blackhawk Manufacturing Division.)*

Figure 13-18 Using the bench system in combination with a floor-mounted straightening system. *(Courtesy of Applied Power Inc., Blackhawk Manufacturing Division.)*

holes in the front underbody assembly, the section is straight and in alignment. These fixtures must fit, leaving little room for error. The fixtures are made for specific vehicles. This type can be used with the floor mounted body and frame aligner (see Figures 13-17, 13-18, and 13-19).

Another type of body frame uses a very accurate lazer beam for alignment purposes. Whatever type frame and body alignment is used, the trend is toward more accuracy and less "close enough" or "they will never see it."

After completing the repairs to the underbody, the bare metal must be cleaned and primed with a zinc chromate or a rust inhibitor primer, not a lacquer-type primer. All seams must be sealed, and the assembly should be rustproofed. If the underbody parts are permitted to rust, the whole assembly will be weakened and create hazardous conditions for driving.

1. What is a self-centering gauge?
2. How many gauges should be used to check the unibody?
3. Can the gauges be attached to movable parts?
4. Where is the best place to eye the self-centering gauges, near the damage or at the opposite end of the vehicle?
5. What is a *tram gauge* used for?
6. What is a *datum line?*
7. If obstructions are present, how can a datum line be sighted?
8. What are some indications of a swayed front end?
9. If the door to fender gap is very wide at the bottom and close at the top, what type damage has occurred?
10. Should the type equipment available be taken into consideration when estimating the cost to repair a unibody section?
11. What can be used to prevent a chain from flying when it suddenly breaks or slips?
12. What can be used to prevent damage to a body member when using it for an anchor?
13. If a portable straightener cannot correct all of the damage, what can be used in combination with the straightener?
14. Can too much heat weaken a frame section?
15. Can a badly rusted underbody panel have an effect on the vehicle's operation?
16. Why does straightening or repairing strut suspension require more accuracy?
17. Can the caster be affected by a misaligned cradle?
18. What is used to check the alignment of parts on the new type straightener?
19. Why is it very important to protect the underbody from rusting?

Frame Correction

USE OF SELF-CENTERING GAUGES, TRAM GAUGES, AND MANUFACTURERS' SPECIFICATIONS

The same gauges and system of checking the underbody are used for checking frame damage. Depending on the type of damage to the frame, the first step in checking is the use of the self-centering or centering gauge. Use at least three gauges, four gauges if possible, for better observation. The gauges should be hung on the frame using the same holes on both sides of the frame (Figure 14–1). The gauges can be hung on the top edge of the frame or attached to magnets on the bottom surface of the frame (Figure 14–2). The main point to remember is that the gauges must be attached at the same exact location on the frame or else the readings will be false. Some gauges use adjustable hangers. If one gauge is set at a different height than the other, poor straightening procedures could result.

Check the location of the pointers on the centering gauges from the opposite end of the automobile from where the damage is located. If the pointers are in line, the frame is not swayed.

The datum line must be established to determine whether the frame is sagged or the frame ends are pushed upward or downward. There are several types of gauges that can be used to establish the datum line. The centering bar-type gauge can be used by adjusting the hangers to bring the datum line below the frame for the proper sighting. If the frame is straight, the ends of the bar should line up with each other.

Another type of datum gauge is the magnetic type which attaches to the frame with crossbars and extensions. Each bar has a level bubble, and when properly set all the crossbars will line up if the frame is straight.

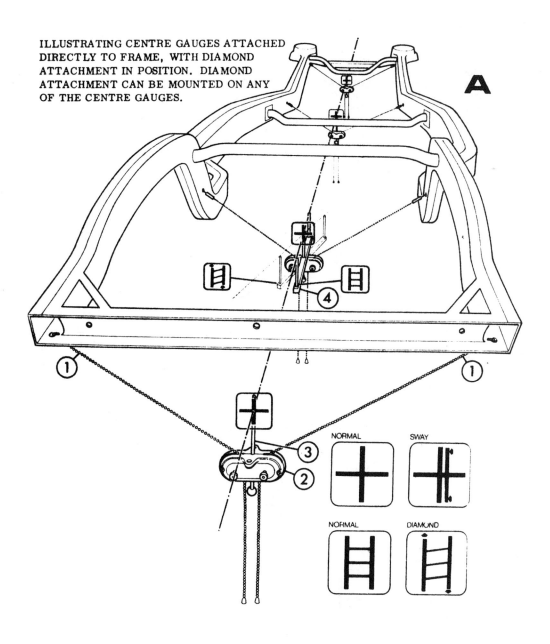

ILLUSTRATING CENTRE GAUGES ATTACHED
DIRECTLY TO FRAME, WITH DIAMOND
ATTACHMENT IN POSITION. DIAMOND
ATTACHMENT CAN BE MOUNTED ON ANY
OF THE CENTRE GAUGES.

A

NORMAL

SWAY

NORMAL

DIAMOND

Figure 14-1 Typical frame gauges. *(Courtesy of Guy Chart Tools Ltd.)*

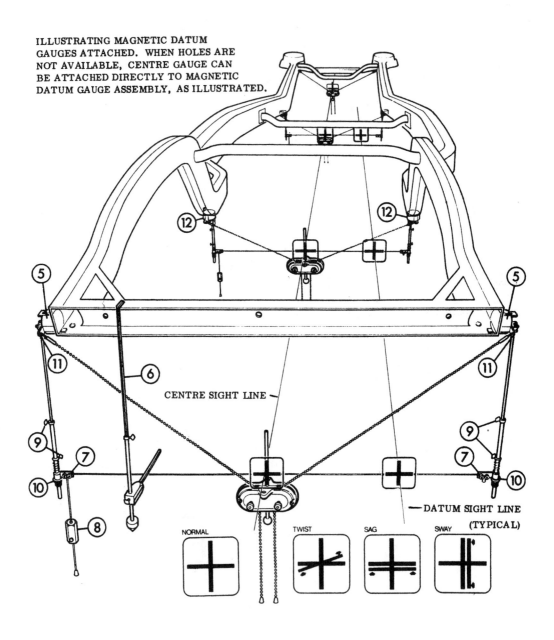

ILLUSTRATING MAGNETIC DATUM
GAUGES ATTACHED. WHEN HOLES ARE
NOT AVAILABLE, CENTRE GAUGE CAN
BE ATTACHED DIRECTLY TO MAGNETIC
DATUM GAUGE ASSEMBLY, AS ILLUSTRATED.

CENTRE SIGHT LINE

DATUM SIGHT LINE

(TYPICAL)

NORMAL   TWIST   SAG   SWAY

Figure 14-2   Typical frame gauges. *(Courtesy of Guy Chart Tools Ltd.)*

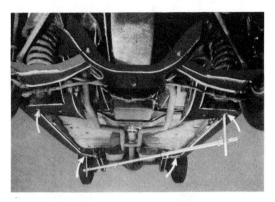

Figure 14-3 Use of tram gauges. *(Courtesy of Applied Power Inc., Blackhawk Manufacturing Division.)*

The tram gauge is used to check the frame using the manufacturer's frame charts as a guide (Figure 14-3). The pointers make it possible to go above or below the obstructions. Check the frame charts for proper placement of the pointers in relation to the bolt holes, bolts, frame edges, or other reference parts (Figure 14-4). The tram gauge can be used to cross-check the frame or to check the frame diagonally. If there is any variation in the tram gauge findings, the frame is damaged.

The tram gauge can be used as a tracking gauge to check whether the wheels are in line with each other. To use the tram gauge, place the two pointers on the inside edge of the rear wheel rim at the center line of the axle. Adjust the pointers to equal length. Place the other pin or point #3 at the center of the front wheel spindle or edge of the wheel. (The wheels must be in a straight ahead position). After getting the gauge set, lock or tighten the thumbscrews and move to the opposite side of the automobile and check. If there is any variation, check the specification chart for the proper wheelbase for the correct length and mea-

sure the gauge to determine which wheel is wrong.

With all of the measurements completed, it can be determined where the damage is located.

Some types of frame damage are listed as follows:

Sag—located at the center of the automobile or the passenger compartment; the frame is lower than it should be as a result of direct impact to the front or rear. A sag is generally visible where the fender and door meet and is characterized by a wide gap at the bottom and a narrow gap at the top. Also, the doors hang and will not latch properly.

Sway—occurs when the front, center, or rear section of the frame is pushed sideways by impact. The hood or trunk will not fit properly and tapered body gaps will be evident. Diagonal measures will have one long and one short measurement.

Mash—the length of the frame is shortened either from the front bumper to the cowl area or from the rear bumper to the rear wheels. Damage and distortion are found in the fenders and hood. There may be collapsing of the coil spring housing. The torque boxes are generally pushed backwards. Rear mash will bulge the quarter panel outward above the rear wheels.

Diamond—caused by one side being driven backward or forward depending on which end is hit. The hood and/or trunk lid will be out of alignment. Buckles may appear in the quarter panel, at the wheel area, or at the roof joint.

Twist—one corner of the frame is raised higher than the other. This condition generally results from an impact from the lower frame upward and may force the opposite side downward.

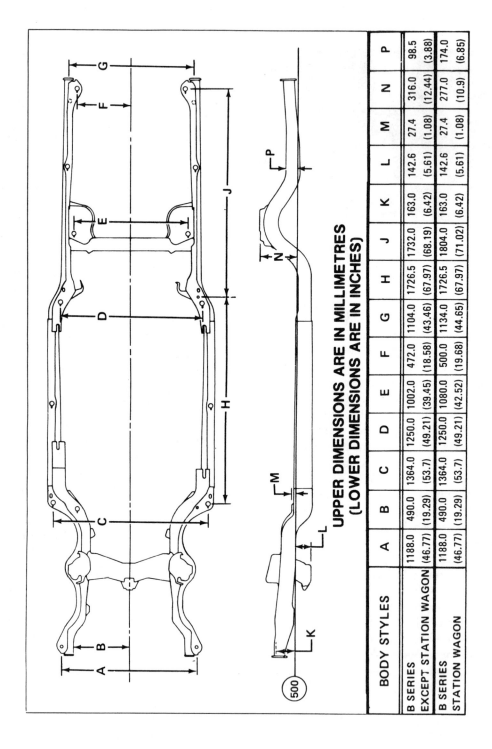

UPPER DIMENSIONS ARE IN MILLIMETRES
(LOWER DIMENSIONS ARE IN INCHES)

BODY STYLES	A	B	C	D	E	F	G	H	J	K	L	M	N	P
B SERIES EXCEPT STATION WAGON	1188.0 (46.77)	490.0 (19.29)	1364.0 (53.7)	1250.0 (49.21)	1002.0 (39.45)	472.0 (18.58)	1104.0 (43.46)	1726.5 (67.97)	1732.0 (68.19)	163.0 (6.42)	142.6 (5.61)	27.4 (1.08)	316.0 (12.44)	98.5 (3.88)
B SERIES STATION WAGON	1188.0 (46.77)	490.0 (19.29)	1364.0 (53.7)	1250.0 (49.21)	1080.0 (42.52)	500.0 (19.68)	1134.0 (44.65)	1726.5 (67.97)	1804.0 (71.02)	163.0 (6.42)	142.6 (5.61)	27.4 (1.08)	277.0 (10.9)	174.0 (6.85)

Figure 14-4 Typical frame dimensions. (*Courtesy of General Motors Corporation, Chevrolet Motor Division.*)

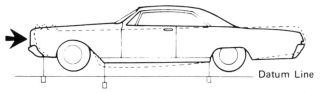

Impact from the front or rear end of the car causes the car to droop near the center.

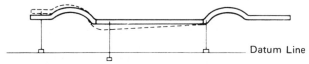

Damage is detected by using three or more gages at key points on the frame. Note center gage is low.

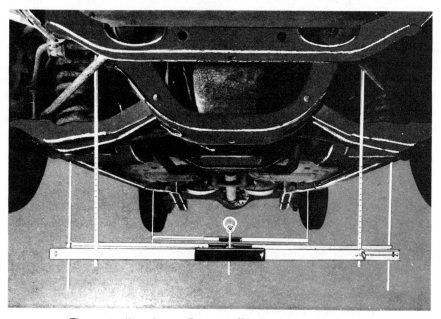

The center line pins are "on center" indicating no side damage present. The horizontal bars are parallel to each other, but the center gage is lower than the other two gages . . . this indicates sag type of damage occurred in the cowl section.

Figure 14-5   Determining a sagged frame. *(Courtesy of Applied Power Inc., Blackhawk Manufacturing Division.)*

Nearly all collisions involve at least two types of frame damage or distortion.

JOB PLANNING

After analyzing the gauge readings, measurement variations, and location of the frame damage, the next step is to plan the repair operation.

In figuring the cost of straightening the frame, an important thing to consider is the amount of time needed to remove the necessary parts to gain access to the damaged area. This is in addition to those parts damaged during the impact.

The number of hookups required to do the job will depend upon what type straightening equipment is available and what type frame is involved. It takes considerable time to change the attachments on certain types of equipment in order to make the different types of pulls. On the other hand, some equipment can make several pulls at one time. The bodyman or frameman must have a knowledge of the different types of frame and a good understanding of what really happened at the time of impact.

USE OF PORTABLE FRAME STRAIGHTENER

The portable frame straightener can be used for straightening some types of frame damage. It can be used at different angles to correspond with the direction of impact.

The automobile must be properly supported on safety stands for easy access to perform the necessary hookups (Figure 14-7). The operator should not stand in the direct line of pull because of the danger of a

chain breaking or a clamp slipping (Figure 14-8). It is recommended that you cover the chains with a blanket to prevent them from whipping due to breakage or slippage. On certain pulls, it is advantageous to have floor anchors or anchor pots to hold the automobile down (Figure 14-9).

The portable straightener exerts a large amount of pressure and if the anchor is not properly placed or the area prepared, additional damage can be created.

When straightening out a mashed frame, if the distance between the frame torque boxes is correct, a pull jack should be used to prevent distortion in that area. (See Figure 14-7 for some of the basic hookups using a portable frame straightener).

NOTE: If heat is necessary, use a neutral flame and heat to a cherry red (not above 650° C (1200° F). Avoid overheating to prevent the formation of weak spots.

USE OF STATIONARY FRAME RACK

The stationary frame rack either floor style, raised ramp, or platform, is used for straightening the more severe and complicated types of frame damage. The ramp or platform model frame and body straightener takes up a lot of floor space which some shops cannot afford to lose. The floor model can be used for other types of work when not being used for frames (Figure 14-10).

With the stationary units, several hookups can be made at one time and at various angles, depending on the type equipment available. Several frame and body pulls can be made at one time, including sideway pulls (Figure 14-11 and 14-12). When using several pulls at one time, the work progresses gradually, and frequent checks of

Gages should be hung to detect the high corners.

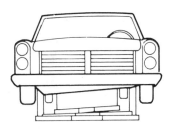

Tilting horizontal bars indicate twist.

When viewed from the side, a twisted frame makes a shallow "X."

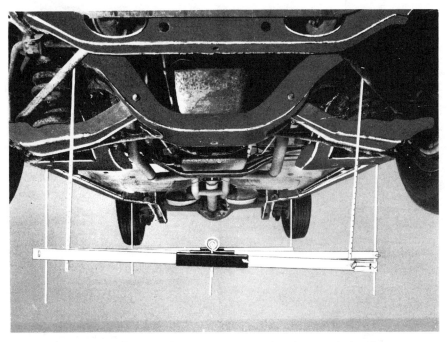

The self-centering frame gage center pins show vertical and horizontal alignment to be okay, but check the position of the horizontal bars. Note that they are tilted . . . twist damage is present as the frame is not level.

Figure 14-6 A twisted condition. *(Courtesy of Applied Power Inc., Blackhawk Manufacturing Division.)*

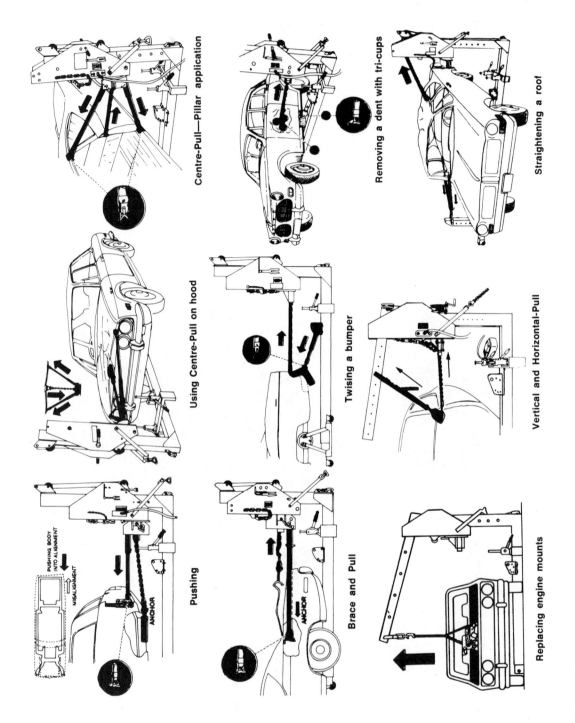

Centre-Pull—Pillar application

Removing a dent with tri-cups

Straightening a roof

Using Centre-Pull on hood

Twising a bumper

Vertical and Horizontal-Pull

PUSHING BODY INTO ALIGNMENT

MISALIGNMENT

ANCHOR

Pushing

ANCHOR

Brace and Pull

Replacing engine mounts

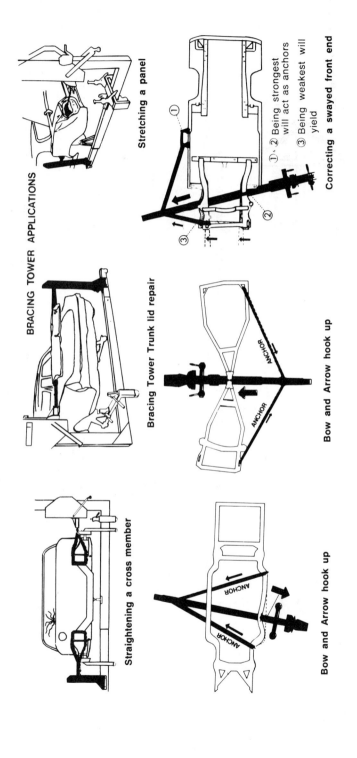

BRACING TOWER APPLICATIONS

Stretching a panel

① ② Being strongest will act as anchors

③ Being weakest will yield

Correcting a swayed front end

Bracing Tower Trunk lid repair

Bow and Arrow hook up

Straightening a cross member

Bow and Arrow hook up

Figure 14-7 A portable frame and body straightener with some applications. (*Courtesy of Guy Chart Tools Ltd.*)

239

proper anchoring procedures distribute the load

Frames and bodies are bent and distorted by collision with a relatively large area of the car bearing the impact. However, the correction procedure utilizes powerful, concentrated loads at key points which can cause local crushing of frame members, etc., if these points are not properly padded to spread the load over a large area. Illustrations of recommended anchoring procedures are shown below for efficient use of the under body anchoring system.

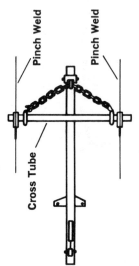

Proper anchoring for a heavy fore and aft pull utilizes the underbody anchoring system as shown here.

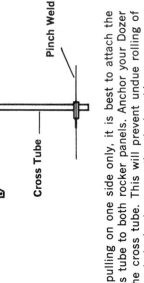

For pulling on one side only, it is best to attach the cross tube to both rocker panels. Anchor your Dozer to the cross tube. This will prevent undue rolling of the underbody clamps on the pinch weld.

Box frames and channel sections should be padded with short pieces of angle iron to prevent damage to the corner of the section when a chain is wrapped around the frame section.

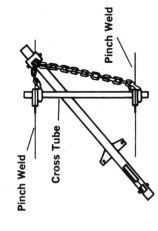

For a diagonal pull, the underbody anchoring system provides attachment to both rocker panels, for better efficiency and less damage. The anchoring loads are spread across both sides of the car.

Figure 14-8 Anchoring procedures for portable frame straighteners. (*Courtesy of Applied Power Inc., Blackhawk Manufacturing Division.*)

Select the combination for <u>YOUR</u> shop

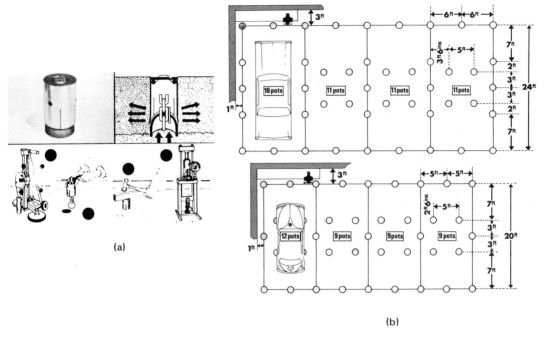

(a)

(b)

(c)

(d)

Figure 14-9 (a) Typical floor anchor pots and installation; (b) typical floor layout of anchor pots; (c) portable frame and body straightener using floor anchors; (d) body tie-downs using floor anchors. *(Courtesy of Guy Chart Tools Ltd.)*

Figure 14-10 A stationary floor mounted frame and body straightener. *(Courtesy of Applied Power Inc., Blackhawk Manufacturing Division.)*

Figure 14-11 Pulling frame and body at the same time. *(Courtesy of Applied Power Inc., Blackhawk Manufacturing Division.)*

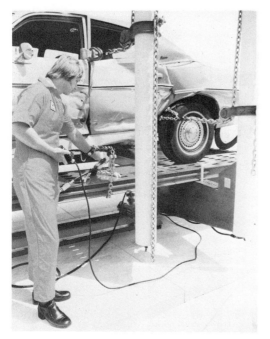

Figure 14-12 Several corrective pulls being made at one time. Uprights can be moved to any position. *(Courtesy of Chief E-Z Liner, Chief Industries.)*

the measurements or gauges are necessary. If the frame or body is overpulled or overcorrected, the correction is sometimes rather expensive (Figure 14-13).

Bodymen using the frame straightener for the first time should limit the work to one or two pulls at one time until some experience is gained. The multipulls require a great deal of skill, knowledge, and understanding of the frame.

Although there are many different types of frame straighteners with new ones being introduced frequently, the basic technique is the same (Figure 14-14). Some units require the moving of heavy posts and rails while others use movable ones. The floor models use movable posts and chains which are attached to rails.

NOTE: It is better to cold work (hammer) the damaged area to aid in straighten-

ing unless the frame is badly kinked. If heat must be used, heat with a neutral flame to a cherry red, at about 650° F (1200° C). Overheating can cause permanent damage and weakness in the heated area.

In cases where chains must be wrapped around the frame, angle iron or plates should be placed under the chain to prevent collapsing the frame. Caution must be used when anchoring the units to prevent damaging other areas of the frame.

When the frame torque boxes are involved, the boxes must be held together to prevent spreading.

NOTE: If the transmission has been shifted during impact, it is advisable to loosen the bolts before force is exerted on the frame.

In areas of severe kinks or wrinkles in the frame, it may be necessary to finish out the metal after the frame is straightened. Access holes or a door may have to be cut in the frame, and the metal straightened; or a small section of a side may have to be cut out and straightened. The pieces are then welded back in position using an electric arc welder or MIG welder rather than an oxyacetylene torch.

REPLACING FRAME SECTIONS

Severely damaged sections of the frame (or unitized body rails) may have to be replaced rather than straightened if the time involved is too great. In some cases, a section is mangled beyond repair, and it would be impossible to restore the section to a likenew condition. Various frame sections are available as replacements such as crossmembers, front sections, side rails, or sections secured from a salvage yard. Before cutting out the damaged section, the ad-

Stretch the chain in the desired direction of the pull. Place a ram foot and chain anchor directly below the chain. Lock the anchors with wedges.

Position ram in the ram foot so it will exert force in the desired direction. Pull the chain tight and lock it in the chain head with the cross pin.

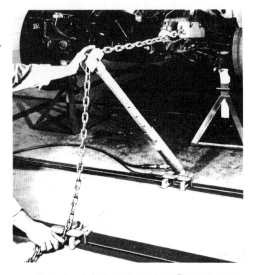

Insert ram foot/anchor into base keeping socket on top.

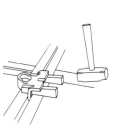

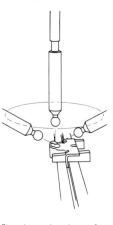

Place the ram into the ram foot at any angle you may need.

Hook the chain into the anchor. The anchor, ram foot and attachment point on the car should be in a straight line in the direction of pull.

Drive wedges toward the socket to lock the chain anchor into position securely.

Figure 14–13 Setting up a frame pull. *(Courtesy of Applied Power Inc., Blackhawk Manufacturing Division.)*

joining frame sections should be straightened and aligned.

Replacing some frame sections involves removing suspension systems, sheetmetal, or even the engine. Before removing the section, a replacement section should be available and should be studied to determine where it should be cut. The damaged section should be cut a little shorter to allow for careful trimming. The new section can be fitted and aligned using the manufacturer's frame or body charts for the proper alignment. The use of centering gauges and tram gauges will be helpful to obtain the correct alignment before welding on the section.

Figure 14-14 Stationary frame and body straightener rack. Rack is lowered at one end to bring the vehicle upon the rack, eliminating dangerous ramps. *(Courtesy of Chief Industries, Automotive Systems Division.)*

The use of the arc welder or MIG is recommended over the oxy-acetylene welder because of the heat factor and distortion.

NOTE: Ford Motor Company recommends using a AWS E6012 electrode for welding or repairing the late model passenger frames.

It is a common practice to install a cut-off frame section secured from a salvage yard. In some northern areas of the country, many vehicles are victims of rusted out frame sections, and these can be repaired by installing used sections. These sections will not present any problems if the job is well planned.

FRAME ALIGNMENT

The frame, like the unitized underbody, provides the vehicle with a strong foundation. The body sheetmetal supports the engine and drive train and to it is mounted the front and rear suspension. Therefore, the frame must be in perfect alignment for proper vehicle handling and for the passengers' safety.

The frame must be straightened before any attempt is made to repair the sheetmetal damage. A swayed frame will force the fenders out of alignment with the hood and possibly prevent the hood frame from closing and locking properly.

Frames with sags may cause doors to close improperly, to bind on the fenders, or even to sag down. Also, a sagged frame will generally affect the vehicle's wheel alignment.

1. What happens if the gauges are not placed in the exact same position?
2. What is *diagonal checking?*
3. What is the most common visible sign of a sag?
4. If the door and fender gap is wide on one side of the vehicle and close on the other, what type damage is it?
5. Should the time to remove additional parts to straighten a frame be figured in the cost?
6. What is the maximum heat to be used on the frame?
7. What is the advantage of a rack-type straightener over a portable straightener?

Questions

8. Should a damaged frame be cut out before or after the replacement section arrives?

9. What can be done to protect the frame from damage when using a wraparound chain?

10. Should the frame be straightened before the new sheetmetal is installed?

Whether an automobile was involved in a front end collision, went off the road, or hit a curbstone, the front wheels should be checked for alignment before returning the automobile to its owner.

Misaligned front ends can cause poor tire wear, poor steering, wandering, and many other problems. Because of the many types of front suspensions used and the variety of alignment equipment available, it would be impossible to describe each and every one of them. Instructions on wheel alignment should be given on the equipment available, using the manufacturer's specifications. The discussion here will focus on the basic principles of wheel alignment as well as the cause and effect of misalignment.

Before any attempt to align a front end is made, a thorough check of the various front end parts should be made. Worn or damaged parts or worn or loose bearings will give a false reading, cause additional tire wear, and lead to a dissatisfied customer.

Front end alignment involves the relationship between the front suspension parts, the front wheel, and the road surface. There are three adjustable angles and two nonadjustable angles in the front suspension, which are designed to properly distribute the weight of the automobile on the moving parts for proper steering. The three adjustable angles are the *caster, camber,* and *toe in and out.*

Front End Alignment

ADJUSTABLE ANGLES

Caster

The caster is the forward or rearward tilt of the top of the wheel spindle when viewed from the side of the automobile (Figure 15-1). If the top of the spindle is tilted back-

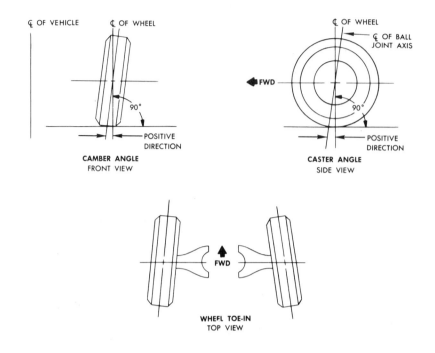

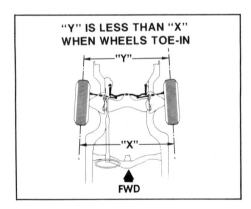

Figure 15-1 Toe-in adjustment. *(Courtesy of General Motors Corporation, Chevrolet Motor Division.)*

wards, the wheel has positive (+) caster, and if the spindle is tilted forward, the wheel has negative (–) caster. Because of the different types of suspension, it is not possible to see the angle of caster without the use of special instruments. The caster adjustments can range from shim types, strut rods, eccentric bolts to slide types, and so on. Each one must be adjusted to the manufacturer's specifications.

The caster tends to stabilize the automobile in a straight ahead position, much the same as a bicycle. The get a better idea of the caster, view a bicycle from the side. If a vertical line is drawn through the center of the front wheel, then a center line extended through the fork until it touches the ground, the point of contact will be ahead of the point of contact from the line through the wheel. This will put the force of the load ahead of the contact with the road. This type setup would have a positive caster.

Some of the later model automobiles are designed with negative caster due to the wider treads on tires and the *steering axis inclination* often referred to as SAI. The steering axis inclination (SAI) or ball joint inclination is the inward tilt of the steering knuckle or spindle at the top from the true vertical line (Figure 15-2). In a solid truck axle, it would be the angle of the king pin. The steering axis inclination, measured in degrees, is not adjustable but will affect the steering if the parts involved are damaged.

On some of the newer strut-type suspensions, the caster angle is built in and cannot be adjusted. When repairing front assemblies on these types of automobile, the underbody must be in perfect alignment to ensure the proper caster alignment.

Many of the caster settings may vary from left to right wheel to compensate for the crown in the roads. If the caster is unequal, the automobile may pull to one side or to the side with negative caster. An automobile with too little caster will cause wandering or weaving whereas excessive caster will cause hard steering.

(a)

(a) Read camber to fractions of a degree on easy to read camber scale.

(b) Read as much as 18° on caster scale. For instance: adjust center of bubble at 9° negative: if center bubble then moves to 9° positive, it records 18° of caster.

(c) Caster correction and steering axis inclination scales located on same vial. Caster correction scale makes it convenient to watch the amount of caster change as caster is adjusted.

(d) Four locating pins to hold the patented Bear Check-o-Matic templates. These locating pins can be easily replaced.

(b)

Figure 15-2 (a) Gauge used for checking wheel alignment; (b) magnetic gauge used for checking caster and camber. *(Courtesy of Applied Power Inc., Bear Manufacturing Corporation.)*

Camber

The camber is the outward (positive) or inward (negative) tilt of the front wheel at the top. This angle is measured in degrees from the vertical and is called the *camber angle*. The camber brings the point of the load inward from the center of the tire. This will put more load on the inner wheel bearing than the outside (Figure 15-3).

Improper or excessive camber will cause the tire to wear on one side only. Excessive camber will cause the outside of the tread to wear more rapidly than the inside or

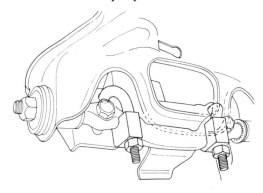

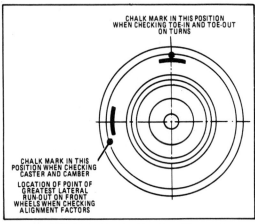

CHALK MARK IN THIS POSITION
WHEN CHECKING TOE-IN AND TOE-OUT
ON TURNS

CHALK MARK IN THIS
POSITION WHEN CHECKING
CASTER AND CAMBER

LOCATION OF POINT OF
GREATEST LATERAL
RUN-OUT ON FRONT
WHEELS WHEN CHECKING
ALIGNMENT FACTORS

Front Wheel Position for Checking Alignment

Figure 15-3 Using a special tool for adjusting camber and caster on some Ford Motors vehicles. *(Courtesy of Ford Motor Corporation.)*

center. Excessive negative camber causes the tire to wear on the inside tread. Unequal camber may cause the automobile to pull to one side. Excessive camber can cause the ball joints and wheel bearings to wear more rapidly (Figure 15-4).

Toe In or Out

The toes, in or out, is the distance between the front and rear part of the front wheels. If the wheels are closer together at the front than the rear, the wheels are toed in. If the wheels are farther apart in the front, the wheels are toed out (Figure 15-5).

The purpose of toe is to ensure parallel rolling of the front wheels. The toe in serves to offset the small deflection of the wheel's suspension system which occurs when the automobile is in forward motion. Excessive toe in or out will cause the wheel to scuff or wear sideways on the treads. (This will appear as a feathered scuff across the treads.) Improper toe setting is one of the major causes of tire wear. Toe in is generally set after the camber and caster has been checked or adjusted (Figure 15-6).

The toe is adjusted by turning the tie rod adjusting sleeves. The alignment specifications can be obtained from the automobile or alignment equipment manufacturers. Some of the things that should be checked before aligning a front end are listed as follows:

1. Check all tires for proper inflation and the same tread wear, not one smooth tire and one with full tread. The tires should be the same size. Check tires for roundness, separations, or bad spots. Check for bent wheels.

2. Check wheel bearings and adjust if necessary.

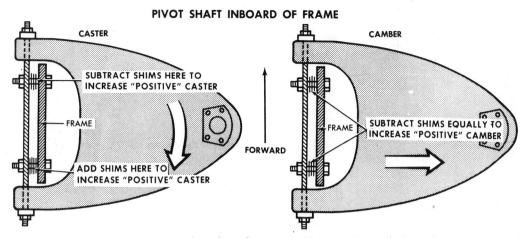

PIVOT SHAFT INBOARD OF FRAME

CASTER

SUBTRACT SHIMS HERE TO
INCREASE "POSITIVE" CASTER

FRAME

ADD SHIMS HERE TO
INCREASE "POSITIVE" CASTER

FORWARD

CAMBER

SUBTRACT SHIMS EQUALLY TO
INCREASE "POSITIVE" CAMBER

FRAME

Figure 15-4 Caster and camber adjustment. *(Courtesy of General Motors Corporation, Chevrolet Motor Division.)*

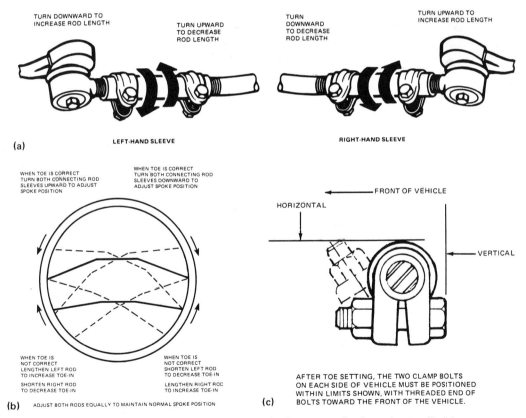

TURN DOWNWARD TO
INCREASE ROD LENGTH

TURN UPWARD
TO DECREASE
ROD LENGTH

TURN
DOWNWARD
TO DECREASE
ROD LENGTH

TURN UPWARD TO
INCREASE ROD LENGTH

(a)

LEFT-HAND SLEEVE

RIGHT-HAND SLEEVE

WHEN TOE IS CORRECT
TURN BOTH CONNECTING ROD
SLEEVES UPWARD TO ADJUST
SPOKE POSITION

WHEN TOE IS CORRECT
TURN BOTH CONNECTING ROD
SLEEVES DOWNWARD TO
ADJUST SPOKE POSITION

WHEN TOE IS
NOT CORRECT
LENGTHEN LEFT ROD
TO INCREASE TOE-IN

SHORTEN RIGHT ROD
TO DECREASE TOE-IN

WHEN TOE IS
NOT CORRECT
SHORTEN LEFT ROD
TO DECREASE TOE-IN

LENGTHEN RIGHT ROD
TO INCREASE TOE-IN

(b) ADJUST BOTH RODS EQUALLY TO MAINTAIN NORMAL SPOKE POSITION

FRONT OF VEHICLE

HORIZONTAL

VERTICAL

(c) AFTER TOE SETTING, THE TWO CLAMP BOLTS
ON EACH SIDE OF VEHICLE MUST BE POSITIONED
WITHIN LIMITS SHOWN, WITH THREADED END OF
BOLTS TOWARD THE FRONT OF THE VEHICLE.

Figure 15-5 (a) Spindle connecting rod adjustment (looking forward); (b) toe and steering wheel spoke alignment adjustments—Ford/Mercury; (c) positioning clamp bolts. *(Courtesy of Ford Motor Corporation.)*

UNDERINFLATION

OVERINFLATION

CUPPING—UNDERINFLATION AND/OR
MECHANICAL IRREGULARITIES
SUCH AS OUT-OF-BALANCE
CONDITION OF WHEEL AND/OR
TIRE, AND BENT OR DAMAGED
WHEEL
POSSIBLE LOOSE OR WORN
STEERING TIE-ROD OR
STEERING IDLER ARM
POSSIBLE LOOSE, DAMAGED
OR WORN FRONT SUSPENSION
PARTS

INCORRECT TOE OR EXTREME CAMBER

FEATHERING DUE TO MISALIGNMENT

Figure 15-6 Tire wear conditions. *(Courtesy of Ford Motor Corporation.)*

3. Check ball joints, control arms, steering joints, springs, or other components for looseness. (Check manufacturer's manual for procedures.)

4. Check shock absorbers.

5. Check stabilizer bar or attachments.

6. Check riding height and load in the trunk. If load is excessive and is always in the trunk, align front end with load.

7. Check rear suspension for broken or sagged springs or other parts.

Replace damaged front suspension parts. Many times during a collision, some parts of the front suspension are damaged. Any parts that show damage should be replaced and not straightened, like tie rod assemblies.

Spindle support damage is hard to detect and if it is received on impact from a collision, it is better to replace the support.

Due to the many different types of suspension, it is advisable to check the manufacturer's manual for proper procedure.

NOTE: In many shops, front suspension repairs are performed by qualified mechanics.

POWER STEERING UNITS

Like the front suspension, the power steering units are often damaged and the repairs should follow the manufacturer's recommended procedures.

1. Before a vehicle can be aligned, what must be done first?
2. What is *caster* and what effect does it have on steering?
3. What is *camber* and how does it affect tire wear?
4. What is *toe in* and how does it affect tire wear?
5. What is *steering axis inclination?*
6. What causes wandering or weaving?
7. What causes a vehicle to pull to one side?
8. Should the front tires be equal in wear and inflation before alignment?
9. Will weak springs change the alignment?
10. What will cause a false reading on the alignment gauges?

Body Service

part
2

The automobile and many trucks contain large amounts of glass for good driving visibility and for viewing the surrounding area. Often, the glass is damaged, cracked, or broken due to collisions, vandalism, and road hazards like stones or other flying objects.

It is hazardous to drive a vehicle with a cracked or defective windshield and many states require replacing the glass if damaged.

TYPES OF GLASS

Todays automobiles contain two basic types of glass, the *tempered* and the *laminated*. Both of these are considered safety glass because they meet the safety standards.

All windshields are made laminated of plate glass which is two thin sheets of glass with a thin layer of plastic in between them. Some of the newer windshield glasses are thinner than before because of a weight-saving factor. Some glass manufacturers have increased the thickness of the vinyl plastic material for greater strength and to increase resistance to penetration.

When this glass is broken because, for example, a person's head hits the windshield, the plastic will hold the broken glass in place and, in many cases, prevent the person from going through the windshield (Figure 16-1). Prior to the use of safety glass, many people were injured by flying glass or sharp jagged pieces.

The windshield glass must furnish a clear, unimpeded view from all angles. Tinted windshields (a light green shade) are available and filter out much of the sun's glare. This is helpful in reducing eye strain, driver tension, and fatigue. If all of the windows in an automobile were tinted, it would reduce the fading of upholstery. Some of the windshields are shaded for

Windshields

chapter
16

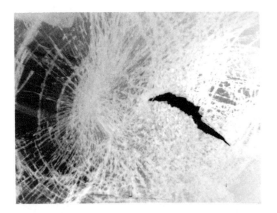

Figure 16-1 A shattered and broken windshield glass. Notice how the broken pieces of glass are still held together by the plastic between the two sheets of glass. Compare to Figure 16-2.

greater protection from the sun's glare and heat. Shaded windshields have a dark band or section across the top portion. Both tinted and shaded windshields cost more than the clear glass but are recommended if the automobile is equipped with air conditioning.

Tempered Glass

Tempered glass is a single piece of heat-treated glass with many times the impact resistance of regular glass of the same thickness. It is used on all glass except for the windshield on the modern automobile. The strength of the tempered glass results from the high compression of its surfaces, induced through rapid heating and then rapid cooling.

When tempered glass breaks, the resulting pieces are small and have a granular texture. The interlocked structure of the shattered glass provides very poor visibil-

ity. This makes it impractical for use as windshield glass, and because the glass does not give, head injuries would be more severe. Because of the surface compression, tempered glass cannot be cut, drilled, or ground after the tempering process.

Tempered glass, for some unknown reason, will shatter if it has been damaged previously or been under stress (Figure 16-2). Chipping an edge or a rock striking it, may cause the glass to break, perhaps months later. Prior to the use of tempered glass, window and rear glass was made from safety sheet glass, and these could be cut and ground by the local glass shop. Safety sheet glass is made in the same way as windshield glass, but it is not optically perfect like the windshield.

Stationary Glass

Stationary glass is generally referred to as glass that does not move. Such glass is used for windshields, rear windows, rear side windows on station wagons, and rear quarter glass on sedans. There are two different methods used to install stationary

Figure 16-2 A broken tempered door glass.

glass, either with gaskets or with adhesive materials.

GASKET-TYPE INSTALLATION

The gasket type of installation was more common in the old automobiles but is still being used today in some automobiles and trucks (Figures 16–3 and 16–4). The glass is fitted in the inner groove or channel of the rubber gasket. The outer part of the gasket has a tab. When installing, the tab is pulled inward over the pinch weld of the glass opening, and this locks the glass in place. Due to the many different types of gaskets used, it would be difficult to discuss them all.

Removal of Necessary Molding

Some of the gasket-type windshields or back glasses use chrome reveal moldings and some do not. Many of the reveal moldings are fitted into another groove in the outer face of the gasket and remain attached to the gasket when the windshield or back glass is removed (Figure 16–5).

Other methods of fastening the chrome reveal moldings are retaining clips attached to the body opening, or bolts and screws. Care must be taken when removing the reveal moldings so as not to damage them. If in doubt as to what method is used to hold the reveal moldings in place, consult the service manual.

Before starting to remove the glass, place protective covering on the dash panel,

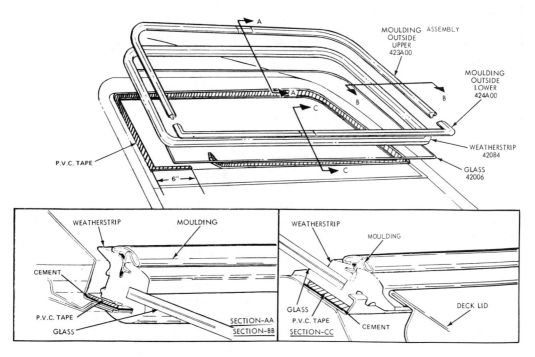

Figure 16–3 Typical gasket or weatherstrip type glass installation. *(Courtesy of Ford Motor Corporation.)*

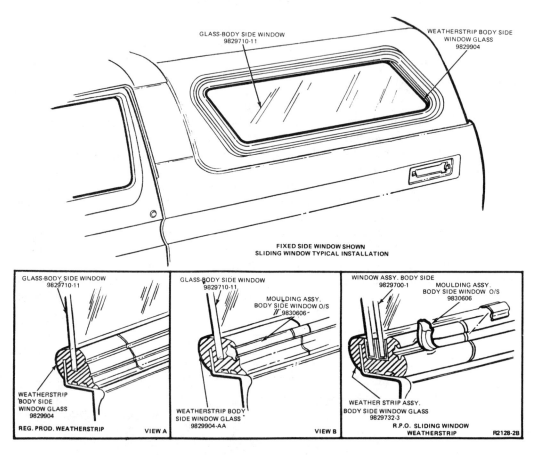

Figure 16-4 Rear side window installation—Bronco. *(Courtesy of Ford Motor Corporation.)*

hood, fenders, seats, or any place that might become damaged or soiled. Remove the necessary parts that may interfere with the glass removal such as wiper arms, inside rear view mirror, garnish moldings, and other parts. Examine the reveal molding, if any, and determine how to remove it.

NOTE: Some moldings are attached to the gasket and are not removed at this time.

On some automobiles, there is a locking tab on the outside of the gasket which must be opened all the way around. Then the glass is loosened up on the outside and inside of the gasket, and the glass is slipped out. Another type uses a locking wedge on the outside of the gasket, and when removed the glass can be slipped out of the gasket. On most gaskets, the tab on the inside of the pinch weld must be slipped to the outside edge. Loosen up the gasket from the pinch weld area on the top and sides of the glass. This can be done with a blunt putty knife or screwdriver while ap-

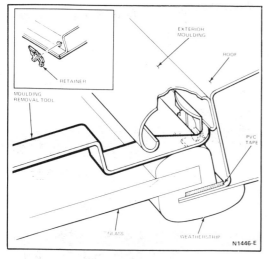

(a)

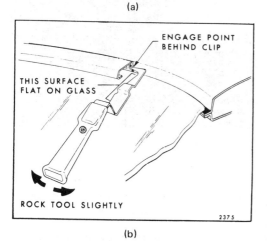

(b)

Figure 16-5 (a) Back window molding-removal tool *(Courtesy of Ford Motor Corporation)*; (b) Molding-removal tool usage procedure *(Courtesy of General Motors Corporation, Fisher Body Division).*

plying outward pressure on the glass. Start at the top center of the glass and work to the left and right evenly to the lower corners. Then the glass can be tipped outward and removed. If the glass is not cracked and is to be used again, care must be taken not to exert uneven pressure to

the glass or hit the glass with the tools (Figure 16-6).

CAUTION: Wear safety glasses and gloves especially if the glass is broken. *Never* use the feet to remove the glass because a serious injury could result if the glass breaks.

Place the glass on a suitably covered bench or table. If the glass was removed for body repairs and not broken, leave gasket (and moldings) intact and store in a safe place.

When the glass is to be replaced, remove the molding from the gasket, if any, and remove the gasket from the glass. Carefully inspect the glass opening in the gasket for chips or foreign material and clean.

NOTE: If glass cracked for no apparent reason and the crack started from the outer edge, check the pinch weld for high or low spots, poor spot weld, or any spot that may have put uneven pressure on the glass. If there is any doubt about the pinch weld being bent or damaged, use the new glass to check the opening.

Figure 16-6 Loosening weatherstrip. *(Courtesy of General Motors Corporation, Chevrolet Motor Division.)*

Before checking the glass, apply a double layer of ¾" (19 mm) masking tape around the outside edge of the glass with ¼" (6.35 mm) extending in on the inside of the glass and a ¼" (6.35 mm) on the outside. This will help to avoid chipping or breaking the glass while checking.

NOTE: Remove the tape after checking the opening.

Clean off old sealer from the opening and install checking blocks as shown in diagram (Figure 16–13). If the blocks are not available, cut pieces from old gaskets. Carefully install the glass on the checking block; avoid hitting the glass on the metal body. With the glass centered, check the relationship between the glass and the pinch weld. The space should be about even around the entire pinch weld. Any variation should be corrected and rechecked with the glass.

Apply a small amount of sealer (non-hardening type) in the glass channel and install the gasket on the glass. Insert a strong cord (Venetian blind cord works well) underneath the inside tab of the gasket. Start from the top of the glass so that the cord meets in the lower center and tape the ends to the inside of the glass. Install molding to the gasket, if applicable. Apply sealer to the base of the gasket. With the aid of a helper, place the glass in the opening and center it. Slowly pull the ends of the cord, starting at the lower center of the windshield, to bring the tab on the inside of the pinch weld. (Figure 16–7). First work the bottom section in, then the sides and the top, working the sections evenly. The glass may crack if it is pulled from one side only.

Be sure the glass is evenly seated in the opening, and the tab is completely pulled inside. Apply some more sealer to the underneath edge of the gasket by the body opening. Remove surplus sealer with a suitable solvent or enamel thinner.

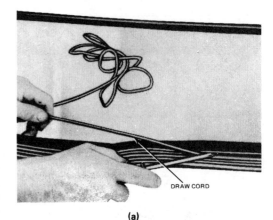

(a)

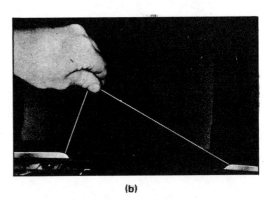

(b)

Figure 16-7 (a) Typical draw cord installation *(Courtesy of Ford Motor Corporation)*; (b) pulling string to seat rubber lip *(Courtesy of General Motors Corporation, Chevrolet Motor Division).*

Reinstall the parts previously removed and remove protective covering. Check the windshield for water leaks. Use a low pressure stream of water rather than high pressure. Thoroughly clean glass and surrounding area.

ADHESIVE-TYPE INSTALLATION

Like the gasket-type windshield, the adhesive type will also vary with the different automobiles. The adhesive-type installation uses an adhesive to hold the glass in place instead of a gasket. One of the advantages of the adhesive-type installation is that the pinch weld of the body does not have to be as exact as in the gasket type because there is no pressure exerted on the glass outside of the reveal moldings.

Some of the materials used as adhesives are: polysulfide, urethane, and butyl rubber. Of the three mentioned, the butyl will stay pliable longer than the other two.

These materials are available through the automobile manufacturer or the local jobber so the methods may vary with the type material used.

NOTE: GM automobiles use both polysulfide and urethane which are not compatible. To determine what type has been used, burn a small piece of adhesive. If the smoke given off is black with very little odor, it is urethane. The polysulfide gives off a very strong, irritating odor with very little visible smoke.

Polysulfide cures or hardens by exposure to air. Water speeds up the curing of urethane. Butyl adhesive does not cure or harden but remains soft, therefore, it can be used again if not damaged when the glass is removed.

Removal of Moldings

The reveal moldings or other trim parts surrounding the adhesive-type glass are held on by a variety of clips and retainers (Figures 16-8 and 16-9). Many of them use a snap or slip-on clip attached to the body by a welded stud or attached by sheetmetal screws. Many types of reveal molding removing tools are available from either the local supply house or from the manufacturer. If there is any doubt about the correct procedure or what type of retainer is used, consult the manufacturer's service manual.

NOTE: On some late model automobiles with certain types of roof covering, the removal of a portion of the material is required when replacing some types of glass.

Removal Techniques

When replacing adhesive-type glass, there are two basic methods—the *short method* and the *long* or *extended method.*

The short method is where most of the adhesive remains in sufficient thickness on the pinch weld, and is in good condition, and can serve as a base for the new adhesive.

The long or extended method is used when the adhesive is defective, sections have been removed for body work or painting, or the old adhesive is not compatible with the new adhesive. The long or extended method involves removing all of the old adhesive.

There are several tools or devices used in cutting the adhesive for the purpose of removing the glass: a steel wire often called *piano wire;* a hot knife, and a cold knife. If the glass is removed for the purpose of body repairs and must be reinstalled, the wire method is the safest. The use of the hot or cold knife may crack the glass in areas where the reveal molding clips are very close to the glass. This is especially true in removing windshields because a small chip may cause the glass to crack.

To remove glass, all of the necessary moldings, wiper arms, inside mirrors, and any other part that may interfere with the removal and installation of the glass, must be removed. If the automobile is equipped with a window defogger and windshield antenna, the leads must be disconnected. Tape the defogger lead to the inside of the

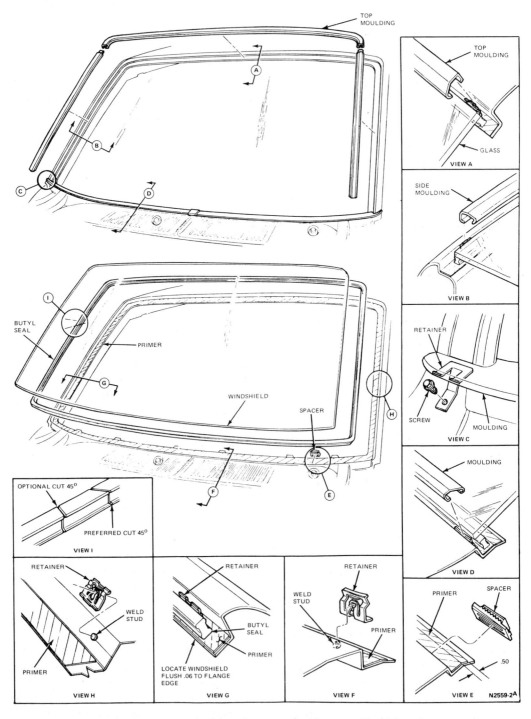

Figure 16-8 Stationary glass-butyl type seals. *(Courtesy of Ford Motor Corporation.)*

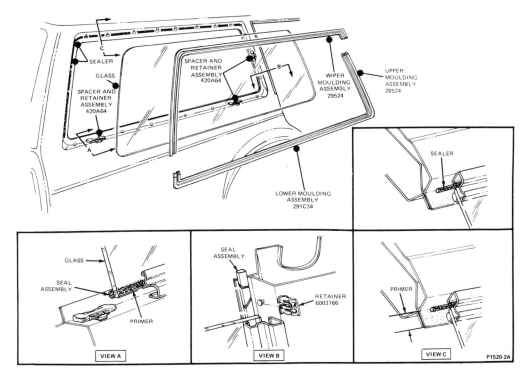

Figure 16-9 Stationary glass-butyl type seals. *(Courtesy of Ford Motor Corporation.)*

glass to prevent tearing it off. The windshield antenna lead should be taped to the outside of the glass to avoid breaking the wire. Protect the area around the glass with protective covers. If the windshield is shattered or badly broken, protect the seats with a cover to keep any glass splinters from being imbedded in the seat covers.

Removing Glass With Wire. To aid in removing glass, cut the surplus adhesive from the edge of the glass to the pinch weld using a sharp knife and remove. Attach one of the wires to a piece of wood (a piece of broomstick works well) to use as a handle (Figure 16-10). Inset the other end of the wire through the adhesive under the glass using a needle nose pliers and attach to another

wooden handle. Pull the wire through the adhesive around the entire glass using a sawing motion and maintaining tension on wire to prevent kinking.

If the short method is to be used, cut the adhesive as close to the glass as possible. If a helper is available, he can hold the wire very close to the glass using a gloved hand. A glove should be worn to avoid injury in case the wire breaks.

A special chemical can be used to soften up the adhesive and make it easier to cut. In some cases involving butyl adhesive, small wooden wedges may have to be inserted in the cut to keep the butyl from resealing itself. After the cut is completed, carefully remove the glass. If the glass is to be reinstalled, place the glass on a covered bench and in some safe area.

Figure 16-10   (a) Cutting adhesive material; (b) one man wire removal method. *(Courtesy of General Motors Corporation, Fisher Body Division.)*

Removing Glass With A Hot Knife.   Cut and remove the surplus adhesive from the edge of the glass to the pinch weld and remove.

Insert knife in the adhesive, keeping the knife as close to the glass as possible and cut around the entire perimeter of the glass (Figure 16-11). Wooden wedges may have

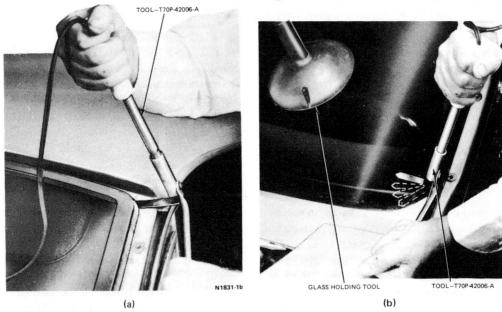

Figure 16-11   (a) Removing butyl type seal; (b) cutting corner seal. *(Courtesy of Ford Motor Corporation.)*

to be used if the adhesive reseals itself after cutting. Be careful not to twist the knife blade as it will break especially after being heated for some time. Use the handle to pull the knife forward. Remove the glass and place it in a safe place or on a covered bench if it is to be used again. Use extreme caution not to crack the glass when cutting in close areas. Be careful not to lay the heat knife on the car surface.

Removing Glass With A Cold Knife. Cut and remove the surplus adhesive from the edge of the glass to the pinch weld. To aid in cutting, spray the adhesive with an adhesive softener. (Avoid spraying chemicals on painted surfaces.) Insert the knife and pull forward with the pull handle and steady the knife. Tip the knife so that the forward edge of the knife actually scrapes along the glass surface.

Spray additional softening solvent if necessary. For faster cutting, sharpen the blade with a file. Continue to cut around the perimeter of the glass. Extreme caution should be exercised when using a knife so as not to crack the glass if it is to be reinstalled. This applies especially when cutting near the molding clips.

Remove glass to a safe area or place on a covered bench if it is to be reinstalled.

Other Types of Glass Removal. On some General Motors automobiles, the back windows are removed to the inside of the automobile rather than to the outside (Figure 16-12). This procedure requires re-

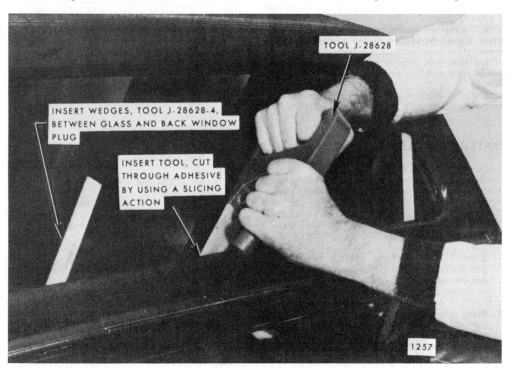

Figure 16-12 Back window removal on General Motors' E body type. *(Courtesy of General Motors Corporation, Fisher Body Division.)*

moval of certain interior trim parts and the use of a special knife.

For this type of glass removal, consult the manufacturer's body service manual.

Installing Glass—Short Method

Before deciding about using the short method of glass installation, make a thorough inspection of the remaining adhesive. There must be sufficient adhesive left in the pinch weld to give adequate clearance between the body and the glass. The adhesive must be tightly bonded to the pinch weld area in order to form a good base for the new material to be added (Figure 16–13).

If rusting has penetrated under the adhesive, it is recommended that the rust be removed or repainted, thus the long or extended method should be used. Allowing the rust to remain will create more serious problems later.

If the original glass is to be reinstalled, remove all traces of adhesive from the glass, either with a razor blade or a sharp putty knife. Remove remaining adhesive with either denatured alcohol or lacquer thinner.

CAUTION: Do not use gasoline or any petroleum product because it will leave an oil film on the glass and prevent the adhesion of the new material. If the glass is a heated type, clean adhesive from glass very carefully to avoid damaging the grids.

Inspect the reveal molding clips for any bent or distorted ones. Replace clips if necessary. The new material to be used will vary depending on the type adhesive on the automobile; either a ribbon or cartridge type can be used. Select the proper type material that will be compatible with the adhesive on the body pinch welds. Remember, butyl is always soft. Use the burn test

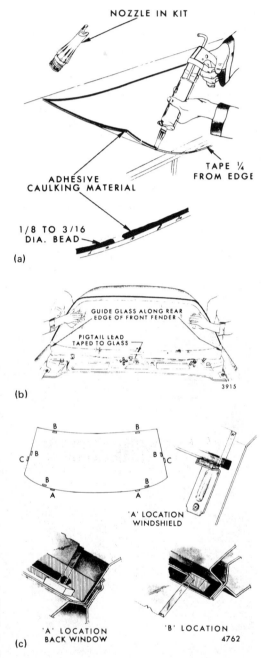

Figure 16-13 (a) Adhesive material application—short method; (b) glass installation; (c) glass spacer installation. *(Courtesy of General Motors Corporation, Fisher Body Division.)*

to determine whether it is a urethane or polysulfide.

Replace lower glass support or spaces where applicable. Position the glass in the glass opening being sure that the gap is equal on both sides and there is ample clearance on the top. Some windshields may vary slightly in size or may require lowering or raising the lower supports or spacers. Apply two pieces of masking tape from the bottom portion of the glass to the body about 6" to 8" (152.4 mm to 203.2 mm) in from the corner and repeat at the top of the glass.

Cut the tape with a razor blade and remove the glass. The tape will help to align the glass when reinstalling it. In windshields containing an antenna, place a piece of butyl about 8" (203.2 mm) from the antenna pigtail. Do not use urethane or primer near the pigtail as it will interfere with the radio reception. Some windshield kits contain suitable material to be used for this purpose.

Apply adhesive primer to the remaining adhesive and to the outer inside edges or the adhesive contact area of the glass, using a lint-free clean cloth.

Depending on the bodyman's choice, the adhesive can be applied to the glass or the pinch weld. Also, some prefer the ribbon-type adhesive and others the cartridge-type heavy bodied adhesive. When the adhesive is applied to the glass using the cartridge-type heavy bodied adhesive, apply masking tape about $1/4$" (6.35 mm) from the outer edge of the inside of the glass on the top and both sides. This will aid in cleanup when the glass is installed.

Apply a smooth bead of adhesive, about $1/8$" to $3/16$" (3 mm to 5 mm) in diameter around the outer end of the glass. On glass with an antenna, do not apply the adhesive within 4" (101.6 mm) on either side of the antenna pigtail or lead.

When using a ribbon-type adhesive, the masking tape is not used. The ribbon should be applied evenly along the outer edge of the glass for good appearance. Do not stretch the ribbon as it will reduce the thickness, especially in the corners. With the assistance of a helper install the glass into the window opening. Place the windshield on the lower spacers or supports with the masking tape tabs lined up. Then, with the door open, place one hand inside the opening and gently lay the glass in position. On rear windows, it may be necessary to use suction cups to control the movement of the glass. Or after the glass is resting on the spacers, one can go inside of the automobile and help lay the glass in place with the masking tape tabs lined up. Press the glass firmly in position to set the adhesive material.

If the adhesive was placed on the pinch weld, a sealed area will appear as a dark line in the glass. The dark line should be completely around the glass, and any light spot will indicate improper seal. When using the cartridge-type adhesive, the adhesive material can be puddled or smoothed out along the edge of the glass. Additional cartridge adhesive can be applied around the entire edge of the glass, except for the antenna area, for additional sealing and smoothed out with a putty knife.

Water test with a fine water spray and do not direct the water directly at the fresh adhesive. Leaks can be corrected by adding additional material in the area. Install the necessary molding and trim parts, connect the antenna or defogger, if applicable. Clean up adhesive and clean the window.

The automobile should remain for about six hours or overnight to allow for the adequate curing of the adhesive. Butyl installations can be taken out as soon as cleanup is finished because the butyl adhesive does not cure.

The Long Or Extended Method of Installation

The extended method is used when the adhesive remaining on the pinch is too thin or has lost part of the bond with the metal or when body repairs are necessary (such as rusted out panels in the glass openings). The remaining adhesive must be removed using a sharp putty knife or chisel (Figure 16–14). This procedure holds true with the following exception. If the original material used was urethane and urethane is being used as the installation material, cut the urethane down as smooth as possible and remove all loose material. The same goes for butyl, if it was the original adhesive and the same material is being used. All loose adhesive or defective material must be removed.

Inspect all of the reveal molding clips; if bent, straighten them. Any other clips that are broken or rusted must be replaced. Install lower support brackets or spacers. The lower spacers should be glued in place with a suitable material. Once again, it is up to the bodyman to determine what type of adhesive material to use. Also, some bodymen prefer to apply the adhesive to the pinch weld or body. Regardless of whatever adhesive or method is used, the glass has to be checked for alignment.

With the lower support or spacer in place, install two rectangular spacers at the bottom, near the supports, and two at the top of the glass opening. These spacers can be held in place by masking tape. With the aid of a helper, put the glass in place and align the sides even with the body. Check the height of the glass at the top. Be sure there is sufficient space between the glass and molding clip if applicable. After aligning the glass, place two pieces of masking tape on the glass and body and two pieces at the top of the glass and body, each about 8" (200 mm) from the sides. Cut the tape with a sharp knife or razor blade and remove the glass. It may be necessary to use suction cups to remove and install the glass. Remove upper spacers used for checking.

When the glass is to be reinstalled, remove all the adhesive with a razor blade or sharp putty knife. Remove the remaining adhesive with alcohol or lacquer thinner.

NOTE: When installing the windshield with the antenna, use a strip of butyl about 8" (200 mm) by the antenna pigtail or lead if the adhesive is urethane.

Ribbon Adhesive. Depending on what brand adhesive is used, the diameter or thickness of the ribbon is very important. If the ribbon is too thick, it may interfere with the replacement of the moldings. Using a thin ribbon may allow the glass to contact the body causing chipping or breakage.

Apply the correct primer (according to the type adhesive used) to the glass and body except where the adhesive is urethane. When applying the ribbon adhesive to the glass, apply it on the outside inner edge, keeping the adhesive flush with the edge of the glass (Figure 16–15). Be careful not to stretch the adhesive especially in the corners. Place the glass in a horizontal position, lower it in the lower spacer, and align with the masking tape tabs. With the aid of a helper with or without suction cups or by reaching inside, lay the glass against the body. Press firmly in place so the adhesive makes good contact all the way around. On some installations, the recommendation is to install a second strip of ribbon adhesive at the bottom of the glass.

For additional insurance against water leaks, the cartridge-type adhesive can be applied around the perimeter of the glass and *paddled* smooth with a putty knife.

FOR EXTENDED METHOD, ENLARGE
NOZZLE BY CUTTING-OUT MATERIAL
WITHIN SCORE LINES

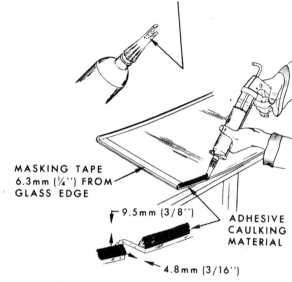

MASKING TAPE
6.3mm (¼'') FROM
GLASS EDGE

┌─9.5mm (3/8'')

ADHESIVE
CAULKING
MATERIAL

(a)

←4.8mm (3/16'')

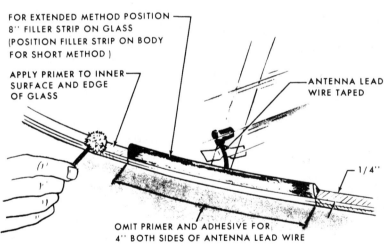

FOR EXTENDED METHOD POSITION
8'' FILLER STRIP ON GLASS
(POSITION FILLER STRIP ON BODY
FOR SHORT METHOD)

APPLY PRIMER TO INNER
SURFACE AND EDGE
OF GLASS

ANTENNA LEAD
WIRE TAPED

1/4''

OMIT PRIMER AND ADHESIVE FOR
4'' BOTH SIDES OF ANTENNA LEAD WIRE

(b)

Figure 16-14 (a) Adhesive material application—extended method; (b) embedded windshield antenna installation. *(Courtesy of General Motors Corporation, Fisher Body Division.)*

Water check with a soft spray of water, but not a direct spray on the fresh adhesive. Install necessary trim parts, connect antenna pigtail and defogger, if applicable.

Cartridge-Type Adhesive. With the lower glass supports in place, cement the flat rubber spacers in place and use only enough cement to attach the spacers. The cement is

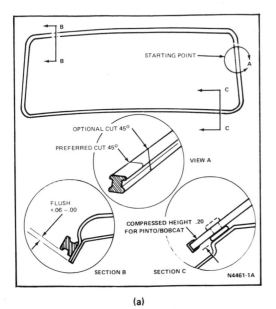

(a)

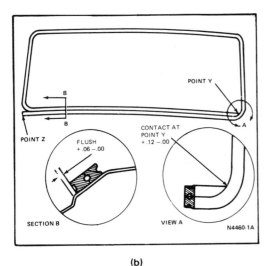

(b)

Figure 16-15 (a) Complete butyl tape replacement (single row butyl); (b) complete butyl tape replacement (double row butyl). *(Courtesy of Ford Motor Corporation.)*

not compatible with the adhesive and could cause a leak. The spacers should provide equal support around the perimeter of the glass and the ones on the side will keep the glass from shifting from left to right. There should be two on the top and one on each side to support the glass and keep it from touching the body.

Apply the masking tape as described in the short method but do not apply the tape to the bottom section. The tape will not only aid the cleanup operation but will give the adhesive a better appearing line. Apply a smooth, continuous bead of adhesive material about $3/8$" (9 mm) high and $3/16$" (5 mm) wide at the base completely around the inside edge of the glass.

With the aid of a helper, carefully position the glass in the opening, using the tape as a guide. Use caution when passing the fender edges to avoid smearing the adhesive. Lay the glass in the opening and use light pressure to make a proper seal between the glass and body. Use a putty knife to smooth out the adhesive and make a watertight seal. Additional adhesive can be added, if necessary.

NOTE: If one chooses, the adhesive can be applied to the body and pinch weld after the spacers are in the proper place.

Glass with embedded antenna (see Figure 16-14b) and using a butyl strip, must have additional adhesive placed at the ends of the butyl strip to ensure a watertight seal. Water check with a soft spray but not a direct water spray on the fresh adhesive. Install necessary trim parts and attach antenna lead and/or defogger lead. Carefully remove masking tape from inner glass by pulling toward the center to make a clean cut edge.

The automobile must remain at normal temperature from six to eight hours to allow for proper curing.

WATER LEAK CORRECTION

Adhesive Type

New and older automobile windshields and rear windows develop water leaks and can be repaired without removal of the glass.

Where the water enters the automobile may be some distance from the actual water leak which is often located between the glass and adhesive or the adhesive and the body. To determine the location of the leak, carefully remove the reveal moldings in the vicinity of the leak, without bending them or chipping the glass.

Use a small stream of water with low pressure and note where the water is actually entering. Another method is to get the glass and adhesive wet and use high pressure air along the inside edge of the windshield. The air will bubble through the defected area. For stubborn leaks, a solution of soap water can be applied to the approximate leak area before using air pressure.

After locating the leak area, trim off the surplus adhesive that extends beyond the edge of the glass (Figure 16–16). Most leaks occur on the top of the windshield or top and bottom of the rear window; or on a station wagon, on the rear side windows. If there are several leaks, it would pay to do the whole top or bottom area rather than just the leak area.

After removing the surplus adhesive, dry the area with air pressure. If traces of oil or grease are present, clean the area with a solvent such as enamel thinner and dry immediately.

NOTE: Some types of windshield sealers require priming of the glass edge and body area.

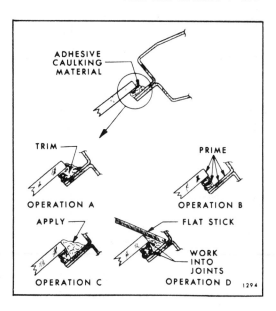

Figure 16–16 Adhesive glass water leak correction. *(Courtesy of General Motors Corporation, Fisher Body Division.)*

Apply cartridge-type windshield sealer along the cleaned area and smooth out with a flat stick or a putty knife. The sealer should be even with the top edge of the glass and tapered back to the molding clip area, working the sealer into the crevices. Water check the area with a very soft stream or spray but do not use any force as it will disturb the sealer. If no leaks are present, reinstall the molding and remove the surplus sealer, if any.

Gasket-Type Glass

Leaks in the gasket-type glass are more common between the gasket and the glass but sometimes occur between the gasket and the body.

Use a water spray to determine exactly where the water is leaking. Mark the area and dry with air pressure. Use a cartridge-type caulking material, often called *bedding compound* or *joint sealer*. This material never hardens and remains soft and pliable.

To apply, trim the nozzle of the cartridge and break the inner seal as directed on the label. To help get the nozzle between the glass and gasket or gasket and body, use a flat pointed piece of wood to make the opening. Place the nozzle alongside of the piece of wood and move forward filling the crevice. Remove the surplus caulking material with a solvent or enamel thinner. Recheck with water using a steady stream.

NOTE: Do not use metal objects to spread the gasket from the glass as they may crack the glass.

Questions

1. What are all windshields made of?
2. What is a *shaded windshield?*
3. What is *tempered glass?*
4. How does tempered glass differ from laminated when it breaks?
5. Can tempered glass be ground or drilled?
6. What is a *stationary glass?*
7. What are the two different types of stationary glass installation?
8. Why is it important to check the glass channel in the windshield gasket?
9. Can a poor spot weld on the pinch weld crack the windshield?
10. When installing a gasket-type windshield, without a locking-type gasket, how can it be pulled in over the pinch weld?
11. What are some of the adhesives used to install windshields?
12. How can you determine what type adhesive was used on a particular GM automobile?
13. What is meant by the *short* and *extended* method of installing glass?
14. What are some tools or devices used to remove adhesive-type glass?
15. How should the vehicle be prepared before removing the glass?
16. What is the danger of using cutting devices for removing glass if the glass is to be reinstalled?
17. What two types of adhesives are used for installing glass?
18. What type of water stream should be used when checking for water leaks?
19. Which type of adhesive does not harden and can be used over again?
20. What is the purpose of using spacers at the bottom of the glass?
21. Which adhesive *cannot* be used near the windshield antenna lead?
22. What two methods are used for locating water leaks around windshields or back windows?

The servicing of door glass or movable glass is an important part of the auto body trade. In many new car agencies, as well as used car agencies, the glass work is generally taken care of by the bodyman. Many times, some parts of the glass mechanism become loose, worn, or misaligned and must be repaired. Door glass must be replaced due to accidents or must be removed in order to straighten the outer panel or install a replacement panel.

Because of the many different types of door glass installations and window control mechanisms, it would be very difficult to mention them all. If it is possible, consult the manufacturer's service manual, but if this is not available, careful thought and observation must be used.

NOTE: Some manufacturers specify that all of the bolts be torqued. When working on door or quarter glass, be careful not to chip or scratch the glass as this may cause it to shatter.

TYPES OF DOORS

There are two basic types of doors, those with an upper door frame which surrounds the glass and those without, called hardtop doors (Figure 17-1 and 17-2). Both of these types use a one-piece glass as compared to other models which use a vent glass assembly and door glass. The window mechanisms in the framed doors are rather simple as compared to the hardtop doors because the upper door frame serves as a guide and support for the glass. Consequently, the framed door needs fewer adjustments for the glass (mainly the tilt of the glass when the glass is moved up or down). The hardtop (HT) door glass, when at the top of the window travel, generally rests up against a soft rubber gasket mounted in the door opening. The glass (whether it has bare edges or a metal strip surrounding the top

Door and Quarter Glass

chapter
17

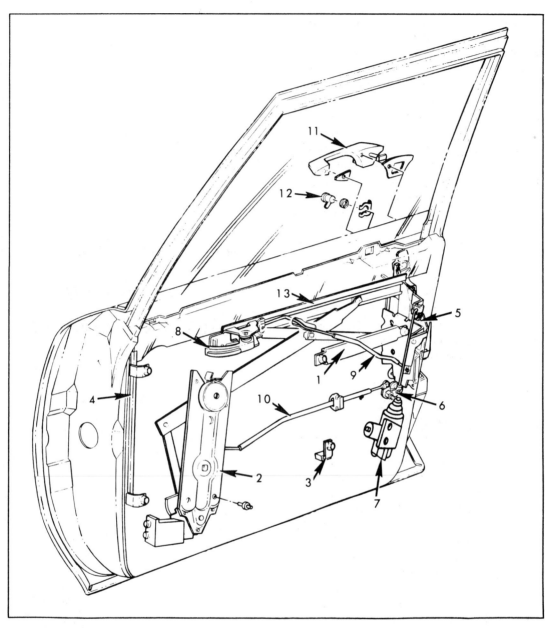

1. Inner Panel Cam	6. Locking Rod Bell	10. Inside Locking Rod
2. Window Regulator	Crank	11. Outside Handle
3. Down Stop	7. Power Door Lock	12. Lock Cylinder
4. Glass Run Channel	Actuator	13. Lower Sash Channel
Retainer	8. Inside Remote Handle	Cam
5. Door Lock	9. Handle to Lock	
	Connecting Rod	

Figure 17-1   Front door hardware—K style. *(Courtesy of General Motors Corporation, Fisher Body Division.)*

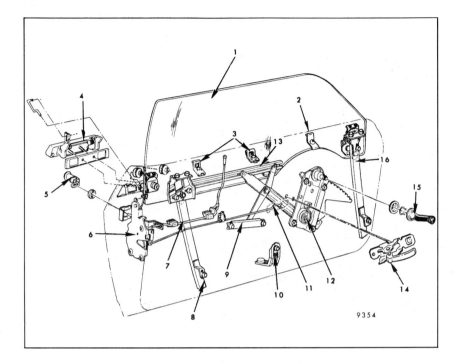

1. Window Assembly	10. Down-Travel Stop
2. Trim Pad Retainer	11. Inside Handle to Lock
3. Trim Support	Connecting Rod
Retainers	12. Window Regulator
4. Outside Handle	13. Lower Sash Channel
5. Lock Cylinder	Cam
6. Door Lock Assembly	14. Inside Remote Handle
7. Inside Locking Rod	15. Window Regulator
8. Rear Guide	Handle
9. Inner Panel Cam	16. Front Guide

Figure 17-2 Door hardware—F styles. *(Courtesy of General Motors Corporation, Fisher Body Division.)*

and side edges) must have means of support and height control when raised up to the limit of travel. These types of glasses or windows, especially those without the metal strip, will break if permitted to come in contact with the drip rail when the door is closed. Water and dust leaks are common in these types, if the glass is not tilted enough to make adequate contact with the upper gasket. On the other hand, if the glass is tilted too far in, this may cause hard door closing and damage to the gasket.

The door glass or windows are attached to the window-lifting mechanism by different methods, depending on the make of the automobile (Figure 17-3). For example, with the bolt through method the lift channel or brackets are attached to the glass by means of bolts through the glass. These bolts have either plastic or rubber washers

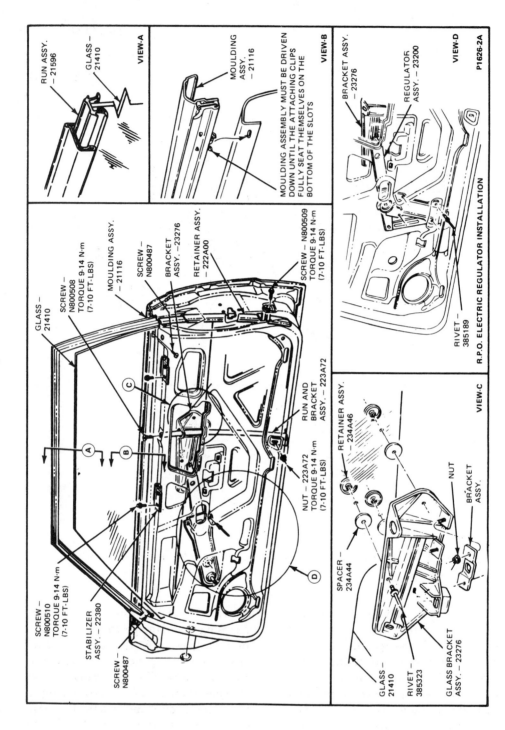

Figure 17-3 Front door window mechanism—two-door models. *(Courtesy of Ford Motor Corporation.)*

or gaskets to keep the bolts or brackets from direct contact with the glass in order to eliminate breakage.

There are also adhesive or bonded types where the lower lift bracket is bonded or cemented to the glass. One model uses a U-shaped channel, with several insulator stays to keep the glass from contacting the metal channel (Figure 17–4). Then the bonding material or cementing material is added. If possible, before removing glass from the channel, measure the distance from the lower front edge of the glass to the front of the sash channel or consult the service manual for the correct location of the glass in the sash channel. The 3M structural adhesive, or similar cement or adhesive, is used for bonding. After mixing the adhesive in proper proportions, apply it to the entire length of the sash channel.

Install spacers and set the glass in the channel in the correct position. Using a heavy-duty cloth tape, tape the sash chan-nel to the glass and let the adhesive cure for at least one hour. After the adhesive has fully cured, apply a thin layer of 3M Super Silicone, or equivalent material, the full length of the bonding adhesive or cement. This is to prevent water from penetrating the adhesive.

Other cemented-type glass may vary in procedure and type of adhesive used. To remove bond or cemented windows from the channel, heat the channel with a torch for one minute and pull off with a pair of pliers. Remove all traces of cement from glass and channel.

CAUTION: Avoid inhaling the fumes.

The oldest method of attaching the glass to the lift bracket or channel is to use the sash channel (Figure 17–5). A rubber seal or tape is put on the lower edge of the glass, then the channel is positioned and driven on the glass with a hammer or rubber mallet. In the event the channel is too loose, shim tape or electrical tape can be used to

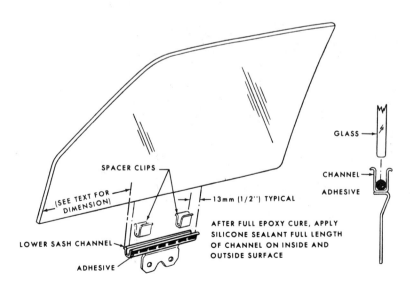

Figure 17-4 Glass to channel bonding. *(Courtesy of General Motors Corporation, Chevrolet Motor Division.)*

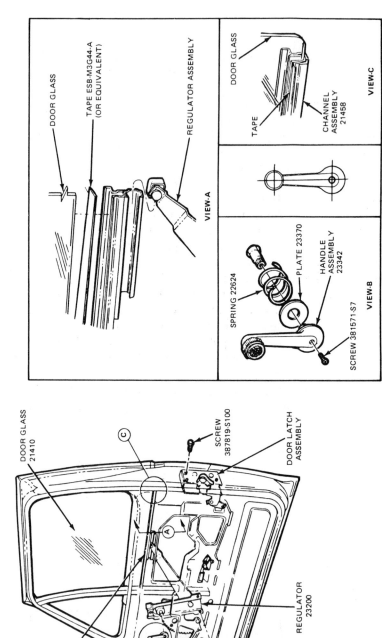

Figure 17-5 Window regulator—removal and replacement. *(Courtesy of Ford Motor Corporation.)*

tighten it. The channel edges can be squeezed together slightly to make a tighter fit.

Many times, the lower bracket which attaches to the regulator breaks off due to rusting or poor spot welds. In this case, the sash channel has to be removed from the glass without breaking it. To remove the channel, special tools are available (Figure 17-6). One method is to place the glass on a soft blanket or several layers of cardboard. Then place a small piece of hardwood about 2" (50.8 mm) wide against the channel and tap the wood with a hammer. Move the wood back and forth along the length of the channel to avoid bending it. In tough cases, a little heat applied with an oxy-acetylene torch on the channel may assist in removing it. Avoid prying off the channel with a screwdriver placed in the channel against the glass. This may chip or damage the glass.

NOTE: Never attempt to weld or braze the channel with the glass in it. The excessive heat will cause the glass to break.

When reinstalling or replacing the glass, the original seal may be unsuitable. A cloth and cork tape, called *window tape,* may be used. The tape is available in various thicknesses with the cloth side of the tape con-tacting the channel. This tape can also be used in the metal strip that surrounds the glass on some models. After installing the strips, the surplus tape is trimmed off with a sharp knife or razor blade.

In order to remove the glass in any door, the interior door trim panel must be removed (see Chapter 20). Each make and model will have different types of trim panels and hardware that must be removed. The more expensive models generally have power windows, lock, and even seat controls mounted in a power panel which is located in the trim panel on the driver's door. The trim panels are either one or two piece with a variety of different types of retainers or attaching devices used to hold the panels to the door frame. Many of the attaching screws or devices are hidden from view, often concealed by plugs or escutcheon plates. Attempting to pry off the trim panel can result in costly damage, and the trim panel may have to be replaced. If possible, consult the service manual for the location of the fasteners.

On some models with a two-piece door trim panel, the upper panel is removed first and then the door glass can be removed. After the trim panel is removed, the insulation panel and/or water shield must be removed. Be sure to install the water shield before replacing the trim panel because water could leak inside the car and damage the trim panel.

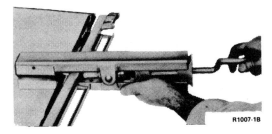

R1007-1B

Figure 17-6 Glass channel replacement. *(Courtesy of Ford Motor Corporation.)*

REMOVAL OF DOOR GLASS

Removing a door glass will vary somewhat between different makes and models. Sedan doors are basically the same as are different makes of hardtop doors.

Some hardtop doors require the removal of the upper window stops, lower lift brackets or bolts, front or rear glass run channel, if required, upper front and rear formed door gasket if applicable, upper glass stabilizers, or any other part or parts (Figure 17-7). Some door glass lift channels are attached by rivets which must be removed to remove the glass.

NOTE: Use caution after removing the lift channel so the glass does not drop inside the door. Also take care when removing the glass from the door in order to prevent chipping or scratching it.

It may be necessary to block up the glass to complete the removal of the necessary

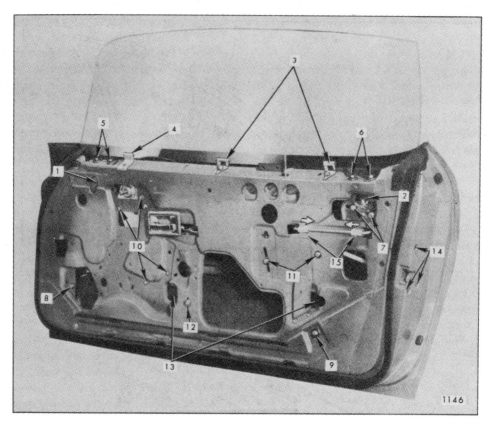

1.	Front Up-Travel Stop Screw	7.	Rear Guide Upper Screws	12.	Down-Travel Stop Screw
2.	Rear Up-Travel Stop Screw	8.	Front Guide Lower Screw	13.	Lower Sash Channel Cam Nut Access Holes
3.	Trim Support Retainer Screws	9.	Rear Guide Lower Screw	14.	Door Lock Screws
4.	Trim Retainer Screws	10.	Window Regulator Rivets	15.	Retainers Inside Locking Rod
5.	Front Guide Upper Screws	11.	Inner Panel Cam Screws		
6.	Rear Guide Upper Bracket Screws				

Figure 17-7 Door hardware attachments—F styles. *(Courtesy of General Motors Corporation, Fisher Body Division.)*

parts. If glass is to be reinstalled, store in a safe place. Tilting the glass may be necessary to remove the guide rollers from the guide channel or from the regulator rollers depending on the type of window mechanism. It is imperative to remember in what order the parts were removed, then observe this order when installing the glass.

When the door is replaced, the new door should be available before removing all of the parts from the old door. Then the parts should be laid out in the order of removal. Reverse the procedure to reinstall the parts, noting what type bolt came from what part. Also, be sure to install the proper spacers or insulators when working on bolt through windows.

Observe the adjustment locations of the various guide channels, front and rear glass movement bolts, and the in and out glass adjustments. This could save a lot of time during reassembly.

The sedan and truck doors do not have the same number of parts to be concerned with when removing the glass as the hardtop door (Figure 17-8 and 17-9). If the inner door trim attaches at the top of the inner door frame or belt line, the inner weatherstrip is attached to the trim panel. On other types of doors, the inner weatherstrip and perhaps the outer must be removed. The strips are attached either by clips or sheetmetal screws.

The regulator arm adjusting channel or inner cam, lock rods, vent glass, and division channel must be removed on some

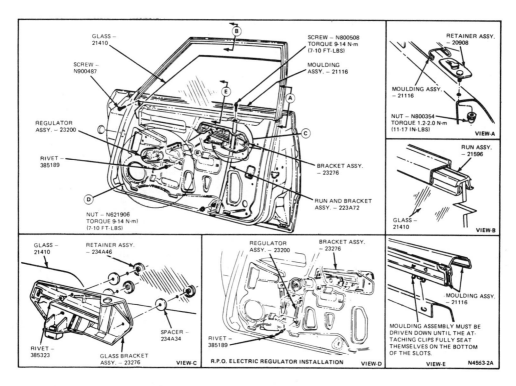

Figure 17-8 Front door window mechanism—four-door models. *(Courtesy of Ford Motor Corporation.)*

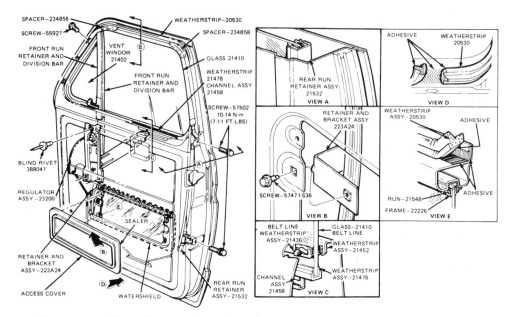

Figure 17-9 Front door window glass adjustment—E-100—E-350. (*Courtesy of Ford Motor Corporation.*)

rear doors. With the glass lowered part way, the rollers can be slipped out of the lower lift channel or sometimes tipped for removal. Other doors may require the removal of one or more vertical guide channels or runs.

NOTE: With window glass lowered, the top edge of glass should be flush with belt line.

CHANNEL ALIGNMENT AND SERVICE

On many doors, the fore or aft adjustment is controlled by the channels. Some windows use a front guide roller in a movable channel that can be adjusted. Others, with a center lift guide, have the forward and aft adjustment as well as the inner and outer tilt of the glass controlled either at the bracket that attaches to the lower sash

channel or where the guide attaches to the inner door panel.

Binding (or stiff operation of the window) can be caused by improper channel adjustment or the lack of proper lubrication of the guide channels. The glass that tips forward (or aft) and binds can be caused by improper adjustment of lower sash brackets, loose channel, cam roller, or stabilized channel out of adjustment.

On sedan doors involving a full or partial length rubber glass run or channel, the glass or the rubber will bind if the channels are too tight or the channel needs lubricating. Some bodymen recommend the use of a dry silicone spray applied to the channel to free up the glass.

NOTE: Do not use oil on the rubber channels. It may cause them to swell and deteriorate.

Doors using a full trim panel sometimes have a set of trim pad brackets at the top of the door to which the trim panel is attached. Setting the brackets too far inward will cause the window glass to bind. Anti-rattle slides or other devices used to keep the window glass from rattling in the down position can cause the glass to bind when raised up.

Quarter Glass

When adusting a door glass to properly align with the edge of the quarter glass, check to see if the fault is in the quarter glass adjustment. To adjust or remove a quarter glass, the rear cushion, back rest, inner trim panel, and water shield must be removed to gain access to the quarter glass attaching devices. Some of the quarter glasses are movable and some are stationary.

On some types of stationary glass and swing-out glass, it is not necessary to remove the seats, depending upon the type and make involved, to service the glass. Just remove the trim panel. The stationary glass can be adjusted by loosening up the retainer bolts or screws and shifting to align with the door glass. Consult the service manual for correct procedures.

The movable quarter glasses operate about the same as the door glass. The up and down movement is controlled by stops. The up stop controls the upper and forward motion of the glass and must be set to obtain the proper spacing between the door and quarter glass. Some quarter glass has two up stops to control the front and rear section of the glass. Like the door glass, the quarter glass has adjustments to control the inward and outward tilt of the glass at the top.

The quarter glasses are removed by different methods depending on the make of the vehicle. Consult the service manual, if available, or make a careful inspection of what is necessary to remove the glass. Be careful not to chip or scratch the glass as this may cause breakage. There is only limited access to most quarter panel inner panels and getting the hands inside the panel is difficult. Care must be taken to prevent accidentally dropping the glass after it has been detached. If the stop appears to interfere with bringing the glass up through the opening, remove it first before detaching the glass from the regulator. On some models, the guide assembly must be removed with the glass.

VENT SERVICE AND ALIGNMENT

Vent assemblies vary depending on the make and model. Some vent windows are friction types and others use a small gear box with a crank handle or are power operated.

The sedan vent assembly is attached to the upper door frame and window opening (Figure 17-10). Many of the assemblies incorporate the forward glass channel or arm. The vent assemblies are held in place by screws through the forward part of the door frame or the top and lower part of the unit. The glass channel or run can be adjusted at the bottom to control the lower travel of the door glass. Also, the channel can be moved in or out to control the tilt of the glass.

To remove most vent assemblies, the lower window stop must be removed and the window lowered to the bottom of the door. The attaching screws are removed, and the inner and outer belt weatherstrip must be removed, if necessary. The upper glass run next to the vent must be brought down so that the vent assembly can be

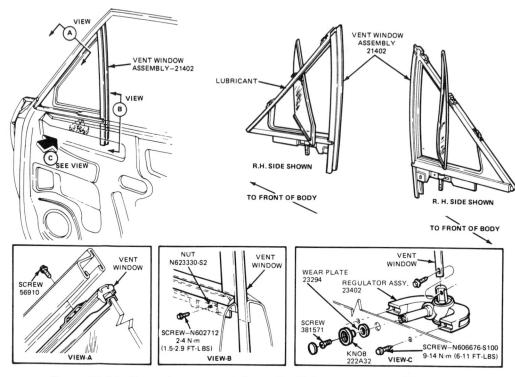

Figure 17-10 Front door vent window—Ford/Mercury. (*Courtesy of Ford Motor Corporation.*)

tipped toward the rear and up. Some vents have to be rotated 90° to permit the adjusting screws to pass through the opening.

NOTE: The vent assembly must be removed in order to take the door glass out in some types of doors.

Doors equipped with gear-type vent controls must be removed first before the vent. The hardtop and convertible vents are attached to the inner door frame by bolts immediately below the vent or in the front part of the door frame. The lower channel is attached by an adjustable screw or stud. The vent can be taken out by removing the lower window stop and removing the attaching vent bolts or studs. The assembly is tilted rearward and upward. The vent may have to be turned to clear the lower adjusting stud through the top of the door.

NOTE: Vent assemblies with a gear box or power-operated unit must be removed prior to removing the vent.

This type of vent assembly must be properly aligned with the windshield post when reinstalled. If the vent is not damaged and must be removed for other purposes, note the bolt locations and measure the gap between the vent and windshield post before removing the bolts.

POWER AND MANUAL REGULATORS

All regulators, either power (electric) or manual, are made to raise or lower the door or quarter glass, and in the case of the vent windows, to move the glass in and out.

There are many different types of regulators, each varying with the make or model of the vehicle. The manual regulators are very similar to the power regulators except the handle crank mechanism is used in place of the electromotor and drive gear. The lift arms are basically the same for any given door.

Some regulators use one lift arm, and some are made with two lift arms, called the X design. This X design uses an auxiliary arm mounted into a cam or stabilizer channel. The cam or stabilizer channel is adjustable so that the glass can be tilted or rocked to make the window glass raise in a parallel position. The single-arm regulators use other methods of operation, that is, adjustment can be made to the lower sash channel if applicable, to the guide channels, or to the stops. Some doors are modeled without adjustments.

Many of the regulators and other parts are riveted in place instead of bolted. Care must be taken not to enlarge the holes when drilling out the rivets. Also there is a danger of hitting the glass if the glass is in the wrong position.

The rivets are removed by first removing the center pin or mandrel, then drilling out the rivets with a 1/4" (6.35 mm) drill bit. When reinstalling the regulator or other parts with rivets, a heavy-duty rivet gun, such as a Marsen 39010 "Big Daddy," is needed. Generally, the 1/4" (6.35 mm) or 1/2" (12.7 mm) in length rivets are used or some other types as recommended by the manufacturer. Be sure the part is held or clamped tightly against the inner panel before setting the rivet.

Window Regulator

Some types of regulators are spot welded to the inner door panel. Be sure to place the window in an up position and secure with tape. Detach the window from the regulator, using the service manual as a guide.

To remove the regulator, center punch visible spot weld marks on the inner panel. Use a spot welder cutter to drill out each weld (Figure 17–11). A small amount of weld may still hold the regulator to the inner panel. Drive a chisel between the regulator and inner panel to separate the regulator from the panel. Depending on the manufacturer, the replacement regulator is generally reattached by U-clips and screws.

Other parts besides regulators are spot welded and can be removed by the same method.

When removing regulators, without removing the glass, the glass must be held up by either heavy cloth tape or wedges to prevent the glass from dropping inside the door and breaking. Consult the manual for the proper procedure for removing regulators; each make recommends specific procedures. Some require the drilling of new holes to remount the regulator with bolts, and some recommend rivets.

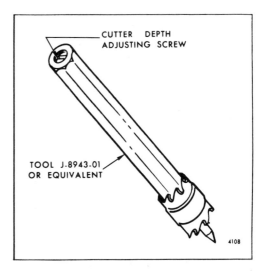

Figure 17-11 Spot-weld cutter. *(Courtesy of General Motors Corporation, Fisher Body Division.)*

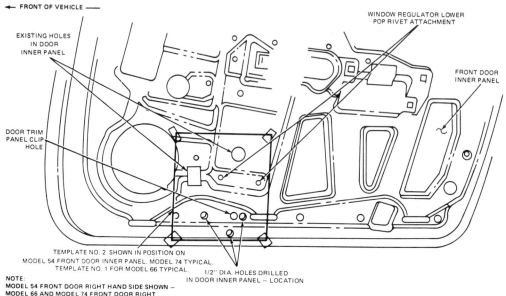

(a)

(b)

Figure 17-12 (a) Power window motor removal—front door—Ford/Mercury; (b) front-window power regulator—Lincoln Continental/Continental Mark VI. *(Courtesy of Ford Motor Corporation.)*

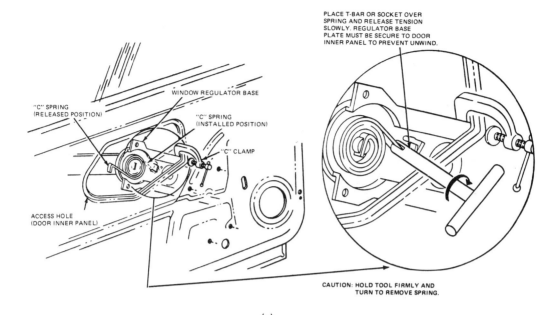

PLACE T-BAR OR SOCKET OVER
SPRING AND RELEASE TENSION
SLOWLY. REGULATOR BASE
PLATE MUST BE SECURE TO DOOR
INNER PANEL TO PREVENT UNWIND.

WINDOW REGULATOR BASE

"C" SPRING
(RELEASED POSITION)

"C" SPRING
(INSTALLED POSITION)

"C" CLAMP

ACCESS HOLE
(DOOR INNER PANEL)

CAUTION: HOLD TOOL FIRMLY AND
TURN TO REMOVE SPRING.

(a)

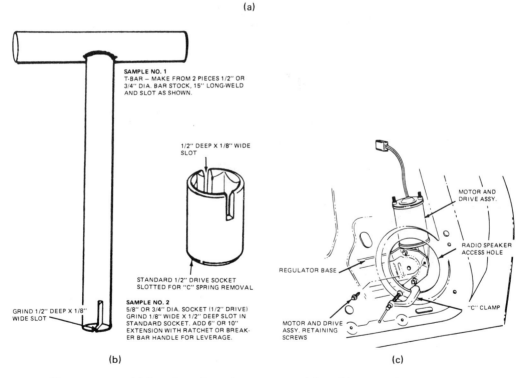

SAMPLE NO. 1
T-BAR — MAKE FROM 2 PIECES 1/2" OR
3/4" DIA. BAR STOCK, 15" LONG-WELD
AND SLOT AS SHOWN.

1/2" DEEP X 1/8" WIDE
SLOT

STANDARD 1/2" DRIVE SOCKET
SLOTTED FOR "C" SPRING REMOVAL

GRIND 1/2" DEEP X 1/8"
WIDE SLOT

SAMPLE NO. 2
5/8" OR 3/4" DIA. SOCKET (1/2" DRIVE)
GRIND 1/8" WIDE X 1/2" DEEP SLOT IN
STANDARD SOCKET. ADD 6" OR 10"
EXTENSION WITH RATCHET OR BREAK-
ER BAR HANDLE FOR LEVERAGE.

(b)

MOTOR AND
DRIVE ASSY.

RADIO SPEAKER
ACCESS HOLE

REGULATOR BASE

"C" CLAMP

MOTOR AND DRIVE
ASSY. RETAINING
SCREWS

(c)

Figure 17-13 (a) Regulator base clamping—model 36; (b) counterbalance spring removal tool; (c) regulator motor removal—model 36. *(Courtesy of Ford Motor Corporation.)*

Power regulators require more care when servicing because of the counterbalance springs (Figure 17-12). On some Ford Motor Company models, such as the Fairmont and Thunderbird, the counterbalance spring of the regulator must be released before removing the regulator motor. The regulator is positioned to a large access hole in the inner door panel and clamped to the panel with a C-clamp (Figure 17-13). Using a special tool, the spring tension is released. After servicing the motor, the regulator is clamped to the inner panel and the spring reinstalled in its same position. Failure to remove the spring can cause damage to parts and hands.

On some General Motors models, the regulator can be secured by drilling a hole through the regulator gear and back plate, then a screw or bolt with a nut is installed to lock them together. Then the motor can be removed safely and without damage to the hands.

NOTE: Be sure to remove bolts or screws after installing the motor.

On some General Motors models, with-

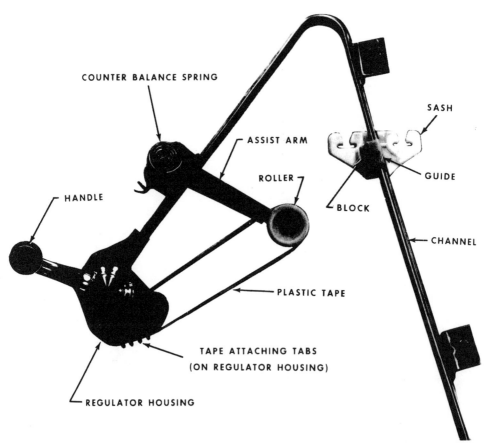

Figure 17-14 Coupe door manual window regulator—other regulators similar (Chevrolet Citation). *(Courtesy of General Motors Corporation, Chevrolet Motor Division.)*

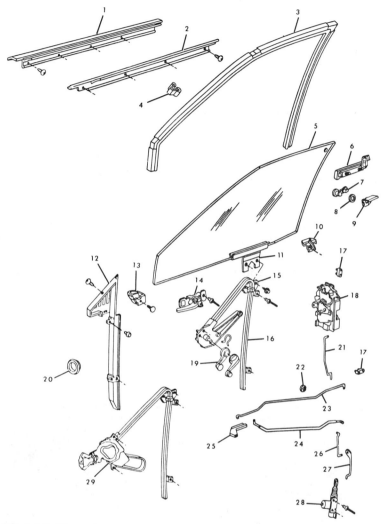

1. Door Belt Reveal Molding with Integral Sealing Strip
2. Outer Belt Sealing Strip (Styles without Belt Molding)
3. Window Glass Run Channel Assembly
4. Window Guide Clip
5. Door Glass
6. Outside Handle
7. Lock Cylinder
8. Lock Cylinder Gasket
9. Lock Cylinder Retainer
10. Rear Inner Panel Belt Sealing Strip Filler
11. Lower Sash Channel Assembly
12. Glass Run Channel Lower Front Retainer
13. Front Inner Panel Belt Sealing Strip Filler
14. Lock Remote Control Handle Assembly
15. Regulator Sash
16. Manual Window Regulator Assembly
17. Over Slam Bumper
18. Lock Assembly
19. Window Regulator Handle
20. Electrical Conduit Hole Plug
21. Outside Handle to Lock Rod
22. Inside Locking to Lock Rod Shoe (Guide)
23. Inside Locking to Lock Rod
24. Lock Remote Control to Lock Rod
25. Inside Locking Knob
26. Lock Cylinder to Lock Rod
27. Locking Actuator to Lock Rod
28. Electric Lock Actuator
29. Electric Window Regulator Assembly

Figure 17-15 Chevrolet Citation door parts. *(Courtesy of General Motors Corporation, Chevrolet Motor Division.)*

out a counterbalance spring, removing the motor will cause the window to drop to the bottom of the door. Before removing, tape the glass in the up position or use blocks. Consult the manuals for specific procedures on the model and make involved.

A new type regulator which is being used by General Motors Citation uses a lightweight tape drive regulator (Figure 17–14). The types used for coupe and sedan doors, either manual or electric, are of different lengths and must be cut to the correct size. The regulators are riveted to the inner panel and must be drilled out (Figure 17–15).

For further information concerning re-placing the tape, consult the General Motors Chevrolet Citation service manual.

STATION WAGON REAR GLASS

The station wagon glass operation is similar to the door mechanism, either manual or powered. The glass can be adjusted from side to side and in and out to maintain proper contact with the sealing gasket (Fig-

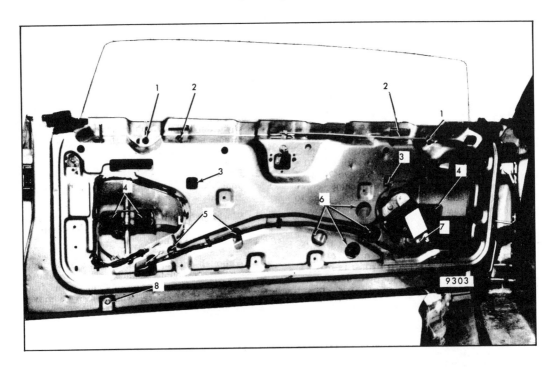

1. Up-travel Stop Attachments	3. Sash Channel Cam to Glass Attachment
2. Belt Trim Support Retainers	4. Guide Plate to Glass Attachments

5. Inner Panel Cam Attachments	7. Motor Rivet
6. Regulator Rivets	8. Torque Rod Retainer Attaching Bolt

Figure 17–16 Typical tailgate assembly. *(Courtesy of General Motors Corporation, Fisher Body Division.)*

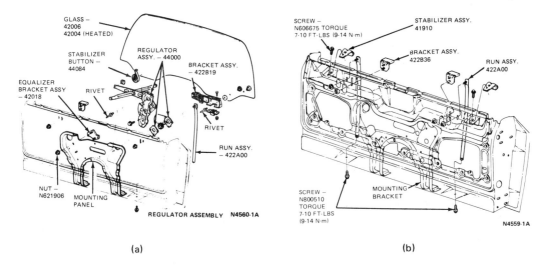

Figure 17-17 (a) Back window regulator assembly; (b) back window glass run assembly. *(Courtesy of Ford Motor Corporation.)*

ure 17-16). Also, the height can be adjusted by means of stops with the top of the glass being parallel with the glass or body opening.

CAUTION: When removing the regulator motor, drill a hole through the regulator gear and backing plate, install bolt or screw and nut. The lift arms are under tension and injury can result if the arms are not secured.

Like the door regulators, the tailgate regulators are riveted to the inner panel (Figure 17-17). When reinstalling, rivets or bolts can be used to refasten the regulator. Consult service manuals for correct procedures for servicing tailgate glass.

Questions

1. What are the two basic types of door constructions?
2. Which type of door gives the door glass the most support?
3. Which type door requires more window adjustments?
4. How are the door glasses attached to the lift channels on many of the modern automobiles?
5. What is the purpose of insulator stays in the lift channnel?
6. Without special tools available, how can the sash channel be safely removed from the door glass without breaking it?
7. What material is used to attach the lower sash channel to the door glass?
8. What are some of the problems that exist when removing an unfamiliar door trim panel?
9. What is the danger that exists after the lift channel has been removed from the glass?

10. What is the purpose of using upper window stops?

11. What can be used to free up the window in the channels?

12. What controls the up and down movement of the quarter glass?

13. What controls the in or out movement of the vent assembly on a hardtop door?

14. What is the purpose of the window regulator?

15. What controls the tilt of the glass in an X-type arm regulator?

16. What fastening device is used to attach the regulator to the inner door panels on many of the late model automobiles?

17. What precautions must be used when removing some types of regulator motors?

18. What is the new type window regulator called?

19. What must be done before removing GM tailgate power regulator motors?

The door lock apparatus consists of several systems that operate the door lock or latch. There is the outside door handle and/or linkage, if applicable, the inside remote control or inside door lock operating mechanism including the linkage, the outside door lock cylinder and/or linkage, if applicable, and the inside locking rod either manual or power operated.

Several different types of outside door handles are used depending on the make of the vehicle (Figure 18–1). These include the push button and the lift type (Figure 18–2). On the push-type handles, the button makes direct contact with the lock lever which releases the mechanism to open the door.

Most of the outside door handles activate the lock mechanism by means of one or more rods (Figure 18–3). With the window raised, the handles can be disconnected by removing the interior trim panel and water shield to get access to the attaching hardware and linkage.

Some door handles are attached by means of screws or bolts, but some are riveted to the outer door panel. When removing or disconnecting the linkage rods, care must be used not to damage the retaining clips or bushing. Some of the causes of malfunction in the operation of the outside door handle are worn bushings, bent or incorrectly adjusted rods, or the lack of lubrication of the handle, linkages, or latch, and worn latches.

The inside remote mechanisms are generally the pull type, but there are many variations (Figures 18-4 and 18-5). The remote mechanisms are connected to the lock by one or more rods and are accessible by removing the interior trim panel and water shield. Depending on the make, the remote mechanism is attached by either bolts, screws, or rivets. Because of the length of the rods, they are supported or held in place to keep them from getting

Door And Trunk Lock

chapter 18

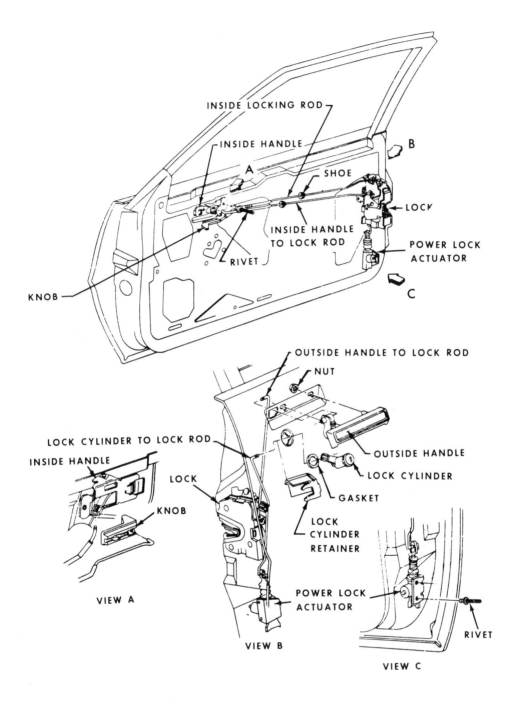

Figure 18-1 Front door locking system. *(Courtesy of General Motors Corporation, Chevrolet Motor Division.)*

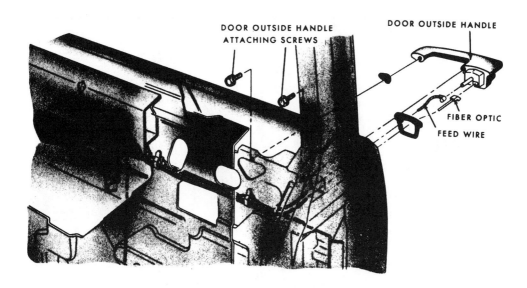

(a)

PUSH·BUTTON

RETURN SPRING

SEALING WASHER

RETAINER

ATTACHING
SCREW LOCATIONS

(b)

SEALING
GASKET

LOCK
CYLINDER
ASSEMBLY

BOTTOM DRAIN HOLE

RETAINER

LOCK
EXTENSION

(c)

Figure 18-2 (a) Illuminated lock cylinder; (b) outside push-button handle disassembly; (c) door lock cylinder removal. *(Courtesy of General Motors Corporation, Fisher Body Division.)*

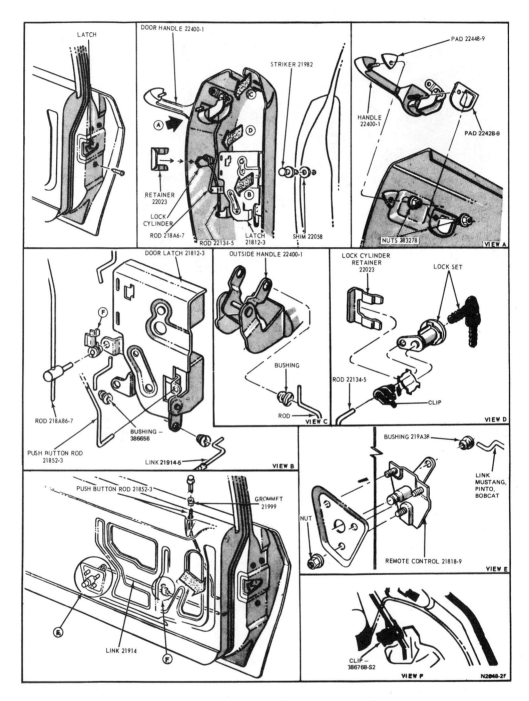

Figure 18-3 Door latch and striker installation—Pinto/Bobcat. *(Courtesy of Ford Motor Corporation.)*

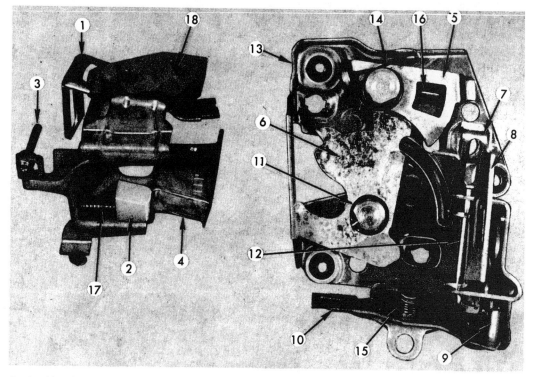

1. Locking Lever
2. Sliding Shoe
3. Intermittent Guide Pin
4. Lock Back Plate
5. Detent Lever
6. Fork Bolt
7. Intermittent Lever
8. Push-Button Lever
9. Transfer Lever
10. Remote Control Lever
11. Spring Tension Washer
12. Push-Button Pin
13. Lock Frame
14. Detent Return Spring
15. Push-Button Return Spring
16. Lock Silencer
17. Sliding Shoe Pin and Spring
18. Overcenter Spring

(a)

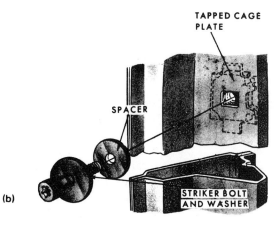

(b)

Figure 18-4 (a) Rear door lock—B and C styles; (b) door lock striker installation. *(Courtesy of General Motors Corporation, Fisher Body Division.)*

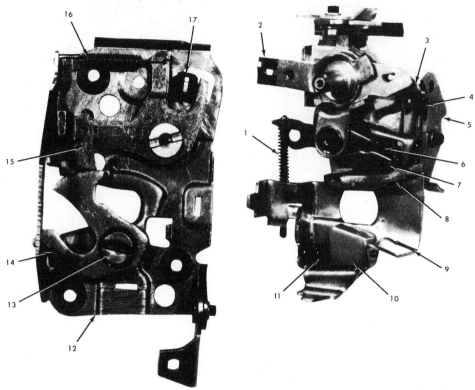

1. Push-Button Pin and Return Spring
2. Locking Lever
3. Overcenter Spring
4. Spring Clip
5. Remote Lever
6. Push-Button Lever
7. Intermittent Lever
8. Upper Ramp
9. Backplate
10. Sliding Shoe
11. Sliding Shoe Pin and Return Spring
12. Lock Frame
13. Spring Tension Washer
14. Fork Bolt
15. Detent Lever
16. Detent Return Spring
17. Detent Silencer

Figure 18-5 Typical front door lock assembly—Chevrolet Citation. *(Courtesy of General Motors Corporation, Chevrolet Motor Division.)*

caught in the regulator arms. The rods are connected with clips or bushings which must be handled with care when they are removed or replaced.

The outside lock cylinders are generally held in position with a spring-type clip which is accessible after the interior trim has been removed. The cylinder is either directly connected to the latch or connected by means of a rod.

On some of the vehicles, as optional equipment, all latches can be locked at one time by means of a power cylinder operated from the driver's door control panel (Figure 18-6). The door key will only operate on one lock at a time.

Some makes have an interior push rod or button to lock the doors. The doors cannot be opened from the inside if they are locked, which is a safety device especially

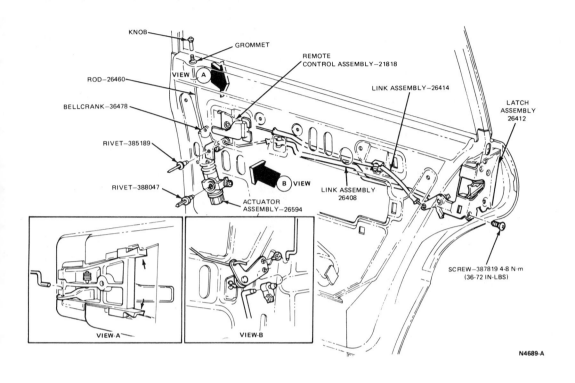

KNOB

GROMMET

REMOTE
CONTROL ASSEMBLY—21818

ROD—26460

VIEW A

LINK ASSEMBLY—26414

BELLCRANK—36478

LATCH
ASSEMBLY
26412

RIVET—385189

B VIEW

RIVET—388047

LINK ASSEMBLY
26408

ACTUATOR
ASSEMBLY—26594

VIEW-A

VIEW-B

SCREW—387819 4-8 N·m
(36-72 IN-LBS)

N4689-A

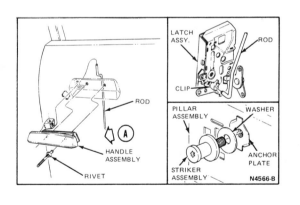

LATCH
ASSY.

ROD

CLIP

ROD

PILLAR
ASSEMBLY

WASHER

HANDLE
ASSEMBLY

STRIKER
ASSEMBLY

ANCHOR
PLATE

RIVET

N4566-B

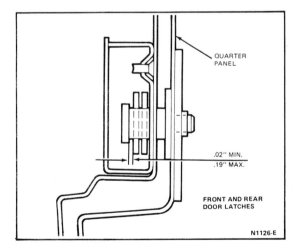

QUARTER
PANEL

.02" MIN.
.19" MAX.

FRONT AND REAR
DOOR LATCHES

N1126-E

Figure 18-6 (a) Rear door latch mechanism—Fairmont/Zephyr; (b) door latch striker assembly; (c) door latch striker adjustment. (*Courtesy of Ford Motor Corporation.*)

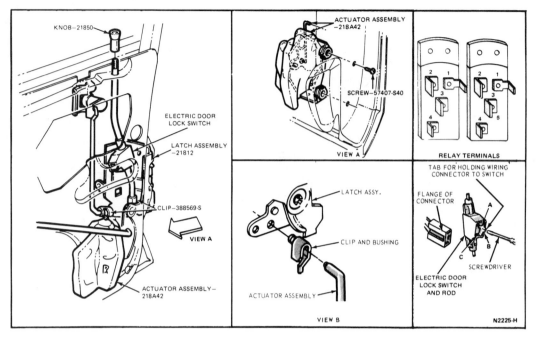

(a)

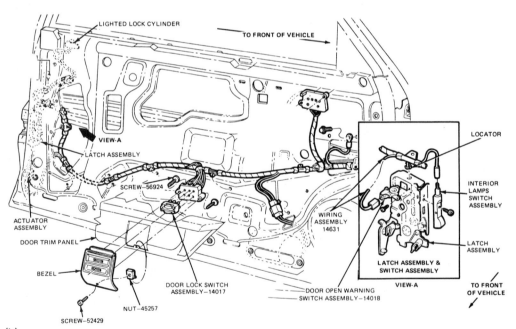

(b)

Figure 18-7 (a) Power door lock actuator, switch and relay—Granada/Monarch; (b) front door power locks wiring—Thunderbird/Cougar XR-7 (low series). *(Courtesy of Ford Motor Corporation.)*

useful with small children in the rear seat.

The power units are either bolted or riveted to the inner door frame (Figures 18-7). Failure of the power unit to operate could result from a poor electrical connection. Check the wiring with a test lamp to determine whether the current is reaching the power unit.

Trunk or hatch locks operate with a key or from a dash switch (Figure 18-8). Depending on the make of vehicle, some are adjustable while others are riveted in position.

STATION WAGON LIFT AND SWING-OUT GATE

There are many variations of gate assemblies used on station wagons (Figures 18-9 and 18-10). Some wagons use a lift and swing-out tailgate. Adjustment or proper function of the locking mechanism is very important in order to prevent the gate from dropping down when opened. This type of gate has one permanent pivot or anchor which is in the lower left. When used as a lift gate, the upper left anchor is disengaged. When used as a swing-out gate, the upper left anchor is locked and will pivot. Sometimes, through body damage or defective linkage or latches, the upper left anchor will become unlocked or will not lock properly. Some of the problems come from the lack of proper lubrication.

Some of the older models use a rod or switch that prevents the gate from being opened unless the gate glass is rolled completely down. This prevents the glass from being broken.

If the problem cannot be solved, it is advisable to consult the service manual remembering that each make uses a different type of locking mechanism.

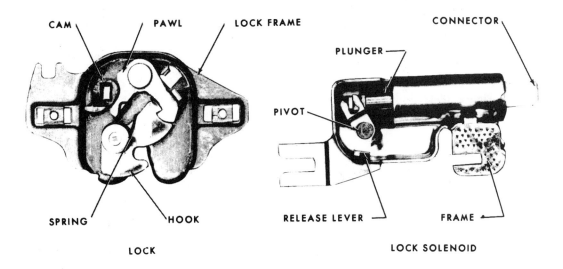

Figure 18-8 Typical rear compartment lid lock and solenoid. (*Courtesy of General Motors Corporation, Fisher Body Division.*)

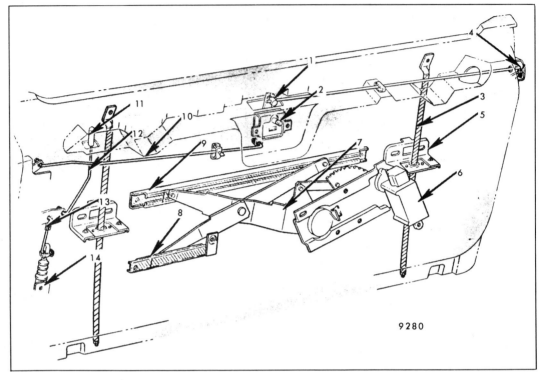

9280

Fig. 7-119 - Tailgate Lock Synchronization Rods

1. Left Upper Remote
   Synchronization Lock
   Rod
2. Remote Control
3. Guide Tube
4. Left Upper Hinge
   Lock

5. Guide Plate Assembly
6. Motor, Window
   Regulator
7. Tailgate Window
   Regulator
8. Tailgate Inner Panel
   Cam

9. Tailgate Glass
   Regulator Cam
10. Right Upper Remote
    Locking Rod
11. Knob Door Inside
    Locking

12. Tailgate Inside
    Locking to Lock Rod
13. Rod Tailgate Lock to
    Power Actuator
14. Electric Lock Power
    Actuator

Figure 18-9 Tailgate lock synchronization rods. (*Courtesy of General Motors Corporation, Fisher Body Division.*)

NOTE: When servicing locks that require the removal of the trim and water shield, be sure to reinstall and seal the water shield to prevent damage to the trim panel.

Regardless of what type lock or latch is involved (the striker pin, plate, or other type), the proper adjustment of these devices is important for proper locking operation (Figure 18-11). Also, if the striker is out of position in relation to a properly aligned door or deck, the door or deck will have to be lowered, raised, or shifted to lock. The striker should be adjusted so that the door or deck does not have to shift to lock and requires very little effort to close.

A quick way to check is to open the door, deck, or gate and watch the movement of

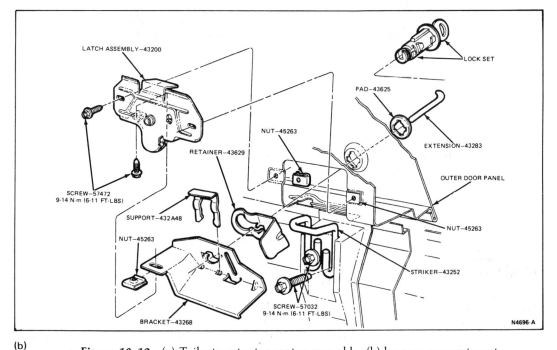

(a)

(b)

Figure 18-10 (a) Tailgate actuator motor assembly; (b) luggage compartment latch and lock—Thunderbird/Cougar XR-7. *(Courtesy of Ford Motor Corporation.)*

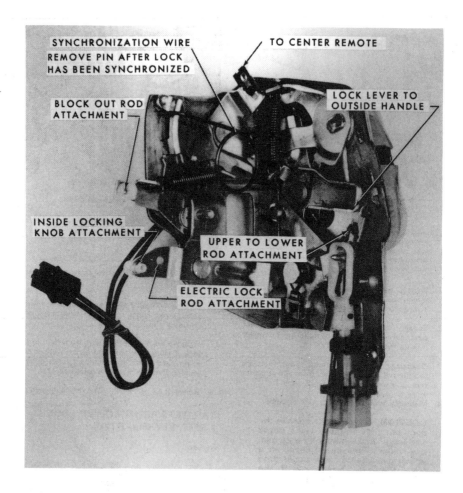

SYNCHRONIZATION WIRE
REMOVE PIN AFTER LOCK
HAS BEEN SYNCHRONIZED

TO CENTER REMOTE

LOCK LEVER TO
OUTSIDE HANDLE

BLOCK OUT ROD
ATTACHMENT

INSIDE LOCKING
KNOB ATTACHMENT

UPPER TO LOWER
ROD ATTACHMENT

ELECTRIC LOCK
ROD ATTACHMENT

Figure 18-11 Tailgate upper right lock and synchronization wire. *(Courtesy of General Motors Corporation, Fisher Body Division.)*

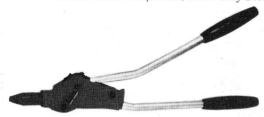

Figure 18-12 Heavy duty riveter used for installing ¼″ (6.35 mm) rivets used for attaching regulators, outside door handles and other hardware or door parts. *(Courtesy of Townsend/ Richline Company, Division of Textron Inc.)*

the unit as it comes off the striker. Adding or removing shims may be required to permit better contact between the lock and striker.

NOTE: When parts are attached by rivets, many of them use a 1/4″ (6.35 mm) rivet. The rivet is removed by drilling out the center of the rivet with a 1/4″ (6.35 mm) drill bit. If the part is to be riveted back in

SNAPO® SPLIT RIVETS

These patented* ¼" blind rivets are used by most American automobile manufacturers to attach the window regulator mechanism to the door or body panel; to attach the nylon glass stops to both the glass and regulator and to attach the latch to the door panel.

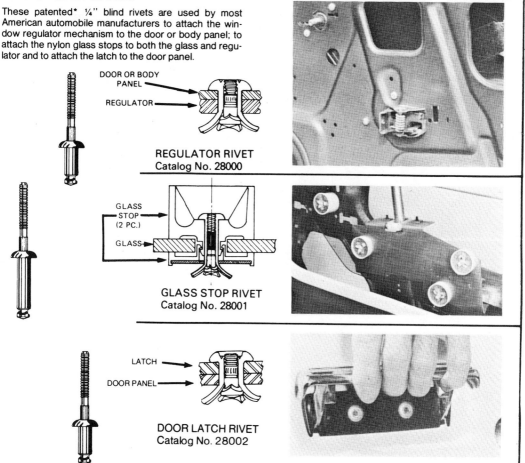

DOOR OR BODY PANEL

REGULATOR

REGULATOR RIVET
Catalog No. 28000

GLASS STOP (2 PC.)

GLASS

GLASS STOP RIVET
Catalog No. 28001

LATCH

DOOR PANEL

DOOR LATCH RIVET
Catalog No. 28002

A heavy duty riveter, such as Catalog No. 04024 (or No. 04012 Richline® HN-80), equipped with special nosepiece No. 04021, is required to properly install the above split rivets.
*Licensed under Townsend Patent No. 3,232, 162 and Huck Patent No. 3,204,517.

Figure 18–13 Split rivets. *(Courtesy of Townsend/Richline Company, Division of Textron Inc.)*

position, use caution not to enlarge the hole when drilling out the rivet. Some manufacturers recommend using a U-nut and bolt or bolt and nut in place of rivets.

A heavy-duty riveter must be used for 1/4″ (6.35 mm) rivets such as the Marsen

39010 Big Daddy made for 1/4″ (6.35 mm) rivets (Figure 18-12 and 18-13).

The 1/4″ (6.35 mm) by 1/2″ (12.7 mm) diameter rivets are generally suitable as replacements but in some cases, the manufacturer may recommend some other type of rivet.

Questions

1. What are some of the causes for lock malfunction?
2. If a power locking mechanism fails to operate, what is the first step in checking the mechanism?
3. How are the lock cylinders held in the door on most automobiles?
4. Why are water shields important in doors?

It has been a few years since the convertible top vehicle has been produced domestically, but on occasion, this type vehicle is brought in for repair or for the purpose of restoration (Figure 19–1). There were several different types of convertible tops used by manufacturers; therefore, it would be difficult to explain the service and repair procedures for all of them.

INSTALL AND ALIGN TOP COVERS AND REAR WINDOWS

The top covering varies depending on the price range of the vehicle. Some are made of vinyl, others of nylon or other similar material. The material, through age and abuse, can become cracked or torn and must be replaced. Some tops are available from the vehicle manufacturer, otherwise the replacement covers can be obtained from mail order catalogs or wholesale parts jobbers. In many cases, complete instructions and the necessary trim parts are included with the cover and most of them are not too difficult to install.

Top covers can be purchased with or without the back windows, depending on the make. On some model convertibles, the rear window must be unzipped before the top is lowered. Avoid leaving tools in the stocking or top storage area as this may accidentally damage the cover.

When removing and installing a top cover, apply protective covers on deck, cowl top, and hood to prevent scratching or damaging the finish. The rear seat and backrest should be removed as well as the side trim panels, if necessary (Figure 19–2).

The following are some of the general steps used for removing and installing a new or replacement cover. These will vary with different makes of vehicles. For the

Convertible Tops

chapter
19

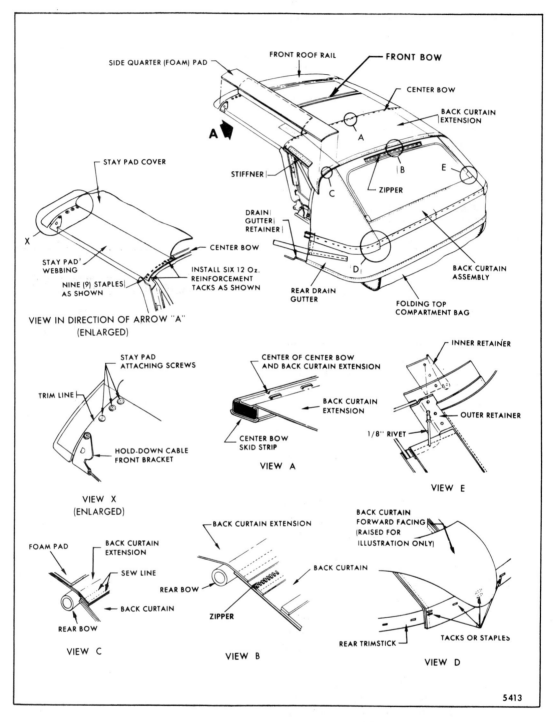

Figure 19-1 Back curtain assembly attachment and reference marking. *(Courtesy of General Motors Corporation, Fisher Body Division.)*

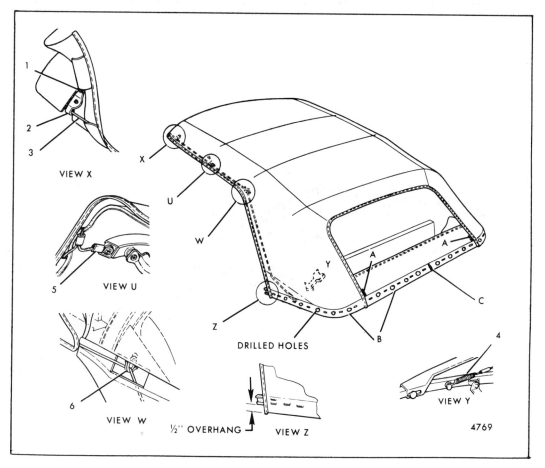

1. Front Attaching Screw
2. Hold-Down Cable Front Bracket
3. Hold-Down Cable
4. Hold-Down Cable Rear Spring (Left Side is Shown, Connect Right Side with Hook Downward to Hold Spring Flat Against Trimstick)
5. Hold-Down Cable Loop Retainer
6. Folding Top Material Hold-Down Cable Retainer

Figure 19-2 Hold-down cable attachment and convertible top reference marking. *(Courtesy of General Motors Corporation, Fisher Body Division.)*

correct, recommended procedures, consult the service manual for that particular vehicle.

The cover is removed by starting with the front bow or rail, also called *No. 1 bow.*

The top is unlatched, and the bow raised far enough to gain access to the underside of the bow (Figure 19-3).

The weatherstrip and retainers in the front and side of the bow are removed in

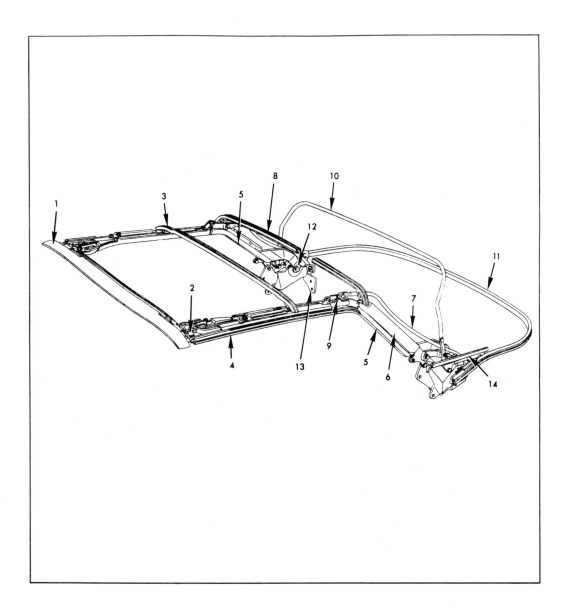

1. Front Roof Rail
2. Front Roof Rail Lock
3. Front Roof Bow and Link Assembly
4. Side Roof Front Rail
5. Side Roof Inner Rear Rail
6. Side Roof Outer Rear Rail
7. Side Roof Rear Control Link
8. Center Bow Assembly
9. Side Roof Rail Set Screw
10. Rear Roof Bow and Link Assembly
11. Rear Belt Rail Trimstick
12. Folding Top Actuator Assembly
13. Main Hinge
14. Folding Top Cover Pressure Bar

Figure 19-3 Inward folding top hardware components. *(Courtesy of General Motors Corporation, Fisher Body Division.)*

order to remove the cover from the front bow. The hold-down cable is detached, if applicable.

NOTE: On some models, the top storage trim is removed from the tacking strip. (The tacking strip screws are also removed.) Remove the window and material leaving the tacking strip. Mark the location before removing; also mark the quarter section before removing from strips.

Remove retainer screws from the second and third bows. Remove the fourth bow mounting and retainer. Some molding strips are opened up to remove the staples. Remove the staples from tacking strip and remove cover (Figure 19–4).

CAUTION: On tops, the control links are under spring tension and could cause injury if the spring is not detached.

When removing covers on some models, an align gauge must be used to stabilize the second, third, and fourth bow (Figure 19–5). When installing a new top, mark the new cover in accordance with marks on the old cover. After marks are lined up with the No. 4 bow, with the top centered on the bow, reattach in reverse order. Some tops are marked to align with the center of the front bow.

It is important, where the sections are cemented, to remove wrinkles and creases before attaching, especially on the front bow.

With the top raised and secured at the No. 1 bow, the rear tacking strips are adjusted and fastened. The rear section should have a neat appearance. Avoid overstretching the material but avoid loose, sagging material.

Adjust the weatherstrip to make the proper contact with the glass and where the strip butts against the windshield frame.

HYDROELECTRIC AND CABLE POWER UNIT

Besides the manual lift–type tops, there are the hydroelectric and electrically driven cable units. The hydroelectric system consists of an electrically driven reversible rotor pump and two hydraulic cylinders with upper and lower hydraulic lines. The pump assembly is generally located behind the rear seat backrest panel and is controlled by a dashboard mounted switch.

To repair or replace the hydroelectric unit, it is necessary to remove the rear cushion and backrest. The top should be in a fully raised position. Disconnect the pump and ground wires. Before removing the hydraulic lines, vent the pump reservoir by removing the filler plug, then reinstall the plug. Most filler plugs are located on the top of the reservoir.

NOTE: The reason for venting the reservoir is to equalize the pressure and reduce the possibility of fluid spraying on the trim and paint when the hydraulic lines are disconnected.

Use clean cloths beneath the hydraulic line connection, disconnect lines, and plug the open filling and lines. Remove the retaining nuts and washers and remove the pump assembly.

If the motor pump has been replaced, fill the reservoir with the recommended fluid; some bodymen recommend automatic transmission fluid. Remove the plug from the lines and connect the lines to the pump. Wipe up any fluid that leaked out while the lines were being connected. Lubricate the grommets and tighten the pump. Connect the motor and ground wires.

Operate the top several times to bleed air from the lines and check fluid level. The fluid level should be within 1/4" (6.35 mm)

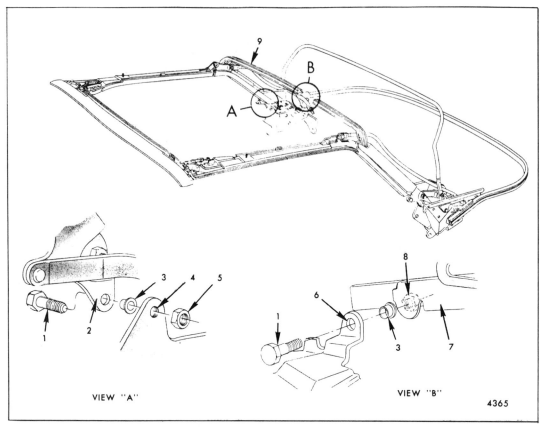

VIEW "A"

VIEW "B"

4365

1. Attaching Bolt
2. Side Roof Outer Rear Rail (Part of Center Bow Assembly)
3. Bushing
4. Threaded Hole in Main Hinge
5. Lock Nut
6. Main Hinge
7. Rear Trimstick (Part of Center Bow Assembly)
8. Anchor Nut (Part of Trimstick)
9. Center Bow

(a)

(b)

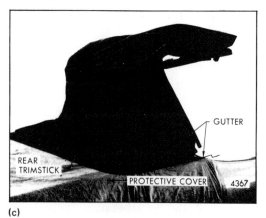

(c)

Figure 19-4 (a) Center bow assembly and rear trimstick attachment; (b) lifting rear trimstick from body; (c) rear trimstick on rear deck of car. *(Courtesy of General Motors Corporation, Fisher Body Division.)*

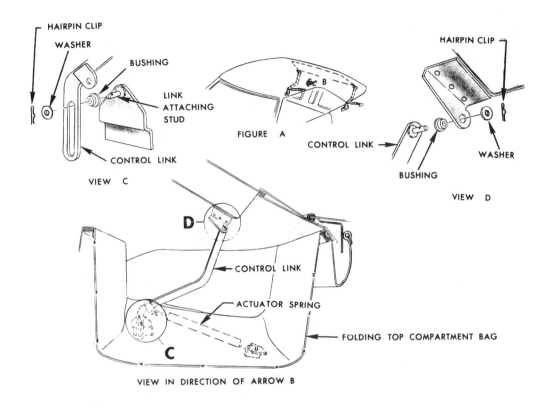

Figure 19-5 Back window guide control link attachment. *(Courtesy of General Motors Corporation, Fisher Body Division.)*

of the plug opening. If the top does not operate properly, the cause may be air trapped in the lines. To bleed the lines, raise the top part way and crack open the lines. Look for small bubbles which are an indication of air in the lines.

Repair or service kits for the pump are available by some manufacturers. If the pump is to be serviced, remove it from the vehicle and drain the fluid into a clean container.

Scribe lines across the motor, pump, and reservoir to aid in correctly positioning the parts during reassembly.

Remove reservoir center bolt and O-ring and remove reservoir cover. Remove bolts that attach valve body to pump body. Remove carefully so as not to lose the check balls. Preferably, use a clean cloth spread on a work bench to avoid losing the small parts. Remove rotors and drive bolts. Clean and inspect parts for wear. Do not soak motor in solvent.

Assemble the parts in reverse order, using new parts and seals as provided in the repair kit, if available. Align the parts with scribed lines and tighten. Fill with clean fluid to within 1/4" (6. 35 mm) of the filler plug hole. Install the pump into the vehicle and connect all lines and wires. Check for operation and refill, if necessary. Wipe up any fluid on the pump or in the area before replacing the seat.

ELECTRIC CABLE UNIT

The electric cable units consist of an electric motor with a gear box attached, two drive cables, and two actuator units which are attached to the top arms (Figure 19-6). The actuator consists of a worm and pinion gear assembly, gear and pinion, and a sector assembly (Figure 19-7).

The electric motor and gear box plus motor relays are mounted in the rear seat back panel. To remove the motor assembly, it is necessary to remove the rear seat cushion and backrest. To remove actuator assembly, lower the top, remove rear seat

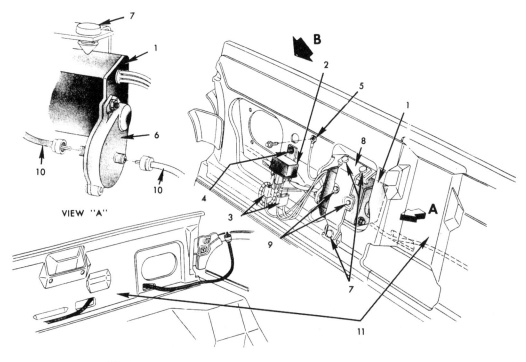

VIEW "A"

VIEW "B"

1. Electric Motor	5. Motor Ground to Seat Back Panel	8. Motor Support
2. Relay	6. Electric Motor Reduction Unit	9. Motor Attaching Screw
3. Electric Motor Connectors	7. Rubber Grommet(s)	10. Drive Cable
4. Relay Attaching Screw		11. Seat Back Panel

Figure 19-6 Folding top electric motor and relay. *(Courtesy of General Motors Corporation, Fisher Body Division.)*

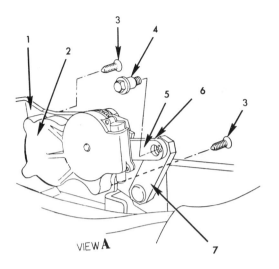

VIEW **A**

1. Main Hinge
2. Top Actuator Assembly
3. Flat-head, Cross-recessed Attaching Screw
4. Shoulder Bolt
5. Actuator Sector Arm
6. Shoulder Bolt Locking Set Screw
7. Side Rail Actuator Link

(a)

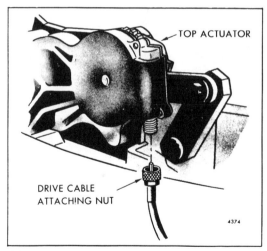

TOP ACTUATOR

DRIVE CABLE ATTACHING NUT

4374

(b)

Figure 19-7 (a) Folding top actuator attachment (view in direction of arrow "A"); (b) drive cable to top actuator attachment. *(Courtesy of General Motors Corporation, Fisher Body Division.)*

and side trim. Disconnect drive cable from actuator assembly and attaching screws. Loosen set screws in side rail actuator links and remove shoulder bolt securing section arm to actuator link. Reinstall in reverse order.

ALIGNMENT

Each make of convertible top may require a different alignment procedure. Some tops

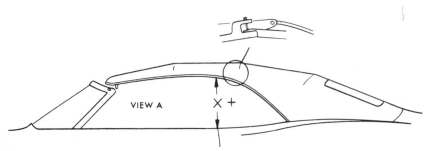

VIEW A

X +

"HIGH SHOULDER CONDITION" CAUSED BY SET SCREW TOO DEEP
LOCATING PIN TOO SHORT

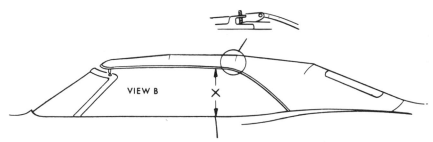

VIEW B

X

"PROPER ADJUSTMENT CONDITION" FOR PROPER SETTING SEE:
"SIDE ROOF RAIL AND LOCATING PIN ADJUSTMENT PROCEDURE"

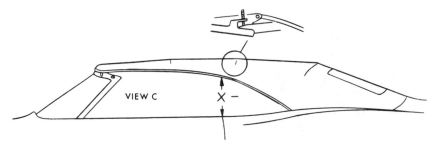

VIEW C

X —

"LOW SHOULDER CONDITION" CAUSED BY SET SCREW NOT DEEP ENOUGH
LOCATING PIN TOO LONG

Figure 19-8   Side roof rail and set-screw adjustment. *(Courtesy of General Motors Corporation, Fisher Body Division.)*

can be aligned by means of a single adjustment while others may require a combination of adjustments.

When the top is raised, the front top rail should align with the guides located on the windshield header or frame. There are different types of guides (such as dowl, pins, or wedges), and some are adjustable. The guide must be aligned in order for the top to lock in position. There are different types of latches or locking hooks. The hooks are adjustable to permit a snug fit when closed and locked.

CAUTION: Do not attempt to lower top unless it is unlocked and the hooks are not in contact with the header. Occasionally, the hooks are not free, and lowering the top results in bent or broken arms (Figure 19–8).

When a top is raised and is off to the left or right of the guides, the problem could be in the main hinge adjustment or control links, depending on the make of vehicle.

When the side roof rails are too high or too low over the side windows, the rail is adjusted by the control link.

On some tops, the side rails are adjusted by means of a set screw adjustment. Because of the different makes and models, a top with major problems in alignment must be carefully examined. The top mechanism should be looked at and the adjustment points located. Then analyze the job in hand and determine what adjustments are necessary. If in doubt, rather than damage the top, consult the service manuals.

Questions

1. Before starting to remove the top covering, what must be done to protect the surrounding area?
2. On some models, what must be used to stabilize the No. 2, No. 3, and No. 4 bow?
3. What must be done first before fastening the cover?
4. What are the two different types of lift mechanism used in convertible tops?
5. Why must the reservoir be vented before removing the hydraulic lines?
6. How can air be removed from the hydraulic lines?
7. How can the motor, pump, and reservoir be reinstalled in the same position?
8. What parts make up the electric cable system?
9. What are guides on the front bow used for?
10. On some tops, what causes the top to shift to one side?

Interior Trim

The interior trim in the modern automobile is made of very durable material or plastic. Many trim pieces are made of formed plastic. These include door trim panels, center post covers, and quarter panel inner trim panels. However, vinyl-covered fiberboard is still used as trim panel.

Each model automobile has available a wide range of interior colors, different materials, and styles, which are made to make them more attractive for sales purposes. The more expensive the model is, the more attractive is the material. The economy model uses less expensive materials.

Because of the large range of materials and types of trim used in the late model automobile, it is impractical to discuss all of the procedures for trim removal and replacing.

Working with interior trim is a major function of the bodyman, and it is his job to safeguard the interior while repairing the body.

NOTE: Because it is necessary to work with the doors opened or removed, the interior trim must be protected from dust, paint spray, and flame from the welding torch.

If the bodyman must work inside the vehicle, especially with white or light colored trim, delicate material seatcovers, or thick light colored floor covering, care must be used not to damage or discolor them. The seats as well as the floor covering should be protected with a clean cover if the repairs call for the bodyman to be in and out of the vehicle numerous times.

The cloths used by the bodyman must be clean — not greasy, solvent soaked, or full of sanding dust. Avoid having sharp objects, such as screwdrivers or any sharp tool, protruding from the pockets.

Shoes must also be clean — not full of grease, sanding dust, or paint specks. Some shops cover the floor mats with newspa-

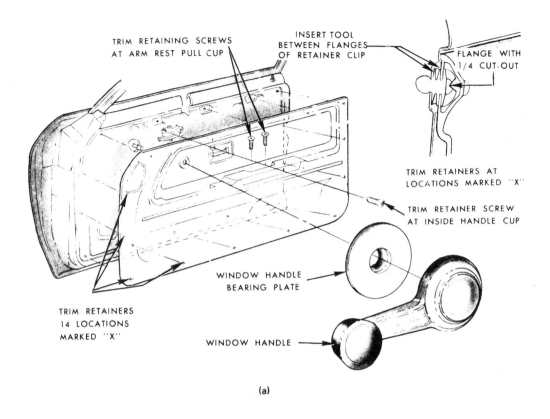

TRIM RETAINING SCREWS
AT ARM REST PULL CUP

INSERT TOOL
BETWEEN FLANGES
OF RETAINER CLIP

FLANGE WITH
1/4 CUT-OUT

TRIM RETAINERS AT
LOCATIONS MARKED "X"

TRIM RETAINER SCREW
AT INSIDE HANDLE CUP

WINDOW HANDLE
BEARING PLATE

WINDOW HANDLE

TRIM RETAINERS
14 LOCATIONS
MARKED "X"

(a)

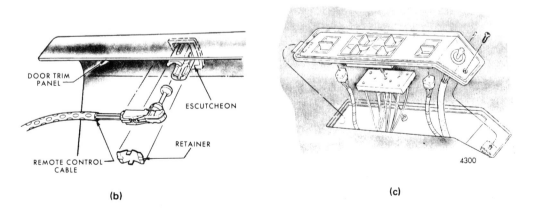

DOOR TRIM
PANEL

ESCUTCHEON

RETAINER

REMOTE CONTROL
CABLE

4300

(b)

(c)

Figure 20-1 (a) Door trim assembly—"H-05, 11, 15 and 77" styles; (b) remote mirror cable attachment—"A-57" style; (c) door armrest switch cover plat and remote mirror cable attachment. *(Courtesy of General Motors Corporation, Fisher Body Division.)*

pers. Never stand cans of solvent, especially lacquer thinner, inside the vehicle or leave solvent-soaked cleaning cloths inside on the seats or floor.

If the interior trim must be removed for the purpose of repairs, store in a safe place away from paint spray or dust.

DOOR TRIM PANELS

The door trim panels are attached to the door by various methods depending on the make of vehicle. Also, there are many different types of trim panels. The procedure for removing the door trim panel will vary somewhat with each make and model.

To remove the trim panel that is equipped with a manual window regulator, the handle must be removed. The handle is held in by either a C-clip, which is removed by a special tool, or a screw which is either exposed or hidden by a metal disc held on by adhesives or plastic plugs (Figures 20-1 and 20-2).

Many vehicles are equipped with pull handles that are secured by rivets, large sheetmetal screws, or by studs (Figure 20-3). Many of these are hidden by a snap-on decoration which can be removed with a flat blade tool. Care must be used when

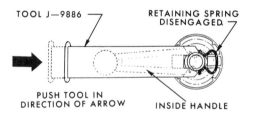

TOOL J—9886

RETAINING SPRING DISENGAGED

PUSH TOOL IN DIRECTION OF ARROW

INSIDE HANDLE

Figure 20-2 Clip retained door inside handle removal. *(Courtesy of General Motors Corporation, Fisher Body Division.)*

removing these escutcheons to avoid breaking off the tabs.

The armrests are either separate from the trim panel or an integral part of the trim panel. The separate armrest is held on by large sheetmetal screws or bolts that are sometimes hidden by a plastic plug (Figures 20-4 and 20-5).

On models with power equipment such as windows and locks, the switch or control panels are mounted in the door trim panels. Care must be used when disassembling the trim panel to avoid damage to the wires and switches. When reassembling, the switches should be checked for operation before the panel is fastened in the trim panel.

In many cases, there are attaching screws for the trim panel underneath the switch panel. There may also be attaching screws in the inside door handle cover or cup.

To remove the trim panel, some of the inside or handles must be removed. Also remote outside mirror controls must be disassembled before removing trim. (Other types are attached directly to the trim panel.) If repairs are necessary to the door, the control must be removed from the trim panel. Be careful not to change the routing of the mirror remote cable (the window glass may catch on the cable).

There may be other options found on trim panels such as stereo speakers or courtesy lights which may have to be removed before the trim panel.

Trim panels themselves are attached by screws, metal or plastic trim fasteners, or clips. Some of the trim panels are attached by clips at the window line or slipped into a strip retainer.

The trim panels are made of vinyl-covered hardboard or molded plastic and can be damaged if not handled properly. The retainers must also be carefully handled. Special tools are used for removing

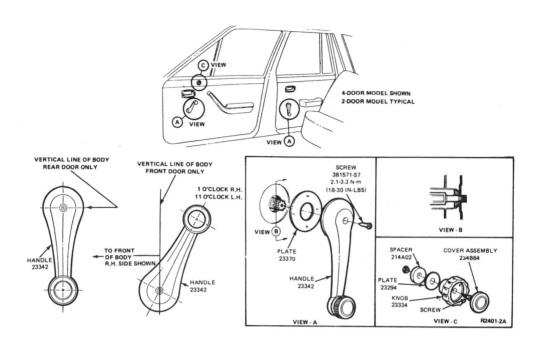

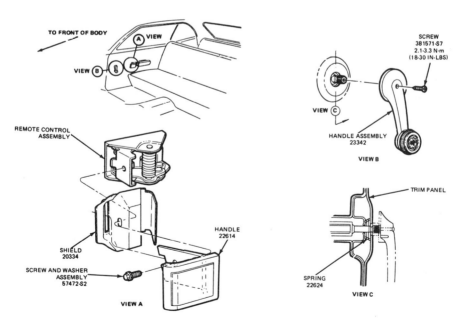

Figure 20-3 Door inside handles. *(Courtesy of Ford Motor Corporation.)*

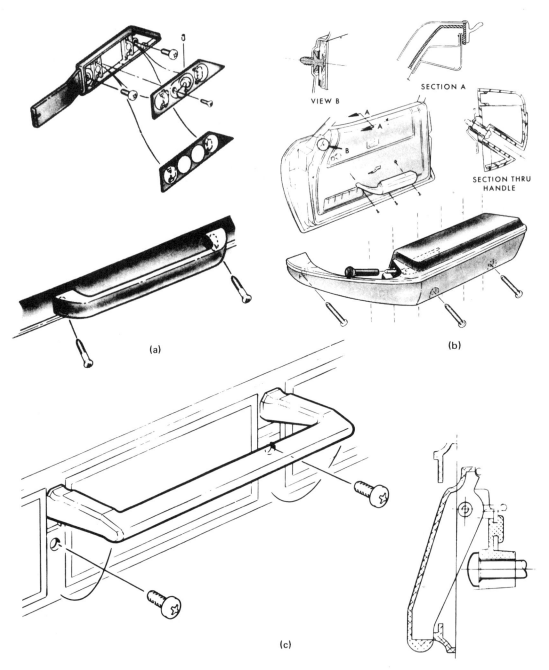

VIEW B

SECTION A

SECTION THRU HANDLE

(a)

(b)

(c)

Figure 20-4 (a) Typical door pull handle attachment; (b) "H-07" door armrest and pull handle—typical attachment for armrests applied after trim installation; (c) typical door pull handle attachment. *(Courtesy of General Motors Corporation, Fisher Body Division.)*

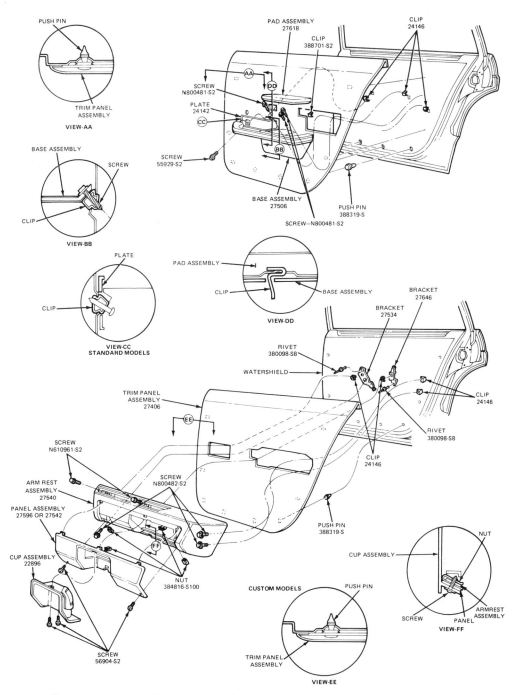

Figure 20-5 Rear door trim panel and armrest—Ford/Mercury. *(Courtesy of Ford Motor Corporation.)*

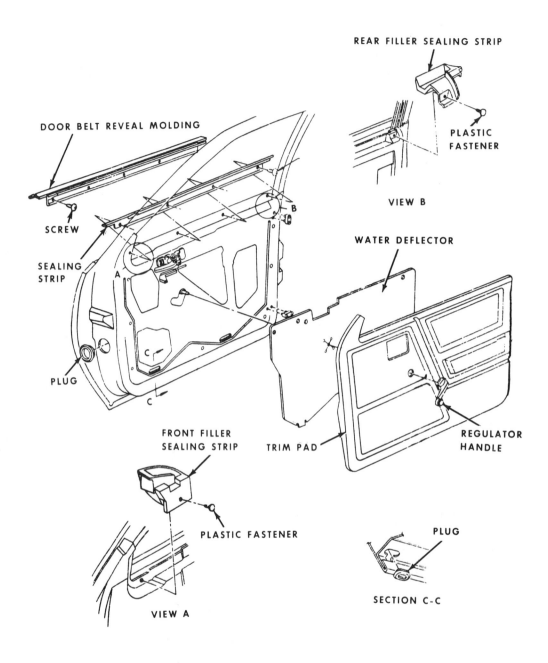

Figure 20-6 Front door sealing components. *(Courtesy of General Motors Corporation, Chevrolet Motor Division.)*

some types of plastic retainers to avoid breaking them.

On some models there are small coil springs behind the trim panel on the window and inside door handle shaft. Be careful not to lose them or forget to put them back when installing the trim panel. They are used to keep the trim panel in close contact with the inside handle for appearance purposes.

On some models the inside lock rod and knob protrude through the trim panel at the top, and the knob must be removed in order to remove the trim.

When reinstalling the trim panel, be sure that the water shield is in place and properly sealed to avoid water damage to the trim panel. The trim panel must be properly aligned and all of the retainers in place. Avoid too much pressure when snapping the panel in place and make sure the panel is attached properly. Replace the screws in the right location. (Figure 20-6).

When replacing the inside handles, don't forget the escutcheon plate behind the handle. Install the handle in the same position as before. If in doubt, check the opposite door for location. After the trim and accessories are in place, check door for operation including the mirror, power window, locks, and so on. Before leaving the vehicle, wipe the trim panel clean as well as the windows and chrome. Avoid leaving fingerprints and trademarks behind.

TRIM PARTS

During the course of body repairs, other trim panels or trim parts must be removed for body repair. The various types of trim parts, such as center post trim covers, quarter trim panels, roof side trim panels,

and others are attached or fastened by many different types of clips and fasteners, such as push pins or interlocking panels (Figure 20-7). If these panels have to be removed without the use of a service manual, examine them for hidden screws or clips and do not exert too much force when trying to detach the trim as the trim may crack or break (Figure 20-8). Some panels require special tools to release the retainer (Figure 20-8).

Place all of the screws and small pieces in a suitable container to avoid losing them. Some of the special clips are hard to replace and time is lost trying to find them or to find something suitable to substitute for the original.

If water seal is used behind the trim panel (as in the quarter trim panel) and is removed for repair, replace properly. A water leak could result in damage to the interior trim.

On many of the two-door models and some four-door models, in order to remove the quarter panel and rear quarter lock pillar trim panels, it is necessary to remove the rear seat cushion and backrest.

REMOVING REAR SEATS

Many times, the trim screws are inaccessible because of the placement of the seats, and some bodymen wonder why the trim panel cannot be removed. The rear seat cushion, except on station wagons, is secured in position by either the cushion frame wire or cushion spring element, locking into a retainer or bracket in the floor pan. Some cushions are secured by sheetmetal bolts which attach the cushion to a floor-mounted bracket (Figure 20-9).

To remove the cushion with floor retainers, push the forward edge of the cushion

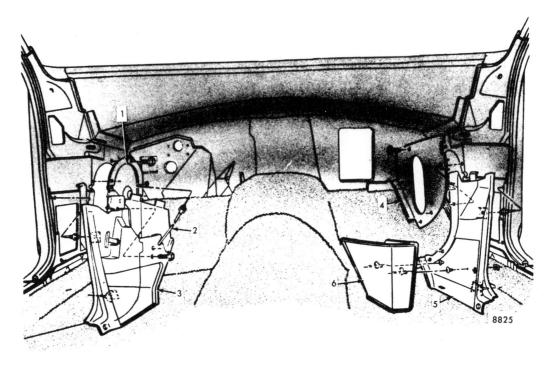

1. Shroud Side Cover
   Assembly (Left Side)
2. Hood Release Cable
   Assembly
3. Shroud Side Trim
   Panel

4. Side Duct Panel and
   Door Assembly (Right
   Side)

5. Rear Shroud Side
   Trim Panel (Right
   Side)
6. Litter Container

(a)

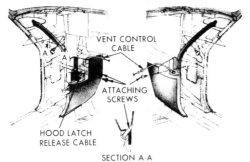

VENT CONTROL
CABLE

ATTACHING
SCREWS

HOOD LATCH
RELEASE CABLE

SECTION A-A

(b)

Figure 20-7 (a) Front end component identification; (b) shroud side finishing panels—E styles. *(Courtesy of General Motors Corporation, Fisher Body Division.)*

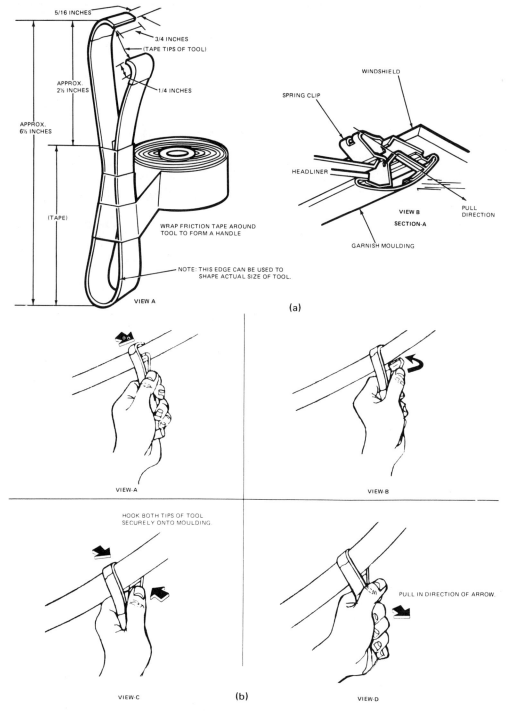

Figure 20-8 (a) Molding section and tool fabrication; (b) molding removal. *(Courtesy of Ford Motor Corporation.)*

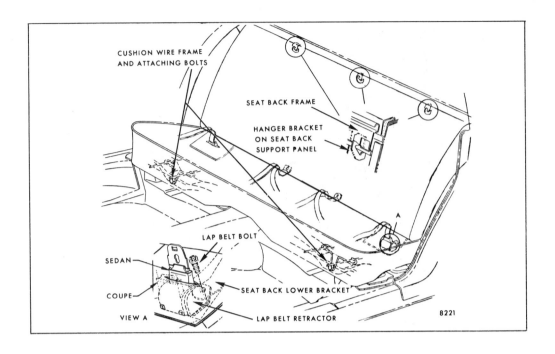

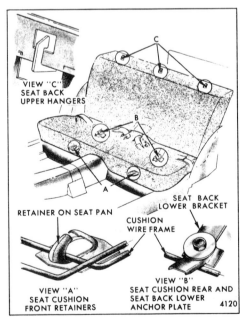

Figure 20-9 (a) Rear seat cushion and back installation—all A styles except station wagons; (b) rear seat cushion and seat back—H-27 styles. *(Courtesy of General Motors Corporation, Fisher Body Division.)*

toward the rear and lift. If the cushion does not disengage, it may be necessary to apply pressure with the knees to release the wire from the retainer. Also, while exerting pressure with the arm, tap the lower front part of the cushion with a cloth-wrapped rubber mallet to disengage the spring wire (Figure 20-10). Place the cushion in a clean safe place on a blanket.

The rear backrest is secured in different ways. Some seats are held in place by lap belt retractor bolts passing through a metal tab attached to the seat. Some rear backrests are secured by sheetmetal bolts that attach a metal cushion tab or a cushion wire loop to a bracket in the floor pan.

On some two-door models, it is necessary to remove one of the armrests in order to remove the backrest cushion. To remove the backrest, pull the bottom of the backrest cushion out and lift up to disengage the backrest from the upper hangers or hooks.

Remove the backrest using care not to damage the interior trim. To install seats, follow procedure in reverse, except lower cushion. Cushion should be pushed back under the backrest and hooked on to the retainers.

QUARTER TRIM PANELS

Quarter trim panels will vary with different makes and models and the procedure for removal will vary. The trim panels are attached by an assortment of clips, screws, and interlocking panels (Figure 20-11). On some models, after the rear seat cushions are removed, the back window garnish molding is removed. The roof side molding is then taken off (using a fabricated special tool) followed by the package tray trim panel and the quarter trim panel.

Many of the trim panels that have removable armrests are rather easy to disassemble and only involve several sheetmetal screws and a few clips. Other armrests are an integral part of the panel.

NOTE: A special tool is required to remove the ashtray assembly on some GM models in order to gain access to the trim panel clips (Figure 20-12).

Many of the quarter trim or finishing panels on the lock pillar require the removal of the door sill trim panel (Figure 20-13). On the front end of the panel (by the quarter panel pinch weld) some trim panels slip over the pinch weld or use a clinch-type finish strip that slips over the edge of the trim panel and pinch weld (Figure 20-13). Without the proper service manual, the trim panels must be examined closely for the best method of removal because many of the retainers are hidden from view (Figures 20-14 and 20-15). This also holds true for any other trim panel, as different ones appear every year with each make or model. Many of the retainers are made of plastic, and all are rather fragile.

HEADLININGS

The headlining or interior trim attached to the roof is either a cloth type held in place by listing wires (or rods) or a formed type. (Figures 20-16 and 20-17). The formed type can consist of one piece or it can have two or more sections joined together by plastic strips. To remove the formed type, a certain amount of hardware and trim pieces must also be removed such as the domelight, sun visors, shoulder belt retractors, or any other hardware (Figure 20-18). Depending on make and model, the windshield garnish molding, roof side trim, rear

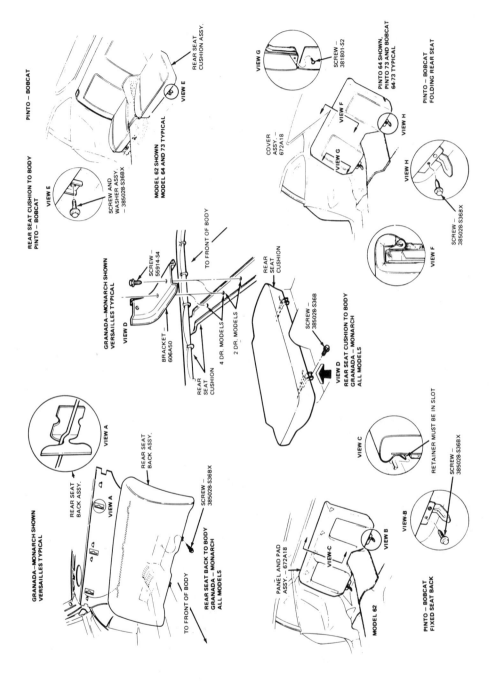

Figure 20-10 Rear seat back and cushion installation—Pinto/Bobcat, Granada/Monarch, Versailles. *(Courtesy of Ford Motor Corporation.)*

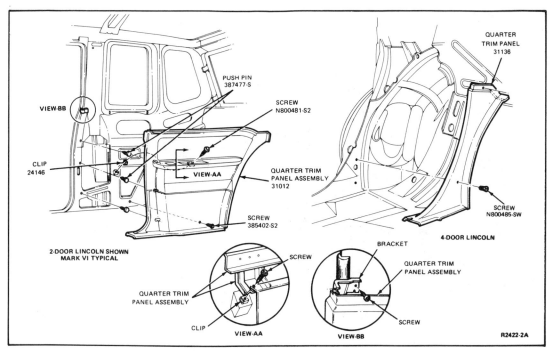

(a)

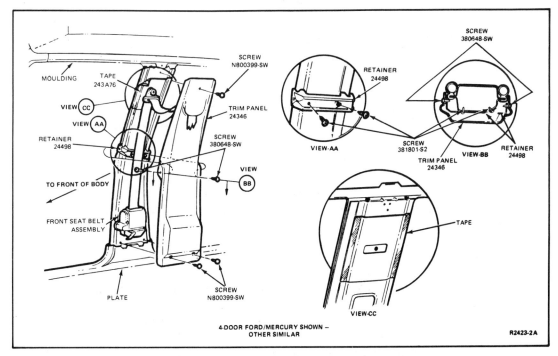

(b)

Figure 20-11 (a) Quarter trim panel—Lincoln/Continental Mark VI; (b) center pillar trim panel—Ford/Mercury. *(Courtesy of Ford Motor Corporation.)*

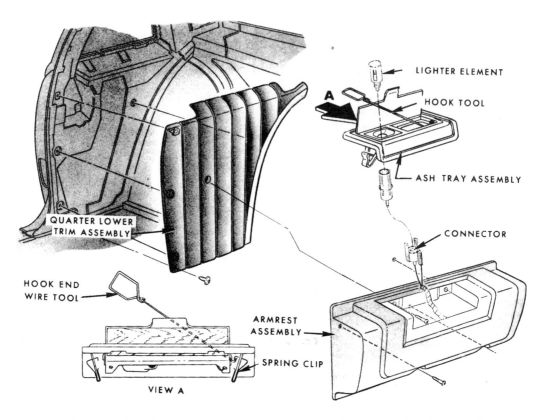

Figure 20-12 Quarter armrest attachment—C and 4BZ37 styles. *(Courtesy of General Motors Corporation, Fisher Body Division.)*

window garnish molding, and at times, the rear quarter trim panels must be removed.

Underneath the trim panels are retainers or clips used to hold the headlining in place. After the retainers are removed, the headlining is shifted to one side and removed.

To install, attach domelight first to hold in position, then install the retainers. Do not bend the edges too far when removing and installing the headlining as it may crack.

Cement with nonstaining adhesive if necessary and install the necessary trim and hardware. There may be other methods of removing and installing formed headlinings. Consult service manuals.

There are various methods of removing and installing cloth headlining using listing wires or rods. The listing wires are used to shape the headlining to the contour of the roof (Figure 20-19). They hold the headlining by means of listing wire pockets or sleeves which are sewn to the back of the headlining at the seams or joints of the lining sections or panels. Each listing wire is color coded to match the color-coded bracket or tab located on the sides of the roof rails.

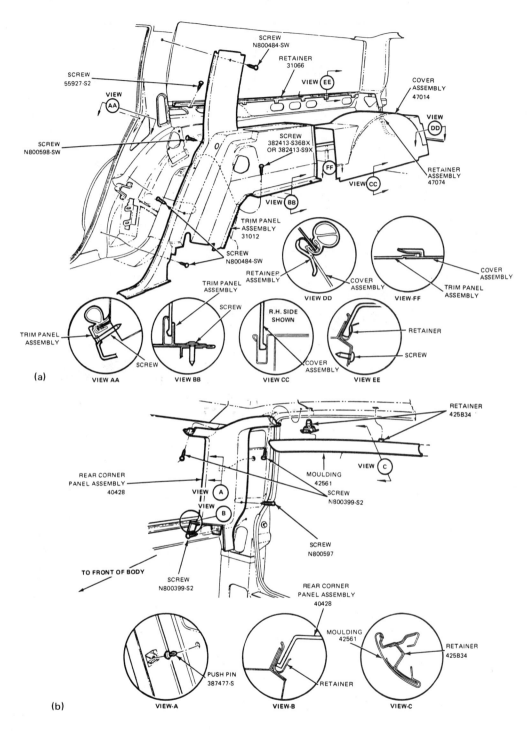

Figure 20-13 (a) Quarter trim panel—Ford/Mercury station wagon; (b) rear corner panel—Ford/Mercury station wagon. *(Courtesy of Ford Motor Corporation.)*

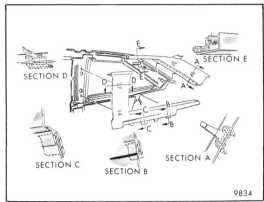

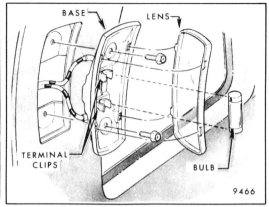

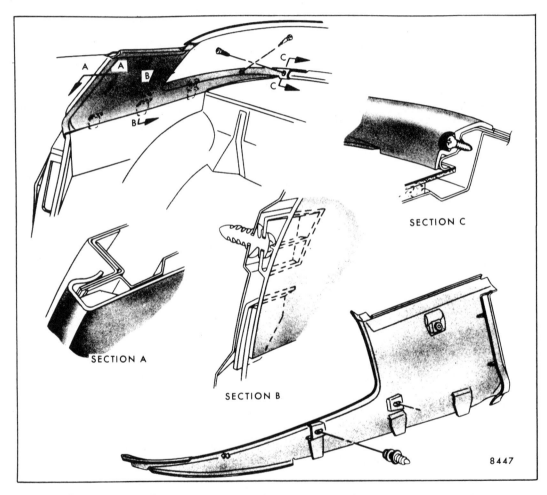

Figure 20-14 Quarter upper trim. *(Courtesy of General Motors Corporation, Fisher Body Division.)*

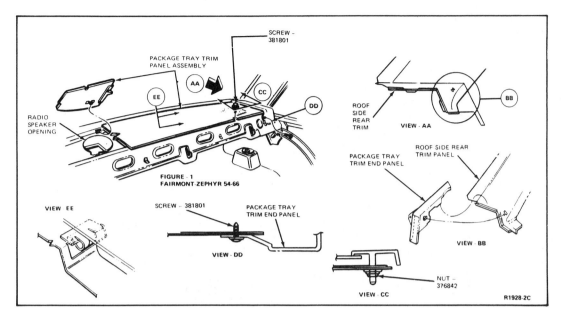

Figure 20-15   Package tray trim panel—Fairmont/Zephyr. *(Courtesy of Ford Motor Corporation.)*

It is very important to install the listing wires in the correct places. This may affect the tightness of the headlining, especially if the wires are of different lengths. The wires are often stabilized in the roof inner panels by means of retainers.

Another type of headlining uses rectangular lugs sewn to the headlining, and these fit into slots located in the roof inner panel. Some headlinings use retaining brackets which are attached to either the front or rear listing wire. In this case, the headlining is drawn securely in the reverse direction to remove wrinkles.

The headlining removal procedure depends on which area of the headlining needs to be removed or partially removed to permit necessary body work. If the headlining is to be changed, the procedure will be different in various makes and models.

Some models require that the windshield and rear window be removed in order to fasten the front and rear ends of the headlining. On other models, where finishing lace or strips are used by the front and rear window, the headlining is cemented in these places. Tack strips are used in the roof extension or rear upper quarter panel, and the headlining is either stapled or tacked in place (Figure 20-20).

On the sides or the roof rail area, the headlining is either cemented to the body or attached to pronged retainers or saw tooth retainers.

Procedure for Removing Headlining

The following is the general procedure for removing headlining. Before starting, cover the front seat with a clean, protective cover. The floor carpet should also be covered if necessary. Place the vehicle in a

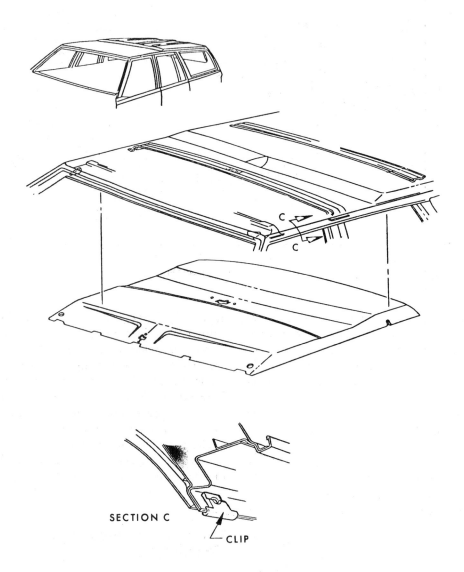

SECTION C

CLIP

Figure 20-16 Headlining front section assembly—B-35 style (A-35 similar).
Courtesy of General Motors Corporation, Fisher Body Division.)

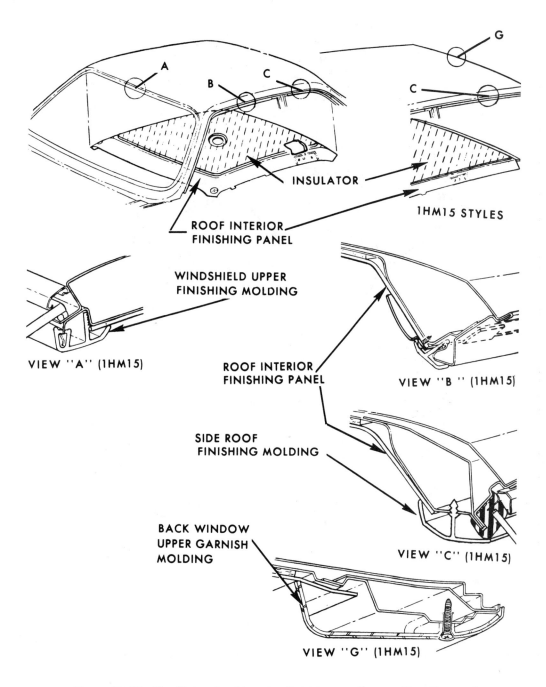

G

A

C

B

C

INSULATOR

1HM15 STYLES

ROOF INTERIOR
FINISHING PANEL

WINDSHIELD UPPER
FINISHING MOLDING

VIEW "A" (1HM15)

ROOF INTERIOR
FINISHING PANEL

VIEW "B" (1HM15)

SIDE ROOF
FINISHING MOLDING

BACK WINDOW
UPPER GARNISH
MOLDING

VIEW "C" (1HM15)

VIEW "G" (1HM15)

Figure 20–17 Headlining (roof interior finishing panel) assembly—H-15 styles.
(Courtesy of General Motors Corporation, Fisher Body Division.)

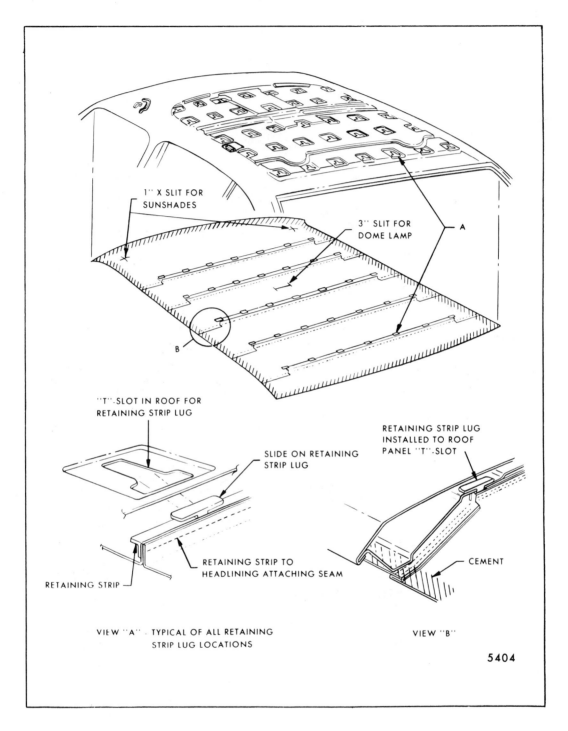

1'' X SLIT FOR SUNSHADES

3'' SLIT FOR DOME LAMP

A

B

"T"-SLOT IN ROOF FOR RETAINING STRIP LUG

SLIDE ON RETAINING STRIP LUG

RETAINING STRIP LUG INSTALLED TO ROOF PANEL "T"-SLOT

RETAINING STRIP TO HEADLINING ATTACHING SEAM

RETAINING STRIP

CEMENT

VIEW "A" - TYPICAL OF ALL RETAINING STRIP LUG LOCATIONS

VIEW "B"

5404

Figure 20-18   Typical cloth headlining installation—K style. *(Courtesy of General Motors Corporation, Fisher Body Division.)*

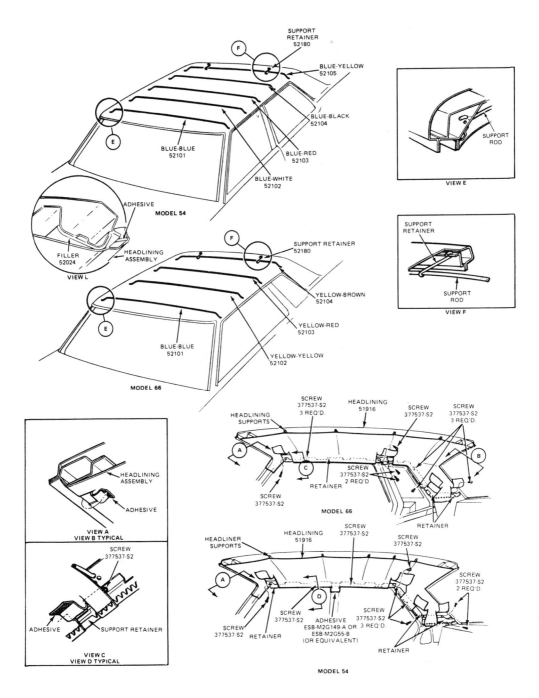

Figure 20-19 Headlining—Granada/Monarch. *(Courtesy of Ford Motor Corporation.)*

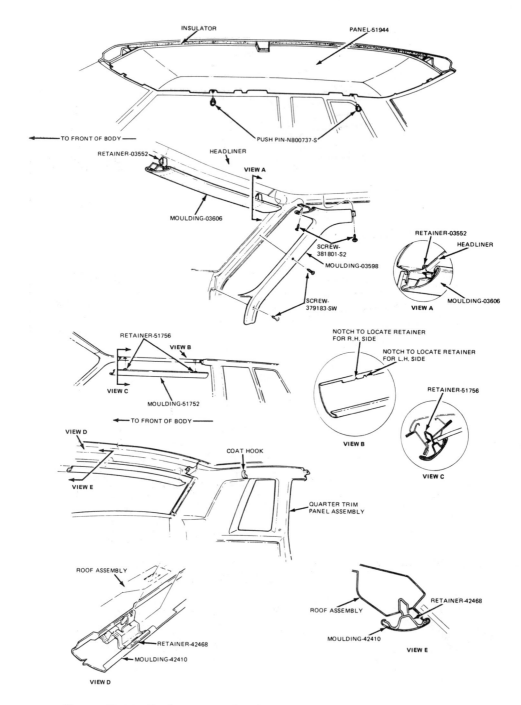

Figure 20-20 Roof trim panel—Thunderbird/Cougar XR-7 w/o sun roof. *(Courtesy of Ford Motor Corporation.)*

clean area to avoid tracking in dirt or grease. The bodyman working on the headlining should wear clean clothes. Remove the necessary hardware including sun visors, shoulder belt retractors, domelight, and any trim necessary such as windshield, back window garnish moldings, and quarter panel roof extensions. Remove staples from windshield area and rear quarter roof panel. If the headlining is to be reinstalled, careful removal of the headlining from the pronged retainers with a putty knife or similar tool is necessary. Avoid tearing material on headlining that is cemented. Starting from the front, first detach the lining from the roof retainer and disengage the listing wires from the roof rails. Continue on to the rear. To keep the material clean, roll the headlining up with the listing wires on the outside. On some models start in the front and then move to the rear and work forward. The direction will depend on the make or model.

Installation

To install a new headlining, place old lining on a clean table and stretch out the new lining. Cut the listing wire pockets the same length as the old lining and transfer the listing wires in the corresponding pockets of the new lining. Install listing wires, one at a time, to avoid mixing them up, especially if the color codes are not recognizable. To install, either the old or new, install listing wires in the reverse procedure from removal. Center the material and be sure that the wires are secured in the retainers. If the wires are not firmly against the roof, they can be adjusted.

Attach headlining at the windshield by staples or cement whichever is applicable to the particular model. Stretch lining and attach at rear window area using the original

method. Be sure that the headlining is tight and without wrinkles.

Attach headlining to the roof rails by the method selected; also the rear quarter section, where applicable (Figures 20-21 and 20-22). Remove all draws and wrinkles and replace necessary trim and hardware. Some new holes must be made to attach the hardware. Check with old headlining, then feel area to locate the proper holes. If lining is satisfactory, clean where necessary including other areas such as dashboard and package tray. If the windshield and rear window were installed thoroughly clean the glass and exterior of the vehicle.

FRONT SEAT SERVICE

There are many different types of front seat assemblies. They vary not only in construction but in style — full bench, buckets, reclining, and the like. Also, there are many different types of seat mechanisms such as manual and four-way manual, and four- and six-way power seats (Figure 20-23).

Many times, front seats must be removed either for repairs or because of body damage. Generally full bench and bucket seats anchor to the floor pan by either bolts or studs at both ends of the seat tracks. To remove the seat, depending on the make or model, requires removing the seat belt or shoulder retractor or anchors. The scuff or sill plates are removed so that the carpet or floor mat can be moved to gain access to the seat track bolts. Some seats can be removed without moving the carpet, but others are unbolted from underneath the floor pan.

Remove seat or lap belts where applicable or unbolt them from floor if seat repairs are not required. Seats that are bolted from the top of the floor pan must be

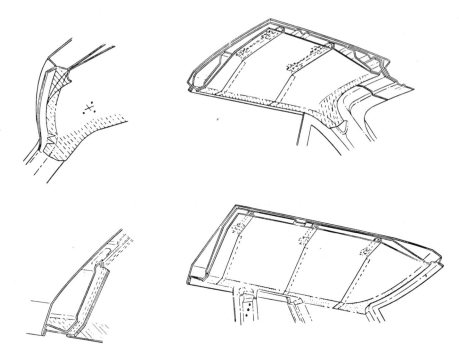

Figure 20-21 Typical trim cement application to headlining. *(Courtesy of General Motors Corporation, Fisher Body Division.)*

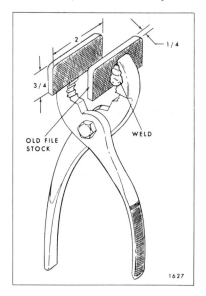

Figure 20-22 Fabric roof cover pliers. *(Courtesy of General Motors Corporation, Fisher Body Division.)*

moved to the maximum forward position and the rear end of the track unbolted. Move the seat rearward to the maximum position and unbolt the forward end of the track (Figures 20-24 and 20-25).

If any electrical components are present, disconnect by tipping the seat backwards to gain access to the connectors. With a helper, remove seat assembly from the vehicle using care not to damage the interior trim. When installing the seat assembly, connect the wiring and be sure to put back any shims that were there before the seat was removed (Figure 20-26). Sometimes shims or even wooden blocks are added to raise the seat assembly to suit the owners liking.

To remove the tracks from the lower cushion, remove the nuts or bolts on both ends of the track by shifting the track for-

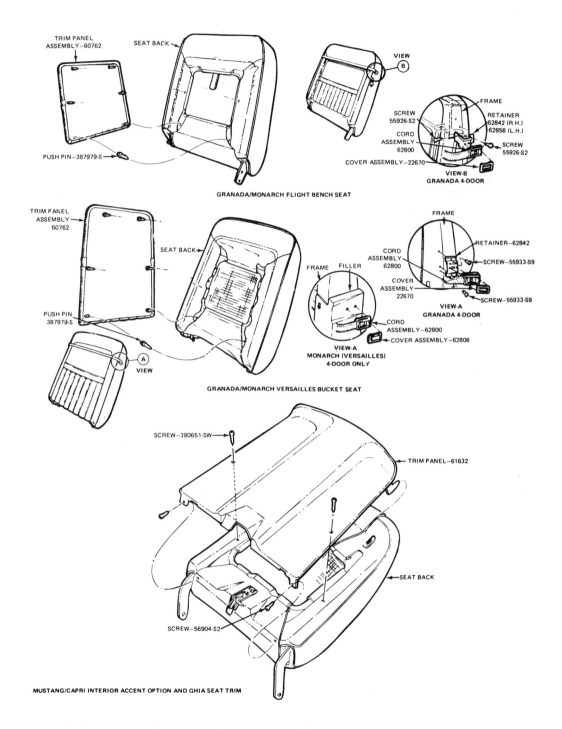

TRIM PANEL
ASSEMBLY–60762

SEAT BACK

PUSH PIN–387979-S

VIEW
B

FRAME

SCREW
55926-S2

RETAINER
62842 (R.H.)
62858 (L.H.)

CORD
ASSEMBLY
62800

SCREW
55926-S2

COVER ASSEMBLY–22670

VIEW-B
GRANADA 4-DOOR

GRANADA/MONARCH FLIGHT BENCH SEAT

TRIM PANEL
ASSEMBLY
60762

SEAT BACK

PUSH PIN
387979-S

A
VIEW

FRAME

CORD
ASSEMBLY
62800

COVER
ASSEMBLY
22670

RETAINER–62842

SCREW–55933-S9

SCREW–55933-S9

VIEW-A
GRANADA 4-DOOR

FRAME   FILLER

CORD
ASSEMBLY–62800

COVER ASSEMBLY–62808

VIEW-A
MONARCH (VERSAILLES)
4-DOOR ONLY

GRANADA/MONARCH VERSAILLES BUCKET SEAT

SCREW–380651-SW

TRIM PANEL–61632

SEAT BACK

SCREW–56904-S2

MUSTANG/CAPRI INTERIOR ACCENT OPTION AND GHIA SEAT TRIM

Figure 20-23 Front seat back—trim panel installation. *(Courtesy of Ford Motor Corporation.)*

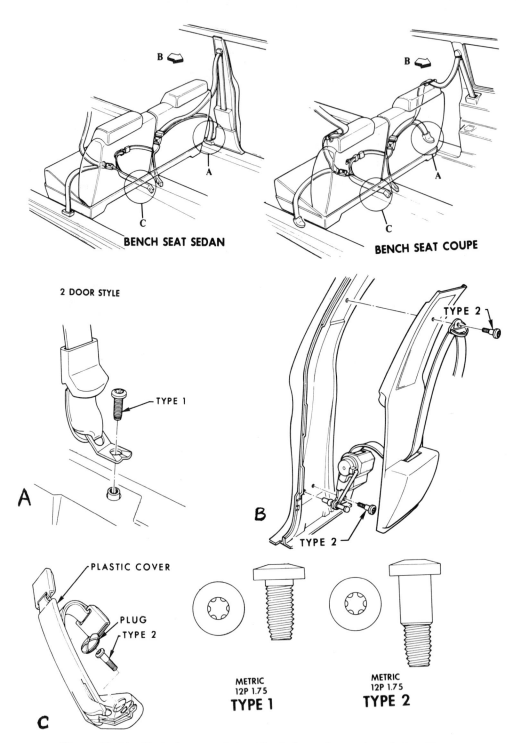

BENCH SEAT SEDAN

BENCH SEAT COUPE

2 DOOR STYLE

TYPE 2

TYPE 1

A

TYPE 2

B

TYPE 2

PLASTIC COVER

PLUG
TYPE 2

C

METRIC
12P 1.75
TYPE 1

METRIC
12P 1.75
TYPE 2

Figure 20-24 Typical seat and shoulder belts with attaching bolts. *(Courtesy of General Motors Corporation, Fisher Body Division.)*

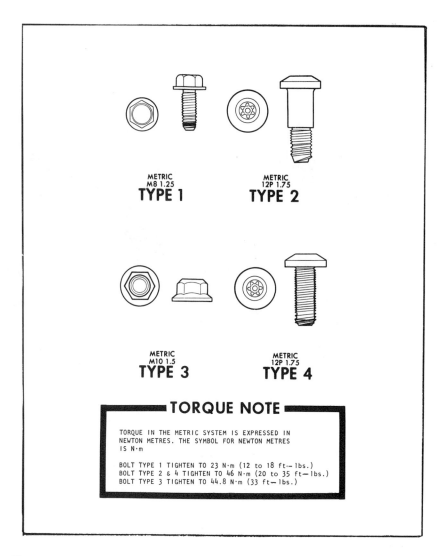

Figure 20-25 Front and rear seat shoulder and lap belt anchor bolts. *(Courtesy of General Motors Corporation, Fisher Body Division.)*

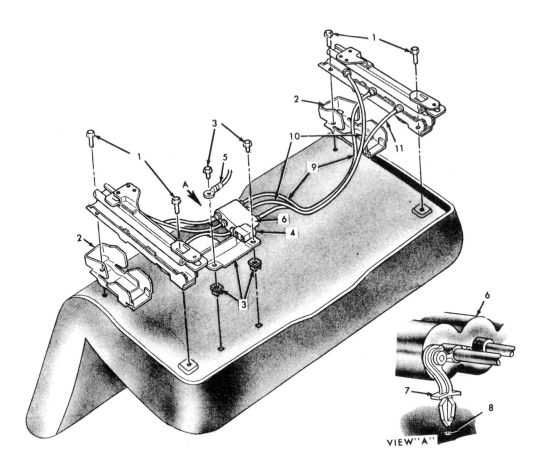

1. Adjuster-to-Seat
   Frame Attaching
   Bolts
2. Adjuster Track Rear
   Covers
3. Transmission and
   Motor Support
   Attaching Screws
   and Push-In Nuts

4. Motor Relay
5. Ground Wire
6. Transmission
   Assembly
7. Transmission
   Stabilizer Support
8. Hole in Seat Frame
   for Stabilizer Support

9. Horizontal Drive
   Cable (Black)
10. Rear Vertical Drive
    Cable (Blue)
11. Front Vertical Drive
    Cable (Red)

Figure 20-26 A, B and C style power six-way seat adjusters—full width seat.
(Courtesy of General Motors Corporation, Fisher Body Division.)

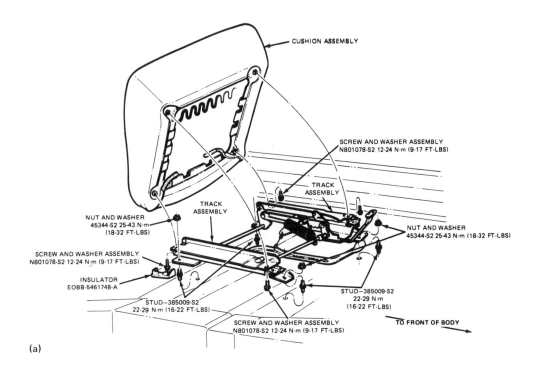

(a)

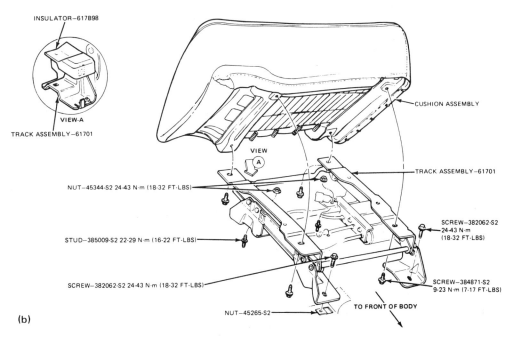

(b)

Figure 20-27 (a) 4-way manual track bucket driver's seat—Mustang/Capri; (b) 6-way power seat tracks split bench—Versailles. *(Courtesy of Ford Motor Corporation.)*

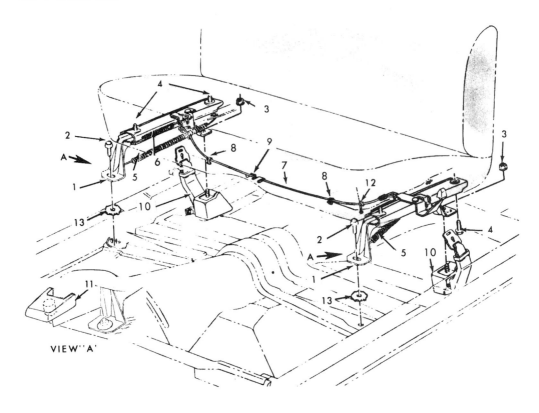

1. Adjuster Assembly	5. Adjuster Assist	8. Locking Wire-to-Seat	11. Adjuster-to-Floor Pan
2. Adjuster-to-Floor Pan	Spring	Frame Hog-Ring	Bolt Covers - Front
Front Bolts	6. Adjuster Lock Bar	Loops	Only
3. Adjuster-to-Lap Belt	Spring	9. Locking Wire-to-Seat	12. Locking Wire Tension
Retractor Nuts	7. Adjuster Locking	Frame Retainer	Hook
4. Adjuster-to-Seat	Wire	10. Lap Belt Retractor	13. Carpet Retainer
Frame Bolts			

Figure 20-28 X style manually operated full width seat and adjusters. *(Courtesy of General Motors Corporation, Fisher Body Division.)*

ward and removing rear bolts or nuts. Then move the track rearward to remove the forward bolts or nuts. With bench seats, the locking wire or rod must be disconnected when removing a track. The manual seat tracks generally require thorough lubrication for proper operation. New tracks may require removal of some of the sharp edges or burrs from manufacturing that restrict the locking mechanism or track movement (Figures 20-27 and 20-28).

Because some of the power seat mechanisms are quite complicated, the service manual should be used for checking the operation, unless it is quite obvious that a cable is bad or the current is not getting to the motor.

Seat Covers

At times, it is necessary to change the seat cover for seat frame repairs or to replace defective covers. To remove cover on front backrest, the head restraint must be removed by the use of a special tool or a thin strip of metal (Figure 20-29). Some restraints just lift out.

With the seat upsidedown on clean blankets, remove side trim covers. Depending on the made and model, remove hog rings on the backrest tab from cushion. Remove lock pin or bolts to separate the

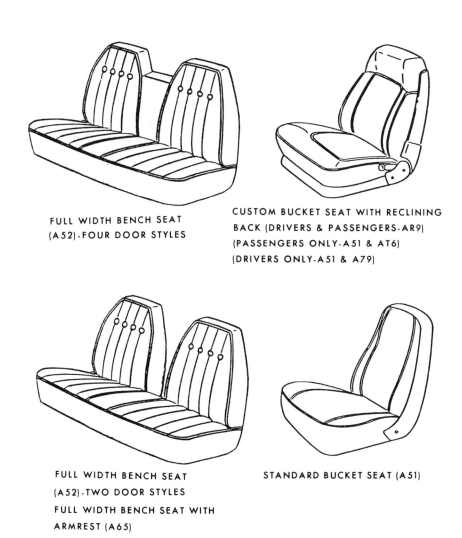

FULL WIDTH BENCH SEAT
(A52)-FOUR DOOR STYLES

CUSTOM BUCKET SEAT WITH RECLINING
BACK (DRIVERS & PASSENGERS-AR9)
(PASSENGERS ONLY-A51 & AT6)
(DRIVERS ONLY-A51 & A79)

FULL WIDTH BENCH SEAT
(A52)-TWO DOOR STYLES
FULL WIDTH BENCH SEAT WITH
ARMREST (A65)

STANDARD BUCKET SEAT (A51)

Figure 20-29   Types of front seat. *(Courtesy of General Motors Corporation, Chevrolet Motor Division.)*

two assemblies. Generally, the covers are attached by hog rings at the bottom of the backrest and slip off the cover.

On some bucket seats, remove the panel on the back of the backrest to expose retainers. On the bench seat cushion and the rear cushion, the covers are attached to the frame by means of hog rings. For addi- tional information, consult the service manual because of the many options on the modern vehicle.

When working on seats, especially those with light colored trim, keep the covers as clean as possible. After the seats are installed, clean up with a suitable cleaner.

Questions

1. What precautions are necessary to prevent soiling interior trim while working inside the automobile?
2. Where should interior trim be stored while working inside the automobile?
3. How are some of the interior door handles held in place?
4. Should the power switches be checked before fastening the trim panels?
5. What methods are used to fasten trim panels to the inside of doors?
6. Why is it important to place all of the small trim pieces and hardware in a safe place?
7. What two methods are used to hold the rear seat cushion in place?
8. Why is it necessary to remove one armrest before removing some rear backrest cushions?
9. What is the result of careless removal of interior trim panels?
10. Name two types of headlining?
11. What are *listing* or *support wires* (or *rods*)?
12. Why is it important to install the support or list wires (or rods) in the correct position?
13. Where should the vehicle be placed before starting to remove the headlining?
14. How are the front seats attached to the floor panel?
15. For what reasons may a seat track not operate?
16. What are hog rings used for?

Many times the bodyman is required to work on vinyl tops either to install a new quarter panel, to replace a torn or worn out top cover, or to add a vinyl top cover to a customer's vehicle.

The vinyl top covers are made of a special material coated with plastic vinyl. They cover the entire roof area or a section of the roof panel. On some models, the vinyl cover is cemented directly to the roof panel. Other models use a foam pad which is cemented to the roof panel, and the vinyl cover is cemented to the foam pad.

The ends of the covers at the windshield and back window opening are held in place by either drive nails, reveal molding retainer clips, and/or adhesive cement. Also, the window reveal molding tends to hold the edge of the cover down (Figure 21-1).

The edges of the vinyl cover below the rear window or edges of the half-covers are concealed by molding attached to clips on welded studs (Figure 21-2). The sides or the drip edge areas are cemented and covered with a drip edge molding or cover. Some use various other methods of securing the edges, depending on the vehicle's make, model, and style (Figure 21-3). Some models use additional trim strips over the vinyl covers for decorative purposes.

In cases involving replacing a quarter panel where the panel joint will be just underneath the edge of the vinyl or if the metal is buckled under the vinyl cover, the cover must be carefully removed. Depending on the area involved, the necessary molding or trim must be removed. Using a heat gun, heat up the edges of the vinyl cover to aid in loosening it from the body panel.

CAUTION: Do not get the vinyl too hot as it may lose its grain texture, blister, or become shiny. Do not use excessive force as the vinyl cover may be torn or stretched.

Remove the cover well beyond the joint of repair to avoid damaging it by either the

Vinyl Top Covers

chapter 21

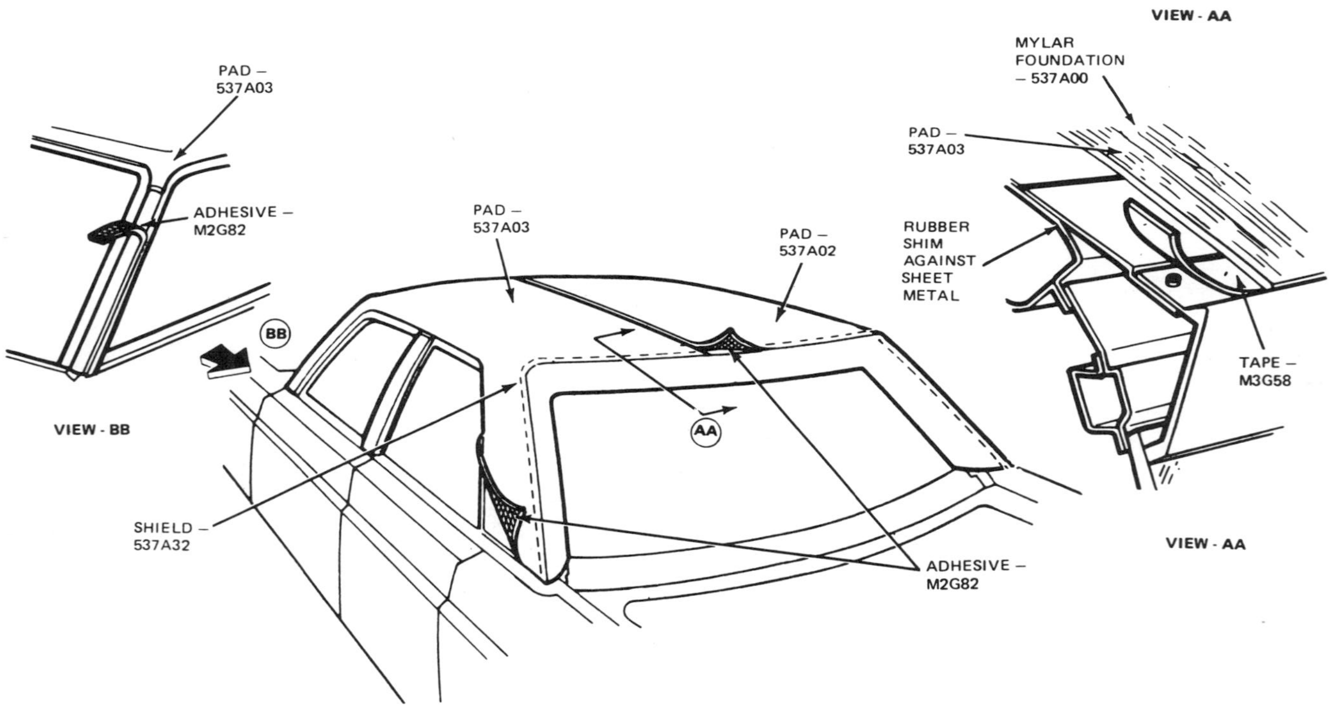

VIEW - AA

TAPE –
M3G58

MYLAR
FOUNDATION
– 537 A00

PAD –
537A03

RUBBER
SHIM
AGAINST
SHEET
METAL

VIEW - AA

PAD –
537A02

ADHESIVE –
M2G82

AA

PAD –
537A03

WITH COVER REMOVED

PAD –
537A03

ADHESIVE –
M2G82

BB

SHIELD –
537A32

VIEW - BB

354

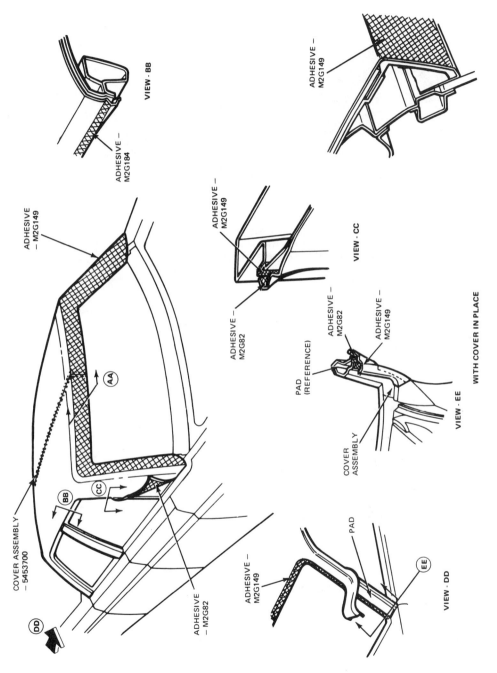

Figure 21-1 Roof outside cover installation—Versailles. *(Courtesy of Ford Motor Corporation.)*

ADHESIVE – M2G149

VIEW - BB

ADHESIVE – M2G184

ADHESIVE – M2G149

VIEW - CC

ADHESIVE – M2G82

COVER ASSEMBLY – 5453700

AA

BB

CC

DD

ADHESIVE – M2G82

ADHESIVE – M2G149

PAD (REFERENCE)

ADHESIVE – M2G82

ADHESIVE – M2G149

COVER ASSEMBLY

VIEW - EE

WITH COVER IN PLACE

ADHESIVE – M2G149

PAD

VIEW - DD

EE

355

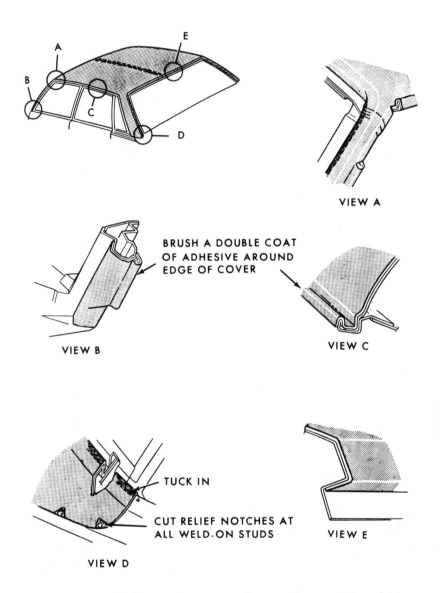

Figure 21-2 Typical fabric roof cover installation. *(Courtesy of General Motors Corporation, Fisher Body Division.)*

torch or power tools. With the vinyl loose, fold it back and insert some clean cloths in the area of the crease to avoid getting sharp creases in the vinyl if the repairs involve a long period of time.

If necessary, cover the edge of the vinyl cover with wet towels or wet asbestos to avoid overheating it.

After completing the body work, the area must be painted. Be sure that the body

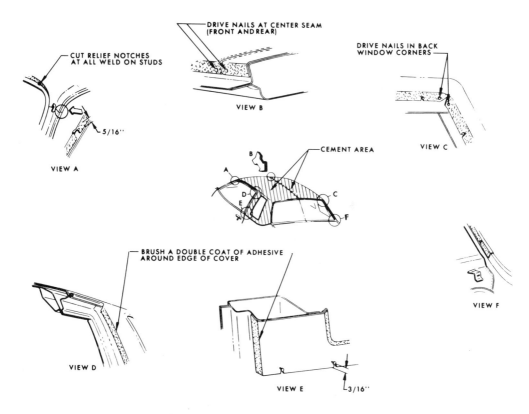

Figure 21-3 Fabric roof cover installation. *(Courtesy of General Motors Corporation, Fisher Body Division.)*

work is smooth as it will show when the cover is replaced.

NOTE: When painting, do not permit surface cleaners or paint solvents to come in contact with the vinyl as it may damage it. The paint must be thoroughly dried because any solvents in the paint will have to evaporate through the vinyl cover and could cause the vinyl to blister.

Apply the recommended adhesive and reattach the vinyl cover in its original position (Figure 21-4). Avoid getting the adhesive on the surrounding area. Mask area if necessary.

Use a heat gun to remove the wrinkles or creases. Hold it 1" to 2" (25.4 mm to 50.8 mm) from the cover and rotate the gun in a circular motion. Avoid overheating the cover. Heat lamps can be used also, but not closer than 18" (457.2 mm) from the surface of the vinyl. Replace necessary moldings and trim.

REPLACING VINYL TOPS

Unroll the new vinyl cover to check for correct fit and to help remove some of the

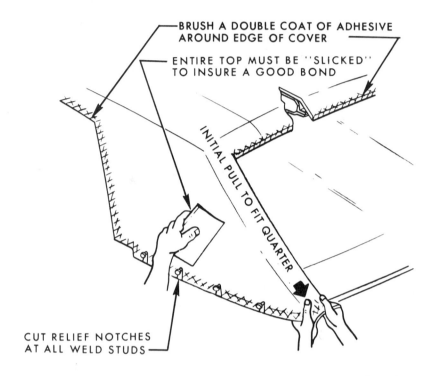

——BRUSH A DOUBLE COAT OF ADHESIVE
AROUND EDGE OF COVER ——

— ENTIRE TOP MUST BE ''SLICKED''
TO INSURE A GOOD BOND

INITIAL PULL TO FIT QUARTER

CUT RELIEF NOTCHES
AT ALL WELD STUDS ——

Figure 21-4 Cementing cover to quarter upper. (*Courtesy of General Motors Corporation, Fisher Body Division.*)

wrinkles. This can be accomplished by placing the cover on a flat table where it is warm or on another vehicle that is covered with a clean blanket or pad.

To replace a vinyl top, remove all the necessary molding such as windshield or back windows, clips from edges of molding were necessary, and any other emblems, nameplates, or weather stripping.

NOTE: Drive nails used to secure the cover edges in the window openings should be removed carefully to avoid chipping the glass and enlarging the nail holes so that they cannot be used again.

Remove or clean off any window caulking or adhesive from window opening and remove the reveal molding retainer clips. Separate the vinyl cover from the edges using a pair of pliers or putty knife. A heat gun can be used on stubborn cases. *Slowly,* pull the vinyl cover from the roof panel using the heat gun, if necessary.

After the cover is removed, clean the top with an adhesive cleaning solvent. All of the adhesive does not have to be removed as long as there is no high spot that will show through the new cover. Any defect in the body or paint should be repaired before installing the new top. Carefully mark a center line on the roof of the vehicle and the center of the top cover on the undersides. In some cases, the seam from the original cover is still visible on the roof; if it is straight, use this as a guide.

Mask the glass area, side window area, hood and deck to prevent adhesive from getting on the painted surface or glass, especially if the adhesive is sprayed on.

The adhesive can be applied by several different methods — with a pressure spray gun, brush, a mohair-type roller. When using a brush or roller, be sure to spread the adhesive evenly. Allow no excessive adhesive buildup.

CAUTION: Use adhesive in a well-ventilated area and avoid inhaling the toxic fumes. Wear a spray mask.

Place the new cover on the vehicle and align the center marks with the center line of the roof. Fold the cover in half lengthways. Apply some adhesive along the center line of roof and the same area of the cover. After drying as recommended by adhesive manufacturer or when the adhesive becomes tacky, place cover on the center line, stretch slightly to remove the wrinkles. Apply adhesive to the roof and cover on one side and apply the cover, working out the wrinkles as the cover is applied. Follow the same procedure for opposite side of the roof.

NOTE: Be careful not to apply too much adhesive in spots as the vapor may be trapped under the cover and cause blisters.

Continue to cement down the quarter section around the body window if applicable. If cover extends around rear window area, notch corners for tight fit; also notch cover for reveal molding studs. Securely fasten all of the edges of the cover, applying two layers of adhesives, if necessary.

NOTE: Cement edges before carefully installing drive nails.

Trim the cover if it extends beyond the edge of the trim molding. Avoid cutting the cover too short. Securely fasten the cover in the drip molding area using a putty knife and apply sealer if originally sealed. Apply drip molding trim cover.

Install balance of molding, ornaments, and weatherstrip, locating the existing holes with an awl. Some covers have two seams which can be applied in basically the same way. This is true for vehicles using half-covers or partials.

If the cover is removed and damage occurs to the foam pad underneath, the pad should be replaced because any defect in the pad will show through the top cover. If a new pad is used, it should be applied before the vinyl cover is added.

After completing the cover installation, remove any surplus adhesive and clean top, windows, and any other area involved. At times wrinkles may appear after a day or two. Some can be removed by the use of a heat gun or an electric household iron and a damp cloth. Set iron on medium and work iron back and forth around the wrinkled area. If the wrinkle is still present, the cover must be loosened and restretched which involves removing trim or hardware in the area. Use care not to tear the cover (Figure 21-5).

VINYL TOP REPAIRS

On occasion the vinyl top cover is damaged with cuts, gouges, or tears. If the damage is minor, it can be repaired with the proper methods, materials, and equipment.

There are repair kits available from the auto manufacturer or through local whole-

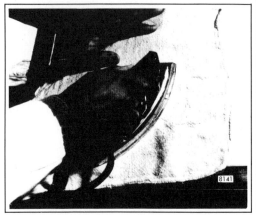

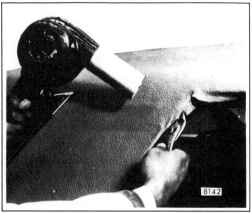

Removing Wrinkles with a Dampened Cloth and Home Type Iron

Loosening Edge of Fabric Roof Cover

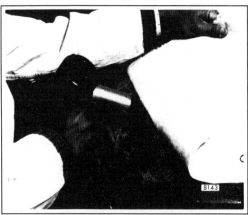

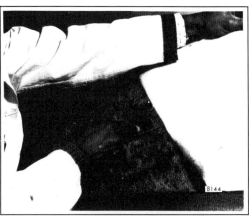

Separating Wrinkled Area from Roof Panel - Heat Application

Separating Wrinkled Area from Roof Panel - Flat-Bladed Tool Application

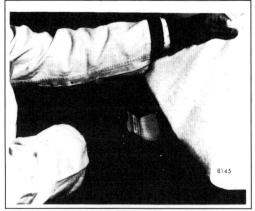

Applying Adhesive to Roof Panel

Cementing Fabric Roof Cover to Roof Panel

Figure 21-5 Removing wrinkles in vinyl top. *(Courtesy of General Motors Corporation, Fisher Body Division.)*

saler. Some of the materials needed are listed as follows:

1. Sharp knife or scapel knife.
2. Applicator or small trowel.
3. Heat gun.
4. Vinyl cleaner or liquid detergent cleaner.
5. Vinyl repair compound.
6. Vinyl repair paint.
7. Silicone mold release.
8. Graining die material or plastic body filler and hardener for substitute.

The grain mold die should be made first using a graining die material or plastic body filler. Use a scrap of vinyl or a spot next to the damaged area and clean it with a suitable vinyl cleaner. Dry the surface thoroughly and spray an area about 6″ × 8″ (152. 4 mm × 203.2 mm) with silicone mold release or equivalent (Figure 21-6).

Using a nonporous surface, mix about an ounce (about 28 grams) of the grain die compound with a suitable hardener. Mix thoroughly and apply to the surface that was sprayed with the silicone mold release, spreading and blending an area about 4″ × 6″ (101.6 mm × 152.4 mm). Cut a 6″ × 8″ (152.4 mm × 203.2 mm) piece of vinyl material of the same grain material and place over the compound with the grain side up.

Place a piece of wood or hard material on top of the vinyl and place a weight on it. Allow to dry for about 15 minutes. After hardening, peel off grain pattern die and trim edges. The die should be sprayed with mold release or silicone.

Vinyl Roof Repair Procedure

The following is a general procedure and may vary depending on the situation.

(a)

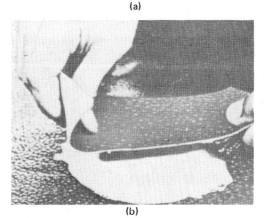

(b)

Figure 21-6 (a) Mixing grain die compound; (b) place vinyl material over die compound. *(Courtesy of Ford Motor Corporation.)*

Clean area around the damaged area with a detergent cleaner or vinyl cleaner and dry thoroughly.

Cut off the loose threads and loose vinyl to obtain a firm clean edge. Apply the patching compound to the cut area. Using a small trowel, work some of the material into the damaged area so it bonds the roof to the edges of the vinyl (Figure 21-7).

Heat the area with a heat gun held about 1″ (25.4 mm) away and move the gun in a circular motion. It takes about 20 seconds to cure and most materials will change from white to translucent. Continue to

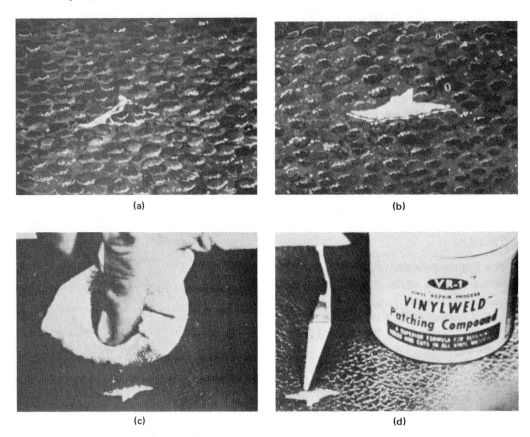

Figure 21-7 (a) Typical vinyl roof damage; (b) vinyl roof damage after trimming; (c) cleaning damaged area; (d) applying patching compound. *(Courtesy of Ford Motor Corporation.)*

build up area and cure with the heat gun.

When the material nears the original surface and is built up slightly above the surface and the last coat starts to harden do not use the heat gun. Trim off the excess to make a level surface and remove any surplus material from the surrounding area (Figure 21-8). Heat area for about 30 seconds until the material turns glossy. Immediately apply the die mold, pressing down to make a good impression. Cool the area with a wet sponge and dry.

Spray on matching vinyl color spray using a sweeping back and forth motion.

The procedure may vary when using different materials.

For procedures for repairing foam pad vinyl covers, consult the service manual. In cases where the vinyl has small scruff marks or where a small piece of vinyl is lifted, a small soldering or wood burner can be used.

Some vinyl can be repaired by carefully melting it with a small point of a wood burning set or by obtaining additional material from a scrap piece of vinyl (Figure 21-9). Spray several coats of vinyl color spray to blend in.

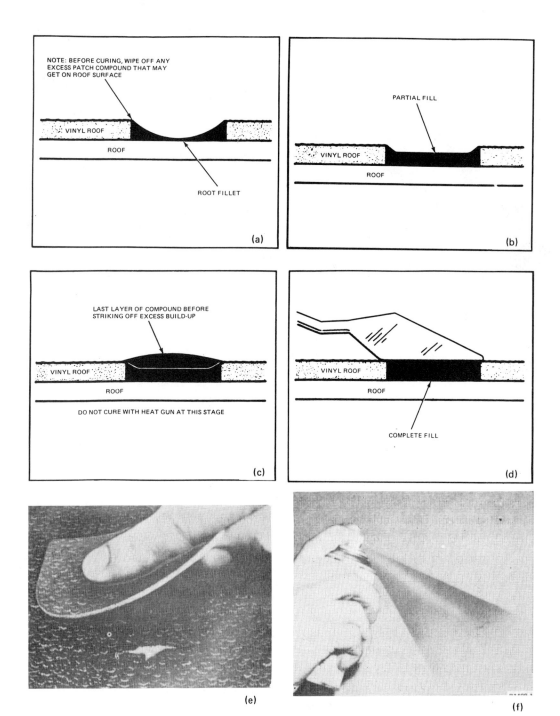

Figure 21-8 (a) Patching compound—first layer; (b) patching compound—intermediate layer(s); (c) patching compound—last layer; (d) leveling surface; (e) applying grain pattern die; (f) spraying repaired area. *(Courtesy of Ford Motor Corporation.)*

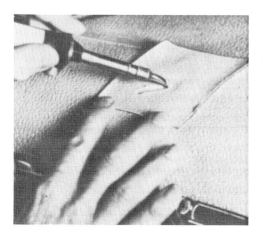 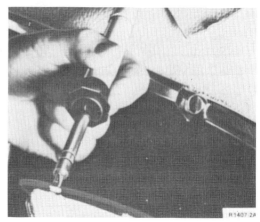

Figure 21-9 Repairing minor defects. *(Courtesy of Ford Motor Corporation.)*

Questions

1. What are the two different types of vinyl top installations?
2. What is the danger of improperly using a heat gun when removing part of the vinyl top?
3. Can reinstalling the vinyl cover over freshly painted surfaces damage the cover?
4. How can some of the wrinkles be removed from a new vinyl cover before it is installed?
5. Does all of the adhesive remaining on the panel after the cover has been taken off have to be removed?
6. Is it important to correct any body defects before installing a new top.
7. Should the surrounding area be protected when spraying the adhesive on the roof panel?
8. Where should the vehicle be placed when adhesive is being used?
9. Can an excess amount of adhesive, improperly dried, cause damage to the vinyl cover?
10. How can small wrinkles be removed after the top is installed?
11. Name some of the material and equipment necessary for repairing vinyl tops?
12. What is a *grain mold?*
13. What is the first step in preparing the area for repair?
14. How can small nicks in the cover be repaired?

WOODGRAIN TRANSFER STATION WAGON

For many years simulated woodgrain transfers have been used on station wagons to enhance their appearance. In recent years, the woodgrain transfers have been used on trucks and other vehicles. These transfers are made of vinyl or similar material with pressure sensitive adhesive on the back for bonding the vinyl to the panels.

Some time in the 1950s, the station wagon and similar vehicles used real wood paneling with generally hard maple wood strips as molding or trim around the edges of the paneling. The later models are trimmed around the edges with either metal moldings, plastic or fiberglas strips.

Transfers differ in shade, gloss, and patterns with each model automobile. A wetting solution is used to aid in applying the transfers.

The panel or surface where the transfer is to be applied must be painted or primed, depending on the manufacturer's recommendation. The transfer should never be applied to a bare metal surface.

Before applying the transfers, depending on what panel is involved, the necessary moldings and hardware must be removed, including side marker lights, outside door handles, and anything which may interfere with the transfer.

NOTE: If a replaced panel is involved, drill all of the necessary holes for molding or trim before applying the transfer.

If the transfer must be removed, start from the outer edges and peel back using a heat lamp or heat gun to soften the vinyl transfer. Remove the remaining adhesive with a transfer removal spray or enamel reducer.

The surface of the panel should be free of wax or grease, then wet sanded with 360 (9/0) or 400 (10/0) grit paper to remove any

Exterior Application

chapter
22

imperfections on a newly painted panel. Clean the surface with a solvent to remove all traces of dust. Some transfers are precut to the right shape. Otherwise, the vinyl transfers are sold by the sheet in rolls.

INSTALLATION METHODS

Two methods for installing vinyl transfers will be discussed, but there are other methods depending on the manufacturer.

The first method of applying a transfer is as follows. Tape a large sheet of suitable paper to the panel so that the top of the paper is aligned with the adjoining transfer or in line with the horizontal molding retainer holes. Mark the front, rear, and bottom edge. Lay the paper on a table or bench and extend the line on the front, bottom, and rear edges about ¾" (19 mm) to allow for going around edges, inside doors, or wheelhouses. Mark or notch paper pattern (or template) to indicate the front end and the inner side of the pattern.

If the transfer has horizontal lines, mark the upper edges of the top lines. Cut out the template along the lines and hold it up against the panel and check for accuracy. Also, be sure that the front part is indicated as well as the inside of the template.

Unroll the new transfer with the paper backing side facing upward, and the grain pattern running from left to right. Position the template on the transfer with the inner side of the template facing upward or outward. If the transfer has horizontal lines, mark the lines on the transfer. Mark the transfer with the cut lines and cut along the lines. Position the transfer on the panel in correct alignment and mark the center on both.

Mix the wetting solution in a clean container about ¼ ounce (.071 liters) of detergent to 1 gallon (about 4.5 liters) of clean water. Obtain a clean, grit-free, sponge and a good 3" × 4" (76 mm × 102 mm) squeegee. Lay the transfer face down on a table and peel off backing paper. Thoroughly wet the transfer adhesive and the body panel with the sponge.

Position the transfer at the center line, align top edges (if transfer has lines, match and align the lines), and press down lightly at the top. Using a squeegee, start in the center and work outward, smoothing and removing all air bubbles.

On large areas, lift the transfer on left or right and squeegee the transfer outward. Follow procedure, working outward first on top, then work toward the bottom. It may be necessary to lift up the transfer and resqueegee. If wrinkles appear, stop and lift up the section and rework. Use additional solution to keep the transfer workable. Cut V-notches in the transfer to facilitate working around corners. If difficulty is experienced on sharp creases or concave surfaces, a heat lamp or heat gun can be used to assist in shaping the transfer.

CAUTION: Do not overheat.

Trim off excess transfer material. Apply trim adhesive to the inside of the door hem flanges or inside edge of the lock pillow or wheel opening and secure edges. Use a heat lamp or heat gun, if necessary, to shape the transfer material around edges and press to secure edges.

Using a sharp knife or razor knife, cut out around the door handle opening, marker light, or other openings. Any small air or moisture bubbles can be removed by piercing with a pin or needle and pressing down firmly. Install the necessary trim and hardware.

The second method uses the same wetting solution and the same preparation.

The transfer with the backing is placed on the panel and taped at the top edge along the molding holes or studs. Be sure that the grain is straight. Line up any lines.

The transfer must have an overlap for inside the door edges, quarter panel opening, and wheelhouses. After positioning, mark and trim the transfer to size. Mark the panel with tape for the transfer location. Soak the vinyl transfer in the wetting solution and thoroughly wet the panel.

Peel the backing on the upper edge of the transfer for about 4" to 5" (201 mm to 227 mm) and apply the transfer to the edge of the molding holes or studs using the tape as a guide. If the transfer has lines, line them up.

Using a squeegee, smooth out the transfer starting from the center outward. Remove the balance of the backing paper from the transfer using the method previously mentioned (Figure 22-1).

Once the transfer is in place with all defects removed, use adhesive to fasten down the edges. Heat if necessary. Install all necessary molding and trim.

If a transfer panel or section is damaged or a small section removed due to body work, the balance of the transfer does not necessarily have to be removed. Clean the entire panel with a recommended wax and silicone remover solvent and wipe clean.

The area can be featheredged and cleaned with solvent. The area can be built up with several applications of primer, letting each coat flash before applying the next coat. If necessary, apply a light coat of glazing putty to help build up the surface in relation to the surrounding area. Sand putty when dry and apply two additional coats of

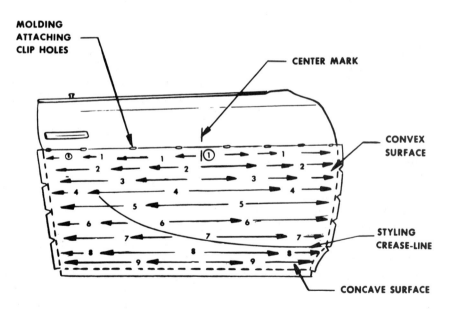

Figure 22-1   Transfer installation sequence (right front door shown). *(Courtesy of General Motors Corporation, Fisher Body Division.)*

primer over the area. Sand entire panel with #360 or #400 grit sandpaper and thoroughly clean panel. Trim transfer film from inner edges of door, quarter panel, or wheel opening and sand edges.

Apply transfers as previously described, matching the lines. Cut out the transfer along the cut lines.

TAPE STRIPES AND DECALS

Many passenger vehicles and trucks have decorative stripes and decals to make them more attractive. Most of the stripes and decals are made of a tough, durable, weather-resistant, solid vinyl with a pressure sensitive backing.

Small or Thin Stripes

If the stripes have to be replaced because of body damage, they can be removed on some vehicles as follows:

1. Clean the area of the stripes and the surrounding area.

2. Remove any parts or trim that overlap the stripes.

3. Remove the stripes by starting from one end and peeling them off the painted surface. If necessary, use a heat gun to soften the vinyl.

   NOTE: Avoid using pointed or sharp tools because they may damage the painted surface.

4. The remaining adhesive can be removed with a rag soaked in 3M woodgrain and stripe remover solvent (or similar material). Some types of enamel reducers can be used providing they do not damage the painted surface.

   CAUTION: Before using any sol-

vents on a painted surface, check the solvent on a hidden painted surface to see whether it will affect the paint.

5. Rinse area thoroughly with soap and water.

Installation of Small or Thin Stripes

Dry Method. Before installing stripes, the painted surfaces including the wraparound flanges on door openings, should be cleaned with a recommended wax and silicone remover. Avoid installing stripes on freshly painted surfaces as the remaining solvent may damage them. Position the stripe on the panel, align the lines with the adjacent panel, and mark with masking tape. Remove inner liner from the stripe, about 1/2 the distance of the panel and tear off liner. Stretch stripe in place but do not push striping to vehicle. Use of plastic squeegee starting from the center of the panel is recommended. Press striping in place, working toward the end of the panel.

CAUTION: Do not use fingers or hands as they may cause creases.

Peal off remaining liner and press into place. Remove premask by pulling at 180° angle. Use heat to mold stripes in recessed and flanged areas with a heat gun and a soft clean cloth.

Large Decals or Stripes

Wet Method. The method of installing large decals and stripes is very similar to the woodgrain installation. The panel or panels must be free of wax, grease, or dust. Wash thoroughly with soap and water. Use wax and silicone remover solvent, if necessary.

Mix a wetting solution using about 1/2 fluid ounce (.142 liters) of detergent soap to 1 gallon (4.5 liters) of clean water in a clean container. A small clean sponge or a spray

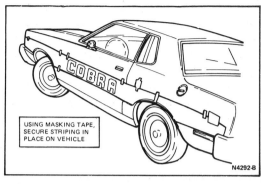

USING MASKING TAPE, SECURE STRIPING IN PLACE ON VEHICLE

N4292-B

(a)

Figure 22-2 (a) Tape striping in place on vehicle; (b) removing stripe; (c) squeeging on tape stripe; (d) removing pre-mask paper; (e) molding striping into recessed area. *(Courtesy of Ford Motor Corporation.)*

REMOVE LINER PAPER BY SHARPLY BENDING EDGE OF STRIPING TOWARD FACE WITH FLICK OF FINGERNAIL.

PEEL LINER PAPER FROM STRIPING.

RIP LINER PAPER OFF AT APPROXIMATE MID-POINT OF PANEL.

N4293-2A

(b)

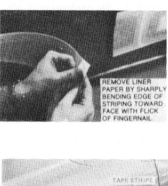

TAPE STRIPE

PLASTIC SQUEEGEE

N4294-1A

(c)

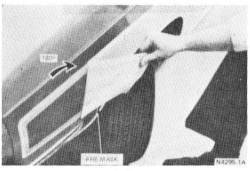

180°

PRE-MASK

N4295-1A

(d)

N4296-1A

(e)

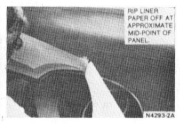

bottle can be used for applying the wetting solution.

Position the decal or stripe and mask with masking tape (Figure 22–2). Remove half of the inner liner and wet the pressure sensitive backing and the panel. Position decal or stripe with characters aligned. Use squeegee and start from the center of the decal and smooth onto the panel. Use overlapping strokes and work toward ends. If air bubbles or wrinkles appear, lift up the decal, rewet and reapply. Remove premask paper carefully, wetting paper, if necessary.

Use a heat gun and clean soft cloth to mold decal to panel recesses and to flanged areas.

Questions

1. On what type surface should the transfer be applied?
2. Should all body and paint defects be corrected before applying the transfer?
3. Should the necessary molding and trim holes be drilled before installing the transfer?
4. If the transfer is available in rolls, is it advisable to make a paper pattern first?
5. What care must be taken with transfers involving lines?
6. What method can be used to remove small air bubbles?
7. How can the edges that go inside the edges of the panel be shaped and attached?
8. Can the transfer be repaired or must the complete transfer be replaced?
9. How can stripes or decals be removed?
10. When using woodgrain and stripe remover, should it be checked first on an inner edge before it is tried on the outer panel?
11. Can stripes be placed on freshly painted surfaces?
12. How should stripes be applied to the surface?
13. What is a *wetting solution?*
14. What is used to smooth out the stripes when applying?
15. How can the stripes be molded to the body recesses?

During many types of collisions, the automotive electrical system is involved in one way or another. The auto body man should have some knowledge of the system, although some parts of it are very complicated.

Generally, some of the lights, either front or back are damaged and must be replaced. Very often, the wiring harness is damaged and must be repaired or replaced. The driver's door on many automobiles contains electrical window controls, automatic locks, and other devices that require removing when the door shell is replaced.

Because of the large variety of different types of systems, it will be impossible to describe them all. When there is doubt about a certain circuit, it is recommended that you consult the service manual.

Automotive Electricity

BATTERY

chapter
23

Battery electrolyte is sulfuric acid. Avoid contact with the skin, eyes, or clothing. Wash hands immediately after working on batteries and keep hands away from mouth. Shield eyes with suitable safety glasses when working near the battery to protect against possible splashing of the acid solution or corrosion in battery area.

WARNING: Keep out of the reach of children.

In case of acid contact with the skin, eyes, or clothing, *flush immediately* with *water for at least 15 minutes*. If acid is swallowed, drink large quantities of milk or water followed by milk of magnesia, a beaten egg, or vegetable oil. Call a physician immediately.

The heart of the electrical circuit is the battery which supplies electrical energy to the ignition system, electrical components, and the starter circuit. The battery, or storage battery, consists of a series of individual cells located in a hard rubber or plastic case.

NOTE: When carrying batteries, use proper carrier straps and keep away from body.

Each cell consists of an assembly of posi-

tive and negative plates containing dissimilar materials and are kept from touching each other by separators. These assemblies are immersed in a solution of dilute sulfuric acid.

All the positive plates are connected

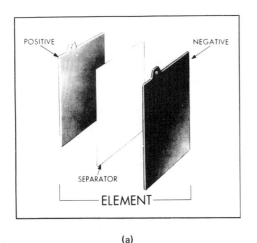

(a)

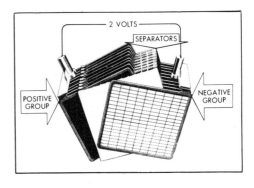

(b)

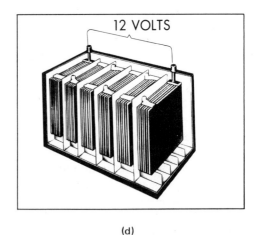

(c)

(d)

Figure 23-1 (a) Battery element (simple); (b) battery element (compound); (c) two volt battery cell; (d) typical 12 volt battery cell arrangement. *(Courtesy of General Motors Corporation, Chevrolet Motor Division.)*

together with a lead strap at the top of the plates. Likewise, all of the negative plates are connected together (Figure 23-1). These groups are connected in series by means of a connector which passes through the sides of the cell partition. Each 12-volt battery will have six individual cells (Figure 23-2). The positive and negative plates are then connected to a positive and negative terminal, either on top- or side-mounted terminals which pass through the case. The side-mounted terminals are supposed to create less corrosion problems with the cable connections than the top-mounted terminal types. The storage battery is an electro-chemical device for converting chemical energy into electrical energy. The battery does not store up electrical energy as believed, but energy in chemical form. The active material within the battery reacts chemically to produce a flow of direct current whenever a demand is placed on the battery from, for example, lights, radio, or starting motor circuit. The chemical reaction between the plates and the electrolyte in the form of dilute sulfuric acid produces the energy or current.

The battery will last a long time and stay charged under normal conditions. Battery failure or poor service can be caused by numerous reasons: leaving the automobile accessories on overnight, below average driving speeds especially at night in heavy traffic, using more current than the generator or alternator can produce, defective charging system, defective regulator which could cause overcharging and overheating of the battery, slipping belts, dirty battery terminals, low electrolyte level, loose hold-downs causing the battery to vibrate. Dirty or corroded terminals that impede the flow of current from the battery or into the battery from the generator alternator is one of the leading causes of an automobile's

failure to start. During cold weather, the battery electrolyte will freeze and buckle the plates unless the battery is kept at full charge. Likewise, the electrolyte level should be kept at the proper height unless it is a sealed-type battery.

Battery Removal and Replacing

Defective and dead batteries must be replaced and the replacement battery should be of equal capacity or as recommended by the automobile manufacturer. A higher capacity battery, with more plates, may be recommended if additional accessories have been added or for better starting during cold weather.

A battery has two ratings: the reserve capacity rating at 80° F (27° C) which is the time the fully charged battery will operate the car with the generator or alternator not in operation; the cold crank rating of 0° F (-18° C) which indicates the load capacity.

When removing the battery, the position of the terminal should be noted unless the battery is a side-terminal type. Remove the ground cable first to avoid the chance of sparking. The fastening device will vary from spring-type terminal ends to side mount bolts. The terminals and battery tray assembly should be cleaned with baking soda (sodium bicarbonate) and water.

CAUTION: Avoid contact with the skin and protect the eyes.

After drying the tray, hold-down parts should be inspected for defects. Inspect terminals for wear, especially the terminal bolts. Install suitable battery and tighten battery down with the hold-down device but don't overtighten. Install battery terminals.

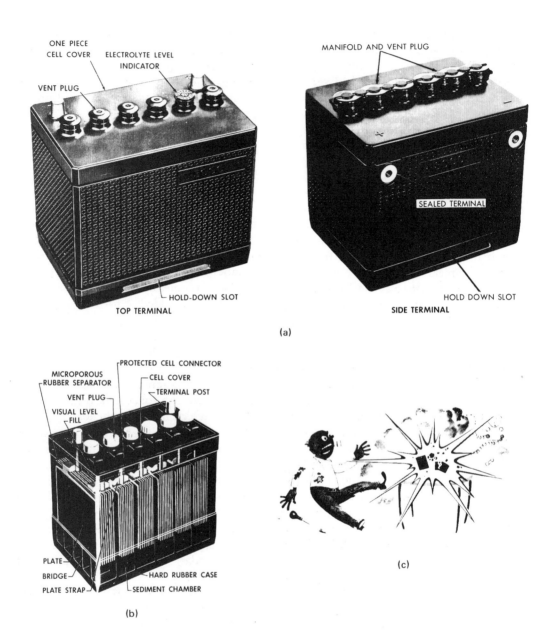

Figure 23-2 (a) Terminals; (b) parts of a typical battery; (c) flame or spark can cause a charging battery to explode. *(Courtesy of General Motors Corporation, Chevrolet Motor Division.)*

Jump Starting

When using another automobile or battery to start a motor caution must be used as this can be dangerous. Before attempting to start, be sure that all of the switches are turned off and put on eye protection. Connect the ends of one cable to the positive (+) terminal of each battery. Connect one end of the other cable to the negative (–) terminal of the charged battery or good battery. Connect the other end of the cable to a good ground such as a motor bracket or bolt on the car being started but not on the negative terminal of the battery.

NOTE: If another car is being used, have the motor idling before connecting the terminals.

CAUTION: The chemical action of the battery produces oxygen and hydrogen which is explosive if exposed to a flame or spark.

Recharging

A dead or discharged battery can be charged providing the battery cells are in good condition. Before charging, remove the ground cable in the event that the charger cables are attached to the wrong terminals. The alternator could be damaged if connected wrong. Check electrolyte level for proper height, add distilled water if necessary. Connect the positive cable of charger, generally red colored, to the positive (+) terminal of the battery. Connect the negative cable to the negative (–) terminal of the battery. Set charger to the proper voltage, either six or twelve volts; set the charging rate and automatic timer. Avoid charging the battery at high rates as this may damage it. Many chargers are marked with a safe charge zone on the charge in-

dicator. Shut off charger before removing cables to avoid sparking and possible explosion.

Important note: On some of the new type sealed batteries, check the hydrometer indicator. If the indicator is clear or light yellow, do not charge the battery, replace it (Figure 23–3).

Battery Test

Batteries can be tested with a hydrometer for state of charge. Depending on the type of hydrometer used, a fully charged battery should have a specific gravity of 1.280 (Figure 23–4). All cells should read within 40 points of each other. A reading of 50 or more points in one cell could indicate a defective cell. If after charging for 20 minutes, the difference still remains, the battery needs replacing.

At times, the specific gravity is within range, but the battery has lost its capacity. In this case, a high rate discharge tester should be used. Consult the service manual for additional information, especially when working on the sealed maintenance-free batteries.

Body Wiring

The automobile contains many different electrical circuits with many accessories such as power windows, seats, locks, and so on. Most of the wires are either standard or solid copper covered with either plastic or rubber coating for insulation. On some of the later model automobiles, metric size wire is used instead of the standard gauge wire. If it is necessary to replace a section of the metric wire, an equivalent size should be used. See conversion chart for low primary cable

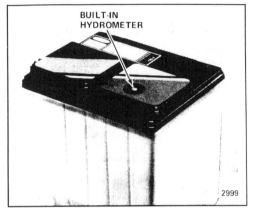

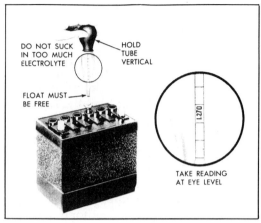

(a)

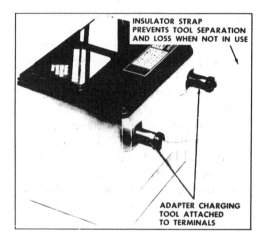

VALUE OF SPECIFIC GRAVITY @ 30°F	FREEZING TEMP. °F	°C	VALUE OF SPECIFIC GRAVITY @ 80°F	FREEZING TEMP. °F	°C
1.100	18	−8	1.220	−33	−36
1.120	13	−11	1.240	−50	−46
1.140	8	−13	1.260	−75	−59
1.160	1	−17	1.280	−92	−69
1.180	−6	−21	1.300	−95	−71
1.200	−17	−27			

(b)

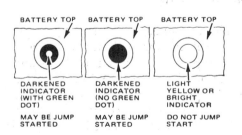

(c)

Figure 23-4 Testing specific gravity of battery; (b) specific gravity and freezing temperature; (c) battery power vs falling temperature. *(Courtesy of General Motors Corporation, Chevrolet Motor Division.)*

Figure 23-3 Typical sealed battery. *(Courtesy of General Motors Corporation, Chevrolet Motor Division.)*

Most of the wires are color coded for ease in servicing or replacing. Wire identification charts or schematics are available for all the late model automobiles. Some charts consist of numbered wires and an accompanying identification index (Figure 23–5).

The numerous circuits are placed in harness form (several wires wrapped with an insulation tape or covering depending on the location). In areas where there is a danger of possible damage or wear, the harness covering is much heavier (Figure 23–6).

The junctions or wire ends are generally shaped into a coded type of plug-in so the danger of connecting the wrong wires together is eliminated. The circuits are protected against excessive loads which might occur due to shorts or excessive overloads. The protection devices are circuit breakers, fuses or fusable links (Figure 23–7).

A short or short circuit occurs when the wire is grounded before reaching its intended source and electrical unit. This happens when the insulation is worn off by abrasion, torn off, or cut by impact, and the copper wire touches part of the body or frame. It could also occur within a wiring harness when the insulation is worn off or melted off due to excessive load. A short circuit on a feed wire before a breaker or fuse can drain the current from the battery (Figure 23–8).

A circuit breaker is a protective device designed to open the circuit when a current load is in excess of rated breaker capacity. The circuit breaker will remain open until the short or overload is corrected. The circuit breaker is used in the heavier demand circuits and will protect the wires from being damaged. The breaker will close when the problem is corrected.

The fuse is the most common type device used to protect the circuits from overload or shorts (Figure 23–9). The main disadvantage of the fuse is that once the fusible link or wire in the fuse is burned or broken, the fuse must be replaced.

The fusible link is used in circuits that are not normally fused such as the ignition systems. Each link is four gauge sizes smaller than the cable which it is designed to protect and is marked with the wire size in the insulation. If the link is damaged, it must be replaced with another link and not replaced with ordinary wire. Consult the service manual for the proper procedure.

The fuses and some circuit breakers are mounted into a fuse block which contains many different sizes for different circuits. For instance, the radio uses a 10-amp fuse while the heater (AC circuit) uses a 25-amp fuse. Most of these blocks are mounted under the dash panel where many of the circuits converge.

Many of these circuits are connected with various type harness connectors and will vary with different automobiles.

One of the problems that occurs frequently in wiring, especially if the automobile has been involved in a collision, is the open circuit. An open circuit is when the current does not reach its destination or returns to ground. An open circuit could be a blown fuse, an open circuit breaker, defective wiring, a break in the wire, or an improper ground. Frequently, a wire is broken within a harness due to impact, or a harness is wedged between two panels.

To check for an open circuit, visually inspect the wire circuit involved. Then start from the source of power (or battery side) and connect the test light to a good ground. Insert the test light probe into the insulation to reach the wire. If the test lamp lights, the circuit is operating to that point.

Circuits involving a circuit breaker or fuse must be checked on the battery side of

Circuit Number	Circuit Color	Circuit Name
2	RED	FEED, BATTERY - UNFUSED
9	BRN	TAIL, LICENSE, PARK AND SIDE MARKER LAMP FEED
14	LT BLUE	LH INDICATOR AND FRONT DIRECTIONAL LAMPS
15	DK BLUE	RH INDICATOR AND FRONT DIRECTIONAL LAMPS
16	PPL	DIRECTIONAL SIGNAL SW, FEED FROM FLASHER
17	WHT	DIRECTIONAL SIGNAL SW, FEED FROM STOP SW
18	YEL	STOP AND DIRECTIONAL LAMP OR DIRECTIONAL LAMP ONLY - REAR LH
19	DK GRN	STOP AND DIRECTIONAL LAMP OR DIRECTIONAL LAMP ONLY - REAR RH
20	LT BLUE	STOP LAMP (ONLY)
22	WHITE	DIRECT GROUND - TRAILER
24	LT GRN	BACK UP LAMP FEED
30	PNK	FUEL GAUGE TO TANK UNIT
32	YEL	MAP LIGHT FEED
37	LT GRN	GROUND, ENG METAL TEMP SW CONTROLLED (HOT)
39	PNK-BLK	FEED, IGN SW, "ON AND CRANK" CONTROLLED - FUSED
40	ORN	FEED, BATTERY - FUSED
41	BRN-WHT	FEED, IGN SW "ACCSY AND ON" CONTROLLED - FUSED
44	DK GRN	I.P. AND LIGHTS FEED (USUALLY LIGHT SW TO FUSE)
45	BLK	MARKER AND CLEARANCE LAMPS (TRAILERS)
46	DK BLUE	REAR SEAT SPEAKER FEED FROM SINGLE RADIO OR RIGHT STEREO
47	DK BLUE	AUXILIARY CIRCUIT (TRAILER)
48	GRAY	TAIL LP - HEADLAMP SW "ON" - OR DIR SIGNAL AND STOP - HEADLAMP SW "OFF" REAR LH
49	DK BLUE	TAIL LP - HEADLAMP SW "ON" - OR DIR SIGNAL AND STOP - HEADLAMP SW "OFF" REAR RH
50	BRN	FEED, IGN SW "ON" CONTROLLED - FUSED
60	ORN-BLK	FEED, BATTERY, CIRCUIT BREAKER PROTECTED
70	PNK	FEED, RELAY CONTROLLED, IGN SW CONTROLLED
76	PNK	FEED, IGN SW CONTROLLED
90	PNK	FEED, CUTOUT SW CONTROLLED, CIR. BRKR. PROTECTED
91	GRAY	WINDSHIELD WIPER - LOW
92	PPL	WINDSHIELD WIPER - HI
93	WHT	WINDSHIELD WIPER MOTOR FEED
94	PNK	WINDSHIELD WASHER SW TO WASHER
95	DK GRN	GROUND, PULSE WIPER SW CONTROLLED
96	BRN	FEED, PULSE WIPER RHEOSTAT SW CONTROLLED
115	LT BLUE	SPEAKER RETURN, RT RR STEREO
116	YEL	SPEAKER RETURN, LF RR STEREO
117	DK GRN	SPEAKER RETURN, RT FRT STEREO
118	GRAY	SPEAKER RETURN, LF FRT STEREO
125	YEL	DOOR JAMB SWITCH
126	BLK	SEAT BACK LOCK FEED
139	PNK-BLK	FEED, IGN SW "ON AND CRANK" CONTROLLED - FUSED
140	ORN	FEED, BATTERY - FUSED
141	BRN-WHT	FEED, IGN SW, "ACCSY AND ON" CONTROLLED
142	BLK	RR COMPARTMENT LID LOCK RELEASE
146	DK GRN	GROUND, TRUNK RELEASE TELL-TALE

Figure 23-5 Chart identifying wires in late model vehicles. *(Courtesy of General Motors Corporation, Fisher Body Division.)*

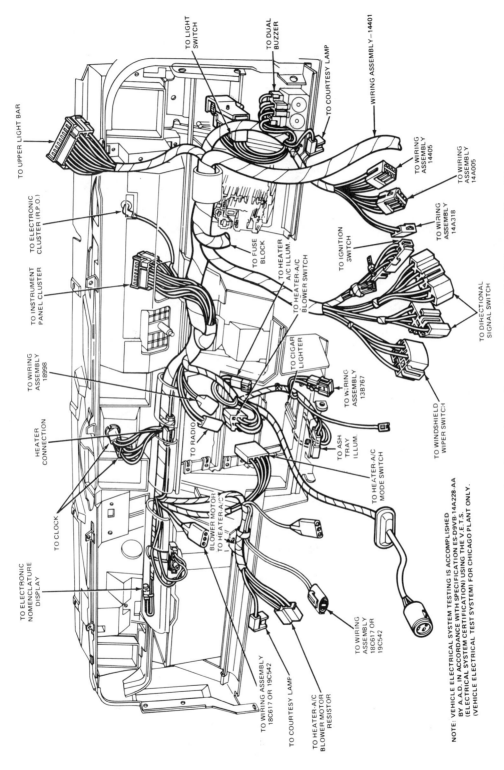

TO UPPER LIGHT BAR

TO LIGHT SWITCH

TO DUAL BUZZER

TO COURTESY LAMP

WIRING ASSEMBLY – 14401

TO WIRING ASSEMBLY 14405

TO WIRING ASSEMBLY 14A005

TO ELECTRONIC CLUSTER (R.P.O.)

TO INSTRUMENT PANEL CLUSTER

TO FUSE BLOCK

TO HEATER A/C ILLUM.

TO HEATER-A/C BLOWER SWITCH

TO IGNITION SWITCH

TO WIRING ASSEMBLY 14A318

TO WIRING ASSEMBLY 18998

TO CIGAR LIGHTER

TO WIRING 13B767

TO DIRECTIONAL SIGNAL SWITCH

HEATER CONNECTION

TO CLOCK

TO RADIO

TO ASH TRAY ILLUM.

TO WINDSHIELD WIPER SWITCH

TO ELECTRONIC NOMENCLATURE DISPLAY

TO COURTESY LAMP

TO HEATER-A/C BLOWER MOTOR RESISTOR

BLOWER MOTOR TO HEATER-A/C

TO HEATER-A/C MODE SWITCH

TO WIRING ASSEMBLY 18C617 OR 19C542

TO WIRING ASSEMBLY 18C617 OR 19C542

NOTE: VEHICLE ELECTRICAL SYSTEM TESTING IS ACCOMPLISHED BY A.A.D. IN ACCORDANCE WITH SPECIFICATION ES-D9VB-14A228-AA (ELECTRICAL SYSTEM CERTIFICATION) USING THE V.E.T.S. (VEHICLE ELECTRICAL TEST SYSTEM) FOR CHICAGO PLANT ONLY.

Figure 23-6 Instrument panel and 14401 wire harness—Thunderbird/Cougar XR-7. *(Courtesy of Ford Motor Corporation.)*

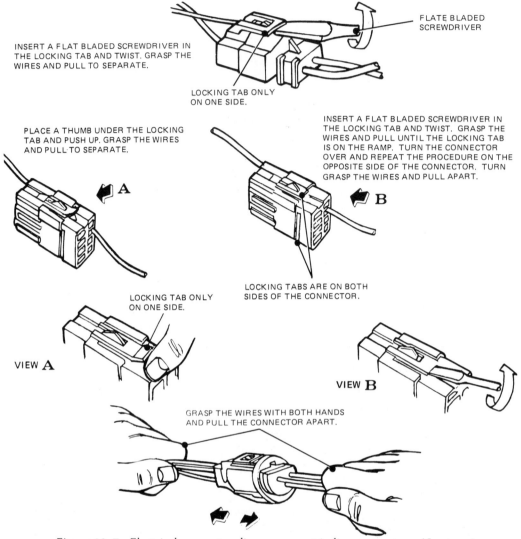

INSERT A FLAT BLADED SCREWDRIVER IN THE LOCKING TAB AND TWIST. GRASP THE WIRES AND PULL TO SEPARATE.

FLATE BLADED SCREWDRIVER

LOCKING TAB ONLY ON ONE SIDE.

PLACE A THUMB UNDER THE LOCKING TAB AND PUSH UP. GRASP THE WIRES AND PULL TO SEPARATE.

A

INSERT A FLAT BLADED SCREWDRIVER IN THE LOCKING TAB AND TWIST. GRASP THE WIRES AND PULL UNTIL THE LOCKING TAB IS ON THE RAMP. TURN THE CONNECTOR OVER AND REPEAT THE PROCEDURE ON THE OPPOSITE SIDE OF THE CONNECTOR. TURN GRASP THE WIRES AND PULL APART.

B

LOCKING TABS ARE ON BOTH SIDES OF THE CONNECTOR.

LOCKING TAB ONLY ON ONE SIDE.

VIEW A

VIEW B

GRASP THE WIRES WITH BOTH HANDS AND PULL THE CONNECTOR APART.

Figure 23-7 Electrical connector disengagement in line connectors. *(Courtesy of Ford Motor Corporation.)*

the breaker or fuse. If the light lights, check on the other side of the breaker or fuse.

For a quicker check, check the wire entering the inoperative unit (Figure 23-10). If the circuit is to the unit, check the ground contact of the units. In many parking lights or taillights mounted in the bumper, the ground contact is lost due to dirt or corrosion. On some units, the connector plugs become corroded or worn thus breaking the circuit. Improper grounds on motors or other electrical units often cause problems. To check, connect a short piece of 12-gauge (3 mm) wire to the unit and the other end to a good ground, preferably bare metal. With the power turned on,

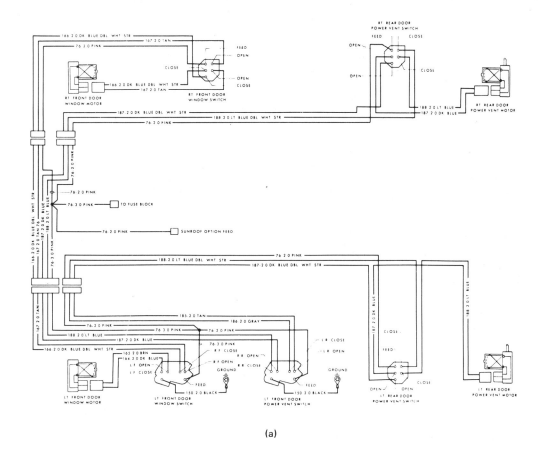

(a)

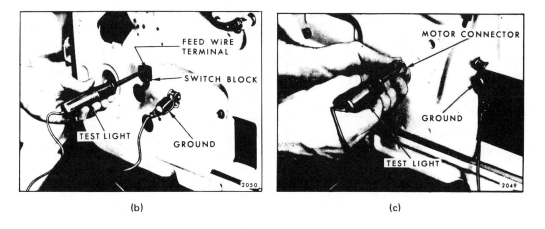

(b)　　　　　　　　　　　　　　(c)

Figure 23-8 (a) Power window and power vent circuit diagram—A styles; (b) checking feed circuit at switch; (c) checking circuit between switch and motor. *(Courtesy of General Motors Corporation, Fisher Body Division.)*

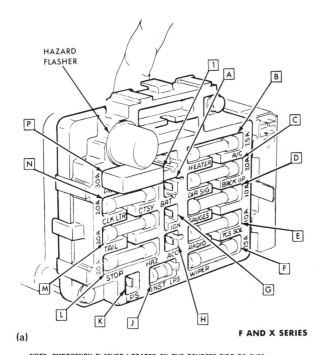

HAZARD FLASHER

1 CIRCUIT BREAKER (F)
A RECEPTACLE-U35
B FUSE-HEATER AIR COND.
C FUSE-DIR SIG AND BACK-UP LAMP
D FUSE-GUAGES
E FUSE-RADIO AND TCS SOL
F FUSE-WIPER
G RECEPTACLE-M15/M20/M21/M61(X)
H RECEPTACLE-ZJ9/ZJ1(X)
J FUSE-INSTRUMENT LIGHTS
K RECEPTACLE-NOT USED
L FUSE-STOP AND HAZARD WARNING
M FUSE-TAIL LAMP
N FUSE-CLOCK, LIGHTER AND CTSY LAMP
P FUSE AND RECEPTACLE-POWER ACCESSORY

(a)   F AND X SERIES

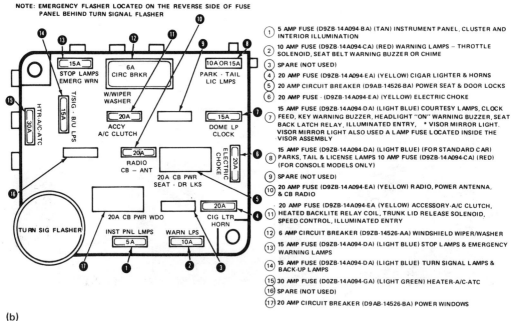

NOTE: EMERGENCY FLASHER LOCATED ON THE REVERSE SIDE OF FUSE
      PANEL BEHIND TURN SIGNAL FLASHER

1 5 AMP FUSE (D9ZB-14A094-BA) (TAN) INSTRUMENT PANEL, CLUSTER AND INTERIOR ILLUMINATION
2 10 AMP FUSE (D9ZB-14A094-CA) (RED) WARNING LAMPS – THROTTLE SOLENOID, SEAT BELT WARNING BUZZER OR CHIME
3 SPARE (NOT USED)
4 20 AMP FUSE (D9ZB-14A094-EA) (YELLOW) CIGAR LIGHTER & HORNS
5 20 AMP CIRCUIT BREAKER (D9AB-14526-BA) POWER SEAT & DOOR LOCKS
6 20 AMP FUSE - (D9ZB-14A094-EA) (YELLOW) ELECTRIC CHOKE
7 15 AMP FUSE (D9ZB-14A094-DA) (LIGHT BLUE) COURTESY LAMPS, CLOCK FEED, KEY WARNING BUZZER, HEADLIGHT "ON" WARNING BUZZER, SEAT BACK LATCH RELAY, ILLUMINATED ENTRY, * VISOR MIRROR LIGHT. VISOR MIRROR LIGHT ALSO USED A LAMP FUSE LOCATED INSIDE THE VISOR ASSEMBLY
8 15 AMP FUSE (D9ZB-14A094-DA) (LIGHT BLUE) (FOR STANDARD CAR) PARKS, TAIL & LICENSE LAMPS 10 AMP FUSE (D9ZB-14A094-CA) (RED) (FOR CONSOLE MODELS ONLY)
9 SPARE (NOT USED)
10 20 AMP FUSE (D9ZB-14A094-EA) (YELLOW) RADIO, POWER ANTENNA, & CB RADIO
11 20 AMP FUSE (D9ZB-14A094-EA) (YELLOW) ACCESSORY-A/C CLUTCH, HEATED BACKLITE RELAY COIL, TRUNK LID RELEASE SOLENOID, SPEED CONTROL, ILLUMINATED ENTRY
12 6 AMP CIRCUIT BREAKER (D9ZB-14526-AA) WINDSHIELD WIPER/WASHER
13 15 AMP FUSE (D9ZB-14A094-DA) (LIGHT BLUE) STOP LAMPS & EMERGENCY WARNING LAMPS
14 15 AMP FUSE (D9ZB-14A094-DA) (LIGHT BLUE) TURN SIGNAL LAMPS & BACK-UP LAMPS
15 30 AMP FUSE (D0ZB-14A094-GA) (LIGHT GREEN) HEATER-A/C-ATC
16 SPARE (NOT USED)
17 20 AMP CIRCUIT BREAKER (D9AB-14526-BA) POWER WINDOWS

(b)

Figure 23-9   (a) Fuse panel—F and X series *(Courtesy of General Motors Corporation, Fisher Body Division)*; (b) fuse panel—Thunderbird/Cougar XR-7. *(Courtesy of Ford Motor Corporation).*

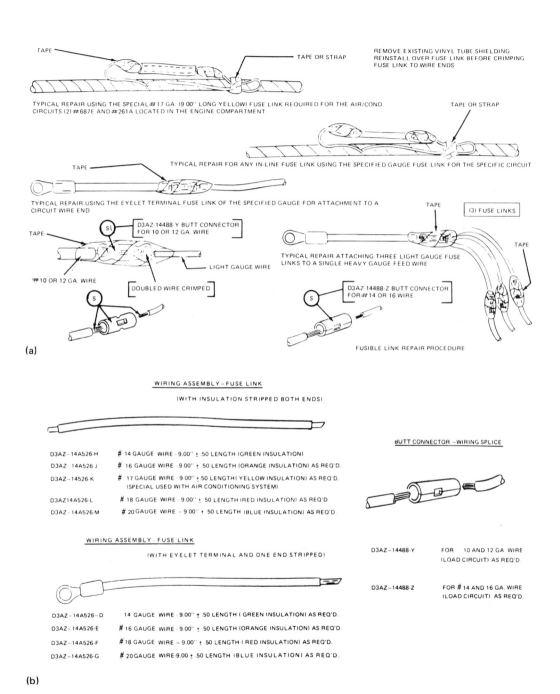

TAPE

TAPE OR STRAP

REMOVE EXISTING VINYL TUBE SHIELDING
REINSTALL OVER FUSE LINK BEFORE CRIMPING
FUSE LINK TO WIRE ENDS

TYPICAL REPAIR USING THE SPECIAL #17 GA. (9.00" LONG YELLOW) FUSE LINK REQUIRED FOR THE AIR/COND.
CIRCUITS (2) #687E AND #261A LOCATED IN THE ENGINE COMPARTMENT

TAPE OR STRAP

TYPICAL REPAIR FOR ANY IN-LINE FUSE LINK USING THE SPECIFIED GAUGE FUSE LINK FOR THE SPECIFIC CIRCUIT

TAPE

TYPICAL REPAIR USING THE EYELET TERMINAL FUSE LINK OF THE SPECIFIED GAUGE FOR ATTACHMENT TO A
CIRCUIT WIRE END

TAPE

(3) FUSE LINKS

TAPE

D3AZ-14488-Y BUTT CONNECTOR
FOR 10 OR 12 GA. WIRE

TYPICAL REPAIR ATTACHING THREE LIGHT GAUGE FUSE
LINKS TO A SINGLE HEAVY GAUGE FEED WIRE

TAPE

LIGHT GAUGE WIRE

#10 OR 12 GA. WIRE

DOUBLED WIRE CRIMPED

D3AZ-14488-Z BUTT CONNECTOR
FOR #14 OR 16 WIRE

FUSIBLE LINK REPAIR PROCEDURE

(a)

WIRING ASSEMBLY–FUSE LINK

(WITH INSULATION STRIPPED BOTH ENDS)

BUTT CONNECTOR –WIRING SPLICE

D3AZ–14A526-H	#14 GAUGE WIRE - 9.00" ± .50 LENGTH (GREEN INSULATION)
D3AZ–14A526-J	#16 GAUGE WIRE - 9.00" ± .50 LENGTH (ORANGE INSULATION) AS REQ'D.
D3AZ–14526-K	#17 GAUGE WIRE - 9.00" ± .50 LENGTH (YELLOW INSULATION) AS REQ'D. (SPECIAL USED WITH AIR CONDITIONING SYSTEM)
D3AZ14A526-L	#18 GAUGE WIRE - 9.00" ± .50 LENGTH (RED INSULATION) AS REQ'D
D3AZ–14A526-M	#20 GAUGE WIRE – 9.00" ± .50 LENGTH (BLUE INSULATION) AS REQ'D.

WIRING ASSEMBLY - FUSE LINK

(WITH EYELET TERMINAL AND ONE END STRIPPED)

D3AZ–14A526–D	14 GAUGE WIRE - 9.00" ± .50 LENGTH (GREEN INSULATION) AS REQ'D.
D3AZ–14A526-E	#16 GAUGE WIRE - 9.00" ± .50 LENGTH (ORANGE INSULATION) AS REQ'D.
D3AZ–14A526-F	#18 GAUGE WIRE – 9.00" ± .50 LENGTH (RED INSULATION) AS REQ'D.
D3AZ–14A526-G	#20 GAUGE WIRE-9.00 ± .50 LENGTH (BLUE INSULATION) AS REQ'D.

D3AZ–14488-Y	FOR 10 AND 12 GA. WIRE	(LOAD CIRCUIT) AS REQ'D.
D3AZ–14488-Z	FOR #14 AND 16 GA. WIRE	(LOAD CIRCUIT) AS REQ'D.

(b)

Figure 23-10 (a) Fuse link service procedure; (b) fuse link and butt connector
identification. *(Courtesy of Ford Motor Corporation.)*

if the unit operates, the fault is in the ground. Door units occasionally lose ground with the body because of either rusted or excessively lubricated hinges.

When repairing front end collisions, make sure that the ground wire, if applicable, is not left off, cut, or improperly reattached.

As previously mentioned, short circuits or shorts cause circuit failure and should be corrected immediately (Figure 23-11). If a short circuit is evident, make a thorough inspection of the circuit involved before replacing a fuse or circuit breaker. Trace the wire as it passes through body openings, over brackets, and any place where the insulation may be worn off. Some wires are difficult to locate because they are under the seats, under floor mats, between the inner and outer quarter panel or front fender skirts. Some shorts are caused by different accessories being added with sheetmetal screws inserted in the wrong place or wires being pinched. It is bad practice to alter the fuse or bypass it because fire may result.

A device, called a *short tester*, is very useful in locating shorts. It consists of two leads with alligator clips for bypassing the fuse or breaker, a 15-amp breaker to replace the existing breaker, and a meter for detecting intermittent electrical current. Follow the procedure as recommended by the equipment manufacturer. Basically, the meter needle will deflect until it nears the short, and the deflector will decrease and deflect in the opposite direction as the short is passed.

Some shorts can be corrected by simply applying electrical tape to the area. Otherwise, the section of the wire must be replaced, and the replacement should be the same size.

NOTE: On some automobiles, aluminum wires are used for some circuits and

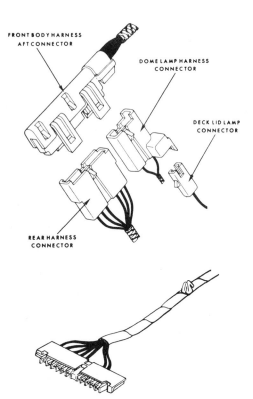

'HARMONICA' TYPE CONNECTOR

LOW PRIMARY CABLE	
GAGE	METRIC SIZE
20	0.5mm^2
18	0.8
16	1.0
14	2.0
12	3.0
10	5.0
8	8.0
6	13.0
4	19.0

Figure 23-11 (a) Front body harness—aft connector—F style; (b) front body harness—forward connector and aft connector on H styles; (c) wire gauge to metric conversion chart. *(Courtesy of General Motors Corporation, Fisher Body Division.)*

WHERE USED	BULB NO.	NO. USED	CANDLE POWER	MODEL
FRONT				
HEADLAMP - 142.0 X 200.0 2B	6052	2	55/65	ALL
PARK & DIRECTIONAL SIGNAL	1157NA	2	3/32	ALL
SIDE MARKER	194	2	2	ALL
REAR				
TAIL & STOP	1157	4	3/32	ALL
LICENSE ILLUMINATION	194	1	2	ALL
SIDE MARKER	194	2	2	ALL
LUGGAGE COMPARTMENT LAMP	1003	1	15	ALL U25
BACK-UP	1156	2	32	ALL
DIRECTIONAL SIGNAL	1156	2	32	ALL
INSTRUMENT PANEL				
ILLUM. (SPEEDO)	161	1	1	ALL
ILLUM. (SPEEDO)	194	2	2	ALL
ILLUM. (GAGES) (U14)	161	2	1	ALL U14
ILLUM. (FUEL GAGE) (LESS U14)	194	3	2	ALL
ILLUM. (GAGES) (U14)	194	2	2	ALL U14
ILLUM. (CLOCK)	194	1	3	ALL
ILLUM. (CLOCK)	194	1	3	U35
ILLUM. (HEATER/A/C CONTROL)	194	1	2	ALL
INDICATORS				
HEADLAMP HI BEAM	161	1	1	ALL
DIRECTIONAL SIGNAL	194	2	2	ALL
OIL PRESSURE	194	1	2	ALL
TEMPERATURE (TEMP)	194	1	2	ALL
GENERATOR (GEN)	194	1	2	ALL (-U14)
BRAKE	194	1	2	ALL
CRUISE	161	1	1	ALL K30
FASTEN BELTS	194	1	2	ALL
CHECK ENGINE	194	1	2	ALL UR3
SERVICE ILLUMINATION				
RADIO DIAL ILLUMINATIONS	1893	1	2	ALL
ASH TRAY	1445	1	.5	ALL U28
HEADER MAP LAMP	211-2	1	12	ALL UF3
UNDERHOOD	631	1	6	ALL
INTERIOR ILLUMINATION				
FLASHER HAZARD		1		ALL
DOME WITH READING LAMP	212	1	6	ALL C75
READING LAMP	1004	2	15	ALL C95
VANITY MIRROR				ALL D34
DOME	561	1	12	ALL (-C95)
COURTESY	906	2	6	ALL U29
FLASHER-DIR. SIGNAL - 2 LAMP				ALL

Figure 23-12 Bulb chart. *(Courtesy of General Motors Corporation, Chevrolet Motor Division.)*

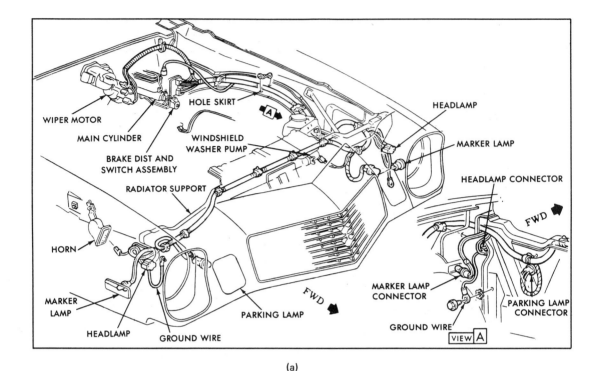

(a)

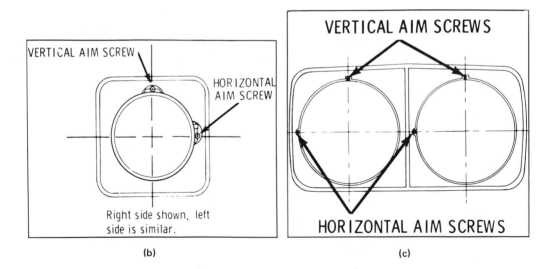

(b)

(c)

Figure 23–13 (a) Forward lamp wiring—F series; (b) two headlamp system aiming screws; (c) four headlamp system aiming screws. *(Courtesy of General Motors Corporation, Chevrolet Motor Division.)*

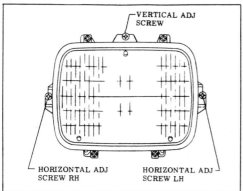

VERTICAL ADJ
SCREW

HORIZONTAL ADJ
SCREW RH

HORIZONTAL ADJ
SCREW LH

−5 x 7 Headlamp System Aiming Screws

Figure 23-14 Typical headlight assemblies. *(Courtesy of General Motors Corporation, Chevrolet Motor Division.)*

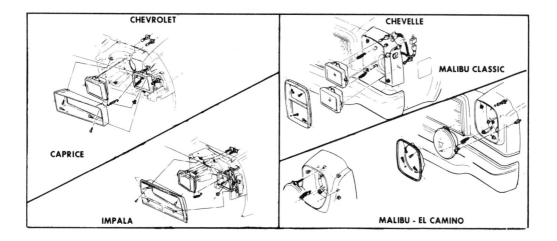

CHEVROLET

CHEVELLE

MALIBU CLASSIC

CAPRICE

IMPALA

MALIBU - EL CAMINO

require a special repair kit which can be secured from the manufacturer.

LIGHTS

After completing body repairs, the headlights and other lights should be checked for operation (Figure 23–12). If the headlights were involved in the repair operation, they should be checked for adjustment in accordance with the state's safety inspection tests.

The headlights are adjusted by a horizontal and vertical screw without removing the headlight door. Many headlight alignment units are available for making the correct adjustments (Figures 23–13 and 23–14).

Parking-directional, tail and brake, and marker light failure is often due to moisture getting into the bulb sockets and causing corrosion of the contact and bulb. Many of these can be sanded but in case of severe corrosion, the sockets and/or bulb should be replaced. Some attempt should be made to waterproof the unit if possible to avoid future problems.

Questions

1. What type electrolyte is used in batteries?
2. In case of accidental spills, what must be done immediately if the electrolyte contacts the skin?
3. What does each battery cell consist of?
4. How many cells are in a 12-volt battery?
5. What are the two different types of terminals?
6. What type energy is stored in the battery?
7. What are some of the causes of battery failure?
8. Will freezing temperatures damage a discharged battery?
9. What are the two battery ratings?
10. Where should the negative end of the booster cable be placed when starting an automobile?
11. Why is a charging battery dangerous?
12. Can a high charging rate damage a discharged battery?
13. How are different wiring circuits identified?
14. How are circuits protected from overload?
15. What is a *circuit breaker?*
16. What is a *fusible link?*
17. Can the fusible link be repaired with any size wire?
18. What is an *open circuit?*
19. How can an open circuit be checked?
20. What causes motors or other units to operate improperly?

Refinishing

part

3

HISTORY OF AUTOMOTIVE FINISHES

Did you ever look at a can of acrylic enamel or lacquer and think how it all started? Before 1923, all the automobiles produced were painted with brushes. The paint used was varnish mixed with a pigment (materials used to make colors) called *lampblack*. Several coats of paint or varnish were brushed on the vehicles. Each coat was dried thoroughly, then rubbed, or sanded with pumice stone (a finely ground volcanic rock) and water before the next coat could be applied. This type painting could take as long as one month, seriously tying up production lines. Because of the slow drying varnish, dust was a problem. These painters were often referred to as *carriage painters*. It was said by Henry Ford, the founder of the Ford Motor Company, "You can have any color new car you request, as long as it is black."

Another problem with this type paint was that within a year, the finish became dull.

In 1923, the Du Pont Company developed a new type paint called *Duco* which was in reality nitrocellulose lacquer paint. Several coats of this new Duco could be applied, and each dried in minutes. The new Duco had a gloss and durability that far exceeded the varnish-type paint. Also, the automotive production line could be speeded up as the bottleneck had been removed. By 1924, Duco was available in 21 standard colors throughout the automotive industry.

Then a new problem developed because each brush painter had to be taught how to use a new piece of equipment, the spray gun.

Although lacquer paints revolutionized the automotive industry, lacquer finishes were not suitable for commerical vehicles. This was due to their brittleness and the

Automotive Finishes Past and Present

chapter
24

necessity of high compound to bring out the gloss.

In 1930, a new finish was developed called *alkyd enamel* which was a synthetic resin finish that could withstand more impact than the fragile nitrocellulose. The drying time was slower than that of nitrocellulose, but a higher gloss finish resulted without the necessity of rubbing as required by lacquer. This new finish was well adapted to use on commerical vehicles. It was immediately adopted by some auto manufacturers and is still used today on trucks and some foreign cars.

In the middle 1950s, a new finish appeared called *acrylic lacquer* which had several times the durability of lacquer. By 1959, General Motors adopted acrylic lacquer as their OEM (original equipment manufactured) finish. This material became popular as a spot repair material because it matched the gloss on either factory enamel or acrylic lacquer.

There was still a need for improving the paint's drying time. In the early 1970s, *acrylic enamel* was introduced to the market and soon was used by some auto and truck manufacturers because of its gloss retention and fast drying properties.

The paint industry is now going through continual change. In 1971, a new type paint, a two-part, air dry finish called *polyurethane* was introduced. This finish has a tougher but flexible film which is superior to any other finish. This paint was primarily used on commercial truck fleets but now it is available as a standard refinish material in a wide range of colors.

The paint industry is rapidly changing with the new antipollution laws and the introduction of new type bodies for fuel economy. The future will see more aluminum, fiberglass, and plastics used in the automobile bodies due to increased environmental regulations.

In recent years, some paint manufactur-

ers introduced an additive to increase durability and drying time and to prevent wrinkling in alkyd enamel. Likewise, a hardener for acrylic enamel is now used to increase the gloss and make it more resistant to chemicals.

With the increased use of flexible plastic around the bumpers and grilles, a different type paint was necessary that could withstand the flexing of the plastic.

The paints used on the production lines and those used in the repair shop are similar but different. The paints, lacquer, and enamel are adopted for use with high temperatures on the production line. The stripped body is painted, then baked at high temperatures. In the repair shop, this high temperature could damage the glass, plastic trim, and other heat-sensitive materials.

Even the primers used serve the same purpose, that is, protecting the bare metal from rust and corrosion, but there is a difference because of the method used. If the same primer used in repair shops was used in the production of new vehicles, the line would slow down because of the extra labor involved.

Whether it is paint, primer, or other paint-like material, all have the three basic components found in paints. These are: binders, pigments, and the solvent or vehicle (Figure 24–1).

Binders are often referred to as the film former or the substance that makes the paint stick. The binders are made of a vast number of materials which give the paint durability, flexibility, adhesion, corrosion resistance, gloss, and other desired properties. Some of the ingredients are natural and man-made such as oils from cottonseed and castor, material resins, methyl, urethane and so on. The binder is a nearly clear or amber-colored liquid with no hiding abilities.

Pigments must be added to give the paint the color. Pigments cannot be used alone

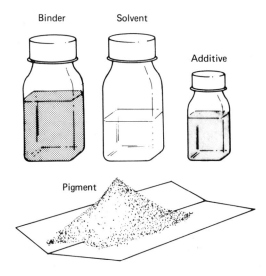

Binder   Solvent

Additive

Pigment

Figure 24-1 Basic components of paint.

settle faster than others. Some pigments are five times heavier than others. Some paints contain varying amounts of metallic flakes or aluminum flakes in various sizes and shapes. Pigment is used for coverage and to improve the strength of the paint film. It also improves the paint's durability and color retention.

Solvents (or vehicle) must be able to dissolve the binders and carry the pigments and binders from the gun to the surface being painted. Some solvents are added during the paint manufacturing process and the rest are added to thinner or reducer for the right spraying viscosity.

In the fifties, acrylic was added to the binder to improve the quality of the gloss and reduce fading. Later came the acrylic enamels with faster drying qualities.

Polyurethane increased the flexibility of the paint film and was chip resistant.

The additives now used could be considered in the binder class. These additives prevent wrinkling, add flexibility and chemical resistance to acrylic enamels, add hardness and quicker drying times to alkyd enamels. In general, they improve the quality of the paints.

because they lack the necessary qualities found in the binders. Pigment is that material found on the bottom of the can after it has been sitting on the shelf for awhile. The pigments will vary in weight because of the different colors used. Some pigments are light and fluffy while some are very heavy. This is why some colors will

Questions

1. What type paint was first used on new automobiles?
2. In 1923, what type paint was introduced that revolutionized the automotive industry?
3. Was this paint suitable for commerical vehicles?
4. About 1930, what new type paint was introduced?
5. During the 1950s, what new paint was introduced that increase durability?
6. What automobile manufacturer adopted this paint as original equipment?
7. What new paint became available in the 1970s which had more durability than the old type enamel?
8. What other paint was introduced in the 1970s that was more flexible and tougher?
9. What is the chief difference between production painting and painting in the shop?
10. What are the basic components of paint and what are they used for?

Preparation Materials and Abrasives

chapter
25

Auto refinishing or painting is perhaps the most important part of the auto body business. Not only do wrecks and minor damage have to be painted, but many automobiles are repainted to enhance their beauty. New and used car dealers repaint automobiles to attract buyers. Also, sometimes the owner gets tired of looking at the same old color. The finish on many automobiles often needs attention because it has been neglected or damaged by weather conditions.

In the body and fender business, an excellent paint job is good advertising. A poor job may turn potential customers away. In many cases, bad body work will be more pronounced by a paint job. The finished job, whether good or bad, will always be on display when the automobile leaves the garage. In today's world, fancy stripes and murals are popular. This means more business for the good painter.

SURFACE CLEANING

One of the first steps in doing a high quality paint job is to properly clean the surface to be painted whether it is just a fender or the complete auto body (Figure 25-1). If the painting is limited to a single panel, it is advisable to clean the adjoining panel also because the painted panel will be compared to the adjoining panels. All of the loose dirt and road film must be removed with a thorough wash job (Figure 25-2). If sand or grit remains on the surface during the sanding operation, deep scratches could result affecting the entire paint job. There would then be extra labor to remove the scratches.

Also, after all of the work is completed, a quick wash job will remove all spray dust or other dust that may have settled on the car while in the body shop. It helps with customer relations. Many times the first im-

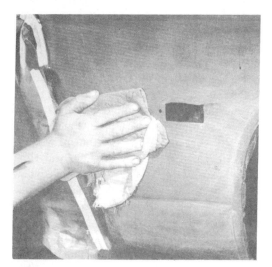

Figure 25-1 Clean the surface to remove particles, oil and film. *(Courtesy of 3M Company.)*

pression the customer has when he sees his automobile after it has been repaired is very important. Washing will not remove wax, silicones, road tar, or other contami-

nents. Failure of some paint jobs can be traced back to improper cleaning of the surface before sanding.

Washing Procedures

1. Rinse the automobile with water to remove loose dirt.
2. Use detergent or car soap, and water; wash a section at a time with a sponge or towel. Start with the top, hood, and deck. Thoroughly cover the entire panel.
3. Rinse soap before it dries on the surface.
4. Wash the sides, including the edges of the wheel opening and around the bumpers and grille.
5. Thoroughly rinse off entire car.
6. Dry the surface thoroughly.

CLEANING WITH CHEMICALS

The surfaces must be chemically cleaned because washing will not remove wax, silicone, road tar, or other contaminents. Select only clean, soft cloths, preferably cotton or a commercial disposable wiper. Select the proper wax and silicone remover and read the instructions on the label. Enamel reducers will not completely remove some waxes, silicones or polishes. Lacquer thinners should not be used as cleaning agents as it may soften the painted surface or damage it. Use only solvents or chemicals made for that purpose. Generally, use the same brand of wax and silicone remover as the brand of paint used in the shop.

Figure 25-2 Washing panel with soap and water. *(Courtesy of 3M Company.)*

Cleaning Procedures

1. Fold cloth into a pad and apply the cleaning chemical or solvent with enough chemical to thoroughly wet the surface.

2. Wet a section of the panel and immediately wipe dry with a clean cloth before the solvent dries. Preferably, wet a section 2 ft. by 2 ft. (609.6 mm x 609.6 mm) or just large enough to wipe dry before the solvent evaporates. If the solvent dries before being wiped, rewet it, as the residue from the solvent can affect the adhesion.

   Change cloth frequently as the cloth becomes saturated with solvents.

3. When cleaning the entire car or just a section, start at the highest point.

   Be sure to get in around drip moldings, cowl vent grille, inside of door edge, hood and deck lids or any place where wax and silicone can hide and cause trouble when painting.

4. Wipe thoroughly around molding or chrome to remove all traces of solvent.

   If some molding or trim can be removed quickly and easily, it is better to remove it now. Then you can be sure of removing any traces of wax and silicone that may be behind the molding.

   NOTE: When dusting an automobile before painting, if all wax and silicone have not been removed, they will be blown out on the panel and then the paint job will be ruined.

ABRASIVES

In preparing a car for painting, the surface must be properly sanded to remove all of the imperfections such as chips, rust, scratches, or ridges left from body repair. Any imperfections remaining on the surface will be magnified by the final color coat.

Removal of these imperfections is done by the use of a wide range of sanding materials, called *abrasives*, which usually are in a disc or sandpaper form. There are several types of abrasives such as aluminum oxide, silicone carbide, emery garnet, and flint. Only aluminum oxide and silicone carbide are used in the automotive repair business while the other three are used on softer materials such as wood.

Aluminum oxide is made by fusing aluminum ore or bauxite with intense heat and melting into a solid block. It is then crushed and graded by size. The granules or grits are extremely tough to withstand the heat of grinding. They can penetrate almost any surface.

Silicone carbide is made in a resistance-type furnace. Pure glass sand (chemicals, silicone oxide), coke, either from petroleum or soft coal, sawdust and common salt are used in the process. The silicone of the sand and carbon from coke combine to form silicone carbide.

After it cools, the material is crushed and screened. The grits or granules formed are hard and brittle and fracture into sliver-like wedges.

The grit size ranges from #16 (4), the largest, to #600, the smallest. The adhesive used and the backing material will vary in accordance with the usage.

Grinding Discs

The grit on the grinding discs range from #16 (4) to #80 (1/0) grit (Figure 25-3). The backing material for grinding discs is made of a fiber-type material which is strong and

Figure 25-3   Different sanding discs: (a) 16 grit, open coat; (b) 24 grit, open coat; (c) 36 grit, closed coat; (d) 50 grit, closed coat. *(Photo by S. Suydam.)*

flexible. The adhesive used is a synthetic resin which is heat resistant due to the action of the grinder.

After the disc is coated with resin, it is placed in the disc by electric static means, then additional resin is added to seal the grit into place.

There are two types of discs — *open* and *closed coat*. The open coat has grits spaced apart. It is used for paint or soft material removal because it will not clog up too quickly. The other type (closed coat) with the grit close together produces a smoother cut with less gouge marks in the metal surface. A #50 (1) or #80 (1/0) grit is used to remove the marks from the #16 (4) disc.

These discs are available in 5" (127 mm) for air grinders and 7" (178 mm) and 9" (229 mm) for larger electric and air grinders.

NOTE: There is a growing use of aluminum in the manufacture of body panels such as hoods. Aluminum is a soft metal as compared to steel and can be damaged by harsh abrasives. For the removal of paint from aluminum, a #36 (2) grit open coat disc should be used. Never use a #16 (4) or #24 (3) grit disc. Avoid removing the metal as much as possible. Use a sharp disc to avoid heat buildup.

Production Paper

Production paper is used for dry sanding and faster removal of materials such as old paint and body filler plastic. Aluminum oxide grits are glued on a paper backing. The grits range from #36 (2) to #100 (2/0) grit and are the open coat type to resist clogging and cut faster. The production paper is available in discs of many sizes, 9" × 11" (229 mm × 279 mm) sheets or precut for different types of power sanders. Many bodymen use a #40 (1 1/2) grit for smoothing body filler and finish up with a #100 (2/0) grit for final shaping and featheredging the paint (Figures 25-4 and 25-5).

NOTE: Use caution when sanding plastic filler or featheredging paint on aluminum hoods or any other aluminum body panel. Aluminum is a soft metal and could be damaged if a #40 (1/1/2) grit paper is used for sanding. Nothing coarser than #80 (1/0) grit paper, preferably with a foam-backed pad, should be used to avoid heat buildup.

Finishing Sand Paper

Finishing sand paper or fine sanding paper is used to prepare to surface to be primed or to sand primer before applying the final paint coats. (Figure 25-6).

Finishing paper is available in two types: wet or dry waterproof paper or a nonclogging dry-type paper. The wet-type paper

Figure 25-5 Sanding area with production paper and sanding block. *(Courtesy of 3M Company.)*

consists of silicone carbide grits bonded with waterproof glue to a special waterproof paper which is tough and durable.

The wet-type sandpaper is available from

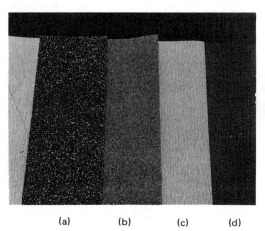

(a)   (b)   (c)   (d)

Figure 25-4 Types and sizes of abrasive paper: (a) 40D production paper for fast removal of plastic filler; (b) 100C production paper for final shaping of plastic filler and featheredging; (c) 220 non-clogging paper for dry sanding; (d) 400 wet or dry paper for fine sanding. *(Photo by S. Suydam.)*

Figure 25-6 Wet sand surface with wet or dry paper and water. *(Courtesy of 3M Company.)*

#80 (1/0) to #600 grit. The most commonly used grits range from #220 (6/0) to #500. The coarser papers are used for sanding primer before the final color coats. The #500 or #600 grit is used to sand dust or imperfections after the final coat and before compounding.

Using water with a wet-type paper speeds up the process, and the sanding residue is washed away. Otherwise, the residue will clog the paper. One of the main objections to wet sanding is that it is messy.

Non-Clogging Paper

This type paper is very popular. The grits are the same size as wet sanding paper, but one size coarser must be used, to get the comparable finish (Figure 25-4, c). Some bodymen object to this type because of the dust produced.

There are several other types of abrasive materials available such as cloth back (for heavy paint removal) belts, preglue, or contact-type disc, but these are not as frequently used.

Questions

1. Why is a thorough wash job an important step in preparing an automobile for a repaint job?
2. Why should the automobile be washed again just before delivery to the customer?
3. Why is it important to rinse off the loose dirt before washing with soap?
4. How large an area can be wet with chemical at one time?
5. Why is it important to carefully remove the wax and silicone from around moldings and trim?
6. What are the five types of abrasives used?
7. What is aluminum oxide made from?
8. What is silicone carbide made from?
9. What is the largest and smallest abrasive grits used in shops?
10. What is meant by *open* and *closed coat discs?*
11. What is production sandpaper used for?
12. What type abrasive material is used on production paper?
13. What type abrasive material is used on finishing sandpaper?

Thinners and Reducers

Thinners and reducers are very important in the spray application of lacquer and enamel paint. These specially developed agents dilute the paint or lower the viscosity, so that the paint can be properly atomized as it passes through the spray gun and is transported in the air stream to the panel surface.

On the panel surface, the thinner and reducer must remain in solution long enough to permit the paint to flow out to a smooth finish. Then these thinners and reducers evaporate as the paint dries and do not remain as part of the dried paint film.

Thinner is a solvent combination used to thin lacquer and acrylic lacquer to spraying viscosity. *Reducer* is a solvent combination used to thin or reduce enamel or acrylic enamel to a spraying viscosity. The viscosity or consistency of the thinned or reduced paint is very important for proper paint application. The viscosity is measured with a No. 4 Ford cup or a Zahn cup and a stop watch. The length of time it takes the cup to empty is recorded. Depending upon the paint manufacturer, enamel generally takes about 22 to 25 seconds and lacquer 18 to 20 seconds.

Although thinners and reducers perform the same function, using a thinner as a reducer could lead to early paint fading or dulling, because the thinner is not balanced with the hardeners and pigments of the enamel paint.

ACRYLIC LACQUER THINNER

Lacquer thinner is a strong solvent, and when added to acrylic lacquer dissolves and thins the binders, vehicles, and pigments. There are three important components in acrylic lacquer thinner: *active solvents, latent solvents,* and *diluents* (Figure 26-1).

Figure 26-1 Different grades of acrylic lacquer thinner. *(Photo by S. Suydam.)*

1. An active solvent is a solvent that acts immediately to dissolve other substances.

2. A latent solvent is a solvent that improves a good solvent but cannot be used alone.

3. A diluent is a resin solvent with more thinning qualities.

These components provide for a balanced thinner (a thinner with the right qualities).

Most of the paint materials are packaged and shipped at as high a viscosity (or consistency) as possible to help in slowing down the settling rate of the pigments or fillers. This is why most paint materials must be thinned or reduced at the time of usage.

The use of bargain or cheap thinners is not a money saver and may result in extra labor or paint failure. Each thinner is formulated for a specific use with the right solvents. A cheap thinner may lack the proper solvent to permit adequate flow and gloss.

Selection of Proper Thinner

Different manufacturers of thinners use various numbers and names for their products, but all are classified in the same way.

The temperature of the shop is one factor to take into consideration when selecting a particular type thinner. A cool or cold shop would require a thinner with a fast evaporation rate. Shops with temperatures of 85° F (29.4 C) or above would require a slow drying lacquer thinner. Normal shop temperatures range from 70° F (21° C) to 85° F (29.4° C).

Another condition which determines the type thinner to use is high temperature with high humidity (moisture content of the air). High humidity during high temperatures causes blushing in lacquer paint. Blushing is caused by rapid cooling due to the fast evaporation of the thinner. This is the result of moisture condensing in the film in the form of minute droplets of water. This will give the paint a milky or grayish look.

Always follow the directions on the paint can label and match the thinner to the paint for best results.

Thinner and Base Coat

The surface to be painted must be considered when selecting the proper type thinner along with shop conditions. The surface could be original acrylic lacquer, enamel, primed or previously repaired sections. If the surface has been previously repaired or coated with improperly cured enamel, the use of a slow drying thinner in a cool shop could cause excessive solvent penetration. Solvents remaining on the surface too long will either soften the base paint or cause the paint to lift. Sand scratch swelling is often the result of penetration of the base paint. See the dicussion of paint problems for more information (page 000).

The use of a very fast evaporating thinner results in poor adhesion to the base paint. Most of the thinner is evaporated in the air stream, and little will reach the surface to permit proper adhesion to the base paint.

Thinner and Top Coat

The right thinner for the job means less work in the end — the smoother the paint, the less time spent in compounding.

Under the right conditions with the right thinner, the paint will flow out upon reaching the surface while the thinner is evaporating. The use of a thinner that evaporates too fast will cause the paint to dry and not flow out. The overall painted surface will have a sandy rough finish and possibly poor adhesion. This type finish will require additional sanding and compounding. If the paint used is a metallic type, the paint will be lighter than normal.

NOTE: Air pressure and the distance between the spray gun and panel are some other factors which affect color match of metallic-type paints.

Using a thinner that evaporates too slowly for shop conditions will cause the paint to run or sag. Excessive solvent penetration of the underneath surfaces could cause sand scratch swelling, and lifting. Metallic-type paint will appear darker than normal because the metallic flakes have settled too deep in the paint film.

Special Thinner or Additives

A special thinner or additive called *retarder* is used to control blushing. This slow drying solvent promotes leveling or flow out of the last coat and a high gloss finish. The retarder is only added to the last coats of prethinned lacquer paint. When using this type solvent, follow the manufacturer's directions concerning the amount to be added to prethinned paint. Excessive amounts of retarder solvent can lead to serious paint problems.

NOTE: When mixing lacquer-type primer-surfacers, check the labels on the thinner can as to whether the thinner is satisfactory for use in primer-surfacer. Very fast or slow drying thinners or those specified as color coat thinners are normally not recommended for primer-surfacers.

ENAMEL REDUCER

Enamel or acrylic enamel reducer, like lacquer thinner, has many different names and stock numbers depending on the manufacturer. Some manufacturers offer a few types or grades of reducer while others have more grades to select from, and some offer an all-weather–type reducer (Figure 26–2).

The reducers are classified according to how fast the solvent evaporates, and the solvents perform the same function in the makeup of the reducers. Both enamel and lacquer paints depend on the evaporation of the solvents for drying, but enamel has an additional stage in drying called *oxidation.* Oxidation is the combining of oxygen with the paint binders. Thoroughly dry enamel or acrylic enamel is practically insoluble in ordinary solvent. Temperature or shop conditions are important when selecting the grade or type reducer to use. The alkyd enamel and acrylic enamel use different types of reducers for the best results as recommended on the paint can label by the manufacturer.

The cool or cold shop needs a fast or medium fast evaporating type reducer. If the paint remains wet too long, it will run or sag. In the case of alkyd enamel, which is

(a)

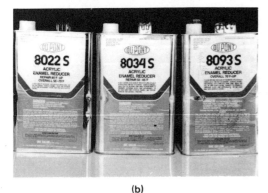

(b)

Figure 26-2 (a) Different grades of reducers for alkyd enamel; (b) different grades of acrylic enamel reducers for different shop conditions. *(Photos by S. Suydam.)*

normally slower drying than acrylic enamel, dust in the air could settle on the wet paint.

When the shop temperature reaches 80° F (26.7° C) or above, a slower type evaporating reducer is necessary. Shop temperatures above 85° F (29.4° C) require a very slow evaporating reducer. If the reducer evaporates too fast, the wet paint film will not flow out, causing a rough film or dryness with little or no luster. This is one of the causes of orange peel. (Refer to the discussion of paint problems for other causes of orange peel.)

The use of the wrong grade reducer is one of the causes for mismatch of metallic-type paints. A slow drying reducer used under cool shop conditions will permit the metallic to settle too deep in the paint film causing a dark color. A very fast drying reducer will cause a light color because the metallic will not have time to level off before the film dries.

Selection of Reducer

Some grades of enamel reducer are recommended for reducing color coats and enamel-type primer-surfacers or primer-sealers. Generally, the fast, medium fast, or all-weather reducers are recommended for primers or undercoats. The slower evaporating reducers are not recommended for primers or undercoats, but for color coats only. Always follow the recommendations on the labels.

Occasionally, a can of paint may recommend one reduction ratio of paint and reducer, but the label on the reducer container may recommend a different ratio of paint and reducer. It would be advisable to follow the directions on the reducer container.

Forced Dry Reducers

Some shops use a drying oven or heating panel to speed up the paint-drying process. Using heat will sometimes cause enamel to wrinkle while drying. This is caused by solvents being trapped below the surface of the paint film. An antiwrinkle additive is available to eliminate the wrinkling problem.

Retarder

Retarders are a special blend of solvent used to control the drying characteristics of enamel or acrylic enamel. It is recommended when shop temperatures exceed 85° F (29.4° C), or it can be added to reducers to slow the drying of the paint film.

Retarder is also used in the last coat of paint to increase the flow out and to dissolve the overspray in the case of spot repairing. It cannot be used alone as a reducer and is used only in small quantities in mixed paints. Follow the label very closely when using retarder to avoid serious paint problems.

Questions

1. What is the purpose of using thinners and reducers?
2. What is *viscosity*?
3. What are the three important components of lacquer thinner?
4. Why is paint packaged and shipped at a high viscosity?
5. What type thinner should be used in a cool or cold shop?
6. What type thinner should be used during high temperatures?
7. What causes blushing?
8. What is the purpose of using retarder?
9. What is the second stage of drying in enamel paints called?
10. What happens if metallic enamel paints dry too fast?
11. What causes wrinkling of the paint film when forced dry?

Primers and primer-surfacers, referred to as *undercoats,* serve two important functions in the refinishing process. First, they protect the bare metal from moisture or rusting and provide adhesion to properly prepared bare metal. This must be a lasting bond that will not deteriorate with time. Color coats will stick to bare metal for a short period of time, then crack and peel off because they lack the proper adhesive qualities.

Secondly, the primers and primer-surfacers provide a surface to which the color coat can adhere. Also, the primer or surfacer must be able to adhere to a properly sanded, painted surface.

PRIMERS

A primer is specifically designed for adhesion to bare metal or previously painted surfaces called *substrate.* A substrate is a surface to be refinished, either an old finish, bare metal, or primer-surfacer. The primer has very little filling quality or content and is normally used on new panels that do not require additional sanding (Figure 27-1). The primer can be used on properly prepared steel, aluminum, galvanized and other substrates. These primers require very little sanding, just a light scruffing to remove any overspray or nibs. Primers are used on commercial vehicles and equipment where the smoothness of the substrate is not important.

As with paint, there are different types of primers, either lacquer or enamel. Zinc chromate primer is used on steel and aluminum to protect the metal from further corrosion. It is used as an overall primer for new commercial bodies. Zinc chromate is also an insulator against corrosion caused by electrolysis (having two dissimiliar metals touch each other). This condition is very common where aluminum trim is attached to steel bodies.

Primers and Primer-Surfacers

chapter **27**

Figure 27-1 Different types of primers for lacquers, enamels, plastic and dissimilar metals. *(Photo by S. Suydam.)*

In the repair procedures, the application of zinc chromate is followed by several coats of primer-surfacer, if lacquer is used as a top coat.

Wash primer or *vinyl wash primer* can be used on fiberglass, steel, aluminum, and certain types of galvanized metal. Wash primer has excellent adhesion and is fast drying.

After applying wash primer, an enamel primer-sealer or enamel primer-surfacer coat is applied. It is not recommended that color coats be directly applied to the wash primer.

Other special primers are available from different manufacturers; for example, primer for polypropylene plastic parts and an epoxy zinc chromate primer recommended under urethane top coats.

PRIMER-SURFACERS

Primer-surfacer is a combination of a primer and filler material called *surfacer*. In the process of repairing body metal, the paint is removed by means of a grinding disc. The grit on the grinding disc leaves many small grooves in the metal. If just a primer were used to cover the bare metal and the color coats were applied over the primer, the grooves would show through. Applying several coats of primer-surfacer to the bare metal along with the proper sanding, produces a smooth metal surface. Small scratches or chips in the painted surface can be filled with primer-surfacer (Figure 27-2). It is not intended to fill deep grooves or scratches. Any imperfection left on the surface will show after the color coats have been applied. Primer-surfacer is worthless unless properly sanded after it has dried thoroughly (Figure 27-3).

The most popular primer-surfacer is the

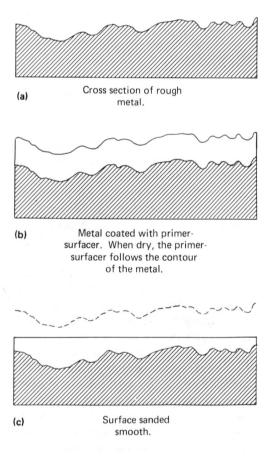

(a) Cross section of rough metal.

(b) Metal coated with primer-surfacer. When dry, the primer-surfacer follows the contour of the metal.

(c) Surface sanded smooth.

Figure 27-2 (a) Cross section of rough metal; (b) metal coated with primer surfacer. When dry the primer surfacer follows the contour of the metal; (c) surface sanded to a smooth surface.

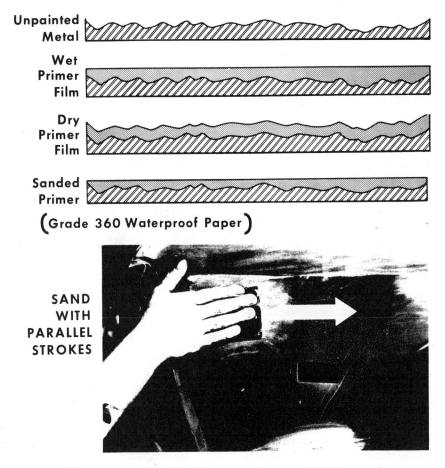

Unpainted Metal

Wet Primer Film

Dry Primer Film

Sanded Primer

(Grade 360 Waterproof Paper)

SAND WITH PARALLEL STROKES

Figure 27-3 Sanding the primer. *(Courtesy of 3M Company.)*

lacquer type. It is available in different colors because some of the color coats are semitransparent, and it would be difficult to prevent the primer from showing through the color coats.

Primer-surfacer can be used over aged enamel surfaces, acrylic lacquer, and bare steel. It is not recommended over uncured enamel, aluminum, and galvanized metal or on an overall refinish. On an overall refinish, a sealer must be applied before the color coats.

Enamel primer-surfacer dries rather quickly and can be sanded after several hours. It has better adhesion, flexibility, and rust resistance than lacquer primer-surfacer. However, it takes longer to dry before it can be sanded.

Some brands of enamel primer-surfacer can be color coated without being sanded if surface smoothness is not required. Therefore it is commonly used on commerical vehicles because it is a time saver. It is not recommended for use under lacquer as lifting may occur. Enamel primer-surfacers are available in various colors.

Application of Primer and Primer-Surfacers

The following is a brief list of basic procedures for the application of primer and primer-surfacers. These procedures will vary with the different manufacturers and surfaces.

Primers

1. Zinc chromate primer
   a. Under enamel or acrylic enamel
      1. Stir thoroughly. Reduce in accordance with the paint manufacturer's directions.
      2. Apply one light to medium wet coat.
      3. Allow to dry at least 30 minutes before applying color coat. Sanding is not required in most cases. Tack wipe to remove overspray.
   b. Under acrylic lacquer
      1. Stir thoroughly. Reduce in accordance with the paint manufacturer's directions.
      2. Apply one light to medium wet coat at 45 lbs (310 kPa) pressure.
      3. Allow to dry — from four hours to overnight. Follow directions on label.
      4. Apply lacquer primer-surfacer.
2. Wash primer or vinyl wash primer
   a. Stir thoroughly. Reduce wash primer with activator or catalyst in accordance with the label.
   b. Apply one wet coat at 40 lbs (276 kPa) pressure.

   c. No sanding required. Let dry for 30 minutes.
   d. Apply enamel primer-sealer or acrylic enamel-sealer before applying color coats.

Primer-Surfacers

1. Enamel primer-surfacers, enamel color coats
   a. Stir thoroughly. Reduce in accordance with the paint manufacturer's directions.
   b. Apply two or three coats medium wet at 45 to 55 lbs (310 to 380 kPa) pressure. Allow each coat to flash before applying next coat.
   c. After four to five hours, dry sand with #320 (9/0) or #400 (10/0) paper.
   d. Apply color coats three to five hours after sanding.
      Alternate: If color coat is to be acrylic lacquer, let dry overnight, sand with #400 (10/0) paper. Apply a lacquer-type sealer. Apply color coats.
2. Lacquer primer-surfacer
   a. Stir thoroughly. Reduce in accordance with paint manufacturer's directions.
   b. Apply two or more medium coats at 30 to 40 lbs (207 to 276 kPa) pressure. Allow each coat to flash before applying next coat.
   c. Allow at least 30 minutes to dry before sanding, depending on shop conditions.
   d. Apply sealer or color coats.

Questions

1. What are the two important functions of primers?
2. Does primer have any filling qualities?
3. What are primer-surfacers used for?

4. Can regular primer-surfacers be used on aluminum or flexible plastic parts?

5. How long should zinc chromate primer dry before applying lacquer primer-surfacer?

6. What is used to reduce wash primer?

7. When can enamel primer-surfacer be sanded?

8. What is the spray pressure of lacquer primer-surfacer?

Sealers

28

Sealers are used to improve adhesion between the substrate (or finish to be painted) and the color coats, to reduce sand-scratch swelling, and provide uniformity of color holdout.

Sealers can be applied over any finish or primer and primer-surfacer. When painting factory-primed new panels, a sealer can be used if no filling is necessary, before the color coats are applied.

Sealers are recommended when applying enamel over acrylic lacquer or lacquer primer-surfacer to reduce the chance of peeling after the color coats have aged (Figure 28-1). Some of the color coats have poor hiding qualities, and primer-surfacers may show through the color coats. A coat of sealer will give a uniform background.

When applying color coats over an area that was spot primed, the primed areas may appear dull or dry while the surrounding areas are glossy. This is caused by the primer being more porous than the old finish. A sealer will give a uniform color holdout and prevent sinking of the color coats. Sealers are not intended to fill in sand scratches or other surface defects. Some colors, like reds and maroons, may bleed through colors like white; that is, a pink or reddish haze may result. A bleeder sealer is applied before the color coats are applied.

Sealers are classified as *clear, universal,* and *primer* and are available in both lacquer and enamel. When applying acrylic lacquer over properly prepared acrylic lacquer, sealing is not required for adhesion, but it will reduce sand scratch swelling and improve color holdout.

USE OF LACQUER SEALERS

Clear sealer

1. Stir thoroughly. Most sealers are sprayed as is, because no thinning is required. Check label.

Figure 28-1 One of the many types of sealers. *(Photo by S. Suydam.)*

2. Apply one to two coats wet, depending on label directions, at 30 to 50 lbs (207 to 345 kPa) pressure. Let each coat flash before applying next coat.

3. After drying for 30 minutes, apply color coats. No sanding except for nibs. Tack wipe to remove overspray.

Universal sealers

1. Stir thoroughly and strain. Most universal sealers require no thinning. Check label.

2. Apply one even medium coat at 35 to 45 lbs (242 to 310 kPa) pressure.

3. Allow to dry 15 to 30 minutes. Remove nibs and tack wipe to remove overspray.

4. Apply top coats within one hour.

Bleeder sealer (Use only when necessary)

1. Stir thoroughly. Thin in accordance with recommendation on label.

2. Apply two medium wet coats at 35 to 45 lbs (242 to 310 kPa) pressure. Allow 15 to 30 minutes drying time before applying second coat.

3. Drying time one hour. Remove nibs and tack wipe to remove overspray.

4. Apply color coats.

USE OF ENAMEL SEALERS

For enamel or acrylic enamel

1. Primer-sealers or nonsanding primer-sealers
   a. Stir thoroughly and reduce in accordance with the recommendation on the label.
   b. Apply one light to medium wet coat at 40 lbs (276 kPa) pressure.
   c. After drying for 30 minutes, remove nibs and tack wipe to remove overspray.
   d. Apply color coats.

2. Recoat sealer for acrylic enamel
   a. Stir thoroughly. Some recoat sealers require no reduction.
   b. Apply two medium wet coats at 30 to 40 lbs (207 to 276 kPa) pressure. Allow 15 to 20 minutes between coats.
   c. Remove nibs and tack wipe to remove overspray.
   d. Apply color coats.

Questions

1. What is the purpose of a sealer?
2. Can sealers help in color holdout or in achieving uniform background?
3. What are some types of sealers?
4. What is a *bleeder sealer*?
5. Do lacquer sealers require thinning?

Putty

Putty is a hard pigment material or solid material with about the same composition as primer-surfacer. It is used to fill in imperfections in the surface that primer-surfacer cannot fill. Even small or shallow scratches in the metal can be filled with putty rather than with body filler. However, putty should not be used as a substitute for body work or to fill in a deep dent in the metal that exceeds $\frac{1}{16}$" (1.6 mm) deep.

Some manufacturers produce a *glazing putty* and a *spot putty*. A glazing putty is used to fill in sand scratches or small nicks. Spot putty, with more pigments, is used for deeper nicks, scratches, or grinding marks. A good quality putty will dry fast, sand easily, and have good color holdout. Poor quality putties are too porous, and some are very hard sanding or shrink too much.

Lacquer and enamel type putties are available. They can not be directly applied to bare metal.

LACQUER PUTTY

Lacquer putty is applied on properly prepared surfaces, preferably over primer-surfacer, but can be applied over properly sanded and aged top coats (Figure 29-1).

1. Apply in thin coats with a squeegee or a flexible putty knife. Work quickly before solvents evaporate. Two or threethin coats are better than one thick coat. Apply only where necessary, not on the whole panel.

2. After drying for thirty minutes to one hour, dry or wet sand using a sanding block for best results (Figure 29-2).

ENAMEL PUTTY

Enamel putties are available for use with enamel primers or primer-surfacers to fill in minor imperfections.

Figure 29-1 Filling surface imperfections. Use "spot" putty. *(Courtesy of 3M Company.)*

Figure 29-2 Block sand the putty by hand only. *(Courtesy of 3M Company.)*

1. Apply in thin coats rather than one heavy coat and only apply where necessary.
2. Let dry for at least one to two hours depending on shop conditions, before sanding.

3. Apply a light coat of primer or primer-surfacer before applying color coats.

The above procedures may vary with the different manufacturers.

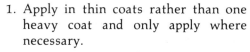

Questions

1. What are putties used for?
2. What is the difference between glazing and spot putty?
3. Why should putty be applied in thin coats?

Masking

Masking means the covering with masking tape, paper, or any other covering material to protect chrome moldings, bumpers, or other surfaces from unwanted paints and/or primers. Improper masking can result in damage to vinyl tops, plastic grilles, upholstery, and any other materials that can be affected by the solvents in the paint. Improper masking can cause unnecessary labor and can damage the freshly painted surface when it is removed. Improper masking can leave obvious signs such as paint on the radiator supports, bumper brackets, door gaskets, tires, and any other area that should not be painted. A good painter or craftsman does not leave these telltale traces when refinishing a panel or a complete car. Time spent in proper masking will save time in cleanup after the job is refinished.

SELECTION OF MASKING TAPE

Masking tape is a waterproof paper gummed on one side. It must adhere to any clean and dry painted or unpainted surface, to chrome moldings, to glass, tires, and any other surface on the automobile (Figure 30–1).

A good quality tape will not be affected by water during the sanding operation and will not leave traces of glue on the finished panel or moldings when removed. Cheaper or economical grades of tape do not have adequate adhesive properties and have a tendency to come loose especially on curved surfaces, permitting paint to get underneath. Likewise, some tapes will leave adhesive on the surface after removal, and the paints will bleed through this type paper. Economical tape and masking paper are not really money savers.

Masking tape is available in various widths from $\frac{1}{8}$" (3.17 mm) to 3" (76 mm).

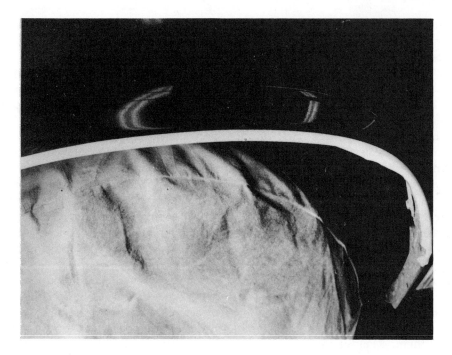

Figure 30-1 Masking chrome for spot repair with masking tape. Note wheel protective cover. *(Photo by S. Suydam.)*

The ¾" (19 mm) width tape is the most popular size used. The narrower width tapes are used for masking nameplates or small trim that cannot be removed easily or safely. Some areas may require wider tape than ¾" (19 mm).

NOTE: Do not leave masking tape on chrome or other areas that are exposed to sunlight or moisture for a long period of time. The tape will not come off or the adhesive will not come off with the tape.

MASKING PAPER

Masking paper is a good quality paper that will not permit paint to penetrate to the surfaces underneath and will not disintegrate when wet. It can withstand handling and will not tear as easily when curved surfaces are being worked on.

Masking paper is available in rolls from 3" (76 mm) to 36" (915 mm) wide with 12" (305 mm) being the most popular width used. Many shops will use 3" (76 mm), 12" (305 mm), and 24" (610 mm) widths to save time when masking an entire vehicle. Newspapers are used in place of masking paper in order to save money, but newspapers are a weak paper especially when wet sanding. They will tear easily and cannot stand air pressure when damp. Paint will bleed through the newspaper and sometimes transfer the ink to the surfaces underneath. If enough paint is applied to newspaper, the paper will stick to the surface underneath. It may be cheaper to purchase, but not cheaper to use, as it takes longer to apply tape to the paper.

Apron or paper dispensers are made to accommodate one or more rolls of paper and tape. The most common size is one with 12" (305 mm) paper and ¾" (19 mm) tape. These dispensers apply tape to the paper as the paper is pulled out. The taped paper is cut to the desired length by the cutter bar on the dispenser. Half of the width of the tape is applied to the paper edge, and the other half is applied to molding or any other area where it is needed.

Proper Procedures for Covering Chrome Parts

Premasking preparation is very important in avoiding problems when the primer or color coats are being applied to the surfaces. It is sometimes quicker to remove chrome molding, emblems, or letters than to mask them. Remove moisture or dirt from behind molding letters or emblems with high pressure air. Remove dirt and moisture from chrome surfaces. When applying tape to chrome or plastic molding, keep as close to the edge as possible but do not touch the painted surface. Press the tape on firmly to avoid getting the paint behind the tape. On small trim, emblems, or letters, narrow tape, ⅛" (3.17 mm) or ¼" (6 mm), is easier to use and can be worked into small areas with a knife. Antenna mast can be masked in several ways after the base or part nearest the paint is covered. Placing two strips of tape on both sides of the mast and pinching the edges together is one way. A tube made from narrow masking paper or a piece of rubber hose can be used. Be careful to mask any chrome that will be exposed to primer and paint.

Masking headlights and some taillights is best done with narrower paper, 3" (76 mm) or 6" (203 mm), if available, because it is easier to fold and work around curves.

Proper Procedures for Lacquer Refinishing

When refinishing a door, hood, or any other body panels, the surrounding area must be covered with masking paper to control overspray (Figure 30-2). It is important to mask gaskets, brackets, rubber bumpers, or parts on the inside edges of the panel to be painted. Door jams are masked to prevent paint from getting into the interior. Door gaskets should be cleaned with lacquer thinner or coated with a thin coat of clear lacquer so the tape will stick to it. The same procedure can be used on trunk gaskets.

NOTE: When removing tape from some types of gaskets, be careful not to pull pieces of gasket with the tape.

Rubber bumpers, brackets, or inner panels under the hood must be covered to avoid being painted. Most radiator supports, grille brackets, or hinges are normally black and should remain black. The same applies to bumper brackets and inner fender panels. Overspray on gaskets or brackets is a clear indication of a careless painter.

When painting hoods or deck lids the windshield or rear window must be completely covered to avoid overspray getting on the glass. The air current will bring the overspray up to the top of the glass, especially if slow drying thinner or retarder is used. The same rule applies to refinishing a roof panel. In addition to several lengths of paper to cover the glass, blankets, sheets, or any other covering should be used to avoid overspray from getting on hood and deck lid. Frames or undercarriage parts should be protected from paint, especially on newer autos.

On large areas to be covered such as windshields, several lengths of paper are

Figure 30-2 Use of masking paper. *(Photo by S. Suydam.)*

necessary to cover the glass: each length of paper should be overlapped. All overlaps and seams must be sealed with tape to prevent paint from being blown under the overlaps. First use masking tape alone along the edges of the chrome moldings, followed by the paper. The paper may have to be pleated or folded when going around a curved edge. If the roof is to be painted, overlap the bottom piece of paper with the top piece to prevent dust and moisture from seeping under the paper. The reverse procedure is used when painting the hood and not the roof. Door glass is masked in the same way as in the case of hardtop models. Each door glass should be masked separately so that doors can be opened for final cleanup.

Proper Procedure for Enamel Refinishing

Masking procedures for enamel or acrylic enamel are similar to lacquer refinishing but with some variations. The alkyd enamel, which dries more slowly, produces overspray that travels further before drying. Consequently, in panel refinishing, the rest of the automobile must be covered with blankets or sheets to avoid overspray from getting on the surfaces. More care must be taken to prevent overspray on interiors or under hood parts because of the higher pressure used for enamels and acrylic enamels, primer, and color coats. Masking in general is more critical when refinishing an enamel or acrylic enamel auto to reduce overspray seepage. Masking overlapped joints is especially important.

NOTE: Some new car and truck dealers cover the engines to prevent overspray and costly cleanup.

Questions

1. What is the purpose of masking?
2. What are some of the features of a good masking tape?
3. Should masking tape be removed before exposing it to the sun?
4. Is newspaper as good as masking paper when wet sanding?
5. Will paint penetrate a good quality masking paper?
6. What should be done to molding or trim before masking?
7. What should be masked on the inside edge of panels?
8. Should under the hood items be protected from overspray?
9. When masking a windshield or large area, should all of the seams be sealed with tape?
10. When spraying alkyd enamel, how much of the automobile should be covered?

CHECKING CONDITION OF OLD FINISH

A thorough examination of the old finish is essential before any surface preparation can begin. The color coats are not made to fill in rough areas and will be only as smooth as the surface and the substrate underneath.

The color coats must have proper adhesion to the surface to which they are applied, and the surface must have proper adhesion to the substrate beneath it. Even if the old finish appears to be in good condition, free of cracks, rust, or any other defects, the use of a magnifying glass may reveal defects invisible to the naked eye. A pitted or rough surface may indicate the presence of rust.

A simple check for adhesion of the old finish is to sand a small spot to the bare metal. If the featheredged substrate has smooth edges and there is no crumbling, the old finish has good adhesion and is suitable for color coats. When the edges keep breaking off, the old finish (all the layers of paint and primer) must be removed until the area can be properly featheredged. (All the material from the entire panel may have to be removed.)

At times, it may be necessary to determine what type paint is on the old surface. When lacquer thinner is used on the surface, lacquer paints will dissolve readily. Acrylic lacquer will dissolve after considerable rubbing. Alkyd enamels, acrylic enamels, and other finishes such as polyurethane will not be affected except if the enamel is uncured. Uncured or unaged enamel finishes will start to blister or lift but will not dissolve. Old finishes with line cracks, crowfeet checks, and crazing are indications of defects that may require the removal of all the material down to the bare metal if the cracks are deep enough.

Surface Preparation

chapter **31**

PROCEDURES FOR OLD FINISH CORRECTION

1. Old finishes with minor defects can be sanded and broken edges or chips featheredged.

2. Old finishes with poor adhesion can be ground off with a disc grinder if the panel or affected area is not too large. Also, areas affected by surface rust must be ground off beyond the rust area.

CAUTION: Use extreme caution when grinding near panel edges, or body opening gaps near bumper, near metallic moldings or trim or any place where the disc may be caught. Many disc grinders are very powerful and could be thrown out of the hand and possibly cause injury to the oper - ator. Also, avoid grinding across sharp ridges or creases as the grinder could cut through the metal. Grind along the ridges. Keep grinder moving at all times.

In many instances, surface rust is confused with rust through, where the metal is completely rusted out. Removing the old finish and rust scale is the only way to determine how severely the metal is affected.

The disc-grinding method for paint removal is good, but careless use of the grinder could lead to more serious problems such as warped panels or grinding through the metal or ridges.

Procedure for Disc Grinding

Start grinding with a #16 (4) grit open-coated disc, moving forward and backward evenly and quickly over the area. Hold the face of the disc at a slight angle to the surface or at about a 5° angle from the surface (Figure 31–1). The #16 (4) grit will

Figure 31-1 Hold disc at a low 5° angle with the surface. *(Courtesy of 3M Company.)*

remove the bulk of the material. Follow with a #50 (1) close coat disc over the same area and a little beyond to remove the #16 (4) grinding marks. An alternate method is to use a #24 (3) or #36 (2) close coat disc to remove most of the #16 (4) grinding marks and gouges and follow with the #80 (1/0) close coat disc for final cleanup. Then the edges are ready for featheredging and metal conditioning. Old finishes that are deeply cracked or checked can be removed by the disc grinder if the area is not too large. Areas with several panels involved with defective finishes can be removed with paint remover.

Paint Remover

Paint remover is another method of removing paint or old finishes from a panel or from the entire car. Safety procedures must be followed due to the chemicals in the paint remover. It is recommended that goggles, rubber gloves, and a respirator be used.

Removal of moldings or other trim on the affected panels is important to avoid paint edges close to trim which cannot be featheredged. Hood and deck lids can be easily removed which will reduce the chance of damaging the adjoining panels if they are in good condition.

Avoid using common household paint strippers as most of them contain wax and must be washed and neutralized.

Use only paint removers designed for removal of automotive and truck finishes. Read the directions on the labels and follow the recommended procedures carefully. One method for paint removal is as follows:

Apply paint remover with a brush and brush in one direction, applying heavy coats. Allow the finish to soften and remove with a putty knife and steel wool. Rinse with water to flush off residue and dry thoroughly. Proceed with featheredging or metal preparations. If the area was previously repaired with body filler, the filler may have to be removed depending on conditions.

Sand blasting is another method for removing the old finish and rust (Figure 31–2). It is a fast method of removing rust from pitted metal that cannot be removed with a disc grinder. The surface is left in an ideal condition for refinishing. The metal must be treated with metal conditioner and primer as soon as possible to prevent the formation of rust. Rust will appear if the metal is allowed to stand even for a very short period of time. Precautions must be taken to avoid damage to chrome, glass, plastic, or any other soft materials. Aluminum panels can be sand blasted, but caution must be used as aluminum will pit very easily. With any type finish removal, the metal will be exposed to rapid rust formation if not primed within a short time.

Figure 31–2 Sand blaster used for removing rust on lower section of fender. Note operator's use of protective headgear. *(Photo by S. Suydam.)*

FEATHEREDGING

Featheredging is the tapering of various layers of paint or old finish and primer to the bare metal into an invisible edge. Improper featheredging can be felt with the bare hand and will be noticeable after the color coats are applied. All chips, scratches, or any other broken areas of the old finish must be featheredged. The painted edges surrounding body-repaired areas must be featheredged. This can be done either by hand or by mechanical means.

Hand Method

After the old finish has been properly cleaned with solvents:

1. Use #220 (6/0) sandpaper with a sanding block or squeegee and cut down the broken edges. The use of water and wet-type sandpaper is faster than dry sanding.

2. Complete featheredging with #320

(9/0), then #400 (10/0), wet or dry sandpaper with a sanding block or squeegee. Be sure to remove all sand scratches left by the coarse paper.

Featheredging without the use of a block or squeegee will leave finger grooves due to the pressure of the finger tips on the paper. The resulting surface will be uneven and will show in the color coats if not corrected.

Mechanical Method

Orbital sanders are commonly used for featheredging. Both electric and air-operated sanders are available, but the air-operated type is the most popular because of its safety and durability.

The orbital sander with the rectangular sanding pad should be held as flat as possible to the surface with just enough pressure to control the movement. The sander must be kept moving in a back and forth motion across the surface of the old finish. Most air-operated orbital sanders can be used for wet sanding and featheredging. These sanders leave circular marks on the old finish that must be removed during the final sanding operation.

The orbital disc sander with a random or nondirectional motion is also used for featheredging and sanding. The random movement sander does not clog the sandpaper as fast as the orbital type and also has faster cutting action. It cannot be used for wet sanding (Figure 31-3).

Areas to be featheredged where several layers of paint and primer must be cut through should be started with #100 (2/0) production paper to cut down the broken edges. Follow with #220 (6/0) paper to finish the featheredge (Figure 31-4). The final step is to use #320 (9/0) or #400 (10/0) wet or dry sanding with a block or squeegee. If the surface is lacquer, #400 (10/0) paper is

Figure 31-3 Duel action sander for featheredging. *(Courtesy of 3M Company.)*

recommended for the final sanding (Figure 31-5).

Featheredging Solvents

A special chemical solvent is marketed to dissolve the edges of lacquer paints. This

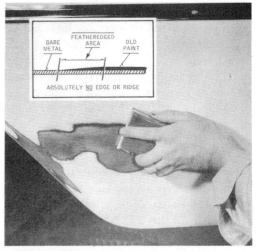

Figure 31-4 Intermediate featheredging. *(Courtesy of 3M Company.)*

Figure 31–5 Final featheredging. *(Courtesy of 3M Company.)*

product will not disturb the primer undercoats if properly used. After the area is properly featheredged, follow with a light sanding with #400 (10/0) and water. Follow the instructions on the label of the can very carefully for the best results.

TYPES OF SANDING PROCEDURES

Basically there are two types of sanding procedures, wet or dry sanding. There are pros and cons with respect to either type procedure, and it is up to the individual to determine which type to use. Also, the particular job and shop conditions will help determine what type to use.

Wet sanding produces a finer finish and quick cutting action. The water acts as a lubricant and washes away the sludge (or ground up paint) and/or primers and prevents the paper from clogging up. Wet sanding requires more cleaning time and

time to remove moisture from body joints and molding. Body shops should have good floor drainage. Wet floors combined with sanding sludge could create a safety hazard. On overall refinishing, a panel is wet sanded, then rinsed off to remove all traces of sludge, even on the inner edges. Then the next panel is sanded. If each panel is cleaned after sanding, the final cleanup job requires less time. If the sludge is allowed to dry on the surface, it is more difficult to remove.

Dry sanding is considered cleaner because no water is used. It requires less cleanup time. However, dry sanding produces more dust, and the sandpaper has a tendency to clog up quicker than in wet sanding. Therefore, in some shops, dry sanding may be more of a problem than wet. Wet-type paper may be used for dry sanding, but it will clog up sooner than dry-type paper. But dry-type paper cannot be used in place of wet paper because the glue and paper backing are not made for water.

Other methods include scuffing, light sanding, overall sanding, and compounding. *Scuffing* is used to remove nibs and imbedded dust in coats of nonsanding primers, sealers, or lacquer finishes when too much dust appears after one coat.

Light sanding is removing gloss and is used to improve adhesion on areas where the old finish is in good condition. This method is often used in two-toning or to correct a color mismatch.

Overall sanding is a thorough sanding of panels or the entire vehicle where the old finish is in poor condition and requires a large amount of time in order to produce a level base for the color coats. This generally involves featheredging, sanding of old finish, and primer-surfacer.

If spot refinishing, the surrounding areas

are *compounded* to remove oxidized paint film and to clean the surface for color coat adhesion. Rubbing compound, as discussed later on, contains an abrasive which produces minute sand scratches to improve adhesion of the color coats. On some vehicles which are factory painted with acrylic lacquer, compounding of the finish and cleaning with solvent will give sufficient adhesion to the color coats. Check the vehicle manufacturer's service manuals for complete instructions.

Use of Sanding Block and Squeegee

Use of a sanding block or squeegee is very important to a good refinish job. Sanding blocks provide a large surface area for featheredging, sanding plastic, and general sanding of the old finish. The block will bridge the defect in the old finish until it is sanded down to a smooth surface. If the sandpaper is used with just the bare hand, the paper will follow the defect, spreading it rather than correcting it.

Standard sheets of 9″ × 11″ (227 mm × 279 mm) sandpaper can be cut or torn to make four sheets of 3″ × 8″ (76 mm × 203 mm) paper to fit the standard sanding block. Attach all four pieces to the block and as one wears out, just tear it off and continue sanding.

Coarse grit production paper is available in precut 3″ × 8″ (76 × 203 mm) sheets. Smooth wooden blocks can be used in place of sanding blocks if none are available.

Squeegees are very useful for sanding the old finish and can be used for featheredging if used carefully. Use the squeegee under the palm of the hand rather than the finger tips to avoid putting grooves in the old finish. When wet sanding, the squeegee is used to remove water after a section has

been sanded and to locate defects or surfaces that require additional sanding.

Sanding Primer-Surfacer

Sanding of primer-surfacer is one of the last steps before the application of sealers and/or the color coats. Because of the heavy pigment in the primers, the surface of dried primer is generally rough or sometimes has a sandy-like texture. The primer-surfacer must be sanded thoroughly to an even surface for color coats. The use of a sanding block or squeegee is recommended to assist in obtaining an even and smooth surface. Primer-surfacers can either be wet or dry sanded after it is thoroughly dry.

Sanding of primer-surfacers before they are thoroughly dried will cause sand scratches, swelling to appear, and additional settling due to the solvents still remaining in the primer-surfacers or solvents that have penetrated the old finish.

Sanding Putties

Putties, like primer-surfacers, must be thoroughly dried before attempting to sand them. The sanding block is recommended when sanding putties to obtain the smoothest possible surface. It is essential that the edges of the putty be sanded off or a ridge will remain that will be easily seen on the completed job. This is one way an inexperienced refinisher can be identified.

Sand with the contour of the panel, never across the contour or body line to avoid low spots or gullies in the panels. After sanding off the putties and cleaning the area, apply several coats of primer-surfacer allowing each coat to flash. Allow sufficient time for the primer-surfacer to dry because the solvents in the primer-surfacer will cause some shrinkage of the putty.

METAL CONDITIONERS

After featheredging the old finish, paint removal, sand blasting, and refinishing new bare metal products, the bare metal must be treated to prevent corrosion and promote adhesion of the primers or primer-surfacers.

Generally, all bare metal must be cleaned with solvents to remove all traces of grease, dirt, or any other foreign material (Figure 31-6).

There are many different brand name chemicals for preparing bare metal. Read the directions very carefully and follow the recommended procedures for each chemical used.

The following is a general description of the procedures for preparing bare metal:

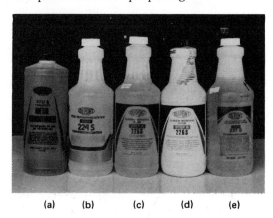

(a)　(b)　(c)　(d)　(e)

Figure 31-6　(a) and (b) Used for preparing bare steel for priming; (c) and (d) used on aluminum; (e) used on galvanized metal. *(Photo by S. Suydam.)*

1. Steel body metal
   a. New bare steel (replacement panels)
      1. Wash with solvents to remove grease, oil, or dirt. (New bare steel panels are shipped coated with grease or oil to prevent rusting.)
      2. Sand bare metal to remove scale and rust. Reclean with solvents.
      3. Mix metal conditioner (made for steel) with water as recommended on the label.
      4. Apply mixture with a brush or clean cloth. Scrub with steel wool or wire brush to remove rust from pits. Work in small areas.
      5. Remove the metal conditioner before it dries on the panel. If it dries before removal, rewet panel and wipe dry.
      6. Apply the recommended primer or primer-surfacer.
         CAUTION: Avoid prolonged contact with skin; wear a pair of rubber gloves. Wear safety glasses or face shield.

NOTE: Some product manufacturers recommend using metal conditioners before applying body filler and some do not. Follow the directions and procedures listed on the labels.

Conversion Coating

Conversion coating is used to improve the adhesion to the bare metal and to make the metal more rust resistant.
CAUTION: Wear gloves and safety shield.

1. Follow the directions on the label. Some conversion coatings are used "as

is" from the container and some are diluted with water.

2. Apply the coating to the surface with an abrasive pad, thoroughly wetting the surface. Work in small areas or in as big an area as can be worked without drying.

3. Leave the coating on the surface for about five minutes to give the chemicals a chance to react. Rinse this area with cold water.

4. Wipe thoroughly dry with clean cloth and air pressure.

5. Apply the recommended primer or primer-surfacer.

ALUMINUM

Because of the energy problem, much aluminum will be used for making body parts. Some manufacturers are using aluminum in hood and deck lids and more will be used in the future as a weight saving factor.

1. Remove grease and dirt with solvents.

2. Lightly sand the surface if surface is oxidized.

3. Dilute conditioner as recommended on the label. (Only use conditioners that are recommended for aluminum.) Scrub with steel wool to remove oxidation.

4. Wipe dry with clean cloth. Rewet if the solution dries before wiping.

5. Apply recommended primer or primer-surfacer to suit the needs of the job.

Alternate Method

Another method of preparing aluminum for finish coats is the two-step method. This will vary with the different products manufactured.

1. Application of cleaner and conditioner
   a. Dilute cleaner and conditioner in accordance with instructions on the label.
   b. Apply conditioner and scrub surface to remove oxide and other surface contamination. Keep surface wet at all times.
   c. Allow several minutes for chemicals to react with surface.
   d. Rinse thoroughly with cold water and dry.

2. Conversion coating
   a. Dilute conversion coating in accordance with the label although some brands are used as is from the container.
   b. Apply conversion coating, wetting entire surface, and allow chemical to react for several minutes.
   c. Flush with clean water and thoroughly dry surface.
   d. Apply the recommended primer or primer-surfacer.

The above procedure may vary with the different manufacturers of similar products.

When working on galvanized steel, zinc die casting, zinc alloys, copper alloys, and other similar metals, the same general procedure is used for these metals as for steel and aluminum, except that a different type chemical is used. Follow the recommendations of the manufacturer for the use of these products.

1. How can it be determined if the old finish has good adhesion to the metal?
2. How can the type of paint used on the vehicle be determined?
3. If the old finish is crazed or line cracked, what must be done to correct the condition?
4. What grit disc is used for heavy removal of painted surfaces?
5. What grit disc should be used for finish grinding?
6. What safety precautions should be used before using paint remover?
7. What type paint remover should be used?
8. What is another method of removing paint and rust?
9. What is *featheredging?*
10. What grit paper is used first to sand out chips in the paint?
11. Why should a sanding block be used for featheredging?
12. What grit paper is recommended for final sanding?
13. What is the difference between scuffing and light sanding?
14. What can be used to locate defects in the surface when sanding?
15. What happens if primer-surfacer is sanded before it dries?
16. What chemical is used on bare metal to prevent corrosion and promote adhesion?
17. What is metal *conversion coating?*
18. How large an area should be treated with conversion coating at one time?

A good air supply is essential in any body and paint shop. The heart of the air supply system is the air compressor, which must be large enough to supply air for all the various types of air-powered equipment when a shop is in full operation. Lost labor and time result if some machines cannot be operated at a given time or at a sufficient air pressure.

Air Systems

AIR COMPRESSOR

Single Stage Compressor

An air compressor is a machine designed to compress air from atmospheric pressure to a higher pressure. There are several kinds of air compressors such as the *piston* type, *diaphragm* type, and *rotary screw* or *jet* compressor. The piston compressor is the most common type used in shops. The diaphragm compressor is a low volume type generally used at home. The rotary screw or jet is a high volume, low pressure compressor used when volume is more important than pressure. It can exert a maximum pressure of 120 psi (828 kPa).

The single stage compressor is a piston-type compressor with one or more cylinders in which the air is drawn in and compressed in a single stroke. The maximum pressure of the single stage usually does not exceed 100 lbs (690 kPa). Single-stage compressors can be used over 100 lbs, but as the pressure rises, the efficiency of the machine decreases and becomes more costly to operate.

Single-stage compressors are generally used in small shops and in homes and are not suited for spray guns or air tools which consume large volumes of air.

Figure 32-1   2-stage, 2-cylinder air compressor.

Two-Stage Compressor

A two-stage compressor has two or more unequal size cylinders in series of two (Figures 32-1 and 32-2). In the first stage, air is drawn into the large cylinder and compressed. The air then passes through a cooling line into the smaller cylinder where it is compressed again to a higher pressure and delivered to a storage tank or to the

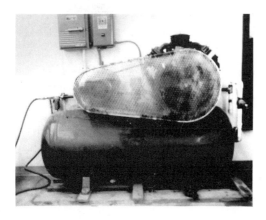

Figure 32-2   2-stage, 4-cylinder air compressor.

main air line. The most common type of two-stage compressor has a maximum output of 175 lbs (1,206 kPa) pressure. Larger shops use compressors that exceed 200 lbs (1,380 kPa) pressure. They often have two or more compressors and hold one in reserve as a standby. The two-stage compressor is more efficient, runs cooler, and delivers more air volume for the amount of current used. Most two-stage compressors are rated at 80 percent efficiency.

Principal Parts of a Compressor Outfit

1. *Air compressor* — pumps and compresses the air.
2. *Motor or engine* — powers or drives the air compressor.
3. *Air storage tank*.
4. *Check valve* — prevents air leaking from tank back through compressor.
5. *Pressure switch* — automatically controls pressure.
6. *Centrifugal pressure release* (on larger models) or *unloader switch* (on smaller models) — bleeds air from cylinders to ease starting.
7. *Safety valves* (several on larger models) — to protect air lines and equipment in event pressure switch fails to shut off after exceeding maximum pressure.

Selection of Air Compressor

In the process of selecting an air compressor, the total amount of air consumption must be known in order to determine the correct size compressor to install. The total amount of air consumption is expressed in cfm (cubic feet per minute) or liters per minute and is the total amount of pressure needed to operate all of the air-powered equipment used in a shop during an eight-hour workday. In addition, plans for further expansion or the purchasing of additional air equipment must be taken into consideration. Allow approximately 10 percent additional air consumption to avoid having a compressor just make it or labor too hard (Figure 32–3).

Next, select the size compressor necessary which is expressed in horsepower (watts); for example, a 10 hp (7,460 watts) compressor output is 26.5 to 35.3 cfm (750 to 1000 liters/minute) with a maximum of 175 psi (1,210 kPa).

Installation of Air Compressor

Where a compressor is installed in the shop is very important to its operation. The life of the compressor could be considerably shortened if it is installed in the wrong place. A compressor should be installed in an area where there is an ample supply of clean, cool, dry air and at least one foot or

Figure 32–3 Rotary jet, high volume, low pressure system.

more away from any wall or obstruction in order to ensure proper air circulation, proper cooling, and accessibility for servicing. Place compressor near but not in the work area to reduce the amount of air piping and loss due to friction (Figure 32–4).

Placing a compressor in the work area where it is exposed to dust and paint will shorten its life. Dust and paint collecting on the compressor will cause it to run hotter. The higher the temperature of the compressor, the lower its efficiency. Also, the air intake of the compressor could become clogged, putting a strain on the motor and cutting down the air input. If the dust or paint gets through the air intake filter, it could damage the compressor. *Extreme* dust conditions could damage the electric motor and could even burn it out.

Care of the Air Compressor

The air compressor is often neglected until the air supply ceases. The compressor's oil supply should be checked frequently and changed every two or three months. A good grade of motor oil should be used, SAE No. 10 for normal conditions and SAE #20 where temperatures exceed 100° F (37.8° C).

The intake filter should be cleaned frequently in accordance with the manufacturer's recommendations. The electric motor should be oiled and the dust cleaned off. Belt tension should be checked out and tightened, if necessary. Keep the compressor and cooler lines free of any accumulations of dust to ensure adequate cooling. Drain water from the storage tank at least once a week. Check safety valves for proper functioning. Check flywheel for tightness.

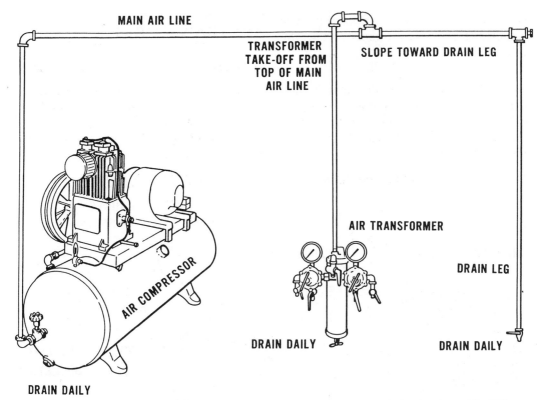

MAIN AIR LINE

TRANSFORMER TAKE-OFF FROM TOP OF MAIN AIR LINE

SLOPE TOWARD DRAIN LEG

AIR TRANSFORMER

DRAIN LEG

AIR COMPRESSOR

DRAIN DAILY

DRAIN DAILY

DRAIN DAILY

DRAIN DAILY

1-1/2 AND 2 HP: 1/2-INCH TO 50 FEET; 3/4-INCH OVER 50 FEET

3 AND 5 HP: 3/4-INCH TO 200 FEET; 1-INCH OVER 200 FEET

Figure 32–4 The compressor system. *(Courtesy of 3M Company.)*

AIR LINES

Proper Layout of Lines and Sizes. The piping should slope back toward the compressor or to a drain leg at the end of the line and at convenient locations to provide for moisture drainage from the air lines. On some large air installations, the main line coming from the compressor may be as large as 2″ (51 mm) in diameter. Small installations with short length of pipe can use smaller diameter (1″) pipe.

NOTE: Some larger compressor installations include a dryer unit next to the compressor to cool and dry the air before it enters the main lines.

Each feeder line coming off the main line should be at least 3/4″ (19 mm) pipe and should come off the top of the main line to reduce moisture in the feeder lines. On each feeder line, where regulated pressure is not required, an air separator should be installed if used for air tools or blowing dust off cars.

Friction Loss. In any air line installation, friction loss must be taken into consideration. The smaller the line and the greater the distance, the greater the friction loss (drop in pressure).

AIR TRANSFORMER

Purpose and Type of Transformers

The air transformer or separator-regulator, attached to the end of the feeder lines, is made to separate the oil, moisture, and dirt from the air and reduce the main line pressure to a desired pressure (Figure 32–5).

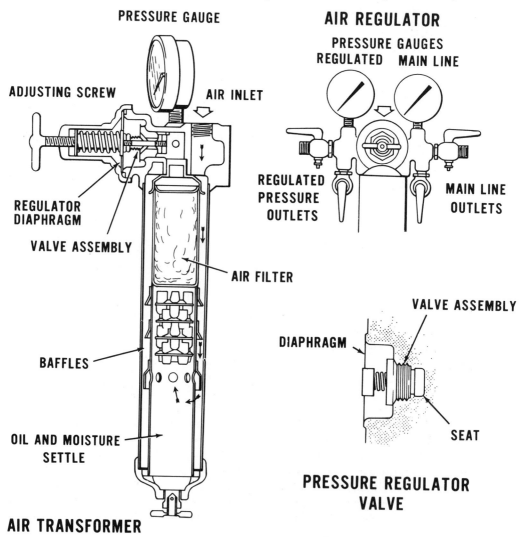

Figure 32-5 Air supply system. *(Courtesy of 3M Company.)*

Construction of Transformer or Separator

The air separator removes dirt, oil, and moisture from the air by means of a series of baffle plates, filter screens, and filter material. The air enters the filter chamber from the bottom and leaves at the top (Figure 32–6). From the filter, the air either goes to the high pressure outlets or to the regulator for pressure reduction. The separator or transformer filter container should be drained once a day in normal use and several times a day when in constant use or under high humidity conditions. Air transformers or separator-regulators are available in all sizes depending on the amount of air consumption. The unit must be large enough to supply adequate air for the equipment being used.

Air Regulator

The regulator is a device used to reduce the main pressure to a desired pressure and maintain the desired pressure with minimum fluctuation due to variations in the main line pressure (Figure 32–8). The pressure must remain constant when spray paint applications are being done even if two spray guns are attached to a regulator at the same time. The pressure is controlled by turning the adjusting knob or handle inward (tighter). Pressure is exerted on the diaphragm by means of a heavy spring. As the diaphragm is pushed down, the needle valve is moved away from the valve seat

Figure 32-6 Air control unit. *(Courtesy of Sharpe Manufacturing Company Inc.)*

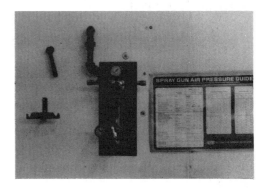

Figure 32-7 Air transformer.

Figure 32-8 Air regulator and hoses.

allowing air to pass from the high pressure to the low pressure portion of the regulator. The more the knob or handle is turned inward, the more air will pass through, increasing the pressure.

Each regulator has two pressure gauges, one to indicate the main line pressure and one to indicate the regulated pressure. Larger transformers or separator-regulators have two regulators attached to one separator. Some shops use a *portable regulator*, which is attached to the high pressure outlet of the regulator, to supply additional regulated outlets. Most regulators are equipped with shut off valves on each outlet.

AIR HOSE

Sizes and Friction Loss

The air hose is used to transfer the air from the regulator or outlets to the spray gun, air tool, or wherever needed. The most common size air hose is the 5/16" (8 mm) inside diameter and is generally available in 25' (635 mm) and 50' (1,270 mm) lengths. The air lines are made of rubber, reinforced with several layers of fabric to withstand high pressure and hard use. Cheap or low quality air hose is generally made of rubber with one layer of fabric and has a tendency to rupture more quickly. Purchasing air hose of 1/4" (6.35 mm) diameter should be avoided because of friction loss.

Friction Loss in Air Hose

Friction loss is the drop in pressure due to the friction between the flowing air and the walls of the hose. For example: a 25' (635 mm) length of 1/4" (6.35 mm) ID at 50 lbs pressure (345 kPa) will lose 16 lbs (110 kPa) pressure. The same length of 5/16" (8 mm) hose will lose 5 lbs pressure (34.5 kPa).

When using air tools or spray guns of high air consumption, the 1/4" (6.35 mm) hose is not large enough and the pressure at the regulator must be raised higher to make up the difference.

Air couplings and fittings are another cause of friction loss or pressure drop in air lines (Figure 32-9). Air lines with 9/16" (14 mm) and 5/8" (15.8 mm) ID have less friction loss but are too cumbersome to be used on small air tools and spray guns.

Figure 32-9 Quick couplers for air lines and tools. *(Photo by S. Suydam.)*

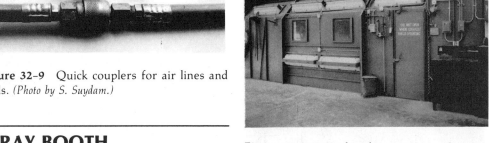

Figure 32-10 Enclosed system spray booth.

SPRAY BOOTH

A spray booth is a totally enclosed room built to confine any exhaust fumes and/or overspray resulting from paint spraying. The booth provides a dust-free area for spraying without interfering with other work in the shop. Dust and paint fumes are a major problem when refinishing.

Types of Spray Booths

Dry Type. In the dry-type spray booth, the overspray and fumes are drawn through a series of filters before being exhausted into the air outside (Figure 32-10).

Wet Type. In a wet-type booth, the overspray and fumes are passed through a series of water curtains or sprays that remove the solids before being exhausted.

In some regions, especially in urban areas, the wet-type spray booth is recommended or required because of air pollution.

There are two different types of air intake systems used in spray booths. One type draws air into the spray booth from the shop area through a set of filters placed in the large doors or walls of the booth. The filters must be changed regularly depend-ing on the amount of time the booth has been used. If the filters become clogged with dust, the dust will be drawn through the cracks and on to the auto while it is being painted. One of the main disadvantages of this booth is that during cold weather, the heat in the shop area is exhausted through the spray booth. (It is advisable to check the local, state, and federal regulations before installing this type spray booth).

The other type booth is an air makeup system where the air is drawn in from the outside and filtered before entering the spray booth. During cool weather, the air is heated to about 75° F (24° C) before entering the spray booth. During extremely humid weather conditions, this heated air is very desirable (Figure 32-11).

On occasion, a shop owner will construct a room of block material or fireproof material to be used as a spray booth with filtered doors or filters and an exhaust fan built in. This construction must meet with any ordinances in that locale.

Figure 32-11 Spray booth controls.

Filter and Exhaust Fan Care

The exhaust and air intake filter should be checked regularly. When exhaust filters become clogged with paint and dust, the amount of air being exhausted will decrease causing excessive fumes and overspray in the booth. Most of the later model spray booths have a safety switch in the filter chamber. If the filters become clogged, the pressure in the filter chamber will become greater than the pressure in the spray booth. The switch will then shut off the air supply and exhaust fan.

The exhaust fan must be checked regularly for spray dust buildup on the fan blades. An excessive amount of spray dust on the blades will cut down the efficiency of the fan and possibly throw it out of balance. Oil pully and motor bearing regularly, if required.

NOTE: Always shut off main fan switch to avoid accidents when working on the fan.

Care of the air intake filter is very important especially if the air is drawn from the shop area. Clogged filters will cause increased exhaust pressure (vacuum) in the booth, and dirt will be drawn in around filters or through cracks. Holes accidentally made in filters will let in dirt when the exhaust fan is running.

Fire Extinguisher Equipment

Many states require that some sort of fire extinguisher equipment be installed in spray booths because of the high explosive nature of the refinishing materials. Dry chemical-type fire extinguishers are most commonly used (Figure 32-12). The dry chemical is discharged through a series of nozzles mounted in the ceiling of the booth and also in the exhaust chamber. This system can be activated either manually or by heat sensors mounted in the system. An alarm bell is generally triggered to warn persons in the booth to leave before the chemical is discharged in the form of a

Figure 32-12 Fire extinguisher for spray booth.

white powder. Immediately, the air supply is shut off and the exhaust fan stops.

Other Controls

Many spray booths are equipped with door switches which shut off the air supply and fan when the doors are opened. This way the fan will not turn on and the air supply valve will not open until the doors are shut. The exhaust damper must be open in order to operate the booth. If accidentally closed, the booth will shut off. An air valve will also shut the booth down if the main line air pressure drops below a certain point.

Lights

The lights are mounted on the outside of the booth because of the explosive paint materials. The glass or windows between the lights and inside of the booth are generally reinforced with wire. Most of the modern spray booths have good lighting and good visibility for spraying.

BAKE OVENS

Some shops install bake ovens in separate places or attach them to spray booths. The controlled heat is good for an enamel paint job which can be ready for delivery in about 30 minutes. The normal drying time would be about 8 hours. The baking temperature varies from 200° F (93.3° C) to 220° F (104° C). Higher temperatures could damage the glass, plastic, or any critical material of the vehicle. This oven uses radiant heat supplied by infrared bulbs.

Another type baking unit is a portable (one that travels on tracks). After the vehicle is painted, the timer is set in the unit to the desired temperature and baking time. The unit travels back and forth on the tracks and shuts off automatically.

Force Dry Heating Units

Force dry temperatures range from 100° F (37.8° C) to 180° F (82.2° C). The paint is dried by heated air passing over the vehicle which speeds up the evaporation of the solvent and increases the oxidation. After force drying the enamel finish, the oxidation is not complete as in the bake oven process.

Small Drying Unit

Units vary from one infrared bulb for drying a small area to larger ones, called *drying panels*, that can be used to heat a large body panel. On some drying panels, several rows of infrared bulbs or all of them can be used depending upon the amount of heat desired.

SAFETY MASKS

Nontoxic Dust Masks

Nontoxic dust masks should be worn when sanding body filler and fiberglass to avoid inhaling the dust. These masks are not intended for use where there is a large amount of paint vapors and inadequate ventilation. These masks are inexpensive and give adequate protection from dust especially when sand blasting.

Spray Mask or Respirator

The respirator is worn where there is a large amount of paint vapor and dust especially involving an overall refinish job. The respirators are made of a soft material to conform with the contour of the face (Figure 32–13). They have either one or two filter cartridges. The respirator with two filter cartridges will give longer service and more adequate air supply. These cartridges filter out all of the paint dust and most of the paint fumes. Some manufacturers of respirators use a wafer or a dust filter that attaches to the cartridge. When painting alkyd enamel, this filter catches most of the paint dust rather than clogging up the cartridge. When the cartridges clog up, install new ones. Do not attempt to clean them.

A good quality respirator must be worn when using urethane paint and any paint additives as many of them will cause irritation of the respiratory system. The respirator must be NIOSH approved. Many of the additives contain isocyanate vapor and mist and a vapor/particulate respirator must be used. The elastomeric additive used for flexible plastic parts is one of the harmful additives.

These respirators should be worn when working with any type chemicals or compounds that have a toxic vapor or odor such as some paint removers.

SPRAY GUN

The spray gun is one of the most important pieces of equipment in the body shop (Figure 32–14). It is a device using compressed air to atomize the refinish materials and apply them to the surface of a vehicle. The refinish material and air are mixed at the air cap in a controlled pattern. The spray gun is a precision instrument and constructed as any precision tool or instrument. With reasonable care, the spray gun will last a long time. Neglect and carelessness cause most of the spray gun problems.

There are two basic types of spray guns. The most common types used in shops are the nonbleeder, external mix, and syphon or suction gun.

Types of Spray Guns

Siphon Gun

The siphon gun or suction gun operates when compressed air, released by the main air valve, flows out of the orifice of the air cup, passes the end of the fluid nozzle, and creates a vacuum in the fluid nozzle. This vacuum, combined with the atmospheric pressure in the fluid or paint cup (or container), forces the fluid or paint up and out of the fluid tube. On siphon-type guns, the fluid nozzle extends out beyond the edge of the air cup. The siphon gun is generally

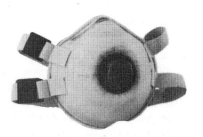

Figure 32–13 Spray paint respirator. *(Courtesy of 3M Company.)*

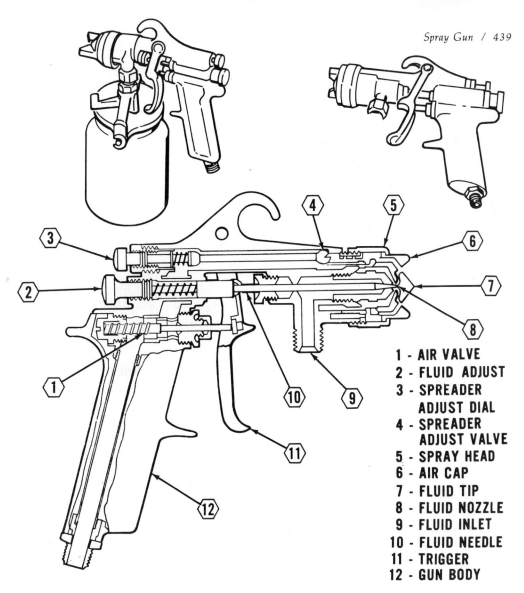

Figure 32-14 The spray gun. *(Courtesy of 3M Company.)*

1 - AIR VALVE
2 - FLUID ADJUST
3 - SPREADER ADJUST DIAL
4 - SPREADER ADJUST VALVE
5 - SPRAY HEAD
6 - AIR CAP
7 - FLUID TIP
8 - FLUID NOZZLE
9 - FLUID INLET
10 - FLUID NEEDLE
11 - TRIGGER
12 - GUN BODY

limited to 1 quart (1 liter) fluid cup or container. Paints and materials of similar consistency can be used in this cup. Heavy bodied materials cannot be used in suction guns.

Pressure Guns

The pressure gun has a closed fluid or paint container, and the fluid nozzle is flush with the air cap. This gun does not depend on vacuum, but instead air is fed directly into the fluid container. A fluid hose connects the container with the fluid connection of the gun; thus, the paint is forced out of the gun's fluid nozzle. This gun is used in production or where large quantities of paint or materials are used at one time or when the same color is used to paint, for example, large trailer trucks. The paint containers range from 1 qt to 50 gal (1 to 227 liters), and the fluid hoses range from 5' (1,524 mm) for the hand-held pressure gun and container to almost any desired length.

Heavy fluids or materials can be used with the pressure gun. One disadvantage of the pressure gun is that it requires large amounts of solvents to clean out the fluid hose especially if the hose is a long one.

Bleeder and Nonbleeder

1. A bleeder gun is designed without an air valve, and the air is discharged from the gun continuously. The fluid or paint is controlled with a valve by means of a trigger. These guns are used with small compressors of a limited capacity and with no pressure-controlling device such as a pressure regulator.

2. A nonbleeder gun controls the flow of air and fluid or paints by means of a trigger. When the trigger is partially depressed, air flows from the air cap. Depressing the trigger further makes the fluid or paint flow. Releasing the trigger will stop the air and fluid.

3. Internal and external mix
   a. Internal mix spray guns mix the air and paint inside the air cap before expelling the mixture. These guns are designed for use in low pressure and with slow drying materials that will not build up in the cap.
   b. External mix spray guns mix the paint and air outside of the air cap and atomize the paint. These are used for almost all fluid and paint materials including fast drying paints.

Construction of Spray Guns

The spray gun is constructed of high quality materials and machined with precision (Figure 32–15). Some parts are made of hardened material to resist wear.

Parts of a Suction-type Gun

1. Air cap.
2. Fluid or paint nozzle.
3. Fluid or paint needle.
4. Fluid control valve.
5. Pattern or spreader control valve.
6. Main air control valve.
7. Gun body.
8. Trigger.

The *air cap* is used to direct the compressed air into the fluid or paint stream to atomize the fluid or paint in the form of a spray. Air caps are made in either conventional or multijet models. The *multijet* air cap is used on the better quality spray gun because it provides for better atomization of the paint, even at lower pressure or higher pressure, uniformity of pattern, and better atomization of more viscous materials such as synthetics. Air caps are available to produce different sizes and shapes of patterns for all types of application (Figure 32–16).

Fluid nozzles direct the fluid or paint into the air stream. The nozzle forms the seat for the fluid or paint needle which shuts off the flow. Fluid nozzles are available in different sizes to handle various types of material.

The *fluid needle* controls the amount of fluid or paint flow. The fluid nozzle and needle can be bought in various combinations to handle different types of materials and to control the amount of fluid or paint.

Figure 32-15 Cut-away of a spray gun. *(Courtesy of Sharpe Manufacturing Company Inc.)*

The *fluid control valve* controls the travel of the fluid needle whcih allows more or less fluid through the fluid nozzle.

The *pattern or spreader control valve* controls the air to the horn holes of the air cap, which in turn control the size of the pattern. By turning the adjusting screw all the way inward (tighten), the air is shut off, producing a small round pattern. The maximum width spray pattern is made by turn-

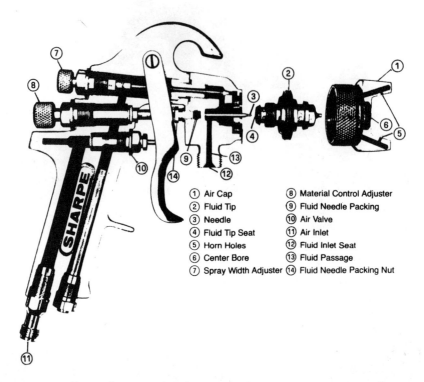

Figure 32-16 Parts of a spray gun. *(Courtesy of Sharpe Manufacturing Company Inc.)*

① Air Cap	⑧ Material Control Adjuster
② Fluid Tip	⑨ Fluid Needle Packing
③ Needle	⑩ Air Valve
④ Fluid Tip Seat	⑪ Air Inlet
⑤ Horn Holes	⑫ Fluid Inlet Seat
⑥ Center Bore	⑬ Fluid Passage
⑦ Spray Width Adjuster	⑭ Fluid Needle Packing Nut

ing the adjusting screw all the way out (loosening) (Figures 32–17 and 32–18).

When the *main air control valve* is depressed, it allows air to flow through to operate the gun's system.

Correcting Defective Patterns

1. Fluttering spray or spitting.
   Some of the causes are loose air cap, loose fluid nozzle and/or gasket, dried out fluid needle packing nut material, loose or dirty cap assembly connection, a crack in the fluid tube, or a clogged vent hole in cap lid (Figure 32–19).
   Corrections: Thoroughly clean gun, oil packing nut, and tighten all parts.

2. Pattern heavy at top or bottom, teardrop shaped.
   Some causes are obstruction in top or bottom of fluid nozzle orifice. Fluid nozzle partially blocked.
   Correction: Clean nozzle and air cap. Rotate air cap. If defects remain, the orifice of the air cap is damaged.

3. Crescent shape is caused by one horn of air cap blocked with dried material or clogged jet.
   Correction: Clean air cap and fluid nozzle.

4. Heavy center pattern is caused by low pressure, fluid or paint too thick, or wrong pattern adjustment.
   Correction: Check fluid mixture with viscosity cup. Readjust pressure and

pattern.

5. Split pattern is caused by air and fluid not properly balanced, pressure too high, fluid too thin.
    Correction: Check fluid mixture with viscosity cup, reduce pressure.

Cleaning and Servicing Spray Guns

Proper care of the spray gun requires very little time and effort if it is done at the right time. A thorough cleaning imme-

Figure 32–18 Air adjustment valve and gauge fits any standard spray gun and is used for increasing air pressure accuracy. The regulator at the control unit is set in relation to the friction loss of the air hose being used. When spraying metallic paints, the correct air pressure is very important for color matching. *(Courtesy of Sharpe Manufacturing Company Inc.)*

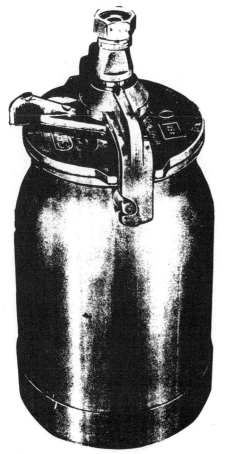

Figure 32–17 Cup and attachment assembly with a "no drip" feature. *(Courtesy of Sharpe Manufacturing Company Inc.)*

diately after using can avoid a lot of the spray gun problems. Immediately after using, remove paint material from the cup and add some clean thinner, reducer, or gun cleaning solvent (Figure 32–20).

NOTE: Never lay the gun on the bench after removing cap because fluid or paint material may flow back in the air passages. Provide a hook to hang the gun on. This prevents the gun from being knocked off the paint bench.

Loosen the cup and air cap a turn or two, place a cloth on the air cap, and pull the trigger. The air will be diverted into the fluid passage and into the cup, pushing the fluid or paint back into the cup. Tighten air cap and pull trigger to flush out the fluid or paint in the fluid passage. Loosen air cap

CONDITION	CAUSE	CORRECTION
RIGHT	Correct Normal Pattern.	No Correction Necessary
 WRONG Heavy Top Or Bottom Pattern	1. Dirty or damaged air cap. 2. Dirty or damaged fluid tip.	1. Rotate air cap 180°. A. If pattern follows air cap, problem is in air cap. Clean and inspect. If pattern is not corrected, replacement is necessary. B. If pattern does not follow the air cap, the problem is in the fluid tip. Clean and inspect the tip for dried paint, dirt or damage. If the pattern is not corrected, replacement is necessary.
 WRONG Split Pattern	1. Air pressure too high for material viscosity being sprayed.	1. Reduce air pressure. 2. Increase material viscosity. 3. Pattern may also be corrected by narrowing fan size with spray width adjuster control knob.

CONDITION	CAUSE	CORRECTION
 WRONG	1. Dirty or distorted air horn holes. 2. Complete blockage of one air horn hole.	1. Rotate air cap 180°. A. If pattern follows air cap, clean and inspect the air horn holes. If horn holes are distorted replacement is necessary.
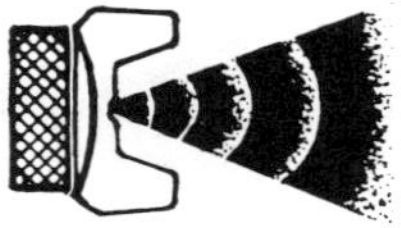 WRONG Gun Spitting	1. Air getting into paint stream somewhere. *EXAMPLE:* Same symptoms as a siphon cup running out of paint.	1. Check and tighten fluid needle packing nut. 2. Tighten fluid tip. 3. Check fluid tip seat for damage. 4. Check siphon tube for crack. 5. Check for poor gun to cup seating.
Air Back Pressuring Into Cup	Excessive Air Blowing Back Into Cup.	1. Tighten fluid tip. 2. Check fluid tip seat. 3. Check for damaged fluid seat on tip or seat in gun head.

Figure 32–19 Spray paint troubleshooting chart. (*Courtesy of Sharpe Manufacturing Company Inc.*)

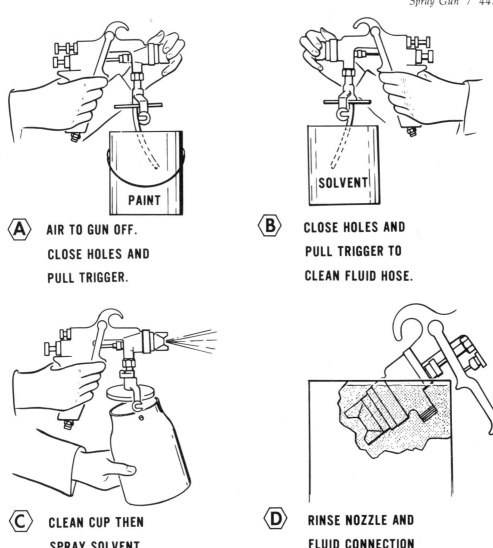

Figure 32-20 Cleaning spray gun. *(Courtesy of 3M Company.)*

again, if necessary, to back flush the fluid passage. Remove the air cap and soak it a few minutes in lacquer or gun-cleaning solvent to loosen up dried paint. Use a soft brush to clean the air cap. The jets can be unplugged using a broom bristle but never use wire, needles, a knife, or anything hard that will distort the jet openings. Do not soak the entire gun in thinner or solvents. This will damage the gun packings and possibly the main air valve. Just immerse the head of the gun below the packing nut on the fluid needle in thinner or solvent. If the fluid nozzle and needle have to be removed, be careful and be sure to reassemble in the proper order. Do not leave out any gaskets or washers (Figure 32–21).

The fluid tube of the cup assembly can be cleaned out with a piece of soft wire with a small wad of fine steel wool attached to it. Dip the steel wool in solvent and run it back and forth through the tube. Rinse out and check for any remaining hardened fluid or paint.

Assemble gun, flush once more, check packing nut, hand tighten only, and store gun with about an inch (25.4 mm) of thinner in the cup. Never store a spray gun without thinner reducer or solvent as the packing will dry out and leak. Oil gun package frequently to keep it soft and pliable.

Proper Spraying Technique

In order to properly spray paint, the first step is to thoroughly mix the paint and thin or reduce the paint as recommended on the paint label. Adjust the air pressure as recommended and spray a test pattern on a piece of cardboard, paper, or scrap metal (Figure 32–22). Do not paint the walls of the building or spray booth. Hold the spray gun perpendicular or at right angles with the surface to be sprayed. The gun should be about 6" to 8" (152 mm to 203 mm) from the surface for lacquer paints or 8" to 10" (203 to 254 mm) for enamel paints. The distance of the gun from the surface to be painted will vary when mist coating,

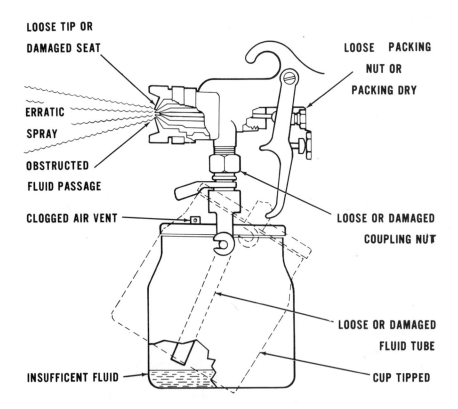

Figure 32-21 Common troubles. *(Courtesy of 3M Company.)*

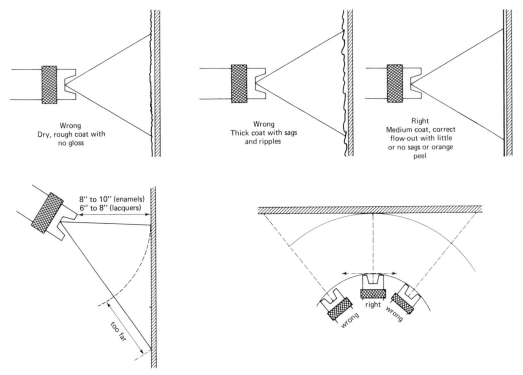

Figure 32–22

blending, or using other types of paint materials.

Hold the gun near the edge of the test material, relax, and with a free arm motion, move the gun forward, squeezing the trigger. Release air, move forward across the panel, pulling the trigger back until the paint comes out. Near the opposite end of the test material, release the trigger, just enough to stop the flow of paint but not the air. Move down halfway the width of the first pass and go back across the test material, overlapping the first pass by 50 percent. As the gun approaches the painted area, pull trigger back again for paint flow (Figure 32–23).

Try several passes or strokes and check for appearance. Adjust or reset the pattern and fluid control for variation. Keep gun moving at a constant speed, not too fast or too slow, always trying to get a wet looking coat. Follow the contour of the test material or body contour.

Poor or insufficient overlapping will cause streaks or dry spots between the passes. Tipping the gun will cause uneven distribution of paint and some wasted paint. The top part of the pass will be well covered, the bottom will have about 50 percent less paint and a dryer looking finish. Holding the gun back too far or going too fast will also cause the film to be dry. Getting too close or going too slow is sometimes the cause for paint sags and runs.

Do not fan the gun, pull back, or turn the gun away from the surface at the end of a pass. This is referred to as *fanning* the gun. The amount of paint at the end is less than

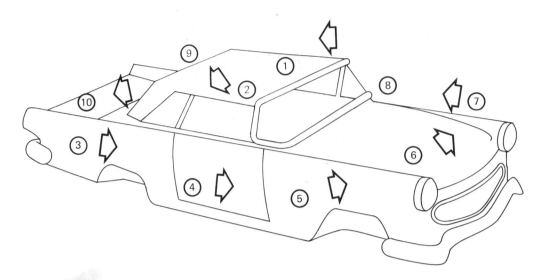

Figure 32-23 Spraying pattern.

the middle, causing dry and uneven paint film. Old or scrap doors, hoods, or deck lids make excellent panels for practice spraying.

Double Coats or Cross Coats. Spray one complete coat in a horizontal direction, overlapping each stroke by 50 percent. Follow immediately with a second coat sprayed in a vertical direction. Or follow with a double coat, spraying one pass in one direction and a second in the reverse direction.

Single Coat. Apply one coat, overlapping each pass or stroke by 50 percent.

Banding. Spray the edge of the panel before spraying the full panel.

Roof, hoods, and deck lid panels. To avoid dryness in the center of the panels, start from one edge and spray toward the center of the panel. From the other side of the car, spray from the center to the opposite edge.

Full paint or Full Bottom. Full paint jobs should be started on the roof; then the lower section of the vehicle is sprayed. The lower section should be started either in the back or front of the vehicle where there is a good breakoff point to start and stop with. Starting in the middle of the vehicle could produce a dry area because the paint may be set up before the rest of the vehicle is sprayed. This condition is more critical in enamel than in lacquer paint jobs.

Questions

1. What is an *air compressor?*
2. Name several different types of air compressors.
3. What is a *single-* and *two-stage compressor?*
4. What are some of the advantages of a two-stage compressor over the single-stage compressor?

5. Name at least five parts of the compressor.

6. What are some things to consider when buying an air compressor?

7. Where is the best place to install a compressor?

8. What is the purpose of sloping the air lines or pipes?

9. What is the reason for branch lines coming off the top of the main air lines?

10. Name two functions of the air separator-transformer.

11. What is *friction loss* in an air line?

12. Which has the greater loss, $\frac{5}{16}$" (8 mm) or $\frac{1}{4}$" (6.35 mm) hose?

13. What are the two different types of spray booths?

14. What are the two different types of air intake systems?

15. List some of the required safety devices in the spray booth.

16. What is the advantage of a bake over?

17. What is the most common type spray gun used in the shop?

18. What is the *syphon principle?*

19. What is a *pressure gun?*

20. What is the difference between a bleeder and nonbleeder?

21. What is the difference between internal and external mix spray gun?

22. Name the parts of the spray gun.

23. What causes a fluttering spray?

24. What causes a teardrop pattern?

25. What causes a crescent-shape pattern?

26. What cause a split pattern?

27. What type brush should be used to clean a spray gun?

28. Why should a spray gun be stored in thinner or reducer in the cup?

29. How should the gun be held in relation to the panel being painted?

30. What is the approximate distance between the gun and the surface to be sprayed for lacquer and enamel paints?

31. How much should each stroke or pass overlap the one before it?

32. What improper spray technique causes dryness in the paint film?

33. What is meant by *fanning* the gun?

Selecting Colors From The Paint Codes

chapter
33

In order to refinish a panel or a complete vehicle, the original color must be duplicated or matched. To do this, first the year and make of the vehicle must be identified. On all domestic vehicles in recent years, an identification number plate is on the left side of the instrument panel. This is visible through the windshield.

On General Motors and Chrysler products, the year is the sixth digit of the identification number. American and Ford Motors vehicles identify the year with the first number after the first letter; for example, A9 would signify a 1979 American Motors vehicle (Figure 33–1).

In 1980, General Motors used an A to signify 1980 models instead of an O. In 1981 Ford, General Motors, and Chrysler started using a 17-digit number with the year being designated as a B for 1981. This is located at the tenth digit of the vehicle identification number. This is the start of a universal identification system for all automobiles and includes the country of manufacture.

The paint codes are located in various places on different vehicles. These codes can be used for selecting colors regardless of the paint manufacturer.

The general location of the paint codes are as follows:

American Motors — a tag on the left side front door or pillar contains the paint code, body style, and other information.

Ford Motors — a tag on the left front door or pillar contains paint code, body style, and other information.

General Motors — a body identification tag on firewall under the hood on most vehicles contains the paint code, body style, and other information.

Chrysler Motors — a body code plate is located on left upper corner of radiator support or left from fender shield or wheelhouse (depending on size of vehicle) and

Figure 33-1 Typical identification plate. *(Photo by S. Suydam.)*

contains paint code, body class and type, and other information.

NOTE:The code is on the left side of the plate, 2nd and 3rd line from the bottom.

Most of the paint color manuals have the location of the paint codes for other vehicles including foreign makes.

Next, after determining the year and make of the vehicle along with the paint code, select the type paint desired (Figure 33-2). General Motors vehicles are usually refinished with acrylic lacquer, although some use water-based paints. The other three major manufacturers use acrylic enamel for cars as well as trucks.

Paints are available in acrylic lacquer, enamel, and acrylic enamel with some truck manufacturers using polyurethane.

In most cases, it is advisable to duplicate the original type paint, but for a small repair job, acrylic lacquer can be used over acrylic enamel. Many painters prefer using acrylic lacquer because it is easier to apply and dries quickly. The letters, OEM, stand for *original equipment manufacturer.*

A color coat/clear coat or basecoat/clear coat is a rather recent method of painting

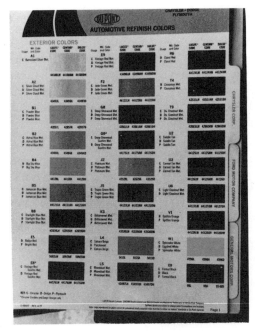

Figure 33-2 Matching vehicle paint codes with paint book for ordering the correct color paints. *(Photo by S. Suydam.)*

and is used on some domestic and foreign vehicles. This involves several coats of highly pigmented paint plus a coat or two of clear. This system of painting involves more expensive materials and extra time so it is advisable to check the type of paint used as OEM finish.

Remember to check with the paint manual for the correct stock number, depending on the brand of paint. In all paint manuals, the code number will be the same, but each paint manufacturer has its own stock number system.

Most paint manuals use color chips and next to their chips are listed the code, the number for acrylic lacquer, acrylic enamel, and enamel.

On some automobiles or trucks, only one type of paint may be listed.

In the later paint manuals, all of the automobiles of one manufacturer are listed together. For example, Ford Motor company could have F, M, L, and T which mean Ford, Mercury, Lincoln, and Thunderbird. In the General Motors section, one color could be listed for Corvette only.

Colors like white and many truck colors are used for several years.

When ordering paint from the wholesaler, it is faster to give the stock number rather than giving the wholesaler the year, code and type of paint. For example, when ordering Du Pont paint, the stock number might be 45322 L for acrylic lacquer, 45320 for acrylic enamel or 45322 for alkyd enamel.

Questions

1. Where are the paint codes generally located on American Motors, Ford, GM, and Chrysler automobiles?

2. When repainting an automobile, is it advisable to use the same type paint as originally finished with?

3. What is color coat/clear coat system?

The area used for color coating, whether it be a spray booth or the shop work area, must be as clean and dust-free as possible.

After all the initial preparation for a refinish job is completed, such as surface preparation, priming, sanding, masking, and other details, the next process is applying the color coats (except when sealing is required).

Using compressed air and gun, remove all dust and dirt from surface, inside body openings, under hoods and inside edges of wheel openings. Clean the entire surface with a solvent or enamel reducer, whichever is recommended by the paint manufacturer. Dirt from the areas under the hood, inside the doors, and deck lid should be removed, including all traces of sanding sludge, primer overspray, and foreign matter. Connect a cable or a chain to the frame or bumper irons to a water pipe or other grounding device to reduce the dust attraction by static electricity. Wet the entire area under and around the vehicle with a fine water spray to control the dust, if possible. Blow the remaining dust off with compressed air and gun. Tack wipe the entire surface with a tack rag. These procedures can be used for almost all of the major refinish or color coat jobs.

NOTE: Thoroughly stir the can or cans of paint to be used or use paint shaker if available. Any pigment not mixed in the paint will cause a color mismatch.

Application of Color Coats

chapter
34

LACQUER OR ACRYLIC LACQUER

Proper Thinners for Colors

The proper selection of thinners for the color coats is very important in order to get the best results. Follow the recommendations on the label of the paint container. Shop conditions must be taken into consideration when making the selection. Although it is possible to use another make of comparable grade thinner, it is not recommended.

Stir thoroughly and add the recommended lacquer listed on the paint label; normally, one part lacquer color to $1\frac{1}{2}$ parts lacquer thinner. Stir thoroughly and strain. The mixture can also be checked for accuracy with a Zahn #2 viscosity cup or other viscosity cup. Acrylic lacquer is approximately 18 to 22 seconds with the Zahn cup.

NOTE: When using diamond flare or any paint with heavy flake, *never* use a strainer of any kind. The paint will lose its glamour effect if some of the flakes are left in the strainer.

With pressure at the gun of 40 to 45 lbs (276 to 310 kPa) hold the gun about 6" to 8" (152 mm to 203 mm) from the surface. Using a wide pattern, spray three to four double wet coats or five single wet coats. Let each coat flash before applying the next coat. If the color is metallic, a wet coat is a must. Dry coats will make the color lighter (Figure 34–1).

For metallic, a mist coat, thinned up to eight parts of thinner to one part of paint, with lacquer retarder added, depending on conditions, is applied with reduced air pressure to obtain the desired results. Air dry overnight or force dry for 30 minutes before compounding and polishing.

Spot Repair

1. Compound well beyond the area to be painted.
2. Wash entire area with solvent or enamel reducer (Figure 34–2). Tack wipe.

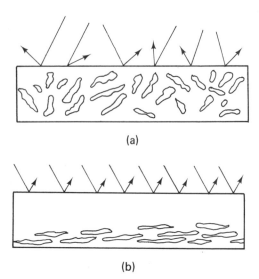

(a)

(b)

Figure 34–1 (a) Dry spray traps metallic particles at various angles near the surface, causing a high-metallic color effect; (b) wet spray allows sufficient time for metallic particles to settle in paint film, causing a strong pigment color effect.

Figure 34–2 Tack wiping surface before painting. *(Courtesy of 3M Company.)*

3. Stir and properly thin the acrylic lacquer. Strain.

4. Hold spray gun from 6″ to 8″ (152 mm to 203 mm) and adjust pressure to 25 to 35 lbs (172 to 241 kPa) at the gun. Adjust pattern to correspond with area to be painted.

5. Spray a single medium coat, let it flash. Follow with three or four wet coats. Extend each coat out slightly beyond previous coat and allow each coat to flash.

6. Mist coat with paint thinner up to eight parts of thinner to one part paint at reduced pressure. Lacquer retarder can be added to aid in melting in the overspray. Extend mist coat well out on the old finish with at least two mist coats.

7. After drying, preferrably overnight, compound and polish (Figure 34-3).

ALKYD ENAMEL

Proper Reduction

Alkyd enamels are generally reduced 25 percent, four parts paint to one part reducer. Some types of reducers are used at 50 percent or two parts paint to one part reducer. Follow the recommendations on the label as to the correct type reducer for shop conditions. Some reducers are not recommended for whites or blacks.

After Final Preparation

1. Remove dust with compressed air and gun. Tack wipe.

(a)

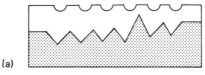

1. Primer-surfacer over sanded metal follows the contours of the metal.

(b)

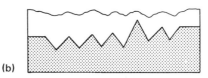

2. Evaporation of solvents will cause shrinkage, and grooves will appear.

(c)

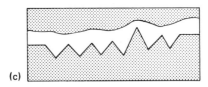

3. Thinner in lacquer causes swelling in primer-surfacer.

(d)

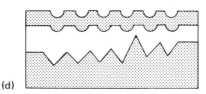

4. Polishing color coat before all thinner evaporates will cause shrinkage, and sand scratches will show.

Figure 34-3 (a) Primer surfacer over sanded metal follows the contours of the metal; (b) evaporation of solvents will cause shrinkage, causing grooves; (c) thinner in lacquer causes swelling in primer surfacer; (d) polishing color coat before all thinner evaporates will cause shrinkage, showing sand scratches.

2. Stir thoroughly. Reduce enamel as recommended on the label and strain.

   NOTE: Some manufacturers recommend the use of a hardener. Follow directions. Enamel with additives has a pot life of three to six hours, depending on manufacturer.

3. Hold the gun 8″ to 10″ (203 mm to 254 mm) from the surface. Vary the pressure from 40 to 60 lbs (276 to 414 kPa) using a wide pattern.

   a. Solid colors

   Apply a medium coat first. Allow paint to become tacky (10 to 30 minutes depending on shop conditions). Tacky means the paint is sticky but will not transfer to the finger. Then apply one full wet coat. If some dry spots are present, mist coat dry areas.

   b. Metallic colors

   Spray a full wet coat and allow to become tacky (10 to 30 minutes). Follow with a light to medium second coat. If streaking or mottling appears after the second coat, partly close the fluid control and apply a dust coat while the paint is still wet. Another method for streaking is to reduce the paint slightly and apply a dust coat while the paint is still wet.

ACRYLIC ENAMEL

Acrylic enamel, like alkyd enamel, will vary in reduction ratio depending on the paint manufacturer. Select the right type acrylic enamel in relation to shop conditions.

NOTE: It is not advisable to use one brand reducer with another brand paint because they are not all compatible.

After Final Preparation

1. Dust with compressed air and gun. Tack wipe.

2. Stir thoroughly. Reduce as recommended on label.

   NOTE: A hardener or additive can be used if desired. The pot life is about three to six hours depending on manufacturer.

3. Use the recommended pressure, ranging from 50 to 70 lbs (345 to 482 kPa) at the gun at 8″ to 10″ (203 mm to 254 mm) from the surface.

4. Apply three full wet coats, allowing the first coat to dry about 20 minutes, and the second coat to flash before adding the third.

Metallics can be controlled by moving back to 12″ to 15″ (304 mm to 381 mm) on the third coat. The edges or overlapping can be melted in with a light coat of reducer.

Spot Repairing Acrylic Enamel

After final preparations, including compounding the surrounding area, follow these procedures:

1. Reduce paint as recommended. Stir thoroughly and strain.

2. Reduce pressure to about 35 lbs (241 kPa) at the gun, at 8″ to 10″ (203 mm to 254 mm) distance; apply a medium coat and let dry for 20 to 30 minutes.

3. Apply three or more medium coats for sufficient hiding, extending each coat out a little beyond the previous one. Allow each coat to flash.

4. Increase the pressure and apply a full wet coat.

5. After flashing, apply a coat of reducer with reduced pressure out beyond the painted area to melt in overspray.

This procedure will vary with different manufacturers.

REFINISHING USING BASE COAT/CLEAR COAT SYSTEM

Some of the domestic and foreign vehicles are finished in a base coat/clear coat system which involves applying several highly pigmented color coats followed with one or more coats of clear. This type finish produces a high gloss and depth to the color, especially metallics. Although enamel is used by the manufacturer, acrylic lacquer is recommended for spot repairing and overall refinishing. Some acrylic enamel systems are available.

Any defects in the base or color coats will be magnified by the clear coats — such as imbedded dust, poorly oriented metallics, and surface imperfections. Application will vary with different manufacturers. Generally, apply four medium wet coats and allow each coat to flash before applying the next. Air pressure at the gun is about 30 to 40 lbs (207 to 276 kPa). Allow last coat to dry for about 15 to 30 minutes before applying the clear coat. Thin clear coat as recommended and apply one or more coats of clear as recommended on the label. If spot repairing, allow to dry overnight before polishing to avoid burning or peeling the clear coat.

HOT SPRAY METHOD

The hot spray method is used for alkyd and acrylic enamel and has the advantage of using less reducer. If used right, one coat is sufficient. The hot spray is also used for spraying enamel in cold shops or during humid conditions.

The paint is reduced by 10 percent or $\frac{1}{2}$ of the recommended reduction, and the paint is heated to 160° F (56° C). If the paint is not hot enough, it will be too thick. Overheating will evaporate some of the solvents in the reducer.

Hot enamel is a little more difficult to spray than cold enamel. The paint should appear slightly dry as it lands on the surface of the panel and then it will flow out. In most cases, if the paint appears very wet immediately, it may run, especially on vertical surfaces.

Application

1. Spray one full wet coat or two medium wet coats. Allow time for the first coat to become tacky.

2. For metallics, a dust coat can be applied while the first and/or second coat is still wet to even off the metallic.

CAUTION: Always use an approved heating device. Do not use an open flame or near an open flame. If an electrical cup is used, unplug the cord before emptying to prevent damage to the cup. Clean heat cup immediately to avoid paint hardening in the cup.

POLYURETHANE ENAMEL

Polyurethane enamel, the newest type paint, is chemical resistant, tough but flexible, impact resistant, and maintains the "wet look" or "just painted look" longer than conventional paints. It is used increasingly on trucks and aircraft.

There are several variations of polyurethane or urethane additives (catalyst) which are added to acrylic enamel. Polyurethane and catalyzed paint dries very quickly and can be taped for two-toning or custom painting in a matter of hours depending on the type paint used and the shop conditions.

Some polyurethane paints are sold in ¾ of a gallon (approximately ¾ liter) and when preparing to paint, three parts of polyurethane should be used to one part activator or catalyst. The mixed paint must be used within six to eight hours, depending on the manufacturer. Mix only the amount necessary and discard what is left over.

CAUTION: The chemicals in the polyurethane and the activator or additives will irritate the eyes, skin, and respiratory system. Avoid coming in contact with vapor or spray mist. Use in a well-ventilated shop and wear a good quality paint mask. Some people will be irritated more by the paint than others. Read label very carefully before using this type paint and the additives.

Before applying polyurethane or other types of catalyzed urethane paint, check the label for the recommended types of primers used in the surface preparation. Mix the paint as directed on the label.

Application

Hold the gun 8" to 10" (203 mm to 254 mm) from the surface. Pressure at the gun will vary from 50 to 70 lbs (345 to 482 kPa) and will vary with solid colors, metallics, and clears.

Solid colors. Spray one full wet coat, allow to dry for 15 minutes or become tacky. Spray second full wet coat.

Metallics. Apply medium wet coat, allow to dry for 15 minutes or become tacky. Apply second medium wet coat. Apply third coat, reduce some types. Light or dust coat to even off. The application of decals or lettering or clear coating should be done within 12 hours. If not, a light scuffing is necessary.

SPECIAL TYPES OF FINISHES

Flexible Plastic

Flexible plastic body parts such as bumpers, stone deflectors, fender extensions, and other body parts cannot be painted with the conventional types of paint. The conventional paints and some primers will crack and peel if applied to these surfaces.

Some paint manufacturers use an additive to give the acrylic lacquer the needed flexibility, while others have a special paint available for flexible plastic parts.

These paints are called *elastimerce* paints or *additive* and must be handled with care.

CAUTION: These paints should be used in a spray booth with adequate respiratory protection. A recommended NIOSH vapor particulate respirator must be used due to the isocyanate vapors and mist created when spraying this type of paint.

Follow the directions on the paint labels because some require special primers and others can be applied on the part without additional priming.

Rigid Plastic Parts

Like flexible plastic, rigid plastic is being used more on the later model vehicles as a weight saver. Prepare and paint as recommended on the paint label. Some manufacturers recommend using a special primer before painting.

Vinyl Paints

Vinyl lacquer paints were originally used as a flat vinyl top coat, as a textured finish, and as a vinyl top restorer. In recent years, it is being used on the rocker panels, lower quarter panels, and front fenders to protect them from stone chips or abrasions. It was originally used on some foreign vehicles and now it is being used on some domestic vehicles. The vinyl lacquer is sprayed "as is" from the can after the proper preparation. Some types can be sprayed with the color coat of the vehicle over top of the vinyl.

Some vinyl lacquer paints require the surface to be sealed with a sealer if the base paint is enamel. Pressure at the gun ranges from 30 to 50 lbs (207 to 345 kPa). Read and follow directions very carefully.

Figure 34-4 Touchup spray gun. *(Courtesy of Badger Air-Brush Company.)*

CUSTOM PAINTING

Custom painting, or the painting of murals on automobiles and vans, is a very involved process which requires a lot of time.

The autobody and paint course as taught in many vocational schools is very long and detailed so that many instructors find it almost impossible to devote much time for instruction and demonstrations on custom painting.

Most instructors give basic lessons on the air brush which is used for painting pin or accent stripes or for touchup. the air brush, due to its size, makes an excellent touchup gun for repairing minor paint defects (Figures 34-4 and 34-5).

Figure 34-5 Air brush with different size cups. *(Courtesy of Badger Air-Brush Company.)*

PAINT PROBLEMS

Defects in the painted surface can be caused by a variety of different things from the metal itself, wrong materials, wrong preparation, and wrong procedures. Below are listed some of the defects encountered by the painter (Figure 34–6).

Rust Under Finish

Appearance — peeling, blistering, or raised spots on the finish.

Possible causes — small fractures in the finish that allow moisture to creep under surrounding finish; many times caused by small stones. Improper preparation when the panel was originally painted. Bare metal exposed to moisture and not chemically cleaned before priming. In severe cases, the metal is rusted through from the inside. Problem usually develops from small holes.

Repair — remove paint and rust in affected area, chemically treat metal, and use a suitable primer. If the panel is rusted through, a welded patch repair is the only solution.

Bleeding

Appearance — discoloration of top coat caused by underneath coat. For example, problem results when painting white over red especially when using alkyd enamels or old lacquers. The white turns to a pinkish color.

Possible causes — solvents from the new paint dissolving old paint, releasing the dyes that come to the surface, most commonly red and maroons.

Repair — after top is dry or cured sufficiently, apply bleeder seal and repaint.

Note: If color is a probable bleeder, a small test area should be tried before painting complete panel.

Blistering

Appearance — small pimples or bubbles on the painted surface. After bubbles break, craters result.

Possible causes — moisture trapped in the paint film, trapped solvents, or using wrong type solvents (not to be confused with dust specks in the paint film).

Repair — sand and repair affected area.

Blushing

Appearance — the paint film becomes hazy or milky. Blacks look grayish. Normally occurs with lacquers or acrylic lacquers.

Possible causes — high humidity and the use of the wrong thinner which traps the moisture in the film.

Repair — add retarder to the last coat of paint and spray a medium wet coat. Using a slower drying thinner in the color coats will help the situation. Avoid fast dry thinners during high humidity.

Crazing, Cracking, or Checking

Appearance — small irregular lines or cracks in the paint, sometimes called *crow feet*.

Possible causes — excessive heavy film of paint applied at one time. Use of wrong type thinner, repainting a previously repainted panel, and solvents penetrating the lower paint film. Extreme temperature changes.

Repair — sand off film to below the depth of the cracks. Repaint, allowing each coat to flash. Avoid applying heavy coat and use recommended solvents.

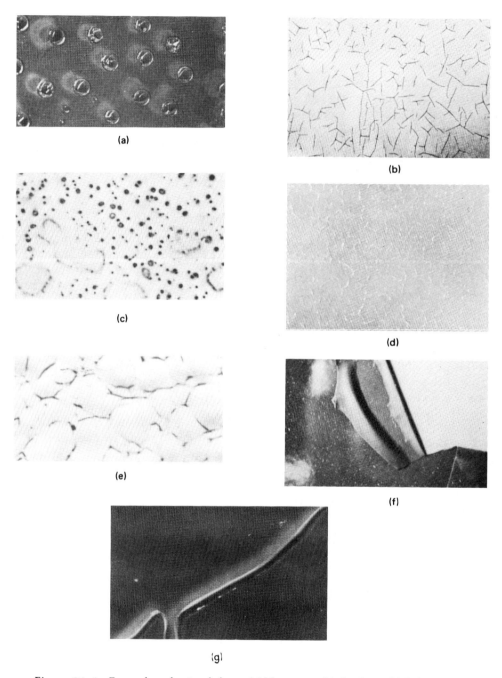

Figure 34-6 Examples of paint defects. (a) blistering; (b) checking; (c) fish eyes; (d) lifting; (e) orange peel; (f) peeling—loss of adhesion; (g) runs, sags, curtains. *(Courtesy of Mac Tools, Inc.)*

Featheredge Cracking

Appearance — primer splitting apart around or along featheredge.

Possible causes — improperly thinned primer, heavy coats of primer, or the application of another coat before the previous one has dried sufficiently. Force drying by air pressure.

Repair — sand affected area. Properly mix primer and apply several coats, allowing each coat to flash.

Fish Eyes

Appearance — small craters in the film as film is being applied.

Possible causes — small specks of silicones or wax remaining on the film before painting.

Repair — if fish eyes are limited or small, add fish eye eliminator to the paint mixture and continue spraying the necessary coats. If fish eyes are severe, remove the new paint before it dries or cures. Properly clean surface with the recommended solvents and repaint the area. Avoid using wax or silicone in the same area as painting and always use clean cloths.

Dulled Finish

Appearance — paint film lacks gloss.

Possible causes — compounding the paint before it dries thoroughly or before the solvents have evaporated. Use of the wrong type thinners. Dry spray caused by the wrong spray techniques. Insufficient paint film especially over primers. Applying wax to paint too soon.

Repair — give paint adequate time to dry, then compound. Use the recommended thinner as stated on the paint can label. Hold gun at proper distance, use correct air pressure and set gun to correct width pattern. Apply medium wet coats and sufficient number of coats for good paint film buildup. Allow plenty of time for paint to dry before waxing, 60 to 90 days under normal conditions.

Lifting

Appearance — swelling or raising of paint film generally after the paint is applied.

Possible cause — using lacquer over insufficiently cured enamel.

Repair — remove damaged film. Prepare and paint area with compatible materials. Follow manufacturers instructions especially when recoating some types of acrylic enamel.

Orange Peel

Appearance — paint film resembles the peel of an orange and does not flow out into a smooth finish.

Possible causes — improper reduction or wrong type. Wrong air pressure.

Repair — lacquer finishes can be compounded after sufficiently drying. In severe cases, the film should be carefully sanded with fine paper before compounding. Enamel finished — after properly curing, the film can be carefully rubbed with a mild polishing compound. Use with care as some polishes will dull the film. Some may have to be sanded and repainted.

Peeling

Appearance — paint film lacks adhesion to the substrate.

Possible cause — improper surface preparation (cleaning and sanding).

Repair — remove all defective paint back to the point where the paint film has good adhesion. Clean and prime area. Sand area, if necessary, and repaint. Use correct thinners.

Plastic Bleed Through

Appearance — discoloration of top coat.

Possible causes — plastic insufficiently cured, applying primer and top coats too soon.

Repair — allow top coat to cure, sand and repaint.

Sags

Appearance — paint film forms curtain-like ridges or paint sliding off the panel.

Possible causes — improper thinners or reducers. Wrong air pressure. Paint film too wet and heavy. Applying another coat before previous coat has set up. Improper spray technique or gun adjustment. Using wrong thinner or reducer for shop conditions.

Repair — while film is still wet, wash off with solvents and repaint. Some runs must be sanded out when film is dry. On occasion, some runs can be smoothed out with the finger or carefully blotted with a piece of paper towel. Use correct air pressure and adjust gun for proper spray. Thin or reduce paint as recommended on the label.

Sand Scratch Swelling

Appearance — enlarged sand scratches caused by the solvents in the top coats, ringlets from an air sander, or swirl marks from a disc sander.

Possible causes — improper preparation such as not sanding out heavy sand scratches with fine paper. Insufficient amount of primer-surfacer applied to the panel. Sanding the primer and painting before the primer has sufficiently dried. Using the wrong thinners or reducers (slow drying solvents in cool shop), allowing the solvents to penetrate the substrate.

Repair — resand area and reprime. Use a squeegee to check for remaining scratches or defects. Apply sealer and paint.

There are many more defects and the cause and cure will vary with each paint manufacturer. For positive results, follow the directions on the paint labels very closely. For best results, stay with one brand of refinishing material and do not mix different brands together.

Questions

1. Before applying color coats, what is involved in the final cleanup and preparation?
2. Why is it very important to thoroughly stir a can of paint?
3. What is the difference between pressure at the gun and pressure at the regulator?
4. In spot repairing, why is it necessary to compound well beyond the area to be painted?
5. How much should enamel be reduced?
6. What is meant by *pot life* when using hardener in enamel paints?
7. Is it advisable to use one brand of reducer with another brand of acrylic enamel?

8. What is the purpose of using clear coat over metallic color coats?

9. Do clear coats magnify defects in preparation and color coat spraying techniques?

10. What is the advantage of using a heat cup for spraying enamel?

11. What are some of the features of polyurethane enamel?

12. What must be added to urethane paint to make it dry?

13. What type of paint should be used on flexible plastic parts?

14. What type paint can be used on the lower body panels to protect them from stone chips?

After painting with acrylic lacquer, the painted surface must be compounded to make it smooth and bring out the gloss. When spot repairing a panel, the area surrounding the spot must be compounded to remove the oxidized film on the old surface.

The compound is made of finely ground pumice, a glassy-like material found in volcanic lava, mixed with an emulsion of oils and water. When the compound is first used, the pumice acts like an abrasive. The pumice is broken down into smaller particles that act as a polish, bringing out the paint's gloss or luster.

In spot repairing, the compound eliminates some of the sand scratches left by the sanding operation. Also, it improves the adhesion of the paint to the old finish by leaving minute sand scratches on the surface after removing the oxidized film.

Compounds are of several different types; for example, hand compounds, fast and medium fast cutting compounds with coarse abrasives, fine or extra fine for hand or machine use, machine compounds, and enamel rubbing compounds. Most of the compounds are white so as not to stain the whites or pastel shades of paint (Figure 35-1).

NOTE: Before compounding and polishing any newly painted acrylic lacquer, be sure that the paint has had sufficient drying time. Overall refinishing or complete refinishing should be allowed to dry overnight or longer if the shop conditions are unfavorable for paint drying.

Compounding And Polishing

chapter **35**

HAND COMPOUNDING

Use a soft cloth, fold it into a thick pad and moisten. Select the desired rubbing compound. Add a small amount of compound to the pad. (Some manufacturers recommend adding water to the compound to form a

Figure 35-1 Rubbing compounds. *(Photo by S. Suydam.)*

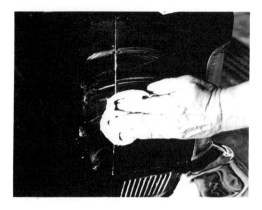

Figure 35-2 Compounding scratches by hand. *(Photo by S. Suydam.)*

creamy paste). Rub on the surface using medium hard pressure, in a back and forth motion, until the area is smooth. Work in a small area and finish it before going to the next area. Using another clean cloth, clean area and check for desired smoothness. It may be necessary to go over the area again to obtain the desired results. Avoid using too much compound at one time as small amounts go a long way.

Hand compounding is generally used for spot painting small areas, removing rub marks and light scratches on painted surfaces, or removing faded paint in preparation for waxing (Figure 35-2).

NOTE: When compounding by hand or machine, it is important not to burn through or rub off the paint on the sharp body lines or styling creases. Apply masking tape on the creases before compounding. After the compounding is complete, remove the tape and lightly hand compound the creases.

Hand compounding is a time-consuming operation, especially when it involves a large area. Therefore, most shops use machines for large areas. Some brands of rubbing compounds are not recommended for machine use because they will remove the

paint too quickly. This could result in having to repaint an area because the paint is too thin. This is espcially true of the fast cut types.

MACHINE COMPOUNDING

Machines are used for compounding and polishing large areas of newly painted autos of acrylic lacquer or restoring the luster on old lacquer and enamel finishes (Figure 35-3). The machines used for compounding and polishing, either electric or air operated, are operated at lower speeds (or rpm) than those used for sanding or grinding. Sanders and grinders can burn the paint because of excessive heat and friction. The compounding wheels or pads are made of short wool nap mounted on a tough canvas like backing pad and are available in several sizes. Some pads are made in shapes of a soup plate with the edges turned upward to avoid burning the paint (Figure 35-4).

Polishing pads are made of lambskin, and the wool is longer. These pads are called

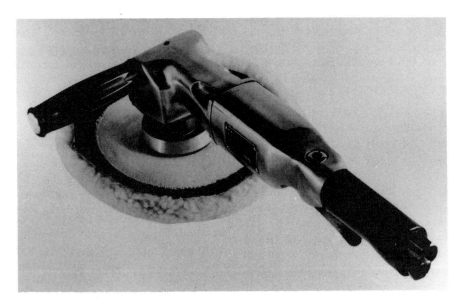

Figure 35-3 Air operated polisher. *(Courtesy of Chicago Pneumatic.)*

high buff or *fine polishing* pads. These pads are not intended to be used for compounding but are used *after* compounding to bring out the luster. They are also used in the application of some waxes and polishes. Another type polish pad is called a *polishing bonnet* which is used over the compound pad and is kept tight with a draw string.

Figure 35-4 Machine compounding. *(Photo by S. Suydam.)*

When compounding or polishing, the machine must be kept moving and only a little downward pressure is used to avoid burning the paint due to heat and friction. Acrylic lacquer will soften with excessive heat causing it to burn or smear when compounding. Compounds are made especially for use by machines, and some extra fine hand compounds can be used if directions on the label are followed.

When machine compounding, work in a small area and avoid letting the compound dry out. The machine compound is applied to the surface with a bristle brush or with a squeegee bottle.

NOTE: Some paint manufacturers recommend that the new acrylic lacquer paint be sanded with #600 grit and water before compounding. Protect the body creases and sharp lines with masking tape to avoid burning the paint off.

The machine should be held tightly, and the pad should be tilted at about a 5° angle from the surface. Avoid tilting the pad too much because the edge of the pad may burn the paint. Keep the machine moving in a back and forth motion with light pressure on the first cut. Compound a small area at a time. When the desired results are reached, move to another area. Do not attempt to compound a large area at one time. Clean the pad frequently to remove residue build-up which is a cause of paint burning or marring. When area is completely compounded, remove residue from the surface.

Install a polishing pad on the machine and go over the surface lightly to remove swirl marks left by the compounding and to bring out the paint's luster. The vehicle should be washed thoroughly with soap and water to remove the remaining residue and dust caused by the compounding. The auto should not be waxed for at least 60 to 90 days depending on the paint manufacturer's instructions.

Old acrylic lacquer can be compounded in the same way to remove dull paint and road film. Before compounding, wash vehicle thoroughly to remove dirt. Remove all traces of road tar with solvent. Immediately after compounding and polishing, a good grade wax or silicone polish should be applied to protect the finish.

ENAMEL PAINT COMPOUNDS

Some compounds are made to be used on enamel paints, either alkyd or acrylic, providing the paint is sufficiently cured. The use of fast cut compounds could permanently dull or remove the gloss on enamel paints. The method and pads are the same as used when compounding and polishing lacquer paints. When preparing to compound old or weathered paint, wash the vehicle thoroughly to remove dirt, then remove all traces of road tar. After compounding and polishing, apply a good quality wax or silicone polish to protect the newly compounded surface. Acrylic enamel can be lightly compounded after 60 days with an extra fine rubbing or polishing compound.

POLISH AND WAX

There are many types of polish and wax available for use. A polish cleaner is a polish with a mild abrasive that serves to remove road film and restore the gloss to the paint. These polishes or polish cleaners will not remove as much weathered paint as rubbing compounds.

Some polishes or polish cleaners are made for hand use, and some can be used with a machine with a lambskin pad or bonnet. Generally, after the vehicle is washed and the road tar removed, the polish is applied to an area or entire surface with a soft cloth. After drying for several minutes (read label), remove polish with a soft cloth such as a cotton undershirt, cheese cloth, or polishing towel. When specified on the label, a machine with a lambskin pad can be used. This is a lot quicker than polishing by hand.

A glaze-type polish is also available for use with machines. Waxes and cleaner waxes are available in paste and liquid form. The cleaner wax, like the polish cleaner, contains a mild abrasive to remove road film and weathered paint. The car should be washed and road tar removed before waxing. Use a soft cloth, slightly moistened, to apply the paste wax. Work in small areas and follow the directions on the label.

FINAL TOUCHES

After the body work and painting operations are completed, one more important step is left; that is, to return the vehicle to the customer in a *clean* condition.

A vehicle that leaves the shop dirty with sanding or compounding sludge inside the door or under the hood, paint on the bumper or chrome, or with a dusty interior because the doors were left open is not the sign of a good craftsman. Remember, the first impression the owner has after seeing his vehicle is very important.

To vacuum and dust the interior, wipe around the body openings, apply a little polish to the bumpers and chrome, clean the wheels and hub caps, and maybe put a little touch up paint here and there will surely pay off in a satisfied customer. If he likes the job, he will recommend the shop to his friends. It is the best advertisement you can have and it is free.

Body and paint work, good or bad, is always on display if the vehicle is on the road.

Questions

1. What can be used to remove oxidized film on paint?
2. What is rubbing compound made of?
3. What can be used on sharp creases to prevent burning the paint on the sharp edges?
4. Can fast cut compound be safely used with a machine?
5. Can a sander or grinder be used for compounding?
6. What are polishing pads made of?
7. Can a dirty, clogged polishing pad damage the painted surface?
8. Before compounding an old car, what should be done first?
9. What is meant by a *polish cleaner?*
10. Can an automobile be waxed immediately after a repaint job?
11. What is meant by the *final touches?*
12. Does this extra work really pay?

Working with Fiberglass

part
4

The use of fiberglass in the making of body parts is expected to increase in the near future. At present, it is used for Corvette bodies, hoods and fender assemblies for trucks and some foreign-made vehicles, recreational vehicles, and some automotive parts.

With the trend toward lighter, weight-saving vehicles fiberglass and plastic are replacing steel for making body parts.

In the past, many bodymen shunned fiberglass repairs, but with more fiberglass around, they might now have second thoughts. It is known that some people are allergic to fiberglass or resins and some have experienced discomfort from the dust. One small advantage of fiberglass is that it does not transmit the force of impact beyond the point of contact like steel does.

Before attempting to work on fiberglass, read the warnings on the label of the materials used. When sanding fiberglass or the resins or when mixing the compounds, a respirator should be worn to avoid inhaling the dust and the vapors. Rubber gloves should be worn when handling fiberglass and resin because these materials may irritate the skin (Figure 36–1). Long sleeve shirts with buttoned collar and cuffs will prevent the dust from getting on the skin. A protective skin cream should be applied to any exposed areas and can be used in place of gloves. If the resin or hardener comes in contact with the skin, wash with borax soap and water. If not available, use lacquer thinner or denatured alcohol. Immediately clean all tools and equipment used with lacquer thinner. Dispose of the leftover mixed material in a safe container. Cover or mask surrounding areas to avoid spilling the resin on the painted surfaces or trim.

CAUTION: For safety sake, use in a well-ventilated area.

Fiberglass is made from molten glass formed into filaments or threads. The fila-

Fiberglass Bodies

chapter 36

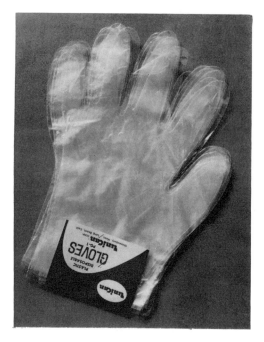

Figure 36-1 Disposable plastic gloves to be worn when mixing and applying resins. *(Courtesy of Unican Corporation.)*

ments are either chopped, formed into mats, or woven into cloth (Figure 36-2). By saturating the fiberglass with resins and curing, a solid panel is formed. Some panels are made by placing the saturated fiberglass into a two-piece mold, heating, and applying pressure. Another method is to spray the chopped fibers and catalyzed polyester resin into a mold and then allow it to cure. Panels can be made by saturating fiberglass cloth or mats with resin and placing them over some shape and then curing. This will be discussed later in the repair of fiberglass.

PAINT DEFECTS

When refinishing fiberglass bodies or panels or repairing scratches or a chipped color

Figure 36-2 (a) Powered fiberglass; (b) chopped fiberglass; (c) fiberglass cloth. *(Courtesy of Unican Corporation.)*

coat, the same procedure is used as when refinishing steel bodies.

(a)

REPAIRING SMALL SCRATCHES OR CHIPS

When the scratches extend into the fiberglass or if a small area is damaged but not shattered, the area can be repaired with fiberglass filler (Figure 36-3).

1. Clean surrounding area of the damage with solvent to remove wax, grease, and dirt.

2. Remove the paint and primer for about 2" to 3" (51 mm to 76 mm) beyond the damage with a #36 (2) grinding disc. Be careful not to remove too much fiberglass. The remaining paint can be removed with a small sanding pad or grinding stones or by hand with #40 (1 1/2) or #80 (1/0) sandpaper. Remove dust with air and a clean cloth.

   Mix fiberglass filler material with the hardener as recommended by the manufacturer (Figure 36-4). Apply filler material, working it into the damaged area and slightly above the contour of the panel.

4. After the proper curing, sand with either #40 (1 1/2) or #80 (1/0) sandpaper to the correct contour.

5. Finish sanding with fine paper as in steel bodies.

CANNED FIBERGLASS

(b)

REPAIRING HOLES

Repairing holes in fiberglass may seem complicated, but it is easier than repairing steel bodies.

Figure 36-3 (a) Fiberglass repair kits *(Courtesy of Bond Tite, Oatey Corporation;* (b) different types of repair material *(Courtesy of Unican Corporation).*

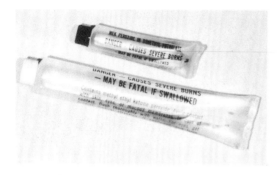

Figure 36-4   Liquid hardener. *(Courtesy of Unican Corporation.)*

When repairing holes, if the underside is accessible, the procedure is a little different from a repair where the underside is not accessible.

Repairing Holes with Underside Accessible

1. Clean area with solvent to remove all traces of wax, grease, or dirt. Remove the paint with a #36 (2) grinding disc about 3" (76 mm) beyond the damaged area.

2. Remove body deadener, dirt, and any foreign material from the underside of the damaged area. Clean with solvent such as enamel reducer or lacquer thinner.

3. Sand underside around damage with #80 (1/0) sandpaper about 3" (76 mm) beyond.

4. Remove fractured fibers with a hacksaw blade or with a #36 (2) grinding disc.

5. Use safety precautions when working with fiberglass resins. Grind a taper on the edges of the hole, about 20°.

6. Cut four or five pieces of fiberglass mat or cloth about 1" to 2" (25 mm to 51 mm) larger than the hole.

   NOTE: Some prefer cloth to mats because it is a little easier to handle when saturated with resin.

7. Next the necessary amount of polyester resin and catalyst or hardener is added as recommended on the label. Using a small paint brush, saturate two pieces of mat or cloth. Two suggested methods: lay mat or cloth on a piece of plastic wrap to apply resin or use a 10" × 10" (254 mm × 254 mm) aluminum baking pan.

8. Apply the saturated pieces to the underside of the hole. Saturate the other three pieces and apply to the outside of the panel and press together. Work out air pockets with a squeegee or a flexible putty knife. The patch should be a little depressed toward the inside. Clean tools and instruments immediately with lacquer thinner.

9. After the proper curing, sand the patch with #40 (1 1/2) paper or grind with #50 (1) disc slightly below the contour of the panel. Fill in with fiberglass filler material to slightly above the contour.

   NOTE: A heat lamp can be used to speed up the curing of the resins and filler. Keep the lamp from 12" to 15" (305 mm to 381 mm) away from the surface. Do not overheat.

10. Sand or grind with #80 (1/0) to correct contour, then finish sand and prepare as steel bodies. Lacquer putty can be used for pinholes or small defects.

Repairing holes with underside not accessible

1. Follow same procedure as before but grind or taper edges around damage to about 30° (Figure 36–5).

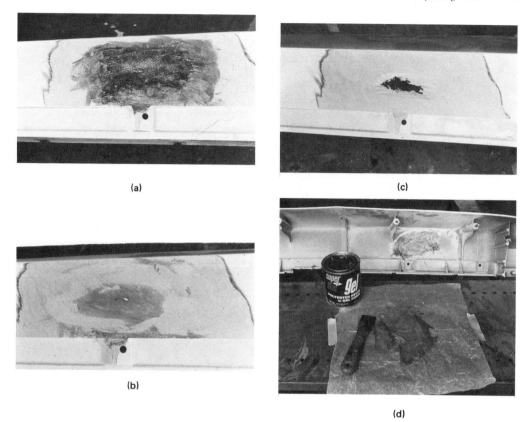

(a)

(c)

(b)

(d)

Figure 36-5 (a) Several layers of cloth placed on the outside of the panel; (b) after sanding or disc grinding, some filler is added to fill in low spots; (c) removing paint and broken fibers from the damaged area; (d) adding several layers of cloth on inside of the panel. *(Photos by S. Suydam.)*

2. Cut three or four pieces of mat or cloth about 1″ to 2″ (25 mm to 51 mm) larger than the damage or hole.

3. Mix the necessary amount of polyester resin and hardener as recommended on the label. Saturate the pieces of mat or cloth with resin.

4. Apply the mat or cloth to the damaged area. Work out air pockets between each layer. Leave center of area depressed slightly.

   Another method is to apply one piece of mat or cloth, depress the center slightly and use a heat lamp to start the curing. When the patch starts to harden, apply the other two or three layers working out the air pockets. This method will prevent the layers of mat or cloth from falling through the hole or sinking too low.

5. After the proper curing, grind with #50 (1) or sand with #40 (1 1/2) paper. Apply fiberglass material to build up area slightly above the contour.

SPLIT OR BROKEN EDGES OF PANELS

Split or broken edges of panels can be repaired without any real problem.

1. Clean area, inside and out as previously described. Grind off paint and cut out the shattered fibers. Grind the edges to a 20° taper and sand inside around the break.

2. Use C-clamp for alignment. If clamps are not possible, use pieces of sheetmetal. Cut and bend sheetmetal to the proper contour and align the edges. The sheetmetal should extend 2" to 3" (51 mm to 76 mm) beyond the break. Drill several holes with 1/8" drill (3 mm) on each end and fasten with sheetmetal screws.

3. After alignment, remove sheetmetal and cover with plastic wrap. Dip screws in paste wax and reinstall sheetmetal. Check again for alignment.

4. Cut three to four pieces of mat or cloth to extend out at least 2" (51 mm) beyond the break.

5. Mix the polyester resin and hardener as directed. Saturate pieces of cloth or mat and apply. Work the pieces into the break and remove air pockets between layers. Use heat lamp if necessary.

6. After proper curing, remove sheetmetal and enlarge screw holes with a drill or small grinding stone. Grind the area with a #50 (1) disc or sand with #40 (1 1/2) paper to slightly below contour.

7. Apply fiberglass filler material to the area and fill in screw holes.

8. When properly cured, sand to proper contour and then fine sand as steel bodies.

9. Remove rough edges on inside and apply several layers of saturated mat or cloth on the inside edge of the break.

REPAIRING SHATTERED AREA

Many times, a section of fiberglass is shattered or badly broken by impact. Rather than replace a complete section, such as a grille opening panel or a fender, it is better to repair it.

If a section is shattered but most of the pieces are available, use the following procedure:

1. Clean with solvent to remove wax and grease. Remove any traces of body deadener or any foreign material and clean with solvent. Remove the paint grind with a #36 (2) disc or sand with #40 (1 1/2) paper about 2" to 3" (51 mm to 76 mm) beyond the damaged area. Carefully remove the paint and dirt from the available pieces. Sand around inside of area with #80 (1/0) paper.

2. The pieces can be fitted in the area by using a canned type fiberglass material. (*Canned fiberglass* is a mixture of chopped fiberglass and resin which is like a very thick paste.) Clamp pieces in place or install a backup piece of sheetmetal covered with plastic wrap.

3. Mix fiberglass mixture with the hardener as recommended on the label. Coat the edges of the pieces and the remaining panel with the mixture and fit into place. Check the contour for correct shape.

4. After properly curing, grind with #36

(1) disc. Cut several pieces of cloth or mat, saturate with resin and apply, working out the air pockets. The pieces should extend about 2″ to 3″ (51 mm to 76 mm) beyond the damage.

5. After proper curing, sand to correct contour and finish for paint.

Another method is to install a backing strip or bond strip behind the shattered area to support the pieces. The bond strip can be attached with sheetmetal screws. Many times, fiberglass pieces can be salvaged from another wreck or picked up in a salvage yard.

1. Prepare as previously mentioned. Cut backing strip to size. Clean and sand strips. Drill holes and fasten strip with sheetmetal screws.

2. Remove strips and apply a layer of canned fiberglass mixed with hardener to the ends of the pieces. Dip screws in wax and reinstall backing strips.

3. After curing, place broken piece into place as mentioned before. Apply liberal amounts of canned fiberglass mixed with the hardener as directed. Make sure that the pieces are bonded to the backing strips.

4. After properly curing, sand or grind off surplus material and check the contour. If the area is solid and strong, use fiberglass filler material to fill in low spots.

5. Where further strengthening is desired, apply one or two layers of cloth or mat saturated with resin extending 2″ or 3″ (51 mm to 76 mm) beyond the damaged area.

6. After curing, sand or grind to contour, adding fiberglass filler material where necessary.

7. Sand filler material and finish sanding as previously mentioned.

Replacing body panels with manufactured panels may require the use of epoxy resin rather than the polyester resin. Epoxy resin is stronger than the polyester (Figure 36-6).

NOTE: The later model Corvette uses a different type fiberglass material from that used in earlier years. The early model used the polyester resin which can be used with the later model if epoxy resin is used for bonding the numerous body panels together (Figure 36-7).

Repair of fiberglass wrecks are a little more complicated because of large scale damage. After removing the damaged materials, the frame, radiator support, and other panels must be in correct alignment before attaching the fiberglass.

Replacing the upper panel which includes the fender tops and hood open on the later model Corvette requires a lot of preparation and alignment.

FIBERGLASS MOLD OR MOLD CORE

To repair a fiberglass panel with some of the pieces missing, even large ones, is rather easy and cheaper than replacing the whole panel. Some panels are large and expensive, and it takes time to get them from the distributor.

Repairing large holes without the use of a mold or mold core is difficult because the cloth or mat will sag and the proper shape will be hard to maintain.

The procedures described in the following relate to a Corvette rear fender section, but the principle can be applied to any type

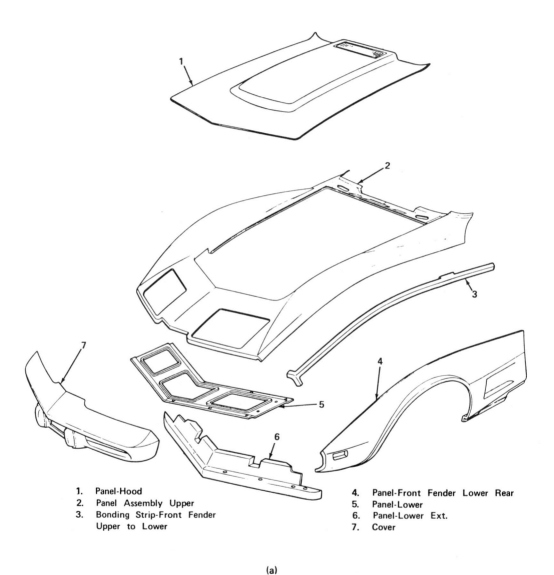

1. Panel-Hood
2. Panel Assembly Upper
3. Bonding Strip-Front Fender Upper to Lower
4. Panel-Front Fender Lower Rear
5. Panel-Lower
6. Panel-Lower Ext.
7. Cover

(a)

Figure 36-6 (a) Front body construction; (b) rear body construction. *(Courtesy of General Motors Corporation, Chevrolet Motor Division.)*

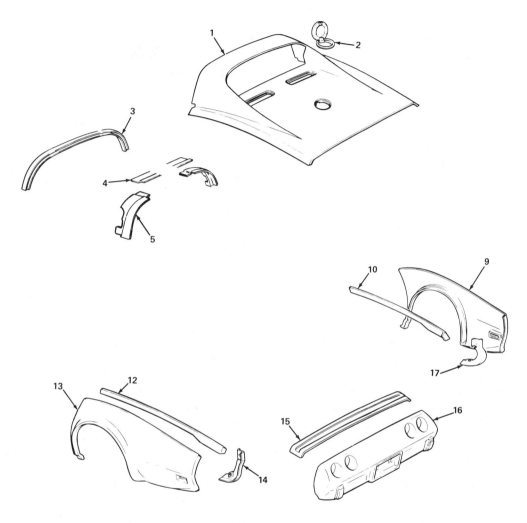

1. Panel-Body Rear Upper
2. Bezel-Fuel Tank Filler Door
3. Reinforcement Roof-
4. Panel-Rear Roof Inner Center
5. Panel-Rear Roof Inner Rear
9. Panel-Rear Quarter-Right Hand
10. Bonding Strip-Body Rear Upper Panel to Quarter Panel-Right Hand
12. Bonding Strip-Body Rear Upper Panel
13. Panel-Rear Quarter-Left Hand
14. Shield-Rear Quarter Panel
15. Bonding Strip-Body Rear Upper
16. Body Rear Lower Panel
17. Shield-Rear Quarter Splash

(b)

Figure 36-6 (continued)

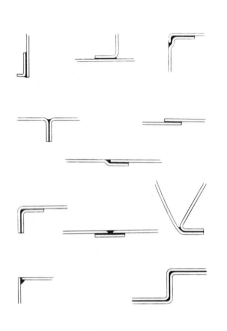

Figure 36-7 Typical body bonds. *(Courtesy of General Motors Corporation, Chevrolet Motor Division.)*

fiberglass panel such as grille panels or hood assemblies for large trucks.

NOTE: Problems may arise with adhesion to the fiberglass body panels or parts, especially on the later models as compared to the earlier models. Although both are supposed to be made of polyester resin, some of them do not accept this kind of filler material. Often, after several hours of drying, if the repair material can be pulled off or cannot be sanded to a fine edge, adhesion is the problem. Epoxy resin should be tried and then polyester filler material can be used to smooth out the contour. Whether polyester or epoxy resin is used, the mold procedure is the same.

The first step in making a mold is to locate an undamaged panel that matches the one that needs repair. A panel from a new vehicle can be used as well as one found in a salvage yard. On the chosen vehicle, mask off an area slightly larger than the damaged area. Put additional masking paper around the area, especially on the low side of the panel, to prevent the resin from getting on the finish (Figure 36-8).

Coat the mold area with a heavy coat of floor wax, leaving the wax wet on the entire surface of the mold area. If the area does not involve a curved surface, a layer of plastic food wrap can be used, which is actually better than wax.

Cut up a number of pieces of continuous filament thin fiberglass cloth, called *fiberglass veil*, into 2" × 4" to 4" × 6" (50.8 mm × 101.6 mm to 101.6 mm × 152.4 mm) pieces. Fiberglass mats or standard reinforcing cloth can be used if the panels do not involve reverse curves.

Mix the resin and hardener in a disposable aluminum baking pan or similar container, following the recommendation on the label.

CAUTION: Avoid contact of the resin and/or hardener with the hands and other areas of the skin. Wear plastic or rubber gloves. Wear safety glasses.

There are two ways to apply the resin and to apply the pieces to the mold area. One way is to place the pieces of veil or cloth on a piece of plastic food wrap or wax paper. Using a cheap paint brush or a long flexible spatula, apply the resin to the cloth. The spatula works well in transferring the saturated pieces to the mold area. Start from one corner of the mold area and place pieces so each edge overlaps with the next one but use just one layer of veil. Work the pieces in around the different curves to get the exact shape of the panel. The smaller

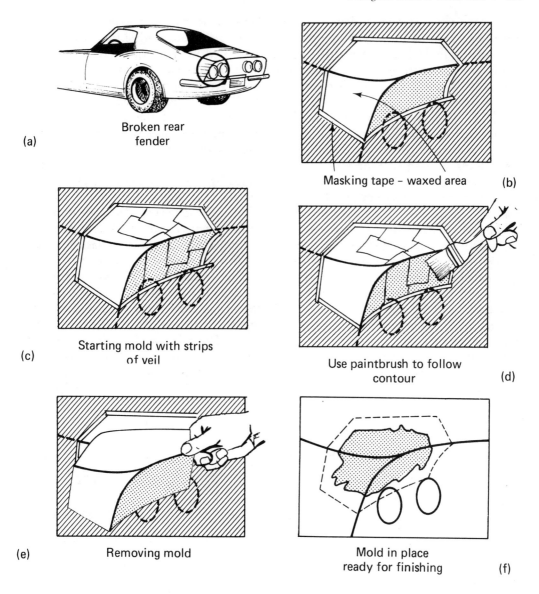

(a) Broken rear fender

(b) Masking tape – waxed area

(c) Starting mold with strips of veil

(d) Use paintbrush to follow contour

(e) Removing mold

(f) Mold in place ready for finishing

Figure 36-8 Making a mold. *(Courtesy of Unican Corporation.)*

pieces of veil can be used around the curves and on the edges. Additional resin can be applied with a brush, brushing in one direction to force the material into the indentations.

The other way is to place the pieces in a pan with the mixed resin and hardener. With gloves on, place the pieces in the mold area. Overlap the edges to form a continuous piece but use only one layer of cloth.

Additional resin can be added with the brush, brushing in one direction only.

After the mold has thoroughly cured, gently work it loose from the panel. Remove the wax, if used, and polish the section of the panel.

NOTE: While waiting for the mold to harden, dispose of the remaining mixed resin in a suitable container. Clean up the other tools and equipment with a resin cleaner and solvent.

Because the mold is larger than the original panel, place the mold under the damaged panel and align. It may be necessary to trim down the edges on some sections for better alignment. The edges of the damaged panel must be cleaned. Grind off the paint down to the fiberglass about 3" (76.2 mm) back from the edge of the hole. Apply a recommended fiberglass adhesive to the edges of the mold and place in position.

After the area is properly prepared (paint and primer sanded off) and the edges beveled, or tapered it is then built up to the desired contour with either mats or cloth saturated with fiberglass resin. Fiberglass filler can be used to smooth surfaces and restore correct contour.

When it is impossible to place the mold on the inside of the damaged panel, the mold must be cut down to the exact size of the hole or missing section. After the damaged panel is prepared or trimmed and the edges beveled, some kind of tabs must be installed to support the mold from the inside. These tabs can be made of bonding strips, pieces of salvaged fiberglass panel, or strips made from fiberglass cloth saturated with resin (Figure 36-9).

The inside sections are cleaned and sanded. The strips or tabs are attached to the inside edge of the panel and are either bonded with fiberglass adhesive or epoxy resin. The tabs can be held in place with either vise-grips or sheetmetal screws while bonding. Remove screws, if used.

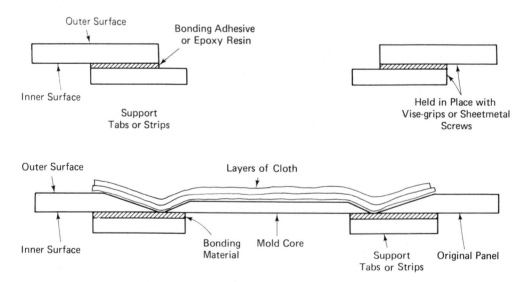

Figure 36-9 Attaching mold core into opening where mold cannot be placed on the underside of panel.

The mold is then placed in position, the edge tapered, and the high spots ground down to make room for additional layers of cloth or mats. Use fiberglass adhesive to bond mold to tabs.

Several layers of resin-saturated cloth or mats are placed over the mold extending about 1½" to 2" (38.1 mm to 50.8 mm) out in all directions beyond the hole. Work each layer down to remove all air pockets. Additional resin may be added with a brush to secure the layers.

After proper curing or hardening of the fiberglass, sand down and use fiberglass filler to finish smoothing the job.

Questions

1. Name some of the precautions that should be followed when working with fiberglass and resins.
2. What is fiberglass made of?
3. How must the underside of the fiberglass panel be prepared for repairing?
4. Why is it important to clean tools immediately after using fiberglass and resins?
5. How much larger should the fiberglass cloth be cut than the spot being repaired?
6. How can broken pieces be held in alignment for repair?
7. What is the purpose of using paste wax on the screws?
8. What can be used to fill in the small depressions in the cloth?
9. When holding broken pieces together with a sheetmetal backing, why is it important to cover the sheetmetal with plastic wrap?
10. What is the purpose of using fiberglass backing strips?
11. Why should epoxy resins be used for installing new panels?
12. Why is it difficult to repair large holes just using cloth?
13. When making a mold from another automobile, why is it important to coat area with wax and mask around area?
14. What is a *fiberglass veil?*
15. What two methods are used to apply resin to the cloth?
16. Will the mold be larger or smaller than the original?
17. If the mold cannot be placed on the inside edge of the damaged area, how else can it be installed?

Estimating

part
5

Estimating is a very important part of the body and fender trade. The margin of profit or loss on a job, many times, depends on the accuracy of the estimate. No shop can continue to operate if the estimates are written carelessly.

Estimates that are too low and are money losers are just as bad as estimates that are too high, thus driving customers away. Estimates are made on small jobs as well as large wrecks, and each one is very important.

One of the first steps in making an estimate is a thorough inspection of the damage or the work requested. A good estimator, appraiser, or bodyman will examine the damage to the vehicle and make mental notes before writing anything on paper.

If the vehicle was in a wreck or has heavy damage, the direction of impact; the amount of indirect damage, and the possibility of hidden damage are some of the important things to take into consideration when making an estimate.

The point and direction of impact is important because a direct head-on collision will have a different effect on the body and frame than a collision where the impact comes from an angle or a sideswipe.

Indirect damage occurs to areas away from the immediate area of impact. For example, if a fender is hit on the front corner, the point of impact will be in front, but the rear section of the fender will be buckled. Also the front edge of the door may be damaged or perhaps even the front door post moved backward causing the door to sag.

Sometimes a vehicle rear bumper is hit on the side and the opposite quarter panel is buckled and the door opening closed up.

Hidden damage is damage not in plain view but hidden by other body parts or by floor mats. Many times, it is not discovered until after repairs have been started, or the

Estimating Auto Body Repair Costs

chapter 37

parts dismantled. Often, some motor parts are damaged but do not appear to be until after dismantling or after the engine is started or the vehicle is running.

When estimating or appraising minor damage, such as a creased door panel, you must determine if any parts must be removed in order to correct the problem and how much time is required to do the job. This is something that is not written in the books. Experience is the best guide.

When examining a vehicle that the customer wants completely refinished, an estimator must assess the condition of the old finish, the number of scratches or digs, the amount of surface rust, or the appearance of small blisters that indicate rusted conditions. The labor and material will vary from job to job and, therefore, a cautious estimator or appraiser must take all of these facts into consideration when giving the customer a price.

The estimating guide is arranged so that the front of the vehicle is dealt with first and then the rear; the outside of the vehicle is discussed before the interior. There are about 30 subsections, for example, front bumper and grille with related parts, cooling and engine, front suspension, and so on. The estimate can be written in the same manner using this book as a guide. It is not advisable to skip from front to rear and back again. Regardless of whether a section requires parts replacement or just labor to correct the damage, keep the estimate in sequence. If a part does not appear in the guide, the price and information should be obtained from the nearest dealer.

Normally, the guide lists the most common parts that are involved in a collision. The guide will refer you to the supplier for information on certain specific items such as the front coil spring, radiator, and some other parts due to the many options or different applications of these parts.

JOB PROCEDURE

After the vehicle is examined closely, the estimator or appraiser, using one of a variety of forms for estimating, will record the damage.

The first step is to record the important data about the vehicle. This includes the year, make, model, identification number, license number, mileage, the paint or color code, and if the interior trim is involved, the interior trim code numbers (Figures 37-1 and 37-2).

Most collision or estimating guides have a section that assists the estimator in properly identifying the year, model, body style, and type of engine, if necessary.

RELATED DAMAGE

Related damage is damage that happened during the time of impact or immediately after. Most of the time, the related damage is not near the point of impact, but a distance from it. For example, during a front end collision, the rear end may swing against a guard rail, causing some damage to the quarter panel. Or, due to impact, the passenger is thrown against the instrument panel.

Sometimes related damage is called *secondary damage* because it was not at or near the point of impact but was caused by the impact.

CHEVROLET IDENTIFICATION

IDENTIFICATION NUMBER OR PLATE LOCATION

VEHICLE IDENTIFICATION

LOCATION – EXC CORVETTE – ON UPPER LEFT SIDE OF INSTRUMENT PANEL VISIBLE THROUGH WINDSHIELD.
CORVETTE – ON LEFT WINDSHIELD PILLAR VISIBLE THROUGH WINDSHIELD.

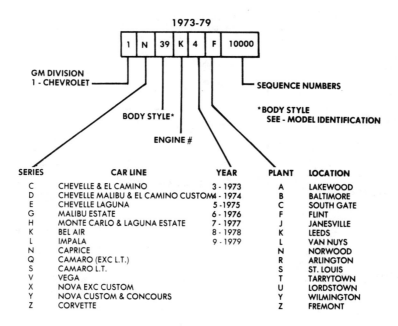

1973-79

| 1 | N | 39 | K | 4 | F | 10000 |

GM DIVISION
1 - CHEVROLET

BODY STYLE*

ENGINE #

SEQUENCE NUMBERS

*BODY STYLE
SEE - MODEL IDENTIFICATION

SERIES	CAR LINE	YEAR	PLANT	LOCATION
C	CHEVELLE & EL CAMINO	3 - 1973	A	LAKEWOOD
D	CHEVELLE MALIBU & EL CAMINO CUSTOM	4 - 1974	B	BALTIMORE
E	CHEVELLE LAGUNA	5 -1975	C	SOUTH GATE
G	MALIBU ESTATE	6 - 1976	F	FLINT
H	MONTE CARLO & LAGUNA ESTATE	7 - 1977	J	JANESVILLE
K	BEL AIR	8 - 1978	K	LEEDS
L	IMPALA	9 - 1979	L	VAN NUYS
N	CAPRICE		N	NORWOOD
Q	CAMARO (EXC L.T.)		R	ARLINGTON
S	CAMARO L.T.		S	ST. LOUIS
V	VEGA		T	TARRYTOWN
X	NOVA EXC CUSTOM		U	LORDSTOWN
Y	NOVA CUSTOM & CONCOURS		Y	WILMINGTON
Z	CORVETTE		Z	FREMONT

1973-75

#
A – 4 Cyl - 140 - 1 Barrel
B – 4 Cyl - 140 - 2 Barrel
D – 6 Cyl - 250
F – 8 Cyl - 307
H – 8 Cyl - 350 - 2 Barrel
K – 8 Cyl - 350 - 4 Barrel
R – 8 Cyl - 400
T – 8 Cyl - 350 - 4 Barrel
X – 8 Cyl - 454
Y – 8 Cyl - 454

1976-77

# VIN CODE	CUBIC DISP.	ENGINE TYPE	CARB. BARRELS	ENGINE OPTION	SERIES USAGE
A	231	V6	2	LD5	A,H
B	140	L4	2	L11	H
C	196	V6	2	LC9	H
D	250	L6	1	L22	A,B,F,X
E	98	L4	1	LY5	T
H	350	V8	4	L82	Y
I	85	L4	1	LX3	T
J	1.6	L4	1	LW5	T
L	350	V8	4	LM1	A,B,F,X,H
L	350	V8	4	L48	Corvette
M	200	V6	2	L26	A
U	305	V8	2	LG3	A,B,F,H,X
V	151	L4	2	LX6	H
X	350	V8	4	L82	Corvette

Figure 37-1 Vital information contained in the serial number. (*Courtesy of Mitchell Manuals Inc.*)

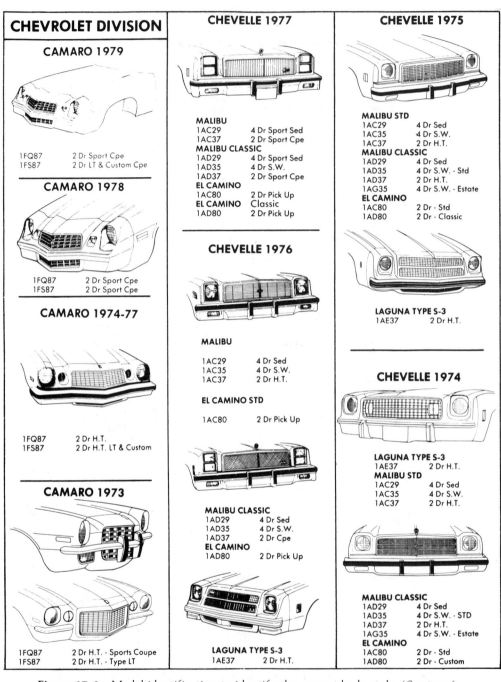

CHEVROLET DIVISION

CAMARO 1979

1FQ87	2 Dr Sport Cpe
1FS87	2 Dr LT & Custom Cpe

CAMARO 1978

1FQ87	2 Dr Sport Cpe
1FS87	2 Dr Sport Cpe

CAMARO 1974-77

1FQ87	2 Dr H.T.
1FS87	2 Dr H.T. LT & Custom

CAMARO 1973

1FQ87	2 Dr H.T. - Sports Coupe
1FS87	2 Dr H.T. - Type LT

CHEVELLE 1977

MALIBU
1AC29	4 Dr Sport Sed
1AC37	2 Dr Sport Cpe

MALIBU CLASSIC
1AD29	4 Dr Sport Sed
1AD35	4 Dr S.W.
1AD37	2 Dr Sport Cpe

EL CAMINO
1AC80	2 Dr Pick Up

EL CAMINO Classic
1AD80	2 Dr Pick Up

CHEVELLE 1976

MALIBU
1AC29	4 Dr Sed
1AC35	4 Dr S.W.
1AC37	2 Dr H.T.

EL CAMINO STD
1AC80	2 Dr Pick Up

MALIBU CLASSIC
1AD29	4 Dr Sed
1AD35	4 Dr S.W.
1AD37	2 Dr Cpe

EL CAMINO
1AD80	2 Dr Pick Up

LAGUNA TYPE S-3
1AE37	2 Dr H.T.

CHEVELLE 1975

MALIBU STD
1AC29	4 Dr Sed
1AC35	4 Dr S.W.
1AC37	2 Dr H.T.

MALIBU CLASSIC
1AD29	4 Dr Sed
1AD35	4 Dr S.W. - Std
1AD37	2 Dr H.T.
1AG35	4 Dr S.W. - Estate

EL CAMINO
1AC80	2 Dr - Std
1AD80	2 Dr - Classic

LAGUNA TYPE S-3
1AE37	2 Dr H.T.

CHEVELLE 1974

LAGUNA TYPE S-3
1AE37	2 Dr H.T.

MALIBU STD
1AC29	4 Dr Sed
1AC35	4 Dr S.W.
1AC37	2 Dr H.T.

MALIBU CLASSIC
1AD29	4 Dr Sed
1AD35	4 Dr S.W. - STD
1AD37	2 Dr H.T.
1AG35	4 Dr S.W. - Estate

EL CAMINO
1AC80	2 Dr - Std
1AD80	2 Dr - Custom

Figure 37-2   Model identification to identify the correct body style. *(Courtesy of Mitchell Manuals Inc.)*

REPAIR OR STRAIGHTENING TIME

As previously mentioned, the time required to straighten a dent or crease is based on where the dent is located and whether or not parts must be removed to gain access to the dent. It is also based on the bodyman's experience working in the trade.

Remember too that to replace a rear quarter panel could involve straightening the wheelhouse, floor extensions, lock pillars, or aligning the adjacents. This is additional time that must be figured in addition to the time to replace the quarter panel.

Another factor to consider is whether or not it is better to replace a panel or to straighten it. This question is usually the subject of much debate.

An experienced bodyman, a true craftsman, will choose to straighten a panel because of his background. He knows it is better to straighten than to replace, whereas an inexperienced bodyman would not know how to assess the relative difficulty of each job.

In addition, there are times when a particular panel must be straightened because a new panel is not readily available, and a vehicle cannot be tied up for a month or better.

Frame and Unibody Straightening

When writing an estimate involving any amount of frame and unibody straightening, more time is needed to determine the necessary labor needed. As described previously, the frame or unibody must be measured and gauges installed to determine where and how severe the damage is. Next,

time must be figured on the removal of the necessary parts needed to straighten the part involved, for example, the exhaust system.

It then must be determined how many pull or push setups are necessary to correct the damage and whether the shop has access to a portable frame straightener or a frame rack when several pulls can be made at one time.

This type of estimating requires a lot of experience and know-how to make an accurate estimate on the total time needed to do the job. If the vehicle is covered by insurance, the estimate or appraisal must be prepared so that it can be backed up with reasonable information and statements in order to get a fair price.

If the shop is not capable of straightening frames or unibodies, it will probably sublet the work to a frame shop. In this case, the frame shop will make an estimate for the body shop which will be added under sublet repairs on the estimate sheet. Some shops sublet or farm out different types of repairs that they are not equipped to do. Auto body shops, depending on the size, farm out, for example, radiator repairs, transmission, radio and tape deck, and windshield repairs.

Estimating straightening time must be considered very carefully. Enough time must be allowed to ensure that the job is profitable.

AMOUNT OF MATERIAL NECESSARY

The materials necessary to complete a job, especially a paint job, is very important because of the rising prices.

Although there is really no definite formula for the cost of materials for a particu-

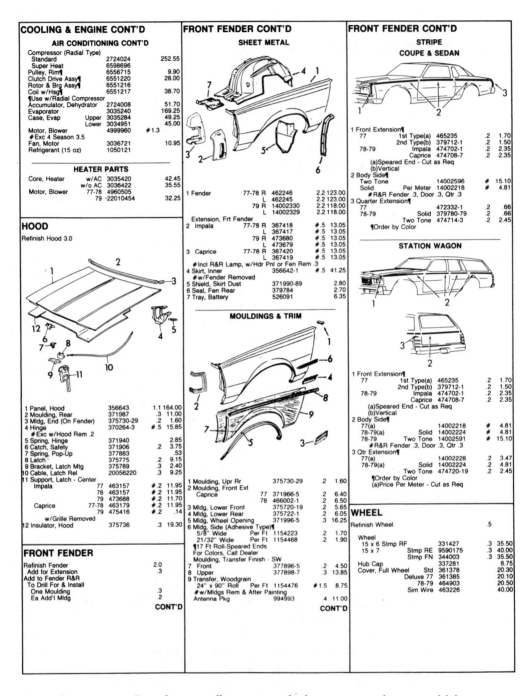

COOLING & ENGINE CONT'D

AIR CONDITIONING CONT'D

Compressor (Radial Type)		
Standard	2724024	252.55
Super Heat	6598696	
Pulley, Rim¶	6556715	9.90
Clutch Drive Assy¶	6551220	28.00
Rotor & Brg Assy¶	6551216	
Coil w/Hsg¶	6551217	38.70
¶Use w/Radial Compressor		
Accumulator, Dehydrator	2724008	51.70
Evaporator	3035240	169.25
Case, Evap Upper	3035284	49.25
Lower	3034951	45.00
Motor, Blower	4999960	#1.3
#Exc 4 Season 3.5		
Fan, Motor	3036721	10.95
Refrigerant (15 oz)	1050121	

HEATER PARTS

Core, Heater	w/AC	3035420	42.45
	w/o AC	3036422	35.55
Motor, Blower	77-78	4960505	
	79	22010454	32.25

HOOD

Refinish Hood 3.0

1 Panel, Hood	356643	1.1	164.00
2 Moulding, Rear	371987	.3	11.00
3 Mldg, End (On Fender)	375730-29	.2	1.60
4 Hinge	370264-3	#.5	15.85
#Exc w/Hood Rem .2			
5 Spring, Hinge	371940		2.85
6 Catch, Safety	371906	.2	3.75
7 Spring, Pop-Up	377883		.53
8 Latch	375775	.2	9.15
9 Bracket, Latch Mtg	375789	.3	2.40
10 Cable, Latch Rel	20056220	.3	9.25
11 Support, Latch - Center			
Impala	77	463157	#.2 11.95
	78	463157	#.2 11.95
	79	473688	#.2 11.70
Caprice	77-78	463179	#.2 11.95
	79	475416	#.2 .14
w/Grille Removed			
12 Insulator, Hood	375736	.3	19.30

FRONT FENDER

Refinish Fender		2.0
Add for Extension		.3
Add to Fender R&R		
To Drill For & Install		
One Moulding		.3
Ea Add'l Mldg		.2
		CONT'D

FRONT FENDER CONT'D

SHEET METAL

1 Fender	77-78 R	462246	2.2	123.00
	L	462245	2.2	123.00
	79 R	14002330	2.2	118.00
	L	14002329	2.2	118.00
Extension, Frt Fender				
2 Impala	77-78 R	367418	#.5	13.05
	L	367417	#.5	13.05
	79 R	473680	#.5	13.05
	L	473679	#.5	13.05
3 Caprice	77-78 R	367420	#.5	13.05
	L	367419	#.5	13.05
#Incl R&R Lamp, w/Hdr Pnl or Fen Rem .3				
4 Skirt, Inner		356642-1	#.5	41.25
#w/Fender Removed				
5 Shield, Skirt Dust		371990-89		2.80
6 Seal, Fen Rear		379784		2.70
7 Tray, Battery		526091		6.35

MOULDINGS & TRIM

1 Moulding, Upr Rr		375730-29	.2	1.60
2 Moulding, Front Ext				
Caprice	77	371966-5	.2	6.40
	78	466002-1	.2	6.50
3 Mldg, Lower Front		375720-19	.2	5.65
4 Mldg, Lower Rear		375722-1	.2	6.05
5 Mldg, Wheel Opening		371996-5	.3	16.25
6 Mldg, Side (Adhesive Type)¶				
5/8" Wide	Per Ft	1154223	.2	1.70
21/32" Wide	Per Ft	1154468	.2	1.90
¶17 Ft Roll-Speared Ends				
For Colors, Call Dealer				
Moulding, Transfer Finish - SW				
7 Front		377896-5	.2	4.50
8 Upper		377898-7	.3	13.85
9 Transfer, Woodgrain				
24" x 90" Roll	Per Ft	1154476	#1.5	8.75
#w/Mldgs Rem & After Painting				
Antenna Pkg		994993	.4	11.00
				CONT'D

FRONT FENDER CONT'D

STRIPE

COUPE & SEDAN

1 Front Extension¶				
77	1st Type(a)	465235	.2	1.70
	2nd Type(b)	379712-1	.2	1.50
78-79	Impala	474702-1	.2	2.35
	Caprice	474708-7	.2	2.35
(a)Speared End - Cut as Req				
(b)Vertical				
2 Body Side¶				
Two Tone		14002596	#	15.10
Solid	Per Meter	14002218	#	4.81
#R&R Fender .3, Door .3, Qtr .3				
3 Quarter Extension¶				
77		472332-1	.2	.66
78-79	Solid	379780-79	.2	.66
	Two Tone	474714-3	.2	2.45
¶Order by Color				

STATION WAGON

1 Front Extension¶				
77	1st Type(a)	465235	.2	1.70
	2nd Type(b)	379712-1	.2	1.50
78-79	Impala	474702-1	.2	2.35
	Caprice	474708-7	.2	2.35
(a)Speared End - Cut as Req				
(b)Vertical				
2 Body Side¶				
77(a)		14002218	#	4.81
78-79(a)	Solid	14002224	#	4.81
78-79	Two Tone	14002591	#	15.10
#R&R Fender .3, Door .3, Qtr .3				
3 Qtr Extension¶				
77(a)		14002228	.2	3.47
78-79(a)	Solid	14002224	.2	4.81
	Two Tone	474720-19	.2	2.45
¶Order by Color				
(a)Price Per Meter - Cut as Req				

WHEEL

Refinish Wheel   .5

Wheel				
15 x 6 Stmp RF		331427	.3	35.50
15 x 7	Stmp RE	9590175	.3	40.00
	Stmp FN	344003	.3	35.50
Hub Cap		337281		8.75
Cover, Full Wheel	Std	361378		20.30
	Deluxe 77	361385		20.10
	78-79	464903		20.50
	Sim Wire	463226		40.00
				CONT'D

Figure 37-3 Page from a collision manual, showing cost of parts and labor.
(Courtesy of Mitchell Manuals Inc.)

lar job, it is up to the bodyman to keep track of the materials used. The cost of the materials will depend on what color or type of paint is to be used. The condition of the old finish will determine how much sandpaper or abrasive will be necessary to correctly prepare the surface for painting. The cost of other materials such as primer, sealer, if necessary, cleaning solvents, and masking material must also be estimated. All too often, materials such as brazing or steel welding rods, grinding disc, welding gas, sheetmetal screws, and bolts are not included when figuring a price for replacing a quarter panel or other panels.

Remember, anything that is used on a particular job had to be bought and should not be given out free.

List Price and Estimated Time

A collision or estimating guide should be used as a reference and not to determine the absolute price. The guide lists the name of the part, the year of the vehicle it will fit, the part number, the estimated time, and the current price. For example, Fender, 1979, part number, 2.2 hours, and price (Figure 37-3).

NOTE: In the front of the estimating guide along with part numbers, there is a notation to help identify a part for either the left or right side or both. For example, a hood hinge for a Chevrolet is listed as 370264-3. The right side is listed first; that is, 370264. The left side hinge would be 370263. Sometimes the number is widely separated, and it would appear as 77R-20051400 and 77L-20047727.

In the front section of the guide, there is an explanation of what the labor includes and what it does not include. For example, to replace a fender includes transfer of the part attached to the fender. It does not include installing moldings or drilling the holes for them, antennas, refinishing, pin striping, decals, and any other necessary parts or operations.

Also, not considered or included are rusted bolts, undercoating, application of rustproofing or undercoating, alignment or straightening of damaged adjacent parts or bolts inaccessible to the bodyman.

Before marking down the hours, check with the estimating guide for more information. The rate that is to be charged per hour will depend upon the geographical region in which the estimate is made. A rate in a large city will differ from one in a rural area (Figure 37-4).

Abbreviations Used in Estimating Guides

When using these guides, the bodyman must be familiar with the abbreviations and the meaning of some of the abbreviations. For example, *R&1* bumper means to remove the part or assembly and install it at a later time without working on the bumper or other part. The bumper was removed to install a new fender or quarter panel. *R&R* means remove and replace a particular part. *O/H* means to overhaul. For example, *O/H a front bumper* would mean to remove bumper assembly, place on bench or floor and replace the necessary part. Abbreviations and definitions of common terms may vary in some estimating guides.

When using the guide, be sure to take notice of all the notations listed in the particular subsection and be sure to list all the parts involved. Some sections, such as quarter panels or doors, are divided into sheetmetal parts, moldings and trim, hardware and glass. Because of the many

Time	$6.00	$7.00	$8.00	$9.00	$10.00	$11.00	$12.00	.50	$13.00	$14.00	$15.00	$16.00	$17.00	$18.00	$19.00	$20.00
6.5	39.00	45.50	52.00	58.50	65.00	71.50	78.00	3.25	84.50	91.00	97.50	104.00	110.50	117.00	123.50	130.00
6.6	39.60	46.20	52.80	59.40	66.00	72.60	79.20	3.30	85.80	92.40	99.00	105.60	112.20	118.80	125.40	132.00
6.7	40.20	46.90	53.60	60.30	67.00	73.70	80.40	3.35	87.10	93.80	100.50	107.20	113.90	120.60	127.30	134.00
6.8	40.80	47.60	54.40	61.20	68.00	74.80	81.60	3.40	88.40	95.20	102.00	108.80	115.60	122.40	129.20	136.00
6.9	41.40	48.30	55.20	62.10	69.00	75.90	82.80	3.45	89.70	96.60	103.50	110.40	117.30	124.20	131.10	138.00
7.0	42.00	49.00	56.00	63.00	70.00	77.00	84.00	3.50	91.00	98.00	105.00	112.00	119.00	126.00	133.00	140.00
7.1	42.60	49.70	56.80	63.90	71.00	78.10	85.20	3.55	92.30	99.40	106.50	113.60	120.70	127.80	134.90	142.00
7.2	43.20	50.40	57.60	64.80	72.00	79.20	86.40	3.60	93.60	100.80	108.00	115.20	122.40	129.60	136.80	144.00
7.3	43.80	51.10	58.40	65.70	73.00	80.30	87.60	3.65	94.90	102.20	109.50	116.80	124.10	131.40	138.70	146.00
7.4	44.40	51.80	59.20	66.60	74.00	81.40	88.80	3.70	96.20	103.60	111.00	118.40	125.80	133.20	140.60	148.00
7.5	45.00	52.50	60.00	67.50	75.00	82.50	90.00	3.75	97.50	105.00	112.50	120.00	127.50	135.00	142.50	150.00
7.6	45.60	53.20	60.80	68.40	76.00	83.60	91.20	3.80	98.80	106.40	114.00	121.60	129.20	136.80	144.40	152.00
7.7	46.20	53.90	61.60	69.30	77.00	84.70	92.40	3.85	100.10	107.80	115.50	123.20	130.90	138.60	146.30	154.00
7.8	46.80	54.60	62.40	70.20	78.00	85.80	93.60	3.90	101.40	109.20	117.00	124.80	132.60	140.40	148.20	156.00
7.9	47.40	55.30	63.20	71.10	79.00	86.90	94.80	3.95	102.70	110.60	118.50	126.40	134.30	142.20	150.10	158.00
8.0	48.00	56.00	64.00	72.00	80.00	88.00	96.00	4.00	104.00	112.00	120.00	128.00	136.00	144.00	152.00	160.00
8.1	48.60	56.70	64.80	72.90	81.00	89.10	97.20	4.05	105.30	113.40	121.50	129.60	137.70	145.80	153.90	162.00
8.2	49.20	57.40	65.60	73.80	82.00	90.20	98.40	4.10	106.60	114.80	123.00	131.20	139.40	147.60	155.80	164.00
8.3	49.80	58.10	66.40	74.70	83.00	91.30	99.60	4.15	107.90	116.20	124.50	132.80	141.10	149.40	157.70	166.00
8.4	50.40	58.80	67.20	75.60	84.00	92.40	100.80	4.20	109.20	117.60	126.00	134.40	142.80	151.20	159.60	168.00
8.5	51.00	59.50	68.00	76.50	85.00	93.50	102.00	4.25	110.50	119.00	127.50	136.00	144.50	153.00	161.50	170.00
8.6	51.60	60.20	68.80	77.40	86.00	94.60	103.20	4.30	111.80	120.40	129.00	137.60	146.20	154.80	163.40	172.00
8.7	52.20	60.90	69.60	78.30	87.00	95.70	104.40	4.35	113.10	121.80	130.50	139.20	147.90	156.60	165.30	174.00
8.8	52.80	61.60	70.40	79.20	88.00	96.80	105.60	4.40	114.40	123.20	132.00	140.80	149.60	158.40	167.20	176.00
8.9	53.40	62.30	71.20	80.10	89.00	97.90	106.80	4.45	115.70	124.60	133.50	142.40	151.30	160.20	169.10	178.00
9.0	54.00	63.00	72.00	81.00	90.00	99.00	108.00	4.50	117.00	126.00	135.00	144.00	153.00	162.00	171.00	180.00
9.1	54.60	63.70	72.80	81.90	91.00	100.10	109.20	4.55	118.30	127.40	136.50	145.60	154.70	163.80	172.90	182.00
9.2	55.20	64.40	73.60	82.80	92.00	101.20	110.40	4.60	119.60	128.80	138.00	147.20	156.40	165.60	174.80	184.00
9.3	55.80	65.10	74.40	83.70	93.00	102.30	111.60	4.65	120.90	130.20	139.50	148.80	158.10	167.40	176.70	186.00
9.4	56.40	65.80	75.20	84.60	94.00	103.40	112.80	4.70	122.20	131.60	141.00	150.40	159.80	169.20	178.60	188.00
9.5	57.00	66.50	76.00	85.50	95.00	104.50	114.00	4.75	123.50	133.00	142.50	152.00	161.50	171.00	180.50	190.00
9.6	57.60	67.20	76.80	86.40	96.00	105.60	115.20	4.80	124.80	134.40	144.00	153.60	163.20	172.80	182.40	192.00
9.7	58.20	67.90	77.60	87.30	97.00	106.70	116.40	4.85	126.10	135.80	145.50	155.20	164.90	174.60	184.30	194.00
9.8	58.80	68.60	78.40	88.20	98.00	107.80	117.60	4.90	127.40	137.20	147.00	156.80	166.60	176.40	186.20	196.00
9.9	59.40	69.30	79.20	89.10	99.00	108.90	118.80	4.95	128.70	138.60	148.50	158.40	168.30	178.20	188.10	198.00
10.0	60.00	70.00	80.00	90.00	100.00	110.00	120.00	5.00	130.00	140.00	150.00	160.00	170.00	180.00	190.00	200.00
10.5	63.00	73.50	84.00	94.50	105.00	115.50	126.00	5.25	136.50	147.00	157.50	168.00	178.50	189.00	199.50	210.00
11.0	66.00	77.00	88.00	99.00	110.00	121.00	132.00	5.50	143.00	154.00	165.00	176.00	187.00	198.00	209.00	220.00
11.5	69.00	80.50	92.00	103.50	115.00	126.50	138.00	5.75	149.50	161.00	172.50	184.00	195.50	207.00	218.50	230.00
12.0	72.00	84.00	96.00	108.00	120.00	132.00	144.00	6.00	156.00	168.00	180.00	192.00	204.00	216.00	228.00	240.00
12.5	75.00	87.50	100.00	112.50	125.00	137.50	150.00	6.25	162.50	175.00	187.50	200.00	212.50	225.00	237.50	250.00
13.0	78.00	91.00	104.00	117.00	130.00	143.00	156.00	6.50	169.00	182.00	195.00	208.00	221.00	234.00	247.00	260.00
13.5	81.00	94.50	108.00	121.50	135.00	148.50	162.00	6.75	175.50	189.00	202.50	216.00	229.50	243.00	256.50	270.00
14.0	84.00	98.00	112.00	126.00	140.00	154.00	168.00	7.00	182.00	196.00	210.00	224.00	238.00	252.00	266.00	280.00
14.5	87.00	101.50	116.00	130.50	145.00	159.50	174.00	7.25	188.50	203.00	217.50	232.00	246.50	261.00	275.50	290.00
15.0	90.00	105.00	120.00	135.00	150.00	165.00	180.00	7.50	195.00	210.00	225.00	240.00	255.00	270.00	285.00	300.00
15.5	93.00	108.50	124.00	139.50	155.00	170.50	186.00	7.75	201.50	217.00	232.50	248.00	263.50	279.00	294.50	310.00
16.0	96.00	112.00	128.00	144.00	160.00	176.00	192.00	8.00	208.00	224.00	240.00	256.00	272.00	288.00	304.00	320.00
16.5	99.00	115.50	132.00	148.50	165.00	181.50	198.00	8.25	214.50	231.00	247.50	264.00	280.50	297.00	313.50	330.00
17.0	102.00	119.00	136.00	153.00	170.00	187.00	204.00	8.50	221.00	238.00	255.00	272.00	289.00	306.00	323.00	340.00
17.5	105.00	122.50	140.00	157.50	175.00	192.50	210.00	8.75	227.50	245.00	262.50	280.00	297.50	315.00	332.50	350.00
18.0	108.00	126.00	144.00	162.00	180.00	198.00	216.00	9.00	234.00	252.00	270.00	288.00	306.00	324.00	342.00	360.00
18.5	111.00	129.50	148.00	166.50	185.00	203.50	222.00	9.25	240.50	259.00	277.50	296.00	314.50	333.00	351.50	370.00
19.0	114.00	133.00	152.00	171.00	190.00	209.00	228.00	9.50	247.00	266.00	285.00	304.00	323.00	342.00	361.00	380.00
19.5	117.00	136.50	156.00	175.50	195.00	214.50	234.00	9.75	253.50	273.00	292.50	312.00	331.50	351.00	370.50	390.00
20.0	120.00	140.00	160.00	180.00	200.00	220.00	240.00	10.00	260.00	280.00	300.00	320.00	340.00	360.00	380.00	400.00
30.0	180.00	210.00	240.00	270.00	300.00	330.00	360.00	15.00	390.00	420.00	450.00	480.00	510.00	540.00	570.00	600.00
40.0	240.00	280.00	320.00	360.00	400.00	440.00	480.00	20.00	520.00	560.00	600.00	640.00	680.00	720.00	760.00	800.00

Figure 37-4 Labor times to dollars conversion table. *(Courtesy of Mitchell Manuals Inc.)*

ROCHE'S GARAGE, Inc.
Tel. 887-5150
Callicoon, N. Y. 12723

Pontiac   SALES and SERVICE

Name_____ Address_____ Phone_____

Car_____Year_____Model_____Mileage_____Ins. Co._____Phone_____

Mfr. No._____Body Style_____License_____Adj_____Policy-Claim No._____

No.	OPERATION	LABOR	PARTS	No.	OPERATION	LABOR	PARTS	No.	OPERATION	LABOR	PARTS
	A-Front Bumper				I-Front Door				S-Trunk Lid		
	Bumper Guards				Mldgs.				Mldg.		
	Bumper Brkts.				Handle				Lock		
	Stone Deflector				Lock						
					Hinge				T-Rear End Panel		
									Floor Pan		
	Radiator Grille				Vent Glass						
	Grille Mldgs.				Door Glass				V-Rear Bumper		
									Guard		
	B-Radiator Assembly				J-Center Pillar				Brkts.		
	Core Support										
	Baffles				K-Rear Door				A-1 Wheel Cover		
	Horn				Mldgs.				Front Wheel		
	Fan Blade				Handle				Frt. Tire. % Worn		
	Fan Belt				Lock				Strg. Knuckle		
					Hinge				Upper Control Arm		
	C-Front Fender, (L)								Lower Control Arm		
	Inner Skirt				Glass						
	Mldgs.								B-1 Frame		
					L-Quarter Panel, (L)				C-1 Tie Rod		
	C-Front Fender, (R)				Quarter Extension				Steering Shaft		
	Inner Skirt				Mldgs.				Steering Wheel		
	Mldgs.								Horn Ring		
					L-Quarter Panel, (R)						
	D-Head Lamp				Quarter Extension				E-1 Fuel Tank		
	Sealed Beam				Mldgs.				Tail Pipe		
	Door										
					Lock Pillar				J-1 Wheel Cover		
	E-Parking Lamp				Wheel Housing				Rear Wheel		
					Quarter Glass				Rr. Tire % Worn		
	F-Hood								Axle Shaft		
	Mldg.				N-Tail Light						
	Ornament				Back-Up Light						
	Hinge										
	Lock				O-Rocker Panel						
					Rocker Mldgs.						
	G-Windshield				Floor Pan						
					P-Roof						
	H-Cowl				Q-Back Window						
	Hinge Pillar										
	Instrument Panel				R-Upper Deck Panel						

SUBLET REPAIRS
Bumper Rechrome
Wheel True Up
Radiator Recore
Towing
Frame

RECAP
Parts_____
Body_____
Paint_____ }
Mech._____ }
(L A B O R)

THIS IS NOT A BILL—
ADVANCE ESTIMATE ONLY

Estimated by_____

Date_____

This estimate is based on the initial inspection. It does not cover additional parts or labor that might be required after the damaged sections have been removed. Occasionally, worn or damaged parts are found after work has been started which were not evident on the initial inspection, in which case you will be notified.

Tax _____

Total _____

S-Straighten A-Align C-Clean P-Paint -*Tinted Glass

Figure 37-5 One type of estimating form. *(Courtesy of Roche's Garage Inc.)*

options nd styles of trim, it is very important to start with the correct model and series for identifying the parts.

Overlap Time

Overlap time is a subject many bodymen hate to hear about and the insurance company always brings up. It describes a situation where one operation overlaps another or a bodyman is paid twice when, for example, two panels must be finished and each must be masked and prepared. Overlap is often encountered when the labor for replacing a panel includes molding; therefore, installing a new molding does not require

'CLASSIC PONTIAC, CADILLAC and BUICK
incorporated

131 Mill Street   Exit 100 on Quickway
Liberty, New York 12754   PHONE: (914) 292-3500

BUICK

NAME John Jones	ADDRESS Calloon Center, N.Y.		PHONE 482-5218	DATE Mar 20,80

YEAR	MAKE Chev	MODEL Van Step	LICENSE NO 123422	MILEAGE 60892	SERIAL NUMBER PS15938585 26

INSURANCE CARRIER	ADJUSTER	PHONE	CAR LOCATED AT

OPERATIONS	PARTS		LABOR		REFINISHING	
1 - Left Side Lower Panel	92	50	10	0	4	0
1 - Left Lower Reinforcement Rail	17	50	5	0		
Repair Inner Panel						
Paint & Material	25	00				
Freight charge	25	00				

INSURED PAYS $_____ INS. CO. PAYS _____

TOTALS	160	00	270	00	72	00
					502	00

INS. CHECK PAYABLE TO_____

The above is an estimate, based on our inspection, and does not cover additional parts or labor which may be required after the work has been opened up. Occasionally, after work has started, worn, broken or damaged parts are discovered which are not evident on first inspection. Quotations on parts and labor are current and subject to change.

WRECKER SERVICE		
TAX 7%	35	14

EST. MADE BY_____   R.O. _____

TOTAL OF ESTIMATE	537	14

AUTHORIZATION FOR REPAIR. You are hereby authorized to make the above specified repairs to the car described herein.

SIGNED   John Jones   DATE Mar 20, 80
J-129718

THE REYNOLDS & REYNOLDS CO ... CELINA, OHIO   LITHO IN U.S.A.

Figure 37-6   A typical estimate. *(Courtesy of Classic Pontiac, Cadillac and Buick Inc.)*

Livingston Manor 439-4242	*Art Sargent Corp.* AUTO DAMAGE APPRAISER Livingston Manor, N.Y. Box 605	N.Y.S. License No. 2981	

ESTIMATE OF DAMAGE

Owner *Justin Jones*	Location	Make *Chevrolet*	Year
Body Type *Van*	Mileage *60872*	Model *Step Van*	I.D. No. *PS159J835526*
License No. *12-3ZZ*	Standard Trans. ☐ Power Str. ☐	Roof ☐	Radio ☐
Color *Green*	Air Conditioning ☐ Cylinder Heater ☐ Tape Deck ☐ Power Br. ☐ Auto Trans. ☐		

REAR CONT'D.	NET	HRS.	PARTS
Bumper Guard		.	
Gravel Shield		.	
Bumper Brkts.		.	
Frame		.	
Tail Pipe		.	
Gas Tank		.	
Hub		.	
Wheel		.	
Tire		.	
		.	

FRONT	NET	HRS.	PARTS	LEFT SIDE	NET	HRS.	PARTS
Bumper		.		Fender		.	
		.		Fender Mldg.		.	
Bumper Guard		.					
Gravel Shield		.		Fender Skirt		.	
Bumper Brkts.		.		Headlamp		.	
		.					
Grille		.		Park Light		.	
				Cowl		.	
		.				.	
		.				.	
		.				.	
		.		Windshield		.	
Baffle Side		.		Door Front		.	
Baffle Upper		.		Door Mldg.		.	
Baffle Lower		.				.	
Horns		.				.	
Core Support		.				.	
Radiator		.		Door Rear		.	
Fan Blade		.		Door Mldg.		.	
		.				.	
		.				.	
		.				.	
		.				.	
Hub		.				.	
Wheel		.				.	
Tire		.		Center Post		.	
Frame		.		Rocker Mldg.		.	
Lwr. Cont. Arm		.		Rocker Panel		.	
Shaft		.		Floor Pan		.	
Knuckle		.				.	
Up. Cont. Arm		.		Quarter Panel	10	.	92 50
Shaft		.		Quarter Mldg.		.	
Frt. End Align		.		*Roof Rail*	3	.	17 50
		.				.	
Steering		.				.	
Tie Rod		.				.	
Str. Wheel		.					
Hood		.					
Lock Plate		.					
		.					
		.					
		.					
Engine		.					

RIGHT SIDE	NET	HRS.	PARTS
Fender		.	
Fender Mldg.		.	
Fender Skirt		.	
Headlamp		.	
Park Light		.	
Cowl		.	
Windshield		.	
Door Front		.	
Door Mldg.		.	
		.	
		.	
		.	
		.	
Door Rear		.	
Door Mldg		.	
		.	
		.	
		.	
Center Post		.	
Rocker Mldg.		.	
Rocker Panel		.	
Floor Pan		.	
		.	
Quarter Panel		.	
Quarter Mldg.		.	
		.	
		.	
		.	
		.	

REAR OF CAR	NET	HRS.	PARTS
Deck Lid		.	
Hinge		.	
		.	
Tail Light		.	
Lic. Light		.	
End Panel		.	
Floor Pan		.	
Bumper		.	

MISC. ITEMS	NET	HRS.	PARTS
Roof Panel		.	
Headlining		.	
Seat		.	
Inst. Panel		.	
Undercoat		.	
Painting & Matl.	*45*	.	
Freight	*25*	.	
Towing		.	
LABOR *13* HRS. @*18*	$ *234*		
PARTS LESS %	$ *110*		
NET & SUBLET	$ *120*		
TAX *7% 4.14*	$ *32*	*48*	
TOTAL	$ *496*	*48*	

The Below Agrees To Make Guaranteed Repairs As Per Appraisal, When Authorized By Owner

A-Align   1-2-New   OH-Overhaul   S-Straighten   R-Repair

THIS IS NOT AN AUTHORIZATION FOR REPAIRS

Figure 37-7 Typical form used by appraisal company. *(Courtesy of Art Sargent Corporation.)*

additional time. Also, the labor for painting two doors at a set time should be less because the total masking time and preparation is less when they are painted together.

KINDS OF ESTIMATES

There are three kinds of estimates, the courtesy estimate, the competitive, and noncompetitive estimate.

Courtesy estimates are ones generally made when the shop knowingly will not get the job but, because an insurance company needs two or more estimates will submit an estimate as a favor or for a small fee.

Also, courtesy estimates are written on vehicles that are total wrecks without question. The estimator will write up to the total list range. If the vehicle is worth $1,500, but the actual loss is $2,000, the estimator will stop at $1,500.

A *competitive* estimate is one that must compete with another shop, and the job will, most times, go to the one with the lower estimate. These are the most accurate types of estimates and must not be too high or the job might be lost. On the other hand, it must not be too low or the shop will lose money on the job (Figures 37–5, 37–6, 37–7).

Noncompetitive estimates are given to a customer who asks the shop's fee for fixing a door or painting the vehicle, for example. These are normally noninsurance type estimates and are generally agreed to on the spot. The price depends on the salesmanship of the estimator.

Questions

1. What is the first step in making an estimate?
2. Is it important to determine the direction of impact when determining the amount of damage?
3. What is *indirect* damage?
4. Why is it important to correctly identify the body style when making an estimate?
5. What is *hidden* damage?
6. When estimating a paint job, what should be looked for?
7. Why is it important to keep the estimate in the proper sequence?
8. What is *related* damage?
9. How is straightening time determined?
10. How is the cost of straightening a frame determined?
11. Should material for painting be carefully figured especially with reference to the color?
12. In most crash manuals, which number is listed first, left or right?
13. Does the estimated labor for installing a new fender take into consideration rusted bolts or undercoating?
14. Is it important to check out all of the notations for a particular part?
15. Name three types of estimates.
16. What type estimate depends on the salesmanship of the appraiser?

Conversion
Tables

appendix

DECIMAL AND METRIC EQUIVALENTS

Fractions	Decimal In.	Metric mm.	Fractions	Decimal In.	Metric mm.
1/64	.015625	.397	33/64	.515625	13.097
1/32	.03125	.794	17/32	.53125	13.494
3/64	.046875	1.191	35/64	.546875	13.891
1/16	.0625	1.588	9/16	.5625	14.288
5/64	.078125	1.984	36/64	.578125	14.684
3/32	.09375	2.381	19/32	.59375	15.081
7/64	.109375	2.778	39/64	.609375	15.478
1/8	.125	3.175	5/8	.625	15.875
9/64	.140625	3.572	41/64	.640625	16.272
5/32	.15625	3.969	21/32	.65625	16.669
11/64	.171875	4.366	43/64	.671875	17.066
3/16	.1875	4.763	11/16	.6875	17.463
13/64	.203125	5.159	45/64	.703125	17.859
7/32	.21875	5.556	23/32	.71875	18.256
15/64	.234375	5.953	47/64	.734375	18.653
1/4	.250	6.35	3/4	.750	19.05
17/64	.265625	6.747	49/64	.765625	19.447
9/32	.28125	7.144	25/32	.78125	19.844
19/64	.296875	7.54	51/64	.796875	20.241
5/16	.3125	7.938	13/16	.8125	20.638
21/64	.328125	8.334	53/64	.828125	21.034
11/32	.34375	8.731	27/32	.84375	21.431
23/64	.359375	9.128	55/64	.859375	21.828
3/8	.375	9.525	7/8	.875	22.225
25/64	.390625	9.922	57/64	.890625	22.622
13/32	.40625	10.319	29/32	.90625	23.019
27/64	.421875	10.716	59/64	.921875	23.416
7/16	.4375	11.113	15/16	.9375	23.813
29/64	.453125	11.509	61/64	.953125	24.209
15/32	.46875	11.906	31/32	.96875	24.606
31/64	.484375	12.303	63/64	.984375	25.003
1/2	.500	12.7	1	1.00	25.4

TORQUE CONVERSION

NEWTON METRES (N•m)	POUND-FEET (LB.-FT.)
1	0.7376
2	1.5
3	2.2
4	3.0
5	3.7
6	4.4
7	5.2
8	5.9
9	6.6
10	7.4
15	11.1
20	14.8
25	18.4
30	22.1
35	25.8
40	29.5
50	36.9
60	44.3
70	51.6
80	59.0
90	66.4
100	73.8
110	81.1
120	88.5
130	95.9
140	103.3
150	110.6
160	118.0
170	125.4
180	132.8
190	140.1
200	147.5
225	166.0
250	184.4

POUND-FEET (LB.-FT.)	NEWTON METRES (N•m)
1	1.356
2	2.7
3	4.0
4	5.4
5	6.8
6	8.1
7	9.5
8	10.8
9	12.2
10	13.6
15	20.3
20	27.1
25	33.9
30	40.7
35	47.5
40	54.2
45	61.0
50	67.8
55	74.6
60	81.4
65	88.1
70	94.9
75	101.7
80	108.5
90	122.0
100	135.6
110	149.1
120	162.7
130	176.3
140	189.8
150	203.4
160	216.9
170	230.5
180	244.0

SI METRIC-CUSTOMARY CONVERSION TABLE

Multiply	by	to get equivalent number of:
LENGTH		
Inch	25.4	millimetres (mm)
Foot	0.304 8	metres (m)
Yard	0.914 4	metres
Mile	1.609	kilometres (km)
AREA		
Inch^2	645.2	millimetres^2 (mm^2)
	6.45	centimetres^2 (cm^2)
Foot^2	0.092 9	metres^2 (m^2)
Yard^2	0.836 1	metres^2
VOLUME		
Inch^3	16 387.	mm^3
	16.387	cm^3
	0.016 4	litres (l)
Quart	0.946 4	litres
Gallon	3.785 4	litres
Yard^3	0.764 6	metres^3 (m^3)
MASS		
Pound	0.453 6	kilograms (kg)
Ton	907.18	kilograms (kg)
Ton	0.907	tonne (t)
FORCE		
Kilogram	9.807	newtons (N)
Ounce	0.278 0	newtons
Pound	4.448	newtons
TEMPERATURE		
Degree Fahrenheit	(°F-32) ÷ 1.8	degree Celsius (C)

Multiply	by	to get equivalent number of:
ACCELERATION		
Foot/sec^2	0.304 8	metre/sec^2 (m/s^2)
Inch/sec^2	0.025 4	metre/sec^2
TORQUE		
Pound-inch	0.112 98	newton-metres (N·m)
Pound-foot	1.355 8	newton-metres
POWER		
Horsepower	0.746	kilowatts (kW)
PRESSURE OR STRESS		
Inches of mercury	3.377	kilopascals (kPa)
Pounds/sq. in.	6.895	kilopascals
ENERGY OR WORK		
BTU	1 055.	joules (J)
Foot-pound	1.355 8	joules
Kilowatt-hour	3 600 000. or 3.6x10^6	joules (J = one W's)
LIGHT		
Foot candle	10.764	lumens/metre^2 (lm/m^2)
FUEL PERFORMANCE		
Miles/gal	0.425 1	kilometres/litre (km/l)
Gal/mile	2.352 7	litres/kilometre (l/km)
VELOCITY		
Miles/hour	1.609 3	kilometres/hr. (km/h)

Temperature scale:

°F	-40	0	32	40	80	98.6	120	160	200	212
°C	-40	-20	0	20	37	40	60	80	100	

NOMINAL WRENCH OPENINGS TO FIT STANDARD BOLTS, NUTS AND SCREWS

THREAD DIAMETER OF BOLT, NUT OR SCREW

Determine the type of bolt, nut or screw and locate the thread diameter below. Then move across to the left hand column to find the wrench size that will fit the bolt head or nut.

Column groups: **AMERICAN STANDARD ASSOCIATION (B18.2.1 and B18.2.2—1965)** covers *BOLTS* (Square/Hex Bolt columns) and *NUTS* (Square Nut, Hex, Heavy columns). **OLD U.S. STANDARD** covers National Coarse Bolts and Nuts, and Cap Screws. **OLD S.A.E. STANDARD** is National Fine Bolts, Nuts & Screws.

NOMINAL WRENCH SIZE — Also width across flats of Bolts, Screw Heads and Nuts	Square Bolt / Hex Bolt / Hex Cap Screw (Finished Hex Bolt) / Lag Screw	Heavy Hex Bolt / Heavy Hex Screw / Heavy Hex Structural Bolt	Square Nut	Hex Flat / Hex Flat Jam / Hex / Hex Jam / Hex Slotted / Hex Thick / Hex Thick Slotted / Hex Castle	Heavy Square / Heavy Hex Flat / Heavy Hex Flat Jam / Heavy Hex / Heavy Hex Jam / Heavy Hex Slotted	National Coarse Bolts and Nuts	Cap Screws	National Fine Bolts, Nuts & Screws
9/32″	No. 10*	—	—	—	—	—	—	—
5/16″	—	—	—	—	—	—	—	—
11/32″	—	—	—	—	—	—	—	—
3/8″	1/4″*	—	—	—	—	—	—	—
7/16″	1/4″	—	1/4″	1/4″	—	—	1/4″	1/4″
1/2″	5/16″	—	—	5/16″	1/4″	1/4″	5/16″	5/16″
9/16″	3/8″	—	5/16″	3/8″	5/16″	—	3/8″	3/8″
19/32″	—	—	—	—	—	5/16″	—	—
5/8″	7/16″	—	3/8″	—	—	—	7/16″	7/16″
11/16″	—	—	—	7/16″	3/8″	3/8″	—	—
3/4″	1/2″	—	7/16″	1/2″	7/16″	—	1/2″	1/2″
3/4″	—	—	—	—	—	7/16″	—	—
13/16″	9/16″	—	1/2″	—	—	—	9/16″	—
7/8″	—	1/2″	—	9/16″	1/2″	1/2″	5/8″	9/16″
15/16″	5/8″	—	—	5/8″	9/16″	—	—	5/8″
31/32″	—	—	—	—	—	9/16″	—	—
1″	—	—	5/8″	—	—	—	3/4″	—
1 1/16″	—	5/8″	—	—	5/8″	5/8″	—	3/4″
1 1/8″	3/4″	—	3/4″	3/4″	—	—	7/8″	—
1 1/4″	—	3/4″	—	—	3/4″	3/4″	1″	7/8″
1 5/16″	7/8″	—	7/8″	7/8″	—	—	—	—
1 3/8″	—	—	—	—	—	—	1 1/8″	—
1 7/16″	—	7/8″	—	—	7/8″	7/8″	—	1″
1 1/2″	1″	—	1″	1″	—	—	1 1/4″	—
1 5/8″	—	1″	—	—	1″	1″	—	1 1/8″
1 11/16″	1 1/8″	—	1 1/8″	1 1/8″	—	—	—	1 1/4″
1 13/16″	—	1 1/8″	—	—	1 1/8″	1 1/8″	—	—
1 7/8″	1 1/4″	—	1 1/4″	1 1/4″	—	—	—	1 3/8″
2″	—	1 1/4″	—	—	1 1/4″	1 1/4″	—	—
2 1/16″	1 3/8″	—	1 3/8″	1 3/8″	—	—	—	1 1/2″
2 3/16″	—	1 3/8″	—	—	1 3/8″	1 3/8″	—	—
2 1/4″	1 1/2″	—	1 1/2″	1 1/2″	—	—	—	—
2 3/8″	—	1 1/2″	—	—	1 1/2″	1 1/2″	—	—
2 7/16″	1 5/8″	—	—	—	—	—	—	—
2 9/16″	—	1 5/8″	—	—	1 5/8″	1 5/8″	—	—
2 5/8″	1 3/4″	—	—	—	—	—	—	—
2 3/4″	—	1 3/4″	—	—	1 3/4″	1 3/4″	—	—
2 13/16″	1 7/8″	—	—	—	—	—	—	—
2 15/16″	—	1 7/8″	—	—	1 7/8″	1 7/8″	—	—
3″	2″	—	—	—	—	2″	2″	—
3 1/8″	—	2″	—	—	—	—	—	—
3 3/8″	2 1/4″	—	—	—	—	—	—	—
3 1/2″	—	2 1/4″	—	—	2 1/4″	2 1/4″	—	—
3 3/4″	2 1/2″	—	—	—	—	—	—	—
3 7/8″	—	2 1/2″	—	—	2 1/2″	2 1/2″	—	—
4 1/8″	2 3/4″	—	—	—	—	—	—	—
4 1/4″	—	2 3/4″	—	—	2 3/4″	2 3/4″	—	—
4 1/2″	3″	—	—	—	—	—	—	—
4 5/8″	—	3″	—	—	3″	3″	—	—
4 7/8″	3 1/4″	—	—	—	—	3 1/4″	—	—
5″	—	—	—	—	3 1/4″	3 1/2″	—	—
5 1/4″	3 1/2″	—	—	—	3 1/2″	3 3/4″	—	—
5 3/8″	—	—	—	—	3 1/2″	4″	—	—
5 5/8″	3 3/4″	—	—	—	3 3/4″	—	—	—
5 3/4″	—	—	—	—	3 3/4″	—	—	—
6″	4″	—	—	—	4″	—	—	—
6 1/8″	—	—	—	—	4″	—	—	—

*Regular square only.

Index